Emotional Intelligence

Theory and Practice

Vikramaditya Ekkirala
Institute of Management Technology (IMT), Nagpur

Smita Singh (Dabholkar)
Institute of Management Technology (IMT), Nagpur

CENGAGE

Australia • Brazil • India • Mexico • Singapore • United Kingdom • United States

CENGAGE

Emotional Intelligence: Theory and Practice

Vikramaditya Ekkirala
Smita Singh (Dabholkar)

ISBN-13: 978-93-5350-319-2
ISBN-10: 93-5350-319-1

Cengage Learning India Pvt. Ltd.
T-303, 3rd Floor
DAV Complex, Plot 3
Mayur Vihar Phase 1
Delhi-110091

Cengage Learning is a leading provider of customized learning solutions with office locations around the globe, including Australia, Brazil, India, Mexico, Singapore, United Kingdom, and United States. Locate your local office at:
www.cengage.com/global

Cengage Learning products are represented in Canada by Nelson Education, Ltd.

For product information, visit **www.cengage.co.in**

Printed in India Third impression 2022

THE DALAI LAMA

FOREWORD

All of us, 7 billion human beings, want happiness and joy; but many face a multitude of difficulties. This suggests a contradiction—no one wants problems, yet we seem to bring them on ourselves. How does this come about? It is because we are subject to emotions without properly using our intelligence. Scientists have lately confirmed that basic human nature is compassionate. However, we are also prone to being swayed by anger and fear. Too often we accept the existence of such emotions without realizing how destructive they can be.

Material development ensures sensory gratification, but its pleasures are short lived when compared to the benefits of a calm mind and a warm heart. On the other hand, what disturbs our peace of mind is giving into emotions like anger, desire, attachment and jealousy. And when our minds are clouded by emotions, they are biased and obscured from seeing the reality of whatever situation we find ourselves in.

If we want to tackle these destructive emotions, it's helpful to understand the various factors that give rise to them. Essentially, they are based on misconceived projections about people and things. Therefore, I believe the purpose of education is to enable us to see through superficial appearances and view the reality beneath.

Unfortunately, modern education does not adequately teach about inner development and so does not equip students to tackle their emotional problems.

This is why 'emotional intelligence' is so important. It gives us a way to handle our own disturbing emotions, and to be more sensitive to the emotions of others. These are skills that can be learned with proper guidance. Nowadays, whenever I can, I tell our Indian brothers and sisters that they already have a thorough understanding of our inner world and the workings of our mind and emotions, although many people neglect this ancient knowledge. One of my commitments is to encourage interest in its revival here in India. I believe that India is a country where it is possible to combine the benefits of a modern education with the benefits of this ancient understanding of the mind.

With this book—a textbook on Emotional Intelligence—the authors have tried to gather the fruits of contemporary understanding of the workings of our emotions, along with practical applications and exercises for tackling them constructively. I am confident that readers, whether they are students, trainers or consultants will find these materials invaluable. Those who learn to tackle their destructive emotions will more readily find peace of mind equipping them not only to be able to use their intelligence more realistically, but also to contribute to happier families, happier communities and therefore a more peaceful world.

I congratulate Dr. Vikramaditya Ekkirala and Dr. Smita Dabholkar for the dedication they have brought to this project. May its benefits spread far and wide.

7 March 2020

PREFACE

This book was written with the primary objective of filling the gap that exists in the landscape of extensive literature on emotional intelligence (EI). This is to portray a comprehensive and realistic picture of emotional intelligence in the form of a textbook, depicting its multiple facets — models, measures, competencies, techniques, contra-indicators, influence, dark side, workplace relevance, domains of application and research insights — designed to meet the needs of diverse audience, i.e. students, researchers, practitioners, educators, trainers and readers of self-improvement literature. One of the important objectives of this book was to present an overview of emotional intelligence — its emergence as a distinct construct, tracking its evolution and roots, analyzing its impact on personality, its role in a variety of outcomes like decision making, relationship management, mental and physical health, and interpersonal relationships at home and work. The constituents and competencies of EI and guidelines for their development form another capsule of valuable offerings given in this book. The physiological and neurological network of emotions and their functions and processes are presented through scientific lens in a lucid style. The dark side of emotional intelligence is also explored in the backdrop of workplace politics and insights from theoretical and empirical research. A critical appraisal of emotional intelligence, its multiple conceptualizations, and their implications on research and practice are presented in a lucid linguistic flavor appealing even to a general reader who may not have any scientific or domain-specific knowledge.

The other objective of this book was to present a comprehensive review of various models and measures of emotional intelligence scanning through the research literature. An emerging area of interest, popularity and research focused in this book is the interface between artificial intelligence and emotional intelligence. Insights from various experiments and research initiatives embedding emotions into artificial intelligence systems and robotic devices are summarized and presented in an articulate style. Specific applications in market research, decision and learning support systems, robotics in healthcare and counter terrorism are also covered. Another important goal for designing this book is to bring together concepts that are closely connected and relevant to emotional intelligence, such as mindfulness, forgiveness, neuro-linguistic programming, and rational emotive therapy. These are immensely helpful in developing emotional intelligence competencies.

One of the unique features of this book is that the content provides insights and guidelines on applications of emotional intelligence in organizationally relevant function-specific domains of customer relationship management, sales and marketing, product design, HRM and behavioral finance. Another important feature is that 25 experts of the industry have provided insights on EI, exclusively for this book.

This is probably the first book to feature analytical insights on emotional intelligence from Hollywood and Bollywood movies. Such insights, presented at the end of each chapter, offer a realistic pictorial projection of the concepts and their practical relevance closest to reality through the dramatized emotional art-form of movies.

The opening caselet of each chapter offers realistic perspectives of practical relevance while illustrative capsules of insightful practices enmeshed in the text project interesting and inspiring tales of contextual relevance. At the end of each chapter, the reader would find links to interesting and valuable video resources on emotional intelligence, and related constructs while having access to application and practice exercises for developing self-awareness and other emotional intelligence competencies. The chapter-end references serve as a valuable resource for researchers and practitioners for further study and exploration of relevant concepts.

To access the online material, visit http://login.cengagebrain.com. Register as a new user or log in as an existing user if you already have an account with Cengage. Click on tab *Find Product With Free Access*, search by ISBN (9789353503192) and download the files.

This earnest and enchanting endeavor has been an insightful journey despite being highly challenging. When we look back in retrospect, we find it to be a rewarding collaborative adventure for both authors. We earnestly hope the readers would find it useful as a resource book, a practice guide and a research companion.

Vikramaditya Ekkirala
Smita Singh (Dabholkar)

ACKNOWLEDGEMENTS

At the outset, I express my gratitude and revered salutations to His Holiness Sri Sripada Srivallabha Swamy, the incarnation of Lord Dattatreya, whose blessings and guidance made this publication possible. I offer my salutations to His Holiness the 14th Dalai Lama for blessing us with his message of Foreword for this book.

I am grateful to my father, Late Dr. Vedavyas Ekkirala for instilling spiritual values and discipline early in my life, which fueled all my constructive endeavors and contributions. I express my gratitude and salutations to my mother, Late Smt. Rani Samyuktha Ekkirala for her love and emotional elixir that nourished my inner being and for instilling in me human values and service orientation, demonstrated throughout her life.

I extend my heartfelt thanks to my employer, the Institute of Management Technology, Nagpur, specifically to its Director, Dr. Subhajit Bhattacharyya for extending valuable support and encouragement by providing paid sabbatical leave for a period of eight months for the specific purpose of writing this book. This facility offered me an invaluable opportunity to focus on this book without any distraction or deviation. The institute also lent its support by providing access to library and online research database resources needed for this book.

I am grateful to the Cengage team for their patience and support in completing this book.

I thank my co-author, Dr. Smita Singh (Dabholkar) for her valuable contribution to this book and for being the initiator of this project in the first place.

I thankfully acknowledge the support of Mr. Aman Mishra (batch 2018-20 of IMT Nagpur) for his creative designs of artwork used in this book; Ms. Rashika Sood (batch 2019-21 of IMT Nagpur) and Ms. Prachi Upneja (batch 2019-21 of IMT Nagpur) for their contribution in the preparation of supplementary learning material for this book. Their relentless efforts and timely support are laudable.

Last but not the least, I acknowledge the contribution of my wife, Sarada Ekkirala in facilitating me in this work, for enabling me to devote extensive time and effort, and for her encouragement, support and patience which made this book possible.

I thank all the readers of this book in advance for being the major purpose and reason behind this effort and endeavor and for the opportunity to enrich myself intellectually and emotionally in this process.

Vikramaditya Ekkirala

It is a blessing to receive a foreword from His Holiness the 14th Dalai Lama. This divine intervention has further strengthened my belief in goodness and kindness.

While writing the chapters, I was constantly getting reminded of various people in my life who clearly demonstrate various EI competencies. Thus, I am acknowledging the very specific attribute in each one of those.

Director of IMT Nagpur, Dr. Subhajit Bhattacharyya for his empathetic leadership and continuous encouragement during this assignment.

If not for Dr. Vikramaditya Ekkirala, my co-author, this book would not have been possible.

I would like to express my gratitude towards:

My father, Dr. Subhashchandra Dhok for demonstrating conscientiousness, my mother, Dr. Ranjana Dhok for her profound ability to empathize, my parents-in-law Mr. Anand Dabholkar and Mrs. Vijaya Dabholkar for their self-management, Mr. Vijay Narain Singh and Mrs. Kusum Singh for their unique display of self-control. My sister, Dr. Aparna Bakshi for her unconditional emotional support.

Dr. Arun Kulkarni and Mr. Vijay Phanshikar, my Gurus, for their seamless demonstrations of EI in everyday activities. Without their support in the crucial years of my life, I would have never stood my ground.

Mr. Vishnu Manohar for demonstrating self-motivation and commitment and Mr. Shyam Pethkar for his mindfulness. Our extended family and friends for their constant support and for demonstrating the value of team capabilities.

Along with these, there are many who have acted like catalysts and as it is said that it is difficult to measure the impact of catalysts, so it is. I am thankful to Dr. Anil Pathak, Ms. Sanchita Kumar, Dr. Santosh Bhave, Mr. Anand Toal, Mr. Girish Deodhar, Dr. Garima Sapre, Mr. Shashank Sharma, Dr. Jasbir Singh Matharu, Mr. Sachin Waikar, Dr. Vibhava Srivastava and Mr. Ashwin Kelkar for extending their help and support in every possible way.

I would also like to acknowledge my students, Aman Mishra (batch 2018-20 IMT Nagpur), for his creative images, and Prachi Upneja and Rashika Sood (batch 2019-21, IMT Nagpur) for their fine demonstration of commitment.

I thank my husband, Dr. Abhishek, a person with high emotional intelligence, for accommodating my work as well as helping me in all the possible ways; my son, Aryan for his steadfast support and daughter, Shriya for being there.

I would also like to acknowledge the Cengage team for their patience and fine sense of professionalism during the period of completing this book.

I am indebted to the following practitioners who willingly provided their insights.

CHAPTER-5

1. **Dr. Arun Kulkarni**, Former Head, Department of Psychology, Rashtrasant Tukadoji Maharaj Nagpur University (RTMNU), Nagpur, India.
2. **Mr. Sharu S. Rangnekar**, Founder, Rangnekar Associates and a Management Guru.
3. **Mr. Amit Waikar**, VP Sales-Asia Pac, Doehler.
4. **Ms. Anu Kumari**, IAS Kerala cadre.
5. **Mr. Abhishek Kumar,** Former DGM-HR, JK Paper Ltd.
6. **Mr. Birender Ahluwalia**, Chief Optimist and Chief Executive Officer, The Positivity Company.
7. **Mr. H. N. Shrinivas**, Advisor TATA Trusts.
8. **Mr. Punyashlok Dwibedy**, IMT Nagpur alumnus (2012–14).
9. **Mr. Amit Saxena**, MD & CEO, Unimoni India (Formerly, UAE Exchange & Financial Services Ltd.).
10. **Group Captain Joy Kurien**, Former Leader Suryakiran Team of Indian Air Force.

CHAPTER-6

1. **Mr. Rajeev Singh**, COO & Business Head - Karvy Fintech - Global Business Services, Hyderabad, Telangana, India.
2. **Mr. Jayasekaran Zen**, Founder and Coach for Zenlp Academy, Master Trainer.
3. **Mr. Raghunath Medge,** President of Nutan Mumbai Tiffin Box Suppliers Charity Trust (NMTBSA), popularly known as the Dabbawalas.
4. **Ms. Barkha Nayak,** Counseling Psychologist and REBT Practitioner.

CHAPTER-7

1. **Ms. Lize Rech**, Program Manager, Middle East, Africa & India, Six Seconds, The Emotional Intelligence Network.
2. **Mr. Bharat Dabholkar**, Ex-Managing Director Publicis India.
3. **Dr. Neeta Verma**, DG - National Informatics Centre, Govt. of India.
4. **Mr. Navaneeth Walter**, Legal consultant.
5. **Dr. S. Senthil Kumar**, Professor-OB & HR, IMT Nagpur.
6. **Dr. Rajendra Nargundkar**, Professor- Marketing, IIM Indore.
7. **Mr. Rahul Yadwadkar**, Leadership Coach, Organization Development (OD) Consultant and Facilitator, certified by ISABS.

CHAPTER-9

1. **Prof. William J. Rothwell**, Professor, Pennsylvania State University.
2. **Mr. Mukul S. Joshi**, PhD, Partner@POASSOCIATES.NET
3. **Dr. Yogesh M. Deshpande**, Professor & HOD, Humanities & Social Sciences, VNIT, Nagpur.

My sincere apologies to those whose names I might have inadvertently failed to mention. I thank them all, nonetheless.

Smita Singh (Dabholkar)

BRIEF CONTENTS

CONTENTS

1

EMOTIONS AND INTELLIGENCE

OPENING CASELET

- Tennis star, Andre Agassi tweeted that we tend to be emotional when we are young which takes toll on our nerves, but with experience, we learn to regulate emotions.

Source: https://twitter.com/hashtag/throwbacktennis?src=hash&lang=en&lang=en

- On one occasion, ace tennis star, Andre Agassi had a bitter experience at tennis court. It so happened that the referee warned Agassi when he heard him uttering an obscenity in low tone. Upset with this incident, Agassi lost focus and started hitting ground strokes into the net and he eventually lost that match. This incident of impulsive behavior does not justify or suggest suppression and display of lesser emotion, but it calls for expression of appropriate emotion. The sense of injustice or the feeling of being obstructed from achieving one's goal may trigger a powerful emotion like anger. Instead, he could have used his anger as a motivator for achieving success rather than allowing the same to influence his temperament resulting in emotional outbursts that were not triggered by any external situation but by the physiology of his own emotions.[1]

Source: Caruso, David and Salovey, Peter (2004). "The Emotionally Intelligent Manager". Jossey-Bass. pp. 6.

- A joint study was conducted by Telegraph and IBM using decades of extensive statistical data, coverage and social media inputs with the use of IBM's artificial intelligence platform, Watson. It was revealed in this study that Andy Murray became more successful as he evolved and learned to control his emotional outbursts over time.

  After analyzing all of Murray's Wimbledon performances in comparison with the number of incidents in which he displayed anger at each tournament, the study found that processing and managing anger rather than wild displays of it can enhance performance.

Source: 1) https://www.telegraph.co.uk/tennis/player-qualities/how-andy-murray-has-harnessed-his-emotions/
2) http://dialoguereview.com/serious/

EMOTIONS

Emotion is a universal language and the first spontaneous human expression. It is the medium through which a newborn declares its arrival into this world and those defying this expression are deemed to be still-born. The communication of an infant through the language of emotion is understood well by the mother, eliciting her response and care. Emotional literacy begins to evolve when an infant learns to express, identify, understand and use emotional knowledge to glide through the civilized world. Research shows that the expression of certain basic emotional information and signals are universal in nature.[2a] Observe a newborn baby emerging with a circuitry to identify and convey basic emotions along with a prodigious potential to comprehend and assimilate. The baby is able to cry or remain composed, recognize its mother by smell and turn its head towards its mother's breast for feed. When the baby is able to see faces of other people, its mirror neural cells start helping in learning and imitating facial expressions. The child then expands his/her capability to discern and communicate emotions through the sensory medium of touch and smell to progressively recognizing the tone and tenor of voice, to simple language and then to exploring alternative scenarios. Ideally, he/she is expected to evolve into a happy and secure individual capable of identifying and labeling a wide array of his/her own emotions, developing an understanding of others' feelings toward different expressions and becoming proficient in expressing and regulating his/her emotions.[2b]

Human life is intricately enmeshed with emotions and the processing of emotional information provides meaning which is beyond the instinctual survival value. Since times immemorial, emotions have been found inseparable from human existence, the study of which is often shrouded in mystery, intrigue and contradictions.

The Concise Oxford English Dictionary (Indian Edition, 2009. Oxford University Press, New York, pp.467) describes the meaning of emotion as, "A strong feeling, such as joy, anger or sadness. Instinctive or intuitive feeling as distinguished from reasoning or knowledge". The Chambers Thesaurus (Allied Chambers India Ltd. 2001, page 250) describes emotion as, "Feeling, passion, sensation, sense, sentiment, ardor, fervor, warmth, reaction, vehemence, excitement, joy, happiness, ecstasy, sadness, sorrow, grief, fear, despair, dread, hate, anger".

Psychologists and philosophers nevertheless, have squabbled for over a century on what constitutes emotion and as to which emotions should be considered basic.

THE COMPLEXITY OF HUMAN BRAIN AND INTELLIGENCE

Human brain is an astounding operating system that sustained its streak of intrigue in sync with the revelations of scientists unraveling the mysteries of its functioning by means of methods like brain-mapping techniques. As against our anchored presumption, brain is anything but a logical computing machine, functioning as per its own habits, bypaths, generalizations, prejudices, and addictions acquired during its evolution over generations. Primitive humans might have been benefited by some of these habits, biases and generalizations for surviving in the wilderness, but the same short-cuts have become a major source of problems for the modern man. Likewise education and socialization might have also caused these imperfections and deficiencies in the brain rather than them occurring out of its own nature. Nevertheless, irrespective of the cause of these imperfections, brain could misleadingly navigate us afar from making judicious and logical decisions.[2c]

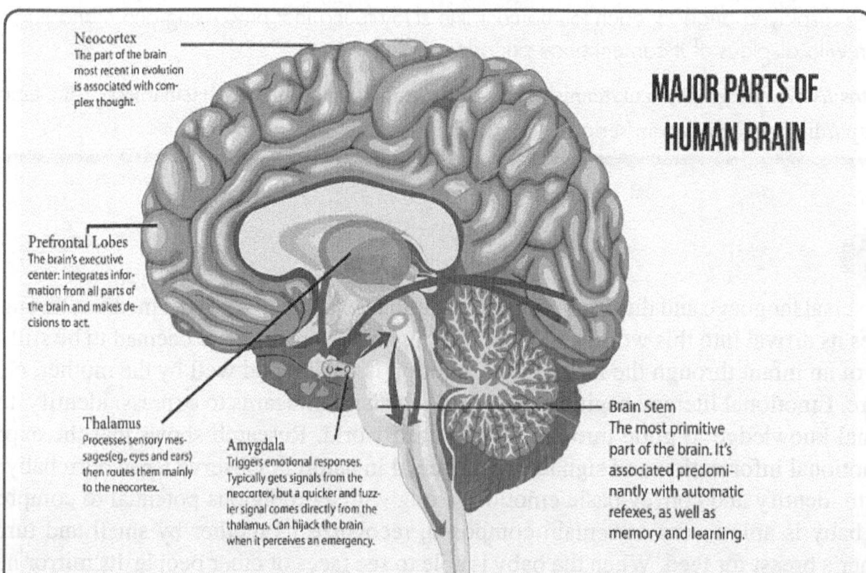

The heritage and origins of human intelligence remain grounded in our genetic code and in the evolutionary narrative of life on earth. It has been evidenced that our intelligence is influenced by various factors, such as our day-to-day encounters, physical as well as mental health, diet and physical exercise, the nature of our relationships, among others. In terms of neurological interpretation, all the factors that influence our intelligence are either tunneled through or regulated by the brain and its neural network spread throughout the human body. Our brain is an evidently amazing component of human body shaping the conscious mind, influencing our self-awareness, and our capability to exercise free choices in courting with the world. Our brain generates and organizes our thoughts, enfranchises our emotions and molds the spiritual aspects of our lives — our perception of meaning and value — enabling us to relate our experiences with appropriate context to derive meaning out of them. Brain provides us insights through the inputs of touch, sound, smell, sight and language to make sense of the world. It serves as a repertoire for memories while regulating heartbeat, rate of perspiration, speed of breath, and other multitudinous functions of our body. The exterior neural fibers of brain are spread through the entire body connecting our internal life with the external world. The neural connections are the source of our intelligence.

The complex, flexible, adaptive and self-reinforcing nature of the brain is responsible for its ability to handle such latitude of functions. After birth, an infant is equipped with just the basic mechanism of neural connections needed for sustenance of life, such as regulation of breathing, heartbeat, maintaining the body temperature and so on. However, an infant can neither perceive faces or objects nor form notions or vocalize cohesive sounds at the outset, instead acquires these abilities by experiencing the world over time as the brain establishes fresh neural connections. The complexity and the expanse of the new neural connections that are formed depend on the richness and variety of the world experiences encountered by the infant. Such complexity is reflected in the structure of the brain comprising more than 10 billion neural cells or neurons and hormones like noradrenaline that stimulate the entire brain.[2c]

THE PARADOXICAL COMBINATION OF EMOTIONS AND INTELLIGENCE

Traditionally emotions were believed to be eruptive forces disrupting logical thinking, and disturbing the rational mind and were therefore, deemed necessary to be controlled. In the early 100 BC, Pubilius Syrus proclaimed that one should regulate and control one's own feelings and should not allow them to control us.[3]

For a long time, the tradition of viewing emotion as inimical to logical thinking wielded considerable influence.[4]

Despite the age-old apprehensions and negative connotations, the study of emotions retained its interest and charm as its challenge and mystery grew over time. It has been a long and intriguing journey of exploration for psychologists, sociologists and management experts who plotted the role of emotions in human endeavors. The role of emotions evolved from survival instinct to a stimulant of intellect; from a disruptive explosive force to a constructive adhesive bonding people; from a powerhouse of passion triggering action to a treasure of compassion; from an offensive and defensive mechanism to the lifeblood of teams, the building blocks of today's organizations. Though philosophers, theologians and dramatists conjectured on the role of emotions for thousands of years, scientific study of emotions in academic psychology is relatively recent.[5] Man's quest for meaningful life set him on the course of exploring the chemistry of the mind to track the core of intellect which is believed to be the propelling force behind the advancement of civilization. In this journey, emotions attracted the suspicious scanner of behavioral scientists who believed them to be negative forces defying logical and rational intellect. But the fact of the matter is that though cognition can be disrupted by emotions, such as anxiety and fear, emotions can also prioritize the cognitive system to attend to what is important and to focus on what it does best in a given mood.[6]

Quest in this direction led to the departure from the myopic perspective of viewing emotions as merely life preserving mechanism of 'fight or flight response'. It was not until the recent past that the influence of emotions on intellect came to be viewed with such profundity that civilized world can ill afford to ignore.

An emotional mind triggers instantaneous action as speed is the essence of its nature, acting faster than the rational mind. The automatic reactions of emotional mind and its rapid decision-making bypassing the rational mind are based on snap judgements aided by perceptions and emotional memory. Feelings guide our actions while sidetracking the lens of analytical and logical thinking. Emotional states have been found to influence one's perception of the world just like the colored glasses, it could be a positive or a negative influence depending on whether we are happy or sad.[7] Accordingly, our perceptions influence our attitudes which in turn influence our behavior. In an experiment, a group of people were made to watch a film with intense emotional content. It was found that frightened people overestimated the risks of accidents, crimes and diseases, while those who were angry made exaggerated judgements of blame. Emotions are also found to be expressions occurring in response to a person's changing relationships, such as one who recalls a happy childhood memory may find the world brighter and joyous.[8] Since emotions track relationships this way, they convey meaning about relationships.[9] By virtue of possessing a wealth of resources of feelings, certain individuals may be emotionally fluent in rapidly and effectively generating emotions and emotion-related thoughts in the same way as a verbally fluent individuals can effectively generate words rapidly.[10] Impulse is the medium of emotion and the seed of all impulse is a feeling rushing to express itself in action. Those at the mercy of impulse — who lack self-control — suffer moral deficiency. Therefore, the ability to control impulse lies at the base of will and character. It is also true that intellect is not effective without emotion which adds flavor and meaning while accessing a memory. Emotion and intellect together contribute to the ultimate cognitive tool. It has been proposed that there are three layers of cognition — emotional cognition, intellectual cognition and a kind of intuition.[11] Some researchers deliberated on an overlap between human emotions and thinking.[12] Others considered emotions themselves as higher order intelligence and believed that "reason without affect would be impotent, affect without reason would be blind".[13] Artificial intelligence researchers have recently considered the value of adding emotions to computers so as to prioritize and direct their processing. In the early 1900, French psychologist, Alfred Binet developed a test to identify the need for special educational interventions for school kids.[14, 15] Simultaneously, a contemporary English psychologist, Charles Spearman worked on general intelligence or *g*.[16, 17] Both of them contributed to the notion that the general ability to solve problems is at the root of all forms of intellectual activity.[18]

EI PERSPECTIVE Two Monks and a Damsel

Once upon a time, two monks were travelling together in a forest. When they reached a river, they sought and reached a shallow place to cross the river. At that moment, a young lady of the night approached them and requested them to carry her across the river as she was afraid of the water current. One of the monks hesitated, while the other agreed and picked her up on his shoulders. When they crossed the river and reached the other side, the monk let the woman down. She thanked him for the help and left on her own way. The monks continued their journey, but the first monk was still ruminating over the other monk carrying the lady of the night on his shoulders. Unable to hold his angst, he protested that the other monk's act was against their spiritual training which forbade them any contact with women let alone a lady of the night. The second monk replied that he already left the lady on the other side while the first monk was still brooding over the incident and was still thinking about her. The relevance of this story to the situations of modern day business has been illustrated through another story. Brown and Joseph ran a business that was still in its infancy. Their business was vulnerable despite promising prospects. Two years ago, the conduct of one of their staff members in an important role was uncharacteristic and damaging, which threatened the very existence of their business. Eventually, the matter got sorted out, the staff member left the service and the business was restored to its normal course. But partners found it difficult to overcome their feelings of anger resulting from a sense of injustice and betrayal. Joseph specifically nurtured an intense hatred as he was unable to forget the betrayal of the ex-staff member. Though he appeared to be normal and calm, he was burning underneath with anger and hatred. Many months later, a business coach, motivational speaker, and trainer met Brown and Joseph. During his conversations with them, the trainer narrated the story of the Two Monks and a Damsel. When the trainer met them again after some time, he found that their business was really moving forward. During the chat, Joseph confessed that the trainer's narration of the story of Two Monks and a Damsel had a profound impact upon him, as it helped him realize that he was only hurting himself by carrying this baggage of anger much longer than it was necessary. He confided that he questioned himself about the utility and benefit of continuing to hold on to the anger and after a rational evaluation, decided to let the matter go forever. When we nurture such feelings of anger, resentment or revenge, we must remember that they were in the long past directed towards other people in specific contexts. It's now time for us to move on as those other people have also moved on having no interest in the subject and as they are also not relevant to us anymore.

Joseph was able to understand that he was unconsciously hurting himself by nurturing and perpetuating his anger long after the incident. He realized that the only way he could stop was by letting go of his anger and resentment.

Source: http://www.emotionalintelligenceatwork.com/resources/the-monks-and-the-lady-of-the-night/

Since then, Spearman's theory of general intelligence (*g*) was significant in the conceptualization of intelligence and became the basis for many IQ tests developed subsequently (e.g., Stanford- Binet Intelligence Scales Fifth Edition, 2003; Wechsler Adult Intelligence Scales Third Edition, 2008).

MULTIPLE INTELLIGENCES AND THEIR MANIFESTATIONS

Since the beginning of theorizing and testing of intelligence, there were debates not only on the nature of intelligence but also on the number of intelligences.[19] Based on the combinations of basic mental processes, it was proposed that 120 different kinds of intelligences existed.[20] Intelligence conceptualized as abstract thinking predicted one or other type of success, but failed to explain a vast amount of variance.[21] As Wechsler noted, "Individuals with identical IQ may differ markedly in regard to their ability to cope with the environment".[22] A study revealed that IQ itself was not a good predictor of job performance, estimating its contribution to be 25 percent in an ideal setting.[23]

Howard Gardner's multiple intelligence theory proposed that individuals differ in their aptitude by demonstrating different types of intelligences varying from person to person. He proposed that the capability of people to process various types of information has evolved in diverse ways which he termed as intelligence.[24] He postulated that a demonstrated aptitude in one type of intelligence does not imply comparable aptitude in another type of intelligence.[24]

An individual may possess a higher degree of spatial intelligence but may have moderate or low level of interpersonal intelligence or vice versa. According to Gardner, these different types of capabilities or intelligences enable people to solve problems or create new things or products that are valued in a society.

Thus, the Multiple Intelligence theory differs from the Western Psychological theory in regards to conceptualizing intelligence as comprising multiple forms rather than confining to a singular form.

EI PERSPECTIVE Intelligence is Not Unidimensional

Henri Poincare was a French theoretical physicist and one of the world's greatest mathematical geniuses. He created the 'Poincare conjecture', one of the most acclaimed unsolved mathematical problems which was subsequently solved in 2002-2003 by Grigori Perelman. Poincare discovered the chaotic deterministic system which became the bedrock of chaos theory of modern times. He is also credited to be one of the founding members of topology as a field. Paradoxically, when this mathematical genius took the IQ test formulated by his friend Alfred Binet, on two different occasions he reportedly scored at ridiculously low levels on both instances, which apparently could be used to brand him as imbecilic. The true measure of intelligence therefore appears to be far beyond and more distinct than a number representing IQ levels.

Source: Landrum, G. N. (1999). "*Eight Keys to Greatness – How to Unlock Your Hidden Potential*". Mumbai: Magna Publishing Co. Ltd.

It is pertinent to cite the examples of idiot savants in this context. Idiot savant is a person with extensive knowledge and/or competence in one subject/area but ignorant about everything else. Cambridge dictionary defines idiot savant as someone who has a mental disability but who is good at doing a particular thing like remembering things. Despite poor performance in common IQ tests, idiot savants might demonstrate extraordinary talents in certain domains. Some such people might exhibit prodigious expertise in playing classical music;[24b] others might be able to flawlessly replicate classical paintings while some may solve incredibly complicated mathematical equations in an unbelievably short span of time. Gardner identified the multidimensionality of intelligence and proposed multiple intelligences as shown in Table 1.1.[24a]

Table 1.1: Howard Gardner's multiple intelligences

Type of Intelligence	Description
Linguistic Intelligence	The ability to learn or use spoken and written language to express complex ideas in the most suitably crafted passages; the ability to converse skillfully with others for obtaining useful information; the ability to use oratory skills through narratives, speeches and motivational appeals to convince and induce others to commit for a course of action; the ability to store information in memory and to explain others in a lucid and convincing manner primarily through oral instructions.
Logical – Mathematical Intelligence	The ability to use numbers to assess the past and present and to predict the future; the capability to maneuver the world of numbers and assimilate their information; the ability to calculate, estimate, and assess the financial impact of activities, processes, and decisions.
Musical Intelligence	The ability to perceive and produce music; capability to understand and appreciate the various nuances of melody, harmony and music; the capacity to comprehend and use the structure of music and its various manifestations.
Bodily – Kinesthetic Intelligence	Traditionally, physical abilities were applied in occupations like agriculture, hunting, fishing, defending against enemies, etc. This type of intelligence is also manifested in the abilities of athletes, craftsmen, artisans and surgeons who put their bodies to use in carrying out their professional work. Volleyball and basketball players and people engaged in other games develop their expertise and use their reflexivity and bodily skills to perform in their respective domains.

(Continued)

Spatial – Visual Intelligence	The ability to form mental images of spatial forms and navigate through them or working with them in various ways. For instance, the spatial visual intelligence is manifested in capabilities of a pilot, an astronaut, a mariner or boater, sculptor, painter, and designer of tools and products. The relevant occupations associated with this type of intelligence are architecture, aerospace, design, cyberspace, etc.
Interpersonal Intelligence	The knowledge of others' motivations, sensitivity to others' personality, emotional make-up and working styles, anticipating the reactions of others and the ability to work effectively with others. This includes leadership and followership abilities, negotiation and mediation skills.
Intrapersonal Intelligence	Self-awareness, awareness of one's own feelings, motives, needs and emotions and using this knowledge to achieve personal goals. The 'knowledge of self' can be applied across domains but cannot be easily assessed due to the subjectivity of its nature. However, this ability is of enormous help to individuals in creating a working atmosphere congenial to themselves and to others.
Naturalist Intelligence	The ability to differentiate, distinguish and discriminate between various plants, animals, rocks and cloud formations, and tidal configurations. Primitive man was indeed endowed with this kind of intelligence more for sustenance and survival. Environmental scientists and geotechnical engineers, mining engineers are some of the professionals associated with this kind of intelligence.

Similarly, prodigies possess remarkable talent in one field coupled with normal abilities in all other domains. Both idiot savants and prodigies appear to possess highly developed cognitive functioning in specific areas relative to other spheres of functioning. Gardner holds that such domain-specific higher levels of performance reveal the existence of modular intelligence systems.

Gardner observed that individuals who showed significant talent in diverse domains like music, athletics, chess and entrepreneurship possessed capabilities in these domains which need to be accounted for in the concept of intelligence. [25 a]

Therefore, Gardner did not delve into the issue of creating psychometric instruments while developing Multiple Intelligence theory, but synthesized the research findings of anthropology, evolutionary biology, neuroscience and psychological studies and laid down several criteria for identification of a unique intelligence.

THE PHYSIOLOGY AND CHEMISTRY OF EMOTIONS

Candice Pert of the National Institute of Mental Health discovered the close alliance between emotions and neuro-peptides — the protein molecules that play the role of communication channels as they spread news about various parts of the body throughout the human physiological system like messenger molecules.

EI PERSPECTIVE True Measure of Greatness

As narrated by biographer Sulloway, Charles Darwin was of shockingly average intelligence as believed by his own father and his teachers. Similarly, many authors opined that Thomas Alva Edison was awfully average, as revealed by the normal measure of intelligence. Likewise, Walt Disney was unable to progress beyond the high school level of education and could not even retain his job as a cartoonist beyond a week due to his alleged incompetence. Consider Picasso as a case in point who was deemed a dull student by his

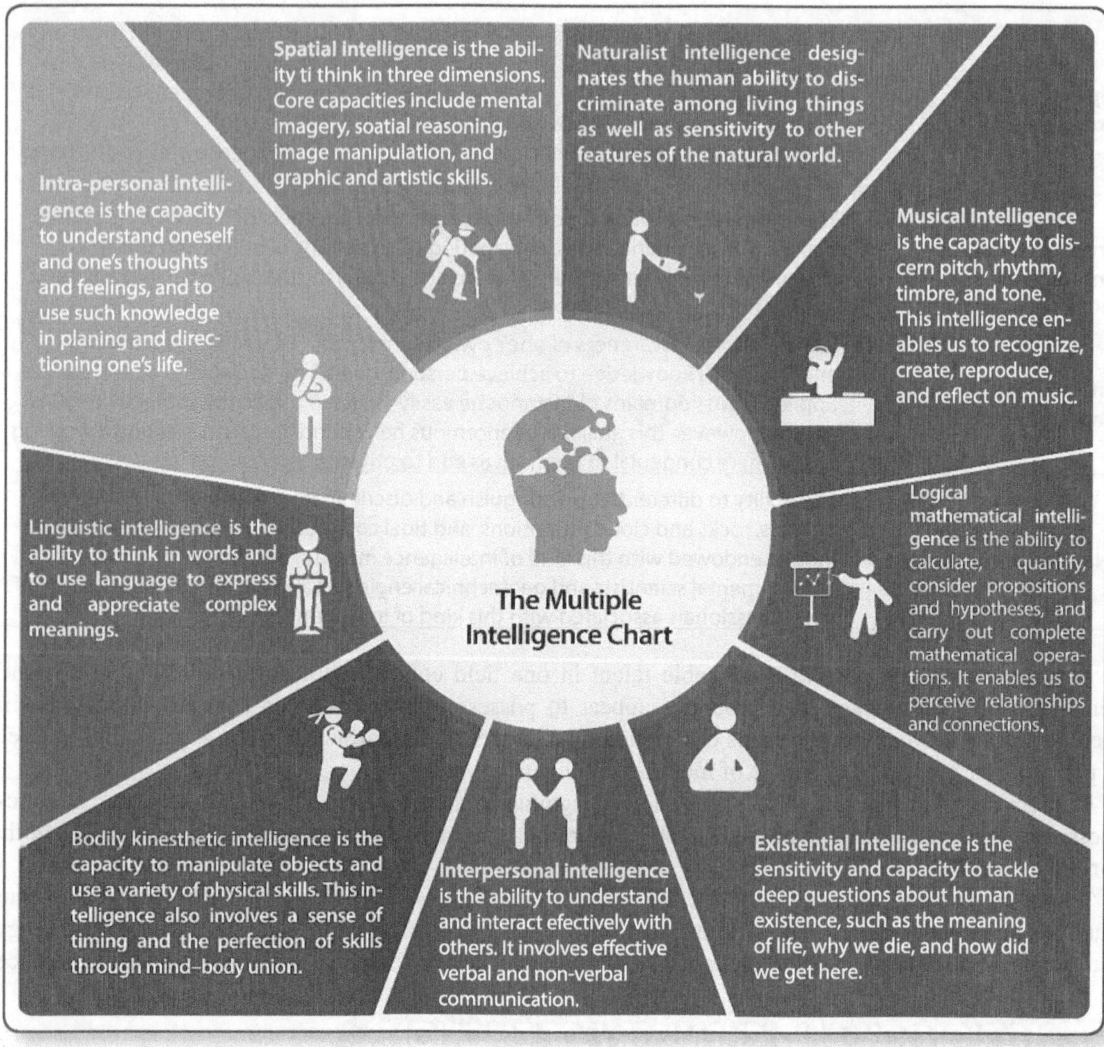

teachers and could hardly make it through grammar school. The famous, successful automobile czar, Honda was a pathetic student who often failed in tests and was unable to qualify for engineering school. The great scientist Albert Einstein is no exception in this respect and had twice failed the entrance tests for art school. The famously successful technocrat, Bill Gates was nevertheless bright but the qualities that made him the world's wealthiest person were his drive, entrepreneurial competence and venturesome nature apart from his work-values.

Sources: 1) Landrum, G.N. (1999). "*Eight Keys to Greatness: How to Unlock Your Hidden Potential*". Mumbai: Magna Publishing Co., Ltd.

2) Sulloway, F. J. (1996). "*Born to Rebel: Birth Order, Family Dynamics, and Creative Lives*". New York: Pantheon Books.

Pert explores the enigmatic interconnection between mind and body at the sub-atomic level and the process that transforms information into matter as well as the bodily chemistry of blending it into consciousness, in her book, *Molecules of Emotion*.[25 b]

According to the American Heritage Dictionary of English Language (Fourth edition, 2000), emotion is "A mental state that arises spontaneously rather than through conscious effort and is often accompanied by physiological changes".

Physiologically, the limbic system located in the temporal lobe of our brain is responsible for carrying out emotions like fear and love. The network of limbic system works together to process emotional information in order to make sense of the world. Serotonin and dopamine are the neurotransmitters which act as chemical messengers to send signals across the limbic network. Various regions of the brain receive these signals, assess and interpret them enabling us to recognize objects and situations. These signals help to evaluate situations and objects for emotional content, make split second assessment of risk or reward and guide our behavior. The limbic system is located under cerebrum, the largest part of our brain and comprises components like the thalamus, hippocampus and amygdala. The sensory inputs from various channels like our eyes or ears are first routed to the thalamus and then they simultaneously travel to the amygdala (the emotional center) and also to the neocortex — the logical brain — through independent routes. This multichannel transmission enables amygdala to respond instantaneously even before the thinking brain (neocortex) analyses the information through its circuit scanners, perceives the complete picture and finally makes its most appropriate response. The amygdala can initiate instantaneous emotional responses using this shortcut route while a parallel echoing circuit begins between amygdala and neocortex.

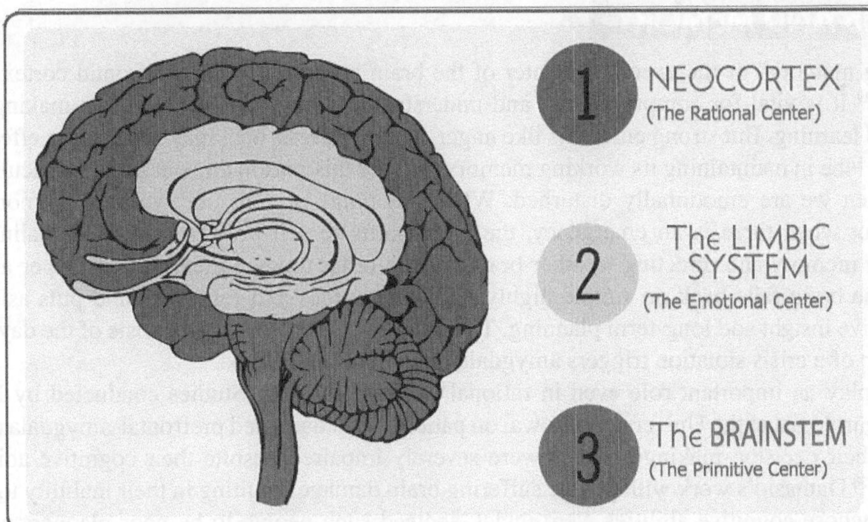

The Three Key Centers of Brain

Thus amygdala can trigger us to immediate action, while the slower but wise neocortex offers a well thought out plan for reaction. Emotions and feelings which directly travel to amygdala for immediate response include life-preserving responses to fear, anxiety, threat to life, etc. Neuroscientist LeDoux's sensational research on amygdala's role in processing of threats helped in understanding heightened responses to threats in anxiety disorder patients. He studied about how the information on a stimulus flows through the brain and how it controls behavioral responses through the sensory network to the amygdala. In anatomical context, LeDoux found that the emotional channel can act independent of the neocortex. Therefore, certain emotional memories can be formed unconsciously, while some emotional reactions can be triggered eclipsing the cognitive brain entirely.[26] This study gave impetus to the notion that there are two different routes for sensory traffic to travel to the amygdala, the first being the short cut as the faster subcortical pathway for intense behavioral responses for countering threats and the second and much slower one being the longer and smoother road for analytically processed information to travel.[27] His work showed how the brain detects and responds to threats, and how memories about such experiences are formed and stored through cellular, synaptic and molecular changes in the amygdala.[28] Thus the almond shaped amygdala becomes a hard disc that can store memories and screenplays of past responses that can be enacted by us without realizing why we do so because the short cut from thalamus to amygdala completely bypasses the neocortex. As an archive of emotional memory, the amygdala scans sensory inputs and relates the current happenings with past memories to find similar "match" of events and then commands reactive response before full information of the event is analyzed. In this manner, we become prisoners of our past. The amygdala is also responsible for several emotional expressions, such as love, fear, anger and sexual desire. Several studies revealed that stimulation or surgical alteration of the amygdala leads to changes in emotional responses. It was found that electrical activation of amygdala caused aggression, while surgical removal triggered indifferent or abnormal emotional reactions. Any damage to the amygdala, therefore, may trigger abnormal emotional responses, and overstimulation may cause excessive reactions. When the amygdalae of monkeys were removed in an experiment in 1939, the researchers found those monkeys exhibiting bizarre behavior patterns. They found that such monkeys became fearless, hypersexual and were either devoid of emotion or displayed irrationally aggressive behavior.

EMOTIONS AND MEMORY

Our "working memory" or the executive center of the brain is located in the prefrontal cortex just behind the forehead.[29] It is vital for comprehension and understanding, planning and decision making as well as reasoning and learning. But strong emotions like anger, anxiety, stress, etc., may hamper the effectiveness of the prefrontal lobe in maintaining its working memory. It is for this reason that our thinking faculties become paralyzed when we are emotionally disturbed. When our mind is calm, the working memory functions at its best. But when there is an emergency, the brain shifts to self-protection mode, stealing resources from working memory and directing to other brain sites in order to keep the senses in hyper alert. During emergency, the brain falls back on simple highly familiar routines and responses and puts aside complex thought, creative insight and long-term planning. The focus is on the present, the crisis of the day. Therefore, our perception of a crisis situation triggers amygdala into emotional hijack.

Emotions play an important role even in rational decision making. Studies conducted by Dr. Antonio Damasio, a neurologist at the University of Iowa, on patients with damaged prefrontal-amygdala connections showed that their decision-making abilities were severely impaired despite their cognitive abilities or IQ being normal.[30] Damasio's work with people suffering brain damage resulting in their inability to experience emotion, but whose cognitive abilities were intact, showed such people to be poor planners and decision makers . They spent inordinate amounts of time making trivial decisions and had difficulty holding jobs and maintaining relationships. Based on his research, Damasio made a strong argument on the importance of emotions in adaptive decision making. His *somatic marker hypothesis* and associated research convincingly showed that an individual's cognitive processes and emotions must interact to allow that individual to make good decisions. Somatic markers are bodily feelings connected with emotions like the association of rapid heartbeat with the emotion of anxiety or of nausea with the emotion of disgust. According to his research, somatic markers have a strong influence on decision-making. The hypothesis has been tested in experiments using the Iowa gambling task, an activity intended to simulate decision making in real life. This task is extensively used in the research of cognition and emotion. This can be illustrated further with the case of a patient of Dr. Damasio who was a brilliant corporate lawyer. Some years earlier, this man was diagnosed with a small tumor in his prefrontal lobes. Surgery was successful except that the surgeon accidentally cut the circuits connecting the lawyer's prefrontal with amygdala. The results were puzzling and dramatic. On one hand, the lawyer had no discernible cognitive defects. On the other hand, he became inept at work, lost his job and was unable to keep another. He thought like a computer, was capable of taking all steps in decision making process but was unable to evaluate different alternatives and make a decision.[26] He ended up being out of work, his wife left him, and he lost his house. The lawyer went to Damasio for help. Looking over the results of his neuropsychological tests, which were all normal, Damasio was baffled at first. Then one day, he noticed that when he asked an innocent question, "When should we have our next appointment?", the lawyer was capable of giving him the rational pros and cons for every possible hour for the next two weeks but had no idea which of those hours was best. Damasio then realized the flaw that the lawyer had no feelings about his thoughts and hence had no preferences. His conclusion was that our mind is not designed like a computer to give us a neat print-out of the rational arguments in favor of and against a decision in life, based on all the previous occasions we faced a similar situation. Instead, the mind does something much more elegant, it weighs the emotional bottom line from those previous experiences and delivers answers to us as a hunch or a gut feeling. As discussed earlier, the amygdala is the brain's emotional memory bank, repository of all our moments of triumph and failure, hope and fear, indignation and frustration. The entire incoming sensory information is scanned for threats and opportunities by matching the current happenings with the stored memories of our past experiences. John Gottman, a psychologist at the University of Washington, carried out the most detailed analysis ever done of the emotional glue that binds couples together and the corrosive feelings that can destroy marriages. In his laboratory, couples' conversations were videotaped and then subjected to hours of microanalysis to unravel the sub-terrain of emotional currents at play. Gottman charted the emotional ecology of marriages with such precision that in one study, he was able to predict which couples seen in his lab would divorce within three years with 94 percent accuracy, a precision unheard of in marital studies.[31] Emotions thus have been found to be an alloy in the cognitive, intellectual, social and behavioral processes of human mind, the absence of which results in severe impairment of these processes and associated functions.

THE ORIGINS OF EMOTIONAL INTELLIGENCE

The earliest reference to the liaison between emotion and intellect can be found in the works of Spinoza who believed that emotion and intellect together contribute to the ultimate cognitive tool.[32] According to him, there are three layers of cognition, emotional, intellectual and a type of intuition. Later, researchers proposed that the development of intellect cannot be isolated from emotions as our performance in the process of 'doing' is influenced by our subjective feelings about the action.[33]

Thorndike suggested the existence of a social intelligence, which involved "the ability to understand and manage men and women, boys and girls to act wisely in human relations".[34] However, social intelligence could not be distinguished from verbal intelligence,[35] though subsequently, some attempts were made to operationalize social intelligence.[36] Emotional intelligence could have a more distinct brain locus in the limbic system and its cortical projections in comparison to social intelligence.[30, 37] It is broader in comparison to social intelligence in that it also includes reasoning about internal emotions that are relevant for personal growth, in addition to reasoning about emotions in social relationships.[38]

Traditionally, mind was considered to be comprised of three components, *cognition* [thought], *affect* [including emotions] and *motivation* [conation], which were studied independent of each other.[39] Intelligence has been defined as, "The ability to grasp and reason correctly with abstractions (concepts) and solve problems".[40] However, concepts like wisdom, prudence, social intelligence, practical intelligence and emotional intelligence have increasingly narrowed the distinction between emotion and cognition. It was held that the adaptive processing of emotionally relevant information is a part of intelligence.[41]

Howard Gardner's concepts of intrapersonal intelligence (the ability to know one's own emotions), and Interpersonal intelligence (the ability to understand others' motivations and intentions) provided a foundation for later models of emotional intelligence.[25]

It has also been suggested that there is another kind of intelligence besides rational intelligence known as experiential intelligence, which is closely connected to emotions and operates on the basis of past experiences.[42] Experiential intelligence has been found to be similar to the concept of practical intelligence.[43] There was another proposition that there are three components of emotion, cognitive–experiential, behavioral–expressive and physiological–biochemical.[44] Regulation of emotions was viewed by some theorists as the fourth component of emotion.

The Sommerville study, a forty-year investigation involving four hundred and fifty boys, found that IQ had little relation to their performance at work or in their lives while the biggest difference was in their ability to handle frustration, control of emotions, and learning to get along with other people. Around two-thirds of these boys were from welfare families, while one-third of them had IQ below 90.[45]

EI PERSPECTIVE RIGHT VERSUS LEFT BRAIN ORIENTATION

Generally, subordinates and followers are inclined to be predominantly left-brain oriented in that they are highly structured, organized and analytical in their approach constituting 85 percent of people in the Western world, who tend to feel constrained to operate in uncertain environments. Left-brain orientation isn't inferior or undesirable by any means, but such people are differently oriented as it makes them less competent beyond the confines of structured systems.

On the other hand, the other 15 percent people are inclined to be largely right-brain dominant and such type of people are termed as visionaries who could integrate both the big picture and the miniscule detail at the same time. Such people are immensely perceptive and insightful as they are not unidimensional in their focus. They may be introverts who can be extroverts as needed and those who could spot opportunities beyond the numerical analyses.

Source: Landrum, G. N. (1999). *"Eight Keys to Greatness: How to Unlock Your Hidden Potential"*. Mumbai: Magna Publishing Co., Ltd.

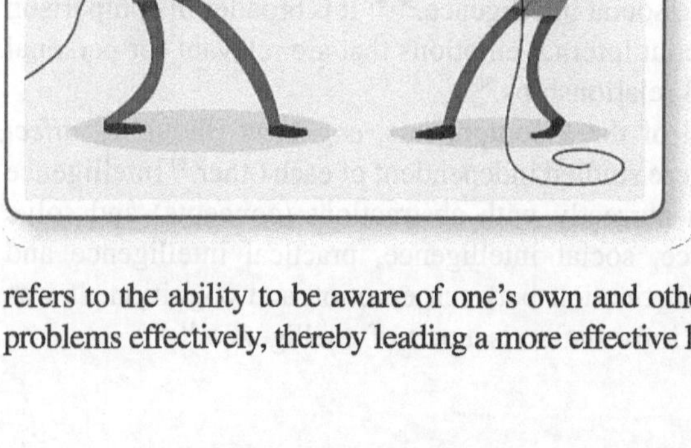

The earliest formal mention of emotional intelligence appeared in 1966 in a German article titled (translated in English) "Emotional Intelligence and Emancipation" by Leuner, which explains that adult women rejected their social roles because of hypothesized low emotional intelligence.[46] The term *Emotional Intelligence* was formally coined and defined as, "The ability to monitor one's own and others' feelings and emotions, to discriminate among them and to use this information to guide one's thinking and actions",[41] and it was empirically demonstrated as to how emotional intelligence could be tested as a mental ability.[47]

The apparently paradoxical term 'emotional intelligence' — conjoining 'emotion' and 'intelligence' — refers to the ability to be aware of one's own and others' emotions and the ability to use emotions to help solve problems effectively, thereby leading a more effective life.

The power of emotion is a double-edged sword like the forces of nature, such as electricity and water which need to be harnessed, regulated and channelized for constructive purposes. We cannot imagine civilized human life without electricity and water. Similarly, there cannot exist a civilized world and an effective human life without the power of emotion, which is an integral part of our physiology, psychology, work, personal and social lives as well. Emotional intelligence provides the key to unlock infinite human potential towards actualizing the purpose of human life in its true meaning and spirit. The relevance of emotional intelligence can be appreciated better by comparing and contrasting the construct with the condition called Alexithymia.

Alexithymia and Emotional Intelligence

Alexithymia is a condition characterized by one's inability to understand or express emotions. According to Daniel Goleman, people with this condition cannot find words for their feelings and even reported absence of any feelings or fantasies and their dreams are devoid of any color. In other words, such people do not have any emotional experiences in their life to talk about as they appear ignorant of the language of emotions.[26]

Harvard psychiatrist, Dr. Peter Sifneos coined the term *alexithymia* and described such patients as those who felt themselves to be different and hailing from an alien world and living in a society dominated by people endowed with feelings.[48] Scientists theorized that such condition may be either due to:

1) a malfunctioning in the brain's right hemisphere; or
2) due to the left hemisphere being overactive; or
3) the messages of emotion get blocked due to the damage of communication system (corpus callosum) between the right and left sides of the brain.[49]

Early studies reveal that the deficiency in the corpus callosum can be found in patients having adverse childhood experiences. Indeed, the emotional state of parents becomes an important determinant of a child's emotional development as infants who have not developed their speaking abilities depend on the validation or feedback for their facial expressions in the form of emotional expression from the parent.

When there is no feedback or when there is incorrect feedback due to the parent's neglect or indifference to a child's facial expression, the child's facial expression in turn is invalidated including the child's emotions as well. The parent's inability to identify, differentiate and recognize their child's emotional expressions can influence the child's ability to understand and respond to the emotional expressions of others.

A person with the condition of alexithymia will obviously be very low on emotional intelligence.[50] Sometimes alexithymia may also manifest when a person suffers an injury to the brain.

EI PERSPECTIVE Thomas Keller's Reaction to Criticism

Thomas Keller is a reputed chef with popularity and fan following spread throughout the world. He has been credited with numerous awards for his contribution and has authored multiple titles that became bestsellers. He is reported to have bagged three Michelin stars simultaneously for two separate restaurants and happens to be the only American chef to receive such recognition.

Once a restaurant reviewer of *The New York Times* published a scathing and devastating criticism about the food he sampled at Keller's restaurant, 'Per Se' in New York between the fall and winter of 2015. Paradoxically, Per Se was named "the best restaurant in New York city" by the same newspaper just four years earlier.

Thus the most accomplished chef and restaurant owner in the world responded to this criticism with an honest and humble apology to his guests. His apology was published in his blog on February 1, 2016. He conveyed that his team assumed responsibility for the poor quality of dishes prepared at Per Se and promised improvement. While acknowledging that his team did not rest on past laurels, Keller expressed his belief in continuously striving to do better for himself and his team, for their profession and for their guests in particular. He acknowledged that his team was motivated and dedicated to utilize all the expertise at their command and the opportunity to do well by working harder.

In his reply to the guests, he reiterated that his team would spare no effort to provide the guests with the best experience possible. He expressed deep regret for not being able to live up to the expectations of the guests and for not meeting the standards of quality while sincerely apologizing for the same.

Viewing in perspective: In such situations, the usual and common response could have been to question the competence of the critic while attacking him with counter criticism. But doing so would surely be a lost opportunity to grow. In perspective, it is therefore prudent to learn from experience and try to swallow our pride when we become target of tough criticism.

How is this connected to emotional intelligence?

Emotional intelligence is the ability to identify and interpret emotions and use such information to guide our actions and behavior. Criticism is a bitter pill to swallow irrespective whether you are a successful entrepreneur or a committed employee. Especially when you invest your best efforts and hard work in a precious accomplishment of your life, it would be extremely painful to witness someone destroying what you have built. But the fact remains that criticism is more often than not based on facts even if it is not expressed properly. We have two choices when responding to a critical feedback. The first one is to set aside our own feelings about the issue and to think logically and derive valuable lessons from the incident. The other alternative is to allow our emotions to take control and react to the situation. There is no need to guess which option would be beneficial to us in the long run.

It is not to advocate for tolerance of even the severest and bitter criticism, preaching to follow the monks' way of life. Though, it is equally important to stress the need to deliver criticism constructively in a dispassionate and objective manner. When we became target of criticism, it is important to set our emotions aside and look for insights to learn from this alternative perspective even when criticism is delivered inappropriately. It is also essential to ponder over the ways and means of using such feedback to improve ourselves as individuals and as team players.

Source: https://www.inc.com/justin-bariso/how-emotionally-intelligent-people-handle-criticism.html

Alexithymia has been found to be associated with eating disorders, panic disorders and post-traumatic stress disorder.[49]

Alexithymia and disorders of autism spectrum have a common condition, lack of emotional connection, and those with this disorder are unable to interpret or exhibit social cues. Clinical psychologists report that individuals with alexithymia disorder show limited capacity for empathizing with the emotional states of others.[51, 52] This emotional incapacity often leads them to report unspecified medical problems when in fact they experience emotional distress which is known as *somaticizing* in psychiatric terms—mistaking an emotional pain for a physical ache.

Treatment for Alexithymia

For someone with alexithymia, the process of developing their emotional literacy and awareness could be a struggle. First and foremost, it is essential to be patient with people affected by this condition by avoiding punishing or criticizing their emotional unresponsiveness.

Symptoms of Alexithymia

The symptoms of alexithymia center on the inability to understand the intricacies of feelings and emotions for both themselves and other people. These symptoms include:

- Inability to recognize various types of feelings
- Lack of understanding about the causes of feelings
- Inability or difficulty in expressing feelings
- Difficulty to recognize facial cues in others
- Lack of imagination
- Narrow thinking style
- Highly sensitive to physical sensations
- Inability to control impulses
- Outbursts which are explosive or disruptive in nature
- Lack of connection, detachment or temporary connection with others
- Struggling to identify and label feelings and difficulty to discriminate between feelings and the physical sensations
- Trouble in describing feelings to other people
- Restricted imagination and, therefore, finite or absence of fantasies and limited dreams
- Lack of awareness of happenings in their own mind; and a very concrete way of thinking.

Source: Elsie Divinagracia, MPH, March 22, 2017. https://blog.cognifit.com/alexithymia/

It is necessary to explain your emotional needs in briefer terms, "*I'm feeling tired, I don't want to cook. Let's get take-out for dinner*". Or try and help them to label emotions, "*You look angry. Is something bothering you?*"

Help of a mental health professional is essential, who often focuses on helping the person to label emotions and to appreciate a range of feelings through self-reflection and relating the experiences of others.

Writing a daily journal, reading stories or books with emotional content, practicing creative arts (e.g. dance, acting, music, or painting), undergoing skill-based and group therapy, and various relaxation practices can help in developing emotional skills.

Thus many studies have shown that the condition of alexithymia is negatively associated with or inversely proportional to emotional intelligence.

EMOTIONAL AWARENESS

Sigmund Freud aptly concluded that most of the emotional life is unconscious. But the moment emotional reactions are brought into the searchlight of (self) awareness, they can be intelligently evaluated and behavioral responses can be altered accordingly. Just as someone cannot violate traffic rules and cross the stop-line in the presence of a policeman, in the same manner, one cannot be emotionally hijacked when under the scrutiny of self-awareness and self-regulation. Thus emotional self-awareness is the foundation of intelligent evaluation and regulation of emotions which have a significant positive influence on our behavioral response mechanism besides enhancing our emotional and physiological well-being.

Emotional intelligence as a field of study is vast and diverse, encompassing myriad disciplines, such as:

- *Biopsychology* (focused on the influence of brain, neurons, and nervous system on our thoughts, feelings, and behaviors).
- *Cognitive psychology* (dealing with internal states of mind)

- *Clinical psychology* (concerned with the assessment and treatment of mental illness, abnormal behavior, and psychiatric disorders)
- *Behavioral psychology* (focused on theory of learning with the fundamental premise that all behaviors are acquired through conditioning)
- *Personality psychology* (branch of psychology focusing on the study of thought patterns, feelings, and behaviors that make each individual unique)
- *Social psychology* (provides insights on social behavior while focusing on group behavior, social interactions, leadership, non-verbal communication, social influences on decision-making, etc.)
- *Positive psychology* (scientific study of human potential to thrive and actualize; processes and practices to enhance the quality of life experiences and positive emotions)
- *Anthropology* (study of human beings and evolution of human behavior in societies; study of the norms and values of societies)
- *Neuropsychology* (study of the structure and function of the brain in relation to specific psychological processes and behaviors)
- *Organizational behavior* (study of the behaviors of individuals, work groups and the organization itself in the organizational context)

The field of emotional intelligence is truly expansive but emotional illiteracy is prohibitively expensive for individuals, groups, organizations and communities. The cost of this illiteracy is to be paid in the currency of toxicity in workplaces, relationships and in personal as well as social lives of people at large. This book is an attempt to combine research insights and conceptual framework of emotional intelligence with practical applications and exercises serving as an illustrated and comprehensive guide.

PLAN OF THE BOOK

This book attempts to distill the essence of research and practices on emotional intelligence and present them to the broader audience of industry professionals, students, trainers and consultants serving as a companion and practice guide while providing insights into and conceptual foundations of the subject.

Each chapter begins with an opening caselet while several insightful capsules (EI PERSPECTIVE) of episodes/ illustrative incidents are interspersed in the text exemplifying its content. Chapter synthesis is provided at the end of each chapter followed by key terms. The chapter-end exercises include review questions, an application-based question, activity beyond the book, links to video resources and a self-assessment instrument for each chapter. These are followed by analysis of three Hollywood movies for each chapter, ending with the chapter references.

Chapter 1 provides the introduction to the subject of emotions traversing through the domains of multiple intelligences, the physiology and chemistry of emotions while throwing light on the impact of emotions on memory, and the origins of emotional intelligence. Research insights have been textured in lucid and application-oriented style. The chapter also discusses the phenomena of alexithymia and its relationship with emotional intelligence while concluding with the relevance of emotional intelligence.

Chapter 2 opens up with a discussion on the ubiquitous nature of emotion while chronicling the evolution of the concept of emotional intelligence. It addresses the question of whether individuals high on emotional intelligence are more successful and discusses the relevance of emotional intelligence for individual effectiveness and life satisfaction specifically in their daily life — in the spheres of romantic/ marital relationships, health and well-being, psychological stress and troublesome behavior. The chapter also explores the impact of emotional intelligence on workplace performance. Most importantly, the chapter provides insights into the influence of emotional intelligence on leadership. The issue of emotional labor and the strategies — individual and organizational — to counter its effects are discussed in detail. The pitfalls of emotional intelligence — its adverse impact on creativity, realistic feedback, taking tough calls, risk-taking, and leadership — and the manipulative tactics associated with it are deliberated. The issue of trainability of emotional competencies is also explored in detail. The chapter ends with exploration of the dark side of emotional intelligence — how people with Machiavellian orientation and endowed with high emotional intelligence competencies tend to misuse their emotional intelligence to serve their self-promoting agenda through manipulation and emotional exploitation of others.

Chapter 3 covers various definitions of emotional intelligence while addressing the question of whether emotional intelligence is a form of intelligence and provides theoretical foundations of the construct while scrutinizing its major models — ability and mixed models. It provides an overview of various measures of emotional intelligence and major findings and outcomes of research in the domain while presenting the criticism raised in various quarters against emotional intelligence and the arguments and neurological evidence in support of the construct.

Chapter 4 addresses the interface between personality and emotional intelligence while exploring specific linkages with Big-Five Inventory, the Jungian typology of personality and the dimensions of Enneagram theory of personality. Diverse postulations and arguments on emotional intelligence as a component of personality, as a distinct construct independent of personality and extent of overlap between the two domains are presented. The chapter concludes with practical insights into the transcendence of preferred personality orientation toward ideal strategies using varied personality behaviors for self-actualization by applying the Enneagram emotional competencies framework through a process, termed as 'Awareness to Action'.

Chapter 5 showcases description and insights on the constituents and components of emotional intelligence under the clusters of self-awareness, self-regulation, motivation and social competence (empathy and social skills). The competencies associated with each of these clusters which can be developed by individuals to enhance their emotional intelligence quotient are illustrated.

Chapter 6 focuses upon developing emotional intelligence competencies, detailing the practices and strategies for enhancing the EQ. It illustrates various techniques and practices including Mindfulness, the practice of Forgiveness, Neuro Linguistic Programming, and Rational Emotive Therapy, by means of which emotional intelligence can be developed in individuals and teams.

Chapter 7 provides insights and guidelines on specific applications of emotional intelligence in organizational context in the functions of customer relationship, sales and marketing, product design, HRM and behavioral finance.

Chapter 8 is dedicated to contemporary and emerging field of artificial intelligence and its interface and relation with emotional intelligence as well as discussing the efforts and possibilities of incorporating emotions into the mediums of artificial intelligence. Applications of artificial emotional intelligence in the domains of Market Research, Decision-making, Decision Support Systems, Learning Support Systems and Robotics are illustrated and presented. Specific AI interventions like Robotics in training children in the autism spectrum, deployment of robots in healthcare, counterterrorism and multi-agent systems are illustrated.

Chapter 9 presents a global perspective of emotional intelligence while detailing the status of emotional intelligence across various regions in the world.

CHAPTER SYNTHESIS

Emotion is the universal language of human expression and our lives are intricately enmeshed in emotions. The seemingly paradoxical term emotional intelligence dispels the traditional notion that emotion is a disruptive force derailing rational processes. We have come to view emotion as a helpful mechanism for cognitive processes, departing from the narrow perspective of viewing emotions as life-preserving primitive response mechanism of 'fight or flight'. Emotional mind is characterized by speed and instantaneous reaction as feelings guide our actions sidelining the analytical and rational thinking. Emotional states have been found to influence one's perception of the world and thereby one's attitude and actions as well. Emotions also track relationships and positively influence cognitive processes. Impulse is the seed of emotions and those who are under its influence, lack self-control. The ability to control impulse is the base of will and character. Emotions and intellect together contribute to the ultimate cognitive tool. Historically, intelligence was perceived to be unitary in nature in terms of general ability of problem solving based on Spearman's theory of general intelligence. But some researchers found that individuals with identical IQ differed in their ability to cope with the environment. This raised the curtain to the existence of multiple intelligence, deviating from the traditional notion that intelligence constituted a single set of abilities. Howard Gardner identified the multidimensionality of intelligence and proposed eight types of intelligences. He proposed that individuals may differ in their aptitude in exhibiting different types of intelligences.

According to the American Heritage Dictionary of English Language (Fourth edition, 2000), emotion is, "A mental state that arises spontaneously rather than through conscious effort and is often accompanied by physiological changes".

Physiologically, the limbic system located in the temporal lobes of our brain is responsible for processing emotional information through its network of neurotransmitters so as to interpret it to make sense of the world. The sensory inputs simultaneously travel to neocortex, the logical brain as well as to amygdala, the emotional center. The emotional center can initiate direct and instantaneous response, bypassing the logical brain, if it perceives any threat in the content of sensory inputs. Thus, the amygdala may encourage us to act immediately while the slower but wiser neocortex comes out with a well thought out plan for reaction. Amygdala stores emotional memories and matches the sensory inputs it receives with these memories to assess the risk of perceived threat and accordingly initiates immediate response. Therefore, when the amygdala was surgically removed from monkeys, they were found to exhibit bizarre behavior and fearlessness. The working memory (located in the prefrontal cortex) is hampered during emergency when emotional response by amygdala diverts resources to meet the emergency. Hence during crisis, the brain falls back on simple and highly familiar routines and responses avoiding complex thought processes. It is for this reason that our thinking faculties are paralyzed when we are emotionally disturbed. Studies conducted by Dr. Antonio Damasio found that emotions play an important role in rational decision making. An individual's cognitive processes and emotions must interact to allow that individual to make good decisions. John Gottman, a psychologist at the University of Washington, developed a system to predict the success and longevity of marriages by analyzing the couples' emotional language. Emotions thus have been found to be an alloy in the cognitive, intellectual, social and behavioral processes of human mind, the absence of which results in severe impairment of these processes and associated function. The origins of the concept of emotional intelligence are reviewed. Several concepts like social intelligence, practical intelligence, prudence and wisdom and finally, emotional intelligence have narrowed the gap between emotion and cognition. The term *emotional intelligence* was formally coined and defined as, "The ability to monitor one's own and others' feelings and emotions, to discriminate among them and to use this information to guide one's thinking and actions". It was empirically demonstrated as to how emotional intelligence could be tested as a mental ability. The power of emotion is a double-edged sword like the force of electricity and water which need to be harnessed, regulated and channelized for constructive purposes. The relevance of emotional intelligence can be better appreciated by comparing the construct with the condition called Alexithymia. Alexithymia is a condition characterized by one's inability to understand or express emotions. People with this condition lack words for their feelings, report no feelings or fantasies and seem to be emotionally illiterate. A person with this condition will obviously be very low on emotional intelligence. There are various methods for treating people with this condition. Apart from seeking the help of a mental health professional, writing a daily journal, reading stories or books with emotional content, practicing creative arts (e.g. dance, acting, music, or painting), undergoing skill-based and group therapy, and various relaxation practices can help in developing the ability to label emotions and gradually increase their emotional skills. Patience is the key in this process. Thus, the condition of alexithymia is negatively associated with or inversely proportional to emotional intelligence, as revealed in several studies.

Sigmund Freud aptly concluded that most of the human emotional life is unconscious. But when emotions are brought under the searchlight of (self) awareness, they can be intelligently evaluated and accordingly, the behavioral responses can be altered. Just as someone cannot violate traffic rules and cross the stop-line in the presence of a policeman, similarly, one cannot be emotionally hijacked when under the scrutiny of self-awareness and self-regulation. Thus emotional self-awareness is the foundation of intelligent evaluation and regulation of emotions which have significant positive influence on behavioral response mechanism besides enhancing emotional and physiological well-being.

Key Terms

Emotional literacy
Emotional cognition
Impulse
Intellectual cognition
General intelligence (*g*)
Binet intelligence scales
Wechsler adult intelligence scale
Linguistic intelligence
Logical mathematical intelligence
Musical intelligence
Naturalist intelligence
Bodily-kinesthetic intelligence
Interpersonal intelligence
Intrapersonal intelligence
Intelligence quotient (IQ)
Limbic system
Amygdala
Neocortex
Emotional memory
Working memory
Prefrontal cortex
Somatic markers
Adaptive decision making
Emotional intelligence
Affect
Motivation
Prudence
Experiential intelligence
Alexithymia
Corpus callosum
Autism spectrum
Emotional incapacity
Empathy
Somaticizing
Biopsychology
Cognitive psychology
Behavioral psychology
Personality psychology
Social psychology
Positive psychology
Neuropsychology
Clinical psychology
Emotional illiteracy
Organizational behavior

Review Questions

1. Describe Howard Gardner's conceptualization of multiple intelligences.
2. Explain in brief the physiological track of emotion.
3. "*Emotions have been found to be an alloy in the cognitive, intellectual, social and behavioral processes and associated functions*". Elaborate.
4. What is the role of emotions in rational decision making?
5. Compare social intelligence and emotional intelligence.
6. Analyze and compare various interpretations of intelligence.

Application-based Exercise

Sharad (your close friend) and his wife Meena are thinking about divorce after being married for just a year. You want to help the couple and therefore decided to talk to Meena. Upon asking her, "What disturbs you the most as far as Sharad is concerned?", she replies, "There are other things too, but primarily, I am not able to come to terms with his (Sharad's) one major problem. He simply doesn't express his feelings ever. He cannot read my face and doesn't seem to understand me. He gets very impulsive and never feels any warmth for people around him".

1) Do these symptoms tell you something about Sharad's condition?
2) Can you relate this with any concept discussed in the chapter?

Activities beyond the Book

1. How many happy moments can you recall from your childhood (between the age of 5 and 12 years). Can you write them down in your journal for reflection?
2. During the last 24 hours, did you make an effort to make someone happy around you? Recall and recount the experience.
3. Make a list of at least three of your emotional strengths. Choose one and explain why it is important for leaders to have competence in that area. (50-75 words).
4. Make a list of at least five stressors in your personal life and five stressors in your work life. Mark an E for each item you can eliminate, an R for each stressor you can reduce the strength of, and a C for each item you can learn to cope with. For the stressor marked with an E or an R, record any ideas you have on how to eliminate or reduce them in a short sentence.

Video Resources

1. **Ten-month-old Mary's passionate response to her mother** singing Rod Stewart's "My Heart Can't Tell You No", took the Internet by storm and has gained over 26 million views. Mary's overwhelming reaction to her mother's emotional rendition reminds us how directly our mirror neurons mimic the emotional states of those around us, especially for children, who soak up their parents' emotions like sponges.
   Link: https://www.youtube.com/watch?reload=9&v=xI7rLiC-DgY
2. **The power of saying thank you (TED talk) – Laura Trice**
   Link: https://www.youtube.com/watch?time_continue=5&v=ag-Oyn8vIPE
3. **Why aren't we all good samaritans? (Ted talk) – Daniel Goleman**
   Link: https://www.youtube.com/watch?time_continue=2&v=r3wyCxHtGd0
4. **Falling in love is the easy part (TED talk) – Mandy Len Catron**
   Link: https://www.youtube.com/watch?time_continue=34&v=3aYWvujaT6M
5. **The divided brain – McGilchrist: RSA Animate**
   Link: https://www.youtube.com/watch?v=dFs9WO2B8uI
6. **Nine types of intelligence. Which is yours?**
   Link: https://www.youtube.com/watch?v=jVQitvk1Xtk

7. **Emotional memory – Shawn Hayes. TEDx Sacramento 2012**
   Link: https://www.youtube.com/watch?v=RNuARPcb5FA
8. **Enhancing memory: The role of emotion – Jim McGaugh and Larry Cahill, University of California**
   Link: https://www.youtube.com/watch?v=dZxGi8eMaw0
9. **Introduction to the human brain – Suzanne Stensaas, University of Utah, Salt Lake City**
   https://www.youtube.com/watch?v=_aCCsRCw78g
10. **Putting emotions into the science of consciousness – Joseph LeDoux: Copernicus Center for Interdisciplinary Studies, 2018**
    https://www.youtube.com/watch?v=b6Ab34llQYc
11. **Hypothalamus and limbic system: UBC neuroanatomy – Dr. Claudia Krebs**
    https://www.youtube.com/watch?v=ErpxEwlWww4
12. **The Magic of emotional touch – Dr. Katalin Gothard, University of Arizona. Public Science Lecture Series of the National Academy of Sciences, Engineering and Medicine**
    https://www.youtube.com/watch?v=LbVFNvzPF1c
13. **You aren't at the mercy of your emotions: Your brain creates them – Lisa Feldman Barrett TED Talks, San Francisco, California December 2017**
    https://www.youtube.com/watch?v=0gks6ceq4eQ
14. **Right brain vs. left brain – Michael Gazzaniga, Dartmouth University. Scientific American Frontiers**
    https://www.youtube.com/watch?v=82tlVcq6E7A

SELF-ASSESSMENT INSTRUMENT

Gardner's Multiple Intelligence Test
Multiple intelligence test based on Howard Gardner's model is available and freely accessible at the following web-link. This instrument may help to ascertain the type of one's dominant intelligence. The description of each type of intelligence and the matching roles, typical tasks and learning styles are also described in detail.

https://www.businessballs.com/self-awareness/howard-gardners-multiple-intelligences-7/#multiple%20intelligences%20tests

Self-report scale: Barratt Impulsiveness Scale

This is a 30 item self-report scale, named as Barratt Impulsiveness Scale (Patton, Stanford, and Barratt, 1995),[53] measuring the characteristic impulsiveness in individuals. People who are unable to control impulses may have trouble harnessing their emotions. They are likely to act on their emotional impulses without considering the consequences. This test helps in assessing one's impulsiveness. The internal consistency of the scale as measured by Cronbach's alpha ranged from .79 to .82 in samples of students, psychiatric clients and prisoners (Patton et. al., 1995).[53]

Correlational studies showed that high impulsivity as assessed by this scale was related to greater physical aggression (Harmon-Jones, Barratt, and Wigg, 1997),[54] greater impulsive aggression (Stanford, Greave, and Dickens, 1995),[55] poorer reading accuracy (Barratt, Sanford, Kent, and Felthouse, 1997;[56] Harmon-Jones, et al., 1997), poorer reading comprehension, and more risk taking (Sanford, Greve, Boudreaux, and Mathias, 1996).[57]

Receptivity to Functional (beneficial) Criticism

Please provide your honest responses to the following statements by marking the appropriate box that best describes your reaction to functional criticism that is beneficial to you:

	Yes	No
1. I would attempt to switch the topic	☐	☐
2. Make it sound like I figured it out	☐	☐
3. I would attribute a hidden agenda to the critic	☐	☐
4. I would stay calm and pay attention	☐	☐
5. I would attempt to maneuver the critic by playing out the sensitive role of an injured	☐	☐
6. I would ridicule the person criticizing me	☐	☐
7. I would blame and denounce the person criticizing me	☐	☐

Acceptance of criticism or denial of criticism entirely or in part is peripheral. The degree of your receptivity to criticism lies on your attitude and reaction towards it. You may prefer to intuitively disregard, reject, or divert it based on your attitude and perception.

Scoring Key

The following responses imply receptivity to functional (constructive) criticism:

1	2	3	4	5	6	7
No	No	No	Yes	No	No	Yes

Analysis of Select Movies

1. ***Rain Man (1988)***

   Directed by Barry Levinson and produced by Mark Johnson, winning four Oscars, *Rain Man* is an inspiring movie demonstrating in-depth awareness of mental health, and is renowned for painting the portrait of autism on public canvas. This hilarious timeless movie tracks the remarkable journey of two brothers, Charlie and Raymond Babbitt, acquainting with disabilities in the process. Raymond is an autistic savant endowed with an amazing memory and inimitable mathematical abilities.

   The younger sibling Charlie Babbitt is a dealer in rare cars who lands himself in a financial mess caused by his extravagant lifestyle and frequent liquidity crisis. When his estranged and rich father dies, he goes home for the funeral, but is utterly disappointed to know that his affluent father did not bequeath him anything significant in his will other than a pocket watch and a 1949 Buick Road-master convertible which are in perfect condition. On the contrary, his father's wealth is willed to Charlie's long-lost autistic brother, Raymond. Though Charlie had separated from his father in the long past, he was nevertheless unhappy. Throughout his life, Raymond was confined in an East Coast Institution for developmental disabilities. He is an autistic genius who is severely impaired in majority of mental tasks and domains but immensely talented in others. He is unable to engage with people very well and has wrapped himself in order and predictability to make sense of the world around him. For this reason, Charlie finds it hard to resolve the monetary issues. Therefore, Charlie kidnaps Raymond from the institute in order to persuade and allure his brother to part with the inheritance, but sooner finds it challenging to deal with his brother's peculiar habits as well as persistent and repetitive announcement combined with flashes of conspicuous genius. The brothers commence their long journey across the country in their father's elegant car — Buick Roadmaster convertible. Paradoxically, this trip leads them to empathy, love and a sort of atonement for Charlie. This is a smooth engaging road movie which depicts a true picture of autism.

Despite Raymond's immersion with self and his obsession for routine conditioned by peculiar apprehensions, he also demonstrates the prowess beyond that of genius. Though he is incapable of establishing emotional connection with people around him, he could memorize the telephone directory from "A" to "G" within a few hours and look at a stack of matches and calculate their total number accurately.

During this adventure tour, Charlie starts developing fondness for his brother, knowing and understanding him despite being aware that normal relationship isn't possible with him. The viewers get to witness the incredible mathematical skills of a genius. We can also see the contribution of Susanna, Charlie's girlfriend, in abetting Charlie to develop a heart amid all these happenings.

This movie helps us to comprehend and appreciate people in autism spectrum while connecting with them. It also helps to introspect, as normal human beings, our evolution in terms of our emotionality, bonding, empathy, understanding and acceptance.

2. ***What's Eating Gilbert Grape? (1993)***

The movie was directed by Lasse Hallstrom and produced by Bertil Ohlsson. It's a story of a young man, Gilbert Grape and his family of five living in a small shabby old house built by his father, who committed suicide seven years ago. Bonnie, Gilbert's mother, grew pathologically obese due to an eating disorder resulting from severe depression and the agony of her husband's suicide. She secluded herself to eating and watching television and never came out of the house since her husband's death. Due to his mother's immobility, Gilbert had to shoulder the responsibility of caring for his autistic younger brother and his two sisters, Amy and Ellen, by working at a small grocery store, while leading a life of vacuum.

The film depicts as to how multiple forces exert enormous pressure on Gilbert. As the eldest male member of the family he is bound by social pressure to assume responsibility for the care of the entire family. Gilbert unknowingly camouflages his true self under a macho image while trying to abide by the social norms. Such people have a strong conviction to dissociate themselves from feelings like fear, uncertainty, and loneliness, which are condemned by the society as inappropriate for males. In line with the proposition of researcher @Pollack, societal expectations compelled Gilbert to shoulder the family burden by himself and his nervousness in seeking external help lead to his despondency and depression. Despite Gilbert's love for his family and the warmth offered by his small group of friends, they hardly made him happy as seen through most of the film. Gilbert was consistently preoccupied in tending to his autistic brother, Arnie and his own broken family, which left no space for his social life. He had to keep a close watch Arnie, constantly trying to protect him from potential risks of bullying and punishment by unsympathetic neighborhood. In a sense, he played the roles of both the parents simultaneously, since his father was no more and his mother was immobile due to extreme obesity.

Oblique in the film is the question as to who was afflicted with the most severe disability among all the characters — is it the autistic Arnie, or his near-dead mother who lost all interest in life after her husband's demise, or the father whose depression drove him to suicide, or Gilbert himself whose life is tethered with Arnie who is ever dependent on him. While trying for an answer to this question, one may find Arnie to be the one with the least disability as he is delightfully ignorant of his disability which makes him immune to frustration, despair, depression and hence not impacted by his disability. Arnie's autism precludes his understanding of others' feelings, social expectations and his ability to form relationships. He is engaged in his own gleeful world, a phenomenon referred to as 'mind blindness' by psychologists. On the contrary, Arnie's disability affects the entire family by way of generating negative feelings of fear, disappointment, anxiety and despair.

In times of crisis or in challenging situations, the general reflective reaction is to escape pain. When there is no escape route from tough and uncontrollable situations, the victim resorts to emotional detachment as exhibited by Gilbert in the movie. He often ponders over his predicament and deliberately tries to moderate his dialect. His miserable family life, disinterest in relationships beyond family, and his emotional reaction to his relationships demonstrate his downright denial of the world surrounding him. He also deprives himself the truthfulness of identifying and accepting his own emotions. Gilbert goes through the motions of life in utter disregard for his feelings and emotions. Despite his sincere love for his brother Arnie, he keeps branding him as "retarded" while showing his vexation toward his behavior and portrays his mother as a "walrus" to Tucker. He keeps his family relationship at arm's length as a coping mechanism for his emotional dilemma. He deprives himself of the joy and involvement in family occasions, while his dishonesty with his family about his real feelings expands the gap between them further. He swallows his hunger due to his subconscious concern for his mother's eating troubles and avoids eating with the family, which also reflects his dejection with his entire family. This is evident from other instances in the movie, where he warmly relishes eating elsewhere, such as the breakfast with Becky's grandmother or the dinner of chicken hosted for him by Mrs. Carver.

The brighter side for Gilbert is Becky who is independent by nature and nourishes him through her understanding of diverse situations and her empathetic sensitivity to others. Becky succeeds in establishing an emotional connect with Gilbert. There is a scene in which Arnie bluntly questions Becky that she is an uninvited guest to his birthday party while Gilbert confronts him saying that he's rude. This is noteworthy considering Becky's reply when she says, "Its ok, he's just being honest". This shows her empathy and understanding. This gesture of Becky helps Gilbert to learn and develop affectionate acceptance of people close to him while accepting his own status in life. This is a crucial headway in his progression towards masculine maturity. Subsequently, on Arnie's eighteenth birthday Gilbert expresses his regret and seeks the forgiveness of his family as a requital for his past behavior. He lovingly longs for his mother Betty whom he missed for long in the past and does something that he impetuously avoided earlier, introduces his mother to Becky, setting aside his self-reproach. Becky establishes an empathetic connect with Betty and shares a compassionate understanding with her.

After the death of Bonnie, her children choose to burn their parental house as a mark of reverence and affection for their mother as also to avoid the attention of bystanders. The house is depicted in the movie as an analogy for the family — dilapidated and plummeting both internally and superficially. Symbolically, no sooner their house is incinerated, the family is relieved from their distresses and blemishes signifying a therapeutic and visible depiction of the process of despondency and tribulation.

This film has become ageless in its appeal on account of its pragmatic and authentic portrayal of banished individuals battling affliction and misery while embracing infirmities. The competing values of self-interest and altruism are realistically presented eliciting the viewer's empathetic reaction and acceptance. Despite increased awareness of psychological illnesses, the afflictions of intense depression and compulsive eating disorders elicit unwelcome social response and are proscribed and misinterpreted even today. The township in the movie never showed any compassion or affinity towards Grape family, but rather ridiculed them time and again. Such a perilous misconception about psychologically sick people and the ill-treatment meted out to them was also responsible for Bonnie's state of progressive deterioration. Benevolent companions and supportive family would surely make a positive contribution towards the well-being and recovery of such people.

@ Pollack, W. S. (1999). The sacrifice of Isaac: A new psychology of boys and men. Society for the Psychological Study of Men and Masculinity Bulletin, 4, 7–14.

3. ***Antwone Fisher (2002)***

Directed by Denzel Washington and produced by Todd Black and others, the movie is centered around Antwone Fisher, a midshipman in U.S. Navy, who is volatile and explosive young man with a record of aggressive behavior. He was orphaned in childhood, as his father died before his birth and his young mother Eva Mae Fisher was jailed when she gave birth to him. Thereafter, he was placed in an orphanage supposedly until the release of his mother from jail, but his mother did not claim him after her release. Antwone Fisher was therefore sent to foster home run by Mr. and Mrs. Tate, where he suffered ill-treatment, physical and emotional assault at the hands of Mrs. Tate, apart from being molested by her grown-up daughter, Nadine. Eventually, he leaves his foster home at 14, lives on the streets for a couple of years and finally, joins the U.S. Navy intending to make his life worthwhile. His brutal and belligerent childhood was responsible for his ill-temper which caused him to fight a colleague. This resulted in his demotion, a fine upon him and 45 days of his confinement to a ship. In addition, he was directed to undergo psychiatric treatment. Accordingly, he meets Dr. Jerone Davenport, who tries to uncover Antwone's feelings by getting him to unveil his inner turmoil which was vehemently resisted by him initially. But slowly he starts trusting Davenport and progressively confesses the suffering caused by his distressing childhood. While still getting into altercations, Antwone cultivates positive feelings toward his Navy colleague, Cheryl and succeeds in establishing a relationship with her. Davenport attempts to analyze the nature of Antwone's feelings for Cheryl with an intent to deploy them in the process of his development. In due course, Antwone reveals to Davenport about his childhood sexual abuse and makes Cheryl aware about his therapeutic counseling. Davenport counsels Antwone to search and locate his family enabling him to resolve his troubles from the past. He convinces Antwone about the need to conclude, ending his ordeal forever. Despite his initial resistance, Antwone goes in search of his family with the help of Cheryl. But he collapses when Davenport informs him about concluding his counseling sessions. Davenport felt that Antwone needs to advance in his journey of self-exploration all by himself. Fisher is awash in a flood of grief and deprivation as he broods over similar instances of abandonment from his past. Eventually, he ruminates on the inevitability of finding his parents to resolve his emotional ordeal. First, he meets with Tates in their household and challenges them questioning their acts of abuse during his childhood. Mrs. Tate finally repents and discloses the name of Antwone's father as Edward Elkins. Through his aunt, Antwone also gets to know the whereabouts of his mother and finally proceeds to meet with her, which results in Antwone finding atonement, ending his turmoil as he forgives her and decides to move on. Upon his return to the kinfolk of Elkins at their home, a feast awaits him and finally, he gets reunited with his long-lost family.

In the end, when Antwone thankfully acknowledges Davenport's help and support, he surprisingly reciprocates the same stating that he was himself indebted to Antwone. Davenport reveals that he was fighting his own inner problems and his counseling sessions with Antwone helped him challenge his own inner torments and dragons.

The movie holds its spotlight on Antwone's critical threshold limits that trigger his discord and his hands-on mechanism to cope with his internal dissonance is his current reactionary behavior. It shows how Antwone's emotional sores and unresolved issues from his past act as pressure points that trigger his current behavior. The absence of a supporting edifice of family and the problems of abandonment, self-condemnation, external locus of control, and childhood sexual abuse are highlighted. The issues of Antwone's internal discord that induce him to battle the fountainhead of his dissonance at each of the relevant events are well-presented. Every incident that echoes his disgraceful past acted as a switch that activated toxic behavioral event. Davenport demonstrates that all of us have choices and eventually, the master switch to the quality of our life rests in our ability to make right choices. While upholding Antwone's right to be furious, Davenport expounds the need to regulate his emotions and funnel such energy in a meaningful way to benefit himself. The movie is a narration about braving the past and learning from the present; a demonstration of the power of bonding and resilience. Finally, the film highlights a young man's autarchy and his adventurous expedition from disgrace and discord to pardon and coherence.

Other Related Movies

1. **Blade Runner** (1982) directed by R. Scott.
   A science-fiction film that poses the question, How do we know that we are human and if we are human, what does it mean to be human?
2. **Anger Management** (2003) directed by Peter Segal and produced by Revolution Studios.
   When an annoying passenger and a case of mistaken identity causes Dave Buznik to lose his temper on an airline flight, he is sentenced to anger management classes. Buznik learns his therapist is the passenger, who proves to have a rather interventionist style of therapy.
3. **Robot** movie
   The scene where Chitti (the robot) saves a girl from fire.
   Link-1: https://www.youtube.com/watch?v=ZlpPoiUt7D8
   Link-2: https://www.youtube.com/watch?v=0VHNgqjvx4c&t=13s

References

1. Caruso, D. and Salovey, P. (2004). "The Emotionally Intelligent Manager". San Francisco: Jossey-Bass.
2. a. Ekman, P. (1973). "Darwin and facial expression: A century of research in review. New York: Academic Press.
   b. Grimes, S. (2016). "What is emotion analytics and why is it important?". https://www.mycustomer.com/marketing/data/what-is-emotion-analytics-and-why-is-it-important
   c. Carter, R. (2010). "Mapping the mind". London: University of California Press.
3. Syrus, P. (c. 100 BC/1961). "Sententiae". In Duff, J. W. and Duff, A. M. (Eds.), "*Minor Latin Poets*". Cambridge, M.A: Harvard University Press.; Salovey, P., and Mayer, J. D. (1990). "*Emotional intelligence: Imagination, Cognition and Personality*". 9 (3): 185-211.
4. Woodworth, R. S. (1940). "*Psychology*". Fourth edition. New York: Henry Holt.
5. Lazarus, R. (1991). "*Emotion and Adaptation*". New York: Oxford University Press.
6. Easterbrook, J. A. (1959). "The effects of emotion on cue utilization and the organization of behavior". *Psychological Review*, 66: 183-200; Mandler, G. (1975). "Mind and emotion". New York: Wiley: Simon, H. A. (1982). Comments. In Clark, M. S. and Fiske, S. T. (Eds.), "*Affect and cognition*" (333-342). Hillsdale, NJ: Erlbaum.
7. Bower, G. H. (1981). "Mood and memory". *American Psychologist*, 36: 129-148.

8. Ekman and Davidson (1994). "*The Nature of Emotion*". New York: Oxford University Press.
9. Schwarz, N., and Clore, G. L. (1983). "Mood, misattribution and judgments of well-being: Informative and directive functions of affective states". *Journal of Personality and Social Psychology*, 45: 513-523.
10. French, J. W. (1951). "The description of aptitude and achievement tests in terms of rotated factors". *Psychometric Monographs*, (No.5); Thurstone, L. L. (1938). "Primary mental abilities". *Psychometric Monographs* (No.1).
11. Spinoza, B. (1677). "Ethics". In Curley (Ed.), "*The Collected Works of Spinoza*". Princeton: Princeton University Press.
12. Ellis, A. (1962). "Reason and emotion in psychotherapy". New York: Lyle Stuart.
13. Mowrer, O. H. (1960). "Learning theory and behavior". New York: Wiley; Tomkins, S. S. (1962). "Affect, imagery, and consciousness". *The Positive Affects*, 1, Springer, New York.
14. Binet, A., and Simon, T. (1911). "A method of measuring the development of the intelligence of young children". Lincoln, IL: Courier.
15. Binet, A., and Simon, T. (1916). "The development of intelligence in children". Baltimore, MD: Williams & Wilkins.
16. Spearman, C. (1904). "General intelligence, objectively determined and measured". *American Journal of Psychology, 15*, 201–293.
17. Spearman, C. (1927). "*The Abilities of Man*". London, UK: Macmillan.
18. Perkins, D., and Tishman, S. (2001). "Dispositional aspects of intelligence". In Collis, J., Messick, S. and Scheifele, U. (Eds.). "Intelligence and personality: Bridging the gap in theory and measurement". Mahwah, NJ: Erlbaum.
19. Neisser, U., Boodoo, G., Bouchard, T. J., Boykin, A. W., Brody. N., Ceci, S. J., Halpern, D. F., Loehlin, J. C., Perloff, R., Sternberg, R. J. and Urbina, S. (1996). "Intelligence: Knowns and Unknowns". *American Psychologist*, 51: 77-101.
20. Guilford, J. P. and Hoepfner, R. (1971). "*The Analysis of Intelligence*". New York: McGraw Hill.
21. Terman, L. M. (1921). Second contribution to "Intelligence and its measurement: A symposium". *Journal of Educational Psychology*, 12: 127-133.
22. Wechsler, D. (1940). "Non-intellective factors in general intelligence". *Psychological Bulletin*, 37: 444 – 445.
23. Hunter, J. E. and Hunter, R. F. (1984). "Validity and utility of alternative predictors of job performance". *Psychological Bulletin*, 76(1): 72-93._
24. Gardner, H. (2006). "*Multiple Intelligences: New horizons*". New York, NY: Basic Books.
    a. Gardner, H. (2004). "*Changing Minds*". Boston: Harvard Business School Press.
    b. Sloboda, J. A., Hermelin, B. and O'Connor, N. (1985). "An exceptional music memory". *Music Perception*, 3: 155-169.
25. a. Gardner, H. (1983). "*Frames of mind: The theory of multiple intelligences*". New York, NY: Basic Books; Gardner, H. (1999). "*The disciplined mind: What all students should understand?*". New York, NY: Simon & Schuster.
    b. Pert, C. (1997). "*Molecules of emotion*". New York NY: Simon & Schuster
26. Goleman, Daniel (2013). "*Emotional Intelligence: Why it can matter more than IQ*". New Delhi: Bloomsbury Publishing India.
27. LeDoux, J. E. (1994). "Emotion, memory and the brain". *Scientific American* (SciAm) 270:50-57.
28. LeDoux, J. E. (2002). "*Synaptic Self: How our brains become who we are*". New York: Viking.
29. Selemon, Lynn D. et al. (1995). "Prefrontal Cortex". *American Journal of Psychiatry,* 152.
30. Damasio, A. R. (1994). "*Descartes' error: Emotion reason and the human brain*". New York: Avon.
31. Gottman, John (2003). "*The Mathematics of Marriage*". MIT Press. ISBN 978-0-262-07226-7.

32. Spinoza, B. (1677). "Ethics". In Curley (Ed.). "*The Collected Works of Spinoza*". Princeton: Princeton University Press.
33. Dewey, J. (1944). "*Democracy and Education*". New York: Free Press. (Original work published 1916).
34. Thorndike, E. L. (1920). "Intelligence and its uses". *Harper's Magazine*, 140: 227-235.; Thorndike, E. L., and Stein, S. (1937). "An evaluation of the attempts to measure social intelligence". *Psychological Bulletin*, 34: 275-285.
35. Cronbach, L. J. (1960). "*Essentials of Psychological Testing*". (2nd edn.), New York: Harper & Row.
36. Legree, P. J. (1995). "Evidence for an oblique social intelligence factor established with a Likert-based testing procedure". *Intelligence*, 21: 247-266.
37. LeDoux, J. E. (2000). "Emotion circuits in the brain". *Annual Review of Neuroscience*, 23: 155-184.
38. Mayer, J. D., Caruso, D. and Salovey, P. (1999). "Emotional intelligence meets traditional standards for an intelligence". *Intelligence*, 27(4): 267-298.
39. Hilgard, E. R. (1980). "The trilogy of mind: Cognition, affection, and conation". *Journal of the History of the Behavioral Sciences,* 16: 107-117.; Mayer, J. D. (1995). "A framework for the classification of personality components". *Journal of Personality*, 63: 819-877.
40. Schmidt, F. L. and Hunter, J. E. (2000). "Select on intelligence". In Locke, E. A. (Ed). "*The Blackwell Handbook of Principles of Organizational Behavior*", 3-14. Oxford: Blackwell.
41. Salovey, P. and Mayer, J. D. (1990). "Emotional intelligence". *Imagination, Cognition and Personality*, 9 (3): 185-211.
42. Epstein, S. (1991). "*You're Smarter than You Think: How to develop your practical intelligence for success in living*". New York: Simon & Schuster.
43. Sternberg, R., Wagner, R. K., Williams, W. M. and Horvath, J. (1995). "Testing common sense". *American Psychologist*, 50: 912-927.
44. Dodge, K. D. (1985). "A social information processing model of social competence in children". In Perlmutter, M. (Ed.). "*Cognitive perspective on children's social and behavioral development: Minnesota symposium on child psychology*". 18 (pp. 77-125). Hillsdalc, NI: Erlbaum.
45. Snarey, J. R. and Vaillant, G. E. (1985). "How lower and working class youth became middleclass adults: The association between ego defense mechanism and upward social mobility". *Child Development*, 56(4): 899-910
46. Leuner, B. (1966). "Emotional intelligence and emancipation", *Praxis der Kinderpsychologie und Kinder-psychatrie*, 15: 196-203.
47. Mayer, J. D., DiPaolo, M. T. and Salovey, P. (1990). "Perceiving affective content in ambiguous visual stimuli: A component of emotional intelligence". *Journal of Personality Assessment*, 54: 772-781.
48. Sifneos, Peter (1991). "Affect, Emotional Conflict, and Deficit: An Overview". *Psychotherapy and Psychosomatics* 56, pp.116 – 122.
49. Becerra, Rodrigo, Amos, Andrew and Jongenelis, Steven (2002). "Organic alexithymia: a study of acquired emotional blindness". *Brain Injury*, Vol. 16 (7) 633-645.
50. Bermond, Bob, Vorst, Harrie C. M. and Moormann, Peter P. (2006). "Cognitive neuropsychology of alexithymia: Implications for personality typology". *Cognitive Neuropsychiatry*, Vol 11 (3) 332-360.
51. Krystal, H. (1979). "Alexithymia and psychotherapy". *American Journal of Psychotherapy, 33*: (1).
52. McDougall, J. (1989). "*Theatres of the Body. A Psychoanalytic Approach to Psychosomatic Illness*". New York: Norton.
53. Patton, J. H., Stanford, M. S. and Barratt, E. S. (1995). "Factor Structure of Barratt Impulsiveness Scale". *Journal of Clinical Psychology*, 51, 768-774.
54. Harmon-Jones, E., Barratt, E. S. and Wigg. C. (1997). "Impulsiveness, aggression, reading, and the P300 event-related potential". *Personality and Individual Differences,* 22, 439-445.

55. Stanford, M. S., Greave, K. W. and Dickens, T. J. (1995). "Irritability and impulsiveness: Relationship to self-reported impulsive aggression". *Personality and Individual Differences,* 19, 757-760.
56. Barratt, E. S., Sanford, M. S., Kent, T. A. and Felthouse, A. (1997). "Neuropsychological and cognitive psychological substances of impulsive aggression". *Biological Psychiatry,* 41, 1045-1061.
57. Sanford, M. S., Greve, K. W., Boudreaux, J. K. and Mathias, C. W. (1996). "Impulsiveness and risk-taking behavior: Comparison of high-school and college students using Barratt Impulsiveness Scale". *Personality and Individual Differences,* 21, 1073-1075.

2

WHAT IS EMOTIONAL INTELLIGENCE?

OPENING **CASELET**

Emotion and Love

This is a story about a man who was so annoyed with his three-year-old daughter that he punished her for wasting a roll of gold-wrapping paper during the ongoing decorative arrangements before Christmas. Times were tough for the family, things were running on a tight budget as resources and money were scarce. The man was enraged and maddened when his daughter used up the wrapping paper in her attempt to decorate a box that was intended to adorn the Christmas tree. Despite the annoyance of her father, the little girl however struggled into the night to pack the gift box. The next morning, she brought the gift box that she decorated and packed in all her earnest and gave it to her father saying, "Daddy, this is my gift of love to you".

The father of the little girl was so embarrassed by his earlier reaction of annoyance and felt repentant and apologetic. He took the gift box presented by his little girl and opened it only to find it empty! His anger knew no bounds as he shouted at the girl, tightly gripping her arm saying, "Don't you know to keep something in the gift-box when you give someone a present? Is this how you ridicule and poke fun?" The poor little girl was taken aback and started crying. She looked at her father with tears in her eyes and wailed, "Oh, Dad! It is not an empty box that I gave you. I blew my love-filled kisses into the box. They are all exclusively for you, Daddy".

The father of the girl was inundated in guilt and remorse. With tears of regret in his eyes, he embraced the little girl in a warm hug and begged for her forgiveness.

The story goes on that a few days later, the girl dies in a freak accident. It is also said that the little girl's father kept the gold-wrapped gift box presented by his daughter by his bedside for many years. Whenever he felt overwhelmed by grief, he would take out an imaginary kiss and remember the love of the child who had put it there.

Each of us as human being are endowed with golden gift boxes filled with the kisses of love and affection from our kith and kin, near and dear ones and God. There is no other possession more valuable and precious than this. Let us not destroy the fragrance of such unconditional love with the vicissitudes of our impulsive reactions flooded with negative emotions.

— Unknown author

Emotion is a multifarious and ubiquitous force encompassing every facet of our life and sculpting our relationship with the world through its powerful influence. Such is the influence of emotion — enormous and powerful — that the power of a heavy-duty hydraulic machine or an earth-moving equipment pales in comparison. Everything that we do in our life is driven by emotion — motivation to achieve or inspiration to dedicate for a cause; desperation to perform or trepidation of failure and retribution; risking life as a soldier on the enemy-lines driven by patriotic fervor; or sacrificing life in the nation's freedom-struggle. Even the acts reflective of negative emotions like anger, hatred, vengeance, jealousy, or destruction, including acts of killing people, are driven by intense emotion. Similarly, the acts of love, compassion, empathy, kindness, gratitude, patriotism and sacrifice are also products of intense emotion. Emotions are inevitably and inseparably engrained into our psyche as involuntary reflexive mechanism commonly shared by the entire human race. Our emotions are televised on our faces through expressions like frowns, smiles, raised eyebrows, winks, scowls, anguish, etc. Emotions are also broadcasted through our auditory channel — our voice — by means of shouts, cries and laughter. Facial expression indeed is a channel of non-verbal communication system delivering social information. People afflicted with certain mental illnesses including autism spectrum disorders are trained to identify, perceive and label specific emotional displays in different facial expressions so that they are able to communicate and connect with others.

In his book, "The Expression of the Emotion in Man and Animals",[1] Charles Darwin had written that emotions were inherited by man, through the ages, from his animal ancestor. According to him, emotions in today's humans are caused by archaic parts of our nervous system and therefore, each emotion has a specific and congruous biometric imprint. We have inherited emotions as evolutionary antiquity which helped us survive in the ancient times and now have acquired permanent residence in our biological system and for this reason, they became universal in nature. More often than not, emotions are presumed to be beastly reflexes incompatible with and inimical to reasoning and logic. The internal conflict between emotion and logic is best reflected in the annals of human evolution and it defines us as human. Emotion without reasoning and logic makes man an emotional animal and rationality without emotion is a machine devoid of feelings and choices.

E. L. Thorndike, an eminent psychologist with expertise in education, learning and intelligence stated that humans are endowed with different types of intelligence. He named one of such forms as social intelligence, or the adeptness at comprehending and managing people and the ability to act judiciously in human relations.[2] Similarly, David Wechsler, the inventor of the Wechsler Adult Intelligence Scale (WAIS), had also mooted both cognitive and non-cognitive constituents of intelligence. He later conjured that the non-intellective ingredients of intelligence, such as affective, personal and social factors were indispensable to forecast one's ability to succeed in life.[3] Early thinkers like Thorndike and Gardner have led the way for present day proponents of emotional intelligence (EI). Individual theoretical models postulate emotional intelligence as belonging to either of the two schools of research — ability or mixed models. Ability models conceptualize emotional intelligence as mental ability or a type of intelligence, whereas mixed models combine mental ability with personality traits, dispositions and attitudes like self-confidence, optimism and well-being.[4]

The concept of emotional intelligence was contrived in 1985 by Wayne Leon Payne in a Ph.D. thesis in the U.S.A., who surmised emotional intelligence as an ability that involved a creative relationship with fear, pain and desire. The process of adapting to the environment in which we live requires and includes both cognitive and non-cognitive constituents. The non-cognitive components of intelligence include emotional, personal and social factors essential for success in life. Concepts like social skills, interpersonal competency, psychological maturity and emotional conscience, social development, social and emotional learning and personal intelligence are used in exploring the dimensions of emotional intelligence.

Interest in emotional intelligence gained momentum owing to the explosive popularity of the book by Daniel Goleman[5] that captured the attention of researchers, practitioners and trainers, a privilege enjoyed by few fields of psychological investigation. Enthusiastic proponents proclaimed that emotional intelligence is an elixir of sustained corporate and individual excellence in performance that can be nurtured and developed in individuals and groups unlike rational intelligence [IQ]. Goleman[6] remarked that, "Nearly 90 percent of the difference" between successful performers and average ones at work can be attributed to emotional intelligence. One of the articles in a research journal observed that over 85 percent of outstanding performance of successful leaders is accounted for by emotional intelligence, adding that it is the EI and not the IQ that predicted outstanding performance at work.[7]

Reuven Bar-On, Director of the Institute of Applied Intelligences in Denmark and a consultant to several institutions in Israel, developed an emotional intelligence measure using the term "Emotion Quotient" for the first time. His model focused on the potential for performance and success as against the performance or success itself and hence, regarded as process-oriented rather than outcome-oriented model (Bar-On, 2002).[8] Bar-On postulated that in general, people with above average emotional quotient are more effective in handling environmental challenges and pressures. On the other hand, he observed that people deficient in emotional intelligence could be deprived of success apart from encountering emotional difficulties. People who are unable to cope with their environment are usually found to be low on their scores for subscales of reality testing, problem solving, stress tolerance, and impulse control. Bar-On's proposition is that both emotional and cognitive intelligences contribute in equal measure to an individual's general intelligence, which in turn indicates the potential of an individual to succeed in life.[8]

Notwithstanding its popularity, emotional intelligence attracted the critical scanner of scientific community[9] which questioned its scientific validity and measurement in the light of a flood of diverse theories, models, and measures.[10] Nevertheless, emotional intelligence gained popularity in the industry as it claimed to positively impact academic achievement, occupational success and satisfaction, emotional health and adjustment,[11] performance at work,[12] and leader effectiveness,[13] despite being an emerging field of investigation.

ARE INDIVIDUALS WITH HIGH EMOTIONAL INTELLIGENCE MORE SUCCESSFUL?

Goleman's initial publication which claimed that emotional intelligence could be as powerful as or even more powerful predictor than IQ at times,[5] triggered a spate of research on the predictive power of emotional intelligence beyond the IQ. The claim of earlier research that IQ accounted for only 10–25 percent contribution to job performance was responsible for claims about emotional intelligence being powerful and its consequent popularity to a significant extent.[8] Furthermore, the findings of longitudinal studies upheld the importance of emotional intelligence. One of such studies, conducted on 450 boys, has shown that IQ was insignificantly relevant for success on job and in life while highlighting the significance of one's ability to handle frustration, regulate emotions and maintain harmonious relations with others.[14] Though this study did not directly focus on emotional intelligence, certain themes like the ability to understand and regulate emotions of others addressed by the study were the main constituents of emotional intelligence. Despite the research support favoring the contributory role of emotional intelligence in cognitive-based performance beyond the general intelligence, current propositions have been more astute on incremental advantages of EQ over IQ.[15, 16]

Emotional intelligence by itself is perhaps not a strong predictor of job performance as accentuated by scholars like Goleman[17] as well as Mayer and associates.[18] Instead, EI is like a fountainhead of emotional competencies which are in fact strong predictors of performance on the job.

EI PERSPECTIVE Effect of Non-Verbal Expressions

Renowned psychologists Howard Friedman and Ronald Riggio conducted an interesting research in 1981. Their research revealed that expressions which are totally non–verbal could have considerable impact on people. For instance, take the case of three strangers sitting across and facing each other in silence for a couple of minutes. Among these three people, the one who is apparently high on emotional expressivity broadcasts his or her mood or emotional state to the other two persons without even speaking a single word to either of them.

Source: Goleman, D., Boyatzis, R., and McKee, A. (2001). "Primal leadership: The hidden driver of performance". *Harvard Business Review,* December, 2001 (R0111C).

Goleman endeavored to highlight and clarify the connection between IQ and EQ and their respective domains of influence on performance, in his subsequent work.[19] He elucidates that IQ performs the function of categorizing the types of jobs individuals are competent to hold and hence, it is a strong tool to predict the kind of jobs that individuals can take up and their probability of success. On the other hand, emotional intelligence has the power to predict the probable candidates for success on the job given their IQ levels being relatively same. The predictive power of IQ in identifying outstanding performers pales significantly in cases where individual applicants in a small pool are compared for selection at top-level jobs. In all such cases, emotional intelligence will be a relatively stronger predictor of potential outstanding performers. Goleman conjectured that when identical scores of above-average IQs are shown by individuals in a pool of applicants, their levels of emotional intelligence would alone be able to differentiate the highly successful ones on the job.

EMOTIONAL INTELLIGENCE IN DAILY LIFE

It is evidently true that individuals need to constructively maneuver the geography of emotional terrain and deftly deal with the emotional dynamics to traverse the social pathways with ease. Some researchers have hypothesized that emotional intelligence may envisage social well-being and enable adaptive social consequences.[20] Lower levels of emotional intelligence may befriend relational conflict and instability.[21] Significant research evidences the impact of emotional intelligence on everyday life. Emotional intelligence was found to be a good predictor of life satisfaction,[22] while it was reported that individuals with higher emotional intelligence plausibly use a tailored defensive style and therefore showed nourished psychological adjustment.[23] Emotional intelligence was also found to be associated with higher probability of paying attention to health and fitness, reciprocity and bonding with family and friends, and acquiring and preserving objects connected with memories of loved ones.[24] It was also estimated to be strikingly connected with elevated levels of parental love and affection,[25] enhanced positive interpersonal relationships equally among children, teenagers and adults.[26]

Influence of Emotional Intelligence on Romantic and Marital Relationships

Close personal relationships between marital and romantic partners are inclined to be emotionally enriched positively while being exposed to relational conflicts to a significant extent.[27] The stability of marital and romantic partnership and its perceived satisfaction depends upon the emotional abilities of the couple and their effectiveness in dealing with emotionally loaded contexts and conflicts. As indicated by research, couples proficient in constructively reassessing unpleasant interactions have higher marital satisfaction and fulfilment than those couples reporting lower satisfaction.[28] Most of the studies indicate that couples require high emotional intelligence and significant knowledge of managing emotions in order to understand and appreciate their own and their partners' emotions. It was found in one of the earliest empirical studies on marital relations that people with significant emotional literacy reported lower degree of difficulty in forgiving an offense caused by their partners than people with lower emotional understanding apart from being happier in their relationship.[27] In comparison, people with lower emotional knowledge were apparently more prone to attack their partners and expound the hurt and distress of their partner as bitterness. In a study, it was found that couples reported greater unpleasantness in their relationship when both members had lower levels of emotional intelligence scores compared to couples who both scored high on emotional intelligence.[29] A study conducted to investigate the relationship between emotional intelligence and romantic love among 100 newly married couples showed that spouses with higher emotional intelligence scores were happier and satisfied with their marital relationship.[30]

Emotional Intelligence, Health and Well-being

Researchers contended that emotionally intelligent individuals who are proficient in exhibiting, comprehending, and directing their emotions, while being skilled at handling daily stressors, should also be healthier — both physically and psychologically — than those with lower levels of emotional intelligence.[31] Research indicates a moderate alliance between emotional intelligence and health-related comportment. Positive emotions affiliated to emotional intelligence may have latent beneficial effects on the immune system, enabling effective management of stress and minimizing fatalistic emotions and depression.[32] Predominantly, emotional intelligence seems to be strongly associated with mental health rather than physical health, with the extent of association contingent upon the measure.[33] Self-report measures of emotional intelligence have been found to be associated with happiness,[34] optimism and mood.[35] Negligible research shows that emotional intelligence is associated with life satisfaction after controlling for IQ and personality.[36]

EI PERSPECTIVE Gratitude is an Important Emotion of 2019

The Gratitude Movement attracted widespread attention throughout the world, as its proponents anticipate 'gratefulness' to become the most valued emotion of the year 2019. Fatigued of living by the stupefying dictates of modern world that linked success with happiness, people are seldom contented or savvier. Nevertheless, the situation is changing of late.

Contrived gratitude

A spurt of interest has been there in the subject of gratitude. The following happenstances serve as witness to this phenomenon, gratitude has attracted 15,131,049 Instagram posts, while gratitude-journals garnered 198,975 posts! Also, the 'walls of gratitude' are being set up at many public places. When you search for 'gratitude journal' on the net, Google generates over 8.9 million entries, while Amazon shows listings of over 8,000 books.

An entire department is dedicated to the study of gratitude, compassion and other subjects connected to positive psychology at the University of California, Berkeley. Scientists have been increasingly emphasizing the need for deliberate and intentional gratefulness. It is believed that creating gratitude lists lead us to genuine reflection while directing our attention toward good things rather than the bad ones in our lives. According to life coach, Ranjini Woodhouse, most of us spend a lot of our time brewing negative thoughts and most of the stressbusters that we work upon usually enhance our stress to higher levels. She concedes that spending just five minutes a day to heartfully thank the Universe for all that we are endowed and bestowed with and being grateful for the same would alleviate and rejuvenate us within a matter of minutes. The caveat is that such a practice needs to be a conscious one and a daily ritual as well. A truly interesting book, *Thanks! How the New Science of Gratitude Can make you Happier,* is based on extensive research by Robert Emmons, a renowned psychologist at the University of California, Davis. His research showed that life satisfaction and individual well-being significantly increased by writing a regular gratitude journal of concise contemplations on instances and occurrences for which we are thankful.

According to Emmons, gratitude is all about directing attention to positive happenings in our lives rather than magnifying the bad things happening to us. Motivational speaker and life coach, Shiv Khera, exemplifies that focusing on the benedictions of life attracts unbounded positivity. He emphasized on gratitude as an aid to lead a life devoid of guilt, regret and hostility.

Finally, he posited that gratitude essentially needs to be made a part of our life more in the present times than ever before. He believes that sincere and thankful acknowledgement for what we possess or receive in life helps us to cope up and unwind in times of stress. Gratitude helps us to rejuvenate ourselves by focusing on the brighter side of life and by enumerating all our blessings.

Reflect on Daily Patterns

Patternity.org was established by an art director and photographer Anna Murray, and a product designer Grace Winteringham, with the sole purpose of inspiring people to live their life with positivity through pattern research, design and experience. In their well-written book, *Be Great, Be Grateful,* they present the doctrine of well-being, emphasizing the need to pause and reflect on our daily patterns of living and thinking and to be grateful for every experience. Murray explains that people perceive modern life to be stupefying and they search for happiness as something external that one needs to struggle to acquire but ironically happiness lies in being habitually grateful. Their book comprises insights into and illustrations on journal writing to help us to take time each day, to pause and admire moments of life. Of late, science has been investigating the influence of gratefulness on certain aspects of health like patterns of sleep and also upon fruitful human relationships, finding positive correlations.

The effect of 'Thank You' Notes

A study published in *Psychological Science* found that people underestimate the effect of receiving a 'thank-you' note. The study involved a group of 100 participants in writing letters of gratitude to people they truly felt thankful to.

The study found that people consumed less than five minutes to write thank you notes. Hence it is apparently evident that people did not need to think hard about whom to thank or about the reason for being thankful. The attention of the participants in the study was then drawn to the fact that generally people do not pay attention to many positive things around them on a daily basis.

Probably, the best way to begin a new year or a new phase of life is by being our own teacher of gratitude by adopting the following strategies:

Be Your Own Gratitude Guru

- Direct your attention to big as well as small acts of gratitude
- Contemplate and determine your gratitude practice for this year
- Practice gratitude on daily basis as a ritual either by actions or by writing a journal about ten things for which you are grateful.
- Changing your feelings and mental ambiance by making gratitude your dominant attitude would raise your positive vibration.

— Teri Cole, Gratitude Guru

Source: Walia, Nona (2019). *Times of India*. January 6, 2019.

Psychological Stress and Emotional Intelligence

Research has reinforced the assertion that emotional intelligence significantly predicts the effect of stressful events, both in real life[37] and in experimental contexts.[35a] An appraisal of EI research[38] indicates that greater scores on different self-report measures of emotional intelligence are associated with fewer daily annoyances, lower subjective weariness, lesser occupational stress, and fewer symptomatic problems in a wide variety of contexts. This shows that people who can analyze the nature and sources of their feelings and are adept at regulating their emotions are usually less likely to crumble under pressure of experimental or real-life stressors. Such people are more likely to take concrete and committed steps towards restoring their emotional balance and resolving their problems. Adaptable survival actions for minimizing the impact of stressful experiences would reduce the prospects of contracting health problems related to chronic hyper-activation of physiological stress-response systems.

Emotional Intelligence and Troublesome Behavior

In a study involving college students, self-report violent and trouble-prone behavior was found to be inversely correlated with emotional intelligence to a significant level which remained the same even after factoring out the influences of intelligence and empathy.[39] Lower levels of emotional intelligence were found to be significantly correlated with possession of more self-improvement books,[24] increased use of prohibited drugs and liquor and enhanced participation in the acts of violence and vandalism.[24, 40] In a study involving 15 male adolescent sex offenders, it was found that sex offenders find it difficult to recognize and label their own feelings and those of others — the most important constituents of emotional intelligence.[41]

EMOTIONAL INTELLIGENCE AND ORGANIZATIONAL OUTCOMES

Emotional bonds act as the glue that truly bind, strengthen and maintain organizations, rather than their legal, financial or spatial dimensions.[42] Emotional management and rules of emotional expression pervade workplace culture and norms in today's organizations.[43] In several research studies, the feelings of managers were found to be useful predictors and indicators of organizational performance.[44]

Emotional Intelligence at Workplace

As elucidated above, enhanced levels of emotional intelligence may have been proven to be useful in numerous domains of life, but the most documented literature on its utility and functionality centers around the organizational workplace.

EI PERSPECTIVE The Soft Hardcore General

General Omar Bradley rose from the position of commanding an infantry division in Louisiana through commanding the largest American combat force in the battlefield to become the first Chairman of the US Joint Chiefs of Staff. This marvel man had never raised his voice or spoken in an unpleasant tone in his lifetime, seldom changing his soft and plain spoken demeanor. He was identically at ease with prime ministers and heads of state as well as with the platoon sergeants, showing similar attention and interest in what they communicated. Bradley was branded as the "Soldier's General" on account of his habit of quietly showing up anywhere at the deployments in an unescorted jeep, without any fanfare or maybe he looked like a soldier draped in secondhand short battle jacket, olive-brownish pants and infantry boots. But he continued to be tagged affectionately as the "Solder's General" throughout the war and he never stopped earning it.

He never admonished or censured anyone but just made notes on his writing pad that he carried with him. Narrating his experiences in his book, *A Soldier's Story,* Bradley remarked, "Unless you value the lives of your men, unless you feel what they are going through, you are unfit for command". He had the dexterity and capability of positioning himself in others' shoes. Many people were rattled by General George Patton's grandiosity and demeanor — his sirens, armored scout cars and the habit of whooping it up. But Bradley was never affected and his comment on his superior was, "Well that's George's style". Surprisingly, when their roles were reversed in Europe, Patton served Bradley with unmatched commitment. When Bradley rectified one of the battle plans of Patton, he shouted with conviction, "You are right Brad... Goddammit you're always right".

Bradley's serene but determined and unwavering leadership was the reason he was selected to command the American First Army in the assault on the Normandy beaches on June 6, 1944. When actor Karl Malden was playing Bradley's role in the movie "Patton", he met the General for his advice on portrayal of his character. Malden asked the General, "What do you do when you get mad?". Bradley replied by saying, "I don't do anything differently". Malden persisted by asking, "Don't you raise your voice?", to which the General replied, "Nope. Never needed to".

Source (**1**)*:* Hansen, C. B. (1947). "General Bradley as seen close-up". *New York Times Magazine*, November 30. P. 14.
Source (**2**)*:* Bradley, O. N. (1951). "*A Soldier's Story*". Henry Holt and Company.

Cary Cherniss, a researcher, justified workplace as the logical context for assessing and developing emotional intelligence competencies with the following reasoning:[45]

1. The domain of emotional intelligence constitutes an essential component of competencies needed for success in most of the jobs.
2. Numerous people join the workforce without possessing the competencies essential for successful performance at their job.
3. Organizations have the inducement and resources to provide training to their employees in emotional intelligence.
4. Most of the adults spend major part of their wakeful time at work.

Organizational interest in the professional application of emotional intelligence is reflected in the manner in which they embraced the notions and ideas of emotional intelligence. For instance, The American Society for Training and Development published an elaborate book of guidelines for helping people at workplace.

These guidelines aid in developing emotional intelligence competencies which differentiate outstanding performers against the median ones.[46a] Manila University conducted a study across 100 bank employees and found that IQ scores accounted for job performance to a minimal extent, while EQ contributed to the extent of 27 percent.[46b] A rare and exclusive longitudinal study spanning over a period of 60 years was conducted on a thousand individuals with high IQ scores, following them from childhood to retirement. The study showed that individuals who were self-confident in their early years were most successful in their careers.[46c] In a worldwide study, 286 different job behaviors were analyzed to ascertain relevant job competencies. It was found that 18 out of the 21 competencies needed to differentiate good performers from average performers were related to emotional intelligence.[46d]

An emotionally perceptive employee is sure to harvest significant rewards upon inducing positive affect in others at work.[47] It was demonstrated in a study that top management team of a company sharing a positive emotional outlook contributed to four to six percent higher earnings per share (market-adjusted) in comparison to the earnings of companies whose management team comprised of diverse emotional outlooks.[48] Team-level emotions have been found to impact the team's morale and mood, influencing its performance as a team.[49] Workplace emotions have been found to influence judgment, satisfaction, helping behavior, creative problem solving and decision making.[50] Emotional intelligence in individuals facilitates and induces them towards engagement in collaborative conflict resolution practices[51] besides the dependence of workplace relationships on emotional regulation.[52] The desire to suppress emotions and engage in purely rational pursuits in the workplace was found to be contributing to decision-making failures and creation of an atmosphere of mistrust.[53] In the absence of emotion, rational thinking cannot happen.[54] Beyond making us feel good, positive emotions have been found to expand our thinking, help generate innovative ideas, and encourage us to consider a range of possibilities.[55] A gallop study of two million employees at 700 companies found that people with good bosses are four times less likely to leave their jobs than those with poor bosses and their productivity depended on their relationship with the immediate supervisor and boss.[56] Effective supervisors are enriched in their ability to sense their subordinates' feelings and manage their emotions resulting in enhanced trust and good working relationship. Real-time mood and emotion at work was found to predict job satisfaction to a measurable extent.[57] Job satisfaction is defined as, "A pleasurable or positive emotional state resulting from the appraisal of one's job or job experiences".[58] Satisfaction is an emotional connection binding people to organizations rather than a variable inducing them to perform organizational tasks.[59] Research indicates that emotionally intelligent people show greater satisfaction at work.[60] The poor linkage between job satisfaction and performance may be due to excessive reliance on cognitive appraisals[50f, 57] ignoring emotional elements. The key to success is in an individual's ability to perceive, identify, understand and manage emotions, as evidenced by a considerable body of research. The impact of emotional intelligence on productivity and frugality at workplace is an active area of interest for practitioners and researchers. Many studies captured the commercial value of emotional intelligence as a criterion for hiring people. In a study involving partners of a multinational consulting firm, it was found that the partners scoring above the median on emotional intelligence competencies contributed $1.2 million more to the profits of the firm compared to the other partners.[61] Similarly, The Government Accounting Office of the USA has reported to the Congress, the estimated annual saving of $3 million in costs on account of using Bar-On's Emotional Quotient Inventory (EQ-i) in selecting program recruiters by the US Air Force.[62] The US Air Force experienced a three-fold increase in their effectiveness in selecting successful recruiters from those who scored high on emotional intelligence. According to an estimate, the US industry was losing to the tune of $5.6 to $16.8 billion annually on account of its failure to follow the training guidelines introduced to enhance emotional intelligence at the workplace.[63] This study reported a higher impact of training in emotional and social competencies of employees when such programs adopted the guidelines established by the researchers in comparison to other programs which did not follow their guidelines as a consequence of which those companies were losing money.[63]

Empirical studies provide evidence in support of the link between EI and non-cognitive pay-offs that might be classified under "positive organizational citizenship" category. These pay-offs include job dedication;[64] customer orientation;[65] interpersonal sensitivity and pro-social tendencies;[66] altruistic behavior, career commitment and affective commitment to the organization;[67] altruism and compliance;[68] satisfaction with other group members and with the communication within their group;[66] and affective tone in negotiations.[69]

EI PERSPECTIVE IDEO's Creative Teams and Emotional Intelligence

IDEO is a renowned firm in the industrial design space, whose inventive teams are credited with designing the first mouse of Apple Computers, toothpaste tube of 'Crest' and the Palm V personal digital assistant. Constantly under the pressures of customer deadlines, budgetary demands, the company has to deliver ingenuous, creative, and elegant product designs fulfilling the human needs within the engineering constraints. Therefore, the nature of the firm's work essentially demands higher levels of emotional intelligence at the group level. IDEO has a strong conviction about the efficacy of diverse teams and their creative friction in delivering the best designs as against the outcome of ingenuous individuals in solitary pursuit. Hence the creative teams at IDEO flourish. In their study, researchers Druskat and Wolf found that the group norms at IDEO supported emotional intelligence at multiple levels.

Firstly, at team to individual member level; then at the team to itself level; and in the next level, team to outside entities. At the first level, IDEO's teams are fully aware of the emotions of individual members and they are proficient in regulating them. To illustrate the same, here we mention an instance in which a designer was irked by a marketing member's insistence on applying a particular logo to his product, which the designer felt would visually impair the product. In the product meeting, the leader of project team sensed something that wasn't right as the designer was apparently secluded. He then initiated a dialogue and led through a negotiated settlement to the satisfaction of both the members. During brainstorming sessions, the members usually break the norm of judging and rejecting ideas violating the rule. In such situations, members confront one another against such practice in a hilarious but forceful manner by pelting with foam toys or call the name of the member immediately. Such gestures tend to be indirect and subtler in the presence of a client in the meeting. IDEO teams also display maturity in emotional intelligence at the group level. Teams solicit continuous feedback from sources that are internal and external to the organization in order to maintain high levels of self-awareness. Their practice of working in close coordination with clients is noteworthy. It is imperative that the team modifies the designs when it finds that the same is not fulfilling customer expectations. As a part of regulating group-level emotions, the company provides avenues for team members to vent out their stress through fun-filled playful encounters by shooting soft projectiles using finger blasters (toys) placed around the premises. When frustrated, members can pick up these finger blaster toys and start shooting to relieve their stress. Truly, the company's culture embraces free emotional expression and therefore it may sometimes be the case that someone who is angry or upset may stand up and shout or scream.

The company also allows people to work on fun projects, such as crafting the holiday card or creating the "tourist stop" displays visible to visitors, so that employees can work on them when they feel the need for a break. Lastly, team norms are in place at IDEO to ensure awareness of the interests and needs of people outside the organization and to enable teams utilize such awareness for establishing relationships with those external entities and individuals.

Source: Druskat, V. U. and Wolff, S. B. (2001). "Building the emotional intelligence of groups". *Harvard Business Review,* March 2001 (R0103E).

Another important force in the dynamics of organizational reality is change. Change being the order of today's turbulent world, the ability to perceive and understand the emotional impact of change on self and others remains a pre-requisite for coping with a dynamic change. In order to manage change effectively, leaders first need to be aware of and be able to manage their own feelings of anxiety and uncertainty.[70] Studies have shown that EI influences willingness to change.[71] A study conducted in 2014, across 178 respondents in 27 service management teams at a restaurant found that greater levels of psychological safety are linked with higher degree of team cohesion and performance.[72]

Emotional Intelligence and Leadership

Leadership has been and continues to be one of the most important and practically relevant constructs which is deeply associated with emotional intelligence. Despite innumerable conceptualizations and theories, two distinct forms of leadership viz. the transformational and transactional leadership, dominate the current research concerning the interface of leadership with emotional intelligence.[63] Transformational leaders exert inspirational influence on followers triggering higher levels of motivation and commitment to higher-order goals, while developing their capabilities and orienting them to subordinate their self-interest to the interests of the group. Transformational leadership was postulated to comprise four dimensions, idealized influence, inspirational motivation, intellectual stimulation, and individualized consideration.[73]

EI PERSPECTIVE Maria Montessori

Maria Montessori, the acclaimed emancipator of education metamorphosed from an ordinary medical doctor into an ingenious and progressive educator when she was assigned to teach a group of imbecile and uneducable children. Unwilling to accept her as an equal counterpart of medical system, such a challenge was thrown at her. Not yielding to the pressure and unwilling to allow defeat to overpower her, Montessori accepted the challenge and within a few months transformed the children into pupils proficient in reading and writing at normal levels at par with regular students. She became so energized and motivated that she left her regular job and returned to school. She pioneered the Montessori Method of education that eventually reformed and transformed the learning process.

Through one of her maxims "Education is social engineering", she presented the quintessence of her breakthroughs — excellence and nobility are learned by focused hard work and tenacity and not acquired as inheritance.

Source: Landrum, G. N. (1999). "*Eight Keys to Greatness — How to Unlock Your Hidden Potential*". Mumbai: Magna Publishing Co. Ltd.

In contrast, transactional leaders accentuate work standards, compliance, rewards, sanctions and competition to influence and induce employee performance.[73] Scores of studies found that transformational leadership enhanced job effectiveness and satisfaction,[74] group performance[75] and enhanced the effort of subordinates in comparison with transactional leadership.[76]

Leadership researchers postulated that effective transformational leaders must invariably be endowed with the competencies of emotional and social intelligence, which play a significant role in inspiring employees and establishing strong relationships. There is an abundant body of research establishing strong correlations between transformational leadership and emotional intelligence. The level of emotional intelligence as measured by the Bar-On Emotional Quotient Inventory was found to be significantly related to transformational leadership style in a study involving individuals in managerial positions.[63] Daniel Goleman, author of groundbreaking works on emotional intelligence, trainer, researcher and consultant, strongly advocated that leaders must essentially be emotionally intelligent so as to improve their ability to manage their own emotions to elicit the trust of employees, sense employees' feelings, foresee workplace problems and promptly intervene to resolve while sharpening their perception of political and social conventions within their organization.[19]

EI PERSPECTIVE Leading in Times of Crisis

In the context of leaders' dispositions, the relevance of resonance cannot be ignored. Despite research advocating the traits of optimism and buoyancy in leaders in general, their conduct is expected to be grounded in rationality and pragmatism specifically during situations of managing crisis.

In this context, it is apt to ponder the reaction of Bob Mulholland, Senior VP and Head of the client relations group at Merrill Lynch, to the crisis situation when terrorists attacked New York on September 11, 2001. Holed-up in the office in Two World Financial Center, Mulholland and his staff could feel the building vibrating and shaking when they saw thick black smoke puffing out of a cracked hole in the building exactly on the other side of theirs. Naturally, people were terrified as some of them ran desperately between windows, while others were benumbed with dread. Some were anxious about the well-being of their relatives who worked in the World Trade Center. Even in such a situation, Mulholland was aware that he should get into action and lead people from chaos and crisis to peace and security, guiding them at each step and insuring their risks and apprehensions.

First, he began disengaging people from their state by procuring and providing them information on their relatives working in other floors and the building across which they eagerly sought. He also convinced them of the availability of ample time for everyone to escape.

Next, he pacified each person of the petrified crowd individually assuring safe escape from the building and directing them to follow him down through the stairs, leaving the elevators untouched.

All the while, he remained composed and resolute but refrained from restraining the emotional responses of people. Thankfully, because of his efforts everyone escaped before the collapse of the towers.

The story of Mulholland's leadership continues further. Realizing that this incident would individually affect his clients, he and his team contrived a way for an emotional connect with their clients through his financial consultants. The consultants called each one of their clients and inquired about their safety and well-being and about their kith and kin as well. According to Mulholland, it was not a situation to transact usual business with clients and therefore, the primary focus was to make their clients know that they truly care for their well-being. Bob Mulholland had boldly accomplished one of the most important leadership functions of emotional significance. He enabled himself and aided his people to discover meaning in the face of crisis, turmoil and confusion. To achieve this, he had harmonized with the collective emotional reality and effectively communicated the same with all the stakeholders eliciting their trust and compliance to his direction and guidance. Mulholland's words and deeds actually mirrored people's true feelings and fulfilled their emotional needs.

Source: Goleman, D., Boyatzis, R. and McKee, A. (2001). "Primal leadership: The hidden driver of performance". *Harvard Business Review,* December, 2001 (R0111C).

Much prior to the advent of emotional intelligence, the Ohio State University leadership studies found that most effective leaders were those who were able to connect with members of their group with warmth and establish a rapport of mutual trust and respect at the workplace.[77] Such finding is not unusual in the light of many researchers' claims that efficacious leadership basically lies on the leader's capability to resolve intricate social irritants and problems arising in organizations.[78]

EMOTIONAL LABOR

In the year 1983, Arlie Hochschild[79] coined the term 'emotional labor' to describe the specific dispositional behaviors of service personnel surpassing their physical and mental duties. Behaviors like demonstrating genuine concern for the needs of customers, displaying a smile on the face, and making positive eye contact are essentially important for perceived service quality. Such type of behaviors that become essential components of employees' performance are termed as emotional labor. Emotional labor becomes highly challenging for employees while interacting with angry or aggressive clients, or unpleasant people. The challenge lies to a great extent in the requirement to hide one's true emotions and acting out 'smiles' and displaying pleasant expressions despite encountering negative or critical feedback. Organizations accord strategic importance to service orientation towards external customers and also to colleagues and internal clients as well. In the context of increasing service-oriented dispositions adopted by marketplaces, appraising the impact of emotional labor and devising mechanism to counter its toxic effects assumes significance. The importance of authenticity in all our communications has been emphasized by many people. But such a notion and practice conflicts with the need of organizations requiring customer service personnel to mask their emotions and display positive emotions to make customers happy, giving rise to emotional labor.

EI PERSPECTIVE Emotional Labor at Work

In her book titled "*Fast Food Fast Track*", author Jennifer Parker Talwar portrays the practices and techniques adopted by the managers of New York's fast food chains like McDonalds and Burger Kings to inspire and encourage positive emotions in employees in order to stifle and subdue their negative feelings and moods. They are persistent in harking back at employees to drop their problems at home and tune-in their good moods while they are at work.[a]

The practice of modeling emotion to serve business interests has now become ubiquitous. According to authors, Ritzer and Bryman, such practice is considered indoctrination toward 'Disneyization' or 'McDonaldization' of organizations. Otherwise stated, these business titans induce their staff to display emotions that meet the rigorous standards of the Dreamland experience or that of Big Mac. They model the way in which their staff display emotions, and also structure the process and effort that is required to make such expressions look right.[b, c]

Sources: a) Talwar, J. P. (2002). "*Fast food fast track*". Boulder, Colorado: Westview Press. P. 113.
b) Ritzer, G. (1993). "*The McDonaldization of society*". Thousand Oaks, California: Pine Forge Press.
c) Bryman, A. (1999). "The Disneyization of society." *Socialogical Review,* Vol. 47 (1): 25–47.

Implications of Emotional Labor for Employees

Employees engaged in emotional labor control their feelings to meet the expectations of their job roles and to achieve their organizational objectives. Practically, this implies that such people may (a) express only positive feelings, or (b) conceal or regulate their negative feelings. People may exercise one of the following behavioral choices while dealing with negative emotions:

- Display the emotion they do not truly experience or feel.
- Conceal the true emotions they feel or experience.
- Generate an emotion which is appropriate for the situation.

This can be achieved by using the following two techniques:

1) **SURFACE ACTING**: Imitating or mocking-up an emotion by employing feigned body language and artificial verbal communication. Wearing a smile combined with a soft tone of voice helps in displaying emotions which are not felt or for hiding felt emotions.

2) **DEEP ACTING**: Controlling emotions by redirecting them with a belief that one is truly happy and enjoying such interactions. Instead of pretending, we truly convince ourselves to believe that we are not experiencing any negative reaction or emotion. The continuous practice of displaying unrealistic emotions appropriate for the job, irrespective of one's true feelings, may often lead to an emotional conflict between real emotions and those displayed to others in the performance of jobs. Some psychologists believe such emotional conflict to be detrimental, leading to emotional exhaustion, burnout and high levels of stress and may even result in an experienced disconnect in close personal relationships. However, certain other studies did not find any connection between emotional conflict and emotional exhaustion.

EI PERSPECTIVE Emotional Plight of Flight Attendants

In her popular book, *The Managed Heart: Commercialization of Human Feelings*, sociologist Arlie Russell Hochschild demonstrates the extortionate effect of emotional labor on flight attendants while illustrating the regimentation of emotional display by the flight attendants of a major airline. She narrates as to how they had to fulfil the expectations of the airline's alluring advertisements captioned as 'Fly me, you'll like it' schemed to captivate and thrill new clients. The tenderness of smile and expression is expected to be genuine in terms of triggering the feeling and conveying the intent. In the midst of chaotic commuter services, time constraints, tumbles, flirty, intimidating and offensive clients, and the sensual comments, attendants are expected to respond with a smile and understanding. Some of them took the job to their heart by truly feeling what they expressed and struggled through 'deep acting' as they experienced tough emotional labor. As these flight attendants engrossed themselves deeply in their roles, they became disconcerted about their individuality and identity, specifically their sexuality. Few others performed their job as a stage role trying just to appear right and not exerting beyond 'surface acting'. Such employees repelled the employer's endeavors to in-depth indoctrination.

They could veer and swap between various moods and emotions like smile, chuckle, and compassion as contextually needed. Nevertheless, such surface acting could fall off as well under the pressure of a break-down due to rage, vexation or revolt.

Source: Hochschild, A. R. (1983). *"The Managed Heart: Commercialization of Human Feeling"*. Berkeley: University of California Press.

Such inconsistency in research findings can be explained by a popular proposition stipulating that individuals differ in their ability to articulate inauthentic or fictitious expression of emotions.

Some people may be committed and capable of identifying with the values of organization with regard to positive emotional communication, making them better prepared to express desirable emotions. In general, cheerful and pleasant people might be better equipped to turn-off negative emotions more easily than others.

The potential negative effects of emotional labor can be minimized by assessing the extent of emotional labor in our work and practicing detached involvement in our jobs, while following various stress management strategies and techniques.

Individual Strategies to Counter Emotional Labor

- **EXPRESSING AUTHENTIC AND POSITIVE EMOTION:** We should never forget that we need not manage our emotions at work at all times. We have the freedom to be authentically ebullient jovial, positive and exuberant. This eliminates the need to deal with either stress, emotional exhaustion or burnout.

- **USING HUMOR:** Humor lightens the seriousness in perception of a situation enabling those handling emotional labor tasks to take a different view of the situation and retaining their sense of control. Hilarity also facilitates the release of negative emotions arising out of tense situations while laughter helps us in experiencing positive emotion, removing the prospect of draining resources in managing negative emotion.
- **DEVELOPING FRIENDSHIPS AT WORK:** Research has evidenced that people who befriend colleagues at work are likely to be more satisfied with their work-life. Friendships at work facilitate close communication, understanding and sharing that result in minimized impact of emotional stressors.

EI PERSPECTIVE The Attorney and the Raisins

This is a story about an attorney who fought fierce court battles vigorously defending his clients who were embittered by the injustices meted out to them. His career was enflamed by anger and outrage which invigorated his commitment to pursue his cases with fiery arguments, burning midnight oil, researching and preparing for them. Deeply moved by his clients' problems, he relentlessly worked hard through sleepless nights scheming his legal strategies.

The attorney, on one of his vacations, met a meditation instructor and sought her guidance on meditation. He was taken aback when she gave him a few raisins and asked him to eat one of them slowly with focused attention and guided him to concentrate on the moment. She instructed him to feel and relish the opulence of every moment and sensation in the entire process. She guided him step-by-step to focus on feeling the sensations from the moment he lifted the raisin to his mouth to the gush of flavors as he chewed and the sounds that accompanied his eating. He was so absorbed in the process that he submerged himself in the richness of experience from his senses. He was then instructed to bring the same focused attention and concentration to his breathing while relieving his mind from the flood of thoughts by letting them out. He was surprised to find the voices in his mind quietening after he continued focusing and meditating on his natural breathing for the next fifteen minutes. With this exercise, he felt being tuned into a Zen-like state, instantly refreshing his mind with tranquility and serenity which he liked so immensely that he made it his daily habit.

This type of activity is termed as mindfulness meditation. Directing our full attention to our senses results in calming our mind from its habitual babble. Brain scans taken during mindfulness meditation showed that it subdued the brain circuits from self-focused mental gabble which gives us immense relief .• Neuroscientist Davidson explains that engrossment or concentration brings our mind back from roaming state to focus on a specific activity due to which we are likely to disable the circuits of its habitual patterns. He adds that one cannot brood over self while engrossed in a formidable task. This is why people develop a passion for adventure sports and mountaineering where one is totally engrossed and consumed, as Davidson explains. Potent concentration elevates the sense of joy and peace.

•Farb, Norman A. S., Segal, Zindel V., Mayberg, Helen, Bean, Jim, McKeon, Deborah, Fatima, Zainab and Anderson, Adam K. (2007). "Attending to the present: Mindfulness meditation reveals distinct neural modes of self reference". *Social Cognitive and Affective Neuroscience*, 2 (4): 313–322.

Source: Goleman, D. (2013). "*Focus: The hidden driver of excellence*". New Delhi: Bloomsbury Publishing India, Pp. 48.

- **PRACTICING MINDFULNESS:** More often than not, we engage our mind in thinking about our regrets, failures, and future. Mindfulness practices enable us to dislodge our baggage of emotional stressors by non-judgmental focus on the present moment. Mindfulness practices help us achieve a balanced or neutral state of mind, eliminating stress levels and emotional exhaustion. A study published in the *Journal of Applied Psychology* confirmed that people practicing mindfulness interventions experienced lower levels of emotional exhaustion and enhanced levels of satisfaction.[80]

Implications of Emotional Labor for Organizations

It is an overriding concern for organizations to take notice of this infestation and initiate proactive steps to assist employees, helping them deal with the effects of emotional labor. Organizations should objectively assess the impact of emotional exhaustion and burnout periodically along with their regular employee appraisals. It is also essential to seek expert advice in dealing with the effects of emotional labor in organizations.

Organizational Strategies to Counter Emotional Labor

The following strategies may help address the challenges of emotional labor:

- **CREATING AN ENABLING AND CARING CULTURE:** A culture of openness, receptivity, and tolerance creates a sense of belongingness and caring among employees working in service delivery roles which are demanding. In a study of 334 employees at a service firm, organizational support was found to reduce the impact of emotional labor on employee satisfaction and performance.[81]

Supportive culture may include, amongst other things, doing the following:

1) Connecting and reaching out when in need of help
2) Voicing concerns and feelings honestly without any apprehensions
3) Developing reliable friendships at workplace
4) Make use of training to help in getting better in service delivery roles
5) Take part in decision-making process in order to feel in control

- **TRAINING FOR EMOTIONAL INTELLIGENCE:** Despite the multi-million dollar budgets for skill-based job-training, most employees in the hospitality sector learn to manage emotions on their own. Training might reduce the incidence burnout and emotional exhaustion among employees, which adversely affect their performance. Emotional intelligence training may enhance employees' abilities in the areas of using and managing their own emotions as well as the emotions of others with whom they interact.
- **PROVIDING PSYCHOLOGICAL SAFETY:** Psychological safety may be defined as the ability to demonstrate and apply one's self without being apprehensive about adverse consequences on self-image, status or career.[82]

EI PERSPECTIVE Emotional Independence

This is a story of a man who regularly traveled by bus to his workplace, every morning. Day in and day out, this man had to encounter the bus driver who was habitually harsh with a sullen demeanor. Passengers had to invariably encounter this resentful bus driver who was always blunt and rude while addressing the commuters. But this particular passenger, mentioned at the start of this narration, was always polite and courteous in his responses to the pungent and repugnant driver despite his rude behavior. One of his co-passengers asked him as to why he was putting up with such an intimidating behavior of the driver. In reply, he stated that he was asserting his independence by refusing to let the driver command or influence him on how he should react to his demeanor. He had in fact exercised his emotional independence.

Source: Joseph, P. T. SJ. (2007). "*EQ and Leadership*". New Delhi: Tata McGraw-Hill Publishing Company Ltd., pp.85.

People experiencing psychological safety at their workplace have a sense of kinship and a feeling of being valued. They rarely feel apprehensive about facing rejection from coworkers. People working in customer service roles face considerable uncertainty in the situations experienced by them. Comfortable and unconstrained work environments promoting spontaneity aid in minimizing the level of uncertainty in service delivery encounters and the resulting emotional strain and drain. A study conducted across 178 respondents in 27 service management teams at a restaurant in the year 2014, found that greater levels of psychological safety are linked with higher degree of team cohesion and performance.[72]

PITFALLS OF EMOTIONAL INTELLIGENCE [83]

Having discussed a multitude of positive effects concerning emotional intelligence in the above sections, the pertinent question that remains to be answered is whether higher levels of EQ are always beneficial. Despite the dearth of evidence on the adverse effects of emotional intelligence, it is logical to be cautious with a 'single-size-fits-all' approach or with the assumption that more of a good thing is always better. In general, there is a downside to every human disposition or attribute and almost everything is good at moderate levels. In the following sections, some of the not-so-favorable effects of higher EQ are explored.

- **Minimal Levels of Creativity and Innovation:** Emotional quotient is negatively correlated with certain traits that are inclined with creativity and innovation. Certain traits reflecting low EQ like artistic impulsiveness, dissidence, belligerent impetuousness and a volatile (vacillating up and down) personality have long been associated with creativity. It may be possible for creative people to be emotionally intelligent by building relations, following established processes and working with others, but the desirable levels of nonconformity and unconventionality that challenge the status quo and drive change would be severely hampered in them. Creative people may be molded into conforming and contented people with serenity and stability in their persona and relationships.
- **Inhibiting Feedback:** Emotionally intelligent people are expected to be at ease in giving and receiving negative feedback, but it might be an extremely difficult task for highly empathetic and interpersonally sensitive people. On the other hand, some people with high EQ may become insensitive to negative feedback while trying to maintain high levels of emotional balance through self-regulation. Undeniably, it could be immensely difficult to shake up people with high EQ scores as they are usually serene, accommodative and optimistic.
- **Inhibitive of Tough Calls:** Though high EQ levels are desirable in people at entry-level positions, mid-level management jobs and followers and senior leadership roles demand capabilities required to make tough calls, make unpopular decisions and drive results even at the expense of strained employee relations. Besides, senior-level leaders and executives are expected to demonstrate entrepreneurial capabilities in pursuit of growth and to drive innovation. Such an orientation requires people to be bold, cold-blooded and unhesitant in taking unpopular decisions which the high EQ people are unlikely to demonstrate as they are focused more on getting along than getting ahead.

- **Risk Aversion:** People need to perform a difficult balancing act between risk-taking and risk-avoidance, risk and reward in most of the innovative business endeavors. Since high EQ is associated with conscientiousness, emotionally intelligent people predictably chose to play safe avoiding risky choices and making measured decisions resisting impulses. Since EQ corresponds to self-regulation, a high degree of self-control turns inimical leading to perfectionism and risk avoidance.
- **Manipulative Tactics:** Stretching emotional intelligence farther can encourage people to use manipulative tactics to influence others for own advantage. Such tactics may involve excessive use of social skills, emotional communication devoid of logic and transactional elements. Such manipulative tactics using EQ drive people to become excessively persuasive in order to pursue their personal agenda. On similar lines with charisma, EQ is also regarded as a positive trait while at the same time, it can be applied in exploitative ways and used for achieving unethical goals as well.
- **Ideal Managers and Pathetic Leaders:** Emotional intelligence is the most desirable and chameleonic ability and it is intelligible that people prefer to be rated high on EQ rather than scoring low. But infatuation with high EQ would surely produce happy, emotionally stable and diplomatic employees who dabble along zealously following rules rather than driving change and innovation. They would be anything but visionary leaders and change agents, making for great followers and good managers.

CAN EMOTIONAL INTELLIGENCE BE ACQUIRED?

The question of whether emotional intelligence can be acquired and developed has become one of the most contentious features of emotional intelligence. Strong proponents of developmental school of emotional intelligence like Goleman contend that genuine and ideal training programs can help people, for instance, in changing from being pessimists to optimists within a few weeks.[17]

On the other hand, equally opposing arguments contend that, logically, emotional intelligence cannot be acquired or learned. Such contentions emanate from personality theory (specifically the trait theory) and neurological evidence. The proposition that personality traits are shaped by the genes which persist from childhood to adulthood and remain steady over time is strongly evidenced in the research.

EI PERSPECTIVE Michael Jordan

When he was in his freshman college year at the University of North Carolina, the acclaimed Michael Jordan was disheartened and disillusioned with college basketball so much that he once decided to quit and headed back home. By providence, he was brought back by the assistant coach and his life changed thereafter. Eventually, the magical moments of his transformation emerged in a game played at the end of that season in 1982, during the finals against Georgetown University. The scores were tied and Jordon had the ball in his hands when the last few seconds of the game were left to be played. He played the shot hitting the net, winning the national championship for North Carolina and the court reverberated with the shouts of student body chanting "superman, superman" at Jordan and thereafter his life changed like never before.

Forever thereafter, Jordan insisted that he had the ball in his hand whenever the game was on wire as he believed at heart that he could make it happen. He did not merely think that he could do it, but he knew and believed that he could. As the German philosopher Friedrich Nietzsche aptly said, "Power accedes to those who takes it" and Jordan took it into his hands whenever he laced up to race.

Such a belief and attitude transformed him into the most fascinating basketball player and living legend. Jordan became a legend on account of the college shot that he took when the game was on wire, and he told a reporter that he became fearless after that shot.

Source: Landrum, G. N. (1999). "*Eight Keys to Greatness — How to Unlock Your Hidden Potential*". Mumbai: Magna Publishing Co. Ltd.

Despite the traits being ubiquitous and enduring, they evidently pursue a developmental path. Between the age of late adolescence and thirty years, traits of neuroticism, extraversion and openness to experience are inclined to decrease, but agreeableness and conscientiousness tend to increase. These traits are enduringly sustained throughout the adult life span, despite a more gradual shift in this trend as one advances in age.[84] Hence as proposed by trait theorists, it may be possible to train people in emotional intelligence, changing certain attitudes and behaviors, but bringing in enduring and deep change in personality is extremely difficult.

Since personality traits are so strong, any change brought about in behavior or attitude may be peripheral and interim in nature.[85] There is also a neurological explanation to the argument concerning the extent of learnability of emotional intelligence competencies.

Research has shown that it is possible to identify distinct type of intelligence (other than the IQ) by analyzing the PET (Positron-emission Tomography) scans of patients with lesions in certain parts of the brain, specifically the amygdala and the pre-frontal cortex.[86] Given the premise that emotional intelligence is evidently different from cognitive intelligence since it does not involve neocortical connections (which can be acquired or enhanced by learning), it can plausibly be concluded that EI skills cannot be learned or developed.

Apparently, the contention that emotional intelligence is genetically shaped and therefore is stable rather than dynamic in nature is endorsed by the neurological support for emotional intelligence to a certain extent. Acknowledging the role of genes in shaping emotional intelligence, Emmerling and Goleman[87] highlighted the fact that geneticists themselves accepted nature's ability to mold gene expression.

EI PERSPECTIVE From Task focus to People focus

An episode narrated by the famous researcher, Richard Boyatzis to another popular researcher, author and trainer, Daniel Goleman is discussed here. There was a manager who joined an Executive program as a student for improving his skills in developing relationships. He hailed from an engineering background which influenced his thinking and approach to perform a job. Whenever a task was entrusted to him, he could only visualize the task, its components and structure but was never able to focus on the people he worked with, in the process of accomplishing the task.

Given his persona and approach to work, his learning objective and agenda became clear. He had to expend his time thinking about and perceiving how the other person feels and thinks. To practice developing this competence in a low risk environment outside his work, he started coaching the members of his son's soccer team. Here in this coaching engagement, he had opportunities to focus on the feelings and perceptions of the players whom he trained and in the process, he trained himself to acquire the skills of developing relationships.

Source: Goleman, D. (2013). "*Focus: The hidden driver of excellence*". New Delhi: Bloomsbury Publishing India, Pp. 174.

They also questioned the common misbelief that developing emotions was an effortless and unchallenging exercise. They contended that the pursuit of developing emotional intelligence demands undiluted commitment, sustained effort, and involvement of the person at the deepest level. Finally, they supported their contention with research findings from a longitudinal study of the Weatherhead MBA program, which found that emotional intelligence was developed to the extent of 50 percent in a span of seven years after the completion of the program.[88] These researchers cited support from neurological research which evidenced that the emotional centers of the brain — the amygdala and pre-frontal cortex among others — may undoubtedly possess the plasticity to change.[89]

THE DARK SIDE OF EMOTIONAL INTELLIGENCE

A self-seeking individual with Machiavellian orientation may have a high degree of emotional intelligence capabilities which may be used for identifying and manipulating others' weaknesses for own advantage. In extreme cases, people with antisocial personality disorder may be equipped with social skills enabling them to exploit others despite their imperfections in other domains of emotional functioning.[90a]

Different types of counterproductive behaviors at workplace like deceit, or imposture, subversion, sexual harassment and vandalism may be attributed to some extent to dysfunctional emotional responses.[90b]

There is an increasing inquest in the recent years on the use of socio-emotional intelligence for opportunistic and exploitative purposes toward self-aggrandizement through covert use of emotional manipulation.[91]

An emotionally astute individual is adept at judicious use of emotional knowledge for attaining multiple goals including self-progression, similar to a cognitively intelligent individual's ability to swiftly discern options and draw insightful conclusions.[92] With this perspective, individuals high on emotional intelligence may be likened to the character of Iago in Shakespeare's novel Othello, who is described as one who regulates and controls his own emotions and also a manipulator of others' emotions.

EI PERSPECTIVE Napoleon Bonaparte

Colonel Napoleon Bonaparte transformed into the world's greatest military prodigy and the battle of Lodi in Italy provided the context for the same. At the age of 24, Napoleon fought a battle that he was predicted to fail. Many years later, he wrote about his revelation and vision elucidating that the battle of Lodi was the inflexion point for his energy and surge to glory and fortune. Thereafter, Napoleon started believing himself to be a superhuman paragon as a result of which he envisioned and nurtured ambitions of greatest accomplishments.

He fought a strong army of 70,000 of combined forces in April 1796 with his 30,000 soldiers. He drove his soldiers into exerting superhuman effort and won a decisive victory outplaying the conventional warfare and martial maneuvers against all odds and logic. Thereafter, enflamed by an internal transformation, he developed a strong conviction that he was an invincible superhuman unconquerable by mortals.

He started to translate his convictions into actionable behavior. In addition to the battleground, the French political arena turned out to be a fertile ground for Napoleon's capabilities and ambitions to establish himself as an indomitable ruler. Napoleon was enthroned as the First Consul of France within three years, despite his Italian descent. Thereafter, in another five years, he was proclaimed the Emperor and within the subsequent five years, Napoleon defeated all of the European powers.

Sources: 1) Markham, Felix (2010). "*Napoleon*". New York: Penguin Books
2) Landrum, G. N. (1999). "*Eight Keys to Greatness — How to Unlock Your Hidden Potential*". Mumbai: Magna Publishing Co. Ltd.

People high on emotional intelligence and adept in modulating their own emotions and those of others may be compared with Iago.[50c, 64, 93]

Scarce resources trigger increased competition in archetypal organizations in which case, emotionally intelligent individuals might apply their skills and emotional competencies in the furtherance of their own self-interest at the workplace, albeit at the expense of others. Emotionally intelligent individuals may be motivated to behave strategically in pursuit of self-interest given their ability to regulate their own and others' emotions. Strategic behavior implies specific goal-directed or goal-oriented behavior.

EI PERSPECTIVE Practices Promoting Positive Behavior

- Louisiana based healthcare provider, Ochsner Health System, adopted a system termed by them as "the $^{10}/_{5}$ way" that was practiced by all their healthcare staff. This practice requires the healthcare staff to make eye contact and smile if they are within 10 feet of someone. When they are within 5 feet of somebody, they are to wish that person by saying hello. As a result of this practice, Ochsner witnessed a surge in patient satisfaction and an increase in patient referrals.
- With the objective of identifying positive actions and encouraging employees towards right deeds, Zappos put into practice an employee recognition program termed as "Wow". Employees at any level can bestow a "Wow" prize carrying a cash bonus of up to $50, to any other employee found doing something remarkable. All such "Wow" awardees become eligible for a "Hero" trophy for which the awardees are selected by top executives. Heroes receive many privileges like covered parking slot for a month, a Zappos gift card of $150 with full ceremonial fanfare and a hero's cape. Such small rewards could be strong emblems of civility and positive behaviors.
- A successful restaurant chain owner in Manhattan, Danny Meyer has a stringent policy of intolerance for incivility among his staff. He is unhesitant in firing even the most talented and accomplished employees for their uncivil behavior. Accomplished but impudent chefs won't survive at his restaurants as they pollute the atmosphere by spreading bad vibes. Mayer is convinced that his customers can smell and feel the pungent dish of employee incivility despite such behaviors happening in the kitchen.
- It has been a few years since Cisco conducted an elaborate exercise of assessing and quantifying the cost of incivility. The company presumed that incivility among its employees would be extremely low on account of its consistent reputation as a great place to work. When the company estimated the cost of incivility among its employees at $12 million despite its reputation, the revelation led to realization. To counter the incivility, the company instituted Cisco global workplace civility program.

Source: Porath, Christina and Pearson, Christine (2015). "The price of incivility". *Harvard Business Review,* January-February 2013 (R1301J).

It is a fact that job seekers regulate their emotional and body language to communicate effectively and influence hiring decisions to their advantage in interviews.[94] Some researchers cautioned against exploitative and manipulative tactics of emotionally intelligent people.[95] Recovery agents and collection staff show displeasure and anger while collecting dues,[96] while employees in service delivery roles wear smiles and exhibit enthusiasm to enhance perceived quality of service.[97] "Emotional labor" denotes managing emotions in tune with the requirements of a job. In a similar fashion, employees may also regulate their emotions in pursuit of self-interests.

As early as in the year 1959, Goffman[98] explored the social interactions of people involving expressions and behaviors directed to influence the perceptions of others. Goffman's research has already explained how some people were adept at regulating their emotions with the intent of strategically affecting the behaviors and attitudes of others, much before the advent of emotional intelligence. It is imperative that people skilled in emotional management could apply such expertise to their gainful advantage in promotion tournaments in the context of organizations characterized by competitive workplaces.[99] The abilities of perceiving emotions of self and others, and utilizing emotional intelligence to facilitate thinking are essential pre-requisites of focused attention on strategic goals.

Individuals high on emotional intelligence may judiciously deploy their emotional abilities, focusing only on people whose attitudes and behaviors facilitate or impede their goals while ignoring others who are not relevant in context. Those competing for organizational positions to advance their careers predictably use emotional intelligence to discern targeted people, including their managers and key subordinates, for an edge over their rivals while ignoring less influential ones. Emotionally intelligent people are capable of consciously configuring their emotions to concoct favorable perceptions about themselves and such people could use their emotional intelligence to fortify their connections with supervisors. A subordinate may, for instance, discover a sign of despondency in the face of a supervisor and offer to help by seeking to know the cause of distress in an empathic demeanor. Empathizing with a supervisor can establish an emotional connect which may be beneficial to the subordinate in other situations.[100] An apparently spontaneous and instinctive behavior serves a strategic purpose. Though individuals convey emotions that are expedient and conducive to their objectives, their demonstration may diverge from their innate feelings.

EI PERSPECTIVE CEO Fires an Employee in Public

On a cloudy Friday afternoon in August 2013, Tim Armstrong, the CEO of AOL, attended a crowded conference for the second time that week, at the company's headquarters in Manhattan. There were more than a hundred employees of his news subsidiary, 'Patch' in attendance and several hundred more telephonically joining the meeting. In his prior visit two days earlier, Armstrong announced that he was committed to honor his earlier assurance to AOL's shareholders to make Patch profitable by the year-end and that he would meet the AOL's Board the next day to chalk-out a plan and he would be back at Patch on Friday to announce the plan. So, employees were expecting that he would be breaking serious news. At the current gathering, the employees of Patch were tensed as they anticipated that making Patch profitable would entail mass layoffs — that may include people in the room — which would be announced in this meeting. Armstrong began his speech by announcing that he was going to ask people to leave though not meaning to be in a harsh demeanor but for leading Patch towards enduring success. In a heated tone, he said that people may blame him for everything that went wrong for Patch and that he wouldn't care if the press wrote against him. He directed each one of them present in that room to commit themselves to the company completely. It was then that suddenly something unusual happened. Armstrong interrupted himself and asked Abel Lenz, the creative director of Patch to put his camera down right then. Thereafter, he declared in a high-pitched voice that Abel was fired. The entire room became silent for a few seconds. Finally, Armstrong started to speak again contradicting people's assumption that AOL neglected its commitment to Patch. He stressed that such an assumption was absolutely baseless.

Such words of motivation usually charged up everyone in that room, but that didn't happen because people were shocked by what Armstrong had just done. Quickly as the news spread, hundreds of thousands of people outside of AOL's headquarters felt the same sense of shock. A leader's actions set the emotional tune for the organization affecting the morale of its employees. For hapless Armstrong, his aggressive and impulsive act of firing Lenz completely sabotaged the commitment he expected to induce in Patch employees. As Maya Angelou said, "People will forget what you said and did, but they will never forget how you made them feel". Few days thereafter, Armstrong apologized to Abel Lenz in private and then to all AOL employees in public. But by then, the news was broadcast in the mainstream channels including Yahoo and the Daily Mail. Some people felt that the public firing was like a bad-tempered CEO's move, likening with the acts of popular and demanding CEOs, such as Steve Jobs or Larry Ellison. But most people near and far perceived it as an unwarranted and humiliating act by a leader. People wondered what went wrong with Tim Armstrong and speculated on what kind of a CEO fires a hapless employee in front of all his colleagues and what was going on at AOL?

Sources: **(1)** Top Five Emotional Intelligence Moments of 2013 by Travis Bradberry https://www.forbes.com/sites/travisbradberry/2014/01/08/top-five-emotional-intelligence-moments-of-2013/#223911ab710e

(2) The Cost of Winning: Tim Armstrong, Patch and The Struggle to save AOL by *Nicholas Carlson*. November 7, 2013.

(3) https://www.businessinsider.in/THE-COST-OF-WINNING-Tim-Armstrong-Patch-And-The-Struggle-To-Save-AOL/articleshow/25355140.cms.

In strong competitive organizational contexts and cultures promoting and rewarding competitive performance, people most likely adopt winning as a primary aspiration regardless of risk or expense, similar to the happenings at Enron[101] and at Salomon Brothers.[102]

People search for cues from rivals to discern their relative position in competitive situations. They deploy emotional scanners on the faces and kinesics of rivals for any signs of predictable competition or collaboration as mirrored in their body language[103] and for any signs of rivals' focal agenda, i.e., either to get along or to get ahead.[104] An emotionally astute individual plausibly understands the significance of emotional gesticulation in bargaining contexts with rivals and would be able to identify the possibility of integrated solutions. Typically, when people gain power in organizations, they are likely to perceive others as channels to be used for achieving their goals.[105] People vested with high power in organizations typically use negative emotional expression due to uninhibited expression backed by high interpersonal power.[105] However, any capability or competence for that matter, can be used either for constructive or for destructive purposes as well; for achieving organizational objectives or to serve individual agenda of people in power. Same is the case with science and scientific discoveries as well — using the power of science for the welfare of people at large or for destructive purposes like war or sophisticated exploitation and loot. Frankly speaking, even professional managerial capabilities could be deployed for engaging in organizational politics and power plays for securing individual dominance over resources or for accumulating power or for serving personal interests of an individual at the cost of a larger group. Even emotional intelligence is a powerful tool which could be used for individual, group, organizational and societal well-being and for actualization of human potential or for exploitative purposes.

Emotional intelligence is a distinct and valued construct that can be plotted, nurtured and developed and is relevant for application in a wide variety of settings in workplace. Its positive impact on leadership effectiveness, change and crisis management, stress management, team building, organizational and individual performance and a host of applications in human resource management has been evidenced.

Being an emerging area of scientific investigation, the terrain of emotional intelligence remains unexplored to a great extent.[106] The influence of culture and gender upon emotional intelligence and its conceptualizations remain significantly unexplored.[107] The experience and articulation of emotions are influenced by the norms domiciled in culture.[108] In collectivistic cultures like India, people may subjugate and control the expression of emotions in the interests of their group or society, while it may be entirely different in individualistic cultures.[109]

Another area of concern is the heterogeneity reflected in diverse approaches to emotional intelligence which justifies the need for a clear conceptualization and universal definition.[110] In the interest of clarity and universality in its application, it is necessary that the term "emotional intelligence" be confined to abilities at the intersection of emotions and intelligence, specifically restricted to abilities applied in reasoning about emotions and the use of emotions to enhance reasoning.[21]

Further research is wanting in the areas of conceptual unanimity, measurement rigor, and culture-specific dimensions of emotional intelligence. Research evidenced thus far indicates that emotional intelligence has a promising role in the current corporate context of collaborative structures and work teams. And the EI's ability to provide immunity from stress, burnout, work-life imbalance and emotional labor is immensely relevant in today's corporate world. It is increasingly becoming evident that emotional intelligence is a valuable resource to fight the web of inexplicable corporate and social trauma resulting from the dynamic and unpredictable change unleashed by the context of competitive warfare in this modern business world.

Chapter Synthesis

Emotion encompasses every facet of our life shaping our relationship with the world. Everything that we do — both good and bad — is driven by emotion. We televise our expressions of emotions on our faces and auditory channels. Emotion without reasoning and logic makes a man an emotional animal and rationality without emotion is a machine devoid of feelings and choices. Thorndike named one form of intelligence as social intelligence. Wechsler mooted both cognitive and non-cognitive constituents of intelligence. The concept of emotional intelligence was first contrived by Leon Payne in a Ph.D. thesis. Daniel Goleman's book triggered interest in emotional intelligence and gained explosive popularity. Reuven Bar-On developed an emotional intelligence measure by using the term "Emotional Quotient" for the first time. Despite the popularity, emotional intelligence attracted the critical scanner of research community which raised questions on its scientific validity and measurement. In spite of tall claims on the predictive power of emotional intelligence, research evidence was mixed, and contemporary theorists became watchful. Several studies found support for positive influence and utility of emotional intelligence in various aspects of daily life, such as life satisfaction, health and fitness, reciprocity and bonding, romantic and marital relationships, and psychological stress. It was also found to be negatively correlated with troublesome behavior. Emotional intelligence was also found to be associated with positive workplace behaviors and outcomes like economic value addition, creative problem solving, decision making, good judgement, job satisfaction, helping behavior, collaborative conflict resolution practices, team morale and mood, help generate innovative ideas, and longer tenure with the organization. Several studies found EI to be an essential ingredient in managing change and effective leadership behaviors specifically transformational leadership style. Even the Ohio State University studies on leadership, undertaken much prior to the advent of emotional intelligence, found support for emotional dimensions of leadership.

The concept of emotional labor was coined and described by Arlie Hochschild as a phenomenon where employees in service delivery roles display positive emotions even when the clients are most aggressive or unpleasant, suppressing their true emotions. Emotional labor is characteristic of service roles but its adverse impact manifests in emotional exhaustion, stress and burn-out. Various individual and organizational strategies have been advocated to minimize the adverse impact of emotional labor.

Despite the findings about the positive effects of emotional intelligence, several pitfalls and concerns have been brought out by the researchers and theorists. EI is negatively correlated with creativity and innovation which is associated with certain traits like artistic impulsiveness, volatility and dissidence which in turn are opposite traits of emotional intelligence. Emotionally intelligent people may find it difficult to give and receive negative feedback, while possessing a tendency to avoid risks and might also convert their EI skills into manipulative tactics for exploitative purposes.

Another issue that was extensively debated concerns the learnability of emotional intelligence skills. From the personality theory and neurological perspectives, it is argued that personality is shaped by the genes which persist from childhood to adulthood and remain relatively stable over time. Since emotional intelligence also comprises certain personality traits, it is contended that emotional intelligence training may change certain attitudes and behaviors peripherally, but bringing about enduring change is extremely difficult as personality traits are so strong. This contention was countered by geneticists' acceptance of nature's ability to mold gene expression. Furthermore, it was demonstrated by a longitudinal study that emotional intelligence is indeed learnable with deepest level of commitment, sustained effort and involvement of the person undergoing the training.

Another insight concerns the dark side of emotional intelligence. A self-seeking individual with Machiavellian orientation having a high degree of emotional intelligence may use it for identifying and manipulating others' weaknesses for personal gain. Individuals high on emotional intelligence may deploy their emotional abilities on people whose attitudes and behaviors facilitate or impede their goals. However, any capability for that matter can be used for both constructive and destructive purposes; either for achieving organizational goals or to serve individual agenda. Similar is the case with scientific inventions as well, applying the power of science for the welfare of people at large or for destructive purposes like war and sophisticated loot.

Emotional intelligence is a distinct and valued construct that can be plotted, nurtured and developed and is relevant for application in a wide variety of settings in workplace. Being an emerging area of scientific investigation, the terrain of emotional intelligence remains unexplored to a great extent.

Further research is required in the areas of conceptual unanimity, measurement rigor, and culture-specific dimensions of emotional intelligence. Research evidenced thus far indicates that emotional intelligence has a promising role in the current corporate context of collaborative structures and work teams. And the EI's ability to provide immunity from stress, burnout, work-life imbalance and emotional labor is immensely relevant in today's corporate world.

Key Terms

Social intelligence
Ability model
Mixed model
Psychological maturity
Emotional conscience
Social well-being
Psychological adjustment
Psychological stress
Optimism
Mood
Subjective weariness
Non-cognitive pay-offs
Positive organizational citizenship
Altruistic behavior
Interpersonal sensitivity
Affective commitment
Psychological safety
Team cohesion
Transformational leadership
Transactional leadership
Idealized influence
Inspirational motivation
Intellectual stimulation
Individualized consideration
Compliance
Emotional quotient inventory (EQ-i)
Emotional labor
Dispositional behaviors
Surface acting
Deep acting
Emotional exhaustion
Authentic emotions
Mindfulness
Artistic impulsiveness
Manipulative abilities
Machiavellian orientation
Visionary leaders
Conscientiousness
Position-emission tomography (PET)
Promotion tournaments
Intrinsic behavior
Emotional scanners
Collectivist cultures
Collaborative structures

Review Questions

1. How does emotional intelligence influence our daily life, our romantic and marital relations?
2. Examine how emotional intelligence influences psychological stress, health and well-being.
3. In what ways does emotional intelligence influence workplace behavior and leadership phenomenon?
4. What is emotional labor and what are its consequences? Suggest strategies for individuals and organizations to deal with emotional labor.
5. What are the likely adverse effects of high emotional quotient?
6. Is emotional intelligence hereditary, part of personality or acquired? Discuss whether people can be trained in emotional intelligence competencies.
7. Explore the dark side of emotional intelligence. How can emotional intelligence be applied for opportunistic and exploitative purposes through emotional manipulation?
8. What is your take on emotional intelligence as valid and useful which can be developed and applied for constructive purposes by individuals and organizations? Justify your arguments.

Application-based Exercise

Emotion versus Reason in Judgement

You might have encountered many situations in which you are pulled in one direction by your rational mind while you are wobbled in another direction by your emotional mind. In such situations of a tug of war between your rational mind and emotional mind, writing down the arguments of each of the opposing sides of the issue would be of immense help. Such a written checklist provides clarity of thought, enabling you to consider the significance of emotions without being unduly influenced by them.

You can create the list by making two columns — using the left one to record the inclinations of your emotions and the right side for the advice of rational mind — enumerating the course of action preferred by your emotion and intellect. Scrutinize this written information to weigh the pros and cons of each side ensuring that neither reasoning nor emotions are dominating your choice and masking your judgement. Over-reliance on reason would be mechanical and insensitive, while being driven by emotions would blind your common sense. Reducing the rational versus emotional arguments into a written-down checklist compels you to think both ways and appraise the situation logically and passionately.

Therefore, whenever you face a predicament, dilemma or tricky situation or when you feel stressed due to a persistent problem, confine yourself to a quiet place, arrange your thoughts on the issue and write down the 'reason vs. emotion' list of alternatives on a sheet of paper. Make this a habit until you master the technique and gain independence from the skewed influences of pure intellect or unalloyed emotion. When you have the list before you, the issues become threadbare and transparent, making it simpler for you to decide whether you should go by the counsel of emotional or that of rational parts of your mind in each situation.

Activities Beyond the Book

Self-Awareness through Journal of Emotions

1. By sundown each day, write down all the emotions and feelings that you have encountered and felt throughout the day in a notebook. Also mention the causes and triggers of each emotion that you experience, however small or insignificant it may be.
2. Review your emotional record after a month and see if there are any patterns emerging. For instance, you may find that you experience specific emotions more frequently than the others like feeling stressed or depressed most of the time or being irritable consistently. Also analyze if you are experiencing similar emotions time and again recurrently, arising on account of the same reason or source. For instance, stressed out due to deadlines, social interactions, sense of insecurity or low self-esteem, etc.
3. Through this analysis of your emotions, you will be able to identify some possible solutions or modifications that you may institute in your approach, behavior, disposition, or inner state to mitigate or lighten your anxiety or stress. You may also uncover strategies to work through other negative emotions so as to minimize their impact on your efficient day-to-day functioning.

Video Resources

1. **The Explainer: Emotional Intelligence**
   Link: https://www.youtube.com/watch?reload=9&v=bcLf_Ozw4lc
2. **Keys to Leadership – *Richard Boyatzis***
   Link: https://youtu.be/54IKJbSoR0w
3. **Leadership and Compassion – *Daniel Goleman***
   Link: https://youtu.be/TnTuDDbrkCQ
4. **The Power of Empathy: TEDx Middlebury – *Helen Riess***
   Link: https://youtu.be/baHrcC8B4WM
5. **The Light and Dark of Emotional Intelligence: TEDx Plymouth University – *Alison Bacon.***
   Link: https://www.youtube.com/watch?v=xqPJKtFI42U
6. **Emotional Intelligence: How to Control your Negative Emotions & Thinking – *Skillopedia.***
   Link: https://www.youtube.com/watch?reload=9&v=6-IfiKkHkr8
7. **The Birth of Emotional Intelligence in India: TEDx CRCE – *Sneh Vaswani.***
   Link: https://www.youtube.com/watch?v=1enO9bD514g
8. **Emotions – The Hidden Messages: Positive revolution – *Bonnie Kelly*.**
   Link: https://www.youtube.com/watch?v=B-ieqbSSrnY
9. **Emotional Intelligence: From Theory to Everyday Practice – *Marc Brackett*,** Yale University.
   Link: https://www.youtube.com/watch?v=e8JMWtwdLQ4
10. **How to make stress your friend: TED talk – *Kelly McGonigal***
    Link: https://www.youtube.com/watch?time_continue=15&v=RcGyVTAoXEU

Self-Assessment Instruments

Are you assertive, aggressive or passive?

Scores of individuals are confused about what it means to be assertive. Usually people lack clarity on the distinction between being aggressive and being assertive. Throughout each day, at all times, you would have a preference to react in a specific manner towards other people and external conditions. Such reactions can be categorized as either assertive or aggressive or still further as passive forms.

Your choice of response may be that you are adopting one of the above types of behavior all the time, usually or react aggressively at times with some people and passively with others on other occasions. However, sometimes you may feel that you should have responded in a different way, regulating your emotions and reactions. In such situations, the important prerequisite for changing your behavioral response is to comprehend the distinction between these types of behavioral responses.

Reflect on the following statements and check the box that reflects periodicity of your behavioral response (i.e. always, frequently, sometimes, and never):

Sl. No.	Description	Always	Frequently	Sometimes	Never
1	I feel threatened when people question my opinions, ideas or conduct.				
2	I am keen on leading a calm and undisturbed life and do not enjoy stirring up things.				
3	I can boldly seek anything that I want with conviction even at the risk of annoying others.				
4	I earnestly strive to pursue mutually advantageous results or positive outcomes for all.				
5	I prefer to be in charge of all my situations and steer through them.				
6	I can turn down the requests and demands of my counterparts and aides but have trouble refusing someone who can exert power or influence over me.				
7	I find it hard to remain composed while interacting with furious people.				
8	I am inclined to toe the line of majority, as I feel it is significant to ensure that others hold me in good esteem.				
9	I can regulate my emotions and stand fast in challenging situations.				
10	I feel compelled to concur with some people who have the canniness to make me feel inferior and deficient, despite my aversion to do so.				

Sl. No.	Description	Always	Frequently	Sometimes	Never
11	I could be temperamental and unstable when situations are not in my favor.				
12	I believe that my view is as important as that of others who wanted to express their views.				
13	I become furious when I sense that others are exploiting me, and I make them aware of it.				
14	I go a long way to avoid dissent with co-workers or associates to maintain congenial work environment which I feel is essential for good teamwork.				
15	I can endure a painful situation and speak my mind sincerely in a straightforward manner.				
16	When troubles pop-up, I would spontaneously accept responsibility for them.				
17	I do everything that I feel is needed with the belief that ends justify means.				

Scoring:

Questions	Choice of your response	Your disposition
7, 13, 5, 11, 17	Always or Often	Relatively **Aggressive**
1, 8, 2, 10, 6, 14, 16	Always or Often	Relatively **Passive**
9, 4, 12, 3, 15	Always or Often	**Assertive**

The type of behavioral response that you generally adopt (Aggressive, Passive or Assertive) would impact your job / occupation, your counterparts or associates and all those who form a part of your life. Hence, it is important for you to know your behavioral style.

Analysis of Select Movies

1. ***Good Will Hunting (1997)***

   Directed by Gus Van Sant and produced by Lawrence Bender, the film bagged two Oscars. This film is an account of a man's challenges in self-discovery and endeavors to position himself in this world. The movie takes us through the journey of Will Hunting, who is compelled to undergo psychological treatment in lieu of jail sentence. Guided by Sean, the therapist, Will traverses through self-discovery, reinventing himself. He realizes his self-worth through self-awareness while identifying his values and prioritizing them. The crux of the movie is the impactful encounters between a twenty-year old middle-class genius Will and a patently worn out mature therapist, Sean. Both are intensely impacted, unsettled and inspired by their relationship. The impact is such that they relinquish the pleasure of their old ways, leave their household and their town toward uncharted territory.

An inherently brilliant youngster, Will Hunting devours solving challenging puzzles that apparently other college students couldn't discern, while working as a janitor at MIT. Nevertheless, Will's childhood is beset with abuse and despair and so he is distraught despite his incredible intellect. Will successfully combats his misery and despondency through regular sessions with his therapist, Sean, and reconstructs his disarrayed life. This movie is worth watching for those looking for an inspiring, hilarious if you're looking for an uplifting, humorous masterpiece.

Despite the fact that Will can solve the toughest mathematical problem at the theoretical level, his own life seemed to be controlled by chaos theory as is referred to in mathematical terminology. While working as a janitor at MIT during the day, Will loiters around the bars and liquor joints with his vagabond buddies gulping beers and stirring brawls. Undoubtedly, it is his negative emotions as against his intellect, which control his life. It is no wonder that Will gets detained by police for an offense of onslaught, though not for the first time for such offence. His emotional imbalance and volatility often land him in prison. Nevertheless, the court of justice makes an unusual offer to Will, due to the helpful intervention of Professor Lambeau. Will is granted a conditional probation subject to his compliance with two requisites. The first condition is that Will studies mathematics under the guidance of Professor Lambeau and the second one requires him to attend therapeutic counseling sessions. Will accepts these conditions in order to avoid being jailed. He is guided by the counselor to identify his invisible potential while discovering that his gifted skills and abilities transcend beyond his intellect. He realizes the real significance of love and finds a girl who enables him to appreciate the true import of love. On the other hand, the story focuses on Will's self-exploration leading him to self-awareness — knowing himself beyond his persona as an intelligent working-class man that he is.

Deprived of a family, Will is raised up in foster home with an abusive and alcoholic father. People at large seldom grow up in perfect families and therefore it is essential that everyone learn to acclimatize with any type of family environment and continue to grow despite confronting toughest of situations. It is hard to comprehend that someone as dazzling as Will is not being able to attend any school whatsoever. Despite his ingenuity, Will's capabilities remain incognizant, blemished and unutilized without proper education. His crude family history acts as a deterrent to his motivation to pursue his education while being deficient to afford the same. He doesn't even believe that he is worthy of better things in life. The stereotyped contexts in this film are subdued by the emotions reflected in the narrative. The core element of this film is the emotional discourse that affects the inner most sensitivities of our hearts apart from probing the deep seated and unspeakable segments of life. Other important expositions of the film are trust, faith and love and the emotions associated therewith. Will finds closure for his quest in life and succeeds in finding meaning after permitting his girlfriend access to his unguarded emotional persona while accessing her true love.

However, despite its significance, education by itself is not an end in itself. In a way, the movie illustrates that life dedicated to education and devoid of positive emotions associated with love, faith and trust results in meaningless and disconsolate existence.

2. ***Charlie Bartlett (2008)***

The film is directed by Jon Poll and produced by Sidney Kimmel and others. Charlie Bartlett grows up without the support of a father, and battles with attention deficit hyperactivity disorder (ADHD), a sustained ailment typified by impetuous behavior, indifference, and hyperactivity. During his stint at public school, he discovers that he is not alone in this metal turmoil and many other kids suffer from various deep-seated disorders. These kids start seeking Charlie's counsel on their problems ranging from family problems, issues of their physical appearance, to sexuality and other problems bothering them. Despite his initial unorthodox methods of helping the kids solve their problems, he gradually gains insights through experience which enables him to find his veritable vocation.

Charlie Bartlett is the son of a single mother who is under the regular treatment of a therapist and has many prescriptions for psychological medications concerning her mental condition. He is shunted out of many private high schools owing to his escapades, such as crafting fake IDs and the like, in the course of his endeavors to become popular. Thereafter, he joins a public school and to tide over his concentration troubles, he obtains a prescription for the drug, "Ritalin" used in the treatment of attention deficit hyperactivity disorder. When he learns about the popularity of Ritalin among college kids, he decides to join hands with the brats to sell the drug.

Charlie is shown to be engaged in regular interaction with majority of students in his school ranging from well-known sports kids to the outcasts plagued with acute nervous disorders and self-destructive dispositions. He succeeds in subduing a school ruffian by counselling him on managing his anger. This incident triggers Charlie's popularity and sooner other kids start queuing up for his counseling in a temporary office set up by Charlie in a rest room at the school. Predominantly, most of the students approaching him for counseling and treatments are the ones neglected by their dual-career parents and overstretched teachers. Charlie looks into their symptoms and prescribes medicines based on the prescriptions obtained by him from other therapists by faking the same symptoms while consulting them. He also dispenses anti-depressants that he and his mother didn't need, and thus he becomes the unofficial psychological counselor cum pharmacist at the school. Charlie's popularity reaches its pinnacle and then plummets when one of the kids had an overdose of medicines prescribed by him. Realizing the unintentional harm caused due to him, Charlie pledges to discontinue medication while continuing with 'office hours' for students. Though the student community is annoyed by this decision, they continue to consult Charlie and talk to him about their problems. In fact, Charlie comes to the aid of many of these students by lending his ear and patiently listening to their problems and made himself a cult-figure of sorts. While Charlie is far from being a professional counsellor, he puts in his best efforts in this task. In a way, he seems to be overcoming his own psychological problems by empathizing with others' troubles and tribulations and trying to resolve them. At the end of the movie, Charlie is found assisting a kid in staging a play on the plight and problems of a high school student. Incidentally, the same kid who became critical due to overdose of drug prescribed by Charlie, happens to be staging the play. The movie closes with the scene showing Charlie attending an interview for a fiercely competitive internship position at a reputed psychiatric clinic.

3. ***It's a Wonderful Life (1946) Movie Analysis***

The movie, produced and directed by Frank Capra, is based on the story, The Greatest Gift, by Philip Van Doren Stern. It turned out to be one of the most adored movies in the U.S., where it became customary to watch it during Christmas time. The movie was nominated for five Academy Awards and the American Film Institute declared it as one of the 100 best American films ever made.

The storyline of the movie is about George Bailey, a psychologically defeated man burdened by financial liabilities and disappointment with himself as an individual. When he contemplates suicide, an angel alights from the sky and takes Baily along the journey into the timeline of his life, enabling him to realize the true worth of himself and his life. In the concluding part of the film, there is a noteworthy scene showing George dashing off to his town in celebration. He returns home, locks his family in the warmth of a strong embrace, cuddling and caressing them alongside a Christmas tree.

This movie articulates the importance of accepting our life as it actually is and the way it unfolds as against how we wanted it to be.

Like many others in this world, George never had an opportunity to accomplish his goals and aspirations. He continues to run his father's business of extending small loans to the local townsmen. But George was never happy as he couldn't find an escape to his dull and uninteresting life as he perceived it to be. The contentment derived from helping his family and the community of his town is the only saving grace for him. Nevertheless, George's small finance company saved the townsfolk from the exploitative and outrageous mortgage costs charged by the greedy local moneylender, Potter. In fact, George happens to protect the residents of the entire town from bankruptcy.

When George was on the verge of leaping down from a high bridge, an angel named Clarence emerges and saves his life. The angel guides George in the review of his actions during his entire lifetime which have immensely benefited many people in the town. While recalling and visualizing his past actions, George discovers the magnitude of goodwill that he earned by helping and supporting many people in his town and realizes that he could fall back upon his reputation. As a consequence of this insight, George comes back to his home with renewed energy and appreciation for all the little things in his surrounding — including the frustrations and stress factors — and the love of his family and his kin. In reality, many people have reported such revelation while narrating their near-death experiences. It would in fact be remarkable if we could help people through some kind of treatment to internalize such appreciation for life without having to face close-to-death situations. Fortunately, there appears to be a solution available in the form of Cognitive Behavioral Therapy (CBT), which aids distraught people in developing such awareness and appreciation for life. The therapy enables such people to realize the value of their lives and transform them as magically as the angel in the movie which helped George to discover in retrospect, the true value of his life.

Cognitive behavioral therapy guides people to adopt a time-plan for various activities while recommending them to be continually engaged in work, recreation or social events. In general, when someone commits suicide, we often wonder why such people were blinded from seeing and appreciating the value of many good things in their lives while succumbing to certain traumatic or adverse events and situations. Such depression and emotional distress hijacks one's mind, overpowers one's thoughts and triggers a surge in self-destructive drives and actions. Needless to say, if only such people show patience and await tough situations to complete their circuit and pass, they would realize how unrealistically their problems were magnified and workable solutions are possible to find with effort and patience. When people get out of depression, they redirect their attention toward the brighter side of their life, such as their achievements, family, long lost friends, small joys and so forth.

In the movie, the angel assumes responsibility for re-directing the attention of George Bailey toward all the good things in his life. The significance of George's life is rooted in his committed efforts and actions to insulate his townsmen from perpetual indebtedness and exploitation. He was unable to appreciate the same as he could not accept his life as it was. Acceptance is the key to unearth the real purpose and meaning of our life which lies beneath the realities of our life and not in our aspirations or accomplishments. Notwithstanding our past or present, our life has its own importance in terms of its influence and impact on others' lives. Our insurmountable challenges, disappointments, failures, abuses, and the emotional pain of losing our near and dear might keep us anchored in the past or entrenched in anxiety about the future. When this happens, we get blinded to our present life and become insensitive to the world surrounding us. Our life becomes truly wonderful only when we accept the same and experience the present. It is essential to realize that our present state of affairs or our life situations are precisely as they ought to be, given the specific edification our life is intended to offer and the objective behind its odyssey.

REFERENCES

1. Darwin, C. (1872) 2005. *"The Expression of the emotion in man and animals"*. Stilwell, KS: Digireads. com
2. Thorndike, E. L. (1920). "Intelligence and its uses." *Harper's Magazine,* 140: 227–235.
3. Wechsler, D. (1940). "Nonintellective factors in general intelligence." *Psychological Bulletin,* 37: 444–445.
4. Mayer, J. D. (1999, September). "Emotional intelligence: Popular or scientific psychology?" *APA Monitor,* 30: 50. [*Shared Perspectives* Column] Washington, DC: American Psychological Association.
5. Goleman, D. (1995). *"Emotional intelligence."* New York: Bantam.
6. Goleman, D. (1998a). "What makes a leader?," *Harvard Business Review,* 76: 93–102.
7. Watkin, C. (2000). "Developing emotional intelligence." *International Journal of Selection and Assessment,* 8: 89–92.
8. a. Bar-On, R. (2002). *"Bar-On Emotional Quotient Inventory (EQ-I): Technical Manual."* Toronto, Canada: Multi-Health Systems.
   b. Hunter, J. E. and Hunter, R. F. (1984). "Validity and utility of alternative predictors of job performance." *Psychological Bulletin, 76* (1): 72–93.
   c. Sternberg, R. J. (1996). *"Successful Intelligence."* New York: Simon and Schuster.
9. Mathews, G., Zeidner, M., and Roberts, R. D. (2002). *"Emotional intelligence: Science and myth."* Cambridge, MA: MIT Press.
10. a. Cooper, R. K., and Sawaf, A. (1997). *"Executive EQ: Emotional intelligence in leadership and organizations."* New York: Grosset / Putnam
    b. Gottman, J. (1997). *"The heart of parenting: How to raise an emotionally intelligence child."* New York: Simon and Schuster.
    c. Salerno, J. G. (1996). *"The whole intelligence: Emotional quotient (EQ)."* Oak Bank: Noble House of Australia.
    d. Segal, J. (1997). *"Raising your emotional intelligence."* New York: Holt.
11. Elias, M. J., Zins, J. E., Weissberg, R. P., Frey, K.S., Greenberg, M. T., Haynes, N. M., Kessler, R., Schwab-Ston, M. E., and Shriver, T. P. (1997). *"Promoting social and emotional learning: Guides for educators."* Alexandria V.A.: Association for Supervision and Curriculum Development.
12. Abraham, R. (1999). "Emotional intelligence in organizations: A conceptualization." *Genetic, Social and General Psychology Monographs,* 125(2): 209–224.
13. Day, D.V. (2000). "Leadership development: A review in context." *The Leadership Quarterly Yearly Review of Leadership,* 11(4): 581–614.
14. Snarey, J. R. and Vaillant, G. E. (1985). "How lower and working class youth become middle-class adults: The association between ego defense mechanisms and upward social mobility." *Child Development,* 56 (4): 899–910.
15. ibid
16. Lam, L. T. and Kirby, S. L. (2002). "Is emotional intelligence an advantage? An exploration of the impact of emotional and general intelligence on individual performance." *The Journal of Social Psychology,* 142 (1): 133–143.
17. Goleman, D. (1998b). *"Working with emotional intelligence."* New York: Bantam Books.
18. Mayer, J. D., Salovey, P., and Caruso, D. (1998). "Competing models of emotional intelligence." In R.J. Sternburg (Ed.), *Handbook of Human Intelligence* (Second edition). New York: Cambridge University Press.

19. Goleman, D. (2001). "Emotional intelligence: Issues in paradigm building." In Cherniss, C. and Goleman, D. (Ed's.) *The Emotionally Intelligent Workplace*. San Francisco: Jossey-Bass.
20. Mayer, J. D., Roberts, R. D. and Barsade, S. G. (2008). "Human abilities: Emotional intelligence." *Annual Review of Psychology*, 59: 507–536.
21. Mayer, J. D., Salovey, P., and Caruso, D. (2008). "Emotional intelligence: New ability or eclectic traits?" *American psychologist*, 63: (6), 503–517.
22. Palmer, B., Donaldson, C., and Stough, C. (2002). "Emotional intelligence and life satisfaction." *Personality and Individual Differences,* 33: 1091–1100.
23. Pellitteri, J. (2002). "The relationship between emotional intelligence and ego defense mechanisms." *The Journal of Psychology Interdisciplinary and Applied,* 136(2): 182–194.
24. Brackett, M. A., Mayer, J. D., and Warner, R. M. (2004). "Emotional intelligence and the prediction of everyday behavior." *Personality and Individual Differences,* 36 (6): 1387–1402.
25. Mayer, J. D., Caruso, D. R., and Salovey, P. (1999). "Emotional intelligence meets standards for traditional intelligence." *Intelligence,* 27: 267–298.
26. a. Rice, C. L. (1999). "*A quantitative study of emotional intelligence and its impact on team performance.*" Unpublished master's thesis, Pepperdine University.
    b. Rubin, M. M. (1999). "*Emotional intelligence and its role in mitigating aggression: A correlational study of the relationship between emotional intelligence and aggression in urban adolescents.*" Unpublished dissertation, Immaculata College, Pennsylvania.
27. Fitness, J. (2001). "Emotional intelligence and intimate relationships." In Ciarrochi, J., Forgas, J. P. and Mayer, J. D. (Eds.). *Emotional intelligence in everyday life*. Philadelphia: Psychology Press.
28. Mathews, G., Zeidner, M., and Roberts, R. D. (2012). "*The Psych 101 Series: Emotional Intelligence* 101." New York: Springer.
29. Brackett, M. A., Warner, R. M., and Bosco, J. S. (2005). "Emotional intelligence and relationship quality among couples." *Personal Relationships*, 12: 197–212.
30. Zeidner, M., and Kaluda, I. (2008). "Romantic love: What's emotional intelligence (EI) got to do with it?" *Personality and Individual Differences*, 44(8): 1684–1695.
31. Bar-On, R. (1997). "*The Emotional Quotient Inventory (EQ-i): Technical manual.*" Toronto, Canada: Multi-Health Systems.
32. a. Dawda, D., and Hart, S. D., (2000). "Assessing emotional intelligence: Reliability and validity of the Bar-On Emotional Quotient Inventory (EQ-i) in university students." *Personality and Individual Differences*, 28: 797–812.
    b. Slaski, M., and Cartwright, S. (2002). "Health, performance and emotional intelligence: An exploratory study of retail managers." *Stress and Health*, 18: 63–68.
33. Schutte, N. S., Malouff, J. M., Thorsteinsson, E. B., Bhullar, N., and Rooke, S. E. (2007). "A meta-analytic investigation of the relationship between emotional intelligence and health." *Personality and Individual Differences*, 42(6): 921–933.
34. Chamorro-Premuzic, T., Bennett, E., and Furnham, A. (2007). "The happy personality: Mediational role of trait emotional intelligence." *Personality and Individual Differences*, 42(8): 1633–1639.
35. a. Mikolajczak, M., Roy, E., Luminet, O., Fillee, C., and de Timary, P. (2007). "The moderating impact of emotional intelligence on free cortisol responses to stress." *Psychoneuroendocrinology*, 32 (8–10: 1000–1012.
    b. Petrides, K.V., Pita. R., and Kokkinaki, F. (2007). "The location of trait emotional intelligence in personality factor space." *British Journal of Psychology,* 98: 273–289.
36. Ciarrochi, J. V., Chan, Y. C., and Caputi, P. (2000). "A critical evaluation of the emotional intelligence construct." *Personality and Individual Differences,* 28(3): 539–561.
37. a. Ciarrochi, J., Dean, F. P., and Anderson, S. (2002). "Emotional intelligence moderates the relationship between stress and mental health." *Personality and Individual Differences,* 32: 197–209.

b. Mikolajczak, M., Menil, C., and Luminet, O. (2007). "Explaining the protective effect of trait emotional intelligence regarding occupational stress: Exploration of emotional labor processes." *Journal of Research in Personality,* 41: 1107–1117.
38. Keefer, K. V., Parker, J. D. A., and Saklofske, D. H. (2009). "Emotional intelligence and physical health." In Stough, C. Saklofske, D. H. and Parker J. D. A. (Eds.). *Assessing Emotional Intelligence: Theory, Research and Applications,* New York: Springer.
39. Mayer, J. D., Caruso, D. R., and Salovey, P. (2000). "Selecting a measure of emotional intelligence." In Bar-On R. and Parker J. (Ed's.) *The Handbook of Emotional Intelligence.* San Francisco: Jossey-Bass.
40. Trinidad, D. R., and Johnson, C. A. (2002). "The association between emotional intelligence and early adolescent tobacco and alcohol use." *Personality and Individual Differences,* 32: 95–105.
41. Moriarty, N., Stough, C., Tidmarsh, P., Eger, D., and Dennison, S. (2001). "Deficits in emotional intelligence underlying adolescent sex offending." *Journal of Adolescence,* 24: 743–751.
42. Rafaeli, A. (1996). "What is an organization? Who are the members?" In Cooper C. L. and Jackson S. E. (Eds.), *Creating tomorrow's organizations: A handbook for future research in organizational behavior,* pp.121–139. New York: Wiley.
43. a. Wichroski, M. A. (1994). "The Secretary — Invisible labor in the work world of women." *Human Organization,* 53(1): 33–41.
b. Yanay, N., and Shahar, G. (1998). "Professional Feelings as Emotional Labor." *Journal of Contemporary Ethnography,* 27(3): 346–373.
44. a. Staw, B. M., and Barsade, S. G. (1993). "Affect and managerial performance: A test of the sadder-but-wiser vs. happier-and-smarter hypothesis." *Administrative Science Quarterly,* 38: 304–328.
b. Staw, B. M., Sutton, R. I., and Pelled, L. H. (1994). "Employee positive emotion and favorable outcomes at the workplace." *Organizational Science,* 5: 51–71.
45. Cherniss, C. (2000). "Social and emotional competence in the workplace." In Bar-On R. and Parker J. (Ed's.) *The Handbook of Emotional Intelligence.* San Francisco: Jossey-Bass.
46. a. Cherniss, C. and Adler, M. (2000). "*Promoting Emotional Intelligence in Organizations.*" Alexandria, Virginia: ASTD.
b. Singh, D. (2001). "*Emotional intelligence at work: A professional guide.*" Delhi: Response Books.
c. Holahan, C. K., and Sears, R. R. (1995). "*The gifted group in later maturity.*" Stanford: Stanford University Press.
d. Spencer, L. M., and Spencer S. M. (1993). "*Competence at work: Models for superior performance.*" New York: Wiley.
47. Isen, A. M., and Baron, R. A. (1991). "Positive affect as a factor in organizational behavior." *Research in Organizational Behavior,* 13: 1–54.
48. Barsade, S. G., Ward, A. J., Turner, J. D. F., and Sonnenfield, J. A. (2000). "To your heart's content: The influence of affective diversity in top management teams." *Administrative Science Quarterly,* 45: 802–836.
49. Totterdell, P. (2000). "Catching moods and hitting runs: Mood linkage and subjective performance in professional sports teams." *Journal of Applied Psychology,* 85: 848–859.
50. a. Brief, A. P., and Weiss, H. M. (2002). "Organizational behavior: Affect in the workplace." *Annual Review of Psychology,* 53: 270–307.
b. Ashforth, B. E., and Humphrey, R. H. (1995). "Emotion in the workplace: A reappraisal." *Human Relations,* 48: 97–125.
c. George, J. M. (2000). "Emotions and leadership: The role of emotional intelligence." *Human Relations,* 53: 1027–1055.
d. Fisher, C. D., and Ashkanasy, N. M. (2000). "The emerging role of emotions in working life: An introduction." *Journal of Organizational Behavior,* 21: 123–129.
e. Ashkanasy, N. M., and Daus, C. S. (2002). "Emotion in the workplace: the new challenge for managers." *Academy of Management Executive,* 16(1): 76–86.

f. Weiss, H. M., and Cropanzano, R. (1996). "Affective events theory: A theoretical discussion of the structure, causes and consequences of affective experiences at work." In Staw B. M. and Cummings L. L. (Eds.), *Research in organizational behavior*. Greenwich, CT: JAI Press.
51. Jordan, P. J., and Troth, A. C. (2002). "Emotional intelligence and conflict resolution: Implications for human resource development." *Advances in Developing Human Resources*, 4(1): 62–79.
52. Martin, J., Knopoff, K., and Beckman, C. (1998). "An attention to bureaucratic impersonality and emotional labor: Bounded emotionality at The Body Shop." *Administrative Science Quarterly*, 43: 429–469.
53. a. Ekman, P. (1985). "*Telling lies*." New York: Norton.
b. Ekman, P. (2003). "*Emotions revealed*." New York: Times Books.
54. Damasio, A. R. (1994). "*Descartes' error: Emotion reason and the human brain*." New York: Avon.
55. Fredrickson, B. L. (2001). "The role of positive emotions in Positive Psychology: The broaden and build theory of positive emotions." *American Psychologist,* 56: 218–226.
56. Zipkin, A. (2000). "The wisdom of thoughtfulness." *New York Times*, May 31: C1- C10.
57. Fisher, C. D. (2000). "Mood and emotions while working: Missing pieces of job satisfaction?" *Journal of Organizational Behavior*, 21: 185–202.
58. Locke, E. A. (1976). "The nature and causes of job satisfaction." In Dunnette M. (ed.) *Handbook of industrial and organizational psychology*, pp.1297–1351. Chicago, IL: Rand McNally.
59. Organ, D. W. (1990). "The motivational basis of organizational citizenship behavior." In Staw B. M. and Cummins L. L. (eds.), *Research in Organizational Behavior*, Vol.12, pp.43–72. Greenwich, CT: JAI Press.
60. a. Brackett, M. A., Palmora, R., Mojsa-Kaja, J., Reyes, M. R. and Salovey, P. (2010). "Emotion-regulation, ability, burnout, and job satisfaction among British secondary school teachers." *Psychology in the Schools,* 47(4): 406–417.
b. Kafetsios, K., and Zampetakis, L. A. (2008). "Emotional intelligence and job satisfaction: Testing the mediatory role of positive and negative effect at work." *Personality and Individual Differences*, 44: 717–722.
c. Sy, T., Tram, S., and O'Hara, L. A. (2006). "Relation of employee and manager emotional intelligence to job satisfaction and performance." *Journal of Vocational Behavior*, 68: 461–473.
d. Vigoda-Gadot, E., and Meisler, G. (2010). "Emotions in Management and the Management of Emotions: The Impact of Emotional Intelligence and Organizational Politics on Public Sector Employees." *Public Administration Review,* 70(1): 72–86.
61. Boyatzis, R. E. (1999). "From a presentation to the Linkage Conference on Emotional Intelligence," *Chicago*, IL, September 27, 1999.
62. Government Accounting Office. (1998). "*Military Recruiting: The Department of Defense Could Improve its Recruiter Selection and Incentive Systems.*" Report submitted by Stys, Y., and Brown, S.L.
63. Mandell, B., and Pherwani, S. (2003). "Relationship between emotional intelligence and transformational leadership style: A gender comparison." *Journal of Business and Psychology,* 17(3): 387–404.
64. Law, K. S., Wong, C. S. and Song, L. (2004). "Construct validity of emotional intelligence: Its potential utility of management studies." *Journal of Applied Psychology,* 89 (3): 483–496.
65. Rozell, E. J., Pettijohn, C., and Parker, S. R. (2004). "Customer-oriented selling: Exploring the roles of emotional intelligence and organizational commitment." *Psychology and Marketing,* 21(6): 405–424.
66. Lopes, P. N., Salovey, P., Cote, S., and Beers, M. (2005). "Emotion regulation abilities and the quality of social interaction." *Emotion,* 5(1): 113–118.
67. Carmeli, A. (2003). "The relationship between emotional intelligence and work attitudes, behavior and outcomes: An examination among senior managers." *Journal of Managerial Psychology,* 18(8): 788–813.
68. Carmeli, A., and Josman, Z. E. (2006). "The relationship among emotional intelligence, task performance and organizational citizenship behaviors." *Human Performance,* 19(4): 403–419.
69. Foo, M. D., Elfenbein, H. A., Tan, H. H., and Aik, V. C. (2004). "Emotional intelligence and negotiation: The tension between creating and claiming value." *The International Journal of Conflict Management,* 15(4): 411–429.

70. Bunker, K. A. (1997). "The power of vulnerability in contemporary leadership." *Consulting Psychology Journal*, 49(2): 122–136.
71. Vakola, M., Tsaousis, I., and Nikolaou, I. (2004). "The role of emotional intelligence and personality variables on attitude toward organizational change." *Journal of Managerial Psychology*, 19(2): 88–110.
72. Guchait, P., Tews, M. J., and Simons, T. (2014). "The influence of transactive memory systems and psychological safety on effectiveness of service management teams in a restaurant setting." *Journal of Human Resources in Hospitality & Tourism*, 13(3): 234–252.
73. Bass, B. M. and Avolio, B. J. (1994). "*Improving organizational effectiveness through transformational leadership.*" Thousand Oaks, CA: Sage.
74. Hater, J. J. and Bass, B. M. (1988). "Superior's evaluations and subordinates' perceptions of transformational and transactional leadership." *Journal of Applied Psychology, 73* (4): 695–702.
75. Keller, R. T. (1995). "Transformational leaders make a difference." *Journal of Research and Technology Management,* 38: 41–44.
76. Seltzer, J. and Bass, B. M. (1990). "Transformational leadership: Beyond initiation and consideration." *Journal of Management,* 16: 693–703.
77. Fleishman, E. and Harris, E. F. (1962). "Patterns of leadership behavior related to employee grievances and turnover." *Personnel Psychology, 15,* 43–56.
78. Mumford, M. D., Zaccaro, S. J., Harding, F. D., Jacobs, T. O., and Fleishman, E. A. (2000). "Leadership skills for a changing world: Solving complex social problems." *The Leadership Quarterly, 11* (1), 11–35.
79. Hochschild, A. R. (1983) 2003. "*The managed heart: Commercialization of human feeling.*" London: University of California Press.
80. Hülsheger, U. R., Alberts, H. J. E. M., Feinholdt, A., and Lang, J. W. B. (2013). "Benefits of Mindfulness at Work: The Role of Mindfulness in Emotion Regulation, Emotional Exhaustion, and Job Satisfaction." *Journal of Applied Psychology*, 98(2): 310–133.
81. Duke, A. B., Goodman, J. M., Treadway, D. C., and Breland, J. W. (2009). "Perceived Organizational Support as a Moderator of Emotional Labor/ Outcomes Relationships." *Journal of Applied Social Psychology*, 39(5): 1013–1034.
82. Kahn, W. A. (1990). "Psychological conditions of personal engagement and disengagement at work." *Academy of Management Journal,* 33(4): 692–724.
83. Chamorro-Premuzic, T., and Yearsley, A. (2017). "The Downside of being very emotionally intelligent." *Harvard Business Review,* January 12, 2017.
84. McCrae, R. R., Costa, P. T., Jr., Lima, M. P. de., Simoes, A., Ostendorf, F., Angleitner, A., Marui, I., Bratko, D., Caprara, G. V., Barbaranelli, C., Chae, J. H., and Piedmont, R. L. (1999). "Age differences in personality across the adult life span: Parallels in five cultures." *Developmental Psychology,* 35, 466–477.
85. McCrae, R. R. (2000). "Emotional intelligence from the perspective of the five-factor model of personality." In Bar-On R. and Parker J. (Ed's.) "*The Handbook of Emotional Intelligence.*" San Francisco: Jossey-Bass.
86. Bechara, A., Tranel, D., and Damasio, A. R. (2000). "Poor judgment in spite of high intellect." In Bar-On R. and Parker J. (Ed's.) *The Handbook of Emotional Intelligence.* San Francisco: Jossey-Bass.
87. Emmerling, R. J. and Goleman, D. (2003). "Emotional intelligence: Issues and common misunderstandings." *Consortium for Research on Emotional Intelligence in Organizations.* Retrieved November 17, 2003 from www.eiconsortium.org.
88. Boyatzis, R. E., Cowan, S. S., and Kolb, D. A. (1995). "*Innovations in Professional Education: Steps on a Journey to Learning.*" San-Francisco: Jossey-Bass.
89. Davidson, R., Jackson, D. C., and Kalin, N. H. (2000). "Emotion, plasticity, context and regulation: Perspectives from affective neuroscience." *Psychological Bulletin, 126* (6), 890–909.
90. a. Harpur, T. J., Hart, S. D., and Hare, R. D. (2002). "Personality of the psychopath." In Costa, Jr., P. T. and Widiger T. A. (Eds.), *Personality disorders and the five-factor model of personality* (2nd ed.), (pp. 299—324). Washington, DC: American Psychological Association.

b. Arvey, R. D., Renz, G. L., and Watson, T. W. (1998). "Emotionality and job performance: Implications for personal selection." In Ferris G. R. (Ed.). *Research in Personnel and Human Resource Management*, Vol. 16 (pp.103–147). Stanford: CT: Jai Press.

91. Austin, E. J., Farrelly, D., Black, C., and Moore, H. (2007). "Emotional intelligence, Machiavellianism and emotional manipulation: Does EI have a dark side?" *Personality and Individual Differences,* 43: 179–189.

92. Kilduff, M. Chiaburu, D. S., and Menges, J. I. (2010). "Strategic use of emotional intelligence in organizational settings: Exploring the dark side." *Research in Organizational Behavior,* 30: 129–152.

93. Cote, S., Miners, C. T. H., and Moon, S. (2006). "Emotional intelligence and wise emotion regulation in the workplace." In Zerbe, W. J. Ashkanasy, N. and Härtel C. E. J. (Eds.). "*Research on emotions in organizations,*" Vol.2 (pp.1–24). Oxford, UK: Elsevier JAI.

94. Fox, S., and Spector, P. E. (2000). "Relations of emotional intelligence, practical intelligence, general intelligence, and trait affectivity with interview outcomes: It's not all just 'G'." *Journal of Organizational Behavior,* 21: 203–220.

95. Mayer, J. D. (2001). "Emotion, intelligence, and emotional intelligence." In Forgas J. P. (Ed.), *Handbook of affect and social cognition,* (pp.410–431). Mahwah, NJ: Erlbaum.

96. Sutton, R. I. (1991). "Maintaining norms about expressed emotions: The case of bill collectors." *Administrative Science Quarterly*, 36: 245–268.

97. a. Pugh, S. D. (2001). "Service with a smile: Emotional contagion in the service encounter." *Academy of Management Journal,* 44: 1018–1027.

b. Van Maanen, J., and Kunda, G. (1989). "Real Feelings: Emotional expression and organizational culture." *Research in Organizational Behavior, 11: 43–103.*

98. Goffman, E. (1959). "*The presentation of self in everyday life.*" Harmondsworth, UK: Penguin.

99. Rosenbaum, J. E. (1979). "Tournament mobility: Career patterns in a corporation." *Administrative Science Quarterly,* 24: 220–241.

100. Rimé, B. (2007). "Interpersonal emotion regulation." In Gross J. J. (Ed.), *Handbook of emotion regulation* (pp. 466–485). New York: Guilford Press.

101. Swartz, M. (2006). "*The three faces of Ken Lay.*" May 21. http://www.nytimes.com/2006/05/21/opinion/21swartz.html

102. Lewis, M. (1989). "*Liar's poker: Rising through the wreckage on Wall Street.*" New York: Norton.

103. Frank, R. H., (1988). "*Passions within reason: The strategic role of the emotions.*" New York: Norton.

104. Hogan, J., and Holland, B. (2003). "Using theory to evaluate personality and job performance relations: A socioanalytic perspective." *Journal of Applied Psychology,* 88: 100–112.

105. Keltner, D., Gruenfeld, D. H., and Anderson, C. (2003). "Power, approach, and inhibition." *Psychological Review,* 110: 265–284.

106. Mathews, G., Zeidner, M., and Roberts, R. D. (2007). "*Emotional intelligence: Knowns and unknowns.*" Oxford, England: Oxford University Press.

107. Matsumoto, D., Yoo, S. H., Fontaine, J. R. J., Anguas-Wong, A. M., Arriola, M., Ataca, B., et al., (2008). "Mapping expressive differences around the world: The relationship between emotional display rules and individualism versus collectivism." *Journal of Cross Cultural Psychology*, 39 (1): 55–74.

108. Thomas, D. C. (2006). "Domain and development of cultural intelligence: The importance of mindfulness." *Group & Organization Management*, 31(1): 78–99.

109. Sharma, S., Deller, J., Biswal, R., and Mandal, M. K. (2009). "Emotional intelligence: Factorial structure and construct validity across cultures." *International Journal of Cross Cultural Management,* 9(2): 217–236.

110. Zeidner, M., Roberts, R. D., and Mathews, G. (2004). "The emotional intelligence bandwagon: Too fast to live, too young to die?" *Psychological Inquiry*, 15: 239–248.

3

MODELS AND MEASURES OF EMOTIONAL INTELLIGENCE

OPENING CASELET

Serenity in Death as in Life

Greek philosopher, Socrates spent most his life debating, reasoning and teaching but never allowed the discussions to become pungent, critical or fiery. He would always be in absolute self-control despite the argument progressing critically against him. Hostility and bitterness didn't find place in his life. With commitment to his life motto, Know thyself, Socrates had the conviction that an individual must understand his heart first in order to acquire insight and foresight. He had a keen sense of observation which he applied on himself by observing his own reactions when he was cut across, challenged, or denied of amenities or privileges. He would practice detached observation upon himself by looking at himself objectively as an external examiner analyzing his own mind as to how it worked. He also actively observed others as to how they responded to social stimuli and their attitudes. Socrates always tried to lead his audience into a community of understanding and logic often hauling them out of their bad tempers. With a mischievous humbleness he used to say, "The Oracle chose me as the wisest Athenian because I am the only one who knows that he doesn't know anything". This attitude gave tremendous edge in an argument. Feigning ignorance, he would pester people with questions leading them to make astonishing admissions. Plato, a protégé of Socrates, chronicled the last moments of his master's life on earth, in his dialog, *Phaedo*. According to his narration, Socrates spent the last night of his life discussing philosophy with his young followers as he usually did and on that night the topic was life after death.

Socrates remained peaceful, unperturbed by his debate and his nearing date with death. As the time of his death neared, his friends and students surrounded him trying to prepare themselves to accept the hard reality and witness their beloved teacher drink the cup of poison. A little before the sun was to set over the Western mountains, Socrates asked for the poison cup himself. As instructed by the attendant, he coolly consumed the poison from the cup halting only to admonish his friends for weeping and lamenting as though he was doing something wrong. The last wish of Socrates was about a small obligation that he overlooked. Removing the cloth that covered his face, Socrates told his friend, Crito that he owed a rooster to a person named Asclepius, asking him to ensure that it was repaid. After saying this, Socrates closed his eyes and replaced the cloth over his face. When his friend asked him if anything else was required of him, there was no reply. He passed away silently! It is bizarre to sentence someone to death simply for developing general definitions and interpretations. Socrates died a martyr to his teachings, embracing death with calm and composure.

Sources: (1) Hackforth, R. (1955). "*Plato's Phaedo: Translated with an introduction and commentary*". Cambridge.

(2) Wilso, E. (2007). "*The Death of Socrates*". Harvard University Press.

(3) Sill, S. W. and McCormic, D. (2008). "*Lessons from great lives*". (pp. 151-157). New Delhi: Maverick Business, an imprint of Rave Media.

(4) "*Inspiring people: Fifty who made a difference*". RDI Print and Publishing, Bombay. (1993).

Emotional intelligence encompasses a set of specific competencies relevant to the identification and expression of emotions; understanding of emotions; assimilation of emotions in thought; and regulation of emotions in self and others.[1]

DEFINITIONS OF EMOTIONAL INTELLIGENCE

Emotional intelligence has been defined in multiple ways by different researchers and scholars. Some of these definitions are given below:

***Salovey and Mayer (1990)*[2]:** *"The ability to monitor one's own and others' feelings and emotions, to discriminate among them and to use this information to guide one's thinking and actions."*

***Mayer and Salovey (1997)*[3a]:** *"The ability to perceive emotions, to assess and generate emotions so as to assist thought, to understand emotions and emotional knowledge, and to reflectively regulate emotion so as to promote emotional and intellectual growth."*

***Mayer, Caruso, and Salovey (1999)*[4]:** *"An ability to recognize the meanings of emotions and their relationships to reason, and problem-solve on the basis of them. Emotional intelligence is involved in the capacity to perceive emotions, assimilate emotion-related feelings, understand the information of those emotions, and manage them."*

***Mayer, Salovey and Caruso (2002)*[5]:** *"The ability to perceive emotions, to access and generate emotions so as to assist thought, to understand emotions and emotional meanings, and to reflectively regulate emotions in ways that promote emotional and intellectual growth."*

***Bar-On (1997)*[6]:** *"An array of non-cognitive (emotional and social) capabilities, competencies and skills that influence one's ability to succeed in coping with environmental demands and pressures."*

***Bar-On (2000)*[7]:** *"An array of emotional and social knowledge and abilities that influence our overall ability to effectively cope with environmental demands."*

***Goleman (1998)*[8]:** *"The capacity for recognizing our own feelings and those of others, for motivating ourselves, and for managing emotions well in ourselves and in our relationships."* His framework has five branches, self-awareness, self-regulation, motivation, empathy and social skills.

***Boyatzis, Goleman, and Rhee (2000)*[9a]:** *"Emotional intelligence is observed when a person demonstrates the competencies that constitute self-awareness, self-management, social awareness, and social skills at appropriate times and ways in sufficient frequency to be effective in the situation."*

***Cooper and Sawaf (1997)*[10]:** *"The ability to sense, understand, and effectively apply the power and acumen of emotions as a source of human energy, information, connection, and influence."*

***Six Seconds Team (1997)*[11]:** *"The capacities to create optimal results in your relationships with yourself and others."*

***Maurice Elias (2001)*[12]:** *"The set of abilities that we like to think of as being on the other side of the report card from the academic skills."*

***Martinez (1997)*[13]:** *"An array of non-cognitive skills, capabilities and competencies that influence a person's ability to cope with environmental demands and pressures."*

***Bradberry and Greaves (2009)*[14]:** *"Your ability to recognize and understand emotions in yourself and others, and your ability to use this awareness to manage your behavior and relationships."*

***Chris (2009)*[15]:** *"EQ is achieving self- and social mastery by being smart with core emotions."*

***Weisinger (1998)*[16]:** *"The intelligent use of emotions: you intentionally make your emotions work for you by using them to help guide your behavior and thinking in ways that enhance your results."*

The term "Emotional Intelligence" was first used by Salovey and Mayer[2] who postulated that emotional intelligence comprised three categories of adaptive abilities, (1) appraisal and expression of emotion; (2) regulation of emotion; and (3) utilization of emotion in decision making and problem solving. The first category consists of the components of appraisal and expression of emotion in self and in others. The second category has the components of regulation of emotion in self and in others. The third category, utilization of emotion, includes the components of flexible planning, creative thinking, redirected attention, and motivation.

EMOTIONAL INTELLIGENCE AS A FORM OF INTELLIGENCE

A three-dimensional criterion is generally used for determining a construct as a true form of intelligence, conceptual, co-relational and developmental.

1. The first criterion specifies that any intelligence should mirror mental accomplishment rather than showing non-intellectual attainments or preferred ways of behaving,[17] and that such accomplishment should measure the concept in question.
2. The second criteria stipulates that an intelligence should comprise similar and closely related abilities but distinct from the mental abilities specified by existing and established intelligences.[17a, 18]
3. The third rule entails that intelligence should develop with age and be based on the work of Binet and Simon[19] as reviewed by Fancher,[20] and other researchers.[21]

Mayer and his associates declared that emotional intelligence fulfils the standard criteria of intelligence enumerated above and therefore it is scientifically considered as intelligence.[4] Firstly, emotional intelligence can be operationalized as a set of abilities. Secondly, it meets the stipulated correlational criteria — the abilities defined by emotional intelligence are interrelated while corresponding to existing intelligences and also showing some unique variance. Finally, the abilities of emotional intelligence develop with age and experience.

MODELS OF EMOTIONAL INTELLIGENCE

Following the Salovey and Mayer's conceptualization of emotional intelligence, two categories have emerged, the ability models and mixed models.[22] A clear distinction was brought out between models conceptualizing emotional intelligence as a mental ability and broader mixed models focusing on adaptive emotional traits and dispositions, personality factors and mental abilities. Ability models conceptualized emotional intelligence as a form of intelligence in which emotion and intelligence (as traditionally defined) are alloyed in unison.[3]

Thus, emotional intelligence is defined as a set of abilities that make thinking more intelligent and enables a person to think intelligently about emotions.

In comparison, mixed models describe a composite conception of emotional intelligence comprising mental abilities, attitudes, dispositions and traits.

Trait is a behavioral disposition and not an ability even though a trait like extraversion may depend on social skill, or results in same, whereas mental abilities may include understanding the feelings of another person. Personality traits like extraversion involve dispositions to behavior, whereas intelligence comprises organismic abilities to behave.[17b] Extraversion, self-confidence, low anxiety and social perceptiveness are essential to maintain good relations with others but do not form a part of intelligence even though all of these correlate with intelligence.[17c]

Mayer and Salovey clarified the distinction between emotional intelligence and traits and talents while defining the construct as, "Traits can be defined as characteristic or preferred ways of behaving [e.g., extroversion, shyness]; talents as non-intellectual abilities [e.g., skill at sports]....we distinguished a mental skill that could be legitimately called emotional intelligence [e.g., being able to figure out one's own and others' emotions] from preferred ways of behaving [e.g., being sociable, or warm]".[3a]

Therefore, as opposed to a valued trait, emotional intelligence is considered as real intelligence.[17c]

Ability Model of Emotional Intelligence

Ability models regard emotional intelligence as an unalloyed form of mental ability and thus an unblended form of intelligence. Mayer and Salovey's 1997 model[3a] is a mental ability model, while their original model of 1990,[2] Goleman's[11] model and several other conceptualizations are considered as broader mixed models.

EI PERSPECTIVE **Kevin Roberts on Emotions**

The author of the famous book, *Lovemarks: The Future beyond Brands,* and ex-CEO of Saatchi & Saatchi, Kevin Roberts proclaimed that he always trusted his emotions. He shared his strong conviction that invoking emotion would attract the best people to work for you, the best clients to excite you, the best associates and loyal customers.

Source: Roberts, K. (2005). "*Lovemarks: The future beyond brands*". London: powerHouse Books.

Mayer and Salovey[3] postulated a revised model of emotional intelligence in 1997, which gives more emphasis to the cognitive components of emotional intelligence and conceptualized it in terms of its potential for intellectual and emotional growth. The revised model consists of four branches, (1) perception, appraisal, and expression of emotion; (2) emotional facilitation of thinking; (3) understanding, analyzing and employing emotional knowledge; and (4) reflective regulation of emotions to facilitate emotional and intellectual growth. In this revised model of emotional intelligence, Mayer and Salovey introduced a hierarchy of abilities ranging from the lowest branch concerning relatively simple abilities of perceiving and expressing emotions to the highest level of conscious and reflective regulation of emotions. They suggested that emotional intelligence is partly innate and partly learned from life experiences. Several research studies[24] found that the component parts of the Salovey and Mayer model [2] are highly related to each other and that emotional intelligence was associated with various adaptive characteristics, such as optimism and better life outcomes like higher grade point average and better supervisor ratings. There is an adequate empirical demonstration to confirm that emotional intelligence could be tested as a mental ability.[25]

Mixed Models of Emotional Intelligence

Mixed models combine together emotional intelligence factors and characteristics with other personality traits, attitudes and dispositions which are not concerned with either emotion or intelligence. Daniel Goleman[23] postulated a theory comprising many important correlates of emotional intelligence, expanding it to include many skills specific to self-management, communication and social skills. He presented the adaptive value of controlling impulses, soothing one's anxiety, avoiding depression, maintaining optimism, directing anger appropriately, responding well to emotional reactions in others, non-judgmental listening and speaking, resolving conflicts in relationships, and showing concern and helpfulness towards others. Goleman's view of the adaptive nature of emotional intelligence is adeptly captured by his notion that cognitive intelligence may help individuals gain admission to settings, but it is emotional intelligence that determines how successful they are within these settings. He defined emotional intelligence to include abilities to motivate oneself and persist in frustrations; to control impulses delaying gratification; to regulate moods and keep distress from inundating the ability to think; to empathize and hope.[23] Goleman's model[26] postulated five domains or dimensions of emotional intelligence that comprised twenty-five competencies. Three dimensions — self-awareness; self-regulation, and motivation — describe personal competencies, such as knowing and managing emotions in oneself. Two dimensions, empathy and social skills, describe social competencies, that is, knowing and managing emotions in others. Subsequently, these twenty-five competencies were collapsed into twenty, and the five domains into four, (1) self-awareness; (2) self-management; (3) social awareness; and (4) relationship management.[9] Goleman postulated a set of emotional competencies under each of the four domains of emotional intelligence.

As against instinctive talents, emotional competencies are acquired and developed through conscious learning to enhance the quality of performance outcomes. Goleman asserts that inborn general intelligence determines an individual's prospects of developing emotional competencies. He adds that clustering competencies under various domains in his model followed a synergetic pattern, reinforcing each other rather than grouping them at random.[9]

Anchored in Goleman's model and its associated competencies, many measures were subsequently developed. Some of such measures include the Emotional Competence Inventory (ECI),[27] the Emotional Intelligence Appraisal (EIA); [28] and the Work Profile Questionnaire — Emotional Intelligence Version (WPQei).[29a]

Contradicting Goleman's conceptualization of emotional intelligence, Mayer, Salovey and Caruso noted that Goleman's book on emotional intelligence started with their own earlier version of emotional intelligence but progressively included other personality traits and attributes.[30] They further added that since Goleman's book partially contained their theory, some researchers mistakenly believed that such composite conceptualization of emotional intelligence was endorsed by Salovey's work. Goleman's conceptualization was referred by some researchers as a "mixed model" of emotional intelligence encapsulating cognitive and non-cognitive processes.[31]

Bar-On defined emotional intelligence as, "An array of non-cognitive competencies, and skills that influence one's ability to succeed in coping with the environmental demands and pressures".[6] His self-report instrument emotional quotient inventory (EQ-i) assesses five domains of emotional intelligence, 1) *Intrapersonal EQ* comprising emotional self-awareness, assertiveness, self-regard, self-actualization, and independence; 2) *Interpersonal EQ* including empathy, interpersonal relationship, and social responsibility; 3) *Adaptability* consisting of problem solving, reality testing, and flexibility; 4) *Stress management* comprising stress tolerance and impulse control; and 5) *General mood* entailing happiness and optimism.[6]

The model of Bar-On combines mental abilities with other characteristics like personal independence, self-regard, and mood which are considered distinct from mental abilities.[22] Many attributes of this model, such as reality testing, stress management, and impulse control, seem to stretch beyond what generally constitutes emotion or intelligence.[32]

Cooper[33] conceptualized emotional intelligence as comprising emotional self-awareness, emotional awareness of others, interpersonal connections, resilience, creativity, compassion, and intuition among other areas, and developed an index called the EQ Map. Cooper and Sawaf defined emotional intelligence as, "…The ability to sense, understand, and effectively apply the power and acumen of emotions as a source of human energy, information, connection, and influence". The Four Cornerstone model of emotional intelligence given by them relates to specific skills and tendencies in the realm of direct knowing, exploration and application. They proposed four dimensions namely, emotional literacy, emotional fitness, emotional depth, and emotional alchemy.[10] Emotional literacy includes knowledge of one's own emotions and how they function; emotional fitness includes emotional hardiness and flexibility; emotional depth involves emotional intensity and potential for growth; and emotional alchemy includes the ability to use emotion to spark creativity.[25]

Petrides and Furnham[34] postulated trait EI comprising self-judged adaptability, assertiveness, social competence, and stress management as, "A constellation of behavioral dispositions and self-perceptions concerning one's ability to recognize, process, and utilize emotional information skirting empathy, impulsivity, and assertiveness as well as elements of social intelligence and personal intelligence".[35]

Comparison of Ability and Mixed Models

The ability models of emotional intelligence were found to be distinct from avowedly analogous constructs as they differ from cognitive intelligence in reflecting experience and learning about emotional processes like memory.[22, 36] Initial evidence suggested that the ability model seemed to be independent of and dissimilar to existing personality traits, unlike the mixed models.[37]

The measures of emotional intelligence based on mixed models significantly overlap with personality traits,[22] both conceptually and empirically.[38] The characteristic of emotional intelligence as a distinct construct of scientific rigor may have been significantly compromised by the inclusion of non-ability dimensions.[39] Mayer and Salovey's ability model[3a] of emotional intelligence, which underwent refinement since its development, gained acceptance among researchers.[40] However, among the corporate community and in workplace training space, Daniel Goleman's model which is focused on applied and learnable competencies, seems to have captured the center-stage gaining significance and popularity.

Ability or Mixed Models – Which is superior?

A considerable debate and discourse is there among researchers on which of the two models in emotional intelligence literature –ability or mixed – accurately and truly represents the concept of emotional intelligence.

EI PERSPECTIVE How to identify a person with high EQ

The passengers of British Airways are provided with the following guidelines and hints for identifying a person with high EQ:

- We gain their respect and friendliness
- We feel geniality and respect for them
- People who do not indulge in power play
- People skilled in networking
- People who are aware of what they want and are able to express the same with clarity
- People who can be firm and tough without jeopardizing relationships.
- People who can recall your minute personal details.
- People who do not perceive mistakes as failures but as information.
- People with openness to opportunities and who are optimistic of the result.
- People who look out for win-win solutions.

Source: Pickles, H. (2000). "I feel therefore I am". *Business Life,* July/August: 37-41.

Proponents of the ability model contend that mixed models are not unalloyed and authentic form of emotional intelligence, while research based on ability measures illustrated that emotional intelligence is a perceptible and well-defined construct with significant validity and additional variance attributable to performance outcomes.[41] But advocates of mixed models criticize the ability model for rigorously concentrating on conventional and intelligence-based psychometric standard. These proponents contend that many theorists advocated expansion of the conventional conception of intelligence to include many relevant capabilities which have traditionally been kept beyond the scope of intelligence. In support of this contention, researcher Howard Gardner observed that typical standard intelligence tests do not predict success in school or in life, as is the case with mixed model of emotional intelligence.[42]

MEASURES OF EMOTIONAL INTELLIGENCE

Corresponding to the development of various models of emotional intelligence, numerous instruments of its measurement have emerged. An overview of various measures of emotional intelligence encompassing both the ability as well as mixed models is presented below. The measurement approaches consist of ability or performance-based measures, self-report measures, and informant report measures.

The Nature of Ability / Performance-based Measures

This approach uses a performance-based measure by asking the respondent to solve a problem or respond to a question. For instance, if one wants to assess how well the respondents perceive emotion, then one may show them pictures of faces displaying various emotions and then ask them to identify and label the emotional expression. Ability-based or performance-based testing is considered as gold standard in intelligence research because intelligence conforms to the true capacity of good performance in mental tasks, not just one's assumption or conviction about such capacities.[17a, 18]

Description about Self-Report Measures

Self-report measures require the respondents to endorse a series of descriptive statements, indicating the degree to which they describe or do not describe themselves. Self-reported abilities and traits rely on the individual's self-perception. These measures provide accurate measurement of the ability or trait in question when the respondent's self-concept is accurate. In cases where the respondent's self-concept is inaccurate, the self-report measures yield information only about the person's self-concept rather than the actual ability or trait.

The ability measures, on the other hand, capture facets of respondent's actual intelligence, in comparison to self-report measures.

The Nature of Informant / Observer-report Measures

Informant reports are ratings about the target individual on certain indicators gathered from target's friends, acquaintances, spouse and others, based on their overall understanding of that target. The other forms of informant reports could include assessment by peers. These measures require an observer to assess the target on observable signs and symptoms over a brief period (e.g., during an interview or over the course of a day) or over long period (e.g., several months). This method yields information about how the target is perceived by others.

Ability / Performance Measures

Multi-factor emotional intelligence scale (MEIS)

Based on the Mayer and Salovey model[3a] of emotional intelligence, Mayer, Caruso, and Salovey[4] developed a performance-based measure called Multi-factor Emotional Intelligence Scale (MEIS). The scale has twelve ability measures grouped into four branches, (1) perceiving, (2) assimilating, (3) understanding, and (4) managing emotions. The first branch consists of four tests assessing the perception and appraisal of emotion in the form of stories, designs, music, and faces. The second branch, on the other hand, comprises two tasks that assess the ability to assimilate emotions into perceptual and cognitive processes, while the third branch has four tasks assessing the ability to reason about and understand emotions. Finally, the fourth branch consists of two tasks that assess the skills of participants in managing their own emotions and emotions of others. The nature and content of these tests range from stories, designs, musical scores, faces, scenarios and short vignettes depicting real-life episodes, especially selected to invoke emotional responses. There are three alternative procedures for scoring of the test — *consensual scoring*, *expert scoring* and *target scoring*.[1]

- *Consensual scoring:* This technique is based on the evaluation by an assortment of judges who assess the scores individually in isolation in the first stage. The individual evaluations of judges are then collated to arrive at an overall rating or measure. In the event, if the group accepts that a particular face or vignette or music displays a happy or sad emotion, then the same becomes the correct response.
- *Expert scoring:* Certain stimuli reflected in facial expression, musical passage or pictorial design or vignette are examined by experts in the field of emotions (e.g., psychologists, psychiatrists, philosophers, and so forth). These experts use their judgment and deduce the emotion expressed in such stimulus. The respondent (the person who takes the test) gets credit for the ratings that correspond to those given by the experts engaged for the purpose.
- *Target Scoring:* The test taker assesses the emotion portrayed by a target (artist, photographer, musician, and so forth) while they were engaged in the activity (e.g., writing a poem, playing a musical score, painting, sculpting, photography, etc.). Then a set of emotion rating scales are used to match the emotions conveyed by the stimuli to those reported by the target. It is believed that the target is more informed than the outside observer[6, 31] and is used as the criterion for scoring the judges' responses.[43]

Research shows that MEIS is reliable, distinct, and is related to important life outcomes despite certain inherent weaknesses like extensive time taken by the test, absence of satisfactory sub-scale reliability, limited empirical support and scoring problems.

EI PERSPECTIVE

Developing Emotional Competence based on EI Test

An e-commerce team was falling apart with apparently no zeal or passion left for the project while extensive energy got depleted in the play of blame-game and search of scapegoat for failure. There was a team leader named Janet, who wasn't the source of these problems, but it is up to her to sort out the issues and turn the situation around toward positivity and productivity.

It was revealed in an emotional intelligence test that Janet's score was poor in the dimension of 'using emotions'. Accepting the results was fundamental to Janet's advancement. She had to direct her attention towards the effect her low score had on her performance and capitalize on her strengths to enhance her abilities in 'using emotions'. By means of extensive counselling and intense discourse, she was motivated and abetted to conquer her negative feelings while building on positive ones, and to develop the competency of 'using' emotion. Researchers associated with this case, who authored the source material of this episode, claimed significant accomplishment by Janet in terms of achieving significant positive outcomes for her organization through excellent performance which was highly appreciated by her managers.

Source: Caruso, D. R. and Wolfe, C. J. (2001). "Emotional intelligence in the workplace". In Ciarrochi, J., Forgas, J. P. and Mayer, J. D. (Eds.). *Emotional Intelligence in Everyday Life*. Philadelphia: Psychology Press. P. 150.

Mayer-Salovey-Caruso emotional intelligence test (MSCEIT) v- 1.1

MSCEIT (pronounced as *miskeet)* version-1.1 developed by Mayer, Caruso, and Salovey[31] is a refined and shortened version of MEIS, enhancing the convenience of its administration and contains twelve subscales. Certain tests based on music, stories, biased feelings and other subtests under branch four that were there in the earlier version of MEIS were omitted from this scale.

MAYER-SALOVEY-CARUSO emotional intelligence test (MSCEIT) v-2

With only two sub-tests within a given branch, MSCEIT version 2 is a 141-item scale that varies significantly from the MEIS. Each subset has lesser number of items than those in MEIS or MSCEIT [Version 1.1]. This version employs both consensus scoring and expert scoring that is obtained from 21 members of the International Society of Research on Emotions.[5] Specific tasks are used to measure each subset of abilities (perception, facilitation of thought, understanding, and regulation). By rating the intensity and nature of emotion expressed in various pictures, the 'perception of emotion' factor is measured. The dimension of 'facilitation of thought' is measured by rating the inputs of respondents on analogues between emotions and physical sensations (e.g., light, color, and temperature) and between emotions and thoughts. The dimension of 'understanding emotion' is measured by asking the respondent to describe how some emotions can combine with other emotions or transform into other emotions (e.g., anger changing to rage). The 'regulation of emotion' factor is assessed by the respondent's choice of effective techniques for managing self and others. The measure provides six types of scores, an overall emotional intelligence score (expressed as an emotional intelligence quotient, or EIQ), two area scores (experiential emotional intelligence, or EEIQ and strategic emotional intelligence, or SEIQ) and four branch scores of emotional intelligence, i.e. PEIQ (perceived emotions); FEIQ (facilitating thought); UIEQ (understanding emotions); and MEIQ (managing emotions). Individual scores are expressed in reference to a standard with mean score of 100 (average score of general population) with a standard deviation of 15. Besides, the manual offers qualitative ratings matching with each numeric score. For instance, a person with an overall EIQ score of 69 or less would be categorized as 'considerable development,' while another individual with an overall score of 130 or more would be rated 'significant strength.'[5]

Emotional accuracy research scale (EARS)

EARS has 96 items testing the perception of emotion branch of the Mayer and Salovey's model of emotional intelligence.[3a] This test is identical to MEIS in that it contains stories, vignettes and mood related items, as its means of assessment and the measure was developed prior to MEIS.[43, 44]

Informant / Observer Report Measures

Emotional competence inventory (ECI)

Developed by Daniel Goleman, this instrument combines the emotional competencies identified on the basis of his own model and an earlier measure titled 'Self Assessment Questionnaire' developed by Richard Boyatzis for assessing the competencies of managers, executives, and leaders.[27]

The ECI (Version 1) comprises 25 competencies grouped into five higher order clusters. It has 110 items measured on a 7-point Likert scale. The measure comes in two forms, i.e. self-report and multi-rater (360 degree) assessment by manager, direct report and peers on a series of behavioral indicators of emotional intelligence. Subsequently, these 25 competencies were collapsed into 20 with the five domains reduced to four, leading to a substantial revision of ECI.[9a] The four higher order constructs of ECI [Version 2] consist of (1) Self-awareness — emotional self-awareness, accurate self-assessment, self-confidence; (2) Self-management — emotional self-control, trustworthiness, conscientiousness, adaptability, achievement orientation, and initiative; (3) Social awareness — empathy, service orientation, and organizational awareness; and (4) Relationship management — developing others, influence, communication, conflict management, visionary leadership, catalyzing change, building bonds, teamwork and collaboration. The ECI [Version 2] comprises 73 items measured on a 6-point Likert scale. Each of the respondents are required to assess themselves or the other person on the behaviors that are usually displayed or typical of the individual on a scale of 1 to 7 for each item reflecting the competencies. Two ratings are generated for each competency — one is the self-rating score and the other being the total of others' ratings (computed by averaging the ratings of all others).[9a] Each respondent can be classified within the range of self-rating and others' ratings.

This test became popular in the field of human resource management despite the scarce information on its psychometric properties.

Self-Report Measures

Bar-on emotional quotient inventory (EQ-I)

The EQ-i is a self-report measure developed by Reuven Bar-On for individuals aged 16 years or above. This measure was designed to determine an individual's emotional and social intelligence based on behaviors reflecting emotional and social competences. The EQ-i was not designed to measure personality traits or cognitive abilities, but to assess an individual's ability to succeed in managing environmental pressures and demands.[45]

Bar-On's EQ-i[6] consists of 15 subscales of emotional intelligence which define five higher-order dimensions.[7] The five main scales and subscales are (1) Intrapersonal EQ — emotional self-awareness, assertiveness, self-regard, self-actualization, and independence; (2) Interpersonal EQ — empathy, interpersonal relationship, social responsibility; (3) Adaptation — problem solving, reality testing, flexibility; (4) Stress management — stress tolerance, and impulse control; (5) General mood — happiness, and optimism. The Bar-On inventory also contains four validity indicators that measure the extent to which people are responding randomly or distorting their responses to appear favorably. The published version of EQ-i comprises 133 brief items and employs a 5-point Likert scale ranging from 1 (very seldom/not true for me) to 5 (very often/often true of me).

The total scores are transformed into standard scores with a mean of 100 and standard deviation of 15, similar to the IQ scores.[45b] Several versions of the EQ-I were developed by Bar-On for use by different types of population and also in varying contexts. Some of these versions are 'the EQ-interview' (to be completed after the self-report), 'the EQ-i Short' (a 52-item version of the original), the 'EQ-i:125' (a 125-item version of the original which excludes the negative impression scale), 'the EQ-i Youth' version (for children and adolescents aged between 7–15 years), and the 'EQ-360 Assessment' (multi-rater instrument to be used alongside the regular self-report EQ-i for a more comprehensive assessment). The original version of EQ-i is also available in several languages, including Spanish, French, Dutch, Danish, Swedish, Norwegian, Finnish, and Hebrew.[45b] The Bar-On EQ-i is a comprehensive measure classifying each respondent based on the range of their EQ scores. This assessment can be applied in a wide range of settings and contexts which includes corporate, educational, clinical, medical, research, and preventative settings. The instrument has been translated into 22 languages, and normative data have been collected in more than 15 countries.[7] Analysis of the measure can be found in several empirical studies.[34, 46]

Schutte self-report inventory (SSRI)/ Self-report emotional intelligence test (SREIT)

Developed by Schutte and associates, the SREIT is a 33-item self-report instrument measuring emotional intelligence on a 5-point Likert scale.[24b] Respondents are advised to mark their choices to questions pertaining to their adaptive propensity toward emotional intelligence on a scale of 1 to 5 with "1" representing strong agreement and "5" representing strong disagreement. This measure is based on the revised framework of Salovey and Mayer's 1990 model of emotional intelligence. Though it does not cover the entire domain of trait emotional intelligence, it is based on the three-dimensional construct of Salovey and Mayer's 1990 model and assesses the ability to adaptively recognize, express, regulate, and harness emotions in self and in others.[24b] The test provides a measure of general EI as well as measures of EI sub-factors. This measure has been criticized for its inadequacy in mapping with the Salovey and Mayer model of emotional intelligence. Such criticism emanated from the fact that the original 62 items of the measure were mapped into the initial model of emotional intelligence proposed by Salovey and Mayer. The factor analysis of the original 62 items translated into a single factor, 33 item scale establishing structural validity. This did not precisely echo the principles of the model.[21] However, this measure has been extensively used in the research literature. The scale showed good criterion validity significantly predicting the year-end GPA for a group of college students while differentiating between groups of people on their levels of emotional intelligence.

Trait meta-mood scale (TMMS)

The 30-item self-report TMMS was developed to assess trait-related dimensions of mood including attention to one's own feelings, clarity of feelings, and mood repair which is also called mood regulation.[47] Originally, 48 items based on those developed by Mayer and associates[48] were factor analyzed and grouped into three domains, attention to emotion; emotional clarity; and mood repair.[47] Finally, 30 items with highest loadings on each factor were selected for the subscales reflecting the three mood domains — attention to feelings, clarity of feelings, and mood repair. A confirmatory factor analysis supported the choices for the three subscales. There are 13 items for the first sub-scale, Attention to Feelings; 11 items measuring the sub-scale of Clarity of Feelings and 6 for the third scale, Mood Repair. Respondents rate themselves on each item using a 5-point scale on which 1 denotes "strongly disagree", 2 denotes "somewhat disagree", 3 signifies "neither agree nor disagree", 4 represents "somewhat agree", and 5 symbolizes "strongly agree". This scale was not intended to provide a global score and the scale does not cover the entire domain of trait emotional intelligence. Salovey and associates found that high scores on mood repair subscale were associated with less depression, more optimism, and less distress; high scores on the clarity of feelings subscale were related to less ambivalence in emotional expression, less depression, less neuroticism, and less distress; and high scores on the attention to feelings subscale were linked to more private and public self-consciousness, less depression, and less repressive-defensiveness, but also more neuroticism. Additionally, individuals scoring high on the clarity of feelings subscale were more likely to rebound from a negative mood. This pattern of results shows that the subscales measure the same basic construct to some extent, but also exhibit some divergent validity among the subscales.[47]

Wong and Law emotional intelligence scale (WLEIS)

Wong and Law[49] developed a 16-item, four- dimensional self-report measure in tune with Mayer and Salovey's four-branch ability model of emotional intelligence.[3a] The scale measures four dimensions, *Self-emotion appraisal* [SEA], *Others' emotion appraisal* [OEA], *Use of emotion* [UOE], and *Regulation of emotion* [ROE]. Self-appraisal of emotion is the ability to understand one's own emotions and to express them naturally. The second dimension is the ability to perceive and understand others' emotions. Use of Emotion is the ability to apply one's emotions to facilitate conduct, while regulation of emotion is the ability to regulate one's emotions. The higher order construct of EI is theorized to account for the relationships between these four lower-order branches. Each dimension is assessed with four items on a 7-point Likert Scale.

Wong's emotional intelligence scale (WEIS)

This measure was developed by Wong, Law and Wong[50] based on the four branches of Mayer, Salovey and Caruso[22]. This is a 40-item forced choice emotional intelligence scale with paired scenario items for Chinese respondents. WEIS has two parts. The first section has 20 scenarios and the respondents are expected to select an option under each scenario which is best descriptive of their reaction for that scenario. The second section has 20 different pairs of abilities and the test-taker is required to select one out of each pair which best describes his/her strengths. The following four ability dimensions of emotional intelligence are fundamental to this scale:

1. Appraisal and expression of emotion in self
2. Appraisal and recognition of emotion in others
3. Regulation of emotion in the self
4. Use of emotion to facilitate performance

Results of an exploratory study indicate[51] acceptable convergent validity with the self-report emotional intelligence of Wong and Law and discriminant validity with Big-Five personality dimensions and mental intelligence.[49]

Emotional intelligence appraisal (EIA)

Developed by Travis Bradberry and associates of TalentSmart research team, the EIA is a 28-item scale measuring the four main components of Daniel Goleman's model of emotional intelligence (self-awareness, social awareness, self-management, and relationship management).[28] This measure uses a 6-point frequency scale ranging from 1 indicating "never" demonstrating a behavior to 6 signifying "always" exhibiting a behavior. The scale provides an overall EI score along with individual scores for each of the four components of emotional intelligence. This measure is available in three different versions (variants) — a self-report version (Me Edition); the 360 degree assessment format (MR Edition) and a variant for intact group (Team Edition). The emotional intelligence appraisal measure was found to predict job performance among middle and senior level managers to a significant extent.[52] Another study of 12,000 employees across all industries, job-classes and levels found that this measure was a significant predictor of job performance, apart from demonstrating additional criterion validity for the ME edition of the EIA.[28]

EQ Map test

The EQ Map test developed by Cooper and Sawaf,[10] consists of over 250 items grouped into five components encompassing 21 EI factors. The five components are Current environment, Emotional Literacy, EQ competencies, EQ values and beliefs, and EQ outcomes. This model provides the context for practicing emotional intelligence and its outcomes. The 21 EI factors are grouped under five components. The Current Environment includes life events, work pressures, personal pressures; the second component, Emotional Literacy, comprises emotional self-awareness, emotional expression, and emotional awareness of others; third component, Emotional Competency, comprises intentionality, creativity, resilience, interpersonal connection and constructive discontent. The fourth component, EQ values and beliefs, consists of compassion, outlook, intuition, trust radius, personal power and integrity; and the last component, EQ outcomes, consists of general health, quality of life, relationship quotient and optimal performance.

Trait emotional intelligence questionnaire (TEIQue)

As a part of a research program at London Psychometric Laboratory in the University College, London, the TEIQue was designed by K.V. Petrides.[53] The TEIQue is based on the trait emotional intelligence conceptualizing EI as a personality trait, located at the lower levels of personality hierarchies.[34, 35] Over the years, various forms of the test were developed and validated.[54] Presently, multiple versions of TEIQue are available in more than 20 languages. Empirical studies using various TEIQue forms and versions have been reported by several research studies.[35b, 54a, 54c] There are various versions (forms) of this measure, which are summarized as follows:

- *TEIQue full form:*
  The TEIQue full form is a self-report inventory measuring trait emotional intelligence. The latest version of the long form comprises 153 items, producing scores on 15 subscales, four factors, and a global trait emotional intelligence. The 15 subscales comprise adaptability, assertiveness, emotion perception (self and others), emotion expression, emotion management (others), emotion regulation, impulsiveness, relationships, self-esteem, self-motivation, social awareness, stress management, empathy, happiness and optimism.
- *TEIQue short form:*
  This version has 30 items based on the full form, measuring overall trait emotional intelligence. There are two items representing each of the 15 facets chosen on the basis of their correlations with their respective facet scores.[55, 56]
- *TEIQue child form:*
  This version was designed for children of 8 to 12 years of age in collaboration with Stella Mavroveli. There are 75 items to be responded on a 5-point scale measuring nine distinct facets.[57]

Work profile questionnaire – emotional intelligence (WPQei)

This self-report instrument developed by Cameron has 98 items measuring seven components of his model of emotional intelligence. This instrument measures competencies that are crucial for employees to manage their emotions at work and help in effective work performance.[29a] These components are similar to those in the instrument of Goleman's model.[26] Originally, this measure had 98 items which were revised to 84 on the basis of a confirmatory factor analysis.[29b] The measure is based on the following seven components:

- *Innovation:* Interpreting one's creative style and assessing the ability to effectuate creative solutions to business problems by self or through others.
- *Self-awareness:* Knowledge of one's own strengths and weaknesses coupled with a strong desire to improve one's capabilities.
- *Intuition:* Gut feeling, aptitude for predicting outcomes with insufficient information, ability to use instincts coupled with information in decision making.
- *Emotions:* Identifying, comprehending and interpreting one's own feelings and emotions and regulating their influence on others.
- *Motivation:* Striving for achievement with energy, initiative and persistence.
- *Empathy:* Showing interest in others and paying attention to their opinions, problems and concerns.
- *Social skills:* Ability to build relationships and communicating effectively.

The instrument provides a score (out of 10) for total emotional intelligence and a score for each of the seven competencies (out of 10).[29] All items are scored on a 5-point rating scale from "1" (never) to "5" (always). Fifty-six (56) items have the positive structure whereas 42 items have the reverse structure. The original version was first translated from English into Turkish and then translated from Turkish into English.[29b]

Workplace Swinburne University EI test (Workplace SUEIT)

The workplace SUEIT scale comprises 64 items measuring workplace emotional intelligence on a 5-point Likert scale.[58] It gives a global score as well as scores on five factors representing a set of related abilities for dealing with emotions in the workplace effectively. These five factors are (1) emotional recognition and expression (in oneself) — the ability to identify one's own feelings and emotional states, and the ability to express those inner feelings to others; (2) understanding emotions (external) — the ability to identify and understand emotions of others and those that manifest in external stimuli; (3) emotions direct cognition — the extent to which emotions and emotional knowledge are incorporated in decision-making and/or problem solving; (4) emotional management — the ability to manage positive and negative emotions both within oneself and others; (5) emotional control — how effectively emotional states are experienced at work and emotions like anger, stress, anxiety and frustration are controlled. Participants are instructed to indicate the extent to which each statement is true of the way they typically think, feel and act at work.

Style in the perception of effect scale (SIPOAS)

The SIPOAS developed by Bernet is a 93-item measure based on the premise that the basis of EI is the ability to address feelings in the most expeditious and judicious manner without difficulty.[59] This measure predicts the respondent's preferred style of perception of affect out of the three styles — body-based, evaluation-based and logic-based perception of affect. Bernet found that the body-based perception of affect was correlated with superior mental health, awareness of small bodily changes, social skill, contentment and creativity.

Genos emotional intelligence inventory (Genos EI)

The Genos EI inventory postulated by Dr. Gillies Gignac comprises 70 items measuring the frequency in the display of emotionally intelligent behaviors on seven dimensions, 1) Emotional self-awareness; 2) Emotional expression; 3) Emotional awareness of others; 4) Emotional reasoning; 5) Emotional self-management; 6) Emotional management of others; and 7) Emotional self-control. Responses are scored on a 5-point Likert scale.

The scale produces an inconsistency index score, two socially desirable responding scores, a total emotional intelligence score, and seven subscale scores. The Genos EI inventory was specifically designed for workplace settings. Therefore, the items within the Genos EI inventory and the corresponding reports have high workplace relevance.[60] The multiple versions of this measure are described as follows:

- *Genos EI Inventory Concise Version* comprises 31 items providing individual scores for all the seven subscales as well as a total EI score. Apart from being a shorter form, the reliability levels of subscale scores for this concise version just fulfill the minimal standards for research.
- *Genos EI Inventory Short Version* has 14 items designed to provide a single total score of emotional intelligence. This version was designed strictly for research purposes.

Workgroup emotional intelligence profile (WEIP)

Jordan and associates[61] designed this measure to sketch the emotional intelligence of individuals in workgroups. The scale comprises 27 items measuring seven facets organized into two broad dimensions [*intrapersonal* and *interpersonal]* on a 7-point Likert scale. This is a self-report measure designed to capture emotional intelligence of individuals in teams. The WEIP6 comprises two dimensions of emotional intelligence, *Ability to deal with own emotions* (Scale 1: 18 items) and *Ability to deal with others' emotions* (Scale 2: 12 items) discerned by the authors. Scales 1 and 2 are delineated into five subscales. Scale 1 is composed of three subscales, (a) *Ability to recognize own emotions; (b) Ability to discuss own emotions;* and *(c) Ability to manage own emotions*. Scale 2 is composed of two subscales, (a) *Ability to recognize others' emotions* and (b) *Ability to manage others' emotions*. Teams emotional intelligence is measured by calculating the average scores of the WEIP6 for all team members.

Group emotional competence (GEC) inventory

The GEC inventory is conceptualized by Vanessa Druskat and Steven Wolff who applied emotional competence concepts at the group level.[62] Their research has demonstrated that GEC norms enhance the effectiveness of the group, by way of building social capital which in turn facilitates involvement in effective task behaviors and processes.[63] The instrument contains 57 items that measure the nine dimensions of group emotional intellegence (GEI).[64]

Emotional intelligence scale [EIS]

The emotional intelligence scale postulated by Van der Zee and associates[65] is a 5-point Likert scale consisting of 85 items measuring 17 subscales. The scale seems to have a three-factor structure comprising empathy, autonomy, and emotional control. The reliabilities of internal consistency for most of the subscales were found to be relatively low, below the mark of 0.50. Congruent with the conceptual distinction between trait and ability emotional intelligence, the authors found that the EIS is related to personality traits, but not to cognitive ability.

Constructive thinking inventory (CTI)

The constructive thinking inventory is a 5-point rating scale based on Epstein's[66] Cognitive-experiential self-theory. The theory states that people basically have two adaptive systems – an "experiential system" that learns from life experiences, and a "rational / intellectual system" that functions on conscious reasoning. The CTI professes to measure the effectiveness of the experiential system.

The scores on this test are entered into a software program and protocols are run to obtain the score report with a profile of results. This test assesses work performance, social skills, emotional and physical well-being and many other abilities/ states, which are either unrelated or weakly related to intellectual intelligence. The CTI scores have been found to augment intelligence in the prediction of academic performance measured by the GPA (grade point average) to a significant extent. This instrument is also used for diagnosing beliefs and thinking patterns to be helpful in psychotherapy and counseling. The CTI has been found useful in developing coping skills in drug abuse victims at treatment centers. It is also used in employee selection, training and counseling at various levels. The test is useful in selecting students during college admissions and also in the counseling of high school and college students. This test provides scores for the Global Constructive Thinking Scale, six scales and 15 sub scales. The Global Constructive Thinking Scale is composed of items from several other scales and provides a general score. There are six main scales at the next level (Emotional Coping, Behavioral Coping, Personal Superstitious Thinking, Categorical Thinking, Esoteric Thinking, and Naive Optimism) measuring the basic ways of thinking (constructively or destructively). The main scales comprise subscales, which identify the specific thoughts and thinking patterns that make up the main scales. This information helps in interpreting the scores on the main scales and in accurate diagnoses for counseling and psychotherapy for correcting maladaptive beliefs and ways of thinking.

Levels of emotional awareness scale (LEAS)

The levels of emotional awareness scale developed by Lane and associates is a self-report measure assessing the respondents' awareness of emotions in self and others.[67] This measure is based on the hierarchical theory of emotional intelligence, particularly the five sub-levels of emotional awareness — physical sensations, action tendencies, single emotions, blends of emotions and blends of these emotional experiences.[68] The scale comprises 20 scenarios involving two people and an emotion-eliciting situation. Respondents should specify how they would feel in the given situation and how the other person in the scenario would feel in the same situation. Each scenario gets a score ranging from 0–5 (corresponding to the Lane and Schwartz theory of emotional awareness).[69] The participant receives a score for self (awareness of emotions in oneself), for others (awareness of emotion in others), and a total emotional awareness score (an average of self and other).[67]

There are many other measures of emotional intelligence which have not attracted much attention in the wider scientific literature.[1]

CRITIQUE OF EMOTIONAL INTELLIGENCE

A raging argument claims that emotional intelligence may be nothing more than a fixation, a rage or infatuation associated with business and education. The volcanic growth and popularity of emotional intelligence reveals a distinct pattern, typically characteristic of fads as claimed by Murphy and Sideman.[70] According to them, these characteristics are (1) a fast track of growth; (2) unrealistic and flattering claims and assurances beyond credible levels; and (3) incitement of fierce positive as well as negative reactions. These researchers argue that usually such fads go through a natural lifecycle. They claim that initial attraction and infatuation fades away leading to a sharp decline though the fad may re-appear after many years or even decades. While strong proponents are highly optimistic of the prominence and permanence of emotional intelligence, critics believe that the concept would have a short life span. Numerous peer-reviewed journal articles currently deal with key issues of emotional intelligence, such as test development; EI and corresponding cognitive abilities and personality; and endorsement of EI measures against measures of social functioning and adaptation. Despite research on emotional intelligence being exposed to a flood of criticism, the domain may still possess significant scientific foundation sufficient to be categorized as a tenable and acceptable branch of psychological science.[1] Nevertheless, there are many problems in assessing the scientific contribution of emotional intelligence research at the broader level.[1]

Problems with Definitions and Conceptualizations

Topping the list of problems is the absence of a universal definition of emotional intelligence. There is no clarity as to whether emotional intelligence is cognitive or non-cognitive, whether it is associated with implicit or explicit knowledge of emotion, whether it is an aptitude or a process of adaptation to social and cultural environment.[71] Secondly, there is uncertainty about the manner in which emotional intelligence is measured as multiple measures fail to converge. There is a diverse range of conceptions, and definitions, each creating its own operational measure of the construct. Thirdly, the psychometric imperfections of various measures of emotional intelligence have decimated their practical utility. The existing measures do not meet the levels of confidence necessary for making real-world decisions as they suffer deficiency of validity evidence.[72] Additionally, certain programs intended for developing emotional intelligence may tend to be deficient in the articulation of theoretical foundations and matching methodological relevance.[73]

Debate on Emotional Intelligence as a Form of Intelligence

The definition of emotional intelligence has been questioned on several counts.[74] It is argued that monitoring one's own emotions does not require any special kind of intelligence since it is only a question of where to focus one's attention — outwards on external world or inward observing the content and processes of one's own consciousness. Inward focus involves introspection. This argument is based on the premise that people have discretionary control on focusing their minds. On the other hand, the ability to interpret others' emotions does not constitute intelligence but simply paying attention to others and being aware of one's own emotions so as to empathize with others. Another issue is with discriminating among emotions which is argued to be a learned skill just like the case of identifying a given emotion. Similarly, the question of whether someone uses his/her proficiency in the course of everyday life is not in the intelligence domain. The definition of emotional intelligence is criticized that it includes a combination of disparate habits, skills or choices rather than characteristics of intelligence. It is argued that there is no common integrating element in emotional intelligence that includes introspecting about emotions, self-regulation, emotional expression, non-verbal communication with others, empathy, planning, creative thinking, etc.

The Concern about 'Reasoning' with Emotion

Another concern was with reference to 'reasoning with emotion' forming a part of the definition of emotional intelligence. It is contended that one cannot reason with emotion. It is claimed as a contradiction since emotion and reason are divergent cognitive processes performing separate and distinct psychological functions. Reasoning is a voluntary process guided by the conscious mind and is a means of acquiring and endorsing one's knowledge. In contrast, emotions involve robotic instinctual processes based on subconscious values and knowledge. Emotions represent a repertoire of beliefs and subconscious judgements about situations, objects or people, based on one's values. Therefore, emotions are manifestations of robotic value judgements.[75] Each emotion mirrors a particular kind of value judgement like fear is a reflexive response to the judgement of threat and anger is an involuntary response to the judgement of being offended or aggrieved. It is argued that since emotions are robotic reactions based on beliefs and values vaulted subconsciously, they are not conjured to be valid evaluation of reality as one may have fallacious beliefs or illogical values. The psychological function of emotions is not to acquaint with the world but to make automatic assessment and motivate action. Emotions are robotic reactions of the subconscious mind and as such, they cannot be instruments of knowledge. Emotions form a part of experience and perceived tendencies for action. Positive emotions influence the felt tendencies to pursue, acquire, or preserve the appraised object, while negative emotions result in feeling a tendency to escape, hurt, or wreck the appraised object. This is not to conclude that all emotions need to be acted on. We have the power of reason to evaluate the propriety of an action or alternative actions in a given situation. Therefore, one cannot reason with emotion, but could only reason about it. In other words, reason being the voluntary and agile component of one's mind, should be in control, failing which one is at the mercy of momentary emotions. Advocates of EI might concur with this proposition and argue that despite wide verbal connotations in its definitions, emotional intelligence truly means being intelligent about emotions, i.e., discerning their nature and their alliance with reason, and the need for introspection. Even if this is the purported conceptualization of EI proponents, they are referring to intelligence (the ability to grasp abstractions) applied to a particular life domain, i.e., emotions but not a type of intelligence. As intelligence could be applied to a host of life domains, it does not imply that multiple intelligences exist. The appropriate word generally used to explain the mastery of a person in a particular domain is skill as against intelligence.

Emotional intelligence defined in multitude of dimensions with a diverse range of perspectives left little scope for a common scientific, valid, robust, and consistent construct. Many personality traits and behavioral dispositions are mixed with a few socio-emotional abilities and are labeled as a model or form of emotional intelligence.[30]

The criticism leveled against emotional intelligence by some research scholars is summarized as follows:[74, 76]

1. The concept is so dynamic that its definitions are constantly changing, some of which are all-inclusive with no unanimity among different scholars.
2. 'Reasoning with emotion' is included in one of the definitions which is paradoxical, as one cannot 'reason with emotion' which is an involuntary process, based on subconscious values and knowledge.[75]
3. Intelligence can be applied to multiple domains, including emotions which denoted application of intelligence but not distinct intelligence.
4. Intrinsically, there is no conflict between reason and emotion.[75]
5. Emotional intelligence adds little or nothing to the explanation or prediction of some common outcomes.
6. The wide range of emotional intelligence measures are diverse and change continuously.
7. The claims of Daniel Goleman with respect to emotional intelligence are unsubstantiated by verifiable and accessible research evidence.

Responding to the above criticism, Ashkanasy and Daus proposed the following:[77]

1. Mainstream research on emotional intelligence should be separated from early attempts to convert social intelligence into a workable model. Emotional intelligence may be instrumental in developing social relationships and enhancing interpersonal skills, but it is markedly distinct from the other constructs in its family including social and spiritual intelligences.[78] Despite the historical amorphous footprints of social intelligence, it is unreasonable to predict that emotional intelligence research would falter similarly, since its conception is rooted in the theories of emotion.
2. As emotional intelligence is in its stage of development, there is a considerable discourse, but it is a desirable and hardy trend in a scientific process.[79]
3. Critics focused their censure mostly on the propositions of a select group of research, failing to differentiate the conceptualization of other schools of research.[3c, 79, 80]
4. Emotional intelligence is used by industrial and organizational psychologists and researchers in organizational behavior as an instrument to understand and predict behavior. It is neither a re-packaged version of social intelligence nor a substitute for intellectual intelligence.[40a]
5. Emotional intelligence is discernible from other forms of intelligences while being positively related to existing intelligences. It is manifested in different degrees among individuals, resulting in some people being more endowed with it while others are less so. Emotional intelligence can be enhanced over a person's life span through conscious efforts and training.

Criticism on other aspects of emotional intelligence include the following:

Measurement Issues

In line with the categorization of theories of emotional intelligence, the measures have also acquired the category status of either ability or mixed models apart from assuming different forms, such as the self-report, other-report or performance-based measures.

- **Inaccurate self-report measures:** Self-report measures require the respondents to rate themselves on the extent to which a particular statement closely describes them. The accuracy in the ratings of self-report measures depends on the authenticity of respondent's self-concept. In the event that the respondent's self-concept is inaccurate, the self-report measures would then be measuring the reported self-concept and not the actual attitudes, thoughts and behaviors of the individual.[81, 31]
- **Informant-report measures and reputation effect:** Informant measures seek the inputs of individuals familiar with the subject about whom the data is collected. Such third person is asked to rate the subject (the person with whom they are familiar) on certain statements indicating the extent to which they describe the subject. Relatively, informant measures may be more accurate as they are less likely to measure self-concept of the subject. However, other-report measures were criticized of measuring the reputation of the subject as against their true self and as such were found to be less reliable in evaluating internal cognitive styles and capabilities.[82]
- **Performance measures (ability measures):** Performance measures evaluate intelligence level by requiring the individual to perform certain cognitive tasks or activities. Customarily, performance measures are treated as the "gold standard" of intelligence testing as they directly relate to the true capability to perform well at intellectual assignments. In other words, having the respondents perform intellectual tasks demonstrates their true competence while self and other report forms of testing capture the beliefs of respondent about those competences.[17b] But there are others who believe that despite being less direct in measurement, self-report measures are not affected by reliability and scoring problems that are inherently associated with performance measures.[83]

In terms of usage, self and other report measures are generally used with mixed models, and performance measures are adopted within the ability model of emotional intelligence.

Emotional Intelligence and Personality Traits

Parallel to the contentious discourse concerning the conceptualization of emotional intelligence, there is an ongoing debate on the most accurate method of measuring the construct. Apprehensions crowded over the validity of self-report measures as some researchers asserted that self-report measures of emotional intelligence did not claim any additional credit for outcomes in life criteria beyond the credit attributable to traditional tests of intelligence and personality.[45a, 84] On the other hand, findings by other researchers show that self-report measures of emotional intelligence have in fact shown additional predictive power over and above that of standard personality measures, but self-report measures weren't the ideal choice to explain the additional variance.[85] Davies and associates conducted an extensive psychometric evaluation of emotional intelligence using an array of measures of EI.[86] This study found low reliability and validity for most of the measures of emotional intelligence while finding strong correlations between self-report measures and conventional personality factors. A comparative study of self-report and performance-based measures of emotional intelligence revealed that self-report measures vigorously correlated with personality measures, while performance measures moderately correlated with personality and well-being.[41] Another finding of this study was the absence of convergent validity between the performance and self-report measures, i.e., the measures were found to be unrelated. Additionally, performance measures showed high discriminant validity when compared to personality measures but the self-report measures did not indicate the same.

SUPPORT FOR EMOTIONAL INTELLIGENCE

Despite encountering extensive criticism, emotional intelligence continues to attract the attention of researchers, trainers, and academicians.

EI PERSPECTIVE Scars of Bad Temper

Once there was a little boy who was highly intelligent but had a bad temper. He was unable to control his anger, which was creating problems at school as well as in the social circle. His parents were worried about his growing ill temper. After a serious thought, one day, the boy's father gave him a bag of nails and instructed him to drill a nail into the oak wood back-fence of their house each time he lost temper. On the first day, the boy hammered 37 nails into the wooden fence. But gradually, he learned to regulate his anger and the number of nails he drilled into the fence declined in the next few weeks.

The boy realized that controlling his temper was easier than drilling those nails into the fence. Ultimately, he reached a stage when he never lost his temper at all. He was so glad for his accomplishment of gaining control over his anger that he went and told his father about it. His father was equally happy but encouraged the boy to start pulling out one nail from the fence for each day he was able to hold his anger in check.

As the days passed, the boy was able to pull out all the nails one by one and informed his father that there were no more nails in the fence. The father then held his son's hand and taking him around the fence he said, "Well son, you have done very well in controlling your temper, but if you look at the fence with the gaping holes, you will realize that the fence will never be the same".

"Same is with the things you utter in the fit of rage or anger. Your words leave a scar upon others just like these holes. You may inflict a knife into the body of a man and pull it out, despite tendering innumerable apologies to the other person for such of your acts, the wounds still remain. Inflicting oral wounds on the psyche of the other person is as bad as the physical one".

Verbal injuries inflicted in a fit of rage destroy relationships and friendships of lifetime, which are more valuable than our urge to vent out our ill temper.

Emotional competencies have been found to hold the key for unlocking human potential while acting as a remedy to emotional toxicity plaguing the workplaces as well as human life in modern day. The following justifications in favor of emotional intelligence may be relevant:

Multi-dimensionality of Emotional Intelligence

Individual emotional intelligence constructs have been found to be connected meaningfully to external criteria.

An extensive body of evidence shows strong correlations between various scales of emotional intelligence and outcomes credibly associated with social-emotional effectiveness.[87] The subscales of MSCEIT as well as other measures of emotional intelligence were found to correlate with the measures of well-being and social engagement.[85, 88]

Structured Developmental Path of Emotional Intelligence

An extensive body of literature on socio-emotional development in children existed much earlier to the advent of emotional intelligence.[89] Apparently, there existed a robustly defined progressive indicators of emotional development starting with straightforward expressions and adaptive behaviors of an infant. Such progression evolved into judicious self-regulation and sensitivity to the social and cultural environment.[90]

Neurological Evidence for Emotional Intelligence

Despite the disparaging viewpoints on emotional intelligence, neurological evidence provides credence to the proposition that emotional intelligence is a distinct capability independent of IQ. The case of Phineas Gage is the earliest and most popular case study in this arena.

Mr. Gage was a notable, hardworking and hospitable person working with explosives in building railroads. Once, he survived a ghastly accident in which an iron bar pierced through the front of his head due to an explosion. Despite his magical recovery with his memory, intellect, speech, sensation and movement intact, his behavior changed radically. His emotions and responses turned erratic, he became reckless and impatient when anything contradictory to his desires was suggested. Contemporary neuroimaging techniques applied on Phineas' skull revealed that the iron road pierced the bilateral ventromedial area of his prefrontal cortex.[91] Neocortex is primarily the base for IQ components of intellectual abilities like verbal fluency, spatial logic, and abstract reasoning. The constituents of emotional intelligence were found to remain mostly as a neurological network connecting the limbic areas for emotion (amygdala and its accordant networks) to the prefrontal cortex (the executive center of the brain). Concussions to this area were found to produce deficiency in the abilities of emotional intelligence.[92] Specifically, patients suffering ventromedial prefrontal lesions (frontal lobe syndrome) retained their intellectual abilities while experiencing acute affliction to their personal and social decision making.

EI PERSPECTIVE Pilot Bob Hoover's reaction to a deadly mistake

Famous test pilot Bob Hoover was at an air show being held at Brown Field in San Diego, in the year 1989. The adventurous test pilot was taking some risk-seeking visitors on a flight trip in his Shrike Commander, a small piston-powered plane. They got more thrills than they expected. When the plane flew at an altitude of 300 feet, it lost all its power and control as it started nose diving to the earth yielding to its gravitational pull. Bob Hoover maneuvered the plane to crash land safely into the side of a gorge by cutting its speed. The aircraft was badly damaged but he walked out safely along with his two passengers. He was puzzled as his mind was swirling around the question as to what caused the failure. While waiting on the hill side for the rescue team, he walked back to the plane and checked the fuel. He found the fuel tank filled with jet fuel instead of gasoline.

A ground crew member who serviced this plane mis-fuelled it wrongly assuming the piston engine plane to be a turboprop. A simple mistake of filling the wrong fuel but could have been fatal. After returning to the air strip, Bob Hoover went to meet the man who was responsible for his close encounter with death. The young man was drowned in guilt and crying in pain for his mistake which caused the destruction of an expensive aircraft apart from nearly causing death of three people. Anyone can imagine the anger of a meticulous and famous pilot like Hoover. Everyone expected an explosive attack on the mechanic for his recklessness in handling the plane, but Hoover did not lambast or castigate the mechanic.

Keeping his arm around the mechanic's shoulder, Hoover consoled him saying that there was none in this world who hadn't made a mistake. He expressed confidence that the mechanic would never repeat that mistake again and asked him to refuel Hoover's aircraft the very next day adding that no one else in the field would touch his plane, except the mechanic himself. He reposed faith in him.

Source: 1) https://www.squawkpoint.com/2014/01/criticism

2) Hoover, B. (1997). "*Forever Flying*". New York NY: Pocket Books

Such people felt incapacitated to plan their day's schedule or their future while struggling to choose their friends, partners and activities. As a result, such patients started exercising disadvantageous choices which they were unknown to have made in their life prior to their brain injuries. They were also incapable of learning from their prior mistakes while being deficient in their ability to process emotional gestures and messages as well as failing to cope with environmental and social requirements.[91]

The research study of Davidson and associates using PET scans (positron-emission tomography) found that abnormal activity in the amygdala resulted in heightened negative emotions.[93] However, the medial pre-frontal cortex, which produces neurons inhibiting the activity of amygdala, mediates this abnormal activity. Therefore, the ability to regulate negative affect apparently lies in the circuit between the amygdala and the medial pre-frontal cortex. Studies conducted on patients afflicted with amygdala lesions show the indispensability of amygdala in recognition of emotions through facial expressions and in assessing the trustworthiness of a person. Moreover, the neural connections which cause the inability to interpret facial expressions overlap with those associated with decision making. Therefore, researchers conclude that deficiencies in the abilities of emotional processing could adversely impact social decision making.[91]

Neuroscience researchers emphasize that their findings do not support one model of emotional intelligence against the other, but they validate the prevalence of certain emotional abilities constituting a type of intelligence which is distinct from the standard intelligence or IQ.[91] Similarly, affectional neurological studies found support for the main constituents of emotional intelligence that are common across different models. For instance, the competency of recognizing emotions in others and managing one's own emotions effectively are common constituents of emotional intelligence across different models.

Such neurological studies focusing on the roots of emotions constitute an emerging area of investigation, and substantial work remains yet to be done in this field. Nevertheless, neurologically differentiating cognitive intelligence from emotional intelligence accords credence to emotional intelligence as a construct distinct from IQ.

Chapter Synthesis

The term emotional intelligence was first used by Salovey and Mayer who proposed that it is comprised of three categories of adaptive abilities, namely (1) appraisal and expression of emotion; (2) regulation of emotion; and (3) utilization of emotion in decision making and problem-solving. Following this, two categories of conceptualization have emerged in the domain of emotional intelligence — the ability and mixed models. Ability models conceptualized emotional intelligence as a form of intelligence. In comparison, mixed models describe a composite conception of emotional intelligence comprising mental abilities, attitudes, dispositions and traits. Mayer and Salovey[10] postulated a revised model of emotional intelligence in 1997, which gives more emphasis to the cognitive components of emotional intelligence and conceptualized it in terms of its potential for intellectual and emotional growth. The revised model consists of four branches, (1) perception, appraisal, and expression of emotion; (2) emotional facilitation of thinking; (3) understanding, analyzing and employing emotional knowledge; and (4) reflective regulation of emotions to facilitate emotional and intellectual growth. Mayer and Salovey's model is considered as ability model, while all other postulations of emotional intelligence including that of Daniel Goleman, Bar-On and many others are considered as mixed models. Mixed models combine together emotional intelligence factors and characteristics with other personality traits, attitudes and dispositions. There is a considerable debate and discourse among researchers about which of the two models in emotional intelligence literature — the ability or mixed — accurately and truly represents the concept of emotional intelligence. Corresponding to the development of various models of emotional intelligence, numerous instruments of its measurement have emerged. The measurement approaches consist of ability or performance-based measures, self-report measures, and informant report measures. Ability/performance based measures ask the respondent to solve a problem or respond to a question. Self–report measures require the respondents to endorse a series of descriptive statements, indicating the degree to which they describe or do not describe themselves. Self-reported abilities and traits rely on the individual's self-perception. Informant reports are ratings about the target on certain indicators gathered from the target's friends, acquaintances, spouse and others, based on their overall understanding of that target individual. The other forms of informant reports could include assessment by peers. These measures require an observer to assess the target on observable signs and symptoms over a brief period (e.g., during an interview or over the course of a day) or over a long period (e.g., several months). This method yields information about how a person is perceived by others.

A raging argument claims that emotional intelligence may be nothing more than a fixation, a rage or infatuation associated with business and education. Arguments criticizing emotional intelligence are centered around the following issues:

1. Absence of a universal definition of emotional intelligence.
2. Lack of clarity on whether emotional intelligence is cognitive or non-cognitive, whether it is associated with implicit or explicit knowledge of emotion, whether it is an aptitude or a process of adaptation to social and cultural environment.
3. Uncertainty about the measurement of emotional intelligence as multiple measures fail to converge.
4. The psychometric imperfections of various measures of emotional intelligence have decimated their practical utility.
5. Certain programs intended for developing emotional intelligence may tend to be deficient in the articulation of theoretical foundations and matching methodological relevance.
6. Monitoring one's own emotions does not require any special kind of intelligence since it is only a question of where to focus one's attention, outwards on external world or inward observing the content and processes of one's own consciousness.
7. EI includes a combination of disparate habits, skills or choices rather than characteristics of intelligence. There is no common integrating element in emotional intelligence that includes introspecting about emotions, self-regulation, emotional expression, non-verbal communication with others, empathy, planning, creative thinking, etc.
8. Emotions cannot be reasoned about. Reasoning is a voluntary process guided by the conscious mind and is a means of acquiring knowledge. In contrast, emotions involve robotic instinctual processes based on subconscious values and knowledge and are based on robotic value judgements.
9. Even if EI is referred to as intelligence (the ability to grasp abstractions) applied to a particular life domain, i.e., emotions, it cannot be categorized as a type of intelligence. Since intelligence could be applied to multiple life domains, it does not imply that multiple intelligences exist.

In response to the criticism against emotional intelligence, some researchers proposed the following justification in support of the construct:

1. Emotional intelligence is multidimensional
2. An extensive body of evidence shows strong correlations between various scales of emotional intelligence and outcomes credibly associated with social-emotional effectiveness.
3. Studies on socio-emotional development in children existed much prior to the advent of emotional intelligence. There were robustly defined progressive indicators of emotional development starting with straightforward expressions and adaptive behaviors of an infant. Such progression evolved toward intelligent and judicious self-regulation and sensitivity to the social and cultural environment.
4. Neurological evidence provides credence to the proposition that emotional intelligence is a distinct capability independent of IQ. The case of Phineas Gage is the earliest and most popular case study in this arena.
5. The research study of Davidson and associates using PET (positron-emission tomography) scans found that abnormal activity in the amygdala resulted in heightened negative emotions. However, the medial pre-frontal cortex, which produces neurons inhibiting the activity of amygdala, mediates this abnormal activity. Therefore, the ability to regulate negative affect apparently lies in the circuit between

the amygdala and the medial pre-frontal cortex. Researchers concluded that deficiencies in emotional processing capabilities could adversely impact social decision making.

6. Neurological studies focusing on the roots of emotions constitute the emerging area of investigation, and substantial work remains yet to be done in this field. Nevertheless, neurologically differentiating cognitive intelligence from emotional intelligence accords credence to emotional intelligence as a construct distinct from IQ.

Key Terms

Ability models
Adaptability
Assertiveness
Autonomy
Behavioral disposition
Cognitive processes
Consensual scoring
Criterion validity
Depression
Emotional alchemy
Emotional control
Emotional depth
Emotional expression
Emotional fitness
Emotional hardiness
Emotional intensity
Emotional literacy
Empathy
Expert scoring
Impulses
Impulsiveness
Informant measures
Instinctual processes
Intentionality
Interpersonal EQ
Intrapersonal EQ
Involuntary response
Mixed models
Mood regulation
Mood repair
Non-cognitive competencies
Non-intellectual abilities
Non-judgmental listening
Optimism
Performance measures
Psychometric standard
Psychometric imperfections
Relationship management
Resilience
Self-awareness
Self-management
Social awareness
Social intelligence
Social perceptiveness
Social skills
Sub-conscious judgments
Target scoring
Value judgments

Review Questions

1. **What is the criterion adopted for determining a construct as a type of intelligence?**
2. **How are the ability models of emotional intelligence different from the mixed models?**
3. **Compare and contrast ability measures, self-report measures and observer-report measures. Which type of measures are accurate and why?**
4. **What are the constituents and competencies underlying Goleman's emotional competence inventory (ECI)?**
5. **Explain the Bar-On model of emotional intelligence.**
6. **What are the grounds of criticism against the construct of emotional intelligence?**
7. **Is emotional intelligence a fallacy and fad or an authentic and useful phenomenon?**
8. **What evidence does neuroscience offer in support of emotional intelligence?**

Application-based Exercise

Seeking Feedback

Request your colleagues / subordinates / or associates for a feedback on your behavior and interactions with them on the following:

1. Recount two of my attributes or qualities that you immensely adore in a manager or colleague or associate.
2. Illustrate two attributes/ qualities/ traits/ behaviors that I should acquire or develop to become more productive and competent.
3. Recall and illustrate two incidents of my emotional reaction during which you felt it challenging to face and deal with me.
4. Narrate any of my behaviors which baffled others so much that it left them puzzled about whether I was truly aware of the impact of my behavior on others.

Activities Beyond the Book

Identifying emotions and monitoring behavior

1. Prepare a checklist of all the emotions that you might possibly feel or encounter every day in your life on regular basis, for example, joy, enthusiasm, confidence, fear, anxiety, depression, etc.
2. Keep a track on your emotions and watch for distinct configuration of behaviors associated with these emotions, the blueprints of emotional behavior. Over a period of time, develop a list of emotions you experience and the behavior that follows triggering you towards action. You would then have identified the behavioral costumes worn by different emotions.
3. Examine the above list to identify any particular archetype, design or specific pattern. Assume for instance that you are scared of powerful people, and therefore you tend to stay away from people in positions of or with authority. When you encounter such people, you might feel highly stressed or terrified.
4. Seek feedback from your colleagues or close associates with whom you have a trusted relationship or close affinity. Inquire them about your behavior when you are infuriated, nervous or despondent. You might for example become highly critical or scornful in your interactions or in the course of discussions at meetings.

Such analysis would provide you sufficient inputs on your behavioral response patterns in the course of experiencing various emotions. This way the emotion-behavior connection could be found so that the underlying real cause can be explored by analyzing past memories.

Video Resources

1. **Emotional Intelligence and Leadership – *Peter Salovey***
   Link: https://youtu.be/0k8TcF-3ofY
2. **Emotional Intelligence Tests: How to Measure Emotional Intelligence and EQ? – *Rachael Green***
   Link: https://www.youtube.com/watch?v=6xSl-RIVMm8
3. **An assessment of emotional intelligence**
   Link: https://www.youtube.com/watch?v=3GqDeuV_Olw

4. **Measuring Emotional Intelligence –** ***Travis Bradberry***
   Link: https://www.youtube.com/watch?v=vY3zKY5A0kM
5. **Why You Should Measure Your Empathy and Emotional Intelligence –** ***James Doyle,*** **JAMSO**
   Link: https://www.youtube.com/watch?v=l6Vbey1dPvA
6. **Emotion Measurement in Natural Settings through Everyday Devices – Daniel McDuff, Microsoft, 2017**
   Link: https://vimeo.com/202639579
7. **How is EI Measured? –** ***Dr. Robert Tett***
   https://www.sigmaassessmentsystems.com/ei-measured/
8. **Emotional Intelligence Test Review –** ***EQ Academy***
   https://www.youtube.com/watch?v=e_cMvzg470k

SELF-ASSESSMENT INSTRUMENT

Self-Efficacy Profile

The following instrument profiles your self-efficacy considering five characteristics, namely inner strength; concentrated vigor and drive; tenacity and determination; strong sense of empathy; and social and interpersonal competence. Be honest in your responses as the results are anyway confined to your own access and information intended for individual development. Think about each of the statements that follow and assign them points as indicated below, depending on the degree to which each statement applies to you:

If it is most characteristic of yourself	5 points
If it is fairly true of you	4 points
If it is somewhat true in your case	3 points
If you occasionally feel or behave this way	2 points
If you rarely feel or behave this way	1 point

1. I can connect and relate with people ... ... ☐
2. When I commit to do anything, I surmount all kinds of hurdles ... ... ☐
3. I am comfortable and grounded in most social settings ... ... ☐
4. I derive immense pleasure from what I do ... ... ☐
5. I am persistent and resolute in the face of adversities and failings ... ... ☐
6. Others recount a positive connect and affinity with me... ... ... ☐
7. I feel that I can achieve anything that I decide to take up ... ... ☐
8. I embrace challenges ... ... ☐
9. I believe myself to be internally resourceful and strong ... ... ☐
10. I am passionate about whatever I do ... ... ☐
11. I develop cordial and unreserved relationships with others ... ... ☐
12. Others pay attention to me when I am talking ... ... ☐

13. I earn the respect of others ... ... ☐
14. I do not undertake to perform anything unenthusiastically or apathetically ... ... ☐
15. I would not give up something on account of challenges I face ... ... ☐
16. I do not quit when I encounter difficulties ... ... ☐
17. I interact with others effortlessly ... ... ☐
18. I can handle tensions effectively and get along well with others ... ... ☐
19. People listen to my arguments even if I do not win them all the time ... ... ☐
20. I am truly enthusiastic about my work ... ... ☐

Scoring

Enter your scores for each statement against its item number in the following table:

Item No.	Score	Item No.	Score	Item No.	Score	Item No.	Score	Item No.	Score
7		4		2		1		3	
8		10		5		6		11	
9		14		15		13		12	
18		20		16		17		19	
Total									
Characteristic	A		B		C		D		E

Characteristic-A: **Inner Strength**
Characteristic-B: **Focused Energy and Drive**
Characteristic-C: **Tenacity and Determination**
Characteristic-D: **Strong Sense of Empathy**
Characteristic-E: **Social and Interpersonal Competence**

High scores indicate the domains of your strengths while lower scores point out to the weaker domains of your self-efficacy.

Note: The highest possible score in any domain is 20 points, while the lowest score is 5 points.

Analysis of Select Movies

1. ***The Breakfast Club (1985)***
Written and directed by John Hughes and produced by Ned Tanen and John Hughes, *The Breakfast Club* portrays five divergent adolescents from different high school groups. On a Saturday morning,

this group of riff-raff teens landed up together in custody, offering the viewer realistic narratives from teenagers' lives. We could immediately notice such types as rebels, nerds, athletes, popular girls, and weirdos that we usually encounter. The film deals with diverse cliques or leagues of uncommon teens strongly inclined to retain their identity of being unique or unconventional. With a demeanor typical of teenagers, these youngsters occasionally exhibit assiduous indifference to everything that repudiates their identity. As each of the kid characters in the film confront the dread of denial or disapproval by their parents and associates, they tend to seclude and sequester themselves into a distinct clique or archetype. These individual kids are also concerned that the bonds of friendship among the Breakfast Club would not sustain beyond their stay at the detention center. Their apprehension is rooted in their perception that the diversity of their social grouping is fairly strong to hold them aloof in exclusivity.

Every individual kid has his or her own frustration to handle that adversely impacts their psychological well-being. As we can see in the movie, John hails from a contemptuous home, Brian attempted suicide in the past, and Andrew's impulsive behavior of intimidating others is a consequence of his father's emotional abuse. The movie deals with the predicament of people skilled at masking their own freaky side. It explores the interspace between those who are apparently doing fairly well and those who are on the verge of breaking down.

At the detention center, these kids initially spend their time conversing and squabbling with each other. But they unmask themselves over a period of time, disclosing their emotions with others in the detention center. Apparently, all of these kids face enormous stress from their peers and each of them is in the grip of intense anxiety about their future. They find each of them to be having a pathetic kinship or association with their respective parents. Claire's parents use her as a punch bag to get even with each other amid their altercations. Likewise, John's parents assault him physically and verbally, while Allison's parents scorn and neglect her. Similarly, Andrew's father shoves him to the peak, particularly in wrestling. Brian's parents, on the other hand, constantly corner him, pushing him to get higher academic grades. Each one of these kids realize that notwithstanding their dissimilarities, all of them are apparently dealing with identical troubles. In the course of their detention spread over nine odd hours on that Saturday, these kids metamorphose from perfect strangers to intimate friends. Each of them felt their detention day to be a memorable occasion despite the fact that the friendships they formed there in a few hours may disband once they return to their real world. During their collective stay, they found many opportunities to analyze their feelings. They discovered emotions that guided them towards in-depth understanding of their lives and the powers that exert influence on the lives of others.

Towards the end of their detention, the group entreats Brian to complete the essay for everybody. Brain completes the essay and drops it in the library to enable Vernon to read the same after they left. When they were just about to go their own individual ways, students realized that each of them is a brain, an athlete, a basket case, a princess and a criminal, at the same time.

2. ***The Pursuit of Happyness (2006)***
   Directed by Gabriele Muccino and produced by Steve Tisch and others, *The Pursuit of Happyness* is a stirring narrative based on the true story of a San Francisco salesman, Chris Gardner battling to shape the future of himself and his five-year old son, Christopher. His girlfriend Linda deserts him, leaving the responsibility of caring for Chris and raising him on his shoulders. Eventually, Chris's perseverance bears fruit and he gets selected for an unpaid internship in a cruelly competitive program of training stock brokers. In the absence of pay or any other earning, Chris and his son get dislodged from their apartment and are constrained to spend the nights on streets, shelters for the destitute, and sometimes behind the locked doors of a metro station toilet. Chris Gardner overcomes his impediments and succeeds in becoming Wall Street celebrity owing to his self-confidence and the motivation derived from his son's love and trust reposed in him. The characters in the movie display profound

emotions while depicting their constructive role. The significance of emotions, values, relationships, attachments, and resilience are depicted in opulence and are well-presented in the movie.

Using instances from the life of Chris Gardener, the movie exemplifies that whosoever is self-driven and resolute, would accomplish his or her own pursuits of happiness. On the other hand, the film illustrates that happiness is not a destination to be pursued but a state of mind that comes from within — our inherent ability to experience happiness irrespective of external situations — in exercising our choice to be happy or otherwise with our own self and our incitement and ability for it. Chis Gardner and his son had to fight tough battles to accomplish their aspirations demonstrating that fortune favors the brave. Despite the deprivation of a shelter for himself and his son and finding no place to go, Gardner never entertained or exhibited defeatist suicidal tendencies or escapist attitudes. And he never thought of getting his son into a foster home even during his testing times. The intimate ties between the father and the son are illustrated in a touching manner, accentuating the vital role of parental support, care and concern in the emotional and psychological development of the child. In our experience, we might find scores of men leaving their kids in circumstances significantly less arduous than those faced by Chris. Despite having the choice of leaving his son with his mother, Chris refrained from disregarding his parental responsibilities even in the absence of a steady income. His steely tenacity in the face of unforeseen and abrupt challenges and his steadfast pursuit of happiness through his chosen path are phenomenal to say the least.

The affectionate and emotional expression reflected in the words of Christopher addressing his father, "You're a good papa", during their stay at the shelter home are truly touching. Even though Chris isn't immaculate, his commitment to shield his son and care for him are manifested through many emotionally enriched situations and depictions in the movie. Tangible expressions of embraces, pecks and other emotional moments between the father and son duo symbolize their deep-seated and profound relationship. In the movie, Chris asks his son to trust him over and over again, and as a father he establishes his credibility of being trustworthy.

As an inspiring parent, Chris exhorts his son to create a wish list for his birthday and gifts him a basketball thereafter but berates him on his errant shots into the hoop saying that basketball is not his cup of tea. Nevertheless, living up to his dad's expectations when Christopher hits a negligent shot, Chris remedies his mistake by contradicting him saying that his son couldn't let others decide about what he isn't good at. He emphasizes that his son should not allow anyone else, including his own father to undermine his abilities. He goes on to motivate his son to go after his dreams and achieve them irrespective of what others think about his abilities. Father and son duo spend an agonizing night at a deserted public transport station in the San Francisco Bay Area. Chris takes his son through a make-believe journey backward in time into the age of dinosaurs imagining that his bone-density machine as a time-travel gadget. His son happily joins him in his fantasy journey and imagines going into a cave which in reality is a public rest room where the duo was constrained to stay that night. Chris looks at his innocent son falling asleep on his lap, while tears roll down his face as he holds the toilet door shut with his leg. This incident in the film is a remarkable depiction of a father's commitment to provide his son the comfort of a mother's lap regardless of harsh realities of the world.

In the end, Chris secures an interview for a momentous internship as stockbroker at Dean Witter. Albeit he had to attend the interview without a proper dress with his face and hair peppered in paint, appearing like a vagabond released from an overnight lock-up. However, he looked at the opportunity rather than an excuse to postpone the interview. Despite the odds and competitive contenders, Chris succeeds in bagging the offer which was apparently beyond his reach.

It was a conditional offer in which the final job is offered to the intern who gets the maximum revenue in a span of six months. Hence there is a mad rush in that everyone was competing to procure maximum business, while each of them slogged by working late hours trying to sign new clients. But Chris had to look after his son and therefore could not allocate more than six hours a day to his internship while all others worked for nine hours. He was constrained to be efficient in managing his time as he had to do in six hours what others did in nine hours. Despite struggling to save every minute of his time during the first two months, he wasn't able to improve his revenue figures in the chart. Eventually, Chris succeeds in selling all the scanners but had to shell out almost the entire money to pay taxes and is barely left with twenty odd dollars in his bank account in the end. Nevertheless, he remains energetic to come back, protecting his son while retaining his trust. He has been a loving, honest and caring father while being humble enough to accept his mistakes before his son. This movie is rich in insights into emotional awareness, expression of appropriate emotions, emotional regulation, empathy, using emotions to facilitate understanding and thinking, and the value of relationships and bonding.

3. ***The Shawshank Redemption (1994)***

The movie is directed by Frank Darabont and produced by Castle Rock Entertainment. In general, most of the human folk would have felt despondent at some point in their life, incarcerated by life's events beyond their control. There could be situations in which we lose hope of dawn overwhelmed by a feeling of being trapped in an inescapable burrow while in the midst of obscurity. Such gloom and despair have the power to destroy our convictions, while impairing our attitudes and behaviors.

This film galvanizes emotions while projecting the importance of anticipation, hope, camaraderie, endurance and persistence in a high security prison context. Enriched with a flow of quintessential emotions ranging from anger to tears, loathsomeness to empathy, the film traverses through the rugged lives of Shawshank's inmates. The movie depicts the vivacity, grit, perseverance and hope of Andy in defiance to his twenty-year jail sentence and the miserable life in prison. Surprisingly, a strong bond of friendship transcending agony and distress develops between Andy and Red which finally culminates into an opportunity for possible deliverance. The movie is all about unyielding perseverance amidst helplessness and despair; friendships and bonding developed over years of common suffering; managing hostilities, animosities and the wicked. A whole lot of people could compare themselves with the predicament of Red who gives up all his hopes of being freed from prison during his lifetime. On the contrary, Andy demonstrates the power of emotional connect with family and friends as anchors of hope delivering us from misery and suffering. Apparently, there is also a loud and clear message that incarceration is not caused by the prison fences as much as by our mindset, beliefs and disposition towards freedom. The Shawshank penitentiary is more about the chemistry of our minds than the locale. The character of Andy demonstrates liveliness, emotional self-regulation, empathy, hope, faith, and search for meaning and purpose of life. Andy shows his zest for life despite agonizing prison conditions, whereas most of other prisoners live like animals in desperation. He constantly looks out for opportunities to negate the run-of-the-mill experience of jail life and always finds an escape from negativity. Paradoxically, he discovers his freedom in prison through perseverance, hope and meaningful pursuits when all others give up on hope. The movie ends with an overwhelming conclusion accentuating the expositions of companionship, conscientiousness, warmth and ardor.

References

1. Mathews, G., Zeidner, M., and Roberts, R. D. (2002). "*Emotional intelligence: Science and myth.*" Cambridge, MA: MIT Press.
2. Salovey, P., and Mayer, J. D. (1990). "Emotional intelligence." *Imagination, Cognition and Personality,* 9 (3): 185–211.
3. a. Mayer, J. D., and Salovey, P. (1997). "What is emotional intelligence?" In Salovey P. and Sluyter D. (Eds.). "*Emotional development and emotional intelligence: Educational implications,*" (pp. 3–31). New York: Basic Books.

b. Mayer, J. D., Salovey, P. and Caruso, D. (2004). "Emotional intelligence: Theory, findings and implications." *Psychological Inquiry,* 60: 197–215.
c. Salovey, P., Woolery, A., and Mayer, J. D., (2001). "Emotional intelligence: Conceptualization and measurement." In Fletcher, G.J.O. and Clark, M. S. (Eds.). *Handbook of social psychology: Interpersonal processes*. Oxford, England: Blackwell.
4. Mayer, J. D., Caruso, D., and Salovey, P. (1999). "Emotional intelligence meets traditional standards for an intelligence." *Intelligence*, 27(4): 267–298.
5. Mayer, J. D., Salovey, P., and Caruso, D. (2002). "*Mayer-Salovey-Caruso Emotional Intelligence Test (MSCEIT),*" *Version 2.0.*Toronto, Canada: Multi-Health Systems.
6. Bar-On, R. (1997). "*The Emotional Quotient Inventory (EQ-i): Technical manual.*" Toronto, Canada: Multi-Health Systems.
7. Bar-On, R. (2000). "Emotional and social intelligence: Insights from the emotional quotient inventory." In R. Bar-On and Parker, D. A. (Eds.). *The handbook of emotional intelligence: Theory, development, assessment, and application at home, school, and in the workplace* (pp.343–362). San Francisco: Jossey-Bass.
8. Goleman, D. (1998). "*Working with emotional intelligence.*" New York: Bantam Books
9. a. Boyatzis, R. E., Goleman, D., and Rhee, K. (2000). "Clustering competencies in emotional intelligence: Insights from the emotional competence inventory (ECI)." In Bar-On R. and Parker, J. D. A. (Eds.). *The handbook of emotional intelligence: Theory, development, assessment, and application at home, school, and in the workplace* (pp.343–362). San Francisco: Jossey-Bass.
b. Goleman, D. (2001). "An EI-based theory of performance." In Cherniss Cary and Goleman Daniel (Eds.), *The Emotionally intelligent workplace: How to select for, measure, and improve emotional intelligence in individuals, groups, and organizations* (pp.27–44). San Francisco, CA: Jossey-Bass.
10. Cooper, R. K., and Sawaf, A. (1997). "*Executive EQ: Emotional intelligence in leadership and organizations.*" New York: Grosset/Putnam.
11. Six Seconds Team (1997). "*Getting Started with Emotional Intelligence,*" from www.6seconds.org
12. Elias, Maurice (2001). "*A View on Emotional Intelligence and the Family*" from http://www.edutopia.org/maurice-elias-emotional-intelligence-and-family
13. Martinez, M. N. (1997). "The smarts that count." *HR Magazine,* 42(11): 72–80.
14. Bradberry, T. and Greaves, J. (2009). "*Emotional intelligence 2.0.*" San Diego, CA: TalentSmart.
15. Chris, G., (2009). "*A New Definition of Emotional Intelligence,*" from http://www. cbsnews.com/8301-505125_162-31147813/a-new-definition-of-emotional-intelligence/_
16. Weisinger, H. (1998). "*Emotional Intelligence at Work.*" In. San Francisco, CA: Jossey-Bass Inc
17. a. Carrol, J. B. (1993). "*Human cognitive abilities: A survey of factor analytic studies.*" New York: Cambridge University Press.
b. Mayer, J. D., and Salovey, P. (1993). The intelligence of emotional intelligence. *Intelligence,* 17: 433–442.
c. Scarr, S. (1989). "Protecting general intelligence: Constructs and consequences for interventions." In R. L. Linn (Ed.), *Intelligence, measurement, theory, and public policy* (pp. 116–134). Urbana IL: University of Illinois Press.
18. Neisser, U., Boodoo, G., Bouchard, T. J., Boykin, A. W., Broody, N., Ceci, S. J., Halpern, D. F., Loehlin, J. C., Perloff, R., Sternberg, R. J., and Urbina, S. (1996). Intelligence: Knowns and unknowns. *American Psychologist,* 51: 77–101.
19. Binet, A., and Simon, T. (1905). "Applications des methods nouvelles au diagnostic du niveau intellectual chez des enfants normaux et anormaux d'hospice et d'éole primaire." *L'Annēe Psychologique,* 11: 245–336.
20. Fancher, R. E. (1985). "*The intelligence men: Makers of the IQ controversy,*" (p.71). New York: W.W. Norton.
21. Brown, B. (1997). "Raw scores of cognitive ability are real psychological variables: IQ is a hyperspace variable." In Shipman V. C. (Chair). *IQ or Cognitive Ability?* Symposium presented to the 9th Annual Convention of the American Psychological Society, Washington, D.C.

22. Mayer, J. D., Salovey, P., and Caruso, D. (2000a). "Models of emotional intelligence." In Sternberg R. J. (Ed.). *The handbook of intelligence*, (pp.396–420). New York: Cambridge University Press.
23. Goleman, D. (1995). "*Emotional intelligence*." New York: Bantam.
24. a. Malouff, J. M., and Schutte, N. S. (1998). "Emotional intelligence scale scores predict counselor performance." Presented at the *Conference of the American Psychological Society,* Washington, D. C.
 b. Schutte, N. S., Malouf, J. M., Hall, L. E., Haggerty, D. J., Cooper, J. T., Golden, C. J., & Dornheim, L. (1998). Development and validation of a measure of emotional intelligence. *Personality and Individual Differences,* 25: 167–177.
 c. Schutte, N. S. & Malouff, J. M. (1998). "*Measuring emotional intelligence and related constructs.*" Levinston: Mellen Press.
25. Mayer, J. D., DiPaolo, M. T., and Salovey, P. (1990). "Perceiving affective content in ambiguous visual stimuli: A component of emotional intelligence." *Journal of Personality Assessment*, 54: 772–781.
26. Goleman, D. (1998b). "*Working with emotional intelligence.*" New York: Bantam.
27. Boyatzis, R. E. (1994). "Stimulating self-directed change: A required MBA course called Managerial Assessment and Development." *Journal of Management Education, 18,* 304–323.
28. Bradberry, T., Greaves, J., Emmerling, R., Sanders, Q., Stamm, S., Su, L. D., and West, A. (2003). "*Emotional Intelligence Appraisal Technical Manual.*" TalentSmart Inc.
29. a. Cameron, A. (2004). "Work Profile Questionnaire-Emotional Intelligence (WPQei) User's Guide." *Emotional Intelligence Personality Team Roles.* Oxford: The Test Agency Limited.
 b. Apaydin, C., and Anafarta, A. (2012). "Factorial validation of the seven-component model of the Work Profile Questionnaire Emotional Intelligence (WPQei) in a Turkish educational setting." *Journal of Instructional Psychology,* Vol. 39 (3): 159–170.
30. Mayer, J. D., Salovey, P., and Caruso, D. (2008). "Emotional intelligence: New ability or eclectic traits?" *American psychologist*, 63: (6), 503–517.
31. Mayer, J. D., Caruso, D. R., and Salovey, P. (2000). "Selecting a measure of emotional intelligence." In R. Bar-On and Parker, J. (Ed's.) *The Handbook of Emotional Intelligence.* San Francisco: Jossey-Bass.
32. Mayer, J. D., Salovey, P., and Caruso, D. (2000b). "Emotional intelligence as zeitgeist, as personality, And as a mental ability." In Bar-On Reuven and Parker, D. A. (Eds.). *The handbook of emotional intelligence: Theory, development, assessment, and application at home, school, and in the workplace* (pp. 92–117). San Francisco: Jossey-Bass.
33. Cooper, R. K. (1996/1997). "*EQ map interpretation guide.*" San Francisco: AIT and Essi Systems.
34. Petrides, K. V., and Furnham, A. (2001). "Trait emotional intelligence: Psychometric investigation with reference to established trait taxonomies." *European Journal of Personality*, 15: 425–448.
35. a. Petrides, K. V. and Furnham, A. (2000). "On the dimensional structure of emotional intelligence." *Personality and Individual Differences,* 29: 313–320.
 b. Petrides, K. V., and Furnham, A. (2003). "Trait emotional intelligence: Behavioral validation in two studies of emotion recognition and reactivity to mood induction." *European Journal of Personality*, 17: 39–57.
36. Cote, S., and Miners, C. T. H (2006). "Emotional intelligence, cognitive intelligence, and job performance." *Administrative Science Quarterly*, 51: 1–28.
37. Van Rooy, D. L., Viswesvaran, C., & Pluta, P. (2005). An evaluation of construct validity: What is this thing called emotional intelligence? *Human Performance,* 18(4): 445–462.
38. Mathews, G., Emo, A. K., Roberts, R. D., and Zeidner, M. (2006). "What is this thing called emotional intelligence?" In Murphy, R. K. (Ed.), *A critique of emotional intelligence,* 3–36. Mahwah, NJ: Lawrence Erlbaum.
39. Schultea, M. J., Ree, M. J., and Carrettab, T. R. (2004). "Emotional intelligence: Not much more than g." *Personality and Individual Differences*, 37 (5): 1059–1068.
40. a. Daus, C. S., and Ashkanasy, N. M. (2005). "The case for an ability-based model of emotional intelligence in organizational behavior." *Journal of Organizational Behavior,* 26 (4): 453–466.

b. Spector, P. E., and Johnson, H. A. M. (2006). "Improving the definition, measurement, and application of emotional intelligence." In Murphy, K. R. (Ed.), *A critique of emotional intelligence* (pp. 325–344). Mahwah, NJ: Lawrence Erlbaum.

41. Brackett, M. A. and Mayer, J. D. (2003). "Convergent, discriminant, and incremental validity of competing measures of emotional intelligence." *Personality and Social Psychology Bulletin, 29* (9), 1147–1158.
42. Gardner, H. (1999). "*Intelligence Reframed.*" New York: Bantam Books.
43. Mayer, J. D., and Geher, G. (1996). "Emotional intelligence and the identification of emotion." *Intelligence*, 22: 89–113.
44. Geher, G., Warner, R. M., and Brown, A. S. (2001). "Predictive validity of the emotional accuracy research scale". *Intelligence,* 29: 373–388.
45. a. Dawda, D., and Hart, S. D., (2000). "Assessing emotional intelligence: Reliability and validity of the Bar-On Emotional Quotient Inventory (EQ-i) in university students." *Personality and Individual Differences*, 28: 797–812.
    b. Bar-On, R. (2002). "*Bar-On Emotional Quotient Inventory (EQ-I): Technical Manual.*" Toronto, Canada: Multi-Health Systems.
46. Palmer, B. R., Manocha, R., Gignac, G., and Stough, C. (2003). "Examining the factor structure of the Bar-On Emotional Quotient Inventory with the Australian general population sample." *Personality and Individual Differences,* 35: 1191–1210.
47. Salovey, P., Mayer, J. D., Goldman, S., Turvey, C., and Palfai, T. (1995). "Emotional attention, clarity, and repair: Exploring emotional intelligence using the Trait Meta-Mood Scale." In Pennebaker, J. W. (Ed.), *Emotion, disclosure, and health* (pp. 125–154). Washington, DC: American Psychological Association.
48. Mayer, J. D., Mamberg, M., and Volanth (1988). "The experience and meta-experience of mood." *Journal of Personality*, 56: 453–486.
49. Wong, C. S., and Law, K. S. (2002). "The effects of leader and follower emotional intelligence on performance and attitude: An exploratory study." *The Leadership Quarterly,* 13(3): 243–274.
50. Wong, C. S., Law, K. S., and Wong, P. M. (2004). Development and validation of a forced choice emotional intelligence for Chinese respondents in Hong Kong. *Asia Pacific Journal of Management*, 21(4): 535–559.
51. Wong, C. S., Foo, M. D., Wang, C. W., and Wong, P. M. (2007). "The feasibility of training and development of EI: An exploratory study in Singapore, Hong Kong and Taiwan." *Intelligence*, 35(2):141–150.
52. Bradberry, T. (2002). "*Emotional Intelligence and leader job performance.*" Unpublished Manuscript.
53. Petrides, K. V. (2009). "*Technical mjanual for the Trait Emotional Intelligence Questionnaires (TEIQue).*" London: London Psychometric Laboratory.
54. a. Furnham, A., and Petrides, K. V. (2003). "Trait emotional intelligence and happiness." *Social Behavior and Personality*, 31: 815–823.
    b. Pérez, J. C. (2003). "Adaptación y validación espa nola del Trait Emotional Intelligence Questionnaire [TEIQue] en población universitaria." *Encuentros en psicología social,* 1: 278–283.
    c. Petrides, K. V., Frederickson, N., and Furnham, A. (2004). "The role of trait emotional intelligence in academic performance and deviant behavior at school." *Personality and Individual Differences*, 36: 277–293.
55. Cooper, A. and Petrides, K. V. (2010). "A psychometric analysis of the Trait Emotional Intelligence Questionnaire-Short Form (TEIQue-SF) using Item Response Theory." *Journal of Personality Assessment*, 92, 449–457.
56. Petrides, K. V. and Furnham, A. (2006). "The role of trait emotional intelligence in a gender-specific model of organizational variables." *Journal of Applied Social Psychology*, 36, 552–569.
57. Mavroveli, S., Petrides, K. V., Shove, C., and Whitehead, A. (2008). "Validation of the construct of trait emotional intelligence in children." *European Child & Adolescent Psychiatry*, 17, 516–526.

58. Palmer, B. R., and Stough, S. (2001). "Workplace SUIET: Swinburne University Emotional Intelli*gence Test – Interim technical manual.*" Melbourne: Organizational Psychology Research Unit, Swinburne University.
59. Bernet, M. (1996). "Emotional intelligence: components and correlates." *Toronto: Annual Convention of the American Psychological Association.*
60. Gignac, G. E. (2008). "*Genos Emotional Intelligence Inventory: Technical Manual.*" Sydney, NSW. Genos Press.
61. Jordan, P. J., Ashkanasy, N. M., Härtel, C. E. J., and Hooper G. S. (2002). "Workgroup emotional intelligence scale development and relationship to team process effectiveness and goal focus." *Human Resource Management Review*, 12: 195–214.
62. Druskat, V. U., and Wolff, S. B. (1999). "The link between emotions and team effectiveness: how teams engage and build effective task processes." *Academy of Management Best Paper Proceeding, Organizational Behavior Division, 1999.*
63. Druskat, V. U., and Wolff, S. B. (2001a). "Building the emotional intelligence of groups." *Harvard Business Review*, 79 (3): 81–90.
64. Druskat, V. U. and Wolff, S. B. (2001b). "Group emotional competence and its influence on group effectiveness." In Cherniss C. and Goleman D. (Eds.), *Emotional competence in organizations*: 132–155. San Francisco: Jossey-Bass.
65. Van der Zee, K., Schakel, L., & Thijs, M. (2002). The relationship of emotional intelligence with academic intelligence and the big five. *European Journal of Personality*, 16: 103–125.
66. Epstein, S. (1992). "Coping ability, negative self-evaluation, and overgeneralization: Experiment and theory." *Journal of Personality and Social Psychology*, 62: 826–836.
67. Lane, R. D., Quinlan, D. M., Schwartz, G. E., Walker, P. A., & Zeitlin, S. B. (1990). "The Levels of Emotional Awareness Scale – a cognitive-developmental measure of emotion." *Journal of Personality Assessment*, 55: 124–134.
68. Lane, R. D. (1991). "*LEAS Scoring Manual and Glossary.*" Tucson, Arizona: University of Arizona.
69. Lane, R. D. and Schwartz, G. E. (1987). "Levels of emotional awareness: A cognitive-developmental theory and its application to psychopathology." *American Journal of Psychiatry, 144,* 133–143.
70. Murphy, K. R., and Sideman, L. (2006). "The fadification of emotional intelligence." In Murphy. K. R. (Ed.). *A critique of emotional intelligence: What are the problems and how can they be fixed?* (p. 283–299). Mahwah, NJ: Lawrence Erlbaum Associates Publishers.
71. Zeidner, M., Matthews, G., and Roberts, R. D. (2001). "Slow down you move too fast: Emotional intelligence remains an "elusive" intelligence." *Emotions*, 1, 265–275.
72. Zeidner, M., Matthews G., and Roberts, R. D. (2004). "Emotional intelligence in the workplace: A critical review." *Applied Psychology: An International Review, 53*, 371–399.
73. Zeidner, M., Roberts, R. D., and Matthews, G. (2002). "Can emotional intelligence be schooled? A critical review." *Educational Psychologist, 37*, 215–231.
74. Locke, E. A. (2005). "Why emotional intelligence is an invalid concept." *Journal of Organizational Behavior*, 26: 425–431.
75. Peikoff, L. (1991). "*Objectivism: The philosophy of Ayn Rand.*" New York: Dutton.
76. a. Landy, F. J. (2005). "Some historical and scientific issues related to research on emotional intelligence." *Journal of Organizational Behavior*, 26: 411–424.
    b. Van Rooy, D. L., and Viswesvaran, C. (2004). "Emotional intelligence: A meta-analytic investigation of predictive validity and nomological net." *Journal of Vocational Behavior*, 65: 71–95.
    c. Barchard, K. A. (2003). "Does emotional intelligence assist in prediction of academic success?" *Educational and Psychological Measurement*, 63: 840–858.
    d. Brackett, M. A., and Mayer, J. D. (2003). "Convergent, discriminant, and incremental validity of competing measures of emotional intelligence. *Personality and Social Psychology Bulletin*, 29: 1147–1158.

77. Ashkanasy, N. M., and Daus, C. S. (2005). "Rumors of the death of emotional intelligence in organizational behavior are vastly exaggerated." *Journal of Organizational Behavior*, 26: 441–452.
78. Lopes, P., and Salovey, P. (2001). "Emotional intelligence and social-emotional learning: assessing emotional intelligence and developing skills and flexibility." *CEIC Review*, 10: 10–13.
79. Jordan, P. J., Ashkanasy, N. M., and Härtel, C. E. J. (2003). "The case for emotional intelligence in organization." *Academy of Management Review,* 25: 195–197.
80. Van Rooy, D. L., (Chair). (2004). "Emotional intelligence: practical questions for I-O psychologists." *Panel discussion presented at the 19th Annual Meeting of the Society for Industrial and Organizational Psychology, Chicago*. (CD of proceedings available from The Digital Record, Inc., Alexandria, V. A).
81. Paulhus, D. L., Lysy, D. C., and Yik, M. S. N. (1998). "Self-report measures of intelligence: Are they useful as proxy IQ tests?" *Journal of Personality,* 66: 525–554.
82. Funder, D. C. and Dobroth, K. M. (1987). "Differences between traits: Properties associated with inter-judge agreement." *Journal of Personality and Social Psychology, 52,* 409–418.
83. Roberts, R. D., Zeidner, M., and Matthews, G. (2001). "Does emotional intelligence meet traditional standards for an intelligence? Some new data and conclusions." *Emotion, 1,* 196–231.
84. Newsome, S., Day, A. L., and Catano, V. M. (2000). "Assessing the predictive validity of emotional intelligence." *Personality and Individual Differences, 29,* 1005–1016.
85. Saklofske, D. H., Austin, E. J., and Minski, P. S. (2003). "Factor structure and validity of a trait emotional intelligence measure." *Personality and Individual Differences*, 34, 707–721.
86. Davies, M., Stankov, L., and Roberts, R. D. (1998). "Emotional intelligence: In search of an elusive construct. *Journal of Personality and Social Psychology, 75,* 989–1015.
87. Day, A. (2004). "The measurement of emotional intelligence: The good, the bad and the ugly." In Geher, G. (Ed.), *Measuring emotional intelligence: Common ground and controversy* (pp. 245–270). New York, NY: Nova Science Publishers.
88. Lopes, P. N., Salovey, P., and Straus, R. (2003). "Emotional intelligence, personality, and the perceived quality of social relationships." *Personality and Individual Differences*, 35, 641–658.
89. Denham, S. A. (1998). "*Emotional development in young children.*" New York: Guilford Press
90. Saarni, C. (2000). "The social context of emotional development." In Lewis M. and Haviland J. (Eds.). *The handbook of emotion* (2nd ed., pp.306–322). NY: Guilford.
91. Bechara, A., Tranel, D., and Damasio, A. R. (2000). "Poor judgment in spite of high intellect." In R. Bar-On and J. Parker (Ed's.) *The Handbook of Emotional Intelligence.* San Francisco: Jossey-Bass.
92. Damasio, A. (1999). "*The Feeling of What Happens: Body and Emotion in the Making of Consciousness.*" New York: Harcourt.
93. Davidson, R., Jackson, D. C., and Kalin, N. H. (2000). "Emotion, plasticity, context and regulation: Perspectives from affective neuroscience." *Psychological Bulletin, 126* (6), 890–909.

4

PERSONALITY AND EMOTIONAL INTELLIGENCE

OPENING CASELET

What is the Metal of People with Mettle?

- Eminent leaders and people with demonstrated achievements rarely fret over small things. Great people focus their attention and direct their efforts and energy towards issues and events of extensive and far-reaching consequences. Sam Walton was criticized on his face at his first job as store manager of J.C. Penny's by his own boss that he can't make a career in retailing because of his incompetence in handling paperwork. History is witness to Walton's success in building Wal-Mart as the world's largest retail chain as he declined to bother about his skills at paperwork.
- Ironically, the creator of the most popular cartoon characters in the world — Mickey Mouse, Donald Duck, Goofy, and Pluto — the legendary Walt Disney was in fact terminated as a cartoonist by a city newspaper in Kansas. He was removed from his first job as a cartoonist purportedly due to Disney's artistic incompetence. Disney knew that the art of succeeding in the business of cartoons, animation industry or in any creative field requires more than artistic competence. He simply refused to give up on his goal or even to be diverted, rejecting others' judgement of his competence.
- Once a reporter quizzed Albert Einstein, the great scientist, about the distance to the moon from the earth. The scientist's unhesitant reply was that he doesn't want to overload his mind with such insignificant information. Einstein added that he knew the sources of such information when he needs it and he had other important things to think about which require an uncluttered mind.
- Ted Turner never wrote a business plan when he launched CNN.
- Frank Lloyd Wright notoriously refused to panic or brood over the agonizing details while making his monumental architectonic masterpieces.
- Michener battled a career in teaching when he had a brush with death in a deadly air accident on the New Caledonia Island of South Pacific leaving him metamorphosed into a bestselling author. Despite passionately nurturing a dream to become a writer since his childhood, Michener couldn't leapfrog from being a school teacher to a writer until his near death experience in that plane accident.

  Escaping death so narrowly and reviewing his life, Michener was convinced that life itself is too short and important to ignore. He decided to take things into his hands and make the best of the rest of his life. He started forthwith writing his novel, *South Pacific*. After a year's hard work, when he submitted his manuscript, the same was rejected as unacceptable and he was told on his face that he couldn't write. His agent deserted him with the contention that he had no future as a writer.

  Nevertheless, Michener persisted in the pursuit of publishing his work. Finally, when his book was published, he was awarded the Pulitzer Prize for literature in the year 1948. The man who was condemned as incompetent writer subsequently wrote and published forty-three books, which became bestsellers and many of them being made into movies.

Source: Landrum, G. N. (1999). "*Eight Keys to Greatness.*" Mumbai: Magna Publishing Co. Ltd.

WHAT IS PERSONALITY?

Personality is ascribed to the thoughts, emotions and patterns of behavior unique to an individual. It is an abstract concept encapsulating an individual's actions, emotions, and motivations. It is an enduring bundle of habits, traits and characteristics of a person which remains stable over long periods of time under normal circumstances. Notwithstanding the commonality of personality traits, every individual tends to be unique in personality.

The term personality is derived from the Latin word *persona* meaning the mask that actors use in a stage-play. Hence the word *persona* came to be referred to as external appearance and public face that is projected to people surrounding us. In the light of the source from which the word *personality* is derived, it may be reasonable to conclude that an individual's perceptible and external characteristics seen by others could be referred to as personality. An individual's personality can also be analyzed in terms of the impression the person makes on others — the way an individual appears to be. Another perspective postulates that a person's character is clothed in personality, its visible dimension influencing others. But personality is not just confined to the visible aspects of a person or our appearances and masks that we wear or the roles that we play but decisively more than and beyond that. The term personality includes many invisible human and emotional qualities and attributes in addition to the apparent physical characteristics at the surface level which together represent the construct.

Personality may also be used to denote lasting attributes and features which are generally stable and enduring. It may vary according to the influence of contextual factors, for instance, a person who is generally calm and stable may turn nervous, unstable and volatile at times. Therefore, personality may manifest differently in different situations. However, despite its contextually dynamic nature, personality is generally immune to drastic and farfetched changes in the short term. Thus, it can be reasonably concluded that personality comprises persistent and distinctive cluster of traits and peculiarities that are situationally reflexive.

Definitions of Personality

Personality has been defined by different psychologists and researchers. Some of their perspectives on what constitutes as personality are recounted herein below:

Pervin and John:[1] Personality is a set of psychological traits and mechanism within the individual which was organized, relatively endured and influenced his or her interaction with the adaptation to the environment.

Alport:[2] Personality consists of dynamic organization traits that determine how a person adjusts himself uniquely to environment and includes seven categories, bio-physical, bio-social, unique, integrative, adjustment, differentiate essential and omnibus.

Van Wagner:[3] Personality is composed of the distinctive and enduring patterns of feelings, thoughts and behaviors unique to an individual.

Raymond B. Cattell:[4] Personality is that which permits a prediction of what a person will do in a given situation.

Feist and Feist:[5] Although no single definition is acceptable to all personality theorists, we can say that personality is a pattern of relatively permanent traits and unique characteristics that give both consistency and individuality to a person's behavior.

McCrae and Costa:[6] Personality can be defined as the ways in which individuals differ in their attitudinal, interpersonal, emotional, experiential and motivational styles.

Attributes of Personality

The above definitions provide us some clues on the constituents of personality. They lead us to conclude that traits and the pattern of thoughts and emotions play important roles in its structure. The other basic features of personality include:

- *Consistency in display:* Usually there is an identifiable sequence and constancy for behaviors wherein people behave and conduct themselves in certain homogeneous ways in diverse situations. Such patterns can be categorized and labeled.
- *Psychological and physiological structure:* Personality is influenced by physiological and biological needs and factors which have their origins established in the mother's womb while being influenced by heredity and social environment. Attitudes, values, emotions and feelings constitute the psychological structure of personality.
- *Influence on behaviors and actions:* In addition to its impact on our environmental response mechanism, personality also induces us to behave or react in certain ways.
- *Multiple forms of manifestation:* Apart from behavior, personality is also reflected in our thoughts, feelings, interactions and relationships.

Despite multiple conceptions and definitions of personality most of them center on the structure and pattern of characteristics and attributes that enable us to speculate and describe an individual's pattern of behaviors. Interpretation of personality can anchor around a cluster of influences spanning from genetic causes of personality traits to environmental influences and life experiences which play important roles in carving an individual's personality. Environmental influences in the development and articulation of personality include factors like parenting, social setting and culture.

PERSONALITY TRAITS

Personality has been investigated using diverse postulations, such as trait, psycho-dynamic, behavioral, humanist and type theories. Trait theory is one of the cardinal and popular personality theories extensively in use which describes personality in terms of the mechanism that is fundamental to behavior. Traits are distinct composition of behaviors or predispositions to feel and act in specific ways, which differentiate individuals on the basis of the type of their behavioral form.[7] This proposition is supported and evidenced in research. Costa and McCrea's longitudinal study of American adults found that the personality pattern of an individual at 30 years of age predicted that individual's personality at 80 years of age for majority of people.[8]

Many proponents of trait theory postulated their frameworks and prototypes of personality based on the traits reflected in personality inventories through factor analyses. Hans and Sybil Eysenck's personality framework, for instance, delineated two factors of personality that are hereditarily influenced, i.e., introversion-extroversion, and stability-instability.[7] Another contemporary and popular trait-based framework of personality is the "Big Five" personality factor model.

The Big-Five Personality Factor Model

The Big Five Personality Factor model or the Five-Factor model is an empirically extracted framework of personality based on the early research of Gordon Allport, Raymond Cattel and Hans, Sybil Eysenck and Odbert. The model posits that personality can be partitioned into five major dimensions or factors, openness, conscientiousness, extraversion, agreeableness and neuroticism.[9,10] The five dimensions of the model are referred to as the acronym of OCEAN. The dimension of *openness* refers to the propensity or predisposition to open mindedness, curiosity, flexibility and creativity. The factor *conscientiousness* reflects predisposition towards reliability, efficiency, self-control, coherence, contemplation and forward-looking nature. The dimension of *extraversion* represents a tendency for amiability, geniality, kindness, firmness, agility and positivity. The factor *agreeableness* refers to an inclination toward generosity, forgiveness, loyalty, trustworthiness, sympathy, accession and sacrifice. *Neuroticism* represents a tendency to experience anxiety, stress, inhibition, bitterness, volatility, shyness, irrationality, despondency and deflated self-esteem.[9,10,11] Each of these factors are plotted on a continuum and individuals are rated between the two extremes of each dimension. Accordingly, the factor of *Openness* assesses the extent to which a person is open-minded as against close-mindedness and the extent thereof, apart from creativity and the ability to understand and communicate emotions of self. *Conscientiousness* represents regulation of impulses, goal directed behavior and task completion. *Extraversion* signifies being spirited and enthusiastic and energetic as against being passive and lethargic, and *Agreeableness* refers to benevolence and sociability as against being unfriendly, solitary, and egoistic. The factor of *Neuroticism* assesses emotionality — the contrasting elements of emotional balance and cohesion as against contrasting elements of negative emotionality.[12] Personality theorists posit that the traits of big five comprise a genetic component to a significant level.[13] These five personality characteristics are proposed to be universal — i.e. possessed by all — while each of these are being assessed in relation to other people, measuring their frequency and intensity in terms of one's thoughts, feelings and behaviors. Hypothetically, two persons may be categorized as 'agreeable' (maintaining good relations with others is important for such people), but they may be remarkably different in the extent of their agreeableness. As against attributes which are either present or absent in an individual, the five personality traits exist on a continuum from the lowest level to the highest degree and individuals fall between the two extremes of each dimension.

The Big Five Inventory:

The Big Five Inventory (BFI) is an instrument designed to assess the big-five personality factors of extraversion, agreeableness, conscientiousness, neuroticism, and openness. This measure has 44 items measuring all the five personality trait dimensions on a 5-point Likert scale ranging from "1" (strongly disagree) to "5" (strongly agree). The sum of ratings for all the items in each subscale gives the score for each personality trait.

EI PERSPECTIVE

Open Awareness is the Key for Creative Breakthroughs

Marc Benioff, the CEO of Salesforce, once shared his belief with noted researcher, trainer and author, Daniel Goleman, that we need to give our permission for new ideas to emerge on the canvas of our conscious mind without which they wouldn't appear from the shadows of clouds. He recalls his own experience during his tenure at Oracle as its Vice President, when he took a break for a month and went on a holiday to Hawaii. When he was relaxing, new ideas and prospects emerged opening up opportunities and new directions for his career.

During that time, when his mind was open and at rest, Benioff could comprehend and foresee possible opportunities in cloud computing space.

This triggered his decision to leave his job at Oracle and start 'Salesforce' in a rented accommodation and promote and develop cloud computing, a concept which was then revolutionary. Salesforce became a pioneer in the domain that become a lucrative industry generating billions of dollars in revenue.

In comparison, a researcher or scientist with an unflinching commitment and resolve to validate his own hypothesis, ignoring and disregarding contradictory findings — rejecting unexpected findings as error or noise — might miss out on more prolific discoveries and productive theories.

Openness combined with mindfulness creates a stage for the emergence of creative discoveries and unanticipated breakthroughs. Such open awareness is devoid of aggressive advocacy, skepticism or evaluation. It is just non-judgmental, objective and open-minded receptivity that opens up our minds to new possibilities and ideas.

Source: Goleman, D. (2013). *Focus: The hidden driver of excellence.* New Delhi: Bloomsbury Publishing India, Pp. 41.

THE MBTI PERSONALITY CLASSIFICATION

Carl Gustav Jung, a Swiss psychiatrist postulated that human behavior is predictable and consistent and it can be categorized into predetermined groups based on individual preferences and predispositions.[14] The Jungian theory posits that people are born with specific personality dispositions and preferences, categorizing individuals on the basis of the following dimensions and factors associated therewith:

1. Polar attitudes of extraversion and introversion
2. Comprehending functions of sensing and intuition
3. Decision making functions of thinking and feeling
4. Preferential processes to deal with external world, judging and perceiving

The fourth dimension was incorporated by the mother-daughter duo, Katharine Briggs and Isabel Briggs Myers who built on Jung's theory of personality type. They developed the personality classification instrument known as the Myers-Briggs Type Indicator or MBTI.[15] The MBTI taxonomy comprises individual preferences on the four personality dimensions on their respective dyadic scales, given as follows:[16]

1. Orientation or favored approach for transacting with the external world:
   Preference for *Extraversion* or focus on external world, people or events as against *Introversion* or focusing internally, contemplating, and reflecting.
2. Favored manner of collecting information or perceptual process:
   Preference for *Sensing* or being watchful and vigilant using the five senses for gathering information in contrast to using *Intuition* or exploring patterns and connections, using imagination, focusing on big picture and identifying alternatives.
3. Choice or preferred ways in the process of making decisions:
   Thinking or logical, objective and analytical approach as against *Feeling* or anchoring decisions in person-centered values, preferring harmony and keeping others' interests in perspective.
4. Predisposition or attitude preferred for dealing with the external world:
   Judging or organized, orderly and methodical with a dislike for surprises in contrast to *Perceiving* or being flexible, yielding, adaptable and spontaneous.

The combination of preferred choices emerging out of the above classification produces 16 different types of personality, categorizing each individual on one trait from each of the four pairs.

EI PERSPECTIVE The Amalgam of Greatness

Accomplished people augment their choices by courageously facing and doing things that they detest or by becoming the opposite of what they are, through acclimatization. People may improve by exploiting their strengths, but aspiring for greatness requires victory over weaknesses. Evidently our strengths can develop and reinforce each other, whereas our weaknesses carry with them seeds of potential self-destruction. Conquering weaknesses would therefore enable us to surmount the unidimensional orientation typical of us and transform the world around us into an oyster. All types of personality characteristics and orientations manifest on a continuum from opulence to paucity. Hence it hardly matters whether an individual is an introvert or an extrovert, or for that matter a Type A or Type B oriented. What matters is the degree of at which one is plotted on those dimensions. In other words, it is not about mutually exclusive polar categorization but the extent of our extroversion or introversion, or the level of Type A or Type B orientation and our position on these dimensions. An individual's common tendency is to operate in any manner between the two extremes of morbid timidity (acute introvert like Howard Hughes, the high profile movie producer, director, business tycoon, engineer and pilot famous for high-risk and reticent behavior) and audacious verbosity (acute extroversion like Margaret Mead, the cultural anthropologist, author and speaker in mass media who served as President of American Association for Advancement of Science). Similarly, our decision making may range from highly emotional (intense 'feeling' type like Mother Teresa) to scrupulously rational (intense thinking type like Bill Gates).

Great people have the ability to navigate between the two extremes as the situation demands, which defines their ingenuity. Typically, individuals get stuck in their habitual preference, but creative savants are flexible and springy. Hughes, the immensely shy introvert, became an extraordinary speaker when he addressed the Congress and beat his enemies by boldly doing what he detested.

Despite being a public figure, Margaret Mead made her imprint by living in seclusion in the wilderness of New Guinea. By adapting themselves, great people operate at a superior pedestal than those anchored in a single orientation. Marrying the opposites of our self and integrating them could be critical for enduring success and greatness. Such a versatility can be developed by traversing across the continuum to places where the needs and situation meet each other. Extroverts are extrinsically dynamic and therefore feel motivated when they are in the company of people, but they find it hard to carry out research in a library by going into isolation. James Campbell, the father of mythology and popular writer, who was an extrovert, did the same. He withdrew from the world and spent four years in isolation in the mountains reading Greek classics. It was challenging for an introverted and shy Hitler to face millions of people and speak, but he did the same which enabled him to take control over Germany. It is immensely challenging for an introvert to face and speak to strange audience, but research shows many introverts to be great speakers as was the case with Karl Marx, Howard Hughes, Ayn Rand, and Mother Teresa.

Source: Landrum, G. N. (1999). "*Eight Keys to Greatness.*" Mumbai: Magna Publishing Co. Ltd.

The MBTI is a 100-item personality measure eliciting responses of people on their preferred ways of feeling and action in certain situations and categorizing them on the following four dyadic dimensions:

1. Extroverted (E) or Introverted (I)
2. Sensing (S) or Intuitive (N)
3. Thinking (T) or Feeling (F)
4. Judging (J) or Perceiving (P)

Jung proposed that we can comprehend individual differences and semblances by blending the preferences of people. Universally, people chose a particular way of doing things as against another. Jung's typology contends that none of the preferences are better than the others and that we need to honor and respect them for what they are. Several studies have established the reliability and validity of MBTI as an instrument for identifying personality types.[17] Consequently, the Myers-Briggs Type Indicator (MBTI) has become the world's most extensively applied personality assessment measure.[18] However, it should be borne in mind that personality type is only one way of looking at humankind and therefore it constitutes one of the features of personality. Every individual having a preference for ENFP (Extroverted, Intuitive, Feeling and Perceiving) happens to be identical in many ways and also different in many other respects.

TRAITS AND EMOTIONS

Many people have a built-in predisposition to experience certain emotions and moods more consistently than others. Some may experience the same emotion differently and also at different intensities. For instance, researchers Larsen and Diener[19] compared the dispositions of two cricketers, Harbhajan Singh and M. S. Dhoni. They analyzed that one of these players was effortlessly stirred-up and enticed while the other remained unprovoked, calm and unmoved, apparently displaying no emotion.

EI PERSPECTIVE

How do Leaders Cope with Anxiety from Childhood Abuse?

The callousness and hardheartedness exhibited by some of the famous leaders have been found to be connected to their childhood distresses and antagonistic or disconcerting relationship with their parents. Margaret Thatcher, the former British prime minister reportedly did not have any communication with her mother after her 15th year, while she admired her father.[a] The attitude of leaders like Mahatma Gandhi, Lenin, Stalin, and Hitler towards authority was reportedly ambiguous, and therefore, they had close relationship with one parent while being isolated or estranged from the other. During his childhood, Stalin was reportedly beaten up brutally by his inebriated father while his mother adored him dearly.[b] Such people use power as a means of countering their anxiety resulting from accumulated childhood tensions. Exercising power also serves them as a protective guard providing relief through control and predictability.[c]

Sources: **a.** Gardner, H. (1997). "*Leading minds: The anatomy of leadership.*" London: Harper-Collins. P. 226.
b. Burns, J. M. (1978). "*Leadership.*" New York: Harper and Row.
c. Marcus, G. E. (2000). Emotions in Politics. *Annual Review of Political Science*, 3: 221-250.

Presumably both differed in their affect intensity, i.e., in the intensity of their feelings and in the expression of their emotions. People with high affective intensity tend to feel both positive and negative emotions more strongly and intensely than others. They are overwhelmingly despondent when grief-stricken and overtly cheerful when happy.

Traits of Eminent Personalities

Napoleon Bonaparte and Mother Teresa
– *Personal magnetism / Charm or charisma*

Mao-Tse-Tung and Babe D. Zaharias – *Competitive edge*

Margaret Mead and Martin Luther King Jr.
– *Self-assurance / Self-reliance / Poise / Confidence*

Fyodor Dostoevsky and Bill Gates
– *Initiative / Doggedness / Dedication/ Drive*

Albert Einstein and Sigmund Freud
– *Instinctive imagination / Inborn perceptiveness / Intuitive Vision / Spontaneous foresight*

Karl Marx and Anne Rice – *Nonconformity / Rebellion*

Marie Curie and Ted Turner
– *Adventurous / Courageous / Daring / Venturesome / Enterprising / Risk taking*

Walt Disney and James Michener
– *Persistence / Perseverance / Purposefulness / Tenacity / Diligence*

Source: Landrum, Gene N. (1999). "*Eight Keys to Greatness.*" Magna Publishing Co. Ltd., Mumbai.

The Marriage of Emotional Intelligence and Personality

Emotional intelligence and personality are entwined as a fabric texture. Emotional quotient (EQ) and personality reciprocally reinforce each other. Development of EQ is influenced and shaped by our personality type, while emotional quotient impacts and transforms the development of our personality type. Our personality type reflects our innate predisposition, whereas the nature of emotional quotient is a transformable competence. It is relevant here to dwell on positive affectivity (PA) which implies a positive emotional disposition or an inclination to experience positive emotional states. Positive affectivity is similar to extroversion, a distinguishing trait of outgoing people who are sociable and outspoken. Conversely, individuals with high negative affectivity (NA) are inclined to experience negative emotions more frequently and intensely.[20] Such individuals are inclined to be distraught, anxious, melancholic and dejected as they tend to focus on the negative side of life and be engrossed therewith.

Overlap of Emotional Intelligence with Big Five Personality Factors

The association between emotional intelligence and personality has been widely discussed and debated in literature, while it remains as one of the most extensively researched topics. Nevertheless, the magnitude of the alliance between these variables is diverse across various studies as results were contingent upon the measures of emotional intelligence.[21] Many empirical investigations established a significant association between emotional intelligence and personality.[22] Various postulations of emotional intelligence, specifically mixed models of Bar-On and Daniel Goleman, have been found to have a significant affiliation with personality theory. The components and sub-factors of both these models of emotional intelligence have been found to be indistinguishable from the dimensions of prior postulations of personality theory. The sub-factors of Bar-On's model, such as empathy, interpersonal effectiveness, impulse control, assertiveness, reality testing and social responsibility have been studied and measured as personality dimensions by well-known personality inventories. As an illustration, we find that some measures like empathy, flexibility, interpersonal effectiveness, self-acceptance, self-assurance and self-control are contained in the personality inventory, the California Psychological Inventory (CPI). Similarly, Bar-On's emotional intelligence scale, emotion quotient inventory (EQ-i), was found to correlate significantly with Revised NEO Personality Inventory (NEO-PI-R) which measures the big five personality factors. Specifically, the correlations were immensely significant between emotional quotient inventory (EQ-i) and neuroticism, conscientiousness, extraversion and agreeableness factors while being moderately significant with openness factor of the Big Five personality dimensions.[23] Another measure from the mixed model family of emotional intelligence, the Emotional Competence Inventory (ECI) of Goleman, was found to be significantly correlated with three factors of the Big Five personality model namely, conscientiousness, openness and extraversion.[24] Moreover, many competencies of Goleman's emotional intelligence model have been vastly researched under the domain of personality psychology including those like self-confidence, empathy and self-control.[25] To a significant extent, the superior predictive validity of self-report emotional intelligence measures may be attributed to their extensive overlap with contemporary constructs like those of the Big Five personality model. Obviously enough, clones for the factors of anxiety or neuroticism would predict the same constructs of corresponding personality dimensions.[26]

Emotional intelligence was found to be strongly correlated with agreeableness, conscientiousness, extraversion, and neuroticism factors of personality but moderately correlated with the factor of openness to experience.[23] In another study, it was found that emotional intelligence was significantly related to openness, experience, extraversion and conscientiousness dimensions of personality when Goleman's (1998) Emotional Competence Inventory (ECI) was used for the study.[24] In a comparative study of ability EI scale, MSCEIT, personality measure, and NEO-PI-R, significant correlations were found between personality factors of openness and agreeableness and emotional intelligence.[23] Several studies revealed that extraversion factor of

Big Five personality domain had a positive association with emotional intelligence. This finding is logically imperative given that extravert people are characteristically outspoken, self-assured, energetic, sociable, adventurous and enthusiastic.[10, 27] Evidently, extroverted individuals are more optimistic and expectant having a predisposition and inclination to experience positive feelings and emotions. Consequently, such people are emotionally intelligent as they are agile, genial and gregarious possessing relational skills to connect with others in addition to the awareness and understanding needed to regulate their own as well as others' emotions.[10, 28, 29] In essence, extraverted individuals are inclined to demonstrate their feelings and emotions fluently and voluntarily in contrast to introverted people.

Similarly, people high on agreeableness are found to be compassionate, unselfish, magnanimous, genial and kind-hearted.[10] Such people with high agreeability were found to be high on emotional intelligence.[10, 21a, 29] This finding is in sync with the notion that people high on the personality characteristic of agreeableness are inferred to be positive, confident and competent to engage in constructive interpersonal relationships while effectively discerning, exhibiting and modulating emotions.

Likewise, individuals with high scores on conscientiousness are prolific, dependable, accountable and meticulous.[10] Highly conscientious people score higher on emotional intelligence.[30] Therefore, conscientiousness is positively associated with emotional intelligence.

People with high scores on neuroticism are apprehensive, antagonistic, susceptible, nervous, volatile, and dysfunctional.[10] They are predictably low on emotional intelligence because of their propensity to experience negative temperament and their inability to perceive and regulate their emotions. In comparison, individuals scoring low on neuroticism are competent to effectively direct and modulate their emotions.[29]

Finally, individuals with high scores on openness are aesthetic, thoughtful, veritable, creative and so forth.[10] Such individuals are considered as objective and receptive. They view situations and things from multiple perspectives and are capable of using their emotions in decision-making process. Such people are considered to be emotionally intelligent as endorsed by literature and evidenced by empirical investigations.[21b]

RELATIONSHIP BETWEEN EMOTIONAL INTELLIGENCE AND THE MBTI

In the last fifteen years, there has been an appreciable inquisitiveness among the researchers of personality psychology about the nature of association between the personality type and emotional intelligence. Several studies were conducted to explore if there was any relationship between emotional intelligence and the MBTI personality measure and if there was one, the nature of such connection.[22c, 31, 32, 33] Most of such studies got mixed results but for one study by Thompson, which found a significant and positive correlation between the overall emotional intelligence and the MBTI measures of extroversion and intuition apart from mixed findings on the other dimensions of preferences.[33] This study by Thompson still remains as the most expansive and inclusive research on personality type and emotional intelligence, examining the features of MBTI Form Q and emotional intelligence.

Thompson posits that psychological type is a dynamical system, the nature and design of which is nonlinear, synergetic and self-regulating with countless interactions amongst its numerous components traversing various timescales.[34] According to the dynamical human systems model, there is an emotional element and also a cognitive ingredient influencing every event of perception (perceiving) and decision-making (judging). On the one hand, cognitive ability inhibits an individual's degree of perception (perceiving) and the progress of judging. Emotions, on the other hand, deeply influence what we perceive and eventually, our decision-making preference. This premise and percept apply to all the 16 types of personality and their stages of development.

Jung postulated that sensing is a mental process which enables us to witness what exists. According to him, the psychological function of sensation involves the perception of a physical stimulus as well as internal stimuli of organic processes.[35] Hence, the sensing function is a perceiving process portraying two different roles of obtaining external information (extroverted-Se), and matching such information with the internal database of known information (introverted-Si). The roles of extroverted (Se) and introverted (Si) are iterative with a two-way feedback and control system (modifying the 'sensing' input of each other). Similarly, all the four functions of sensing (S), intuition (N), thinking (T) and feeling (F) perform these dual roles of extroverting and introverting processes functioning in an algorithmic and iterative manner. Consequently, the four functions of sensing (S), intuiting (N), thinking (T) and feeling (F) along with the two processes of extroversion (E) and introversion (I) produce eight function attitudes (Se, Si, Ne, Ni, Te, Ti, Fe, Fi), as portrayed by Jung.[35] Every function attitude is iterative and algorithmic within its respective function as well as with each of the other function attitudes. Consequentially, Thompson posits that psychological type is significantly more sophisticated than the elongated arrangement of functional attitudes.[36] He accentuates that emotional intelligence is a process of directing/influencing the awareness and appraisal of emotions and the ensuing archetypes of action in a manner that ensues beneficial consequences to the individual either in the presence or in the absence of others. The role of emotional intelligence in regulating the effects of transpersonal interactions, thus becomes more complex in terms of magnitude of interactions. In such events, the process of perception and appraisal involve not only the dynamic emotions of oneself but also those of others engaged in such interactions. Therefore, in such events, all the elements belonging to the system of emotional intelligence interact in an iterative and algorithmic manner eventuating a self-reinforcing process of considerable complexity.

Pearman posits that emotional intelligence is concerned with an individual's overall development and not confined to the type, whereas each personality type enhances interpersonal or relational sensitivity in diverse ways.[31(b, c)] He postulated the existence of a relationship between Jung's function attitude types of personality and emotional intelligence competencies proposed by certain EI proponents. Another approach claims that emotional intelligence is concerned with managing our personality (type) as against assessing different personality types on emotional intelligence.[32d] However, this approach considers it worthwhile to discover the nature of differences among the types. Lately, the function-attitude dyads were speculated to match with the four-quadrants of emotional intelligence model such that the Si (sensing introverted) and Ni (intuitive introverted) are concerned with self-awareness; Se (sensing extroverted) and Ne (intuitive extroverted) with the others' awareness; Ti (thinking introverted) and Fi (feeling introverted) are concerned about self-management; while Te (thinking extroverted) and Fe (feeling extroverted) are concerned with relationship management. A study conducted by Barnard and Nel found that highly extroverted individuals (preference on MBTI scale) appeared to score high on nearly all the sub-scales of Bar-On's EQ-I measure of emotional intelligence compared to the scores obtained by individuals with introverted preference.[37] This study revealed that personality preferences are connected with emotional intelligence. The MBTI scores are indicative of presumptions on emotional intelligence which in turn could direct the focus of organizations towards inclusion of emotional intelligence facets in their development plans. Awareness of employees' personality preferences would help organizations in designing relevant training, coaching and mentoring programs for developing the emotional intelligence competencies of employees. The same study further highlighted that employees with higher personality preference for introversion may experience higher levels of stress and eventually, may need supplemental development support for managing emotions at interpersonal and intrapersonal levels.

Why is the Connection Between Personality and Emotional Intelligence Important?

While asserting that emotional intelligence is a distinct construct, EI theorists offer the following explanation for the linkage, connection or relationship between emotional intelligence and personality: It is argued that emotional proficiency or higher degree of emotional competence leads to significant levels of satisfaction and contentment, i.e., emotional disposition is caused by emotional intelligence. Three interpretations are offered by the proponents of emotional intelligence in justification of the linkage between personality traits and emotional disposition.

Firstly, the development of emotional intelligence may be regulated and guided by personality. Individuals who encounter many negative emotions would find it relatively arduous and onerous to acquire mastery and control over these emotions. Secondly, personality is concerned with stability of emotion, thus individuals with high scores on neuroticism may be inclined to experience less stable emotional encounters.[38] Such people may find it hard to understand their feelings with clarity, the reasons for such feelings and the ways in which to regulate them. Finally, the third reason for the affiliation between personality and emotional intelligence is that individuals with ideal personality (characterized by high positive affectivity, low negative affectivity and high self-regard) are generally inclined to be confident of their abilities. As a result, when you seek their inputs on self-reported emotional intelligence levels, such people, being confident, tend to rate themselves higher than their actual levels of emotional intelligence.[39] Considering that there is a moderate to high degree of overlap between self-report measures and personality, it is imperative that abundant caution is exercised in making generalizations from data. When for instance the data shows that people with high scores on self-reported emotional intelligence measure are inclined to have sound mental health, we may conclude that it is the emotional intelligence that ushers us to enhanced mental health. Nevertheless, it might also be fair and logical to contend that people with high EQ would have a good personality as opposed to emotional intelligence predicting superior mental health.[39] As evidenced in research, individuals having good personality and high self-regard have an edge in life.[40]

Emotional Intelligence as an Independent Construct

Personality theory accentuates inclinations driven by emotional volatility, while Mayer and Salovey's[41] ability model of emotional intelligence focuses on skills which can be acquired through learning and experience. Research by Caruso, Mayer and Salovey revealed that emotional intelligence is a construct reflecting ability which is distinct from personality.[42] In their study investigating the association between the variables of emotional intelligence and personality, these researchers used an ability measure of EI and the personality scale of 16PF. Other empirical studies indicate that trait emotional intelligence is more resolutely associated with but distinct from personality, as measured by the Big Five model[43] and is markedly divergent from ability EI. Nevertheless, personality correlates of ability measures of emotional intelligence, especially agreeableness, do exist.[44]

Emotional Intelligence as a Component of Personality

While considering emotional intelligence to be a part of principal personality classifications as against being an independent construct, many studies investigated the extent of convergence between trait emotional intelligence and higher order personality dimensions. Other views considered trait emotional intelligence as a construct of individual difference and accordingly claim that EI is located within the personality space accounting little criterion variance beyond that of personality factors.[39]

Specifically, trait emotional intelligence constitutes patterns of emotional transcriptions located at the lower levels of personality hierarchies.[43c, 45] Primarily, it is related to individual perceptions about their emotional competencies covering the affective facets of personality. Another study found emotional intelligence to be a distinct construct partly because it is established by many personality factors and also since it is positioned at the lower stratum of personality hierarchies.[43] This has laid to rest the notion that emotional intelligence is a refurbished version of personality.

Many correlational studies[46] and behavioral genetic investigations[47] reinforce the arguments for inclusion of trait emotional intelligence into the personality strata structure. On the contrary, the extensive overlap of trait emotional intelligence with personality dimensions, specifically the factors of neuroticism and extraversion, supports the contention that EI is superfluous. The contention that trait emotional intelligence does not decisively contribute to the assessment and prediction of psychological events over and above that of personality dimensions is well supported.[48]

THE ENNEAGRAM THEORY OF PERSONALITY

Emerging from a pre-historic origin, Enneagram is a personality framework and a system of personal growth depicted by an ideogram symbolizing nine personality dispositions and attitudes. These personality orientations reflect patterns of instinctual predispositions influencing individual perception, comprehension, and behavior.[49] The Enneagram unveils the factors influencing human behaviors while offering guidance for individual development towards self-actualization. It is an effective means for enhancing the quality of relationships with family, friends and colleagues.[50] While exploring their inclinations and predispositions, individuals discover and evaluate their value systems and acquire insights into their strengths and limitations. Such insights help people to attune their perspectives towards surpassing their strengths and weaknesses and to work cohesively in congruence with others' growth.[49]

Though the exact origins of the Enneagram are unknown, it is presumed to have been a part of oral tutoring among the secret Sufi tradition of Middle East.[50] It is claimed to have been initiated into the Europe in 1920 by an esoteric proponent of Russia called G.I. Gurdjieff and subsequently, the concept got introduced in the United States in 1960s. American psychologists, Palmer,[51] Riso and Hudson[52] incorporated the emergent philosophy and practice of Enneagram into the existing personality psychology culminating into the current postulations of Enneagram system and practice during the last decades of the century.

The term *Enneagram* originated in Greek where it stands to represent an emblem with nine points depicting the narrative of nine basic types of people.[53] Each of the nine points in the Enneagram symbol denotes a personality orientation or instinctual and recurrent scheme of perception, emotion and behavior. The spatial attributes of the nine-pointed figure ascribe to a configuration of personality kinetics.[51, 52] Every individual has the abilities of all the nine personality orientations but one of the dispositions is predominantly pronounced and exhibited in an individual's outlook, daily exchanges and behavioral dispositions.

According to a researcher, people adopt one of the nine orientations with the misplaced belief that they wouldn't be adored if they failed to assume the specific style in their day-to-day interactions. Self-examination through the Enneagram framework leads to better awareness and acceptance of self as well as others.[54]

Enneagram offers a blueprint for advancing self-perception and personal development enhancing capabilities to establish and maintain enduring and fruitful relationships. The framework also helps people to discover the potentialities and weaknesses of their individual ethos and conventionalities, identify and analyze their vulnerabilities and strive to a belief system reverberating the traits of Maslow's model of self-actualizing people who excel surpassing the boundaries of their self.[55]

The Enneagram Diagram

Enneagram depicts a classification of nine discrete but complimentary personality types depicted by nine points in the geometric diagram, as shown in Figure 4.1. Each point is represented by a number, constituting a personality type, and the distance between adjacent points on the circumference of the circle is equal. The figure comprises an irregular hexagram formed by the points 1– 4 – 2 – 8 – 5 – 7– 1, which are connected in the same sequence. Also, there is a triangle figure formed by the points connected in the sequence of 3 – 6 – 9 – 3.

The Nine Points and Personality Orientations

These two shapes of irregular hexagon and triangle combine to symbolize the nine personality orientations as disintegrated sequence of divergent polar types anticipating integration.

A brief description of each of the nine personality orientations is given below along with the principal impetus for each type — what do people in each type strive to be and the trait or attribute they resist or avoid:[50, 56]

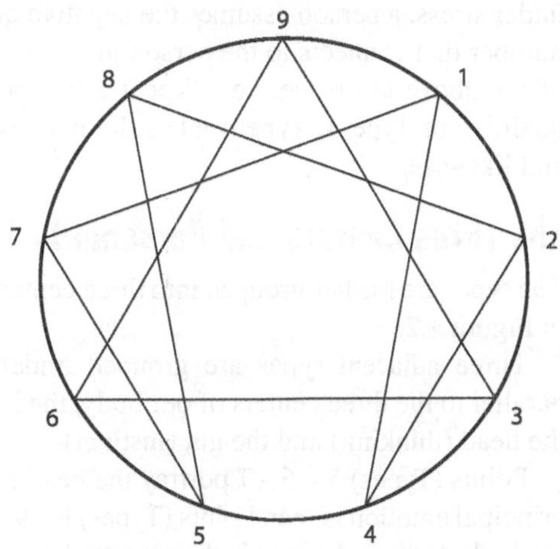

Figure 4.1: The Enneagram Symbol

1. *Perfectionist / Reformer (Type One):* Endeavor to be perfect and work hard so as to avoid becoming careless or irresponsible. They are pragmatic, meticulous, dependable and virtuous. They endeavor to live up to their elevated standards.
2. *Helper (Type Two):* Work hard to affiliate with others. Struggle to avoid being secluded physically or emotionally. They are genial, sympathetic, caring, and responsive to the needs of others.
3. *Achiever / Motivator / Performer (Type Three):* They toil to be exceptionally superior and struggle to avoid being average or undistinguished. They are vigorous, dynamic, positive, confident, and focused.
4. *Romantic / Artist (Type Four):* Strive to be special and distinctive and struggle to avoid being ordinary, conventional or earthly. They are tender, genial, and judicious.
5. *Observer / Thinker (Type Five):* Endeavor to be dispassionate and work hard to avoid being impetuous, temperamental, and unrestrained. They are introverted, inquisitive, rational, and perceptive with a need for erudition.
6. *Questioner / Loyalist (Type Six):* Struggle to be guarded and work hard not to drop their guard and not to become inert. They are dependable, honest, and value commitment to family, friends, groups, and worthy endeavors. Their personality characteristics spread from being unsociable, and shy to being unreserved, plain, and defiant.
7. *Adventurer / Generalist (Type Seven):* Endeavor to work hard and remain enthusiastic and avoid getting disinterested and weary. They are vigorous, active, and positive. They are interested in making a contribution to the world.
8. *Leader / Asserter (Type Eight):* Aspire to be influential and strong, vigorously avoid to be unguarded and susceptible or reliant on others. They are straightforward, independent, self-assured and defensive.
9. *Mediator / Peacemaker (Type Nine):* Endeavor to be tranquil and serene, strive to avoid focusing on themselves or their necessities and desires. They are amenable, responsive, considerate and helpful. They aspire to associate with others and the community around them.

The Wing Styles

The two types adjacent to a given point (type) are designated as wing styles (for instance, Type 9 and Type 2 are the wing styles of Type 1). An individual's personality may alloy with or get colored by the types on either side. For instance, a Type 1 person may have some traits of Type 2 and Type 9, which are on either side of it.

The Relax Type and the Stress Type

Each point on the Enneagram is connected to two other points called arrows. In a relaxed state, a person assumes positive qualities of the number that connects to the person in the sequence of 1 – 7 – 5 – 8 – 2 – 4 – 1 and 3 – 6 – 9 – 3. In other words, Type 1 goes to 7, Type 7 goes to Type 5 and so on. In contrast, when under stress, a person assumes the negative qualities of the number that connects to the person in the reverse direction of the above sequence, i.e., Type 1 takes on the negative qualities of Type 4, Type 4 takes the negatives of Type 2 and likewise.

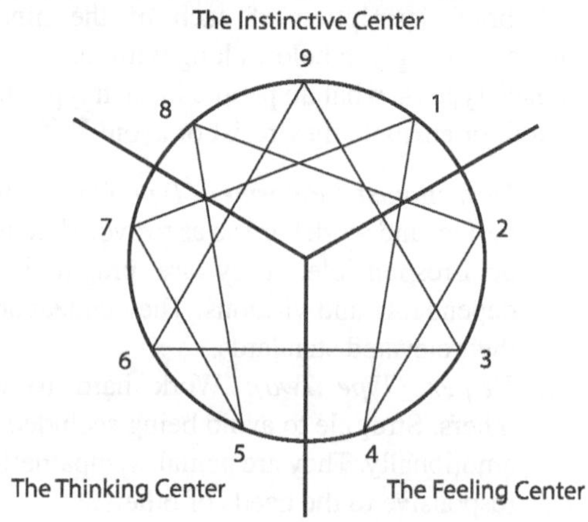

Figure 4.2: The Three Centers

The Three Centers and Personality Types

The types are further grouped into three centers, as depicted in Figure 4.2.

Three adjacent types are grouped under each center parallel to the three centers of our body, the heart (feeling), the head (thinking) and the gut (instinct).

Points (Types) 5 – 6 – 7 portray the head and the related principal emotion is fear. Points (Types) 8 – 9 – 1 symbolize the body (gut) and anger is the affiliated primary emotion. Similarly, points (Types) 2 – 3 – 4 exemplify the heart and the linked central emotion being image. These three centers and the connected personality types and their disposition towards the affiliated principal emotion are detailed as follows:

a) *The Instinctive Center (Paralleled with Gut/Body) with the associated primary emotion of anger:*
   - *The Asserters (Type Eight)* portray a powerful representation of stature and they are not scared to show their anger.
   - *Peacemakers (Type Nine)* are pleasant, congenial, obliging and usually not in affinity with their anger.
   - *Perfectionists (Type One)* follow established behavioral norms and try to improvise the world. They view anger as a flaw in persona and try to control it.

b) *The Feeling Center (Paralleled with Heart) with the associated primary emotion of image:*
   - *Helpers (Type Two)* are concerned about people and take interest in fostering them. They are keen on projecting a loving image.
   - *Achievers (Type Three)* prefer to be projected in positive light in tune within the well-accepted social norms of conduct and behavior.
   - *Romantics (Type Four)* have a persistent need to articulate their self and are keen to be perceived as original.

c) *Thinking Center (Paralleled with Head) with the associated primary emotion of fear:*
   - *Observers (Type Five)* depend on their inherent resources and find security in knowledge.
   - *Questioners (Type Six)* aspire freedom from the shackles of fear by obtaining permission and approval of authority figures or by rebelling against authority.
   - *Adventurers (Type Seven)* are energetic and positive. They avoid all unsavory emotions which includes fear.

Transcending Preferred Strategies and Progression to Ideal Strategies

Each point in the Enneagram reflects a strategy for dealing with the environment which has a bearing on personality. These strategies at each point are outlined as follows:[56]

Strategy at point One – Endeavoring for *excellence / perfection*
Strategy at point Two – Aspiring to be *associated / connected*
Strategy at point Three – Striving to be *extraordinary / outstanding*
Strategy at point Four – Endeavoring to be *special / unique*

Strategy at point Five – Endeavoring to be *dispassionate / detached*
Strategy at point Six – Working towards being *protected / secured*
Strategy at point Seven – Aspiring to be *enthusiastic / excited*
Strategy at point Eight – Endeavoring to be *influential / mighty / powerful*
Strategy at point Nine – Endeavoring to be *serene / peaceful*

Each one of these strategies are available to every individual and at best every person has access to use them as situations demand. But ironically, people are trapped in their familiar and preferred molds of personality types, confining themselves to a favored strategy (referred to as the preferred strategy) irrespective of situational demands. This happens due to a misplaced belief that their preferred strategy is the optimal solution to all types of challenges and problems faced by them. The basic objective of using Enneagram is to motivate people to become aware of the drawbacks of excessive dependence on their habitual and spontaneous strategies and help them to elongate their behavioral choices with enhanced flexibility of alternative actions.[56]

Logically, everyone would be keen to implement the strategies best suited for each situation without clinging to their preferred mode, but frankly, executing it is immensely challenging. Hence the best course would be to progressively enlarge one's preferred strategy to include those behaviors which are yet to get absorbed into our automatic response mechanism. Along this process, people evolve from efficiency-orientation (doing things frugally and faster) to effectiveness orientation (doing suitable and appropriate things frugally and faster), as their preferred strategies broaden to include a wider range of attitudes and behaviors. This awareness and understanding helps in weakening the preferred strategy's hold upon us while we become adept at using other strategies over time on account of awareness, learning and practice.[56]

Enneagram as a Tool for Self-Actualization

The complete potential of an individual's whole self (which is shared by all humans) is epitomized in the form of a circle surrounding all the points in the Enneagram symbol. The number 'Nine' represents entireness or completeness of a circuit, ascendance and revival in many philosophical and mystic traditions which in reference to Enneagram represents the nine personality orientations.[57] Individuals thus progress toward completeness as their own awareness and potential for all the nine type-orientations increase and they start using them. People would then reach out to conflicting personality-oriented people with understanding, and respond to them in benevolent and generous ways, despite past negative experience with them. Furthermore, people will be inclined to display greater confidence in facing diverse situations owing to their renewed and replenished repository of competencies opening up alternative courses of action and decision making. Riso and Hudson, authors of the book titled "The Wisdom of the Enneagram", posit that as we progressively gain insights into the mechanical reactions of our personality, we tend to become less associated with them and experience more freedom in terms of relief from the grip of a personality type and the associated characteristics. They claim that the objective of Enneagram is transcending the personality type.[58]

Applications of Enneagram

There is a significant and copious literature illustrating the nine personality orientations of Enneagram.[51, 52] Case studies have been scripted by Thomson projecting the Enneagram type of Bill Clinton as a Peacemaker (Type 9), Pope John Paul II as a Paragon (Type 1), and the typical American collective psyche as Achiever (Type 3).[59]

Enneagram has been found to be a productive instrument available to academics, trainers, psychotherapists, administrators and career counselors in the appraisal of career-specific competencies, identifying the impediments for students at risk of failure or dropout, and for self-awareness and evaluation.[60] Since its advent in the West, Enneagram's most widespread application has been in organizational development, specifically as an instrument in counseling, team building and building emotional intelligence competencies[61] apart from creating workplaces that are concordant and efficacious.[51, 62]

Many institutions of repute, such as the Stanford University School of Business, U.S. Postal Service, and Central Intelligence Agency have deployed the Enneagram framework in the areas of management training[49] and in behavioral analytics for analyzing the behavior of world leaders.[63] In educational contexts, Enneagram has been applied in effectuating impactful and beneficial teaching methods and in molding the relationships between students and teachers.[64] The fields of nursing and social work have also been drawn to the Enneagram framework owing to its effectiveness and since have used it in human service applications. It's not an overstatement that Enneagram has become a regular topic in today's skill building workshops, self-improvement programs, and conferences.[53] Career counseling centers in colleges have started blending Enneagram into their career assessment interventions for students in tandem with MBTI and Holland personality classification systems.[49] Lastly, it is apt to mention the discourse of Wright and Sayre-Adams on the practicality of Enneagram, a mechanism to uncover higher purpose and meaning in day-to-day interactions and exchanges.[65] Enneagram is used in business settings primarily as a tool of personality taxonomy to acquire knowledge in prevailing interpersonal kinetics at workplaces. The RHETI (Riso–Hudson Enneagram Type Indicator) Enneagram Test comprises 144 statements in pairs with mutually exclusive choices that help people in identifying their archetypes and molds of behavior, feeling and thinking.

EMOTIONAL INTELLIGENCE AND THE ENNEAGRAM

Emotional intelligence has been conceptualized as the ability to regulate feelings and emotions in self and others, to differentiate between them and to utilize such knowledge to direct an individual's thinking and conduct (Salovey and Mayer). It is demonstrated through five elements:

- Self-awareness
- Self-regulation
- Motivation
- Empathy
- Social skills

The first three elements are christened as intrapersonal elements and the last two as interpersonal elements. The Enneagram personality structure and orientation impacts all the above five elements. Therefore, an understanding of one's personality type facilitates in appreciating the plausible consequences of interpersonal and intrapersonal inclinations and propensities of an individual.

The Enneagram Emotional Competencies

Enneagram has been used to exemplify and elucidate the theory of emotional intelligence by authors Tallon and Sikora.[66] They posited that emotional competencies are distinct abilities premised on emotional intelligence which enhance the quality and effectiveness of an individual's interactions with the outside world. They also postulated *The Enneagram Emotional Competencies* as an array of 16 emotional competencies categorized into personal competencies of *Self-Awareness* and *Self-Management;* and social competencies of *Attunement to Others* and *Relationship Building.* The personal competencies, which include *self-awareness* and *self-management*, are concerned with our adeptness at directing and utilizing emotions productively; while the *social competencies* like *Attunement to Others* and *Relationship Building* are associated with our proficiency in identifying the emotional dispositions in others and utilize such knowledge for collective well-being. The following are the 16 *Enneagram Emotional Competencies* postulated by Tallon and Sikora:[66]

Personal Competencies

- Self-awareness
  - Awareness of self
  - Self-confidence
- Self-management
  - Self-control
  - Initiative
  - Adaptability
  - Achievement drive
  - Trustworthiness
  - Resiliency
  - Optimism

Social Competencies

- Attunement to others
  - *Empathy*
  - *Communication*
  - *Political awareness*
- Relationship building
  - Cooperation
  - Influence
  - Leadership
  - Conflict management

The objective of using the framework of Enneagram Emotional Competencies is to gain insights into the impact of emotions on performance and to acquire proficiency in utilizing these competencies to one's own advantage. Such an endeavor is facilitated by comprehending and discerning the association between emotional intelligence and personality orientation. The characteristics, inclinations and constraints of our personality type amalgamate to influence our proficiency in these competencies in a consistent and anticipated manner. It is therefore imperative that we first comprehend our predispositions and molds of behavior before we embark upon enhancing our performance in these segments.[66]

The Awareness to Action Process

Knowledge of our personality orientation and preferred strategies as well as the dispositions and demeanor originating therefrom result in enhanced performance in the areas of the 16 emotional competencies. Such

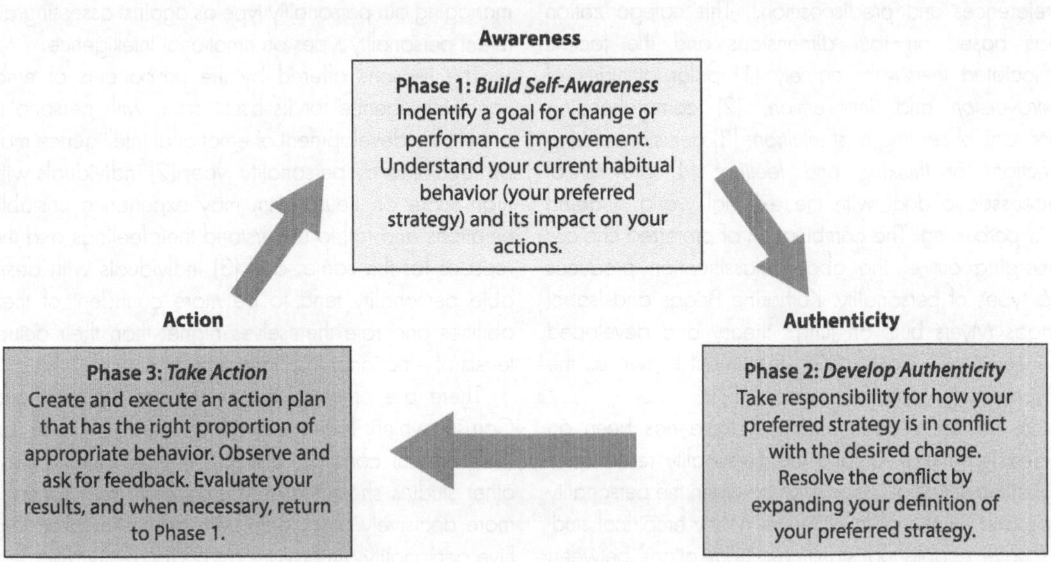

Figure 4.3: The Awareness to Action Process

knowledge or awareness can be transformed into performance by following the three steps of the *Awareness to Action* process in the approach postulated by Tallon and Sikora.[66]

The first step in this process is to firmly set a broader objective of transforming one's competencies followed by determining and implementing clear and actionable steps toward developing effective behaviors associated with a specific competency. This process has been used to educate executives and managers, sales teams and self-help groups about the system.

Developing these 16 emotional competencies is claimed to make an individual a better parent, spouse, coach of a small league, etc. It has also been scouted that there are few pursuits or exchanges which are not improved or developed by the practice of *Awareness to Action Process* and the resultant enhancement in the competencies of emotional intelligence.

Chapter Synthesis

Personality is an enduring collection of habits, traits and characteristics of a person which remains stable over long periods of time and influence the individual's actions, emotions, and motivations. It has been investigated using diverse postulations, such as trait, psychodynamic, behavioral, humanist and type theories. Big Five personality theory is a popular trait-based framework delineating five major factors of personality – openness (curiosity, flexibility) conscientiousness (reliability, efficiency), extraversion (amiability, geniality), agreeableness (generosity, trustworthiness) and neuroticism (anxiety, despondency). A Swiss psychiatrist, Carl Jung categorized personality into predetermined groups based on individual preferences and predispositions. This categorization was based on four dimensions and the factors associated therewith, namely (1) polar attitudes of *extraversion* and *introversion*; (2) comprehending functions of *sensing* and *intuition*; (3) decision making functions of *thinking* and *feeling*; (4) preferential processes to deal with the external world, *judging* and *perceiving*. The combination of preferred choices emerging out of the above classification produces 16 types of personality. Katharine Briggs and Isabel Briggs Myers built on Jung's theory and developed the personality classification instrument known as the Myers–Briggs Type Indicator or MBTI.

In the last decade and half, there has been an increasing interest among the personality researchers about the nature of association between the personality type and emotional intelligence. Many empirical studies have established significant correlations between various components of emotional intelligence, specifically the mixed models, and personality dimensions. Bar-On's EQ-i was found to correlate significantly with Big Five personality measure, NEO-PI-R. Daniel Goleman's emotional competence inventory was also found to be significantly correlated with three factors of the Big Five model. Several studies exploring the association between MBTI and emotional intelligence got mixed results. One perspective viewed emotional intelligence to be concerned with an individual's overall development and not confined to the type, whereas each personality type enhanced the interpersonal or relational sensitivity in multiple ways. Yet another proposition held that emotional intelligence is concerned with managing our personality type as against assessing different personality types on emotional intelligence.

The reasons offered by the proponents of emotional intelligence for its association with personality are (1) the development of emotional intelligence may be regulated by personality type; (2) individuals with high score on neuroticism may experience unstable emotions and fail to understand their feelings and the reasons for the same; and (3) individuals with desirable personality tend to be more confident of their abilities and rate themselves higher than their actual levels of emotional intelligence.

There are other studies by Mayer, Salovey and Caruso which found emotional intelligence as an independent construct distinct from personality. Few other studies show that trait emotional intelligence is more decisively associated with but distinct from Big Five personality dimensions and is markedly divergent from the ability measures of emotional intelligence. Hence to a great extent, this association seems to be measure-specific or model-specific of emotional intelligence. Many studies have postulated that trait emotional intelligence constitutes emotional scripts located at the lower levels of personality hierarchies. A school of research also contends that emotional intelligence does not contribute to decisively predicting psychological events over and above that of personality factors.

The Enneagram is a personality framework and a system of personal growth depicted by an ideogram symbolizing nine personality dispositions and attitudes. Every individual is claimed to possess all the nine personality orientations but one of the dispositions is predominantly pronounced in an individual's interactions and behavior. Apart from the nine types of personality orientations, the framework postulates the concept of 'Wing Styles' (points adjacent to a given type) which implies that an individual's personality type may be colored or influenced by the types on either side of the person's identified personality type. The points are grouped under three centers representing the body/gut (instinct), heart (feeling) and head (thinking). In addition, each point in the Enneagram reflects a strategy for dealing with the environment which has a bearing on personality. The Enneagram is claimed to be an effective means of individuals' progress from their preferred orientation toward proficiency in applying all the nine type-orientations and effectively responding to conflicting personality types in benevolent and generous ways. It is claimed that the objective of Enneagram is transcending the personality type. The Enneagram framework has been applied by trainers, psychotherapists, career counselors and administrators in a wide range of areas. The most widespread area of its application has been organizational development, specifically in counseling, team building, and developing emotional intelligence. Enneagram has also been used to exemplify and elucidate emotional competencies. The framework of Tallon and Sikora, authors of the popular book titled "Awareness to Action", postulated that Enneagram emotional competencies comprise 16 emotional competencies grouped under personal and social competencies. They have laid down a detailed road map and action steps termed as *Awareness to Action* process for developing effective behaviors associated with each emotional competency. It is claimed that developing these competencies would lead to being a better parent, spouse, coach of a small league, etc.

Key Terms

Personality
Extroversion
Openness
Agreeableness
Conscientiousness
Neuroticism
Empathy
Emotional competence inventory
Emotional quotient inventory
Positive affectivity
Negative affectivity
Sensing
Feeling
Thinking
Intuition
Judging
Perceiving
Self-awareness
Self-management
Emotional competence
Enneagram
Self-actualization
Wings styles of enneagram
Behavioral analytics
Career counseling
Skill building
Enneagram emotional competences
Personal competencies
Social competencies
Awareness to action
Myers–Briggs Type Indicator (MBTI)
Mayer–Salovey–Caruso Emotional Intelligence Test (MSCEIT)
Riso–Hudson Enneagram Type Indicator (RHETI)

Review Questions

1. What is personality? Explain its characteristics
2. How would the Big Five personality dimensions influence behavior?
3. Explain the categorization of Jungian typology.
4. 'Emotional intelligence has significant overlaps with personality'. Explain.
5. How can you argue that emotional intelligence is distinct from personality?
6. What is Enneagram? Give an overview of its nine personality orientations.
7. What is the developmental objective of Enneagram and explain its process as an instrument of self-actualization?
8. Explain the Enneagram emotional competencies.
9. How does the Enneagram framework help in developing emotional competencies?

Application-based Exercise

Interpersonal and Professional relationships

Reflect on your professional and personal experience in the past. Recall someone in a position of influence or in a leadership role who was conspicuous by his personal geniality and individual concern for people while functioning as an efficacious leader. In other words, a person who coaches and develops people, while taking tough calls when needed and at the same time nurtures close relationships with people whom he or she leads.

1. Enumerate all the characteristics and attributes of such person, who has become exceptional to work with on account of his qualities and personality. Try to discern and spot some of the attributes and behaviors triggering his/her personal efficacy and social adeptness apart from leadership effectiveness. List out such qualities and characteristics.
2. Assume that you would be appraised and rated by your associates or colleagues on the same qualities and attributes that are discerned and determined above. Estimate the extent or degree to which you would be rated in comparison on the same parameters, i.e., how closely or afar do you stand in relation to the person you had identified.
3. Identify the areas or attributes where you lag in the expected standards of being an effective colleague.
4. Prepare an action plan comprising two to three actionable measures that you can take to acquire/develop those attributes and qualities and put them to use. Miraculous changeover is impracticable but evolutionary and enduring change in character and behavior is possible through small but regular and progressive actions.

Activities Beyond the Book

Reliving the emotions of an agonizing event

The practice of revisiting a past distressing event and reliving the emotions enables us to discover and understand the pattern of our emotional reactions. It is a revelation to observe that our emotional reaction was disproportionately intense in relation to the severity of a distressing event.

Usually we are unwilling to reconnect with grievous or painful emotions, but such experiences offer highly valuable insights for our personal development. Learning to access insights from our emotions is of immense value. The following questions will help us acquire these insights.

1. Identify and focus on an agonizing and distressful event or experience. For this purpose, you need to confine yourself to a calm and peaceful place where you will not be disturbed. Close your eyes and mentally recall the distressful experience that engulfed you in sorrow or hurt you deeply.
2. Attempt to recreate the scenario vividly in graphic detail to the best possible extent. By doing so, you will be able to reach out to your emotions and feel them better.
3. Attempt to recreate the entire dialogue in detail.
4. Make an effort to feel the same emotions that you experienced in the original episode, be it shame, resentment, rage, or hurtful pain.
5. Scrutinize yourself by questioning whether your emotions were apt and congruous to the situation.

You would gain valuable insights following this intervention which will be immensely beneficial to you. For instance, you may learn that you have magnified the adverse effects of the original event which triggered instantaneous negative emotion or feeling, such as shame when the same is unjustified. Possibly such awareness helps in minimizing reactive emotional responses on one hand and mitigating the effect of negative emotions, providing the much needed relief on the other.

Video Resources

1. **Personality and Emotions –** ***Encyclopedia Britannica Films***
   Link: https://www.youtube.com/watch?v=5Uryy9Gr7lg
2. **Predicting Emotional Intelligence from Personality and Values**
   Link: https://www.youtube.com/watch?v=Y_37Y5r8ixo
3. **SYNTHESIS Personality and Emotional Intelligence Test –** ***MySkills***
   Link: https://www.youtube.com/watch?v=__z3drP02g4
4. **Borderline Personality Disorder and Emotional Intelligence**
   Link: https://www.youtube.com/watch?v=c2RyULX14ro
5. **Personal Intelligence and...:Talks at Google –** ***John Mayer***
   Link: https://www.youtube.com/watch?v=RHKYxVjLbkY
6. **Emotional Design Psychology and Personality –** ***Brian Cugelman***
   Link: **https://vimeo.com/257723408**
7. **The Enneagram Narrative in your Life Webinar: Love and Relationships –** ***Terry Saracino***
   Link: https://www.youtube.com/watch?v=fIQpj6ElxsQ
8. **Enneagram and Leadership: Grow in Your Business Based on Your Type –** ***Nick Sonnenberg and Susan Drumm***
   Link: https://www.youtube.com/watch?v=hAowGuWuBx4

Self-assessment Instrument

Self-assessment: Amiability and Disclosure Scale

This instrument assesses your capability of inducing others to disclose their innate feelings and secrets by opening up and confiding in you. In other words, this measure assesses your inclination to listen to others and also other interpersonal skills which induce others to trust you. You should keep in mind that this instrument measures your perceptions and not necessarily the objective reality.

Assign points (as per the key below) to each of the following statements indicating the degree of your agreement or disagreement with the respective statement. Enter your scores in the blank space provided against each statement.

4 = I strongly agree
3 = I slightly agree
2 = I am uncertain
1 = I slightly disagree
0 = I strongly disagree

1. People tell me that I am a good listener ... ... ☐
2. I am sensitive to others' difficulties and am supportive of them ... ... ☐
3. Others feel at ease and comfortable in my company ... ... ☐
4. I hold the trust of others and people share their secrets with me ... ... ☐
5. I can encourage people to talk about themselves by opening up with them myself ... ... ☐
6. I can inspire confidence in others triggering them to open up ... ... ☐
7. Usually people talk to me often about themselves ... ... ☐
8. I pay heed and listen to people who talk to me ... ... ☐
9. I am accommodative and tolerant ... ... ☐
10. I motivate people to share their feelings with me ... ... ☐

Scoring

Total the scores you entered to the left of the statements to arrive at your final score. Women tend to score higher due to higher tolerance for emotional expression in women in society.

A score of 35 – 40 for women and 33 – 40 for men indicates **high levels of disclosure and amiability.** This shows a greater degree of openness in communication as well as reveals an excessive disclosure or an inclination to reveal too much.

A score of 26 – 34 for women and 23 – 32 for men suggests that such people are not inclined to take initiative during their interactions, but are amenable and open to self-disclosure.

A score of 0 – 25 for women and 0 – 22 for men suggests that such people are either unwilling or unable to disclose about themselves or are judicious and choosy in self-disclosure.

Analysis of Select Movies

1. ***Lars and the Real Girl (2007)***

   The movie "Lars and the Real Girl" is directed by Gillespie and produced by Sara Aubrey and others. This is the story of a teenager, Lars, whose mother passed away during his infancy and an absent father who died at the start of the movie. He had a sibling who left the town just after he grew up to be on his own. The gawky and desolate young boy encounters a serene girl made of silicone which is entirely inanimate. However, Lars imagines the girl to be a natural living person and his entire social circle of family, friends and acquaintances join to support his illusion so as to help him resolve his psychological problem. Lars's personality disorder is reflected in his disinclination to associate with his family or to develop intimate relationships. He remains a recluse, unable to express a good deal of emotions. He evades every situation congenial for developing relationships and bonds with others. He remains extraordinarily sensitive to touch, a tendency that is symptomatic of schizoid people. Lars experiences intense anxiety due to his sister-in-law's pregnancy which drives him toward his preferred behavioral response as a mechanism to deal with his predicament. He is found avoiding his sister-in-law Karin's attempts to integrate him into the family as depicted in the scene at the beginning of the movie. He usually covered his neck with an angelic blue hand-knit cloak which he offers to Karin intending to shield her from common cold. It is revealed that this cloak was knit by his mother while she was bearing him in pregnancy. In general, during their childhood, small kids select a specific doll, a blanket or soft cloth as an indispensable belonging during a specific phase. The kids carry such possession wherever they go and literally corrode it while being averse to changing it in any manner, opposing to even washing the object. This peculiarity is termed as 'transitional object' by Winnicott[1] in his theory on its psychological function. It is posited that such an item happens to be the child's first possession identified beyond herself, the first feel of "other than me" which serves a psychological function. In his usual course of development, a person in Lars's position uses the cloak as a transitional object to help him evolve towards connecting with people as distinct individuals.

In the normal course, the cloak would have served Lars as a transitional object which wasn't the case as is apparent from the fact that Lars was still clinging to his cloak that was knit by his mother and he was escaping from every opportunity of connecting with others. Thereafter, he procures a life-sized female doll, names it as Bianca and handles it in the same way as the kids do while playing. He develops a bonding and connects with the doll, treating it as a living human. Trepidation of desertion and abdication – fear of abandonment – was at the root of Lars's dread for developing close relationships with other people. As a coping mechanism, he establishes a bond with Bianca, imagining the doll to be a human. Even while naming the doll as Bianca, he weaves her background with a narration similar to his own past in many ways. To the utter amazement of Gus and Karin, Lars acts as if Bianca is actually eating her food. Thereafter, they consult a psychologist, Dr. Dagmar who instantly understands the predicament of Lars in attempting to find a solution to his psychological problem with the aid of Bianca. While instituting a therapeutic course of action, the psychologist persuades Gus and Karin to support Lars's unrealistic assumptions about Bianca and advises them to tow his line. Furthermore, the entire townsfolk ally in support of the deception of Bianca as a real woman, albeit their grave misgivings. Eventually, Lars uses Bianca as a transitional object and progressively establishes human relations supported by the psychologist as well as the townsfolk and also bonds with Margo, a real young lady interested in Lars. Over time, it becomes inevitable for Lars to realize that Bianca is not totally under his control as he becomes disenchanted with her, his need for a transitional object starts to fade. He crystalizes this realization and starts to detach himself from Bianca by imagining her illness eventually leading to her death. Bianca's death offers an avenue to Lars to mourn the death of his mother despite never knowing her in his lifetime. We can also see that his angelic blue cloak is worn more frequently around Bianca and less often by Lars, during the progression of his association with Bianca. It can be observed that his favorite cloak is missing from his possession around the moment of Bianca's funeral, implying that Lars does not need it anymore as he is prepared to be in the companionship of Margo, the real woman.

The psychologist, Winnicott talks about the need of a holding environment[2] for people like Lars — similar to the physical and psychological support provided by the mother — to cross over to reality. Reacting empathetically, the people of the town en masse offered such vital holding environment to

Lars. According to Winnicott, the function of such holding environment is to guard the baby from the shocks of facing the reality prior to its preparedness for the same. In this emotional narrative, the therapist and the entire townsfolk lend their support to fulfill Lars's need for approval of his delusional premise of Bianca being a real woman. They extended their support either with the complete knowledge about the implications of their action or without it for whatever reason. But such support helped Lars to utilize a living transitional object, aiding him to build relationship with a real girl. Lars was able to establish relationships with other people using Bianca as a means which assisted him in doing away with the doll not needing it any further.

1. Winnicott, Donald. (1953). "Transitional objects and transitional phenomena – a study of the first not-me possession. *International Journal of Psychoanalysis, 34*, 89–97.
2. Winnicott, D.W. (1960). The Theory of Parent-Infant Relationship. *The International Journal of Psychoanalysis,* 41: 585–595.

2. ***Up (2009)***

Directed by Peter Docter and produced by Jonas Rivera, Up is a 3D animated film made by Pixar Animated Studios. The movie presents the tale of a young lad and an aged man who help each other in chasing down their aspirations and desires. While the movie approaches the issues of emotions and attitudes, the diversity in individual perspectives on life is well-presented. Each of the two main characters in the movie illustrates dissimilar worldviews, gloom and despondency as against hope and cheerfulness.

The film depicts complex situations and painful events in the lives of the two people and demonstrates the manner in which each one deals with them. The emotions of grief, frustration, desolation and the emotional competencies of resiliency, steadfastness and modesty are well-projected in the movie.

The movie is all about aging, disappointment and realization about life being complex, chaotic and unmanageable despite our best efforts to change it to the contrary. The movie dwells on the emotional values of benevolence, love and the significance of living each day meaningfully, making it worthwhile.

The summary of the storyline runs thus: The local administration decides to send Carl, an old man, to an old age home. It is then that Carl discovers an opportunity, albeit his last one, to fulfil his late wife's last wish. In pursuit of the same, he fastens hundreds of balloons filled with helium to his house and glides it traversing through the clouds to a dream destination he and his late wife, Ellie, ceaselessly fantasized of visiting. The significance of imagination, intentionality and discharging commitments made in spirit and deed to the near and like-minded are elegantly illustrated in the movie. The bonding and emotions of affection and dedication between the couple, Carl and Ellie, are perceptible across the movie albeit in the absence of verbal dialogue, just by melody. The couple's ordeals and hardships, for instance, the mid-pregnancy miscarriage, strengthen their mutual love, commitment and devotion to each other, triggering a complete range of emotions among the audience.

As childhood friends, Carl and Ellie share a common passion for adventure and a dream to build a house in the aesthetic environs of Paradise Falls in South America. Eventually, Carl falls in love with Ellie and marries her. Early in the movie, we see that Ellie meets with untimely death due to illness abandoning Carl who is intensely attached to her. He tries to retain Ellie's soul through his memories in archives, photographs, keepsakes, mementos and fictive interactions. Carl grows old and is called Mr. Fredrickson by people. He is drowned in the memories of Ellie while repenting for his inability to fulfill Ellie's vision during her lifetime. The movie tracks him and his disorganized and diverse band of a boy, a talking dog and a bird who try to remedy Carl's predicament. Frederickson tries hard to avoid becoming an ill-tempered and sulky old man, while living a lonely life. At this time, a young lad named Russel, a member of the local wilderness adventure society, knocks on his door and walks in. The boy is an optimistic and enthusiastic lad working to win a badge that gets him promoted to senior cadre in his troop working for "helping the elderly". But Frederickson feels rattled by Russel's presence initially, believing that he needed no help whatsoever. However, Russel perseveres with tenacity. Over a period of time, Frederickson develops friendly ties with Russel similar in strength to his bond with Ellie. Contextually, both the lad and the old man need each other's support in their quest to further their aspirations. Younger ones are usually more open and unassailable, but at seventy-eight, Frederickson needs time to open-up to his new association with Russel which eventually facilitates realizing his bygone dream of visiting the waterfall. As he reaches the place, Frederickson discovers an inglorious truth about his childhood friend, shattering his long-held fantasy. Thankfully in the company of his enthusiastic and tenacious new friend Russel, he sails through the rough seas with his support.

In the course of the movie, Frederickson emerges as a real hero by his determination demonstrating that age is not a constraint and it's never behindhand to pursue our escapades and risky exploits. The movie highlights our choices in pursuing creative and fun-filled endeavors that we enjoy, drenching ourselves in happiness.[1] We may align such creative endeavors with our vision, values, and commitments while utilizing opportunities to foster relationships with others.

In summation, Up is a pleasant and touching tribute to the values of companionship, affection, and devotion. It is about finding happiness and joy in small things in our daily lives, which would be no less thrilling than audacious expeditions. The film is delightful and appealing to people of all ages while retaining the equipoise between joviality and distress.

1. Lyubomirsky, S. (2008). *The How of Happiness: A Scientific Approach to Getting the Life You Want.* New York: Penguin Books.

3. ***Dumbo (1941)***

Dumbo is a cartoon movie from Walt Disney productions directed by Ben Sharpsteen and others. The film narrates the account of a baby elephant born to a fervent mother who names him Jumbo, instantaneously enamored by the newborn. But the elephant folk of the circus nickname the baby elephant as *Dumbo*, lampooning and making fun of his enormously–sized ears. *Dumbo* finds himself left out from the circus shows becoming a prey to the persistent intimidation by other animal folks. He also gets separated from his mother who protected him all the while. At this time, Timothy enters the film and befriends *Dumbo* with an intent to help him by encouraging him to accept his oversized ears as a special gift rather than a flaw. *Dumbo* finally learns to accept his flaw and tries using his ears to fly aided by Timothy and his band of bitter crows. Playing the role of a mentor to *Dumbo*, Timothy offers useful hints to perform well in his circus routine while taking care of *Dumbo's* daily upkeep and feeding. *Dumbo* realizes that being different is what makes him exceptional and out of ordinary. His self-acceptance increases dramatically when he discovers his ability to fly with the help of his oversized ears.

Dumbo's tale is akin to many of us when we undermine being different as our weakness. We could progress only when we learn to accept ourselves as we are embracing our uniqueness as our strength. Realistically, this is far from being as simple as stated though it is possible to achieve. If we look at the initial scenes in the film, there is a lot of bullying and ill-treatment meted out to *Dumbo* and his mother, which can as well be related to happenings in real life. Undoubtedly such stereotyping attitudes and practices should always be discouraged and condemned in real life. But looking pragmatically, our well-being truly lies in accepting them as reality and keep moving from the shadow of obscurity towards benignity on the other side. The film presents an eloquent message to the people of all genres demonstrating the transformative power of love amid the complexities of life. The movie triggers diverse emotions in the viewers while appealing to different age groups with an intense and meaningful message.

Essentially, Dumbo showcases the warmth of mother's love and concern for its child. *Dumbo*'s mother is a marvelous defender, guarding her kid against the jibes and scorns of animal folk and others. Adding insult to injury, *Dumbo*'s mother is incarcerated for targeting those bullying her kid as a result of which both get separated forever. But the power of their love and the warmth of their bond sustains them through the dread of their suffering. Despite living in the awful environs of a circus, the mother-son duo find their world in one another. The other message of the movie is self-regard. *Dumbo* initially succumbs to the ridicule and torment of the circus folk for his awkward appearance. However, he regains his composure and learns self-acceptance and self-love before turning his handicap into strength and unique capability which skyrockets him to success.

References

1. Pervin, L. A., and John, O. P. (2001). *Personality: Theory and research.* (8th Ed.). New York: Wiley.
2. Allport, G.W. (1961). *Pattern and growth in personality.* New York: Holt, Rinehart & Winston.
3. Van Wagner, K. (2008, July). *What is Personality?* Retrieved August 3, 2012 from http://jobsource.blogspot.com/2008/07/what-is-personality.html.
4. Cattell, R. B. (1950). *Personality: A systematic, theoretical and factual study.* New York, NY: McGraw-Hill.
5. Fiest, J., and Fiest, G. J. (2009). *Theories of Personality* (7th ed.). New York: McGraw-Hill Higher Education.
6. McCrae, R. R., and Costa, P. T., Jr. (1990). *Personality in adulthood.* New York, NY: Guilford.
7. Myers, D. G. (1998). *Psychology,* 5th Ed. NY: Worth Publishers
8. Costa, P. T., Jr. and McCrae, R. R. (1986). "Personality stability and its implications for clinical psychology." *Clinical Psychology Review,* 6: 407–423.
9. McCrae, R. R., and Costa, Jr. P. T. (1987). "Validation of the five-factor model of personality across instruments and observers." *Journal of Personality and Social Psychology,* 52: 81–90.
10. McCrae, R. R., and John, O. P. (1992). "An introduction to the five-factor model and its application. Special Issue: The five-factor model: Issues and applications." *Journal of Personality,* 60: 175–215.
11. John, (1989). "Towards a taxonomy of personality descriptors." In Buss, D. M. and Cantor, N. (Eds.) *Personality psychology: Recent trends and emerging directions* (pp. 261–271). New York: Springer.
12. Hergenhahn, B. R., and Olson, M. H. (1999). *An introduction to theories of personality.* New Jersey: Prentice Hall.
13. a. Costa, P. T., Jr., and McCrae, R. R. (1988). "Personality in adulthood: A six-year longitudinal study of self reports and spouse ratings on the NEO personality inventory." *Journal of Personality and Social Psychology,* 54: 853–863.
    b. Digman, J. M. (1989). "Five robust trait dimensions: Development, stability, and utility." *Journal of Personality,* 57: 195–214.
    c. Jang, K. L., Livesley, W. J., and Vernon, P. A. (1996). "Heritability of the Big Five personality dimensions and their facets: A twin study." *Journal of Personality,* 64: 577–591.
14. Jung, C. G. (1923). *Psychological types.* New York: Harcourt and Brace.
15. a. Brown, F. W., Reilly, M. D. (2009). "The Myers-Briggs Type Indicator and transformational leadership," *Journal of Management Development,* 28 (10), pp. 916–932.
    b. Knott, K., Taylor, N., Oosthuizen, Y., and Bhabha, F. (2013). "The Meyer-Briggs Type Indicator in South Africa." In Laher, S. and Cockcroft, K. (Eds.), *Psychological assessment in South Africa: Research and applications,* Johannesburg, Wits University Press, pp. 244–256.
16. Myers, I. B., McCaulley, M. H., Quenk, N. L., and Hammer, A. L. (1998). *The MBTI Manual: A Guide to the Development and Use of the Myers-Briggs Type Indicator.* Palo Alto: Consulting Psychologists Press.
17. a. Murray (1990). "Review of research on the Myers-Briggs Type Indicator." *Perceptual and Motor Skills,* 70: 1187–1202.

b. Carlson (1985). "Recent assessment of the Myers-Briggs Type Indicator," *Journal of Personality Assessment,* 49: 356–365.

18. Kennedy, R. B., and Kennedy, D. A. (2004). "Using the Myers-Briggs Type Indicator in career counseling." *Journal of Employment Counseling,* 41(1): 38–44.
19. Larsen, R. J., and Diener, E. (1987). "Affect intensity as an individual difference characteristic: A review." *Journal of Research in Personality,* 21: 1–39.
20. a. Judge, T. A., Locke, E. A., and Durham, C. C. (1997). "The dispositional causes of job satisfaction: A core evaluations approach." *Research in Organizational Behavior,* 19: 151–188.
    b. Brief, A. P., Butcher, A. H., and Roberson, L. (1995). Cookies, disposition and job attitudes: The effects of positive mood inducing events and negative affectivity on job satisfaction in a field experiment. *Organizational Behavior and Human Decision Processes,* 62: 55–62.
21. a. Andi, H. K. (2012). "Emotional intelligence and personality traits: A correlational study of MYEIT and BFI." *International Journal of Academic Research in Business and Social Sciences,* 2 (10): 285–295.
    b. Atta M., Ather, M., and Bano, M. (2013). Emotional intelligence and personality traits among University teachers: Relationship and gender differences. *International Journal of Business and Social Science,* 4(17): 253–259.
22. a. Besharat, M. A. (2010). "The relationship between emotional intelligence and self-efficacy and academic success." *Educational Renovations Journal,* 3 (5).
    b. Saklofske, D. H., Austin, E. J., and Minski, P. S. (2003). Factor structure and validity of a trait Emotional Intelligence measure. *Personality and Individual Differences,* 34(4), 707–721.
    c. Higgs, M. (2001). Is there a relationship between the Myers-Briggs type indicator and emotional intelligence? *Journal of Managerial Psychology,* Vol. 16(7): 509–533.
23. Brackett, M. A., and Mayer, J. D. (2003). "Convergent, discriminant, and incremental validity of competing measures of emotional intelligence." *Personality and Social Psychology Bulletin,* 29(9): 1147–1158.
24. Sala, F. (2002). *Emotional Competence Inventory (ECI): Technical Manual.* Hay Acquisition Company Inc.
25. Mayer, J. D., Salovey, P., and Caruso, D. (2000). "Competing models of emotional intelligence. In R. Bar-On, and J. Parker (Eds.)." *The Handbook of Emotional Intelligence.* San Francisco: Jossey-Bass.
26. Newsome, S., Day, A. L., and Catano, V. M. (2000). "Assessing the predictive validity of emotional intelligence." *Personality and Individual Differences,* 29: 1005–1016.
27. AllPsych and Heffner Media Group Inc., (2011, November 29). *The OCEAN of personality. Retried from AllPsych Online: The Virtual Psychology Classroom: http://allpsych.com/personalitysynopsis/trait_application.html.*
28. Ghiabi, B. and Besharat, M. A. (2011). "An investigation of the relationship between personality dimensions and emotional intelligence." *Procedia – Social and Behavioral Sciences,* 30: 416–420.
29. Shaffer, R., and Shaffer, M. (2005). "Emotional intelligence abilities, personality and workplace performance." *Academy of Management Best Conference Paper 2005,* HR: M1-M6.
30. a. Avsec, A., Taksic, V., and Mohoric, T. (2009). "The relationship of trait emotional intelligence with the Big Five in Croatan and Slovene University student samples." *Psiholoska obzorja,* 18 (3): 99–110.
    b. Md Nawi, N. H., Redzuan, M. and Hamsan, H. (2012). "Interrelationship between emotional intelligence and personality trait of educator leaders." *International Journal of Academic Research in Business and Social Sciences,* 2 (5): 223–237.
31. a. Dulewicz, S. V., Higgs, M. J. (1999). "Can emotional intelligence be measured and developed?" *Leadership and Organization Development,* 20 (5), pp. 242–252.
    b. Pearman, R. (2001a). "Emotional intelligence and psychological type." *TypeWorks,* 39: 5–6.
    c. Pearman, R. (2001b). *Introduction to type and emotional intelligence.* Palo Alto, CA: CPP, Inc.

d. Lawrence, G. (2001). "Emotional intelligence: Does it develop differently in thinking types and feeling types?" *Proceedings of APT-XIV, the Fourteenth Biennial International Conference of the Association of Psychological Type* (pp. 273–280). Minneapolis, MN.

32. a. Torrington, A. (2001). "*Relationship between the Bar-On Emotional Quotient Inventory and the Myers-Briggs Type Indicator.*" Multi-Health Systems, Inc., Technical Report #0018. Toronto, Canada.

b. Farnsworth, R., Gilbert, E., Armstrong, D. (2002). "Exploring the relationship between the Myers-Briggs Type Indicator and the Bar-On Emotional Quotient Inventory: Applications for professional development practices." Paper presented at the *2002 ASAC Meeting*, Winnipeg, Canada.

c. Sitarenios, G. (2004). "*Relationship between the EQ-i, MBTI, and FIRO-B in a corporate sample.*" MHS Technical Report #019. Toronto, Canada: Multi-Health Systems.

d. Maddocks (2004). "How emotional intelligence measures can add value to users of type instruments." British Association for Psychological Type, *Type Face*, 15(1): 14–15.

e. Engstrom, M.C. (2005). "*A study of emotional intelligence as it relates to organizational outcomes beyond what is contributed by personality,*" Loyola University, Chicago, Illinois, unpublished doctoral thesis.

32. Richmond S., Rollins, P., and Brown, J. (2004). "Emotional intelligence and TJ leaders: Openings for growth." *Management and Organizational Development Symposium, Fifteenth Biennial International Conference of the Association of Psychological Type*, Toronto, ON.

33. a. Thompson, H. (2006a). "*The relationship among the BarOn EQ-I scales and the Myers-Briggs Type Indicator Form Q preferences and facets.*" High Performing Systems, Inc., Technical Report 16–06.

b. Thompson, H.L. (2006b). "Exploring the Interface of the Type and Emotional Intelligence Landscapes," *Bulletin of Psychological Type*, 29 (3), pp. 14–19.

34. a. Thompson, H. (1998a). "The Organizational Psyche: Part I: The New Paradigm." *Bulletin of Psychological Type*, 21, *1*, 14–16.

b. Thompson, H. (1998b). "The Organizational Psyche: Part II: The Personality Landscape." *Bulletin of Psychological Type*, 21, *2*, 1–6.

c. Thompson, H. (1998c). "The Organizational Psyche: Part III: The Organizational Landscape." *Bulletin of Psychological Type*, 21, *3*, 28–32.

35. Jung, C. G. (1976). *Psychological types.* (A revision by R. F. C. Hull of the translation by H. G. Baynes). Princeton, NJ: Princeton University Press.

36. Thompson, H. (1996). "*Jung's Function-Attitudes Explained.*" Watkinsville, GA: Wormhole Publishing.

37. Barnard, A., and Nel, E. (2015). "Personality type: Optimizing the development of emotional intelligence." *Problems and Perspectives in Management,* 13 (4): 115–123.

38. Costa and McCrae, (1992c). "Normal personality assessment in clinical practice: The NEO Personality Inventory." *Psychological Assessment,* 4: 5–13.

39. Mathews, G., Zeidner, M., and Roberts, R. D. (2002). *Emotional intelligence: Science and myth.* Cambridge, Massachusetts: The MIT Press.

40. Watson, D., and Tellegen, A. (1985). "Toward a consensual structure of mood." *Psychological Bulletin,* 98: 219–235.

41. Mayer, J. D. and Salovey, P. (1997). "What is Emotional Intelligence?" In Salovey, P. and Sluyter, D. (eds). *Emotional Development, Emotional Literacy, and Emotional Intelligence.* New York: Basic Books.

42. Caruso, D. R., Mayer, J. D., and Salovey, P. (2002). "Relation of an ability measure of emotional intelligence to personality." *Journal of Psychological Assessment,* 79(2): 306–320.

43. a. Petrides, K.V., and Furnham, A. (2001). "Trait emotional intelligence: Psychometric investigation with reference to established trait taxonomies." *European Journal of Personality,* 15: 425–448.

b. Petrides, K. V., Pérez-González, J. C., and Furnham, A. (2007). "On the criterion and incremental validity of trait emotional intelligence." *Cognition and Emotion,* 21: 26–55.

c. Petrides, K. V., Pita, R., and Kokkinaki, F. (2007). "The location of trait emotional intelligence in personality factor space." *British Journal of Psychology,* 98: 273–289.

44. Fiori, M., and Antonakis, J. (2011). "The ability model of emotional intelligence." *Personality and Individual Differences,* 50: 329–334.

45. Pérez-González, J. C., and Sanchez-Ruiz, M. J. (2014). "Trait emotional intelligence anchored within the Big Five, Big Two and Big One frameworks." *Personality and Individual Differences,* 65: 53–58.

46. a. Austin, E. J., Farrelly, D., Black, C., and Moore, H. (2007). "Emotional intelligence, Machiavellianism and emotional manipulation: Does EI have a dark side?" *Personality and Individual Differences,* 43: 179–189.

b. Collins, E., Freeman, J., and Chamorro-Premuzic, T. (2012). "Personality traits associated with problematic and non-problematic massively multiplayer online role playing game use." *Personality and Individual Differences,* 52: 133–138.

c. Petrides, K. V., Vernon, P. A., Schermer, J. A., Ligthart, L., Boomsma, D. I. and Veselka, L. (2010). "Relationships between trait emotional intelligence and the Big Five in the Netherlands." *Personality and Individual Differences,* 48: 906–910.

d. Van der Linden, D., Tsaousis, I., and Petrides, K. V. (2012). "Overlap between general factors of personality in the Big Five, Giant Three, and trait emotional intelligence." *Personality and Individual Differences,* 53: 175–179.

47. a. Petrides, K. V., Vernon, P. A., Schermer, J. A., and Veselka, L. (2011). "Trait emotional intelligence and the dark triad traits of personality." *Twin Research and Human Genetics,* 14, 35–41.

b. Vernon, P. A., Villani, V. C., Schermer, J. A., and Petrides, K. V. (2008). "Phenotypic and genetic associations between the Big Five and trait emotional intelligence." *Twin Research and Human Genetics,* 11, 524–530.

48. Schulte, M. J., Ree, M. J., and Carretta, T. R. (2004). Emotional intelligence: Not much more than g and personality. *Personality and Individual Differences,* 37: 1059–1068.

49. Bland, A. M. (2010). "The Enneagram: A review of the empirical and transformational literature." *Journal of Humanistic Counseling, Education and Development,* spring, 2010. Vol. 49: 16–31.

50. Baron, R., and Wagele, E. (1994). *The Enneagram Made Easy: Discover the 9 types of people.* New York: HarperOne. An Imprint of HarperCollins Publishers.

51. Palmer, H. (1991). *The Enneagram: Understanding yourself and the others in your life.* San Francisco, CA: HarperCollins.

52. Riso, D. R., and Hydson, R. (1996). "*Personality types: Using the Enneagram for self-discovery*" (Rev. Ed.). Boston, MA: Houghton Mifflin.

53. Matise, M. (2007). "The Enneagram: An innovative approach." *Journal of Professional Counseling, Practice, Theory, and Research,* 35: 38–58.

54. Perry, A. K. (1997). "Leading with skill and soul: Using the Enneagram and the Brent Personality Assessment System (Doctoral dissertation, Seattle University)," *Dissertation Abstracts International: Section B. Sciences and Engineering,* 65(10): 5451.

55. a. Maslow, A. H. (1962/1999). *Toward a psychology of being* (3rd Ed.) New York: Wiley (Original work published in 1962).

b. Maslow, A. H. (1970). *Motivation and personality* (Rev. Ed.) New York, NY: Harper & Row.

c. Maslow, A. H. (1971/1993). *The farther reaches of human nature.* New York, NY: Penguin-Arkana (Original work published in 1971).

56. Daniels, D. N. and Price, V. A. (2000). *The essential Enneagram: The definitive personality test and self-discovery guide.* New York: HarperOne.

57. Eckstine, D. (2002). "The couple's Enneagram Questionnaire." *The Family Journal: Counseling and Therapy for Couples and Families,* 10: 101–108.
58. Riso, D. R., and Hudson, R. (1999). *The Wisdom of the Enneagram,* New York NY: Bantam Books,
59. a. Thomson, C. (1993a, August 13). "Bill's soul cries: Why can't we all get along?" *National Catholic Reporter,* p.17.
    b. Thomson, C. (1993b, December 3). "How does one know John Paul II is a one?" *National Catholic Reporter,* p.15.
    c. Thomson, C. (2007, February 2). "Dismantling our trances." *National Catholic Reporter,* p.10.
60. Newgent, R. A., Parr, P. E., and Newman, I. (2002). *The Enneagram: Trends in validation.* Retrieved from ERIC database (ED468827).
61. Ormond, C. H. (2007). "The effects of emotional intelligence and team effectiveness of a newly formed corporate team learning the Enneagram (Doctoral dissertation-Institute of Transpersonal Psychology)" *Dissertation Abstracts International: Section B. Sciences and Engineering,* 68 (04): 2699.
62. a. Colina, T. (1998). "Nine ways of looking at work." *Journal for Quality and Participation,* 21: 56–60.
    b. Kale, S. H., and Shrivastava, S. (2003). "The Enneagram system for enhancing workplace spirituality." *Journal of Management Development,* 22: 308–328.
    c. What makes your boss tick? (1997, December). *Getting Results,* 42: 6–7.
63. "Good leaders understand contributions of different personalities." (1998, June 29). *Business Journal Serving Fresno and the Central San Joaquin Valley,* p. 15.
64. a. Levine, J. (1999). *Enneagram intelligences: understanding personality for effective teaching and learning.* Westport, CT: Bergin & Garvey.
    b. Luckcock, T. (2007). The soul of teaching and professional learning: An appreciative inquiry into the Enneagram of reflective practice. *Educational Action Research,* 15: 127–145.
65. Wright, S., and Sayre-Adams, J. (2007). "Who do you think you are?" *Nursing Standard,* 21: 20–23.
66. Tallone, R. and Sikora, M. (1947/2006). *Awareness to action,* Chicago: The University of Scranton Press.

5

COMPONENTS AND COMPETENCIES OF EMOTIONAL INTELLIGENCE

OPENING CASELET

Adopting a Balanced Approach

Traditionally, intelligence was confined to two varieties of behavior — verbal and logical. Due to this, "ability to understand the meaning of words, concepts and ideas" as well as "ability to understand a problematic situation and apply knowledge to deal with it" were regarded as the vital components of intelligence. Intelligent people were expected to emerge as high achievers in their educational pursuits in various fields, such as engineering, sciences, management and so on. They were also expected to do well in their professional work.

Intellectual ability continues to command respect in human life even today. But this does not mean that the ways in which intelligent people handle various issues would always turn out to be worthy of praise. Let us consider the case of a brilliant professor who has a high level of technical expertise in his field. One of his students, who is pursing B.E. Computer course, has submitted a project report to him for perusal. The student is eager to know his reaction to the report, but the professor has asked the student to wait till the last lecture session is over. Accordingly, the student calls on him during the stipulated time slot. The professor begins his interaction with the boy in a wild tone. He angrily says, "How can you submit such a substandard report? It contains many drawbacks pertaining to adequacy of content, clarity and style of presentation. It seems like you were very casual and careless while preparing the report. Is this the way I taught you to prepare it?" The student feels very much dejected and with a heavy heart says, "Sorry sir, this will not happen again". He then leaves the place without direct eye contact with the professor.

No doubt, the professor was very harsh in his comments, which created a severe upsetting effect on the student. Unfortunately, his brilliance and technical expertise failed to prove helpful in preventing him from attacking the personality of the student, which led to the devaluation of the student's self-esteem. This indicates that he lacked in a personal resource, emotional intelligence, which can be used very effectively in handling oneself and one's emotions as well as others and their emotions appropriately in every interactive situation. If viewed in this light, it can certainly be said that the worth of the professor as a person, who is supposed to create an impact on students in the desired direction, is low. He lacks the ability to relate to others in a cordial way.

The concept of emotional intelligence is based on the notion that emotions are as important as intelligence in human life. It is helpful in creating awareness of one's own feelings and those of others. This is why it prompts us to judge what situation we are in and then act appropriately. By following the tips given in the literature on emotional intelligence, we can always engage in our interpersonal interactions in such a way that they turn out to be satisfying to self and others.

Indeed, it is desirable to strike a balance in using intelligence and emotional intelligence as personal resource, so that it will be possible for us to enrich our life and also do some good to others.

Source: **Excerpt from discussion with Dr. Arun Kulkarni, Former Head, Department of Psychology, Rashtrasant Tukdoji Maharaj Nagpur University (RTMNU), Nagpur, India.**

We all have struggled one time or the other to keep a check on our unruly, disruptive feelings, keeping a cheerful demeanor even when we wanted to cry aloud, keeping ourselves motivated or attending to and getting in sync with feelings of others around us. Honing good interpersonal skills is essential not only at work but also at home. Emotions define whether people accept, reject, approach, avoid, or get involved with others. The more one develops the understanding and management of emotional responses, the more one enjoys an increased sense of comfort and peace in interpersonal relations. Daniel Goleman's framework of Components and Competencies of Emotional Intelligence, as described in his seminal book, *Working with Emotional Intelligence*, provides us with a clear insight into which attributes would one need in order to succeed in life. According to this framework, there are five components of emotional intelligence — *Self-Awareness*, *Self-Regulation*, and *Motivation* in the Personal competence category and *Empathy* and *Social Skills* in the Social competence category.

Another model of emotional intelligence is known as the Six Seconds Model. Anabel Jensen, President of Six Seconds, explains the rationale behind the name Six Seconds. She says, "The organization's name is inspired by the latest research on emotional reactions, which states that it takes around six seconds to identify or recognize the feeling of compassion".

In Daniel Goleman's model of emotional intelligence, under each component, there are several competencies, making a total of twenty-five competencies. Let us first understand what we mean by the term 'competency'.

Competency is defined as, "A capability or ability."[1] "An *underlying characteristic* of an individual that is *causally* related to *criterion-referenced, effective and/ or superior performance* in a job or a situation".

Underlying characteristic means that the competency is a fairly deep and enduring part of a person's personality and can predict behavior in a wide variety of situations and job tasks.

Causally related means that a competency causes or predicts behavior and performance.

Criterion-referenced means that the competency actually predicts who does something well or poorly, as measured on a specific criterion or standard.[2]

A competency study drawing on models from forty companies revealed that strengths in purely cognitive capacities were 27 percent more frequent in the stars than in the average performers, whereas greater strengths in emotional competencies were 53 percent more frequent (Goleman, 1998).[3] Such researches strengthen the need to study the EI framework in detail.

EI PERSPECTIVE — The Gentle Side of a Tough Player

During French Open (Roland-Garros) in the year 2014, Novak Djokovic was in the news not only because he had won the match with 6-1, 6-2, 6-4, but also because of his cordial behavior which was as spectacular as his play.

During the match, when it started raining, his ball boy promptly stood behind him holding an umbrella. On seeing this, Novak, invited the boy to join him on the bench, held the umbrella and offered him a drink.

Source: https://www.joe.ie/sport/video-novak-djokovic-chills-with-ball-boy-during-rain-delay-433680

PRACTITIONER'S INSIGHT — First Impressions, Last... Emotional Intelligence Matters!

When two people interact via writing, talking or even looking at each other, they get a "first impression" based on their previous interaction with what they consider "similar people". For some people, this first impression is very strong and keeps on influencing their further interactions. Some people superimpose this first impression by subsequent interactions. The ability to do so is very important in emotional intelligence.

Every person creating such an impression gives you some pleasure, some pain. If the pleasure is more than the pain, then you like the person and your further interaction with that person is positive. If the pain is more than the pleasure, then you tend to give a negative reaction.

If a person gets a positive initial impression or is able to change the negative impression into a positive approach, the interaction keeps on improving and this creates an impression of a likeable useful person. If the interaction goes the other way, you feel continued difficulty in dealing with the person.

If you are working with a group of people in an organization, this impression plays a key role in your effectiveness in the organization. If majority of people get a positive interaction with you, you get their support and you are more effective in your performance in the organization.

Source: Excerpt from the discussion with Mr. Sharu S. Rangnekar, Rangnekar Associates, Management Guru and author of several bestselling books like '*In the Wonderland of Indian Managers*'.

THE SIX SECONDS KCG MODEL OF EI (1997)

This model of EQ-in-Action begins with three major endeavors — to become more aware (noticing what to do), more intentional (doing what you mean), and more purposeful (doing it for a reason). It believes that emotions are data and defines emotional intelligence as the capacity to blend thinking and feeling to make best possible decisions, which is the key to have a successful relationship with yourself and others.

The three pursuits are explained below:

Pursuit	Competency	Definition
Know Yourself	Enhance Emotional Literacy	Accurately identifying and interpreting both simple and compound feelings.
	Recognise Patterns	Acknowledging frequently recurring reactions and behaviours.
Choose Yourself	Apply Consequential Thinking	Evaluating the costs and benefits of your choices.
	Navigate Emotions	Assessing, harnessing, and transforming emotions as a strategic resource.
	Engage Intrinsic Motivation	Gaining energy from personal values and commitments vs. being driven by external forces.
	Exercise Optimism	Taking a proactive perspective of hope and possibility.
Give Yourself	Increase Empathy	Recognizing and appropriately responding to others' emotions.
	Pursue Noble Goals	Connecting your daily choices with your overarching sense of purpose.

Taken from, https://www.6seconds.org/2010/01/27/the-six-seconds-eq-model/

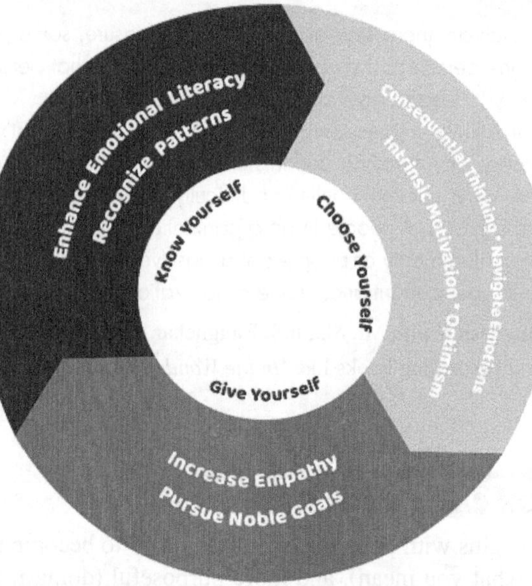

Figure 5.1: Six Seconds Model of EQ
Adapted from Six Seconds website https://www.6seconds.org/2010/01/27/the-six-seconds-eq-model/

THE EMOTIONAL INTELLIGENCE FRAMEWORK

The emotional intelligence framework of Daniel Goleman consists of various competencies. It has two parts, personal and social, and both are vital for success. As one climbs the corporate ladder, these skills become more and more important. Strategies for improving these skills are provided in the next chapter. Although the more recent works of Daniel Goleman have restructured this and present four instead of five skills, as authors, we found that the original five skill framework would be helpful to both first-time readers as well as those who have had some exposure to this concept in the past. The new framework consists of self-awareness, self-management, social awareness and relationship management, as against the previous one which comprised self-awareness, self-regulation/ self-management, motivation, empathy and social skills.

Personal Competence

These competencies determine how we manage ourselves.

Component I – Self-awareness

Knowing one's internal states, preferences, resources, and intuitions

- **Emotional awareness**: Recognizing one's emotions and their effects
- **Accurate self-assessment**: Knowing one's strengths and limits
- **Self-confidence**: A strong sense of one's self-worth and capabilities

Component II – Self-regulation

Managing one's internal states, impulses and resources

- **Self-control**: Keeping disruptive emotions and impulses in check
- **Trustworthiness**: Maintaining standards of honesty and integrity

- **Conscientiousness:** Taking responsibility for personal performance
- **Adaptability**: Flexibility in handling change
- **Innovation**: Being comfortable with novel ideas, approaches, and new information

Component III – Motivation

Emotional tendencies that guide or facilitate reaching goals

- **Achievement drive**: Striving to improve or meet a standard of excellence
- **Commitment**: Aligning with the goals of the group or organization
- **Initiative**: Readiness to act on opportunities
- **Optimism**: Persistence in pursuing goals despite obstacles and setbacks

Social Competence

These competencies determine how we handle relationships.

Component IV – Empathy

Awareness of others' feelings, needs, and concerns

- **Understanding others:** Sensing others' feelings and perspectives, and taking an active interest in their concerns
- **Developing others:** Sensing others' developmental needs and bolstering their abilities
- **Service orientation:** Anticipating, recognizing, and meeting customers' needs
- **Leveraging diversity:** Cultivating opportunities through different kinds of people
- **Political awareness:** Reading a group's emotional currents and power relationships

Component V – Social Skills

Adeptness at inducing desirable responses in others

- **Influence**: Wielding effective tactics for persuasion
- **Communication**: Listening openly and sending convincing messages
- **Conflict management**: Negotiating and resolving disagreements
- **Leadership**: Inspiring and guiding individuals and groups
- **Change catalyst**: Initiating or managing change
- **Building bonds**: Nurturing instrumental relationships
- **Collaboration and cooperation**: Working with others toward shared goals
- **Team capabilities**: Creating group synergy in pursuing collective goals

Source: Taken from Goleman, D. (1998). "*Working with Emotional Intelligence*", Bantam Books.

PERSONAL COMPETENCE

These competencies determine how we manage ourselves.

Self-Awareness

Being aware of the fact that even after achieving splendid success, one needs to remain grounded and humane is quite a clear indication of living in a state of self-awareness, one of the most important but often neglected competence. Stein and Book describe emotional self-awareness as, "The foundation on which most of the other elements of emotional intelligence are built".[4] It is about whether we are aware of our emotions in the first place and how they are impacting what we are doing. It is the ability to understand one's internal states, preferences, resources, and intuitions. Goleman (1998)[5] argues that self-awareness is critical to understand others and to exhibit empathy. The competencies listed under self-awareness, i.e. emotional awareness, accurate self-assessment and self-confidence, help us in understanding whether individuals can recognize their own feelings and thoughts and whether they can identify their strengths and weaknesses. Having too many weaknesses may not necessarily lower our self-confidence but being aware of even a few of our strengths can make us feel confident. Successful people are not necessarily flooded with lot of strengths, but they are quite conscious of whatever their strengths are. More than often, they focus on building further upon those strengths. It doesn't mean they ignore their weaknesses, rather they derive their energy from their strengths, while simultaneously working on their weaknesses.

Some of us would like to spend most of our time having people around, while some may prefer to remain alone; some may be very particular about data and details of any activity they engage in, some may go just by their instinct; some may be making their decisions giving more importance to rationale and logic, while some may make their decisions based on their feelings. Some of us may want to plan our holiday in advance and there are definitely some opposite ones who would be spontaneous in their actions. It is completely fine to have any of these set of preferences as far as one is aware about what one prefers and the challenges and advantages which accompany the preferences. This will enable one to better understand self and others. Many a times, misunderstandings happen because we expect others to be like us and forget the fact that all of us come in different shapes and sizes and that each person does have his or her set of preferences.[6] Fortunately, today there are many tools which can help us understand ourselves better. Some of these tools are discussed in the next chapter.

Emotional Awareness

Individuals who are aware of their current emotions and the reason behind them are people with emotional awareness. They can see the connection between what they are saying and doing and the thought behind it. They are also aware of how their emotions are affecting their performance and have a clear sense of their values and where they want to reach in future. The critical feature of this competence is that people can enunciate their feelings and also choose a socially acceptable expression. Emotional awareness helps one to become more strategic and effective in interacting with his/her surroundings.

We all have had a gut feeling or a hunch some or the other time in our life. Emotional awareness is about being able to understand quite appropriately what exactly is going on inside our body. The decision rules[7] derived from our life experiences reside in the subcortical neural networks that gather, store, and apply algorithms from every event in our lives, creating our inner rudder. This awareness about one's emotions is very essential because it is at the very core of being human.[8] Being fully aware about one's self is a rare feat. For a mortal, it is definitely a challenge, but having said that, not an impossible one to achieve.

Accurate Self-Assessment

The attributes of this competency include being aware about one's strengths and weaknesses. Individuals with this competency have a tendency to reflect and learn from their experiences. They are open to feedback and new viewpoints. They engage themselves in continuous learning, leading to an ongoing process of self-development. During this process, they continuously get insights into the gap between the quantum of knowledge and self. The sense of vastness of the universe and the lack of completeness on their part makes them humble. In their routine transactions and existence, they come across as individuals who prefer to mock about self, which leads to more acceptability in the group they belong to. Absence of ego is a peculiar attribute of this competency. Individuals with this competency believe in having multiple feedback methods and tools.

People who excel in this competency are grounded in reality more as compared to others, and prefer a clear idea of self, as much as possible. Organizations where this competency is intertwined in the culture are learning-oriented organizations. The practical example of this competence is shown in the following Practitioner's Insight box.

PRACTITIONER'S INSIGHT — Knowing One's Strengths - An Essential Element for Success

I have an important global customer who has a regional procurement team based in Jakarta. Recently, a young and talented woman was promoted to head this team. She had a reputation for being extremely aggressive with suppliers, demanding the lowest price for every deal. My first meeting with her did give me precisely the same impression.

In a few weeks, we had our largest fruit supply contract coming up with the same regional customer in Jakarta. I was well aware that my products were priced on the higher side in comparison to what was being offered by other 'not so quality conscious' companies. To make matters worse, one of those competitors was a local Indonesian supplier, while our fruit juice was going to get delivered from another corner of the world. I had to come up with a strategy and fast.

I started asking myself the question, "What needs/requirements does this procurement manager have? What is it that she is looking to acquire or get?" It suddenly dawned on me that this young lady had no prior experience about juices (seasonality; crop cycles; pricing trend; major cultivating regions; etc.). We have a weekly internal document covering all these points since we need to be closest to the actual worldwide situation on fruits. Of course, sharing such a document with my customer was a great risk, since she would be privy to some information which was not easily available. I discussed this issue with my team and my boss, and after a lot of brainstorming, decided that the risk is worth taking.

Still, I was worrying that just by sharing our knowledge, would we be able to differentiate ourselves from our competitors? Traditionally, keeping such an information closely guarded has been the norm of our industry. But on second thoughts, I realized that with the tools that are available today, it will hardly take any time for this smart and professional young lady to gain this knowledge anyway. I went ahead and for three weeks in a row, I kept sharing our internal documents on 'global fruit market updates'. I did not receive anything more than a 'Thank you' every time I shared this information.

On the appointed date of the contract, as predicted, we were 3rd in terms of price and as a standard practice, it meant that there would be no allotment for us. We had lost!

Much to my surprise though, I received a call from the procurement director that same evening. She was not only very courteous in the way she spoke but also quite open in sharing what prices the 1st and the 2nd placed companies had quoted. She went on to say that in her capacity as a regional procurement director, she had the authority to 'add' points to the ranking tally based on individual supplier's 'long-term commitment and partnership approach'. Since my company was the only one that 'clearly demonstrated' this approach to her, she had added these points only to our tally. It meant that we were now at the 1st position and she was willing to offer us the contract if 'we were still interested in taking it.' Are you thinking about miracles? I am thinking about being aware about one's strengths and using them confidently.

Source: **Excerpt from discussion with Mr. Amit Waikar, VP Sales – Asia Pac, Doehler.**

EI PERSPECTIVE — Jamsetji Tata - The One Who Knew His Potential

The Tata group was founded in 1868. Very few organizations have been able to sustain this long. The key reason behind this, according to Harish Bhat, as explained in his book, *Tata Log,* is that all the Chairmen who succeeded Jamsetji Tata, Founder of Tata group, have shared Jamsetji's vision wholeheartedly and never forgot the purpose behind the business. They created wealth but primarily for the people of the nation. This vision has remained like the North Star and provided the right direction to all their endeavors.

Jamsetji was a very determined and confident man, who had tremendous faith in his enterprise. Way back in 1880s, he could foresee a need for steel, it becoming an essential element in nation building. After doing an in-depth study of the industry and having visited places in India which had iron ore deposits, he went to Pittsburgh which was famous for producing premium quality steel to exchange his thoughts with some of the top minds in the metallurgical field. He was warned by many skeptics and critics that his endeavor may not give him the kind of fortune he was envisioning. But he did not budge from his decision and firm-mindedly took the plunge. Such was his accurate understanding of self and the capabilities of his enterprise. Even after the first round of exploration was in vain, as the iron ore and coal required was not available in the area first identified by them, eventually their efforts did lead to fruition. India's first steel plant was established in Jamshedpur in Eastern India. Steel rails from this plant were also used in the British war effort in Mesopotamia, during World War I.

Source: Adapted from the foreword by Harish Bhat (2018), *The TATA Saga: Timeless Stories from India's most Iconic Group*. Penguin Random House India.

Self-Confidence

Individuals with this competency come across as those with surety and self-assurance or a promise. They have the courage to voice their opinions and even if they seem to be unconventional or unpopular, they can fight for the right in their opinion. They are comfortable at making decisions and can operate even in ambiguity and stressful situations. But let us remember that being confident and being rigid are not the same things.[9] Self-confidence is the extent to which we feel sure about our capabilities in a particular situation. It has to do a lot with our prior experiences. Something that we have done in the past and have managed it well, gives a boost to our confidence. But if we have been reprimanded, discouraged or looked down upon; it adversely affects our confidence, our courage to do it again. Has it ever happened with you that you knew the answer to a question, but you still didn't raise your hand? Was it because you lacked confidence? May be because you had tried giving an answer in the earlier session but were ridiculed for speaking incorrect English or lacked logic, or for some other reason? You felt discouraged, insulted or may be embarrassed and that adversely affected you. We have included a chapter on personality and emotional intelligence that you may find worth referring to once again at this juncture. It is interesting to study how genes and environment together shape our personality. Even when one has it in his/her genes, the environment can make or mar one's sense of self-worth. The challenge is not to let oneself get affected by the outside world too much, but at the same time being open to periodic feedback from reliable sources in order to have an accurate self-assessment is a must.

Cognitive psychologists suggest that it increases the thinking abilities, interest, courage, enthusiasm and faith in oneself, which help a person to perform successfully at need.[10] There are quite a few human traits which directly or indirectly relate to self-confidence. A self-confident person perceives himself/herself to be socially competent, emotionally mature, successful as well as optimistic.[11] This competency becomes extremely important as it becomes the prerequisite for everything one wants to pursue. Without self-confidence, it is difficult to sustain oneself.

Self-Regulation

It is about managing one's internal states, impulses and resources. It is the ability to manage one's emotions in a way that one develops a control over what one says and does. It is about controlling the urge to blow up or react, which if not controlled can have long-lasting ramifications. It is therefore extremely important that we learn the art of becoming conscious of the smallest cues that start accumulating within us which may eventually result in an unacceptable overt behavior leading to social embarrassment. The foundation of self-regulation is self-awareness. If one has a fairly clear idea of oneself, it will help him/her to take charge of one's emotions and regulate the same. People high on self-regulation choose how to behave and thus emerge as better managers and leaders. In order to get the work done, one needs to come across as a person whom the co-workers do not dislike working with. One can expect that self-regulated people may have higher chances of becoming preferred co-workers.

Self-Control

Being able to manage the impulse is a key feature of this competency. A person with this competency can remain balanced even in extreme situations. Such a person can think clearly and can remain focused even under pressure. However, lack of this competency can impact one's performance and reputation in a negative way. In the corporate context, this becomes very critical to one's image as a professional, especially while dealing with a setback and managing workload. A common experience is that of losing a potential opportunity to grow in the organization. How does one deal with that? Is it possible to go beyond feeling angry, lost and ditched? Isn't it worth reflecting on what must have led to such an outcome? Taking personal responsibility for one's own performance and mistakes can actually be a great quality to possess. It is essential that one develops self-control. If one shows readiness to accept new challenges and channelizes one's emotions more positively, it can be said that he/she have a fair amount of control on his/her emotions.[12] Many of us are not able to regulate our success, however, more than often, failure and the accompanying sorrow with the setbacks are what we find very difficult to deal with. The ability to think through outcomes before reacting to a situation is critical in determining whether one has developed self-control or not. Practicing consequential thinking, defined as evaluating the costs and benefits of one's choices, can be a great practice.[13] An example in this context can be seen in the following EI Perspective box.

EI PERSPECTIVE When Emotions Win Over Us!

When Indian boxer, Sarita Devi was in Incheon (Northwestern South Korea) for the Asian Games in 2014, she lost her match against Park Ji Na. She was shocked and surprised when her opponent was announced as the winner. At the award ceremony of the 57-60 kg (light weight) category, she simply refused to accept the bronze medal as she was fully confident that she was not the loser. She couldn't hold back when she climbed the podium and burst into tears. When the official finally managed to persuade her to accept the medal, she refused to allow him to put the medal around her neck. After a while, she walked towards Park Ji Na, her opponent who was declared winner, and put the medal around Ji Na's neck. After this, she went back to the podium. The Korean player followed her and pleaded her to take the medal back, but Sarita very warmly refused. Eventually, she relented and kept the medal in her hands and later left it on the podium as she was leaving after the ceremony.

Comment:

"She did what she did at the podium after full twenty-four hours of losing her bout, which means she had the time to think things over. This does not appear natural or spontaneous to me at all", said Adille Sumariwalla, the Indian contingent's Chef de Mission at the Games.

Sources: a) https://www.firstpost.com/sports/minute-minute-account-sarita-devis-refusal-accept-medal-asian-games-1738931.html

b) Das, S. (2016). "*Shadow Fighter*", Harper Sport, p. 119.

EI PERSPECTIVE Drawing a Leaf from The Speaking Tree

A constant guiding inner voice or a conscience is a prerequisite to self-control. This helps us in controlling our mind, our feelings (both positive and negative) and our reasoning. This regulates our desires and we do not get tempted. We resolve better. We neither bask in past glory nor wail over our setbacks. We can thus develop more comfort in dealing with the uncertainties of the future.

Source: Shri Shri Nimishananda (2009). "The Best of Speaking Tree", Volume 5, *The Times of India*, Times Group Books.

Trustworthiness

Trust is defined in the Oxford dictionary as, "A firm belief in the reliability, truth, or ability of someone or something". This trust in action leads to trustworthiness. Individuals with this competency are high on dependability, authenticity, predictability and truthfulness. Even when they make mistakes, they do not hesitate to admit them. When operating as a part of a group, they can muster the courage to challenge any variance in the beliefs displayed by others. They can confidently take a stand and not budge even if it is an unpopular one. This can be a great enabler in achieving success and can impact one's career in a positive way.

Whether we like it or not, we are being observed by people around us constantly, sometimes consciously. People observe our talks, actions and deeds. When they see us performing consistently, always delivering and performing in line with their expectations, we tend to get perceived as being trustworthy. It is an important prerequisite to earn delegation.

In organizational context, what matters a lot is not just how well one can execute one's task but how one comes across as a professional. In order to come across as high on professionalism, one needs to be transparent in one's conduct as much as is required and 'walk the talk'. Only those who do this regularly may come across as trustworthy. For any job to be delegated, seniors do weigh people on these parameters. Similarly, one of the prerequisites for any employee to commit and dedicate her/himself is that s/he considers her/his employer trustworthy. The aspects which are essential to determine whether someone is trustworthy or not can be understood by asking the following questions.

Can we comfortably predict how A would behave in a particular situation? Will A be able to keep the commitment or agreement? Even in your absence, will A deliver what A would in your presence? Has A been honest in the past? Has A delivered high quality work in the past? Can others discuss openly about issues, if any, in the work environment with A and not fear any kind of negative implication?

It is extremely important that in an organizational context, one remains honest and communicates openly and transparently whenever required. Introverts prefer not to interact much with others, they may be interpreted as someone who is secretive and therefore people may misunderstand if they themselves are poor observers of individual behavior.[14] Similarly, with extroverts, there is always a risk of some extra information which need not necessarily be shared, might get revealed because of their outgoing nature. Both, introverts and extroverts are at equal risk of 'may not come across as trustworthy,' if they do not develop an understanding of their preferences and modify their actions/reactions accordingly.

Conscientiousness

Individuals with this attribute are good at meeting commitments and taking responsibility for personal performance. They have internal locus of control and are methodical and watchful in their work. Answerability is an important prerequisite for earning delegation in organization. It can be defined as an appeal from our conscience. It is only when one assumes full responsibility of one's performance that one can propel oneself on the road of success. People with this competency have a belief that success or failure is primarily because of their own efforts and assume that the onus of the outcome is primarily on them. In business, uprightness, honesty and integrity of being conscientious means taking complete responsibility, keeping promises, not being secretive about important and required information and having enough meat to lead self and organization with grit and confidence as well as remaining absolutely unruffled irrespective of any situation.[15]

Adaptability

Individuals possessing this competency are flexible in handling change and are good at multi-tasking and managing even an unplanned change. Flexibility is their key strength.[16] Adaptability, in effect, is about how well and readily you can keep enthusiasm alive.[17] The word enthusiasm has its genesis in Greek word *Entheos* meaning 'from the spirit within'. As Winston Churchill said, "Success is going from failure to failure without loss of enthusiasm." Adaptability, the ability to go with the flow, changing demands and needs, is core to resilience. In today's dynamic world where change comes almost like an avalanche and we are bound to cope with it without having a choice, this competency can impact our career trajectory in a big way. The ability to bounce back when things go wrong is about having an important attribute called flexible optimism. This determines the extent to which one can be comfortable even in adverse conditions and make the most of it. Indian social reformer and independence activist, Bal Gangadhar Tilak wrote *Geeta Rahasya,* while he was serving in jail at Mandalay in Burma. He could convert the isolation and loneliness into solitude because of his emotional adaptability.

In 2004, when Tsunami had surged across the Indian Ocean and disrupted many lives, one of the widely affected islands was Maldives. The Tsunami had shattered many hotels and resorts on this island; two were of Taj Group — Taj Exotica and the Taj Coral Reef. The way the staff handled this unexpected situation is an unprecedented and exemplary tale. Not only it speaks volumes about courage, commitment, and conscientious behavior, it also shows the amount of spontaneous, untaught, and untrained adaptability of the staff of these hotels. They not only helped their guests in moving to safer locations, they remained balanced and positive while fulfilling their respective duties. For example, the head chef made sure that the lunch gets served on time, at 1.00 pm, in spite of battling such a life-threatening situation.[18] Adaptability of this kind is rare and when employees of an organization display it so seamlessly time and again, it gets institutionalized and makes the organization timeless. In the book, *In Search of Excellence*, Robert Waterman and Thomas Peters give many other examples from across the globe. Like many other known management professionals, Marv Adams, Chief Information officer with Ford Motor Company (2000-2006), also believes in the concept of 'Adaptive Organizations'. He states that those learning organizations which not only lead the change but also develop more profound capacity to deal with the ongoing change can be called as adaptive organizations.[19]

Innovation

Individuals with this competency are comfortable with novel ideas, approaches, and new information.

A person who has this competence can think out of the box. Being capable of generating new ideas, being able to look at problems from a different or novel mindset are their key strengths. Believing in the concept of equifinality (in an open system, a given end state can be reached by many ways) is a peculiar feature of a person having this competency. Do you have a relative or friend who is way older than you and yet whom you relate more with? Is s/he more accommodating to your modern choices and way of living and goes overboard in supporting you with your decisions come what may? If yes, you have already understood what kind of competency we are referring to.

In organizational context, this is one of the primary prerequisites. Dr. Santosh Bhave, Director-HR & IR at Bharat Forge Ltd., mentioned during one of his campus recruitment visits, "I am in search of young minds who are high on innovation". At this moment in industry, this is one of those aspects of emotional intelligence that matters a lot. People with the inclination and ability to innovate are comfortable at taking a fresh perspective and can think of seemingly impossible things comfortably.[20] Every organization wants its employees to be change agents. People with this competency also possess the qualities of being able to adjust to new environment and not being judgmental all the time.

Motivation

This competency includes emotional tendencies that guide or facilitate individuals in reaching their goals. Whatever we do, the motives, it involves various mixes of brain chemicals[21]. It is widely known that it is amygdala that general brain circuitry is based in and it is where motivation gets its firm ground. It decides whether one will enjoy one set of activities over the other. Not only this, but it also stores the memory one has of the activities performed in the past, including what one felt during that particular episode and the way one is habituated about it. Emotions can cause motivation and motivation can also cause emotions. Individuals with competencies like being passionate about some objective, not getting affected by the happenings, continuing to volunteer, and initiating and staying hopeful in worst adversities are those whom Goleman called motivated individuals. Motivational theories like Maslow's Hierarchy of Needs Theory, Douglas McGregor's Theory X and Theory Y, David McClelland's Theory of Needs, and Herzberg's Two-Factor Theory are helpful in understanding the concept in detail. Having motivated employees is a challenge faced by many organizations. We will discuss this in detail in the next chapter.

Achievement Drive

Individuals possessing this competency strive to improve or meet a standard of excellence. Being result-oriented is a major characteristic of persons with achievement drive.

David McClelland has dealt with this concept in detail in his research on need for achievement. He states that Need for Achievement (N-Ach) is about an individual's hunger for a substantial achievement.[22] As described by Henry Murray, need for achievement or achievement drive is about the sustained efforts.[23] It is about an insatiable passion for achieving what one wants. People with this competence are highly driven from within to reach their goals. They prefer pursuing challenging goals and take calculated risks. They set venturesome but manageable challenges. Especially in the case of entrepreneurs, taking such venturesome but calculated risks leads to success. They seek clear feedback in order to improve their performance. Having a boss who is low on achievement competency make employees lack clarity in their roles and responsibilities, the bandwidth and the purpose of their job. In such a scenario, employees suffer from lack of corrective inputs in order to improve.

Some lucky organizations have employees who display a high level of achievement drive. Sumant Moolgaokar of TATA was one of them. Harish Bhat, while writing about Sumant Moolgaokar in his foreword for the book, *The Tata Saga*, mentions, "...He used to famously say, "Do not accept second-rate work. Accept the best and ask for it. Pursue it relentlessly and you will get it"". The Tata Sumo vehicle was named after him, combining the first two alphabets of his first and last names. The Practitioner's Insight titled, 'Fighting Internal Battles Everyday' and 'JK Paper- A learning Organization not Just on Paper' are examples about how achievement drive and conscientiousness matters.

PRACTITIONER'S INSIGHT

Fighting Internal Battles Everyday

This is a story of a young lady who decided to quit her corporate job and appear for UPSC exams after her marriage and having a child. She was so determined about what she wanted and why she wanted it that nothing blocked her way. Support systems came up, and it seemed that the entire universe around her conspired to provide whatever support it could. "But even then, the initial days of making people understand my dream and trying to create a buy-in was very tough. But, the toughest part was to stay away from my small child for a long time and getting subjected to speculations and comments from some people who simply failed to understand my decision to quit job, leave my son with my mother so that I could study and prepare myself for one of the toughest exams. After all, I knew that my willingness to achieve my dream will impact my personal life too. But, in spite of all the criticism, I thrived on those strong pillars (support of my family members) who stayed with me in my pursuit of a seemingly unachievable feat," said Anu Kumari, IAS Kerala Cadre.

Source: Exerpt from the talk of Ms. Anu Kumari during her visit to her alma mater IMT Nagpur after having secured 2nd all India rank in UPSC 2017 exam.

PRACTITIONER'S INSIGHT JK Paper - A Learning Organization Not Just on Paper

"We recently took yet another initiative to further nurture the Achievement Drive for our employees so that it may help us in making our organization a *Learning Organization.*"

This initiative was launched in June 2018 and branded as 'Wrong 2 Right'. The concept was to nurture the conscientiousness (taking responsibility for personal performance) and achievement drive (striving to improve or meet a standard of excellence) in our employees by awarding those who admitted their mistakes and took necessary corrective actions. We believe that awareness, acceptance and action are the three important aspects which signify that someone is ready to learn, improve and grow.

We focused on creating an environment where people embrace failure, learn from it and bounce back with success. The senior management at JK Paper Ltd. sponsored this intervention and invited all the employees to participate in this initiative by sharing their learnings from the year 2017-18 by answering the following questions:

1. What is the one mistake you've made in the year 2017-18?
2. What learning did you draw from that particular mistake?
3. What did you do to overcome/rectify/correct that mistake?

The employees were asked to answer the questions in relation to their work/role in the organization. Prize money was also announced for employees, for example, 1st prize worth ₹15,000; 2nd prize worth ₹10,000; 3rd prize worth ₹5,000; and, 10 complementary prizes worth ₹1,000 each.

The panel of assessors of this initiative comprised top management, such as Chief Financial Officer, Plant Heads, VP- Marketing & Sales, and VP-HR. We received very encouraging response from employees across locations and more than 200 entries were received from employees. After assessment, winners were rewarded in a public function. This particular initiative played an instrumental role in taking the *Culture of Excellence* to a new high. The progressive effort led to the strengthening of organizational learning which was showed in the stellar growth of JK Paper in the year 2018-19.

Source: **Excerpt from the discussion with Mr. Abhishek Kumar, DGM - HR, JK Paper Ltd.**

Commitment

For people with this competency, it is very easy to make a personal or group sacrifice for the larger goal of the organization. They can find purposefulness in the larger task. People with this competency offer their services willingly to accomplish the group's purpose. They align their goals with those of the group or organization.

Committed employees are the key drivers of an organization and they go beyond their job descriptions. Such employees display organizational citizenship behavior.[24] They can sustain stress and excel even under pressure and challenging situations. At one federal agency, those employees who experienced the greatest organizational commitment suffered the least from the stress and reported the most satisfaction with their work.[25]

In his book, *Thought Leaders*, Shrinivas Pandit gives many examples of leaders who are high on commitment. Mr. Pramod Chaudhari, Former President of Mahratta Chamber of Commerce, Industries and Agriculture (MCCIA) Pune, India, and Chairman of Praj Group of Industries, is one of them. Shrinivas mentions that Pramod once said, "I don't mind helping a customer even in personal matters, even match-making for his daughter or son, if that gets me closer to him to understand his business needs". Of course, it also goes well with the collectivistic culture of the country where people mostly would not mind such a gesture.[26] Commitment, like many other competencies, is a discretionary behavior that is not a part of an employee's formal job requirements and has a positive implication on the psychological and social environment of the workplace and job performance.[27] One needs to look at the other side of the coin as well. In what circumstances can employees refrain from going extra mile in spite of having the competency? It has been seen that in organizations where employees are not being treated fairly and with dignity, the employees respond in a manner which shows lack of emotional allegiance.[28]

Initiative

Individuals with this competency volunteer to make the most of the opportunities they see ahead of them. They tend to aspire and exert to achieve goals on their own. The unique feature of this competency is that individuals with these kinds of attributes can infuse enthusiasm in others through their enterprising efforts.

Few years back, we had a Management Development Program (MDP) client in the industrial explosives sector. Its HR came down to discuss the impending MDP and insisted that we (trainers) conduct some two–three sessions on 'How to earn delegation'. He was a senior employee with an elaborate experience at hand. He firmly believed that the culture of taking initiatives needed to be expanded in the organization. Employees should be taught to reflect on what can they do to earn more opportunities to contribute. Authors can see a clear link at this point between volunteering for work and success in organization. The authors see a plausible link between 'volunteer for work', leading to 'get noticed', further leading to 'increased interaction for feedback from the subordinates/superiors' and thus increasing the 'chances of getting more and more work' resulting in increased 'chances of growth and development' over others in the organization.

Thus, going beyond the job description is an extremely important attribute of this competency. For people with perceiving type of personality, who are spontaneous in nature (based on MBTI), there may be a possibility that this may come naturally. But there is flipside to it. They need to develop the ability to exert restrain, wherever it is not required, in order to avoid the unwanted side effects. So, at least some level of self-awakening is required in order to use one's preferences wisely. An instance of an initiative backfiring is given in the following EI Perspective box.

EI PERSPECTIVE Initiative That Backfired!

Samya, a young Indian girl got married to a boy called Patrik, German by origin. After marriage, she was staying with her husband and in-laws in Germany. A few months after the marriage, she realized that her in-laws did not have many people visiting them often. So, she decided to throw a surprise party and invited a few of her relatives and her husband's relatives who happened to stay in the same city. The party went well. Patrik who had stayed in India and was aware of the collectivistic culture was appreciative of Samya's efforts. But it didn't go well with her in-laws who felt offended by Samya's gesture.

Sometimes, however good our intentions are, our actions may still get misinterpreted. It is a good idea to think about the outcomes, especially when one is new to a culture.

Source: An illustration given by authors.

Optimism

Individuals with this competency are more driven by the positive outcomes rather than negative. Fear of failure does not bother them much, as they have enough courage to make things happen by taking charge themselves. They are persistent in chasing their goals despite obstacle and setbacks. They have a constructive thought process and can see the brighter side of situations and have a sense of awareness about what can work for them in any kind of adversity. Optimism or positive thinking is a very popular word but equally unpopular in practice. If you look around, you will find enough people who find it absolutely difficult to say anything good about anything or any situation, what-so-ever. They are cynical about everything. Well, why optimism or positive thinking or positivity is not given high regards by many is because it has been presented in an incorrect fashion. It often fails to earn respect from skeptics because it gets interpreted as just saying 'good' to almost everything all the time. Honestly, there is very little harm, if at all any, in this, but optimism is much more than that. According to American Philanthropist and former General Manager at Microsoft, Melinda Gates, "Optimism for me isn't a passive expectation that things will get better, it's a conviction that we can make things better. Whatever adversity may be, no matter how bad it is, we can help people if we don't lose hope and we don't look away."[29]

One of the most popular and widely cited researches in the area of flexible optimism is that of Martin Seligman's studies of insurance salesmen with the MetLife company. He found that new salesmen who were either born with the positivity attribute or were trained optimists sold 37% more insurance in the first two years of their career than pessimists. And during the first year, pessimists quit at twice the rate of optimists.[30]

PRACTITIONER'S INSIGHT

Positive by Choice!

Dr. Martin Seligman, Father of Positive Psychology movement, defines optimism as a way in which we explain events to ourselves. When positive events happen to an optimist; an optimist might state them to be due to personal (I studied hard), permanent (I am capable of studying hard), and pervasive causes (my college encourages hard work and studies). When they undergo a negative event; they explain it as external (I had too much to do), temporary (I usually do well in Math), and situation-specific factors (I am bad only at Math).

A pessimist who undergoes the same event might explain it differently. They attribute a positive event as external (the paper was exactly what I guessed), temporary (it will never happen again), and situation-specific attributes (I was lucky) and explain negative events in terms of personal (I suck at Math), permanent (I am terrible at quantitative studies), and pervasive causes (I won't pass and my life is ruined).

Why is optimism important?

Optimism is linked to work performance, academic performance, athletic performance, in fact, in all walks of life. Optimists also experience more fulfilling relationships. They are better at coping with slings and arrows that life throws at them. They eat better, enjoy better health and are known to recover better from diseases, e.g. heart and cancer episodes.

What prevents us from being optimistic? Let's discuss some myths.

Myths about optimism:

1) Optimists wear rose-tinted glasses and are not realistic
Research seems to suggest that optimists are better at identifying problems and it is this very skill that helps them to correctly identify the source of the problem and rapidly make changes in their lives. A poor health report would spur an optimist to take immediate steps rather than blame self or others. So, optimists are better at identifying both threats and solutions than their pessimist counterparts.
2) Optimists have lesser stress so they can afford to be optimistic:
Research once again suggests that optimists reframe their stressful situation as a challenge. They undergo the same emotional process but like a battle-scarred warrior they bring out their skills, strengths, and resourcefulness to the fore. Taking the same health challenge. They might reframe losing weight as a challenge which invigorates them rather than as a punishment of eating too much fast food. So optimists experience the same negativity but reframe better and faster than pessimists. Some optimists might use humor to change your mindset or cheer up the team.

> What we see is that optimists are approach-oriented rather than avoidance-oriented. They put in a lot of effort to seek information rather than dispute or deny information that is presented to them. Most importantly they ask for help.
>
> *Source:* Excerpt from the discussion with Mr. Birender Ahluwalia, Chief Optimist and Chief Executive Officer, The Positivity Company.

SOCIAL COMPETENCE

The following competencies determine how we handle relationships.

Empathy

Empathy has been defined by psychologists in two ways — (a) empathy is the cognitive awareness of another person's internal states, that is, his thoughts, feelings, perceptions, and intentions; and (b) empathy is the vicarious affective response to another person.[31]

Martin Hoffman (1984; 1987) defined empathy as, "An effective response more appropriate to someone else's situation than to one's own".[32] Empathy is the foundation for positive relationships and the ability and motivation to understand and react to other peoples' fears, challenges, and feelings. People with this competency are conscious about the emotional signals displayed by others.[33] They are attentive while communicating with others, particularly their listening skills are well-developed. They are sensitive to others' standpoints, their unspoken worries or sentiments and can reach out to others by comprehending their needs. A research conducted by Gentry, Weber, and Sadri (Center for Creative Leadership) found that the ability to understand what others are feeling, being empathetic is a skill that clearly contributes to effective leadership.[34]

If one fails to be empathic, there could be multiple issues one is likely to face. For example, people may develop dislike towards such individuals who may come across as insensitive. Poor ability to empathize may lead to serious communication problems. Such people find it extremely difficult to listen because they cannot agree to something being said which is not in line with their thought. Since such people cannot realize that the people working with them have the need to grow, they often fail to provide feedback at all or provide feedback of low quality. People who are low on this competency, rarely provide any recognition or praise as they fail to recognize this need in others.[35]

An interesting research by Feshbach and Feshbach, 1969 and Gibbs, 1987[36] states that empathy has been found to reduce aggression. Another lesser known finding is about empathy's relation to the ability to manipulate people. According to Christie and Geis (1970), who conducted comprehensive study on the 'Machiavellian' personality in the 1960s, effective manipulators are not, as some might think, high on empathy who use empathy to read other people's intentions and then make use of that knowledge against them. In reality, they are weak empathizers and not good at reading other's intentions. Their 'advantage' precisely is that they are poor empathizers and therefore their insensitivity allows them to "bull their way through in pursuit of their own goals. A reference has been made to the movie Blade Runner in this context in the first chapter. "Just a word of caution, we do not want to say that absence of empathy does not doom one to manipulating or killing others," says Martin L. Hoffman. Read the Practitioner's Insight from a senior advisor to TATA Trusts, Mr. H. N. Shrinivas in this context.

PRACTITIONER'S INSIGHT

An Emotionally Intelligent Culture at TATA

Observing successful leaders in my professional career of 40 years, as HR head of large companies, and looking at certain common threads in terms of quality attributes of such leaders, I find that *listening skills* and *empathy* rank very high.

Modern management has successfully taught us how to be articulate and effective in speaking and presenting our thoughts, but there is little training provided regarding how to actively listen with empathy; appreciation, and acknowledgement. So much so, in today's business organizations, we find a large number of managers who are brilliant in presenting their thoughts and impressing the recipient/audience, whereas there are very few people who listen and understand with empathy. Empathy is the ability to share and understand the feelings of others. Understand the full context of a situation and the emotional pulls and pressures involved and putting yourself in the shoes of the person who has gone through an experience; feeling for him and experiencing the pain.

Through empathy, you acknowledge people; you understand the contextual predicaments. Any solution determined in such complex human situations with a touch of empathy shall be realistic, genuine and convincing. So, it works to heal and resolve the conflict. It is this quality that is naturally practiced by some great leaders that puts them on a unique and respectable pedestal.

Empathy helps in building trust relationships. It acts as an enabler in building strong teams that succeed. The quality of empathy in a leader seeks to create a latitude for each member of the team to contribute his best; the diversity of talent and capabilities get integrated into a program, for addressing critical needs of the project on hand, and with this kind of harmonious synthesis, powerful and effective outcomes are delivered.

In the context of HR function, this quality of empathy and active listening, which is the crux of emotional intelligence, plays even a more central role. HR leaders with this strength, can contribute hugely towards interdepartmental harmony through a method of appreciative inquiry to communicate the importance of the contributions being made by each functional specialists, which at times, seem to be coming in conflict with one another. This role of an HR leader helps in driving a performance centric culture and the effectiveness of HR is even more strongly felt by senior leadership. I have noticed managers demonstrating a certain breadth of understanding and relating to the emotional side of conflicts in organizations, effortlessly. This could be the case while addressing an inter-departmental/functional issue, for resolution or it could just be in the process of coaching/mentoring a manager.

The data that appear on paper as the factors that caused it is one part; the other part is the unseen emotions and feelings of people contributing to the situation on hand. Such an understanding comes from practicing empathy, which according to me is nothing but selflessness and objective listening.

Such qualities in senior managers help in building a great culture of performance and loyalty. Employees demonstrate voluntary ownership and commitment towards the company which is very valuable in the context of coping with increasing competitive market challenges and succeeding, besides handling unexpected or sudden crisis situations that organizations face at times.

The unfortunate terror attack on Taj Hotels on 26/11 in Mumbai and the manner in which employees responded is a great example of strong organizational culture, employee engagement and loyalty.

Customers who were trapped inside the hotel narrated stories of how employees on duty saved and rescued them white putting their own life at risk; in the process, some employees even died while facing the bullets of terrorists, but saved their guests/customers. It is this quality of engagement and loyalty of workforce built by leaders with emotional intelligence and empathy that helps build world class organizations with extraordinary levels of performance and service excellence.

Source: Excerpt from discussion on Empathy with H. N. Shrinivas, Advisor TATA Trusts.

Understanding Others

This can be taken as the first stage of empathizing with others. People with this ability not only feel others' standpoints and emotions but take active interest in others' problems, concerns or pain points. They also have a great listening capacity. They prefer to go with the flow and try to search for an opportunity to learn something new in the process. Such people have the unique ability to stretch their senses during each conversation. If someone fails to agree with them, or press them hard against their feelings or stance, they prefer to stay calm and look deeper for meaning. They operate with a mental set that if someone is arguing or not agreeing, it is because they are interested and wish to make things better. They seek to search for a common ground between their objectives and the objectives of those who seem to be in disagreement with them at the moment. They choose not to respond hurriedly, instead practice some restrain and listen more empathetically and patiently. These are some of the important attributes of people with the ability to understand others.[37]

Developing Others

Individuals with this competence recognize and appreciate peoples' core positive areas, achievements, and improvements. They provide beneficial and constructive feedback and help others in identifying their areas for improvement and also have skills to provide coaching and mentoring in order to develop others. At individual level, they are good mentors as they have this innate ability to guide.

When such competencies get converted into organizational values, they further propel growth and development of the organization. By keeping the paramount focus on the continuous development of their employees, organizations communicate a strong message. Such efforts continued over a period of time develop the potential to become a learning organization.[38]

Service Orientation

People with this competency comprehend the needs of others and use that knowledge to create a better fit between their offerings and others' needs. For example, in case of serving a customer, they go an extra mile to understand their unmet needs. This competency revolves around the attribute of being able to serve in the best possible and appropriate way with absolute focus on client/others' satisfaction. The following EI Perspective highlights the importance of service orientation.

EI PERSPECTIVE Taking Service Orientation to A New Height

Once Ishwar Chandra Vidyasagar (a legendary Bengali polymath from the Indian subcontinent, and a key figure of the Bengal Renaissance) was on his way to deliver a talk. He was traveling by train. One of his fellow travelers, who was carrying a suitcase, also alighted the train on reaching the station. On getting down, this traveler started shouting loudly in search of a porter. On seeing this, Vidyasagar approached him and asked about why did he need someone to carry just one suitcase. To this, the man replied that it was against his dignity to carry his luggage. Ishwar Chandra volunteered to carry his suitcase up to the destination. The man offered him some money equivalent to what he would have offered to a porter. To this Ishwar politely replied, "To serve you is my reward".

Source: Anonymous

Leveraging Diversity

Individuals with this competency are able to connect with people from backgrounds different than theirs. They understand that there are other ways which could be different, but worth accommodating and welcoming. They have the ability to convert the differences into an advantage and volunteer to question prejudice, stereotype and narrow-mindedness. Being able to leverage from diversity is multiple steps beyond developing mere sensitivity.

In Spring 2002, Thomas Kochan et al., in their talk on *Beyond McGregor's Theory Y: Human Capital and Knowledge Based Work in the 21st Century Organization*, elaborated on the current challenge in managing diversity. They talked about going beyond efforts to changing attitudes, to focus on building skills, the need to facilitate work in diverse teams and to learn from the variety of backgrounds and knowledge people bring to their jobs.[39] Today, the definition and bandwidth of the term 'diverse' have further broadened and the managers now need to be immensely sensitive about the diversity of their stakeholders.

Diversity enhances an organization's ability to respond to its stakeholders, including customers, with more novel and ingenious products and solutions. However, to fully involve the varied backgrounds, minds, and cultural perspectives within an organization, the leaders and employees should be able to apply this competence of EI called 'leveraging diversity' by cultivating opportunities which creates a common engagement platform for the diverse individuals in the organization. Thus creating, nurturing and leveraging relationships can benefit oragnizations. Beyond creating an inclusive, sustainable and appreciative organizational culture, this will also result in developing novel product designs, bring newer dimensions of service delivery and provide opportunities for customer-facing personnel to address more diverse customer bases. Being able to empathize, organizations can better manage the nature and distribution of rewards and other privileges. People with this competence certainly have big advantage in today's new diverse environment.[40] An example of leveraging diversity in an organisation is discussed in the following EI Perspective box.

EI PERSPECTIVE Diversity Issues at Green Park

Jiten, (name disguised), the owner of Green Park, a logistics company, was seeking Dr. Shoma's consultation (name disguised) on a very unique organizational issue. His organization was a reputed one in the logistics sector and has won several awards and accolades for years. Business had been smooth sailing for last two decades. Recently, he was briefed by his confidant, who is also the HR, that response to one of their policies — reimbursement of the tuition fees of one of the wards of the employees — has not been positive for last 2-3 years. On hearing this, Mr. Jiten was truly shocked and surprised as this very policy had differentiated his company from that of others' for a long time. The HR said that there were some employees who had started feeling left out and had started showing withdrawal symptoms. On analysis, it was found that those employees whose children had now either grown up and were on their own, those who did not have children, singles with not so clear intention to get married, widows, or widowers staying alone were the ones who showed discomfort. These were the employees who were found gossiping or displaying withdrawal behavior. Had the HR been more sensitive to this changing nature of diversity in the organization, he would have done a far better job in designing the roadmap for distribution of organizational benefits, and Green Park would have had lesser bumps.

Source: An illustration given by authors.

Political Awareness

Individuals with this competency can easily understand the power dynamics in an organization. They can identify vital connections and *what* and *who* matters. They have a knack for developing a deep insight into the internal as well as external environment of their job. This competence becomes critical especially in the case of higher-level management and executive positions, where steering through the organization becomes essential for success.

As one moves up in the organization, understanding the underlying issues and politics of the organization becomes increasingly necessary in order to be successful. Picking up the unspoken rules that govern success in organizational politics becomes extremely critical.

Political behavior has been defined as, "Activities that are not required as part of a person's formal role in the organization but that influence or attempt to influence the distribution of advantages and disadvantages within the organization".[41]

Social Skills

Individuals with this competence are adept at inducing desirable responses in others. With the increasing number of persons using social media for communication, it is as if *one's effectiveness on interpersonal skills determine how effective one is at one's written skills.* And therefore, it becomes more important that the millenials and especially, the generation Z understand and hone the social skills not limiting to written skills. The major problem with written skill is that it doesn't provide one with the opportunity to gather cues from other equally or rather more powerful mediums like body language. Sociologists state that there has been a sharp change in the way the young generation is engaged in basic activities like shaking hands, the art of conversation, and dinner etiquette. With the increased amount of diversity in workplaces, conflict will be inevitable and will become one of the key areas requiring effective management. Those who are not good at social skills will find it very difficult to deal with negotiating and to resolve disagreements. The challenge is that if one neglects the importance of developing social skills, there is a possibility that s/he may even become socially impaired to some extent and such individuals would find it difficult to get things done from others due to lack of basic understanding of others, a prerequisite for managing others.

In an Organizational Development (OD) conference in India, William J. Rothwell, a senior professor with Pennsylvania State University, discussed the other important aspects of society which are up for a massive change and the new set of skill sets required to cope with it. These challenges discussed in the last chapter of the book.

Influence

The key attribute of individuals with this competency is that they are persuaders par excellence. They address the most important question in the mind of the audience, What is in it for me? They use all kinds of direct and indirect tactics in order to create a buy-in from the audience. Influence competence is at the center of social skills cluster and is considered very critical in order to make an impact in the social sphere.[42] When we talk about influence in the context of emotional intelligence, it is about influence without authority. Researchers in this field, like Cooper and Sawaf, believe that when we develop a mindset of achieving a goal and give it our best effort, we do make a meaningful and substantial influence irrespective of whether we succeed or not. This means that even if our initiative fails, our sincere efforts create a different variety of influence which can be felt by people around us, even in failure.[43]

People must understand persuasion for what it is; not merely convincing and selling but learning and negotiating. Furthermore, it must be seen as an art form that requires commitment and practice, especially as today's business contingencies make persuasion more necessary than ever.[44]

Communication

Individuals with an ability to communicate effectively can make their point convincingly. As much it is about language, it is also about intentions and attitudes. The ability to have an appropriate body language and paralanguage becomes the key strength of people with this competency. They can listen well, have multiple sources for receiving feedback and can choose appropriate tools during transactions. They prefer open communication and are comfortable at providing or receiving communication and can handle good to worse kind of communication with equal comfort. Indirect or ulterior communication can create big problems in organizations. Any discussion on communication should first start with intrapersonal communication (communicating with oneself).[45] It is advisable that we start with listening to ourselves openly in order to communicate clearly with self and later with others. One can turn inward and listen to the 'little voice' that exists in our mind. This 'little voice' is the sound of our thinking. It is a known fact that we don't always communicate verbally. Whether at a conscious level it is known to us or not, the way we mentally process information influences our interaction with others.

Communication never loses its relevance and significance at any point in time in one's career. In fact, the higher one climbs a corporate ladder, more and more significant it becomes. Along with other leadership functions, in coaching and mentoring, it plays a very crucial role.

According to the study conducted by Albert Mehrabian about where we infer our feelings from, out of the majority of the communication, attitudes and beliefs about what someone communicates, largely (93%) is from the speaker's paralanguage and body language and very less (7%) from the words that s/he may speak.[46] In this case, as major portion of our communication is non-verbal, it is absolutely essential to be high on the ability to understand and interpret non-verbal communication.

As far as the communication in organization is concerned, Ajith Nair, a practice leader with Towers and Watson, has provided a very useful and easy-to-understand framework. He explains what leads to impactful communication in organization and places importance on organizational listening. As stated by him, "Organizational listening refers to a process of deploying listening tools and effectively capturing appropriate employee sentiments at points and frequencies to enable more effective organizational decision making". The three keywords given by him — tools, points and frequency — merit some attention. By points, he means the extent and intensity with which employee opinion needs to be captured with a clear intent, understood and fed back wherever required in the system. By tools, he means the methods, their nature and their place of deployment. By frequency, he means the pace and the number of occasions when the listening takes place.[47] At both individual and organizational levels, mindful communication is a must, says the Zen Master, Thich Nhat Hanh in his famous bestseller, *The Art of Communicating*, in which he lays emphasis on how to listen mindfully and how to express one's fullest and most authentic self. The author leads the reader into a reflective mode and asks us to ponder over issues, such as How do we say what we wish to convey in a way that the other person can hear? Can we envision the benefits of listening with compassion and understanding? Why many people communicate in a manner which is difficult by others to connect with? Is it worth exploring various ways and means to strengthen our relationships by drawing a leverage on our differences and thus accomplishing the objective of effective communication? Undoubtedly, deep listening is the essence of communication. Read the following EI Perspective and Practitioner's Insight to know more about this competency.

EI PERSPECTIVE — On Listening!

In "A leader Who Listens" by Hannah Beech in the June 27, 2005 issue of *Time*, Sun Chao, Mayor of the Chinese city of Xuhui and a constitutional law expert who has instituted town-hall meetings on a wide range of issues in Xuhui city of over 1 million people, comments, "We shouldn't trust ourselves, even if we have the power. We should listen to others' opinions".

Source: Taken from Cutcher-Gershenfeld, J. (2006). "*The Human Side of Enterprise*", Annotated edition. TATA McGraw Hill.

PRACTITIONER'S INSIGHT — Learning Communication Lessons by Being a Part of Student Committee in a B-school

"In our institute, we had several student committees. I volunteered for Corporate Communications Committee (CCC). This committee was in charge of media relations of the institute. Experience with this committee was one of my most important learnings on campus. My day-to-day activities required me to listen openly, speak convincingly and assertively but politely. Our team had to stay connected with all the students on campus so that we could be the first to report the important updates on online and offline platforms. Therefore, we had to maintain good cordial relations with almost everybody. We learned how to control our emotions in a way that they do not hamper our work relations. It was a sudden change from the comfortable life in graduation to this ever demanding and rigorous academic and non-academic activities. We soon developed the ability to adapt to different situations and circumstances. Handling the media and communication of any institution is a very sensitive job in most instances. What goes out can snowball immediately and then the consequences of those news articles do not remain in any one's control. I was directly responsible for the 'Opus', the institute's news magazine. I had to take care of the articles, photographs and interviews. This sense of responsibility brought within me a greater level of adaptability, which I later used during my subsequent job where situations were dynamic and required calm and cool handling. Even later, when I was applying for the doctoral program at IIM Ahmedabad, my ability to communicate mindfully and adapting myself to new situations almost spontaneously became my key strength."

Source: **Excerpt from the discussion with Punyashlok Dwibedy, IMT Nagpur alumnus (2012-14) during an alumni chapter meet.**

EI PERSPECTIVE Jet Airways Hoping to Find A Way

Jet Airways suspended operations in 2019 due to an enormous crippling debt and its inability to secure financing. According to a senior pilot, one of the reasons for the downfall of the airlines was possible lack of transparency in communications between the airline management and the government on funding.

Source: **'The Hitavada', https://www.thehitavada.com/Encyc/2019/4/19/22-000-Jet-employees-still-hope-for-revival-.html**

Conflict Management

Individuals with this competency can manage challenging situations with a tactical approach. They can identify possible disputes, disagreements, contention and can address the same with confidence. Such individuals promote arguments but at the same time they can even harmonize the situation calmly leading to an advantageous win for each of the party involved.

Chris Argyris, an American business theorist, and his colleagues pose a very fundamental question, Why is it that many sharp, proficient managers often fail to learn effectively? Their findings state that great teams are differentiated from mediocre ones on how well they tackle conflict and how they manage the defensive attitude of the team members that invariably accompanies conflict. According to Argyris, each one of us is trained very early in life, on how *not* to get into conflict, may be as a part of acceptable social behavior and in order to come across as a more palatable human. This acquires the status of a defensive routine or a defensive strategy and becomes our 'Mental model,' a term introduced by Peter Senge in his seminal work, *The Fifth Discipline: The Art and Practice of the Learning Organization (Senge 1990)*. These defensive strategies are unclear, counterproductive behavior chosen to avoid interpersonal uneasiness or distress.[48] They get ingrained in us by becoming our daily practices, our habits, which we keep continuing to safeguard ourselves from any awkwardness, shame, embarrassment and risk or danger that comes with revealing our thinking. These defensive routines form a kind of casing around our suppositions, assumptions, and save us from any potential pain but at the same time also prevent us from exploring or reflecting upon the potential causes behind the pain. "The Paradox", says Argyris, "is that when defensive routines succeed in safeguarding us from immediate suffering, they also block the scope from learning how to lessen the reasons behind the suffering in the first place." So having said this, it goes without saying that great teams do not have no–conflict character, but they have people with the competency to understand not only how to negotiate and resolve differences but also have the fine sense to uncover the reasons behind having or not having conflict in the first place.

Leadership

Lao Tzu says, "A leader is best when people barely know he exists, when his work is done, his aim fulfilled, they will say, 'We did this ourselves'". "Leaders, Honor Thy People", is yet another quote by this ancient Chinese Philosopher.

It is widely accepted that teamwork is no accident; it is the by-product of good leadership. Leaders can be people at the top as well as at the bottom. This may surprise the reader a bit if one has not studied Peter Senge's concept of leadership. He definitely includes positional leadership but also expands and introduces a deeper layer and position-less leadership. The basic role of a leader is to help the group achieve its common goal, to maintain it as a unit and to ensure that each individual is at his/her best. Let us stick to positional leadership for a moment. A person is given a leadership role because he has a certain kind of contextual expertise which the organization requires at that moment in time and thereby, expects him/her to positively impact outcomes. This expert, however, needs one important competency and the absence of which can ruin his entire effort. This competency is the skill in managing human relations. This skill is as much important as any other skill. He needs to have functional teams. This is a prerequisite for getting results through teamwork. He needs to be excellent at generating healthy conflicts and one who keeps respect for people as his top priority if s/he is to make things happen in a setting where his fellow members or subordinates are less skilled than s/he is.[49] No style is universally accepted as the best style. It totally depends upon the situation. The ability to observe, understand, predict and accordingly manage using suitable leadership style is the key. In this framework of EI, leadership means to inspire and guide individuals and groups. All leadership theories learned during Organizational Behavior course may come in handy. However, what differentiates a leader is his/her EI.

Daniel Goleman in his seminal article, "What Makes A Leader?",[50] mentioned how emotional intelligence is of paramount significance in the context of leadership. He states that, "Emotional intelligence is the sine qua non of leadership". Although in this chapter, as we look at leadership as one of the competencies of emotional intelligence, several researches along with that of Daniel Goleman's have clearly established a positive correlation between leadership and emotional intelligence.

A research done by Lisa Gardner and Con Stough of Swinburne University of Technology found that, "Effective leaders were identified as those who reported transformational rather than transactional behaviors. However, the significance of transactional leadership has its own place, but it is transformational leadership that one needs to get into in a matter of time, in order to make bigger and more promising impacts. Emotional intelligence correlated highly with all components of transformational leadership with the components of understanding of emotions (external) and emotional management, the best predictors of transformational leadership. Also, the research further discussed the utility of emotional intelligence testing in leadership selection and development.[51]

Leaders become inspirational when organizational members get a feeling that they are a part of a great team and find meaning in the everyday organizational experiences, where people talk about being a part of something bigger and larger than themselves, their experience with the organization stands out as singular periods of organizational life lived to the fullest and where some spend the rest of their lives finding ways to rekindle or recapture that spirit, undoubtedly leader of this organization is a leader we want to refer to. If the leader can create Metanoia, a shift of mind, then it is a leader worth referring to. Individuals with this competence, categorically arouse enthusiasm and can almost spontaneously get people connected to the shared vision and mission. People high on this competency lead as needed, volunteer and operate beyond the defined walls of their job description. They are good at bringing out the best in others and in guiding their performance. Their sense of accountability is highly contagious; and they simply lead by example.[52]

A. P. J. Abdul Kalam (Former President of India and a renowned scientist) had very high regards for Professor Satish Dhawan (Indian rocket scientist). According to Kalam, Professor Dhawan was a leader with a difference, who left an unforgettable impact on him. One particular experience he often shared was that of the launch of SLV3 on August 10, 1979. The vehicle had taken off and the first stage was achieved, as per the expectations. Seeing this, the second stage was initiated. But within a few seconds, the vehicle was seen in a tumbling motion and they finally lost flight over Bay of Bengal. The entire team which had worked tirelessly for so long, immediately got busy in collecting data so that they could gain some insights into the factors which led to the failure of the flight. Meanwhile, Kalam was called by Professor Satish Dhawan to attend a press conference. Before the conference began, Professor Dhawan told Kalam that he himself will handle the press conference and Kalam should be just present with other senior scientists and technologists. The press was more than anxious to know the possible reasons behind the failure. When the conference began, many questions were posed, some thoughtful, some very basic and some critical remarks were also being made. In response, Professor Dhawan said, "Friends today we had the experimental launch of SLV3 to put ROHINI satellite in the orbit. It was a partial success. It is our first mission of proving multiple technologies in a launch vehicle. We have proved many technologies in this launch but still, we have to prove some more. We have tumbled, but not fallen flat. Above all, I realize my team members have to be given all the technological support for the next mission to succeed". Soon, a failure analysis board was formed to investigate the cause. But that is not what A. P. J. wanted to stress upon. It was something more than this.

During the second mission of SLV-3 that took place on July 18, 1980, it was a different story and a different behavior of Professor Dhawan. The entire nation was again anxious to know the fate of the vehicle. At T-0, the vehicle took off and everybody in the office witnessed a textbook trajectory. The mission was successful. Everybody was immensely overwhelmed. The same day A. P. J. was called by Professor Dhawan again, not just to attend but to address the press conference along with the team members.

An important lesson in conscientiousness, taking responsibility for personal performance and inspirational leadership was taught by Professor Dhawan. When successful, the leader should give the credit to the team members but in case of failure, it is absolutely important to take the onus and face the consequences from the front.[53]

EI PERSPECTIVE The Futuristic Leadership at Future Group

Sanjay Jog, Former Head of Human Resources at Pantaloon Retail, expresses his views about Kishore Biyani, Founder of Future Group, in the book, *It Happened In India*. "Kishore Biyani is looked up to for his coaching and mentoring skills and he is a sounding board for the self-managed teams in the organization. His prime purpose is to institutionalize ideation and the execution within teams. One of the most distinguishing characteristics of Kishore Biyani as a leader is, unlike many leaders who look for things that went wrong and try to fix them, he looks for things that worked for the organization and goes onto further building on them. He doesn't mind his people making mistakes, but his worst nightmare is people and teams with absence of creativity, constructive approach and entrepreneurial energy."

Source: Taken from *It Happened in India*, by Kishore Biyani with Dipayan Baishya, Rupa Publications India Pvt. Ltd.

EI PERSPECTIVE Changing Thousand Lives

One of the stories in Sudha Murthy's book, *Three Thousand Stiches*, is about how she brought a sea change in the lives of the Devadasis (Devadasi is a woman who is considered given in marriage to God). These women dedicated to God once held high social status and were well-respected but not anymore. Sudha Murthy decided to bring back the lost honor in the lives of these Devdasis by bringing them in the mainstream of society. The skills which enabled Sudha Murthy comprise two aspects, as stated in the framework. One is initiating change and the other is managing it. In her book, she describes how she failed to even generate any kind of response, when she began with her work with the Devadasis. After reflecting on it and having discussed with her father, she reworked on her strategy of communicating with them, so that they at least listen to what she had to say. It started with change in dressing style in order to strike a chord of similarity and commonness. The outcome of her dogged efforts was that over a period of time, she transformed the lives of almost 3000 Devadasis. A remarkable feat indeed!

Source: Taken from Murthy, Sudha, *Three Thousand Stiches*, Penguin Random House India Pvt. Ltd.
Video link: https://www.youtube.com/watch?v=QZgicTzbPVM

Change Catalyst

Individuals with this competency can comfortably identify the need for change. They can foresee the potential barriers and even remove them.

To be effective in helping their organizations manage change, leaders first need to be aware of and capable of managing their own feelings of anxiety and uncertainty (Bunker, 1997).[54] Change is not only important to initiate but one should also be able to sustain it. John Kotter, in his article on change, states some very basic reasons behind the failure of the change efforts. First reason is not giving enough reasons as to why some change is being brought in and at a particular pace. Second, failure in creating a bigger mass of change agents. Even lack of a vision may become a reason without which a transformation or a change effort may get translated into a series of confusing and incompatible projects that may make employees feel like Alice (of Alice in Wonderland). Or not removing the barriers or blocks to the new vision.[55]

It is important to understand as to why do people resist change? A quite meaningful reasoning provided by Paul Strebel comes to mind. He starts with a very fundamental reason, may be the initiators and those who need to abide by it see change differently. But more importantly, he gives a more humane and empathetic reasoning. He suggests that managers must understand the 'Personal Compacts'[56] – the mutual duties and responsibilities that exist between employees and the organization. He further states that personal compact is a 3D concept — formal, psychological and social. Employees establish their sense of responsibilities, their level of commitment to their work, and the company values by posing questions along these aspects. How organization deals with this determines whether it will be able to sustain the change it has initiated.

Anticipating change and then not falling prey to MAFA (misinterpreting articulation for action) syndrome is the key. For instance, wishing to lose weight and actually losing it are two different things. Being able to initiate change requires one to challenge comfort zones. When most people around us are not even anticipating it, if one goes way ahead of anticipation and volunteers for becoming the change ambassador, s/he is a potential change catalyst. Most of us fear change because of the fear of unknown. People who are passionate change agents may also experience some fear, but they overcome it by gathering more information. They also do not mind sharing the information with others. People who can manage emotions like anxiety and stress are the ones who can sustain the change. The EI Perspective titled, 'Changing Thousand Lives' is an example of how one can be a change catalyst and the following Practitioner's Insight titled, 'The Role of Change Agents in Organizational Communication' is about how change agents impact communication process.

PRACTITIONER'S INSIGHT — The Role of Change Agents in Organizational Communication

As someone who has been at the helm of various organizations for more than a decade, I often find myself posed with the same riddle — How to change the behaviour of my employees. Often this change is not directly linked to their performance; I rely on certain techniques to help drive that change and minimize resistance. I employ a multi-step communication strategy, where each leg of the communication is geared to the audience. Behavioural change, in a large organization requires buy-in from a lot of key stakeholders, the ones who act as change agents. So, the first step is to recruit these change agents and ensure that I have their buy-in. These agents can be a part of the senior leadership itself or often key employees who can influence opinion. It is then the responsibility of these change agents to ensure that there is a tailored communication that reaches each team so that everyone down to the last person in the value chain understands why we are driving a particular change, how it benefits them and the organization as a whole and what is their role in ensuring this change.

Emotional intelligence is a prerequisite to successfully running large organizations with a diverse set of stakeholders. A good leader must understand that not all changes can be driven through carrot and stick rather one has to also employ referent power and foster collaboration.

Source: Excerpt from the discussion with Mr. Amit Saxena, MD & CEO, Unimoni India (Formerly, UAE Exchange & Financial Services Ltd)

Building Bonds

Individuals with this kind of competency are aware that people matter and therefore, they would go an extra mile to not only maintain but nurture relationships with people whom they work with. They maintain a huge pool of informal connections. They believe in keeping people informed. At times, they even make efforts to maintain relations with people who may not be of immediate relevance to them, but could be their potential clients, customers or co-workers. They make an effort to find out what may suit best for self and others, while working in groups. In order to create a bond, trust plays a vital role. It is mandatory that transparency is maintained in order to create mutual trust so that people working with us can trust us, unconditionally in most of the situations.

Freud Luthans and his associates studied more than 450 managers; all of them were engaged in four common managerial activities, i.e. traditional management, communication, human resource management and networking. They were trying to find answers to questions like, what leads to the fast growth of managers in an organization? What activities on the part of employees lead to their growth? They categorized their results in three parts— average manager, effective manager and successful manager. Successful manager was defined in terms of speed of promotion within their organization. Such managers were found spending 48 percent of their time in networking and 28 percent in communication.[57] The remaining was invested in traditional management and human resource management. This finding illustrates the importance of networking and managing social relations in getting ahead in organizations. Both communication and networking are fundamental prerequisites to building bonds.

An introvert who is unaware of the downside of this personality preference, may face challenges while building bonds. Similarly in the case of extroverts, they may need to focus their energies on developing the quality of their engagements with others. They may struggle with this because of the vast number of people in their network. It becomes important for every professional to understand one's natural personality preferences and consciously work on areas for improvement. So it doesn't necessarily mean engaging with numerous people but bringing excellence and sensitivity in whatever number of people one is engaged with. People with this competency have a great ability to stay in touch, beyond business. This comes in handy when they have to reach out for some work. It happens almost without a hitch. Along with technical expertise, maintaining good terms with the stakeholders definitely facilitates ones work at least in today's world where many people do have talent and there is an increased level of competition.

In a research conducted by Wendy Williams and Robert Strenberg at Yale University, the interpersonal skills and compatibility of the group members were found to be the vital determinants of their performance.[58] The findings of the study state that those who were socially incompetent, found it extremely difficult to manage conflicts or convey their messages effectively to others. The group needed social intelligence in order to do well, only having members with individual IQs wasn't enough.

EI PERSPECTIVE Building bonds: *The Russi Mody Way*

Rustomji Homusji Mody, also known as Russi Mody, was one of the extraordinary professionals in the TATA group. In 1939, he joined as an office assistant in Tata Steel and rose to become Managing Director. In 1984, he succeeded J. R. D. Tata as the Chairman of Tata Steel. He was known for his zest for life and for his outstanding human skills. He had an eye for talent and would put in a lot of effort to maintain and develop people working with him. He was known for his caring attitude and it is said that he personally knew the names of several thousand workers in Tata Steel.

Source: Taken from The TATA Saga: Timeless Stories from India's most Iconic Group. Penguin Random House India

Collaboration and Cooperation

The peculiar attributes showcased by individuals with this competency are that they can strike a balance between their task orientation and people orientation. They do not mind sharing their resources and look forward to collaboration. Creating a non–judgmental and friendly atmosphere around them naturally leads to increased cohesiveness in the team. They eagerly explore opportunities for collaborations and easily adapt themselves to the new situation and make effort to nurture it further. It is observed that many a times, teams or groups working together seem to ignore the basic rule of teamwork — they miss the balance between formula of thinking, organizing, defining roles, planning and designing with the solution of implementing, producing, and achieving their desired goals. They simply fail to strike balance between process and product. Every effort one makes in life has two elements, product and process. The product is the final or end state; the process is how you arrive at that end state. It is observed that more than often, organizations lay a lot more attention to product and not so much on process. This creates a lot of trouble. Timely focus on process can save organizations from unwanted and difficult to tackle situations.[59]

Team Capabilities

Individuals with this competency manage their demeanor in such a way that they always come across as pleasant individuals, whom people would like to work with. They offer respect in each of their transactions and give psychological strokes (According to Eric Berne (1971), the Founder of Transactional Analysis, "A stroke may be used as the fundamental unit of social action". Woollams and Brown (1978) have defined stroke as, "A unit of attention which provides stimulation to an individual.") to others, which creates enthusiasm. Although strokes can be positive, negative or neutral. The team goal is of paramount significance and individuals with this competency would exert effort in maintaining the standards set by the group and would go an extra mile to protect the group from any kind of potential threat to its standing.

Chris Argyris states that, "Most management teams break under pressure". He further elaborates, "Teams may function quite well with routine issues. But when they confront complex issues that may be embarrassing or threatening, the '*teamness*' seems to go to pot".[60] One who possesses team capabilities has the ability to sustain the synergy even under pressure.

According to Argyris, most managers find it very challenging to navigate collective inquiry[61] (the art of professional learning by using the power of the collective).

He further explains the reason behind this as, our schooling trains us on never to admit our ignorance, instead most of the systems reward people who are good at giving suggestions and not those who raise concerns about the complex issues. Somehow most of us save ourselves from the suffering of appearing uncertain and ignorant. But the cost is too high. We also may in the process, obstruct any new learning, assuming it to be threatening. Argyris calls this as "skilled incompetence" — teams comprising such people in big numbers who are unbelievably adept at keeping themselves away from learning. Having team capabilities then means, being able to manage this not-so-smooth texture of the team fabric, well. A practical example of importance of team spirit is given in the following Practitioner's Insight box.

PRACTITIONER'S INSIGHT

Flying High on Team Spirit

The Suryakiran Aerobatic Team (SKAT) selects its Pilots, from a pool of professionals, who are among the best qualified aviators. However, to make a cut in the team, in the selection process, apart from professional competence, social skills and emotional quotient / intelligence (EQ/EI) are also given great importance. Sometimes, from this elite pool, pilots don't make it due to lack of EQ/EI. Even during training phase, the leader and supervisors in the team keep a close watch on the flying aptitude and the overall personality of the trainee pilot. Formation Aerobatics being a precise skill with no margin for error, the selection and training process has to be of exacting standards, to ensure flawless displays.

There are two examples in the training period where self-awareness and emotional awareness played a vital role in the team building. One of the trainee pilots realized his own limitation while flying and with help of other experienced members correctly addressed it and became an integral part of the team. In other case, the trainee pilot could not adapt and was inflexible in his approach. This attitude of that young pilot got him terminated from the team.

The members train on each other's wings and apart from synergy and skills, it is 'Blind Trust', in each other's capabilities, that results in stitching together difficult maneuvers in the sky. At times, they fly in extreme close quarters in certain high on risk maneuvers at speeds exceeding 750 kmph and at distances less than a few meters apart.

Once, the team was putting together a new profile for the forthcoming display season and two outer members were being inducted in the nine aircraft team. Both were not getting the synchronization right for a particular maneuver in the sequence resulting in them closing into others' members while changing positions in the sky.

After the second such infringement, that particular maneuver was stopped for flight safety reasons. After a frank and detailed debrief on ground, it was decided that more practice was required before that popular maneuver could be continued in the display sequence.

The two outer members subsequently flew with senior members who groomed and corrected them after any error was made. Once they mastered that particular aerobatic maneuver, the team resumed its full display sequence for the season. Both members showed tremendous self-control to keep their impulses in check and strived to improve and meet the standards of excellence required of the famed aerobatic team.

The team leader had to take timely call for safety of his members during the maneuver and create group synergy to ensure training and display standards were maintained, to culminate the final profile for the display season. The senior members and others pitched in to address the development needs to bolster the abilities of the two new members.

Knowing your own and your team members' capabilities, especially EQ/EI, is vital for each member of the aerobatic team for a successful and flawless display.

Unlike any normal team in any organization which has diverse seniority and skill levels, SKAT has mainly members of similar seniority and skill sets who are motivated and driven to perform at their peak. Hence, the results are guaranteed, but not without emotional intelligence.

Source: **Excerpt from discussion on, "How to Build Team Capabilities" with Group Captain Joy Kurien, Former Leader Suryakiran Team of Indian Air Force.**

Chapter Synthesis

According to the Six Seconds model of EI, emotions are data. Emotional intelligence is an ability to identify and understand our emotions and emotions of others and the ability to use this consciousness to manage our behavior and our relationships. Daniel Goleman's EI framework and EI model by Six Seconds are presented in the chapter. Daniel Goleman claims that EI surpasses IQ, as a determining factor of workplace success. This has been extensively studied by not only Goleman and his associates but also by other scholars and practitioners (Bar-On and Parker, 2000).[62] Goleman's framework starts with self and smoothly progresses towards managing others. It clearly helps one understand how it is absolutely important to look inside, manage the interior dialogue and then create impact on others by managing our interactions.

The framework has five components and each one has a set of competencies which explain the bandwidth of the component. The attributes of these competencies help us understand what it means and how it gets demonstrated. One common thread which runs across the entire framework is the ability to go beyond the minimum. In the personal competence category, the first component of EI is self-awareness. It is about being aware about one's emotional state, knowing one's strengths and limits and about having confidence in self. The next, self-regulation is about how we manage our internal states and how competencies like self-control, trustworthiness, conscientiousness, adaptability and innovation become crucial to this. The chapter further elaborates on the next component of the framework, motivation, essence of which gets captured in achievement drive, commitment, initiative and optimism.

The next competence, presented in the framework, deals with the social arena. It is about handling our relations. Empathy being the most important competency, which gets demonstrated in attributes like understanding what others feel at a particular moment and helping them to overcome their weaknesses. People who have the competence to empathize can see differences as opportunities as they can feel the pulse of the various emotional exchanges and power dynamics within the group.

Further in the emotional intelligence framework, Goleman explains how the skills like being able to influence, communicate with emphasis on listening without bias, managing conflict, being able to see an opportunity ahead of others, being able to work on shared goals and being able to create synergy while doing so, matter.

Key Terms

Equifinality	Strokes
Oculesics	Internal locus of control
Paralanguage	Introverts
Skilled incompetence	Extroverts
Psychological strokes	Appreciative inquiry
Vicarious	Flexible optimism
Mindful communication	Collective inquiry
Metanoia	Organizational listening
Personal compacts	

Review Questions

1. Define competency and explain the term.
2. Empathy is essential. Elaborate on the basis of the emotional intelligence framework provided by Daniel Goleman discussed in this chapter.
3. Explain the Emotional Intelligence model provided by Six Seconds.
4. What do you understand about the term, adaptive organization?
5. List the basic attributes under *building bonds* competency.
6. What do you understand by the term skilled incompetence?
7. Explain the concept of personal compacts.
8. Write a note on learned optimism.
9. Why is communication critical to emotional intelligence?
10. Why do change efforts fail often?

Application-based Exercises

1. Steve Smith, Captain of Australian cricket team, was banned for a year and stripped of captaincy over the ball-tampering issue in 2018. While he was addressing the media over this issue he said, "I don't blame anyone. I am the captain of the Australian team, I take responsibility of what happened last Saturday, in Cape Town". Analyze the response with reference to the concept of leadership as discussed in the chapter.
2. Observe a person in your context. Focus more on non-verbal communication {kinesics, oculesics, paralanguage (in case the other person is speaking), proxemics, chronemics and haptics}. Then try copying that physical state and examine how you feel. This can help in developing empathy.
   - Conduct an interview of a new bride/ groom who has come to new house after marriage to stay with her/his in-laws. Find out, what kind of adjustments she/he was required to make. Also note down what kind of challenges s/he faced while doing this. This will give you some idea of how much readiness is required in order to adapt oneself to a new situation.
   - Do a similar kind of activity with a new entrant in an organization.
     (Suggestion: Try to find a link between the emotional adaptability and the mental and physical adaptability of the person).
3. Interview the owner/ founder/ top manager of an organization in your city and find out if that organization is an adaptive organization.
4. Take a pen and paper. Think of the biggest challenge you faced and overcame in your life. Now start writing. Write in detail about what the challenge was and what was at stake. Now start detailing out the specific steps that you took to successfully meet the challenge. Write down how it shaped you into the person that you are today. What were the strengths that you acquired? What were the values and beliefs that were formed or reinforced? Detail out the thoughts, feelings, and actions before, during, and after the event. You might be able to guess what your attribution style is. If you would like to get an accurate description, you could take this assessment. https://www.authentichappiness.sas.upenn.edu/questionnaires/optimism-test (suggested by Mr. Birender Ahluwalia, Chief Optimist and Chief Executive Officer – The Positivity Company)

ACTIVITIES BEYOND THE BOOK

1. Reflect upon working with a team, particularly when it performed really well. It could be anywhere and any kind of team task. How would you like to describe it? What according to you, was making that team work effectively and efficiently? How was the overall mood of the team? Who were the ones who were guiding the team? What competencies did they showcase? Can you contrast this experience with some other team you were a part of, but the team did not function that well?
The above reflection should help you to find out the distinguishing factors in the team members and the nature and the process of actions taken by them. You may look into the EI framework shared in this chapter to arrive at some basic reasons behind the outcome of the efforts made by the two teams.
2. Attempt a brief summary on one or two most important learning experiences in your life. Reflect on some of the prominent and critical ways in which you have benefited from them.

VIDEO RESOURCES

1. H.H. Dalai Lama on Compassion and Kindness
https://www.youtube.com/watch?v=cAfdMOTs1_0
2. Nick Vijucic's video for Motivation
https://www.youtube.com/watch?v=c3Ffkvb7S3c
3. Ted Talk by Helen Riess on Empathy
https://www.youtube.com/watch?v=baHrcC8B4WM
4. Ted talk on the Power of an Introvert by Susan Cain
https://www.youtube.com/watch?v=c0KYU2j0TM4
5. Daniel Goleman on Emotional Intelligence
https://www.youtube.com/watch?v=pt74vK9pgIA

ANALYSIS OF SELECT MOVIES

1. ***Forrest Gump (1994)***

This 1994 film, starring Tom Hanks and which won six Oscars, is a satire with a difference. Directed by Robert Zemeckis, the movie compels one to reflect upon many aspects of life. It is a classic example in emotional intelligence with reference to competencies like commitment, optimism and conscientiousness, to name a few.

A gripping story of a young boy (Forrest), who even after being tagged as the one with a low IQ, not only sustains but also triumphs not just mundane activities but also situations like that of war! In fact, he emerges as a hero.

Contrasting Forrest's unpretentious simplicity with the revolutions and bitterness of the times, the film is an intelligent commentary on the inanity of smartness. The film presents two scenarios apparently similar but dealt differently. Forrest and his childhood friend and later love of his life, Jenny (Robin Wright) have one important fact in common that they both have a single parent. But not a similar childhood. Forrest's mother is a strong, determined and confident lady who makes her son feel and understand that he is no less than anybody else and that one needs to be optimistic and courageous enough in order to take care of oneself. This positivity gets imbibed in Forrest right in his childhood and even after being tagged as the one with low IQ, he displays wonderful spectrum of personal and social competence in an unpretentious and natural way. The display of his innate integrity is a treat to watch. As against this, Jenny's father comes across as an example of mismanaged self, who is like a nightmare for his daughter. The cluttered destructive response showcased by Jenny's father gets reflected in Jenny's life actions. Most of her life she is wandering to find her lost ground. Unlike Forrest, who stays unruffled by the vagaries of life, Jenny gets torn each time. Forrest carries himself in an upright manner and proves that even with whatever he was blessed with, with faith, positivity, confidence in self, with internal locus of control and solid values, one can weather almost all the storms of life. Lack of these competencies can take a toll over a person despite having a normal IQ.

Many of the scenes are a must watch. In one of the scenes, Forrest as a child and his mother are crossing the road. Initially Forrest is shown to have some problem in walking so he is on a support system which makes him look very different than others and therefore in that scene when very first time the onlookers see him with support mechanism on his legs they keep staring which makes Forrest more conscious of his new look. His mother gives him a good dose of how his self-esteem rests in his own hands and no one can make him feel bad without his consent and that he is absolutely normal and fine, is a scene which stays in one's mind for long.

Another one is when Jenny, as a grown-up girl, comes and stays with Forrest for some time. During this stay of Jenny with Forrest, they share some good intimate time together and then one morning without any prior notice, Jenny leaves. By now, Forrest has even lost his mother, he is all alone. A feeling of absolute loneliness dawns upon him but he chooses to give a constructive response. Instead of surrendering to any destructive addiction like drugs, alcohol, etc., he chooses to run in order to manage his emotions. He is aware of one gift life has given him, the talent of running almost at the speed of wind. He decides to resort to his strength in order to manage his problems. This comes as sharp contrast to Forrest's troop leader lieutenant Dan's (Gary Sinise) response to the challenges of life. After having lost his pair of legs, in the war, the lieutenant succumbs to the pressures and stresses of life and choses to respond with withdrawal and escapism through addiction to alcohol.

A rare display of highest level of the competency, commitment by Forrest for his buddy, Bubba (Mykelti Williamson) also stays for long with the viewers. During the war, Forrest is bent upon rescuing Bubba at the cost of his own life. In the process, he ends up rescuing a couple of other soldiers too; thus, displaying a great sense of compassion and empathy along with the sense of commitment in this case for his friend. Even after Bubba is dead, he keeps in touch with his family and helps them in every possible way, a rare example in life-long friendship and commitment. As a character, Forrest comes across as a highly conscientious person with a strong value system.

2. ***The Intern (2015)***

Directed by Nancy Meyers, *The Intern* is an interesting movie about a retired man who is bored with his life and tries his hand at many a things until he finally earns a job of an intern (senior category) with a web start-up; and about a young and dynamic business woman named Jules. Amongst other emotional competencies, innovation and adaptability get clearly depicted in the movie. It demonstrates that experience is an ageless concept and art and craft of managing emotions is a prerequisite to one's personal and professional success.

The movie starts with a concern which the investors and the fellow staff members of the web start-up, founded by Jules Ostin (Anne Hathaway), have about having a CEO as they feel that Jules is getting overwhelmed by her work. In the process, they also decide to recruit a few interns who would include fresh pass outs as well as experienced persons. They believe that their experience could add a lot of value to the company. Jules feels this is quite an out of the box idea but at the same time unsure about how it may help her organization.

One such intern in the senior category is Mr. Ben Whittaker (Robert De Niro) and to Jule's surprise he gets posted under her. Initially, she seems to be quite uncomfortable with him being around. Ben is a very well–groomed, experienced, go-getter kind of a man and he soon earns his respect and place in Jules life not just as an employee/ intern but as a family member. The way Ben adapts to the new office culture, new gadgets, new people, new role which is way different and also quite below the rank in which he was serving all his life and the way he cheerfully and confidently tackles this change, is worth watching.

Jules is an extremely ambitious and confident woman who tries hard to have it all and how she is about to lose her husband who has left his own illustrious career for her and has chosen to stay at home and look after their daughter. The role-reversal as shown and interpreted by Ben tells us about the commonality in the perceived stereotypes of men and women even today across cultures and countries. The role reversal is a good example in empathy. Also, although he (Jule's husband) gets carried away by his emotions and gets into an extra marital affair, the integrity displayed by him by way of confessing and apologizing to Jules also stays with the viewer for long.

The way Ben transacts from being just another intern in the company to the Mr. Fix-it with his poise and confidence to becoming a mentor if not foster father to Jules is worth watching. The light, peppy and intriguing movie, The Intern, takes us on a ride full of a gamut of emotions, well managed.

References

1. Boyatzis, R. E. (2009). "Competencies as a Behavioral Approach to Emotional Intelligence". *Journal of Management Development*, *28*(9), pp. 749–770.
2. Spencer, L. M. and Spencer, S. M. (1993). *Competence at Work,* Wiley.
3. Cherniss, C. and Goleman, D. (2001). *The Emotionally Intelligent Workplace.* Jossey-Bass.
4. Stein, S., and Book, H. (2000). *The EQ edge: Emotional Intelligence and your success.* Toronto. MHS.
5. Goleman, D. (1998). *Working with Emotional Intelligence,* Bantam Books. (p. 142).
6. Myers, I. B., Mccaulley, M. H., Quenk, N. L. and Hammer, A. L. (1998, 2003). MBTI Manual. CPP.
7. Goleman, D. (2013). *Focus The Hidden Driver of Excellence*, Harper.
8. Hughes, M., Patterson. L. P. and Terrell, J. P. (2005). Emotional Intelligence In Action: Pfeiffer.
9. Senge, P. (1990, 2006). *The Fifth Discipline*. Random House, Business Books.
10. Lam, S. K., Schaub, R. J. and Brown, A. D. (2004). "Laboratory and Field Studies & Group Performance Cognitions". *Journals of Organizational Behaviour & Human Decision Process*, 94(2), pp. 86–101.
11. Goel, M. and Aggarwal, P. (2012). "A Comparative Study of Self Confidence of Single Child and Child with Sibling", *Journal of Research in Social Sciences*, *2*(3), p. 89.
12. Dosunmu, M. S. (2016). Using Emotional Intelligence in the Workplace. Career Development. Vol.33. Issue 1612.
13. Dijk, C. F. V., and Freedman, J. (2007). "Differentiating emotional intelligence in leadership". *Journal of Leadership Studies*, *1*(2), 8–20.
14. Cooper, R. and Sawaf, A. (1997). *Executive EQ*. Orion Business Books.
15. Cooper, R. and Sawaf, A. (1997). *Executive EQ*. Orion Business Books.
16. Serrat, O. (2010). Understanding and developing emotional intelligence. Washington, DC: Asian Development Bank.
17. Cooper, R. and Sawaf, A. (1997). *Executive EQ*. Orion Business Books.
18. Deshpande, R. and Raina, A. (2011). "The Ordinary Heroes of Taj". *Harvard Business Review*.
19. Senge, P. M. (1990, 2006). *The Fifth Discipline - The Art and Practice of the Learning Organization.* Random House.

20. Serrat, O. (2010). "Understanding and developing emotional intelligence". Washington, DC: Asian Development Bank.
21. McClelland, D. C., Patel, V., Stier, D., and Brown, D. (1987). "The relationship of / affiliative arousal to dopamine release". *Motivation and Emotion, 11*(1), 51–66.
22. McClelland, D.C. (1961). "The Achieving Society. New York: Van Nostrand Reinhold.
23. Weiner, B. (1990). "History of Motivational Research in Education". *Journal of Educational Psychology*, 82(4), 616.
24. Goleman, D. (1998) *Working with Emotional Intelligence,* Bantam Books, p. 142.
25. Leong, C. S., Furnham, A., and Cooper, C. L. (1996). "The Moderating Effect of Organizational Commitment on the Occupational Stress Outcome Relationship". *Human Relations, 49*(10), 1345–1363.
26. Pandit, S. (2001). *Thought Leaders*, Tata McGraw Hill.
27. Diefendorff J. M., Brown D. J., Kamin A. M. and Lord R. G., "Examining the Roles of Job Involvement and Work Centrality in Predicting Organizational Citizenship Behaviors and Job Performance," *Journal of Organizational Behavior* (February 2002), pp. 93–108.
28. Brief, A. P., and Motowidlo, S. J. (1986). "Prosocial organizational behaviors". *Academy of management Review, 11*(4), 710–725.
29. Newman Martyn (2016), "Emotional Intelligence and Mindfulness-5 Skills that Work Together". https://martynnewman.com/emotionalintelligencemindfulness-5skillsthatworktogether/
30. Seligman, M. E. P., *Learned Optimism* (New York: Knopf, 1991): 207–17; Miller, S. M. and Seligman, M. E. P., ' The Reformulated Model of Helplessness and Depression: Evidence and Theory', in Neufeld, R. W. J. (ed.), *Psychological Stress and Psychopathology* (New York: McGraw Hill, 1982): 149–79; Peterson, P. and Seligman, M. E. P.,' Causal Explanations as a Risk Factor for Depression: Theory and Evidence', *Psychological Review* 91 (3) (1984): 347–74
31. Hoffman, M. L. (2001). *Empathy and moral development: Implications for caring and justice.* Cambridge University Press.
32. Davis, M. H. (1996). *Empathy - A Social Psychological Approach*, Routledge Taylor & Francis Group.
33. Neale S., Arnell, L. S. and Wilson, L. (2009). *Emotional Intelligence Coaching*. Kogan Page, p. 111.
34. Gentry, W. A., Weber, T. J. and Sadri, J. (2016). "Empathy in the Workplace. A Tool for Effective Leadership (White Paper)", Center for Creative Leadership.
35. Neale, S., Arnell, L. S. and Wilson, L. (2009). *Emotional Intelligence Coaching*. Kogan Page, p. 111.
36. Feshbach, N. D., and Feshbach, S. (1969). The relationship between empathy and aggression in two age groups. *Developmental Psychology*, 1, 102–107. Gibbs, J. C. (1987). "Social processes in delinquency: The need to facilitate empathy as well as sociomoral reasoning". In: W. M. Kurtines and J. C. Gewirtz (Eds.), Moral development through social interaction (pp. 301–321). New York: Wiley.
37. Cooper, R. and Sawaf, A. (1997). *Executive EQ.* Orion Business Books.
38. Senge, P. M. (1990, 2006). *The Fifth Discipline - The Art and Practice of the Learning Organization.* Random House.
39. Cutcher Joel (2006). *The Human Side of Enterprise Annotated Edition*. Tata McGraw Hill. Originally an excerpt from the Contribution to Sloan Student/ Alum dialogue in Course on "Transforming Work, Organizations, and Society" (Sprig 2002).
40. Gardenswartz, L., Cherbosque, J., and Rowe, A. (2010). "Emotional Intelligence and Diversity". *Journal of Psychological Issues in Organizational Culture, 1*(1).
41. Robbins, S. P., Judge, T. A. and Vohra, N. (2017), *Organizational Behaviour*, Pearson Publication.
42. Cherniss, C. and Goleman, D. (2001). The Emotionally Intelligent Workplace. Jossey Bass.
43. Cooper, R. and Sawaf, A. (1997). *Executive EQ.* Orion Business Books.
44. Conger, J. A. (2013). *HBR's 10 Must Reads On Communication*. HBR Press.

45. Cunninggham, S. B. (1992). "Intrapersonal Communication: A Review and Critique", Communication Yearbook 15 (Newbury Park, CA: Sage Publications), pp. 597–620.
46. Belludi, N. (2008). Albert Mehrabian's 7-38-55 rule of personal communication. *Internet. Disponivel em: http://www. rightattitudes.com/2008/10/04/7-38-55-rulepersonal-communication/(consultado em 12 de setembro de 2016).*
47. Human Capital - www.humancapitalonline.com.
48. Weeks, H. (2015). *Delivering Criticism to a Defensive Employee.* Harvard Business Guide to Delivering Effective Feedback. Harvard Business Review Press.
49. Klein, J. (1956). The Study of Groups. Routledge and Kegan Paul.
50. Goleman, D. (2003). What makes a leader *Organizational influence processes, 82*, 229–241.
51. Gardner, L. and Stough, C. (2002). "Examining the relationship between leadership and emotional intelligence in senior level managers", *Leadership & Organization Development Journal*, Volume 23, Issue 2, pp. 68–78.
52. Senge, P. M. (1990, 2006). *The Fifth Discipline - The Art and Practice of the Learning Organization.* Random House.
53. Dr. A. P. J. Abdul Kalam. http://abdulkalam.nic.in/sp181102-4.html
54. Cary Cherniss and Daniel Goleman The Emotionally Intelligent Workplace, Jossey Bass.
55. Kotter, J. P. (1995). "Leading Change: Why Transformation Efforts Fail". *Harvard Business Review.*
56. Strebel, P. (1996). "Why do employees resist change," *Harvard Business Review, 74*(3), 86.
57. Luthans, F. (1988). "Successful vs. Effective Real Managers". *Academy of Management Executive.* pp 127–132, Luthans, F., Hodgetts, R. M. and Rosenkrantz, S. A., (1988). *Real Managers.* Cambridge, MA: Ballinger.
58. Williams, W. M., and Sternberg, R. J. (1988). "Group intelligence: Why some groups are better than others". Intelligence, 12(4), 351–377.
59. Feldman, J. and Mule, K. (2007), Put Emotional Intelligence to Work, ASTD.
60. Argyris, C. (1990). Overcoming Organizational Defenses. New York, Printice Hall.
61. Hargreaves, A., and Fullan, M. (2013). "The power of professional capital". *The Learning Professional, 34*(3), 36.
62. Gardenswartz, L., Cherbosque, J. and Rowe, A. (2010). "Emotional Intelligence and Diversity: A Model for Differences in the Workplace". *Journal of Psychological Issues in Organizational Culture, 1*(1), 74–84.

6

DEVELOPING EMOTIONAL INTELLIGENCE COMPETENCIES

OPENING **CASELET**

The Morning Thoughts

Julia Cameron, author of The Artist's Way a book on creative practice, suggests that the readers should adopt the discipline of 'morning pages', in which she asks the reader to write whatever comes to his or her mind, without giving any space to self-doubt or self-scrutiny. It is based on the principles of here-and-now. This flow-writing of self-expression gradually helps us to clear the clutter inside our mind and if we sincerely practice this every day in the morning, there is a huge possibility that we can slow down enough or get to know ourselves better. She further suggests that it is very important to keep an eye on the bigger purpose or goals we have set for ourselves, and thus put a check on our thoughts.

Source: Theophil, Marguerite (2010), *The Best of Speaking Tree*, Volume 5, *The Times of India*, Times Group Books.

Many bright executives manage everything else except interpersonal relations. Managers who have good technical knowledge but can't manage work pressure have higher threat of bringing their career to a standstill. In such a situation, emotional intelligence (EI) comes into play and helps in achieving organizational success[1]. Before getting into the development strategies and methods for developing EI, we need to answer an important question, can competencies be developed? Since it is often seen that the training programs, in spite of tailor-made content delivery, do not necessarily turn out to be very effective.

Social and emotional learning differs from cognitive and technical learning, and thus requires a different approach to training and development.[2] As stated by Campbell et al.,[3] 'the honeymoon effect' of a typical training program may show improvement immediately after the program, but after a few months, it falls impetuously. During the global search of the literature on emotional intelligence by the consortium, it was found that very few programs were found in various organizations that were aimed at improving emotional intelligence. The impact of these training programs was noteworthy. Depending upon what people aspired for, such as seeking a job, starting new businesses, or finding satisfaction, they were able to achieve it because of the inputs received during the training program. This serves the purpose of any developmental initiative. Having said that, there are two aspects to this — having clarity on how does this change occur, and the questionable sustainability of the change due to the relatively short time periods studied.[4] Has this question crossed your mind that in spite of the inclusion of topics like listening, attitudes, perception, social skills, self-confidence, organizational citizenship feedback skills, communication skills, leadership skills, etc. in almost all behavioral training, why do many people find themselves inept in using these skills effectively?

Daniel Goleman's seminal article on leadership, 'What makes a leader?',[5] is quite an eye-opener. He shares some basic, interesting and widely ignored facts about developing emotional intelligence. Developing emotional intelligence may take some time and it definitely cannot happen merely in a classroom.[6] According to him, emotional intelligence can be developed by targeting the limbic system in our brain. It is generated in the neurotransmitters of the brain's limbic system, which controls our feelings, reflexes and motives.

According to the research referred to by Goleman, limbic system learns best through motivation, extended practice, and feedback. In contrast to this, the other part of the brain, neocortex governs analytical and technical ability. It comprehends concepts and logic. It is this segment of the brain that figures out how to acquire and develop computer skills or ride a bicycle by reading a book. Unfortunately and faultily, it is this part which is targeted by most training programs meant at enhancing emotional intelligence. This has been proved that this may at times have a negative impact on job performance.

Therefore, it becomes extremely important to understand that if we want to really get into developing our emotional intelligence skills, all the training efforts would include limbic system with clarity in mind on how it learns. But there are a few challenges in doing this. First, it requires a lot of time. Certainly, a lot more than a regular training program and also it requires a tailor-made approach. A genuine desire and continuous efforts on the part of the trainee are a must. Without feedback, it will not be of much use since it is absolutely important to know about our level of proficiency from time to time, while we are in the process of acquiring a new skill. Having a structured shadow assessor or a colleague who is capable of providing feedback and is willing to do so informally, may also work to some extent.

In the same article, Goleman gives an insightful example of how to increase, for example, empathy by sharing the story of a Wall Street executive, who makes an effort to increase his ability to empathize. He was a very difficult senior to work with and many a times, people working with him avoided sharing bad news with him, in order to save themselves. When he was confronted with this fact, he was shocked. Later, when he got to know that even his own family members have similar way of dealing with him, he was really taken aback and decided to fix it. With the help of a coach, he started working on it through practice and feedback. As a part of the learning and development intervention, he was sent to a foreign land, where he had absolutely no idea of the language spoken by the people living there. During his stay, he kept reflecting on his reactions to the unknown and his ability to listen and be open in order to understand people who were very different. On his return, his reflective state continued. After several months of this extended practice, feedback from his coach and after having gone through the video tapes of his interaction with his fellow beings, particularly whose ideas didn't match with those of his, he started using on-the-job interpersonal exchanges to the practice of not just'hearing' but also listening. Finally, after his persistent efforts and the feedback and his high level of self-motivation to improve his ability to empathize, there was a noticeable change in the way people started looking at him. This had a positive impact on his performance on the job too.

The advantages of experiential learning for honing leadership cannot be challenged. Top business schools in the world create outdoor exercises that teach group dynamics and team building. Some create an immersion program in real-world projects. This helps the students to grow as a team and hone their interpersonal skills, get involved and thus provide motivation to others working with them to complete a task and address and resolve conflicts, both essential skills of leadership. The 'being' facet of experiential learning benefits the students to hone and develop, a highly ignored, but high-ticket element of managing and leading, i.e. empathy.[7] Next immediate concern is that experiential method needs a significant amount of scarce resource, the trainer's time. Thus, developing EI skill-sets is not a quick process, it requires lot of motivation, best if it is from self, and an experiential approach coupled with lot of extended practice intertwined with feedback.

When new skills are honed or upgraded, the person undergoing this training or upgradation is actually undergoing change. How one can make this change last for long is a challenge.

Intentional change theory[8] (ICT) by Richard Boyatzis also offers some insight. According to Richard, the change process comprises a sequence of discontinuities or discoveries, which operate in a repetitious way in order to produce the long-lasting change at the individual level. The basic premises, or discoveries, as stated by Boyatzis, captured from his theory and further quoted from one of his latest articles,[9] are mentioned below:

a) **The first discovery**: The ideal self and personal vision.
   This means that we need to spend some good time in understanding where we want to see ourself in future. Who do we want to be? Creating an image of a person we want to be is an extremely helpful

technique. This further has three important elements—a mental picture of a desired future; hope that one can make it happen; and one's own core features/individualities, majorly comprising one's strengths; these will be at the core of building one's coveted future. We have often heard this one statement made by Mr. Vishnu Manohar,[10] a famous chef from India known for his world record of 53 hours of non-stop[11] cooking among his other achievements, "Whenever I undertake a challenging task, among my other preparations, I start visualizing the end and try and imagine my feelings at that time in future. This gives me great impetus to march forward with dogged determination. I have experienced time and again that this focus on the end result keeps me my on my toes, till I finally achieve my desired goal". Towards the end of this stage, the person should have a created a personal dream or a vision.

b) **The second discovery**: The real self and its comparison to the ideal self, resulting in an assessment of one's strengths and weaknesses, in a sense, a personal balance sheet
Once the idea of what one aspires to become is clear in the mind, one needs to find out how big is this gap between what s/he is today and what s/he wants to be, the gap between the 'real' and the 'ideal'. To some extent, we all have some fair idea of what we need to change. This can be further enhanced by some reliable feedback. Feedback is also included in Goleman's theory of how to develop emotional intelligence competencies. When one is planning to change, s/he has to have at least an optimal clarity on which aspects of his or her personality s/he values and wants to retain and which should be changed. Whatever aspects of one's ideal and real self are not in sync can be labeled as 'gaps' or 'areas for improvement'. Understanding that gets developed about self, in this process, is called self-awareness, very similar to Goleman's concept of self-awareness. The famous 'boiling frog' phrase is derived from the boiling frog syndrome, implying, "The one who has stopped learning, is dead".[12] It is believed that if a frog is dropped into a vessel of boiling water, it will immediately jump out. But if a frog is put in a vessel containing cool water and slowly the temperature is raised to boiling, the frog will not realize this at all and will be cooked to death. Many factors can lead us to fall prey to this boiling frog syndrome. In order to prevent this, either we should be in a state of awareness and therefore should be able to avoid getting into such a situation, or people around us can help us through guidance and mentoring.

c) **The third discovery**: A learning agenda and plan
One needs to be mindful about how one intends to go about achieving one's goal. To have a road map, the learning agenda with a clear focus on development. This also requires a solid foundation of positive belief or self-confidence that one can make it happen. A learning orientation creates a positive belief in one's ability and the hope of improvement. This results in people setting personal criteria of performance rather than normative standards that merely imitates what others have done.[13]

d) **The fourth discovery**: Experimentation and practice with the new behavior, thoughts, feelings, or perception
Once there is clarity regarding what needs to be done, the next obvious stage is of practice. Also emphasized by Goleman through his concept of 'extended practice'. During this stage, one gets into an experimentation with new behavior. There is a specific emphasis on reflection after practicing the new behavior. This experimentation can be most effective when the environment where practice happens takes place is perceived as safe.[14] This is a very critical factor and again widely ignored. Psychological safety is a prerequisite to any kind of risk-taking behavior. When one starts acting on the new plan towards the desired goals, one is bound to make mistakes, as it has to be a continuous improvement process. The setting in which this takes place needs to be comprised of less chances of embarrassment and without anxiety, fear of failure and related potential negative eventualities.

e) **The fifth discovery**: Trusting, or resonant relationships that enable a person to acquire new learning
Reference groups are the people who are important to a person and with whom that person socializes or mingles in order to provide him/her with a sense of identity. They matter a lot when it comes to providing one with support for his/her effort to change and for providing feedback. If they provide negative strokes (for example, discouraging or hurting comments), there is a chance that one may slip back into earlier ways of behaving. So, the nature of feedback can make or mar our momentum and motivation to change.
According to a series of longitudinal research at Weatherhead School of Management at Case Western Reserve University, people can change the complex set of emotional and social intelligence competencies that constitute the outstanding performers in management and professions. This improvement, as stated by the researchers, lasted for years. This was achieved by students of management studies who undertook a course designed on the basis of **Intentional Change Theory**.[15] Not only students of management studies, but it showed similar results in the executive education program as well, of the same business school. This longitudinal study, done on four classes completing the executive education program, showed that the executives (45–55 years of age), who undertook a course based on ICT improved on self-confidence, leadership, helping, goal setting and action skills. Sixty-seven percent of the emotional intelligence competencies were assessed in this research.[16]
A framework provided by Malcolm Higgs and Victor Dulewicz in their book, *Leading with Emotional Intelligence*,[17] provides a helpful road map for developing EI. This model has six steps, beginning with identifying the need for development, establishing clear development goals, establishing priorities, developing an action plan, implementing actions and ending with monitoring and reviewing.
We will now discuss various strategies and activities to develop the emotional intelligence competencies. At individual level, as stated earlier, development of a competency majorly depends upon the three aspects mentioned above—extended practice, motivation and continuous feedback. In the context of an organization, it majorly depends upon what is the employees' perception of top management's stand on the same. Those activities which are clearly, necessarily led and supported by top management get noticed by the employees and are more likely to be successful.[18]

EI PERSPECTIVE Practice is the Key...

In the book, *The Principles of Psychology*, William James says, "In order to lead a good life, it is necessary to develop good habits, and good habits can be developed only through practice. If we think that we can develop good habits without any practice, we are in for disappointment".

Source: Taken from Mahapragya, (2009), *The Best of Speaking Tree*, Volume 5, *The Times of India*, Times Group Books.

PERSONAL COMPETENCIES

The following competencies determine how we manage ourselves.

Developing Self-Awareness

Knowing one's internal states, preferences, resources, and intuitions

a) Sensitivity training is one of the widely researched and useful tools.[19] An unstructured small group interaction in which individuals get to know about how they are being perceived by others and also about their preferred way of communication, their personal way of thinking which they gather through the feedback from others who participate in the interaction. They are also called T-Groups (for training groups) or laboratory training.

This process definitely needs a trained facilitator who keeps a check on the discussion, ensuring that it should be focused on 'here and now' and not on something else which happened in the past or something about future. The success of this exercise cannot be achieved by meeting just once, the group members should meet more often. This exercise mostly benefits those who are more open to feedback. It increases their self-awareness. It has been observed that mostly, aggressive individuals learn to be friendlier, shy people become more assertive, and curt or rude individuals become more empathetic in the process.

b) Johari Window is a useful theory developed by Joseph Luft and Harry Ingham (the word 'Johari' comprises their first names). According to this theory, personality has four areas. They named these as public area, blind area, the dark area and the private area.[20] What is known to us and to others is public area. What is not known to us but known to others is blind area. It is one of the important areas that we need to work on. The area which is not known to us nor to others is the dark area. The fourth area comprises such information about ourselves which is known to us but not to others, this is called private area. If this is a small part of ourself, it is not a concern because we all can have secrets. But when it exceeds too much, then it can create serious problems. One may come across as secretive. In order to increase awareness about self and to minimize the blind spot (known to others and not known to self) based on this model, one needs to seek at least periodic feedback on how one is perceived as a co-worker, colleague, subordinate, friend, etc. By getting rid of the blind spots, one can get to know how one is perceived by others instead of staying in some false belief about self. Thus, by enlarging the public area and minimizing the blind area, one can understand oneself better. [21]

c) Some old methods high on reliability and validity, that can be used to develop self-awareness are Myers-Briggs Type Indicator (Myers, 1987), Minnesota Multiphasic Personality Inventory (MMPI), or FIRO-B (Fundamental Interpersonal Relations Orientation-Behavior™) (Campbell and Van Velsor, 1985). Career Anchors[22] also helps one to understand one's inclination to a particular type of activity.

d) Peter Drucker's[23] method of Feedback Analysis helps in understanding oneself quite comprehensively. Seemingly simple, this method has a huge potential to reveal one's areas of improvement. The steps suggested by Drucker are — first step, whenever one makes a key or an important decision, s/he writes down what he/she expects will happen. Second, after a period of about 10 to 12 months, one should compare it with the expectations. This, if practiced for a considerable amount time, can help individuals to find their strengths. The outcomes from this activity are as follows:

- One can focus on one's strengths and further build on them.
- One becomes aware of when intellectual pomposity or arrogance is leading to dysfunctional or disabling unawareness.
- One becomes aware of one's bad habits and starts working on them.
- Another outcome is to be able to identify the critical behaviors/manners which matter.
  Drucker makes a very important statement about manners. He says, "Bright people, especially bright young people, often underestimate the power of manners. They fail to realize that manners are the 'lubricating oil' of an organization".
- The next important outcome of the exercise is to identify what *not* to do. He suggests one should focus more on building strengths as compared to working on weaknesses, as a lot more time and energy needs to be invested in improving an incompetence to low mediocrity than it takes to improve from first-rate performance to excellence.
  Besides, we can also do the following;
  i) One can set aside a particular time during the day to 'reflect' upon one's feelings and actions. These reflections can then be recorded in a diary or a log which can be separately maintained for this activity.

ii) Another activity could be using a videotape or an audiotape on oneself in different situations and those tapes could be studied.
iii) In-depth interviewing can also facilitate self-awareness by providing non-judgmental and mirrored interpretations about the learner's thoughts and actions.
iv) Meditation is a tool which can yield several benefits. Mindfulness meditation is regarded as one of the more effective ones. "This technique is designed categorically to help people become more conscious of their inner experience" (Jon Kabat-Zinn, 1990).

Developing Emotional Awareness

First step is to slow down one's activities for a while and start noticing the entire spectrum of emotions one has, starting from positive to negative. This is absolutely necessary if one wants to avoid surprises in future about one's reactions in certain unique situations. Having said this, it is not always an easy and pleasant experience to become aware about one's emotions. It requires some grit, integrity and courage. The Six Seconds KCG model of EI mentioned in Chapter 5 provides steps to understand and develop one's emotional awareness.

Following strategies are helpful:

- Accepting the emotions as they are, without labeling them as good or bad
- Studying the after-effects of the emotions displayed in a given situation and reflecting if one had more options to choose from
- Reflecting upon the 'why' of an emotion experienced. Tracing the trigger/s for the same
- Seeking an honest feedback
- Checking the physical connection with each emotion. Regular practice will make one understand that one can actually start predicting an emotion with the help of the physical signs associated with it and thus leading to better management of emotions[24]

Accurate Self-assessment

Developing an Understanding of One's Strengths and Weaknesses

On a regular basis, we can keep a track of our strengths and weaknesses by keeping records of our continuous/periodic feedback, coaching and the advancement related discussions with mentors. Answering the following questions can help develop one's ability to understand and reflect and eventually, develop a sense of clarity about what should be one's area of focus for development.

- Those aspects of one's job that one finds most interesting and those that one finds most frustrating
- Stating the goals that have been achieved. Listing which aspects of one's personality helped in this process
- Listing those aspects of job that one finds challenging
- Seeking 360 feedback on one's strengths and weaknesses
- Practicing the philosophy popularized by Dewitt Jones — 'improving instead of proving'
- Accepting oneself
- Investing time in taking good care of oneself
- Accepting that one cannot be perfect everytime and at every job
- Practicing self-compassion
- Engaging in positive self-talk
- Talking to a strong supporter
- Surrounding oneself with people with positive mindset
- Acknowledging the completed and well-done tasks

Developing Confidence in Self and Others

A strong sense of one's self-worth and capabilities (individuals and organizations)

How to Develop Self-Confidence

In order to build confidence in self, following steps can be taken:

- Imagining how one wants to be
- Asserting oneself
- Setting small objectives and appreciating self on accomplishing them
- Neither underestimating oneself nor overestimating others
- Replacing negative thoughts with positive ones
- Being patient and considerate with self

Thus by taking charge of one's life, one can begin one's journey to build one's self-confidence.

Along with other tools, we would like to suggest appreciative inquiry (AI)[25] for building confidence in individuals. It is a strengths based positive approach to development. French, Bell and Vohra,[26] in their book, have marked AI as an intervention for teams, groups and total organizations, we would like to suggest its use as a behavioral science intervention for individual improvement as well. What prompted the authors is the underlying assumption of this concept, which is, 'the organization (in this case, the individual included) is a miracle to be embraced rather than a problem to be solved'.[27] With this mind set, when one deals with others, it definitely changes the overall approach and boosts self-efficacy (a more precise facet of self-confidence) amongst employees and creates positivity.

An intervention, appreciative inquiry (AI) developed by David Cooperrider, Frank Barrett and their colleagues, has been defined as, the cooperative search for the best in people, their organizations, and the world around them. It involves systematic discovery of what gives life to a system, when it is most effective and capable in economic, ecological, and human terms. AI involves the art and practice of asking questions that strengthen a system's capacity to heighten positive potential. It mobilizes inquiry through crafting an 'unconditional positive question'.[28] (Cooperrider and Whitney (1999). The basic premise of AI is that we can't overlook problems, we just need to approach them from the other side.[29]

In a study[30] conducted to achieve transformative leader development through AI, it was found that for developing individual capacity by using positively framed questions during the conversations with the participants, the potential leaders were found committing to action and there was a shift in viewpoints, which is an essential element of transformative learning. *Transformational Learning Theory* originally developed by Jack Mezirow is described as being, "Constructivist, an orientation which holds that the way *learners* interpret and reinterpret their sense experience, is central to making *meaning* and hence *learning*".[31] The authors also suggest that AI may enhance a leader's ability to create his or her role afresh through inner work and an inside-out orientation.[32] The basic premises of AI which can be used to build self-confidence are:

1. Appreciating and valuing the best of what is
2. Envisioning what might be
3. Dialoging what should be

AI was a retort to the age-old and dominant use of problem-solving in action research.[33]

The 4D model of AI has the following elements:

- **Discovery:** Finding out what gives life to that individual. What have been the peak moments or experiences in his or her life till date. Exploring the strengths which led to those peak moments. Every individual who needs to build confidence today must have definitely done and accomplished something in the past, however, insignificant it may have been. The assumption is recollecting those episodes and aspects of personality which may have contributed in creating the experience that may boost one's morale.
- **Dream:** After having found some portion of the lost ground, as far as one's confidence is concerned, the person can be coached to create a new vision in relation to the discovered potential, in a less threatening manner.

- **Design:** At this stage, an action plan for the new skill or competence, drawing upon and amplifying the positive core to achieve the newly desired dream/aim (competence), can be developed.
- **Destiny:** Reinforcing the affirmative capability[34] of the individual and enabling it to create and maintain impetus for an ongoing positive change and high performance.

Following strategies will also help in building self-confidence in others:

- Providing decision-making opportunities
- Providing appreciation publicly for even seemingly insignificant accomplishments
- Abiding by the age-old wisdom, appreciating publicly and reprimanding privately
- As a manager one will be required to provide feedback frequently, practicing the principles of Organizational Justice theory will help.[35]
- Creating a positive environment and increased tolerance for mistakes.

EI PERSPECTIVE Building Self-confident Human Architecture

In a newly found B-school, which had the potential to become world class someday thanks to the thought leadership of its Director, few concrete steps were taken to build the self-confidence in its faculty members. The Director made sure that the faculty members were not overwhelmed either by the boss or by stringent rules and regulations. He didn't leave a single stone unturned to boost the confidence in the teachers. In executive training programs, he intentionally made it a point to praise the faculty in the presence of corporate participants attending. He engaged them in meetings and gave them a sense of ownership. In both thought and action, he always kept the institute and the faculty at the top. Internally, faculty members were administrators and were assigned as head in some department and member in another. Their tasks defined their roles. This way, they developed an insight into various activities at the micro level and a sense of the big picture too. Even as they gained confidence in their own abilities, they would develop a certain regard for their colleagues. This organization went on to become IIM Ahmedabad.

Source: Taken from Brick by Red Brick, Ravi Mathai and the Making of IIM Ahmedabad, by TT Ram Mohan.

Self-Regulation

Managing one's internal states, impulses and resources

A physician, a singer, a sportsperson, a teacher, a manager, for that matter any professional may be spending a lot of hours every day in his or her profession, but one is required to manage one's life each moment and in order to even sustain any professional challenges, one needs to be able to manage one's time, talent and energy. It is a good idea to learn how to manage oneself so that one achieves the purpose of one's life, whatever it is. Misinvesting one's resources is the worst thing to do. Each one of us has a limited time to pursue our purpose, which makes a strong case for self-regulation. Clayton M. Christensen in his insightful article titled *How Will You Measure Your Life?*[36] wrote about how important it is to have a strategy for one's life and that cannot come without a well-regulated self.

Increasing Self–Control

Developing impulse control needs recognizing, analyzing, and altering unproductive behavior. It requires emotional self-awareness and readiness to give up the immediate knee-jerk reaction for the strategic benefit of a thoughtful response. The following strategies can be practiced:

- Controlling the breath, counting backwards, and visualizing the way we want to be, prior to an expected anxious moment.[37]

- Engaging in self-talk, such as "This time, I will think before I open my mouth!"
- Reminding oneself again and again that the consequences of impulsiveness may not be worth the immediate gratification of the moment.

By using a strong will to control the spot reactions and compelling urges, one will experience a sense of empowerment and a feeling of liberation. People who develop this competence are found to become more tolerant, better listeners, who have overcome the issue of 'over-talking' and are allowing people to complete their sentences. They may not immediately start replacing their frowns with smiles during each encounter with somebody they are tempted to name 'senseless', but the number of frowns will surely go down. They will be seen as more calm and peaceful souls.[38] In the classic, War and Peace, Leo Tolstoy mentions about two strongest warriors, Time and Patience. The power of these warriors comes from their ability to transform situations, pain, and provide clarity.[39]

"One can make any emotion into a creative force in one's life. Most people do not know what it means for misery to strike in the form of life. But for certain people, when it really strikes, everything that they valued in their life is taken away, and a deep sadness settles. There are many ways to handle this sadness. Some people just sit in the corner and drive themselves mad, making everybody miserable. There are others who, when they become sad, find a way of doing some useful work. Usually, it is people who manage themselves in a constructive way, even when faced with adversities are the ones who may have the potential to become *karmayogi,* (the ones who follow the path of righteousness and believe that right action is a form of prayer in their lives)."[40]

Developing Trustworthiness

To become trustworthy is to refrain from participating in any kind of gossiping or back biting in an organization. One of the students on having received placement offer had one fear, which she was struggling to manage. She said that she was skeptical of working in an organization because she was afraid of 'office politics', which she believed is an inevitable part of an organizational life, at least to some or the other extent. Simple strategy could be to neither initiate any kind of gossip nor join one. It is easier said than done. But it is one of the best strategies to develop trustworthiness. When people around us realize that we would not get engage in loose talk, they feel free to reveal themselves to us. Thus, trustworthiness can be developed by maintaining high standards of interpersonal respect and demonstrating it by not speaking behind one's back.

Few other strategies that can help are:

- Avoiding the usage of innuendo
- Not to overpromise
- Assessing one's limits
- Setting achievable goals and delivering on time
- Staying trustworthy by practicing the above regularly

EI PERSPECTIVE An EI Leader

Mr. Vijay Phanshikar is the editor of The Hitavada, a hundred-year old newspaper in Nagpur, India. He has been its editor for close to three decades, in a volatile industry like print media, staying at the top for so long speaks volumes about the credibility he brings along. His signature remark about someone whom he may look up to is, "S/he has a serif to his/her personality". He used the word 'Serif' to explain elegance, which comes with traits like conscientiousness and trustworthiness.

Source: Author

Developing Conscientiousness

One can begin with seeking feedback from individuals with whom s/he is surrounded with on how they find himself/herself and on how good is the fit between what s/he says and what s/he does. Another strategy could be announcing one's goals publicly, those which are important and achievable. If one meets deadlines, it shows commitment and the ability to prioritize. If this becomes one's second nature, s/he is bound to come across as a conscientious person.[41]

Few strategies are as follows:

- Keeping a daily reminder in place in order to track work progress
- Keeping an eye on time
- Managing tiny/mundane tasks at hand with finesse (includes making one's bed, cleaning cooking platform, keeping one's work station tidy, etc).
- Practicing gratitude on regular basis
- Practicing daily routine and remaining vibrant at non-likable tasks at hand

Nurturing Internal Locus of Control

"This concept denotes whether people believe that they are in control of events, or events control them. Those who have an internal locus of control (internals) believe that they control and shape the course of events in their lives, while those who have an external locus of control (externals) tend to believe that events occur purely by chance or because of factors beyond their own control. Internals, as compared to externals, seek more job-related information, try to influence others more at work, more actively seek opportunities for advancement, and rely more on their abilities and judgment at work".[42]

Becoming More Adaptable and Flexible

Assume that one has a grandmother or a grandfather or someone in the neighborhood who is way older, but one still cherishes his or her company for one simple reason that in spite of the age gap and other differences, one can relate with that person very comfortably. On evaluating, for research purpose, as to why that person is closer and more relatable to us, one can decode the reason behind the bonding. Other people of his or her age would have hung up their boots, but this particular person we are referring to, may not be even thinking about it, as of now. Other people of this person's age may be feeling isolated, while this person is still surrounded with people most of the time. All of this is largely because of one's flexible nature and ability to adapt to the changes happening both inside as well as outside.

One can now easily adopt the similar way of life for himself/herself inspired by the older role model we just discussed. Like in this case, one way is to use fear as a motivator,[43] fear of isolation, abandonment, etc. In the context of organization, one can develop adaptability by:

- Fearing stagnancy and poor growth
- Fearing loss of job
- Gaining more and more information about the aspect one is rigid about
- Seeking support (especially in the case of introverts who do not verbalize a lot)

It is important to understand why an individual resist change or holds onto a rigid approach. It is largely because of lack of trust about the environment. When one is not sure about how s/he would be perceived, one tends not to reveal much and also is not prepared to explore new horizons. At organizational level, creating a culture of trust will enable employees to hone this skill. At individual level, one can check if one is regularly engaging in dysfunctional self-talk like, "I have made mistakes in the past on similar occasions", or "I don't want to experience the comments from my fellow colleagues or supervisors." Such a self-talk negatively affects one's morale and limits one's actions. Step-by-step, one needs to replace such self-defeating talks with more constructive and positive ones like "Let me give it a try", "May be the new experience may not be as bad as I am expecting", etc. Once one develops more flexibility, s/he realizes that it is okay to not be okay all the time. One develops better quality of life, having overcome the barrier mindset of holding oneself tight to certain beliefs and thoughts. By overcoming irrational beliefs, by anticipating change and preparing oneself slowly and steadily for it, by setting small achievable goals and finally stretching oneself, one can develop flexibility. In *Man's search for Meaning*, Viktor Frankl, the holocaust survivor, states, "If one has the *why* of something, one can find ways to do it anyhow".

Developing Innovative Mindset

By making persistent efforts and embracing failure as an integral part of the process, one can develop an innovative mindset. This is possible by being open to change, and by mustering courage. Courage is not an easy game. When one tries something new, amongst the first ten reactions, quarter to ten reactions can be negative and non-supportive. Next, the time gap between planning to take a different route and actually opting for it, should not be very long because there is every chance that our own courage may leave us unannounced because of the ever-changing environment we belong to. Another important aspect is the fear of being ridiculed, or outcasted (at least temporarily). Also, a lot of discipline is required to get into a creative mode. One can read about Thomas Newcomen, who built an atmospheric engine which did a marvelous job of pumping the water out of deep mine or Leonardo da Vinci, one of the greatest inventive genius of all times, both were highly organized, systematic and purposeful innovators. Innovative mindset is a result of a systematic approach and hard work.[44]

Motivation

Emotional tendencies that guide or facilitate reaching goals

In order to work on one's motivation, it is important to develop clarity about what is expected of oneself in the organization and the challenges one is facing to achieve the same. Next, one needs to find what are the satisfiers (motivation givers) one is looking forward to and which can be achieved by overcoming the challenges. Further, one can go back in time and find out when has one experienced personal motivation and checking if some of the elements can be transferred to the new situation that one is struggling to manage. One can try to create a connection between the transferred potential motivating elements and some factors of the work environment in which they can be leveraged on. Discussing this with some mentor (third party), preferably outside the organizational context, may help.[45]

Promoting Self-Motivation Through Training on Achievement Drive

As defined in the Oxford dictionary of Psychology, "Need for achievement or achievement motivation or achievement drive is a social form of motivation involving a competitive drive to meet standards of excellence, traditionally measured with a projective test, such as the 'Thematic Apperception Test (TAT)'. It is believed that those who successfully achieve an objective tend to develop a high need for achievement as compared to those who have not. Those who are successful in achieving a goal develop a high need for achievement while those who are unsuccessful learn to fear failure and avoid situations that threaten their already low self-esteem (Biggs & Moore, 1993, p. 111).

In a classroom set-up, achievement motivation is absolutely critical to learning. Students who believe that their efforts will lead to success, exert and are found to be motivated to learn while others are not so keen. According to the research done by Elliot and Dweck,[46] competence is representative of achievement motivation in the initial years of growing. The students who value themselves as 'competent'in the area of learning will stay motivated to exert for success. The ones who lack this sense of confidence will quit easily.

In young children, activities like storytelling, role play, etc. can boost motivation to achieve.[47] Brier (2006) outlines a series of activities designed to enhance motivation to achieve in classroom learning among students in years 6–8. Activities include storytelling, role play and a homework program.

Activities that can help build achievement motivation are as follows:

1. Individuals can be asked to recall any of the factors that gave him/her a sense of accomplishment.
2. Preparing a list of factors that increase his/her sense of competence and also those that decrease it.

3. Given the fact that failure is an inevitable part of one's life journey, how one handles failure can be a great way of learning how not to let go of one's achievement in case of adversity. This can be a great tool to develop and sustain achievement orientation in individuals.

In achievement motivation training program developed by David McClelland and his colleagues,[48,49] participants go through a series of exercises. To begin with, they get divided into small groups to discuss topics like when did they witness achievement motivation as an important factor. In the next step, participants are made aware of their current level of achievement by making them compose stories and then scoring them to provide them with their level of motivation, based on the whatever element of achievement motivation was present in the story. They further go through several relevant simulations. After this, they are made to create stories filled with achievement thinking until they almost get saturated with it. They further do the same set of things with business situations. Towards the end, the participants develop their individual action plan and at this stage, faculty members intervene in order to help them to increase their achievement motivation.

Developing Achievement Drive: Kakinada Experiment[50]

Achievement drive is about how desperate one is to achieve what one wants. To what extend one wants to stretch or improve.

An experiment was conducted by David McClelland, a well-known behavioral scientist who firmly believed that achievement drive/ motivation can be instilled in an individual through training and experience. He conducted his experiments in three countries including India to imbibe achievement drive in entrepreneurs. In India, it was conducted in Kakinada (in the state of Andhra Pradesh), so was named as Kakinada experiment.

During this program which was aimed at developing the quality of the imagination of the trainees and instigating them to understand and evaluate their own motivational levels, the trainer made the trainees do the following :

1. They were required to seek regular feedback
2. They fetched and studied successful role models in order to learn from them
3. They started planning their winning strategy
4. They were urged to use positive words and phrases even while they talked with themselves.

The result of this program was that those who attended the training showed enhanced performance. Their achievement drive was assessed using Thematic Apperception Test (TAT).

Ability to Develop Commitment in Oneself and in Others

It is important that one develops an understanding of self and accordingly set targets. Many a times, one tends to set a target which is very appealing but seldom knows whether one has the capacity and the bandwidth of resources to dedicate oneself to the given task. So first step could be to fully understand what one wants to commit to, what are the various alternatives available and then analyze how desperately one wants to commit oneself to that activity.

Secondly, people tend to forget that they can operate as a team even in the context of family and so seeking support is not a bad thing. Even in organizations, one can look forward to seeking support from peers in order to stay focused on the commitment. It is important to make one's commitment public so that the environment around knows about it. While one is in the initial phase of building commitment, it may create some turbulence within that individual and/or in the external environment. For example, when one changes radio channels, sometimes due to the change in frequencies, some disturbance may get created. Surviving this change/transit is critical for one's success. Also, even if one does not fully comply with the committed task or activity, which is certainly possible, one should not get dishearten and instead should try to remain focused. Although both regularity and the quantum of activity are necessary to build a commitment ethic, consistency is more important at least in the initial phase while one is building one's ability to commit.

Sorting out step-by-step what is coming in one's way, will also help. The mantra is 'not to give up'. Conducting a habit check, meaning, preparing a list of habits that enable oneself and working on the ones that need to be replaced, is essential.

Positive self-talk is a prerequisite to build commitment. In order to build commitment ethic in oneself or in others, it is also important that even the smallest wins are rewarded or recognized.

Offering respect is of paramount importance when one wants to have a committed workforce. Building a culture of transparency, which in turn creates trust, is vital for organizational growth and development. A culture where intention analysis precedes action analysis, provides a fertile ground to nurture commitment amongst employees.

Developing Initiative Taking Ability in Self and in Others

This is one of the rarest competencies found in any organization. Finding proactive people is like finding a needle in haystack. In order to understand how to develop this ability, let's first focus on what stops one from taking initiative. 'Fear of appraisal' is one of the biggest deterrent. What holds back most people from making an attempt is, 'What if I failed?' 'Will I be ridiculed?' Letting go of this fear is the first step towards developing this competency. Secondly, overcoming 'What will I get from doing this?' mentality. When most employees fail to deliver the minimum, an initiator will undoubtedly get noticed and appropriately rewarded. The learning one acquires in the process of being proactive is immense. It helps one in his/her career growth as it sets one apart from the rest.

It is important that one develops the ability to work in an ambiguous environment. Being able to work in ambiguity is a major attribute of success. In the context of entrepreneurs, taking initiative in ambiguous situations is a prerequisite. To get started, it is not advisable to wait for a perfect moment which in reality may not necessarily arrive. Taking the plunge without waiting for the perfect moment is the key to nurture initiative taking ability in self.

Developing Optimism

As Seligman[51] states, "Being optimistic brings about less depression, better physical health, and higher achievement, at a cost perhaps of less realism". This can be developed by focusing more on the opportunities rather than on the problem. Being grateful, going out of the way to thank others can help one develop optimism. The most important realization is that one has the liberty to choose between one's responses.

Martin Seligman's concept of learned optimism comes as an answer to learned helplessness.[52] Learned helplessness is when people have been conditioned to expect pain, suffering, or discomfort without a way to escape it. Eventually, after enough conditioning, an individual may stop trying to avoid the pain at all, even if there is an opportunity to truly escape it. In order to overcome such strong and rigid conformity to helplessness, strategic efforts to build hope and positivity can be made. For example, a technique called Force-field Analysis, first proposed by Kurt Lewin in 1947, can also be used to develop optimism.

Although it is primarily used for understanding a problematic situation and planning corrective actions, we want to suggest it for developing optimism too.

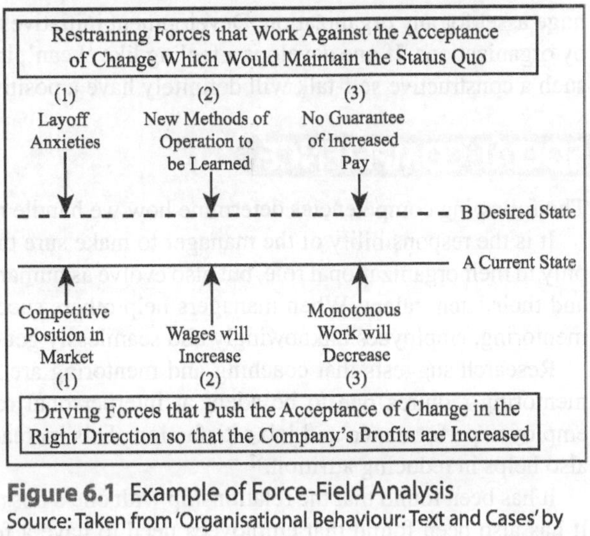

Figure 6.1 Example of Force-Field Analysis
Source: Taken from 'Organisational Behaviour: Text and Cases' by Uma Sekaran

What is force-field analysis? It states that the social phenomenon tends to stabilize at equilibrium points because opposing forces come into balance over time.[53,54] This practice rests on several assumptions; the present state of things (the current condition) is quasi-stationary equilibrium representing a resultant in a field of opposing forces. A desired future state of affairs (the desired condition) could only be achieved by displacing the current equilibrium, moving it to the desired condition — the field forces should be altered — by adding driving forces or by removing restraining forces.[55]

If at any point in time an individual lacks positivity because s/he has got stuck in a seemingly impossible situation, by using force field analysis, one can build optimism, building the persistence in pursuing goals despite obstacles and setbacks.

The following steps can be taken:

1. First, pick up the situation in which you feel absolutely helpless and hopeless. Describe the situation as clearly as possible.
2. Clearly describe the desired state. Where one wants to be.
3. Identify the forces in the field and categorize them into driving and restraining forces. This stage is very critical for the success of this intervention, because only when one has developed a clear understanding of what is in his/her favor and what are his or her restraining forces, one can develop a clear understanding about why the situation is the way it is.
4. The forces need to be examined in order to understand which forces are strong and which ones are weak. (Kurt Lewin suggests that separate force-field analysis could be applied to a few important individual forces too).
5. Steps for moving the equilibrium from the current conditions to the desired condition are as follows:
   a. add more motivators/ driving forces
   b. remove restraining forces
   c. or to do both

One of the most obvious traits one can find in leaders par excellence is what Mihaly, in his book, *Good Business*, calls 'pathological optimism'. Leaders believe that all problems have solutions, having a mind-set of solvability.[56]

When optimism becomes someone's second nature, it will definitely have a huge impact on every aspect of one's life. A lot of research has been done on positive effects of optimism. Positive employees can be a huge asset for any organization. Development initiatives in this area can prove to be a very useful investment by organizations. If one develops a feeling like 'I can', it will transfer onto all the actions one undertakes and such a constructive self-talk will definitely have a positive implication on one's future.

SOCIAL COMPETENCE

The following competencies determine how we handle relationships:

It is the responsibility of the manager to make sure that employees working along with him/her grow not only in their organizational role, but also evolve as human beings. S/he can do this by identifying the strengths and their latent talent. When managers help others succeed by providing them with support, feedback and mentoring, employees unknowingly and seamlessly get converted into leaders themselves.

Research suggests that coaching and mentoring are important roles of a leader. Effective coaching and mentoring requires one to be adept at interpersonal relations. Coaching and mentoring results in better employee performance and job satisfaction. This increases chances of promotion and pay rise go up and it also helps in reducing attrition.[57]

It has been found that the relationship with one's boss plays a vital role in deciding one's career trajectory. It has also been found that employees need to have a feeling that their boss has an understanding of their potential and wants them to succeed. A study conducted by Spherion (a staffing and consulting firm in

Florida) and Lou Harris Associates found that 11 percent of employees, in spite of rating their boss as 'excellent', said they may switch their job in the next year. But 40 percent of those employees, who rated their boss as 'poor', were very keen on leaving. Conclusion, employees with good relationship with bosses are four times less likely to leave their job as compared to those who have poor bosses (Zipkin, 2000).[58]

How to Develop Empathy?[59]

In order to better their productiveness leaders will be required to enhance their ability to demonstrate empathy. To some this may come naturally but to others, it may require a lot of effort. The good news is that like all other competencies even empathy can be developed (Shapiro, 2002).

- Encouraging employees to talk about empathy;
- Encouraging employees to talk to each other and to invest time in each other and thereby demonstrating that they are available to address their concerns, if any;
- Training in active listening skills;
- Training to understand the meaning behind what is being said; going beyond words;
- Creating a culture of sincere perspective taking. This can be much more relevant in the case of expatriates. In diversity rich organizations, this can become a core norm of an organization;
- Creating and nurturing a compassionate culture. A culture of recognizing and rewarding managers displaying compassion should be created;
- Role reversal technique (a role-play activity, especially with the roles reversed) can also be used to understand and develop empathy.

More importantly, in high power distance organizations, empathy can be of much significance.[60]

Another interesting technique to promote empathy is given by Rosenthal.[61] Individuals are shown pictures of actors showing different emotions and they are required to interpret what emotions the actors are expressing. Later, the task goes up on complexity as different parts of each actor's face get concealed.

Empathy is well-defined by Atticus Finch in Harper Lee's, 'To Kill a Mockingbird', "You can never understand someone unless you understand their point of view, climb in that person's skin, or stand and walk in that person's shoes".

Individuals can be instructed to use the following sentences whenever they intend to develop empathy in others. Activities to create empathy in others are as follows:

'I want to tell you something, my only appeal is that please hug me once I have finished doing that'.

'I have been struggling to say something for long, and finally today, I have been able to muster the courage. I sincerely request you to offer patient listening before you say something about it. Can you do that for me'?

'I request you to just offer me your listening for a minute. Let me get rid of that thing in my mind that I have been dying to share with you all these days'.

'What I am going to say, you may not necessarily understand right away, which is fine. Can I request you to not react immediately, can you do this much for me'?

How to Develop the Ability to Understand Others Better?

Whatever we have discussed under empathy applies to this competency too. We can develop the ability to understand others by being more sensitive while providing suggestions and asking questions,

Organizational learning consultants, Charlotte Roberts and Rick Ross suggest a useful technique. First, they emphasize on building faith/ trust in relations and clarity/transparency by becoming mindful about the way we communicate with others. They have suggested following set of statements:[62]

'Here's how I look at this.'

'Here's what I feel, and here's the reason behind it.'

'I suppose that...'

'I arrived at this conclusion because...'
'Shall we check for once if we are building on similar assumptions?'
'Have you taken into account...?'

How to Develop Others?

This is about taking people to those mental heights and confidence levels that they had never imagined for themselves.

This is certainly not a common phenomenon. Few people have the appetite to invest their time and energy in sensing other's development needs and help them grow. This requires a lot of selflessness, time and will. But somebody who works on developing this aspect of his or her personality has for sure carved a different and noticeable trajectory for oneself knowingly, unknowingly.

This includes being on a constant look out for the minute contributions of people around and appreciating them. Thus keen observation and having a highly conscientious personality is a prerequisite. One's mindset needs to be highly optimistic and supportive. One should stay in touch with those whom one wants to develop so that even the unsaid demands are understood. In order to develop others, one should be able to convert most of the interpersonal interactions into learning opportunities. Trusting people and allowing them to try and to make mistakes is also fundamental to developing others. Providing constructive feedback facilitates learning and development.

How to Develop Service Orientation?

Service orientation is a rare competency. Taj group of hotels believe that their employees need to be the customer's ambassadors and not the hotel's.[63] With this shift in mindset, the employees are always concerned about their clients first. One needs to be highly enthusiastic, should possess a go-getter attitude and should always be able to address the anxiety and worries of the clients, even if s/he is unable to provide solutions at times. One can start building this competency by practicing the following guidelines:

- Readiness to go beyond one's job description
- Being able to manage one's ego
- Displaying eagerness and 'want-to-help' body language
- Enthusiasm and smile on the face
- Ready to listen for any length, more critical when registering a complaint from the client
- Always using a polite tone
- Practicing humility
- Maintaining a regular communication with whosoever required
- Responding as quickly as possible
- Always conveying intentions behind one's behavior/ conduct, at least when not being able to deliver
- Never fail to give the impression that customers are important
- Collecting as much information as possible before meeting the client/ customer

EI PERSPECTIVE Pradhan Sevak

India's 2019 Lok Sabha elections were unique in more than one way. One of the campaigns of Bhartiya Janata Party, (a national level party in India) which won the election with a thumping majority, was *Mai Bhi Chowkidar* Me too a Watcher!). Many of the Cabinet Ministers including Prime Minister himself had added prefix, *chowkidar,* to their names on social media accounts. Even during the first-term of the government, the Prime Minister projected himself as *Pradhan Sevak* (chief servant).

This can be an interesting area of research to find out if projecting service orientation has played any role in the winning story of this national party.

Source: Author

PRACTITIONER'S INSIGHT Exemplary Service Orientation in Mumbai Dabbawalas

More than 125 years old Mumbai Dabbawalas is a lunchbox pick and drop system that delivers hot lunches from homes and restaurants to people at work in India, especially in Mumbai. The mode of transport is largely bicycles and railway trains. Prince Charles sent them an all expenses-paid invitation to his wedding. He took care of them during their six-day visit to London. The wedding was attended by Raghunath Medge, president of the Bombay Tiffin Box Supply Charity Trust, and another dabbawala Sopan More.

"Our history is rich with service orientation. Our ancestors were soldiers of Chhatrapati Shivaji Maharaj's able army. Even today, we believe that our strength with which we successfully operate even in case of natural calamities is passed onto us by our ancestors. To serve with utmost dedication is what we believe in. Come what may we don't budge from our commitment. We have been awarded Six Sigma and other certifications without we even applying for it. People have come and studied our processes which are time tested. We have delivered on foot even in heavy rains. To serve is our motto and with each day, we only try to improve it. Most of our dabbawalas are not even educated but they have a spirit of serving which is fully indoctrinated in them and which enables them to deliver their best. We feel humbled by the opportunity given to us by our seniors and derive a lot of satisfaction from what we are able to do."

Source: An excerpt from the discussion with Mr. Raghunath Medge, President, Nutan Mumbai Tiffin Box Suppliers (Mumbai Dabbawala Association)

How to Leverage Diversity?

At organizational level:

"When two men in business always agree, one of them is unnecessary."

– Ezra Pound (Poet)

According to a study, it is estimated that organizations spend $8 billion annually on diversity training.[64] Diversity undoubtedly promotes ideas and learning. When one talks about diversity, one is not just talking about language, religion, race, sexual orientation, gender, age and ethnicity, but also about the entire gamut of human differences. In context of gender, Carol Stephenson, former Dean of Richard Ivey School of Business states,[65] "There should be more women in more boards" she also recommends what companies need to do in order to accomplish this objective. Her study states, "86 percent of boards with three or more women ensure a code of conduct for the organization, compared with 66 percent of all-male boards". Seventy-four percent of boards with three or more women explicitly identify criteria for measuring strategy; while only 45 percent of all male boards do; and 94 percent of boards with three or more women explicitly monitor the implementation of corporate strategy; while 66 percent of all-male boards do. As the research proves, companies with female board members can expect significantly higher returns and better overall financial performance. More female representation also translates into improved risk management and audit control, increased ethical oversight and a broader, more accurate assessment of the company's success. Equally important, with more female leadership, companies are better able to attract more female talent." Companies can take a stalk of the situation by understanding the skills of the current board members they have and fill gaps, if any. Then organizations should proactively find potential women who can fill those gaps.

However hard, people like Carol are trying to make this point and keep substantiating it with solid research, it seems many organizations are still struggling with *Why?*

At organizational level, many of them like McDonald's, Fannie Mae, Sempra Energy, PepsiCo, Freddie Mac, etc., have gone beyond uploading a diversity statement on their websites.[66] Initiatives like strategic initiative in recruiting in order to increase the diversity quotient; development initiatives like organizing leadership development programs; external partnership initiatives like community service outreach; communication initiatives like recognizing and rewarding employees for diversity achievements, circulating newsletters, creating internal websites on diversity; training initiatives like awareness training on organization's diversity initiatives; staffing and infrastructure initiatives like dedicated diversity personnel[67] have become common, at least in organizations which feature regularly in surveys like 'Great Places to Work'.

At individual level, an area of research, mostly termed as 'relational demography', has focused on the effect of working with employees who are demographically similar to them as against with those who are dissimilar. The research finding states that working with dissimilar employees is often associated with negative outcomes.[68] Outcomes like lower commitment to the organization showcase less satisfaction and perceive more discrimination along with other negative behavioral and attitudinal outcomes.

A survey of 785 human resource professionals concluded that the major factor that was strongly related to the success of the diversity training was the perception that the top management believed in it to the core and supported it fully.[69]

In order to mitigate differences and develop a collaborative approach towards working, individuals can use the following intervention.

One may reflect upon one's actions taken in the last one year. Does it show a pattern? Were there any biases playing a role at a subconscious level? Taking feedback from peers/friends and family is also important. If the feedback received from many sources shows that one has a low appetite for people with dissimilar backgrounds, it is wise to get enrolled in a diversity training program as soon as possible. After developing awareness of this fact, the next subsequent step is upskilling in order to become more inclusive and further, be able to draw leverage by creating opportunities through working with different kinds of people.

Other two methods are perspective-taking and goal-setting.[70]

Perspective taking: Write down about what kind of challenges a particular marginalized set of people or people different than us might be facing? If practiced for some time, this has the potential of improving positivity towards those people who at least seemingly appear very different than us.

Realistic goal-setting: As a part of this exercise, individuals can be instructed to set achievable realistic goals in order to develop better inclusion. For example, not supporting inappropriate comments targeted at marginalized or dissimilar group of people.

Both at individual and at organizational level, if leveraging diversity becomes a core competence, then reaching out to the ever-expanding diverse customer base will become more effective. A diverse workforce will lead to increase in the market share too. Besides this, demographic diversity unfolds innovativeness and enhances group decision making and problem solving. This eventually gets translated into competitiveness of the organization.[71]

How to Develop Political Awareness?

Reading group's emotional currents and power relationships

One simple and easy to start with tool can be *direct observation*. Although this may sound simple and easy method, it requires a lot of patience and unbiased state of mind. One can observe other individuals by examining the communication process during team meetings like how they behave and how they address specific situations. By observing, reflecting and studying the errors committed by fellow employees/managers, one can gain insight into *who* matters and *what* matters. One has to have a clarity of thought in what one is looking forward to through the observation to develop political awareness. Somebody who has developed desired level of political awareness can understand the big picture and it can help him or her in networking. Having developed this skill, one can find support from appropriate people who will trust and take one's thoughts seriously. Someone who is good at these skills will subsequently realize that power is not necessarily only with the top and thus people without any designated position can also become very powerful.

Social Skills

Adeptness at Inducing Desirable Responses in Others

Besides other competencies of emotional intelligence, social skills largely depend upon how well we take care of our negative thoughts while interacting with others. We have seen that most of our social relations get spoiled because we are unable to cover are anger, jealousy or other negative emotions appropriately. In order to succeed in organizational role, we need to be great at networking and managing relations.

Developing the Ability to Influence

One of the useful methods to develop influence is to present one's ideas in a rational and logical way. This strategy works in most of the situations. By studying the job structure, culture, and the subject under discussion well before hand, one can share one's insights appropriately. If this is coupled with assertiveness and persistence, it definitely helps. There are nine influence tactics mentioned by Stephen P. Robbins. They are legitimacy, rational persuasion, inspirational appeals, consultation, exchange, personal appeals, ingratiation, pressure and coalitions.[72]

Also spending time with other members of the organization helps, trying to look at issues from others' perspective certainly benefits. One should reflect upon whether one is developing a sense of understanding about those one is working with, without which one cannot truly influence anyone in the long run.

Developing Communication Skills

There are numerous techniques already published on how to develop communication skill. The key is taking the onus of one's communication and practicing mindful communication as much as possible.

A study done by Marshall Rosenberg (2003), a fellow researcher with Carl Rogers, suggests that one can build relations and bring more peace if one practices to isolate observing from judging by adopting non-violent communication.[73] He suggests a four-step model:

- Simply *observing*, being *watchful* (without any kind of assessment)
- Understanding how we *feel* in connection with what we observe
- Understanding the deeper underlying *needs, values and desires* that underlie our and others' feelings
- Skill to make *requests* that might enrich our lives

The fundamental assumption behind this theory is that the human mind has the tendency to classify, compartmentalize and analyze, and in the process, we tend to attach good or bad judging labels when we observe others' behavior. This is quite a damaging/harmful and unfruitful communication in itself.[74]

In order to develop the skill to listen openly, active listening should be practiced. This can be done by:

- Giving our fellow communicators undivided attention
- Picking up cues from their verbal and non-verbal communication
- Taking cognizance of speaker's emotions
- Summarizing what we hear
- Avoiding interruption in the middle

In order to send convincing messages, it is important to choose the communication tools carefully. This is critical in case of employees who are remotely placed. In absence of physical signals, one can be at a disadvantage and can miss the nuances of face-to-face interaction. This becomes even more crucial during difficult conversations. Choosing wisely between the available channels like email, video, instant chat, text message and the way we treat the text, will decide the fate of the communication. One needs to keep in mind that whatever the channel and message, empathy, trust and our genuine concern are the vital components which need to go along with the text.[75]

Genuine gestures can make a profound difference in the way one comes across. For example, making eye contact while greeting people in your office is a simple but widely ignored social gesture. According to Ruthellen Josselson, "These looks do a better job than words. Eyes speak far more than language. They can communicate the spirit of affinity in a better way. Words may lie, eyes cannot".[76] Often one ignores the important part of oculesics (eye-related), non-verbal communication in the daily transactions. Face, not just eyes, is the most important aspect of non-verbal communication. Study by Mehrabian states that only 7 percent of what we communicate consists of the words we communicate, while 38 percent is the paralanguage consisting of the tone, volume, pitch, intonation, pause, etc., and 55 percent of communication is through our body language. Therefore, it is mandatory to hone body language skills as they along with the paralanguage skills contribute a major chunk to the speaking competence.

Listening skill is an extremely important ingredient of communication. This can be done by paraphrasing what one heard. Also paraphrasing the feelings, if possible, along with the meaning. Working on the barriers to communication like lack of focus, daydreaming, selective listening, etc., can be a good beginning. Developing an open body posture, understanding the audience and always addressing the question in the minds of the listeners, "What is in it for me?" are some basic and common methods to improve communication skills.

As defined by Goleman, communication also entails sending convincing messages which means persuading. One can develop persuasive skill by adapting to the following strategy given by Jay A. Conger in his article, 'The Necessary Art of Persuasion'. He states that it is important to establish credibility, frame goals on common ground, vividly reinforce one's position and establish an emotional connect.[77]

Eric Berne's work on transactions called Transactional Analysis (TA), examines the breakdown of communication resulting from crossed transactions. Eric Berne is one of the leading exponents of group therapy and has contributed largely to the initial work on TA. According to this model, although all of us communicate through all the 'mental states' (parent, adult and child), we do have a tendency to mostly communicate through one of them. Our transactions are also classified as either complementary, crossed or ulterior depending upon whether the transactions are happening in compatible or non-compatible ego states. Child–Child, Adult–Adult, Parent–Parent and Child–Parent are termed as compatible ego states. So, when two individuals are transacting, they communicate through a certain 'mental set' and if those two are from compatible ego states, then the transaction is complementary in nature and thus productive. But if the transaction is from non-compatible ego states, then the resulting transaction is bound to be a 'crossed' one and thus rarely productive. In short, TA training is useful in helping individuals engage in effective transactions by minimizing 'crossed transactions'. In the organizational context, Adult to Adult is the most preferred one. TA training enhances competencies like self-awareness, interpersonal sensitivity, empathy and influence. However, one needs to put in a sincere and consistent effort towards this developmental process. There is no 'quick-fix'.

According to a study by Goleman, emotional intelligence vis-à-vis leadership style of executives; it was found that approximately 90 percent of their success was because of emotional intelligence. As against this, unsuccessful executives were found to be rigid (lacked adaptability) and poor in social skills. Because they lacked adaptability, they were inept in managing the changes in the organizational culture. They also lacked[78] listening skills, which automatically affected their receiving feedback for improvement.

Developing Conflict Management Skills

In order to develop conflict resolution skills, one needs to understand what leads or may lead to a conflict. By honing communication skills, majorly the transactional analysis (TA) skills, one can largely evade dysfunctional conflict or successfully manage oneself. Empathy also plays a vital role. If one is able to empathize, one can succeed with ease at developing of this competency. Playing devil's advocate can help and can also save one from the other extreme and equally hazardous state, groupthink. Appreciating differences does magic and can help one in customizing one's communication based on needs of others.

Developing Leadership Competence

Leadership is not about becoming a boss anymore! Developing leadership competence is not a one-time thing.

In fact, management development programs should cater to as many people in the organization as possible and not restricted for select few. The development philosophy should encompass and focus on the unique capacities and potentialities of each individual rather than common objectives for all participants.[79] McGregor emphasizes in his classic, *The Human Side of Enterprise*, that "Outstanding leadership at any level [is] a precious thing". The concept of 'distributed leadership', based on the Theory Y management of McGregor, means that leadership is a process that can be and should be practiced or exercised by individuals across all levels of an organization, while they act independently and collaborate in teams and networks as well.[80]

Warren Bennis in his classic, *On Becoming a Leader*,[81] gives all time relevant guidelines on how to develop leadership competence. He writes that it is absolutely important for a leader to develop his or her self-awareness, should know oneself as fully as possible and also have a clear understanding of the climate in which s/he has to lead. By climate he means the various situations s/he may confront, other people, policies, and a host of other factors. To become a leader, we must understand the rules of the game and know how to play it. His masterstroke idea about developing leadership is that he goes beyond leadership skills. According to him, developing character and vision is the way leaders invent themselves. The second eye-opening concept is of 'Mastering the context'. According to this strategy, one should:

- Become self-expressive
- Listen to one's inner voice
- Learn from right mentors and practice reflection
- Give one's self over to a guiding vision

The other important guideline for developing leadership competence is about understanding through reflection and feedback, what is one's preference. Is one self-reliant and operates in isolation or largely reliant on others and can't function on own? He suggests leaders to develop a balance. He says that most leaders are on the extreme left because they have somehow developed a mindset that they have it all figured out and have a know-it-all attitude. One needs to be mindful of the fact that whatever decisions taken in the capacity of a leader are bound to impact others. Leaders need to be in sync with their people and have an open mind for learning in every situation and be responsible for their own decisions. It is not enough for a leader to do things right; he/she must do the right thing.[82]

He suggests the following:

- Focus has to be on people
- Taking the onus in failure and recognizing others contribution in success
- Avoid playing a blame game
- If one is open for some fun and adventure and if it goes well with one's ego, one can even try having some trusted friend or a consultant to shadow him or her for some time, in meetings, in office, over casual discussions, etc. A lot of content for development can come from this experience.

Leadership development is a continuous process, it never ends. The best method we find is to understand from the subordinates about what does their leader needs to work on.

Peter Senge's concept of leadership is one that we have found has tremendous potential to transform an employee into a leader (not necessarily with a position). From his research over years, he found out that those who could uncover the hidden potential in others and help others grow were not necessarily in a positional leadership. They need not be in occupying a leadership role in a corporate structure with a clear mandate of development but they still could transform people around them primarily because they assumed it is their responsibility to do so and in order to do that, they themselves remained in a continuous learning mode. In order to list the development activities for a leader, one should first ask, Is s/he in a learning mode? Does s/he cultivate a *Shoshin,* a 'beginner's mindset'?

Mahatma Gandhi once remarked, "I suppose leadership one time meant muscles; but today it means getting along with people". In the words of C. K. Prahalad, as mentioned earlier, "Leaders have to play a role of a sheep dog and not a shepherd. A sheep dog has to follow certain rules — it is always behind; it can bark a lot but cannot bite; it cannot lose any sheep; and it should know where it is going".[83]

Becoming a Change Catalyst

When one intends to develop any new competence, change automatically ensues. One needs to visualize the future to some extent and find out what could be the potential hazards of not preparing oneself for the future. As mentioned earlier, fear can be used as a motivation to change and can be quite effective. This kind of thinking will lay the foundation for new behavior to get started. Having done this, one needs to create a road map for development activities or prioritize what needs to be done. If one gets into changing a lot of things together, it may take a toll over the doer and therefore, step-by-step movement will reap more benefits.

Once initiation has happened, one can make more focused efforts on how to sustain the changes, however insignificant they may appear at that stage. This can be done by finding out which goals are seemingly not so difficult to achieve and have considerable impact. Focusing on these goals at an early stage will have multiple advantages. It will provide you with reinforcement and motivation which is a prerequisite to the sustained effort in order to achieve those goals which fall in high effort and high impact category. Periodic review of one's analysis will provide clear and achievable assessment of development priorities.[84]

Building Bonds

Developing bonds is easier said than done. Following strategies can help:

1. Taking genuine interest in those individuals with whom one wants to build a bond
2. Providing support in times when it is really important for the other person
3. At times, being tolerant with his/her behavior (with whom one wants to build a bond) even if it is not according to one's expectations
4. Handling difficult conversations in a responsible way
5. Remembering minute relevant details
6. Practicing gratitude, recognizing and rewarding small achievements
7. Trying to help the individual beyond the minimum
8. Providing space when needed and being available when required
9. Practicing open communication
10. Addressing people with their first names makes a difference

Developing Collaborative Mindset[85]

Employees can be appealed to join the problem-solving process. Asking them to share their ideas and finding out if they are in the flow with whatever they are supposed to do. Do they need help? Are they able to derive any meaning from the discussions? What are they committing themselves to do in order to address the issues on the table and what could be the timeline that they would like to abide by?

Most of the leaders are afraid of interacting with their subordinates on a regular and informal basis. They do not appreciate the employees chit chatting or talking with each other on casual matters during official hours. Most of the time, it is out of fear that they may be discussing him or her as a leader.

A unique practice by a director of a B-school is worth sharing in this context of how to create an enthronement of collaboration and cooperation. The leader made it a point to be at the faculty tea room every day at a particular time, so that he can show it in action by setting a personal example that he very much stands for being together, building bonds and for collaborative spirit. Creating such 'magnet spots', as mentioned by Cooper and Sawaf in their book, *Executive EQ*,[86] is an important tactic used to enhance the collaborative culture. This way, employees do not feel that they will be judged for coming together and for talking to their fellow mates during work hours. There is a possibility of generating fresh perspectives of looking at people or issues through such informal and casual interactions even while being in the office setup.

Collective intelligence, defined as shared intelligence is a natural outcome of collaboration. It has to be cultivated by encouraging people to do what is required vis-a-vis what has been the norm. For example, one of the most important objectives of any organization is to provide the best services to the client. Can that be done by empowering the employee with all the collective intelligence of the office irrespective of his/her location? This calls for heavy investment in the technological infrastructure of the organization, but it is surely worth it. Having said that, the architects of the human process of the organization should not forget where the role of technology ends and where human interface matters. People certainly enjoy working more in places where they know that their opinions and suggestions matter.

Another interesting but widely ignored area of discussion is how are the energies and pressures managed in the organization. If whenever people come together, there is an element (generally initiated from the top) of ridicule or leg-pulling or sarcasm, then people are bound to switch off their mental presence. Thus many meetings become mere meeting of people in a physical setting without their mental presence. In such a gathering, collaboration or cooperation remain only on paper. So when an organizational head is aiming at cultivating a collaborative culture, his/her own conduct and the ability to dissociate people and matter will determine how genuinely s/he intends to achieve his or her aim of creating a collaborative culture. Most organizations end up doing a lip service to this cause. It is a goal easier talked about than achieved.

Physical setting also matters. Many offices today have done away with cubicles and cabins. Instead most of the employees at times including the CEO sits with everybody else and thus collaboration and cooperation has lesser barriers. This doesn't mean that the office place has to be devoid of any private fall-back places or quiet hideaways. Such places provide much required space for reflection and contemplation. Mental spaces need to be carefully and consciously designed, physical will always matter less.

Building Team Capabilities

Mark French (retired Women's Basketball Head Coach for University of California at Santa Barbara),[87] famous for focusing on what his basketball team did well and not on what the opponent did, would keep saying, "Play hard, play together and play smart" before the commencement of the game. After the game, he would be seen talking about what the team did well and what led to their successes.

In order to build team capabilities and collaboration, the following can also be practiced:

- Systems thinking[88] - Most individuals and organizations practice linear thinking not systems thinking. Systems thinking involves looking at the big picture. Business and human actions are also systems and are connected by invisible webs of interrelated actions. When one comes to terms with this reality, it helps in making full patterns clearer and to comfortably see the impact of one or one's unit on the outcome/performance of the team.

In order to further build the team capabilities, one can do the following:

- Instilling energy - This could be required because of lack of motivation and due to lack of clarity of vision.
- Checking the overall morale of the team - Finding out how does the team address issues on most of the occasions.
- Encouraging members to recognize and appreciate each other - This way, strengths can be identified.
- Challenging limited thinking and learning disabilities like, 'I am my position' or 'the enemy is out there'.[89]

MINDFULNESS AND EMOTIONAL INTELLIGENCE

Mindfulness, as defined by Jon Kabat-Zinn (founder of Mindfulness Based Stress Reduction, MBSR) as, "Paying attention on purpose in the present moment and that too non-judgmentally". It has emerged as one of the very effective ways to build emotional intelligence.[90]

It is about possessing the quality of awareness of self, others, and the world around self. Competencies of emotional intelligence like self-awareness (also referred to as self-knowing) can be significantly enhanced by practicing mindfulness. One can start with becoming conscious about subtle physiological reactions in the body and also one's thoughts and feelings, objectively and non-judgmentally.

The purpose of mindfulness is to become conscious to the inner workings of one's mental, emotional, and physical processes.[91] It is about being able to remain fully present of what one is and what one is engaged in, and not overly reactive or overwhelmed by what is going on around.[92] In order to benefit from this practice, it is important to practice it on a daily basis. It is one of many forms of meditation, in which one engages in (1) systematically regulating one's attention and energy (2) thereby influencing and possibly transforming the quality of one's experience (3) in the service of realizing the full range of one's humanity and (4) one's relationships to others and the world.[93] In simple words, it is awareness. Inefficiency and ineffectiveness are common concerns in organizations. One of the major reasons behind these concerns could be the inability to focus. If one practices the above-mentioned way of existing, he/she will naturally become more conscious and wakeful in one's actions too.

One study undertaken by Chu (2009) states, "Mindfulness and EI are similar. They both emphasize people's abilities to perceive, understand and regulate their thoughts and emotions (Donaldson-Fielder and Bond, 2004).[94]

Cultivating Mindfulness: Mindful breathing

Mindful breathing simply means becoming conscious about the in-breath and the out-breath. It so happens that once you become aware about the process of breathing, you get totally consumed by it and any other thoughts will not find any space and the mental discourse will stop. Thinking will slow down and you will not be required to make a conscious effort to do it. The more and more you practice this, less will be your distractions and consequently higher will be your mindfulness. The catch is that we find it easy for a few seconds and after that, we tend to get caught in something as small as, "Oh have I switched off the light in the other room or not?" Once we get distracted, we also get discouraged, and tend to assume that "It is not my cup of tea". We feel that we just cannot develop the habit of being mindful. But the real catch is not to feel demotivated and even while we get up and get going to that other room for switching off the light, we can still be watchful of our in-breaths and out-breaths. More than often, you will agree that the light in the room was actually turned off and the visit was a waste. The more regularly we practice the in-breath and out-breath exercise, the more wakeful we will become and in due course of time, we are less likely to go back and check for the light as we would have done that act enough mindfully to have registered it well in our mind. It is all about how we relieve ourselves from the past and not get anxious about our future. "Mindfulness isn't difficult. What is difficult is to remember to be mindful", said the cognitive scientist, John D. Teasdale. It is in this process of developing the habit that many give up.

As self-awareness is the basic premise of emotional intelligence, knowing our internal states, preferences, resources, and intuitions makes it easier for us to become more aware about ourselves.

Practice of mindfulness is an activity to give a more wakeful, constructive response to a stimulus. It is to make a conscious effort to not go our preferred way or by way of our default setting which may not be the most appropriate one. With more focus and attention when we do what we are doing, we can become more effective.

EI PERSPECTIVE A *Mindful* Prose

"When I dance, I dance; when I sleep, I sleep; yes, and when I walk alone in a beautiful orchard, if my thoughts drift to far-off matters for some part of the time for some other part, I lead them back again to the walk, the orchard, to the sweetness of this solitude, to myself."

Source: Montaigne, Michel de

PRACTITIONER'S INSIGHT

Mind Your Communication

Leo Buscaglia (Felice Leonardo "Leo" Buscaglia Ph.D.), an American author and motivational speaker and a professor in the Department of Special Education at the University of Southern California, said, "Too often we underestimate the power of a smile, a kind word, a listening ear, an honest compliment, or the smallest act of caring, all of which have the potential to turn a life around".

I personally feel that the above quote is apt in real life situations, be it personal or professional.

In real life situations, I observed that people of average intelligence outperform people with the highest levels of intelligence, majority of the time. The reason being that people of average intelligence may be high on emotional intelligence and may be people with high levels of intelligence are mostly high on technical aspects. Research says, 20 percent of employees are successful at workplace because of their product knowledge and 80 percent of them are successful because of EI.

What is emotional intelligence? It is the capacity of recognizing our own feelings and those of others and managing emotions in ourselves as well as in our relationship with others.

With my personal experience, I have come to a conclusion that optimism, empathy, stress tolerance, flexibility, trust, self-awareness, assertiveness and being able to draw leverage from diversity and mindful communication are critical for success at workplace.

I would like to share an incident that happened in the beginning of my career when I was working as a temporary employee at one of the corporates. Though it was a corporate and we did not interact directly with customers, it was an HR policy that we should be professionally dressed every day. There was a dress code which we had to follow. I personally felt that the dress code was overly strict but could not say a word as it was the HR policy.

One day, I noticed that one of the senior employees wore flat slippers to office which was contrary to the dress code. I spoke about this to my colleagues who were also temporary employees like me. We were very angry with the exception given to the other employee. We wrote a very strong email to the CHRO of the organization regarding why was there an exception for the other worker. We also came up with a signed petition, in which we demanded for the following:

1. A more business casual dress code
2. It should not be mandatory to wear suits/blazers during weekdays

Next day, we were called to meet the CHRO. Innocently, we thought that he had called us to discuss the petition, but we were all given slips which asked to leave immediately due to our unprofessional behavior. We were asked to hand over our ID cards, gather our things and leave the premises asap.

Just before we left, the CHRO informed us that the employee who was given exception was an ex-army soldier and was allowed to choose her own footwear in which she was comfortable as she had lost her leg during the war.

It was the moment of reality for each one of us. The following lessons were learned:

1. Impulsive behavior needs to be checked; Need to practice self-control
2. Need to communicate mindfully
3. Need to increase the ability to understand others

Source: **Excerpt from the discussion with Rajeev Singh, COO & Business Head - Karvy Fintech - Global Business Services, Hyderabad, Telangana, India**

Three-step Breathing Space

The three-step breathing space, called AGE (acknowledge, gather and expand),[95] is not entirely different from the first technique mentioned earlier, but is more structured. In the first stage, i.e. **Acknowledge,** one needs to first close eyes and just notice, allowing and acknowledging, not trying to think a particular thing. Just trying to check, what is that one is feeling, what is exactly happening inside, like checking one's own internal What'sapp status. Checking the feelings, impulses, thoughts, etc.

Second stage is called **Gather**. In this stage, one needs to bring one's attention and focus on one's breath for a small portion of time, say a minute for example. One needs to fully focus on each breath, both the in-breath and the out-breath. This precious time has the potential to calm one down and provide some peace in the hullabaloo full days. It is alright if your mind drifts but with a deliberate effort, one can easily get the attention back on track. As mentioned earlier, this will keep happening and one should not feel discouraged, only with practice it will stay for longer time, unruffled. For the poise and peace it brings, it is worth the effort.

Next and last stage is called the **Expand**. In this last stage of three-step breathing space to develop mindfulness, one needs to slowly expand the center of attention from the breath to the body and become more conscious of both breath and body as well as of the difficult or challenging sensations, if there are any. After a few seconds, one can start becoming more conscious of the area surrounding oneself and after a few more seconds, one can open eyes and thus end this exercise.

No amount of reading will help one develop mindfulness. One needs to practice regularly and for quite a long time. This entire exercise is effective when performed even for just three minutes, on a regular basis.

Mindful Eating[96]

It is a simple tool to build Mindfulness.

You can choose a fruit or a vegetable of your choice. Take a small piece in your hand and eat it for as long as 10 min. Chaskalson and McMordie, who created this technique, say that each person can discover unique realizations while doing so, depending upon our past stories and present circumstances. They further state that there is no right or wrong way of doing it. The crucial aspect of this exercise is to reflect on what one actually experienced while eating that small piece of food for a good long time.

They suggest some useful questions for such reflection, such as:

- What was the most striking feature of this exercise?
- How did that piece of food feel on the palm?
- Did you notice its color, shape or odor? What occurred to your mind while doing so?
- Did you look at it closely?
- How did it feel inside your mouth?
- What was the first bite like and the second and third?
- Did you feel an urge to quickly finish it? If yes, how did you resist?
- How did it feel eating just one piece so slowly?
- Anything else?

The above exercise is not for making one realize the details of eating but about paying attention to what was experienced. This exercise builds one's capacity to walk out of the default setting, or automatic pilot mode, as described by Chaskalson and McMordie. Development benefit of the exercise is that one learns that it is good to be able to do things automatically, but the problem is that we start doing a large number of activities automatically, and thus become machine like. There is a threat that we may hardly live in the real sense of the word. Besides that, it may come with a serious disadvantage and actually affect quality of life at both personal and professional levels. When we sit with our family for dinner and watch television or more commonly, move our other unused hand on social media pages, or catch up with all the Whatsapp gossip in the number of groups we belong to, there is a possibility that we may completely miss the facial expressions of our kids who want to share something from their day at school, and possibly need our support. They keep struggling to initiate the discussion and we may unknowingly remain too engrossed in other things while eating on an automatic pilot mode.

In the professional context, we may be running from one meeting to the other and could be completely stressed and thus might overlook a beautiful sunset on the way which could have been a potential stress buster. When we are performing routine jobs like finding out what led our subordinate to perform poorly, we are so used to hearing some or the other reason that we may not pay any conscious heed to what is exactly being said and more importantly, what has not been said. The tone, the body language of that subordinate, could be wanting to share the real reason but we failed to create that space simply because we may have not noticed the cues. All because of being tuned into the automatic pilot.

In *Transactional Analysis*, Eric Berne talks about Life Positions and Life Scripts,[97] which can be connected to this. The 'Life Positions' refers to the specific mindset according to which an individual operates while dealing with others, this is based on certain deep-rooted assumptions made very early in life. When these life positions interact with the environment, we acquire a 'Life Script'.[98] A life script is the temperament we develop right in our childhood based on our early interactions with the people around us. Later in life, we largely interpret an event based on the script. According to Berne, we tend to operate from either of the four life positions, I am OK, You are OK; I am NOT OK, You are NOT OK; I am OK, You are NOT OK; and I am NOT OK , You are OK. People with the first life position are the ones who have a positive life script because they practice empathy. Training in transactional analysis can help people to develop empathy and thus help in overcoming the automatic pilot mode and becoming more mindful.

Besides the above-mentioned advantages of mindfulness, it instills a certain kind of kindliness, gratitude and humility, some of the important ingredients in the recipe of a happy life.

THE POWER OF 'NOW' AND EMOTIONAL INTELLIGENCE

Do you know somebody who always wants to reach somewhere, and no matter where s/he reaches, s/he still wants to reach somewhere else? Being ambitious is a healthy thing if it is coupled with internal harmony and if one does not feel the pressure of it. In most cases, this isn't the case. If one is always focused on becoming, achieving and attaining, there is risk of missing the experience of 'being'. "Realizing deeply that the present moment is all one has and making now, the primary focus of one's life, is developing the power of Now".[99] It is a very powerful technique to quiet one's thoughts.[100] It focuses on building the consciousness to an extent that one learns to live in a state of 'Being' against 'Becoming' and this a very meditative state.

In spite of having the caliber to perform and deliver, many a times, individuals are not able to manage the timeline and ultimately, lose many opportunities in life. This could be because of the invasion of psychological time. "Psychological time is a subjective feeling which is related to the temporal experiences. Nevertheless, psychological time differs from time, because it is non-linear and because it is dependent on the nature of events occurring within a time period not the real time. This is because one's past perpetuates itself as there is lack of presence of mind. The correspondence between psychological time and time, though imperfect, is enough to enable reality testing and normal cognitive and social functioning."[101] Absolute absence of psychological time is not a realistic goal nor is it wanted, but excessive indulgence in the past over future is definitely not the right way to function. This is exactly what we call mismanagement of time because of lack of emotional intelligence. Psychological time performs various important functions which are a prerequisite for sustaining in an ever-changing environment. If one has an idea of the felt pace of the psychological time, one can actually predict the behavior. For example, when somebody develops a feeling of boredom, in that case, the information processing load is below an ideal level for a specific individual. With boredom, the speed of the flow of time slows down. Boredom is an extraordinary mental state which is connected with lowering the efficiency in sensibilities and is correlated with low job satisfaction and overall quality of life. Thus, the feeling of slowing of the flow of time should serve as an alert and should be fixed at the earliest.[102]

Developing the Ability to Stay in the Now

1. Every time you go up and down the stairs, try to focus on each step, every single movement of your body. Try to observe as much as you can. This will keep you away from other thoughts for a while.
2. Develop a habit of asking yourself, "What is going inside me?" Without analyzing this further, just keep your focus and your attention inwards. This is the beginning of the step-by-step process of developing the state of 'being'.
3. If some life situation is bothering you, forget about it for a while and think about your life which is now. If you can segregate the life situation as your thoughts and the life at this moment as real, then you can uncover the power of Now.

'Now' Through Meditation and Yoga

A common and simple technique of meditation is to sit quietly and bring all our attention and focus on our breath. During a long period of time, it is natural for us to get carried away and lose hope to develop meditation skills, as discussed earlier. But the only thing one needs to do is to get oneself back from that thought as many times it happens and refocus on the breath. This leads to the awareness of the present moment, the Now. Later, if this regularity is maintained, many psychological and physical benefits follow.

Jaggi Vasudev, famously known as Sadhguru,[103] explains the science of yoga in his famous book, *Inner Engineering*, as, "Yoga is being in perfect alignment, in absolute harmony, in complete sync with existence".

EMOTIONAL INTELLIGENCE AND FLOW

Viktor Frankl in his famous book, *Man's Search for Meaning*, wrote, "Don't aim at success, the more you aim at it, and make it a target, the more you are going to miss it. For success, like happiness, cannot be pursued, it must ensue…as the unintended side-effect of one's personal dedication to a course greater than oneself".

In Flow, Mihaly talks about a concept called optimal experience. He states that there is certainly a role of fate in our life and by this he means the genes we are born with, the historical period into which we are born, our parents, etc. But in spite of these many factors which are absolutely out of our control, we still experience, although rarely, a sense of control over our actions. At that time, we experience profound happiness and enjoyment. This stays with us for a long time and we often go back to its memory and cherish it too. This is what Mihaly Csikszentmihalyi calls optimal experience, a realization that one has adequate amount of ability to manage a challenge at hand in a 'rule-bound action system' that provides clear signs of how good one is performing. In such a situation, concentration is so intense that there is no attention left to mull over problems or any unrelated thing. In such a situation, one loses the sense of time and self, consciousness seems to disappear. An activity which creates such a state of satisfaction and epiphany is something that people are ready to do for its own sake, without expecting anything out of it. At times, even when it is extremely challenging or dangerous, they still want to go for it.

The smile on the face of a mother when she holds her baby for the first time, or when a writer gets lost in his/her characters and they almost come alive to him/ her, such incidents do not happen necessarily when the external conditions are favorable. Interestingly, there are many incidents shared on different platforms by people who survived concentration camps, terrorist attacks, hijacks, etc., that even during their ordeals, they experienced a sense of enjoyment in seemingly simple and mundane events like sharing one last bread, or listening to a bird when there was no sound of life around, or accomplishing a difficult task, etc. Mihaly developed this theory of *optimal experience* on the concept of *flow* — "the state in which people are so involved in an activity that nothing else seems to matter, the experience itself is so enjoyable that people do it even at a great cost, for the sheer sake of doing it".[104]

As explained by Mihaly, optimal experience is a great thing because

a. It is irrespective of the external environment and
b. It can be created by us
c. In spite of its nature which need not be very pleasant while it is happening,

For example, during a swimming competition, a swimmer must feel completely exhausted in the last few seconds, yet, those moments may become one of the most memorable ones in his/ her life.

The process of developing control over life was and never will be easy for anyone, in fact, it can be very challenging and overwhelming. But if over a period of time, the optimal experiences can help one develop a sense of mastery so much so that one actively participates in deciding the content of life, this comes quite close to what generally gets labeled as happiness.

As a part of coffee-table motivational book, *Bury Your Can't*,[105] a set of people with entrepreneurial thinking were interviewed. One common characteristic was that they all were classic examples of being in a state of *flow* many a times during the course of their life. One of them, Babasaheb Purandare[106] (recipient of Padma Vibhushan, India's second highest civilian award) said that he is addicted to his passion of promoting, celebrating and sharing the lessons from the life of a great Indian warrior king, Chhatrapati Shivaji, and doesn't intend to come out of this stupor. By stupor, he meant a state of trance or lack of self-consciousness, very similar to what Mihaly calls *flow*.

"The defining feature of flow state is the intense experiential involvement in moment-to-moment activity; it can only be achieved on the basis of an individuals' personal effort and creativity".[107] Some may experience *Flow* while cooking, for some, it can come from playing basketball, or from making sculptures, etc. What may lead to a state of *flow* will be different for each of us.

In his book, *Finding Flow*, Mihaly explains the psychology of engagement and how to take ownership of our lives in the major three aspects of our everyday lives, work, leisure and interpersonal relationships. According to the research done by him, people are happiest when they dare to undertake a task that calls for high degree of expertise and commitment and importantly, which are undertaken for their own sake.[108] Read the following small story written by one of the authors on *flow* titled 'The Cooking Platform and Anuradha's Recipe of a Happy Life'.

EI PERSPECTIVE

The Cooking Platform and Anuradha's Recipe of a Happy Life

"This story is inspired by the conversation I had with Anuradha Marudwar, whom I used to fondly address as *Vahini* (word used for sister-in-law in Marathi) and who used to live at a distance of just two houses from my maternal home, around 16–17 years back.

Then, I did not have many friends of my age, so I would spend time with her. It was with her that I realized that friendship and age do not have any correlation. Today, I am lucky to have many good friends who are with me during my thick and thin times. This short episode is a brief conversation with Anuradha *Vahini* in her kitchen.

I used to come back from my college and rush to her place. She was very talkative and at the same time, always available for me. One unique thing about our conversations was that she always kept herself busy in finishing one or the other household chores. During those days, she was not employed anywhere. Her only engagement was doing the household chores which she did cheerfully. Today, she is one of the leading interior designers in Bangalore.

I had developed an image of a homemaker looking at her and felt what a monotonous way of leading one's life it is! I was definitely not dreaming to become one. I was dreaming of a career for myself away from one's house and that too for long hours and in some office.

Once, having observed her for a long time performing the daily ritual of washing the *ota* (i.e. a cooking platform in Marathi) after finishing her cooking, I remarked, "What a boring job it is to wash this stove and clean utensils and then clean the floor!" To this, she smilingly replied, "May be because you look at it with that mindset". I was surprised at her spontaneous remark. I did not understand her fully, so, I asked her to elaborate. She happily explained, "See Smita, every job that one does, becomes monotonous one day. Whether I enjoy doing it or not, I have to do it anyways. But when I do it with a mindset which doesn't have any appreciation for what I am doing, then my attitude and way of doing it gets negatively affected. I feel sorry for myself. Self-pity is a curse in itself. But in contrast to this, when I engage myself in a positive self-talk, I feel energetic. I tell myself, "Oh it's a great day, I am liking this job of cleaning my cooking platform. Today, I have done it quickly and may be even better than yesterday. I love what I do for myself and for my family. I feel positive, energetic and honestly speaking, start enjoying it!" Whatever she said was not just to impress me. I had seen that positive energy and her never-complaining attitude for a long time now. So, I believed her almost instantly.

Although, I thought that I understood whatever she said, it was only later in life that I could actually grasp the deeper meaning and its implications. But because I had witnessed that she practiced what she said, so her sentences got imbibed in my mind.

Source: Author

EI PERSPECTIVE In Search of Happiness

India was ranked 122 in the World's Happiness report 2017.[1] Out of the six basic emotions, one is happiness. India seems to be waiting to become happy and it is going to be quite a wait. The researchers studied countries on the basis of predictors, such as GDP per capita is in terms of purchasing power parity (PPP), the time series of healthy life expectancy at birth, social support, freedom to make life choices, generosity, perceptions of corruption, positive affect and negative affect.

India's rank went down further to 133 among 156 countries in World Happiness Index 2018,[2] published by the UN Sustainable Development Solutions Network. In 2019, India was at 140th position.

In 2020, India is ranked 144.[3]

Many interventions have been initiated at global and local levels. For example, World Happiness Summits are being organized, the U.N. has declared an International Day of Happiness on March 20. Students enroll in happiness courses worldwide and several schools also have redesigned their content and pedagogy towards aligning life-skills with academic learning, etc.

The authors would like the reader to think about what else can be done.

Source: [1]https://s3.amazonaws.com/happiness-report/2017/HR17.pdf
[2]currentaffairs.gktoday.in/world-happiness-index-2018-india-ranks-133-03201853440.html © GKToday
[3]https://happiness-report.s3.amazonaws.com/2020/WHR20.pdf

Question is, How can one regularly get in a state of *flow*? This can happen when one's skill sets and actions or tasks to be accomplished are in sync and one derives absolute pleasure from performing them.

EMOTIONAL INTELLIGENCE AND THE ABILITY TO FORGIVE

"The purpose of life needs to be positive. We aren't born with the purpose of causing trouble, harming others. For our life to be of value, I think we must develop basic good qualities — warmth, kindness, compassion. Then our life becomes meaningful and more peaceful and happier", says His Holiness, the Dalai Lama.[109]

Is forgiveness a popular practice? Is it fully understood by many? It comes across as a very monk-like attribute and we can rarely think of practicing it or implementing it in our day-to-day life at home or at office. But having said that, as mortals, we all struggle with the feelings of hurt and agony. We keep carrying the baggage of negativity all along and more than often mismanage it. Our family, friends and colleagues whosoever has been the source of the wrong-doing that made us suffer, become enemy-like for us and we end up spoiling our relationship with them. Sometimes the harm is irreversible. It is good idea therefore to demystify this concept and see if we can apply some principles which may not only ease our suffering but also make us more positive and freer. Freeing ourselves from that anger would be liberating and that liberation is forgiveness. Forgiveness is giving up the hope that past could be any different.[110] This one thought has immense potential to take a person to a completely new level of realization. It enables us to give up all the grudges and empowers us to focus on constructive issues. "It is about letting go, so that the past does not hold you prisoner" (Oprah Winfrey, 2013).

In order to forgive, empathy has a big role to play. But it definitely has its roots in self-awareness. The awareness of one's pain, suffering and being able to fully assess it leads to the understanding of self. It is only when one has self-awareness that one can progress towards empathy.[111] But before we take our discussion further on how to forgive *others* and why to forgive others and how it matters more today in all walks of life alike, we need to delve a little bit more on self-forgiving. This becomes essential in order to become more confident and focused.

One of the earliest psychological definition of self-forgiveness was proposed by Enright and the Human Development Study Group (1996). They described self-forgiveness as, "Willingness to abandon self-resentment in the face of one's acknowledged objective wrong, while fostering compassion, generosity, and love toward oneself" (Enright et al., 1996, p. 116).[112] Self-forgiveness is releasing negative emotions directed at oneself.

The more we develop insight into our own feelings and experiences, the higher is the possibility that we may understand the feelings and experiences of other people. It is not surprising therefore that often when people score low on the self-awareness component, they also score low on empathy. A major component of forgiveness is empathy. The following EI perspectives are examples of how to practise Forgiveness.

EI PERSPECTIVE Forgiving a Terror Attack

In 2019, at least 50 people were killed and 50 wounded during the terror attack on two mosques in Christchurch, New Zealand. What Farid Ahmad, whose wife Husna Ahmad was killed in the attack, said is a remarkable example in forgiveness. He said that he has forgiven the terrorist and has no negativity against the killer. "I would say to him 'I love him as a person'", he added. "I hope and I pray for him that he would be a great civilian one day", Farid further said.

Source: https://gulfnews.com/world/oceania/update-50-dead-in-new-zealand-terror-attacks-1.1552615420051

EI PERSPECTIVE And Forgiveness Triumphed...The Story of Irène Laure

Irene, a French by origin, who was taught to be a German hater, had seen the World War and had suffered at the hands of Nazis. The last straw that broke the camel's back was when Germans entered Paris in 1940. At a very young age, she became a member of resistance movement. She was a poignant example of a human being wounded by the violence and the war. She and her family suffered along with thousands of fellow countrymen. This led to an ever-growing anger and when anger is not dealt with appropriately, it turns into hatred and the same had happened with Irene.

In 1947, she was invited to attend a conference in Caux, Switzerland. She had assumed that Germans would not be invited for the conference, and so had accepted and reached the venue on the given date. She was shocked and angry to know that 150 Germans were also attending the conference. Her hatred for Germans was so conspicuous that even when a German would stand up for his talk, she and other French people would just walk out. During one such instance, she was stopped by an American Lutheran Minister, Frank Buchman. He asked her a question which made Irene think. He asked, "Is it possible to have a United Europe without Germany?" At first Irene was shocked that anyone could even dare to ask such a question, but on second thoughts, something deep inside questioned her, why not try this? Doing something, may be even unwillingly to begin with, in the larger interest may be worth giving it a try! Still not fully convinced she went through a state of dilemma, To Be or Not To Be! For a long time, she was found inside her room, not interacting much with anyone, pondering over that question, mustering courage to give that thought a space in her mind. Was it even possible? Could she have any feeling for Germans other than hatred? She was totally confused.

During that conference, the day when she was supposed to deliver her address, she happened to share her table with a German lady. It was the kind of moment she had waited for years where she could vomit all the hatred she had maintained for Germans. She talked about how her fellow countrymen and women had become mere skeletons, how her son Louis, suffered, how people who came back from the Nazi camps looked like walking corpse! Irene spoke for long time and kept sharing the horror stories. When she had finally finished, she looked into the eyes of the lady and said one last sentence, "The reason I am telling you this, Madame, is that I want to be free of this hate" (Henderson, 1994).

After a long pause, the German woman began sharing her side of the story. She introduced herself as the widow of that man who was part of a plot to assassinate Hitler. The plot had failed, and he was arrested. He was hanged. While she was in prison her two daughters were taken away to an orphanage. She said she retrospectively realized one thing that they had not resisted enough, early enough and on a scale that was big enough. Because of which, many had suffered terribly. She said, "Because of this, you have suffered terribly. I want to say, I am sorry" (Henderson, 1994, and Piquet, 1985).

After her interaction with that German lady that afternoon when Irene stood up and went to the lectern to deliver her talk, she was a different person. She was a addressing a gathering of almost six hundred people. She said. "I have so hated Germany that I wanted to see her erased from the map of Europe. But I have seen here that my hatred is wrong. I am sorry and I ask for forgiveness to all the Germans present. One cannot forget, one can forgive" (Henderson, 1994).

Her ability to see things differently was a surprise not only to others but to herself too. Her life got a new, refined and a profound purpose. She vowed to spread this message of forgiveness and reconciliation and 1947 onwards, she led a campaign of several months duration through Germany to ask for forgiveness and foster French-German reconciliation.

The war inside the hearts of the survivors had come to an end, finally. Forgiveness triumphed!

Source: **Adapted from Borris- Dunchunstag, Ed.D (2007), Finding Forgiveness, TATA McGraw-Hill edition.**

EI PERSPECTIVE One cannot forget but one can forgive!

In the early hours of February 4, 1997, three monks, who were sleeping a few hundred yards from His Holiness, Dalai Lama's living quarters, were stabbed to death. One of them was a very close friend and confidant of Dalai Lama. The way those monks were murdered, looked like an act of exorcism. Two monks were stabbed fifteen to twenty times in an extremely brutal way. Their blood was all over the room. His Holiness suspected that there could have been five to eight attackers. Cash and Buddhist statues were left untouched. As there was no witness, no one got caught and punished.

When His Holiness Dalai Lama got to know about this heinous act, he was extremely shocked and angry, but soon realized that he should deal with his anger by seeing it clearly. His own teachings in managing emotions came handy. He knew without exception that every situation has the potential to lead us to a new level of compassion. He reminded himself that the atrocity had already happened. It was an irreversible act. He needed to focus on how to handle his anger.

The first step identified by him was to understand the root cause of anger. Second, to become aware of the profound destructive and negative effects anger brings along. To become aware that anger most affects the one who gets angry. He reminded himself that our mind has limitless capacity for improvement even when it comes to managing anger. It is absolutely important to distinguish between beneficial and harmful states of mind in order to fully appreciate values of good states and further nurture them. Anger is truly that one emotion which needs to be dealt with in a way that it reduces the harm and not escalate it further.

As said by H. H. Dalai Lama XIV, "Love and Compassion are necessities, not luxuries. Without them, humanity cannot survive".

Source: Adapted from Borris-Dunchunstang, E. (2010). *Finding forgiveness: A 7-Step Program for Letting Go of Anger and Bitterness.* McGraw Hill Professional.

DEVELOPING EMOTIONAL INTELLIGENCE THROUGH NLP

Neuro-linguistic Programming is popularly known in its short form, NLP. One of the first proponents of this method for developing effective communication can be found in the classic, *Frogs into Princess*, Neuro-linguistic Programming by Richard Bandler and John Grinder. According to them, NLP in one line is, "Knowing what to do and How to do". Joseph O'Conner and John Seymour (1990) have defined NLP as, "The art and science of excellence, derived from studying how top people in different fields obtain their outstanding results". This definition finds some resonance with the concept of EI. And if studied and practiced well, it can surely add to the emotional intelligence of the practitioner.

EI PERSPECTIVE The Boiler Maker's Cool Skills

One story which has stayed with me for long time after having finished reading '*Frogs into Princess*' is the story of a boilermaker who was called to mend a huge broken steamship boiler system. On reaching, the boilermaker listened patiently and asked relevant questions to fill the gap in his understanding of the problem. Later, he went straight to the boiler room. For a while, he observed the web of twisting pipes and listened to the sounds made by the boiler and the steam coming out of it for a few minutes and touched a few pipes. Then as if he had understood the problem, he said something to himself in a low voice and pulled a small hammer out of his kitbag and tapped a red valve just once, that's it. Just after this, the entire system started working fine, and so the mechanic left. Later, he sent a hefty bill of \$1,000 to the steamship owner who complained seeing the amount. He was shocked to see that just for his 15 min visit, the mechanic had charged such a hefty fee. He then requested the boilermaker to provide him with an itemized bill. This is what he received

For tapping with hammer = \$0.50
For knowing where to tap = \$999.50
Total = \$1,000.00

Source: Adapted from Steve Andreas (formerly John O. Stevens) in his foreword to the book, *Frogs into Princes.*

Learning NLP is like learning the language of mind. For example, when we go to a foreign land, it may happen that we ask for service/product A but instead get B. It seems like something got lost in translation. Imagine this kind of misunderstanding happening within ourself with our own subconscious. If what we think we want is different from what is showing up, then there is a need to re-look at what we think we are looking forward to and what we are actually experiencing.

The basic premise of NLP, according to Bandler and Grinder, is that there is a positive motive behind every behavior. Reframing — seeing something that was there all along, but previously unrecognized. Reframing is changing or tweaking the frame of reference and is a popular method in NLP.[113] Read the EI Perspective 'May be' for more understanding.

The six-step model given by Bandler and Grinder is easy to understand and adopt.

1. One needs to identify behavior or a response, something one would rather not prefer to do or feel
2. One needs to interact with that part of self which is creating that unwanted response or behavior. After getting to talking terms with that part, we can seek permission from it for getting started with a conscious conversation. As one creates this first piece of communication, s/he may get to feel some sensation in his/ her body, a mental picture or a voice. On receiving that signal, one must immediately thank that part for responding. This is done with a well thought out logic that if we have been fighting with a particular behavior and now if we want to arrive at solutions, we need to be polite and considerate in the process in order to achieve desired outcomes.
3. After this is done, one should find a positive motive by asking the part a simple question, What does it need? What is that positive thing that it is wanting to do for oneself? The major element which merit attention here is that it is absolutely important to distinguish between the motive or intention of the part/s and the way it is going about it. For example, you tried helping a classmate on the task you thought she is struggling with, but instead, she misunderstood and you felt annoyed. How likely it is that you will help second time? Many people assume that 'shaming' can be used to change behavior. Although the researchers feel that this is not true. The positive assumption — that aspect of self with whom one is struggling to resolve issues with has a positive motive — can help in establishing rapport and therefore, creates more readiness to cooperate.

EI PERSPECTIVE 'May be'

There is an old Chinese Taoist story about a farmer who had a horse and a child. He was considered very fortunate by his neighbors because he had his own horse which he used for plowing and moving around the countryside. One day, his horse ran away. His neighbors expressed concern and felt sorry. The farmer said, "may be". Sometime later, the horse returned with two wild horses. Neighbors were overwhelmed and happy. Farmer again said, "may be". Next day, the farmer's son tried riding one of the new horses and in the process, fell down and broke his leg. The neighbors felt sad and expressed sympathy. The farmer responded, "maybe". After some days, war broke out and the officers from the defense system came to get young boys to enroll in the army. They spared farmer's boy because he was not physically fit. The neighbors saw this as good luck of the farmer and congratulated him. He simply replied, "may be".

The moral of the story being that whatever may be the event, the meaning depends upon the context, the 'frame' in which we make sense out of it.

When we change the frame, we change the meaning. It is great to own two wild horses but if you see it in the context of the broken leg, it isn't. The son's broken leg seems a terrible concern but in the context of war, it becomes a good thing.

This is called reframing, changing the frame in which a person perceives events in order to change the meaning. With the change in the meaning, the person's responses and behaviors also change.

Source: Adapted from Bandler, Richard and Grinder, John, "Frogs and Prince". p 1

4. Next step is to ask one's creative self to provide with three alternative ways to achieve the desired outcome.
5. Get the part with which one is negotiating, evaluate the choices. If they are acceptable, the part needs to give them/it a try. If not acceptable, it is most unlikely that it will cooperate. Creating what Bandler and Grinder call 'winning commitment' is absolutely essential. If the answer is No, it is advisable to go back to step no.4.
6. It is a wise thing to check with other parts of the body/ other people about the new change. When we bring in new behaviors, we may affect some aspects of ourselves and other people (also similar to systems thinking concept).

   Sanchita Kumar, General Manager HR, Haier, in one of her sessions for young executives at IMT Nagpur, said, "It may not be easily believed, but it is true, that even positive changes can have outcomes ranging from not-so-positive to even negative".

The above model is just one model in reframing. There are many models which readers can find in other sources. But this one helps in most of the situations.

Motivation, self-awareness, sensitivity, emotional resilience and influence are important in the context of NLP. Training in NLP can surely help in building EI, but it cannot be taken as a quick fix. Developing NLP skills requires sustained effort over a long period of time. Read the following Insight from a NLP expert titled, 'Programming Self'.

PRACTITIONER'S INSIGHT

Programing Self

NLP is about understanding self and others and that is the commonality between NLP and EI. Understanding NLP can help one develop awareness about self and about others and thus impact social relations.

Neuro-linguistic Programming is about the language of the mind that includes pictures, sounds, feelings, tastes, smells and self-talk. The word 'programming' refers to the way or pattern of thinking and behavior which we all possess rather like a computer program. For example, if one is asked to deliver an impromptu presentation in front of a large audience, one may become very nervous as he/she may not be used to doing this. This is the set pattern or the usual way of responding which has got hardwired in the individual. NLP offers a series of methods, 'techniques', communication tools, approaches and mental processes to facilitate people to alter their patterns of behavior and communication so that they can have more of what they wish to have and less of what they need to get rid of and thus helps them achieve their goals.

NLP also offers an opportunity to study the way one responds in a particular way and why someone else responds in a different way and why one should rethink one's way of doing or responding in a particular way if it is not helping.

The benefits of NLP include:

1. Improving communication
2. Changing our behaviors and beliefs
3. Emulating excellence

NLP basically is about understanding five senses. These five senses can be expressed through VAK — Visual, Auditory and Kinesthetic. Kinesthetic has two sub-classifications — taste and smell.

Visual, auditory, kinesthetic (Feel), taste and smell are the five primary reasons behind our thinking, language and behavior patterns. When we become master at how we see; how we hear; how we feel; how we taste; how we smell, it decides our thinking which in turns promotes language and behavior patterns.

As we train an excellence (an individual) with NLP, the excellence gets awareness in all senses.

As one gets trained well with NLP, EI part of learning becomes a core strength for that person. He/she knows how to stand strong, sensible and moving forward when expected/unexpected emotions hit life.

NLP also has a concept in re-installing new beliefs. "A belief is nothing but the rigid version of feelings." As NLP redrafts and reframes beliefs, rigidity of useless beliefs gets diluted and finds a passage to exit silently without any resistance. As new beliefs are installed in an excellence with NLP, that excellence becomes a new excellence which is what Exactly EI does.

I can summarize this as follows.

"EI is a special subject for emotions and NLP plays an important role in kinesthetic aspect of learning. EI is an umbrella and NLP is the space inside the open umbrella".

Case Studies: 01

Three friends saw a movie. As they came out after watching the movie, first friend said, "The locations are fantastic. Fantastic Visuals!". Second friend said, "Excellent songs". The third one said, "What powerful dialogues. Still does something inside".

This is how people see — Visual, Auditory and Kinesthetic (VAK), which is a preference. As everyone is unique, VAK has its own % for everyone.

Place - Mumbai, India

Case Study: 02

There was a tennis player who was unable to play well in matches. As I observed, he was making more mistakes when he commits his first mistake.

I asked him "What happens inside you when you make your first mistake?"

He replied, "I feel stressed".

"Are you hearing any voices at that time?"

"Yes. Why you are not playing well? The voice inside me said so", he replied.

I understood where he commits mistake.

"How about asking yourself, "How can I play better next time than why am I not playing well?"

He understood how to handle his emotions in a proper direction, and he started winning most of his matches.

Place: Indore, MP, India

Case Study: 003

There was a lady coming out some a counselling session.

"My husband is the worst in the world. I want to get separated."

I asked her, "What is something special about your husband as a person?"

She was taken back for a while but later came up with a reply.

"He is genuine in whatever he does."

I asked her again, "What else?"

She started listing. After she finished her listing, I asked her back, "Now we can talk about getting separated".

She paused for a while and said, "Thanks sir. I guess I require more time to make a decision on this".

Change of beliefs brings change of results.

Place - Delhi, India.

Source: Excerpt from the discussion with Mr. Jayasekaran Zen, Founder and Coach for Zenlp Academy, Master Trainer.

EI AND REBT

As mentioned in the following Practitioner's Insight titled, EI and REBT, REBT is succinctly described by a REBT expert. REBT, as mentioned earlier, was developed in 1955 by Dr. Albert Ellis. Dr. Ellis has been considered as one of the most influential psychotherapists in history. Prior to his death in 2007, *Psychology Today* described him as the 'greatest living psychologist'.[114]

REBT is a kind of psychotherapy, not necessarily for a long duration, that helps you identify negative, self-defeating thoughts and feelings. It helps you challenge the rationality of those feelings and thoughts and helps you replace them with more constructive, productive, and healthier beliefs. It further helps you focus[115] (as defined by Daniel Goleman as today's scarcest resource and the secret to high performance and fulfillment, 'attention') more on how your unhealthy thoughts and feelings create emotional distress and in turn leads to unhealthy actions, behaviors (for example, certain decisions) that interfere with one's personal and professional goals at large.[116] REBT helps one to overcome negative thoughts, beliefs and emotions like guilt, improper anger, and excessive hatred. It also helps one deal with anxiety and depression.

PRACTITIONER'S INSIGHT Emotional Intelligence and Rational Emotive Behavior Therapy (REBT)

According to Epictetus, "People are not disturbed by things, but by views they take on them".

Let's consider an example, recall a situation that you were very disturbed about. You were probably experiencing intense feelings of anger, sadness, guilt, shame, anxiety, etc. Now think, if there were 100 different people in the exact same situation as you, would each one of them feel and react just as you did? Probably, not! Why do you think this difference in how people feel and behave in the same situation exists? You may agree that it is because different people think in different ways, perceive similar situations differently as a result of which they feel and react differently! Hence, external mishaps, such as conflicts, failures, and other people's behaviors don't really cause our emotions and reactions but only trigger our thought process.

Dr. Albert Ellis, Psychologist in New York, extended this philosophy by Epictetus and proposed Rational Emotive Behavior Therapy which suggests that changing thought process can help people feel and behave in ways that helps them progress and reach their goals.

At the root of REBT are scientific explanation, flexibility, non-extremism, logic and realism that lead people to not only deal with specific problems but promotes them to adapt a philosophy to follow.

It is a marvelous tool that aims to teach people how to help themselves to lead a satisfying life and to consistently keep dealing not only with grave disturbances but also day-to-day problems one faces in the process of living. People from all walks of life and varied age groups can use it to help themselves for problems like self-blame, self-pity, anger, guilt, shame, dissatisfaction, depression, hopelessness, anxiety; and behaviors like procrastination, indecisiveness, addictions, compulsiveness, avoidance and withdrawal.

In the last six years of my practice, I have effectively been able to help a lot of my clients reach their goals. I have dealt with clients as young as 10 years and as old as 68 years with problems as simple as an adolescent fighting with their parents and as complex as rape. When clients come for therapy, they generally come asking for solutions — "Please tell me what to do", "Did I make a mistake?", "Is it correct to do this?" To these, I generally respond with a question, "What do you think?" and they always know the answer. Not only are they aware of what their unhelpful behaviors and reactions were, but they also know what they should be doing/should've done instead! So, what the clients really need help with is to be able to actually apply what they know is better. For instance, a student who worked very hard but blanked out in the exam knows that she shouldn't be anxious, yet she blanks out. Even though all her friends, teachers and parents tell her, "Don't stress, be calm", none of them actually tell her how to. And, that's what a REBT practitioner does! REBT gives clients the steering wheel to their own life.

Rational emotive behavior therapy (REBT) is the pioneering form of cognitive behavior therapy — an approach to psychotherapy that focuses on changing thought process. It is a short term, highly structured, action-oriented psychotherapy that teaches individuals to identify, challenge, and replace their self-defeating beliefs with healthier ones that promote emotional well-being and goal achievement. It helps the clients to proactively identify the causes for their emotional disturbances and then learn a concrete, directive approach to uproot these causes. It incorporates the use of a wide range of cognitive, emotive and behavioral techniques toward this purpose. Being a highly flexible therapy itself, it adopts a bio-psycho-social approach to well-being, and hence concepts, techniques and strategies from various other therapies are embedded in the REBT work. It encourages the use of any methods that are found to be useful and helpful and fit the scientific principles that REBT is based on!

REBT is among the worlds' most researched and evidence-based therapies. Research into the outcome and effectiveness of psychotherapy has conclusively established it to be a short and efficacious treatment for a wide range of psychological disorders such as anxiety, depression, personality disorders, etc. It helps people to internalize the philosophy of 'rational thinking for happy living', i.e. adapting thinking patterns that are logical, realistic, factual and helpful for people to live a more fulfilling, goal-oriented life for greater happiness and satisfaction.

Source: Excerpt from the discussion with Barkha Nayak, Counseling Psychologist and REBT Practitioner

Having read the Practitioner's Insight, one must have understood the fundamentals of REBT. The need for this therapy should come from the person who needs it. He or she may not know the name of this particular method but should know that s/he needs to work on self, this realization is a must. For this to happen, one should accept that the performance is going down and that something should be done to fix this. This sense of awareness and accountability towards self-betterment will determine the success or failure of such therapeutic treatments. Managers and seniors who have seen an individual perform well in the past, upon noticing some change, should make an effort to understand if that employee has gathered some negativity or self-defeating behaviors which zap one's vitality. REBT can be of great help to such individuals.

In the organizational context, anger is an emotion which if not properly managed can cause irreparable harm. In business negotiations between two negotiating parties who showed anger and displayed lower levels of compassion for each other, resulted in less willingness to work with each other in future.[117]

Here are some strategies to overcome anger and resentful feelings as suggested by Albert Ellis in his book, *Anger: How to live with and without it.* According to him, anger is mostly brought by oneself, so the first question is, Does one want to keep it or give it up? If a particular person or a particular situation is causing frustration which although not directly but sooner or later and indirectly may be a potential of generating anger, then it needs to be fixed. Increasing one's frustration bearing capacity is another way out if the choice of escaping or moving out is absolutely not possible. Practicing to develop a mindset that some frustration is okay and developing realistic mindset over the tendency to demand that life should be absolutely frustration free. Developing some awareness about the physiological implications of anger on the one exhibiting it will also help oneself in managing it.

It is very essential to manage our anger and other negative emotions like jealousy, narcissism or grandiosity not just at work but also at home.

A certified therapist provides a plan of action which helps the clients to overcome his or her rigid ideas and beliefs. The detrimental effect of holding onto such beliefs is explained by the therapist and the negative thoughts and feelings are replaced with constructive ones. This process of catharsis brings relief from the long and suppressed emotions. REBT is an effective tool to enhance self-management and social skills.

Chapter Synthesis

This chapter reveals a fact that it is possible to develop one's emotional intelligence at any age. But at the same time, it also states a very important pre-requisite that the methodology of learning should be appropriate. Research states that practice, motivation and feedback on how one is performing on the newly acquired skill is absolutely essential in order to develop emotional intelligence. The benefits of Intentional Change Theory, Sensitivity training, Johari window, and Appreciative Inquiry are elaborated in detail.

The chapter further presents a discussion on EI and Mindfulness, the power of living in the Now and how it can be used to help in cultivating emotional intelligence. Inputs on neuro-linguistic programing with an insight from a certified NLP and inputs on REBT from a certified practitioner explain how these techniques make a difference. With the knowledge of Flow, one can find answers to the work and life of many individuals who serve as role models to the society. Importance of forgiveness is discussed at length. The

EI perspectives and Practitioner's Insights provide examples for easy reference.

Methods like mindful meditation, mindful eating, and three-step breathing space are discussed at length. These methods help in sorting the clutter in our mind and help us develop self-awareness, taking responsibility for self-development, monitoring one's thoughts and applying filters for negative ones. Activities and exercises like identifying and working on prejudices, physical exercise, openness for feedback, taking a walk, reading, creating a personal agenda about what you want to accomplish in next few days/ months or years, keeping a journal, are discussed. Simple methods which one can follow on day-to-day basis in order to develop EI like how to take more and more control over your self-talk, how smiling more can help, and what can happen if we imagine success, are discussed in the chapter. Seeking help, at times, from a third party, one who is not engaged with you at an emotional level), cultivating and sustaining beginner's mindset, maintaining a sleep hygiene, trying to address as many people you can by name, trying to clean the clutter in your mind, and making an effort to live in the moment are small activities which have the potential to bring big changes. Even just observing people around us as much as we can, staying context conscious, open and showing interest and eagerness to know more are small steps that anyone can start with. Developing passion for purpose, trying being a fix-it person during a broken conversation can make a difference. Caring and showing it, building on one's preferred communication style, having clear but polite conversations and practicing non-violent communication are some of the small acts with the potential to impact one's developmental journey of EI.

KEY TERMS

Shadow assessor	Negative strokes	Relational demography
Being mindful	Sensitivity training	Direct observation
Psychological safety	Transformative learning	Crossed transactions
Reference groups	Peak moments	Distributed leadership
Mastering the context	Pathological optimism	Theory Y
Magnet spots	*Shoshin*	Beginner's mindset
Psychological time	Automatic pilot	Life Positions and Life Scripts
Catharsis	Optimal experience	Shaming

REVIEW QUESTIONS

1. **Can Emotional Intelligence be developed? Justify your answer.**
2. **Most of the behavioral training programs conducted in a classroom do not necessarily succeed. Explain with a scientific reason.**
3. **Explain the concept of Intentional Change theory given by Richard Boyatzis.**
4. **Explain any two techniques mentioned in the text to improve self-awareness.**
5. **Discuss a strategy to promote self-motivation.**
6. **What is Appreciative Inquiry? Explain its basic philosophy.**
7. **Discuss the strategies to develop optimism.**
8. **Warren has met with an accident and broken his leg. There are chances that he may not be able to walk at all. He is a state-level basketball player. You are his close friend and got introduced to the concept of NLP. Can you try using it? Do you think it can do some good? Can you combine this approach with force-field analysis? Explain how you would do it.**

9. Elan and Jay work in an organization. Jay is a management graduate from a reputed B-school and is posted as Elan's boss. Elan is almost double Jay's age. It has been close to a month since they could have a normal conversation. Somehow, they are not able to communicate with each other. According to you, what must be the challenge faced by both of them? Can you help them using your knowledge of transactional analysis?
10. Discuss the concept 'optimal experience'.
11. Explain the basic premise of REBT.

ACTIVITIES BEYOND THE BOOK

1. Activity to develop an understanding of change: Think of a time when you had to totally change or adopt a new way of doing some task while working with someone. How did you go about it?
2. Activity to develop communication skills: Shirin has been coming late to work for last two weeks in a row. Diya, Shirin's boss, has called Shirin to her cabin to discuss the matter. Role play for 10 minutes. Other students can make notes while the role play is on. The class can share their observations and suggest alternate behaviors.
3. Activity to build self-confidence: Give an example of a situation in which you were very determined. What did you say or do? What can you do to further develop your self-confidence using the inputs from the chapter?
4. Activity to build bonds: In your network, who is the best person at building relationships? Discuss her or his behavior, for example, what does s/he say or do.
5. Activity to build empathy: Observe people on the basis of their non-verbal communication. Check for a potential opportunity to do a role reversal (with your mother/ father/ elder sister/younger brother, etc). Later, reflect upon the gathered insight. Did it help in building empathy to some extent? Document how did it feel to be in that role.
6. Activity to build self-control: Next time you are irritated with somebody, try putting the strategies mentioned in the chapter to use. If you have practiced it already in the past, share the process.
7. Activity to build initiation: Has somebody in college/office taken some initiative in the past? What was the effect on his or her performance? Can you gather at least five such cases? If you see the positive impact, even you can give it a try.
8. Activity to build adaptability: Choose an activity or a person or a situation which you have been struggling for some time to adapt. First and foremost, stop waiting and cribbing, set up small goals and engage in positive self-talks. Share this experience with your close friend or at home and seek feedback.
9. Activity to build influence skills: Next time you are in a group or in a formal meeting where you want to make your presence felt, go fully prepared on the tentative topics which may come up or in case of an official meeting, prepare yourself thoroughly on the topic. Your preparation based on logic and reasoning will help you make a point. Reflect on whether you gave your best or was there some room left for more preparation.
10. Activity to build communication skills using transactional analysis: Observe which ego state you generally communicate from. Analyze if it works well most of the time.
11. Take a routine task and find out how it can be done better with more precision and at a faster rate. Even before you realize it, you will be somewhat engaged in a psychological state, that has the potential to create a feeling of Flow sooner or later.
12. Another Activity to build self-confidence: (Recollecting past success) By recalling a past event when we had managed it successfully and recollecting the positive emotions associated with it. If repeated numerous times,we can feel confident about the skills we used to accomplish that task.

13. Joseph is a homemaker by choice. As a trained content writer, he always wanted to work from home and look after his kids, as he himself had always missed having parents around while he was growing up. His wife, Jasmin is an entrepreneur. For the last two years, somehow Jasmin has started feeling that her husband doesn't give her any time and fails to understand why, even though he doesn't travel like her on everyday basis and run from one meeting to the other. She wonders, what makes him feel so tired? These days, they fight very frequently and their marriage is on the verge of breaking. What kind of help can you provide Jasmin based on either NLP, REBT, or EI knowledge that you have acquired from this chapter?

Video Resources

1. **Inspiring Leadership through Emotional Intelligence by Richard Boyatzis**
   Link: https://www.coursera.org/lecture/emotional-intelligence-leadership/watch-developing-your-personal-vision-including-life-and-career-stages-kVsXd
2. **Jon-Kabat- Zinn's Me MeMe**
   Link: https://www.youtube.com/watch?v=ULJSacYFzzQ
3. **Oprah Winfrey on Forgiveness**
   Link: https://www.huffingtonpost.com/2013/03/07/oprah-on-forgiveness-how-to-forgive_n_2821736.html
4. **Emotion in Education: An Interview with Maurice Elias**
   Link: https://www.youtube.com/watch?v=7K2uSg-_KlI
5. **On Self-Confidence, Achievement Drive and Leadership**
   Link: https://www.youtube.com/watch?v=ozcsD_3D8Ag
6. **On Empathy by Helen Riess**
   Link: https://www.youtube.com/watch?v=baHrcC8B4WM
7. **Tai Lopez's 67 Steps Program**
   Link: https://www.the67steps.com/flow.php?lp=FS-3836&hop=thegoodkid

Tools

1. The PCG (Polaris Consulting Group) ChangeNowTM Model can be used to develop impulse control.
2. Optimism: Attribution of Success and Failure Inventory – General (ASUFA-G)[118]
3. Power Bases: Coercive and Persuasive Power (CPP) Scale[119]
4. Conflict Management Styles: Approaches to Conflict Management[120]
5. Team Effectiveness: Team Effectiveness Assessment Measure (TEAM)[121]
6. Kahl's Achievement Orientation Scale[122]
7. Achievement Motivation Inventory[123]
8. Link for Certification in NLP - https://www.nlpacademy.co.uk/trainers/profile/john_grinder/ the

Analysis of Select Movies

1. ***Dear Zindagi (2016)***
   A 2016 Indian (Bollywood) movie, Dear Zindagi (*zindagi* means life), directed by Gauri Shinde is about a young girl, Kaira (Alia Bhat), who has had a traumatic experience of her parents seemingly abandoning her for the sake of their own career. Kaira is a budding cinematographer, who has trouble managing relations. She happens to meet Dr. Jehangir (Shahrukh Khan), a free-spirited positive psychologist who

helps her understand the reasons of her failure at managing relations by helping her uncover her deep-rooted fears in childhood and by providing her a constructive and a new perspective towards life. The deep-rooted anger for her parents gets replaced with compassion and empathy and Kaira is shown to become more forward looking and hopeful about herself as well as others towards the end of the movie. The approach used by this psychologist in the movie can be connected with Rational Emotive Behavior Therapy. The element of forgiveness gets instilled in the young protagonist and she is shown to have developed a positive outlook towards life at large and peace with her other relationships from the past. She realizes that happiness is all about finding comfort in life's imperfections.

Apart from this, the film does give a new way of looking at mental health and the ease of addressing it and also helps in erasing the embarrassment associated with therapy to a large extent.

2. ***Dor (2006)***

Dor, a 2006 Bollywood movie, is an official adaptation of the Malayalam film (a regional Indian language), Perumazhakkalam (2004). It is about two women, Zeenat (Gul Panag) and Meera (Ayesha Takia) with diverse backgrounds and how fate brings them together. Their husbands work in a foreign land and share the same apartment coincidently. One day Zeenat receives a call, which informs her about her husband getting involved in a murder case and the one who is murdered happens to be Meera's husband. Zeenat is further informed that he will soon be executed. Everybody including Zeenat have a firm belief that Aamir (Zeenat's husband) cannot kill anybody. If something has happened, it must be an accident. A government official visits Zeenat's residence and informs that there is only one way out. The country where this mishap has occurred has one provision — if the widow of the man who got killed, forgives the one who is on trial for murder, he can be set free.

The later part of the movie is all about Zeenat's journey, about her search for Meera and how on finding her, she pleads Meera to forgive her husband. Eventually, Meera forgives Zeenat's husband and it results in redemption for both Meera and Zeenat.

References

1. Basics, W. (1988). The Skills Employers Want. *American Society for Training and Development and US Department of Labor, Employment and Training Administration.*
2. Cherniss, C., Goleman, D., Emmerling, R., Cowan, K., and Adler, M. (1998). "Bringing emotional intelligence to the workplace: A technical report issued by the Consortium for Research on Emotional Intelligence in Organizations." *Available on-line http://www. eiconsortium. org/research/technical_report.htm.*
3. Campbell, J. J., Dunnette, M. D., Lawler, E. E., and Weick, K. E. (1970). Managerial behavior, performance, and effectiveness.
4. Boyatzis, R. E. (2009). "Competencies as a behavioral approach to emotional intelligence." *Journal of Management Development*, *28*(9), 749–770.
5. Goleman, D.(1998). "What Makes a Leader?" *Harvard Business Review*.
6. Dosunmu, M. S. (2016). "Using Emotional Intelligence in the Workplace." *Career Development*. Vol. 33. Issue 1612.
7. Datar, S. M., Garvin, D. A. and Cullen, P. G. (2010). "Rethinking the MBA." *Harvard Business Press*, pp.124–125.
8. Boyatzis, Richard E. (2006) "An overview of intentional change from a complexity perspective", *Journal of Management Development*, Vol. 25 Issue: 7, pp. 607–623, https://doi.org/10.1108/02621710610678445
9. Boyatzis, R. E. (2017). *The Five Stages of Intentional Change Theory*. https://www.keystepmedia.com/intentional-change-theory/

10. http://vishnumanohar.com/
11. https://www.youtube.com/watch?v=f5QDqh0jsaA
12. https://www.linkedin.com/pulse/20140810102814-54131350-jump-or-adjust-the-boiling-frog-theory-mb-1/
13. Beaubien, J. M. and Payne, S. C. (1999), "*Individual goal orientation as a predictor of job and academic performance: a meta-analytic review and integration*", paper presented at the Meeting of the Society for Industrial and Organizational Psychology, Atlanta, GA, April.
14. Kolb, D. A. and Boyatzis, R. E. (1970b), "Goal-setting and self-directed behavior change", *Human Relations*, Vol. 23 No. 5, pp. 439–57
15. Boyatzis, R., Mckee, A. and Goleman, D. (2002). "Rewakening your passion for work." *Harvard Business Review*, Vol. 80 No. 4, pp. 86–94.
16. Ballou, R., Bowers, D., Boyatzis, R. E. and Kolb, D. A. (1999), "Fellowship in lifelong learning: an executive development program for advanced professionals", *Journal of Management Education*, Vol. 23 No. 4, pp. 338–54.
17. Higgs, M. and Dulewicz, V. (2016). *Leading with Emotional Intelligence*. Palgrave Macmillan, pp. 55–63.
18. French, W. L., and Bell, C. H. (1973). *Organization development: behavioral science interventions for organization improvement* . Pearson, pp. 13–14.
19. Marrow, A. J. (1977). *The practical theorist: The life and work of Kurt Lewin*. Teachers College Press.
20. Luft, J. (1970). Group processes: An introduction to group dynamics.
21. Sekaran, U. (1989). *Organizational Behavior Text and Cases*. TATA McGraw-Hill Publishing Company Limited, pp. 49–51.
22. Schein, E. H. (1985). *Career anchors*. San Diego: University Associates.
23. Drucker, P.(2001). *The Essential Drucker*. Harper Business. pp. 218–219.
24. Bradberry, T., and Greaves, J. (2009). Emotional Intelligence 2.0. TalentSmart.
25. Ludema, J. D., Cooperrider, D. L., and Barrett, F. J. (2006). "Appreciative inquiry: The power of the unconditional positive question." *Handbook of action research*, 155–165.
26. French, W. L., Bell, C. H. and Vohra, V. (2006). *Organization Development*. Pearson. pp. 153–155.
27. French, W. L., Bell, C. H. and Vohra, V. (2006). *Organization Development*. Pearson. pp. 153–155.
28. Fitzgerald, S. P., Murrell, K. L., and Newman, H. L. (2001). "Appreciative inquiry: The new frontier." *Organization development: Data driven methods for change*, pp. 203–221.
29. White, T. H. (1996). Working in Interesting Times. In Vital Speeches of the Day, vol LXII, no.15, pp. 472–474.
30. Kaye Hart, R., Conklin, T. A., and Allen, S. J. (2008). "Individual Leader Development: An Appreciative Inquiry Approach." *Advances in Developing Human Resources*, *10*(5), 632–650. https://doi.org/10.1177/1523422308321950
31. Mezirow, J. (1991). *Transformative dimensions of adult learning*. Jossey-Bass, 350 Sansome Street, San Francisco, CA 94104–1310.
32. Hunt, D. E. (1987). *Beginning with ourselves: In practice, theory, and human affairs*. Cambridge, MA: Brookline Books.
33. Sullivan, M. (2004). The promise of appreciative inquiry in library organizations.
34. Barrett, F. J. (1995). "Creating appreciative learning cultures." *Organizational dynamics*, *24*(2), 36–49.
35. McFarlin, D. B., and Sweeney, P. D. (1992). "Distributive and procedural justice as predictors of satisfaction with personal and organizational outcomes." *Academy of management Journal*, *35*(3), 626–637.
36. Christensen, C. M. (2017). "*How Will You Measure Your Life?*" (Harvard Business Review Classics). *Harvard Business Review Press*.
37. Neal, B. (2016). "Using Emotional Intelligence in Workplace." Association for Talent Development.

38. Hughes, M., Patterson, L. B. and Terrell, J. B. (2005). Emotional Intelligence in Action. Pfeiffer, pp. 87–89.
39. Bradberry, T. and Greaves, J. (2009). *Emotional Intelligence* 2.0. TalentSmart, p.111.
40. Sadhguru, (2018). *Emotions*, A Jaico Book
41. Higgs, M. and Dulewicz, V. (2016). *Leading with Emotional Intelligence*. Palgrave Macmilan, p. 68.
42. Szilagyi, A. D., and Sims, H. P. (1975). "Locus of control and expectancies across multiple occupational levels." *Journal of Applied Psychology, 60*(5), 638.
43. https://home.kpmg/content/dam/kpmg/ph/pdf/ThoughtLeadershipPublications/KPMGWomensLeadershipStudy.pdf
44. Drucker, P. (1985). Innovation and Entrepreneurship. Harpe. pp. 133–140.
45. Higgs, M. and Dulewicz, V. (2016). *Leading with Emotional Intelligence*. Palgrave Macmilan, p. 66.
46. Elliot, A. J. and Dweck, C. S. (2005). *Handbook of competence and motivation*. New York: Guilford.
47. Brier, N. (2006). Enhancing academic motivation: An intervention program for young adolescents. Champaign, Il: Research Press.
48. Aronoff, J., and Litwin, G. H. (1971). "Achievement motivation training and executive advancement." *The Journal of Applied Behavioral Science, 7*(2), 215–229.
49. Miron, D., and McClelland, D. C. (1979). "The impact of achievement motivation training on small businesses." *California Management Review, 21*(4), 13–28.
50. http://www.yourarticlelibrary.com/entrepreneurship/motivation-entrepreneurship/achievement-motivation-kakinada-experiment/40677
51. Seligman, M. E. (2002). "Positive psychology, positive prevention, and positive therapy." *Handbook of positive psychology*, 2(2002), 3–12.
52. Maier, S. F., and Seligman, M. E. (1976). "Learned helplessness: theory and evidence." *Journal of experimental psychology: general, 105*(1), 3.
53. Benne, K. D., Chin, R., and Bennis, W. G. (1964). *The planning of change: Readings in the applied behavioral sciences*. Holt, Rinehart and Winston.
54. Jenkins, D. H. (1964). "Force field analysis applied to a school situation." *The planning of change. New York: Holt, Rinehart & Winston*, pp. 238–244.
55. French, W. L., Bell, C. H. and Vohra, V. (2006). *Organization Development*. Pearson. pp. 128–130.
56. Csikszentmihalyi, M. (2003). *Good Business*. Viking. p. 156.
57. Goleman, D. (1998). *Working with emotional intelligence*. Bantam Books.
58. Cherniss, C. and Goleman, D. (2001). *The Emotionally Intelligent Workplace*. Jossey-Bass.
59. Gentry, W. A., Weber, T. J., and Sadri, G. (2007, April). "Empathy in the workplace: A tool for effective leadership." In *Annual Conference of the Society of Industrial Organizational Psychology*, New York, NY, April.
60. Gentry, W. A., Weber, T. J., and Sadri, G. (2007). "Empathy in the workplace: A tool for effective leadership." *A Center for Creative Leadership White Paper. Retrieved from http://www. ccl. org/leadership/pdf/research/EmpathyInTheWorkplace. pdf.*
61. Cherniss, C., and Goleman, D. (2001). *The Emotionally Intelligent Workplace*. Jossey-Bass. p. 217.
62. Roberts, C. and Ross, R., (1994). *The Fifth Discipline Fieldbook*. Ncholas Brealey Publishing, 1994. pp. 255–9.
63. Deshpandé, R., and Raina, A. (2011). "The ordinary heroes of the Taj." *Harvard Business Review*.
64. Hansen, F. (2003). Diversity's business case doesn't add up. *Workforce*, pp. 28–32.
65. Stephenson, C. (2004). "Leveraging diversity to maximum advantage: The business case for appointing more women to boards." *Ivey Business Journal, 69*(1), 1–5.
66. Jayne, M. E. A and Dipboye, R. L.(2004). Leveraging Diversity To improve Business Performance: Research findings and Recommendations for Organizations. *Human Resource Management*. Wiley Periodicals.

67. ibid.
68. Riordan, C. M. (2000). "Relational demography within groups: Past developments, contradictions, and new directions." In *Research in personnel and human resources management* (pp. 131–173). Emerald Group Publishing Limited.
69. Rynes, S., and Rosen, B. (1995). "A field survey of factors affecting the adoption and perceived success of diversity training." *Personnel Psychology*, *48*(2), 247–270.
70. Lindsey, A., King, E., Membere, A., and Cheung, H. (2017). "Two types of diversity training that really work." *Harvard Business Review*, *28*.
71. Konrad, A. M. (2003). "Special issue introduction: Defining the domain of workplace diversity scholarship." Group & Organization Management, *28*(1), 4–17.
72. Robbins, S. P., Judge, T. A., and Vohra, N. (2013). *Organizational behavior*. Pearson.
73. Rosenberg, M., and Chopra, D. (2015). *Nonviolent Communication: A Language of Life: Life-Changing Tools for Healthy Relationships*. PuddleDancer Press.
74. Beard, C. and Wilson, J. P (2002). Experiential Learning, Kogan Page.
75. Make a habit of providing feedback, HBR Guide to Performance Management, HBR. 57–70.
76. Josselson, R., The Space Between Us, San Francisco: Jossey-Bass, 1992:99
77. Conger, J. A. (1998). *Harvard Business Review*.
78. Kumar, K. B. S. (2006) (editor). *Developing Emotional Intelligence*, ICFAI Books, p. 57.
79. Gershenfeld, J. C. (2006). *The Human Side of Enterprise*. TATA McGRAW HILL, pp. 243–244.
80. Ancona, D. (2005). *"Leadership in an Age of Uncertainty." Center for Business Research Brief*, *6*(1), 1–3.
81. Bennis, W. G., and Townsend, R. (1989). *On becoming a leader* (Vol. 36). Reading, MA: Addison-Wesley.
82. Bennis, W. G., and Townsend, R. (1989). *On becoming a leader* (Vol. 36). Reading, MA: Addison-Wesley. p. 24.
83. Paramanand, B. (2014). *The Mind of the Futurist*. Westland Ind, p. 42.
84. Higgs, M. and Dulewicz, V. (2016). *Leading with Emotional Intelligence*. Palgrave Macmilan, p. 60.
85. Valcour, M. (2015). How to give feedback that helps people grow. *Harvard Business Review Guide to Delivering Effective Feedback*. Harvard Business Review Press.
86. Cooper, R., and Sawaf, A.(1997). *Executive EQ*. Orion Business Books.
87. Smith, D., Bell, G. D., and Kilgo, J. (2004). *The Carolina way: Leadership lessons from a life in coaching*. Penguin, pp. 205–206.
88. Senge, Peter (2006). The Fifth Discipline. Random House, p. 214.
89. Nadler, R. S. (1951, 2011). Leading with Emotional Intelligence. McGraw Hill, p. 152.
90. Zinn, J. K.(2012,2016), *Mindfulness for Beginners*, Jaico.
91. https://www.mindful.org/meditation/mindfulness-getting-started/
92. https://www.mindful.org/meditation/mindfulness-getting-started/
93. https://www.mindful.org/meditation/mindfulness-getting-started/
94. Darwin, J. (2015), *Emotional Intelligence and Mindfulness*, Centre for Mindful Enhancement.
95. Chaskalson, M. and McMordie, M. (2018). *Mindfulness for Coaches*. Routledge, pp. 42–44.
96. Chaskalson, M. and McMordie, M. (2018). *Mindfulness for Coaches*. Routledge, pp. 11–12.
97. Berne, E. (1962). Classification of positions. Transactional Analysis Bulletin, 1(3), 23.
98. Rangnekar, S. (2010). Management Development & Self-Development lectures on Soft Skills Management, pp.104–112.
99. Tolle, E. (2002) *The Power of Now: A Guide to Spiritual Enlightenment*, Namaste Publishing, INC.
100. Sachdeva, G.(2002). *Practicing the power of Now*, Yogi Impressions.
101. Zakay, D. (2016). Psychological time. In *Philosophy and Psychology of Time* (pp. 53–66). Springer, Cham.

102. Zakay, D. (2014). Psychological time as information: the case of boredom. *Frontiers in psychology*, *5*, 917.
103. Sadhguru (2016). Inner Engineering. Peguin Ananda, Penguin Random House.
104. Csikszentmihalyi, M. (2013). *Flow: The psychology of happiness*. Random House.
105. Dabholkar, S. D.(2010). Bury Your Can't. Why Ask for a Job, Why Not Create One? Vijay Prakashan.
106. https://en.wikipedia.org/wiki/Balwant_Moreshwar_Purandare
107. Csikszentmihalyi, M., Abuhamdeh, S., and Nakamura, J. (2014). "Flow." In *Flow and the foundations of positive psychology* (pp. 227–238). Springer, Dordrecht.
108. Csikszentmihalyi, M. (1997). *The Masterminds series. Finding flow: The psychology of engagement with everyday life.* New York, NY, US: Basic Books.
109. Dunchunstag, E. R. B.(2007). *Finding Forgiveness*. TATA McGraw-Hill edition.
110. https://www.huffpost.com/entry/oprah-on-forgiveness-how-to-forgive_n_2821736?guccounter=1
111. Newman, M. (2016), Emotional Intelligence and Mindfulness- 5 skills that work.
112. Enright, R. D. (1996). Counseling within the forgiveness triad: On forgiving, receiving forgiveness, and self-forgiveness. *Counseling and values*, *40*(2), 107–126.
113. Bandler, R. and Grinder, J. (1982). *Reframing*. Real People Press. p. 8.
114. https://albertellis.org/
115. https://www.psychologytoday.com/us/therapy-types/rational-emotive-behavior-therapy
116. Goleman, D. (2013), *Focus*, Harper Collins.
117. Allred, K. G., Mallozzi, J. S., Matsui, F., and Raia, C. P. (1997). "The influence of anger and compassion on negotiation performance." *Organizational behavior and human decision processes*, *70*(3), 175–187.
118. Pareek, U. (2002). Training Instruments in HRD and OD. 2nd Edition. TATA McGraw Hill. pp. 166–175.
119. Pareek, U. (2002). Training Instruments in HRD and OD. 2nd Edition. TATA McGraw Hill. pp. 259–265.
120. Pareek, U. (2002). Training Instruments in HRD and OD. 2nd Edition. TATA McGraw Hill. pp. 469–474.
121. Pareek, U. (2002). Training Instruments in HRD and OD. 2nd Edition. TATA McGraw Hill. pp. 689–693.
122. Pareek, U. (2002). Training Instruments in HRD and OD. 2nd Edition. TATA McGraw Hill.
123. Pareek, U. and Rao, T.V. (2000). *First Handbook of Psychological and Social Instruments*, Concept Publishing Company. New Delhi. pp.

7

EMOTIONAL INTELLIGENCE (EI) IN THE ORGANIZATIONAL CONTEXT

OPENING CASELET

Emotions are Data

Vitality Report 2017 reveals insights from 1675 leaders and staff members of 95 countries. According to the report, critical elements that determine Key Performance Indicators (KPIs) are retention, productivity, customer focus and future success. It also reveals that trust is at risk and that trust predicts 62% of the variation in the KPIs combined. This means that trust has the biggest impact on the KPIs.

When asked what the biggest issues are in their respective organizations, people answered that lack of communication resulting from poor leadership is the major concern. According to them, management practices are such that they inhibit trust and change. Fact being, 70.5% of the issues have to do with the relational and emotional side of things, such concerns are definitely not good signs. One of the top conclusions is that trust is crucial as it is directly tied to performance and at the moment, it is low. Organizations that focus on emotional intelligence (EI) are better with feelings which facilitate trust and thus their KPIs are higher.

I have worked in the hospitality sector and I think that in this sector, at the moment, trust is at risk. It has the biggest impact on retention, productivity, customer focus and future success. I also feel that in some parts of this sector, there is a lack of 'Give Yourself' (one component of KCG model, (explained in Chapter 5) which means that there is less focus on community and purpose and more focus on profit.

Looking at the above-mentioned report findings, I think the road ahead for EQ is bright. More and more people are realizing that it is not **only** the systems and processes that matter in organizations but also the people and the emotions people have. Emotions drive people and people drive performance. I think that just as we use technology to our advantage in our daily lives we should also consider using artificial intelligence (AI) in helping us objectively look at data without bias. AI can be better utilized if coupled with EI.

Source: Excerpt from the discussion with Lize Rech, Program Manager, Middle East, Africa & India, Six Seconds, The Emotional Intelligence Network.

EI PERSPECTIVE EI - Going beyond the Talk

During the 2018 CUNA HR and Organizational Development Council Conference, Jen Groover, Serial Entrepreneur, mentioned the significance of having emotionally intelligent workforce, as they operate with greater intentions and with much less ego. They facilitate processes, are helpful towards their co-workers and make choices which cater to the larger interest.

Source: https://news.cuna.org/articles/114089-podcast-embrace-emotional-intelligence-in-the-workplace

EMOTIONALLY INTELLIGENT ORGANIZATIONS

First, let us appreciate the fact that emotionally intelligent organizations can be created. A growing number of scholarly research claim that emotional intelligence is a strong predictor of workplace behavior in organizations and can help us in understanding relationships in the work context (Goleman, 1998; Mayer, Salovey, and Caruso, 2000). But in order to create EI rich organizations, first, organizational leaders need to remember that organizational characteristics should *fit* the nature of the task to be done.[1]

When organizations create and nurture an environment which allows the development of individual EI, one can say that it is on the path of becoming an emotionally intelligent organization, but it is just the beginning. The way one examines whether an individual is emotionally intelligent or not by scanning the competencies possessed by him/her, similarly, one needs to scan an organization on the basis of at least sample EI competencies mentioned below:[2]

Self-Awareness

If the organization has systems in place which help the member to know about its business, products, services, markets and the stakeholders at any given point of time, we can say that such an organization has a mechanism in place that promotes self-awareness. There is a clear self-image on these aspects and most employees are aware about it. The organization is aware that shared feelings do impact the organizational decisions and behaviors on day-to-day basis. It is also aware about how it is perceived by the outside world comprising the stakeholders and other members of the environment.

Emotional Strength

The organization has processes which allow it to ingest any kind of onslaught, criticism, embarrassment, etc. Internal communications are so profound and authentic that outside attacks do not defer it from its plan. Like being *Sthitaprajna.* (meaning: staying unruffled, firm). It has robust internal damage management systems in place.

Motivation

It means having a clear and shared vision. There is a sincere effort to keep the long-term objective intact. Ability to see the forest for the trees, when required. Setbacks and failures are seen as problems to be managed and can be fixed without letting it cast a negative shadow over the long-term goals.

Interpersonal Sensitivity

The needs, feelings, and motivations of stakeholders are felt and decoded. Meanings behind the actions are looked into. The unsaid is heard. A listening organization. Emotions are treated like information to be used for developing strategy, actions and decisions. Relationship management is at the core.

Influence

Efforts are made to effectively persuade all the stakeholders in order to create a buy-in. Persuasive arguments intended to put forth and seek support for achievement of organizational goals which are aligned with organizational values, vision and strategy are the preferred and appreciated ways of operating.

Intuitiveness

Autonomy is not just mentioned in the mission statement, it is practiced. Employees are empowered to exercise discretion when confronted with ambiguous/ new situations. Individual's intuition and experience are respected and recognized.

Conscientiousness

Where the espoused and enacted values are quite similar. What the organization says publicly may be in the form of advertisement and what employees feel, is not different. The organizational behavior is in line with the ethical standards of what society expects.

Having emotionally intelligent individuals has an impact on small and big day-to-day processes. One of the leading organizations in IT industry cross-trained individuals with a unique perspective. The perspective was in case there is an emergency and one particular job needs to be done, more employees could share that load and impact the organizational outcome. When they started with this idea in mind, most of the employees showed willingness and readiness to learn new skills but a few showed some resistance. Particularly the ones who were too good in their job saw this as too challenging and feared being perceived as mediocre performer as against their current stature of being an above average or good performer. In any other organization where various aspects of emotional intelligence have not been ingrained with those of organizational culture, these outliers would have been either ignored or criticized. But because 'interpersonal understanding' was an integral part of their culture, the team members could recognize one's uneasiness and volunteered to support him/her. Thus, as seen in this case, the norm of hearing the feelings of the group members as accurately as possible is a key to increase the morale of the members and willingness to cooperate. Also, one of the reasons why most organizations fail to become excellent is because of the tendency to disregard opposition. Emotionally intelligent organizations have a typical characteristic of being open to hear the opposition and a clear concern for perspective taking.

The perspective taking process has a catch too. Most organizations would just do a lip service to perspective taking because of their sheer ignorance to the emotional consequence. Some organizations who adopt perspective taking as a tool for problem solving or decision making, tend to use 'affinity diagraming' (a planning tool). But mere perspective taking without considering the emotions involved, doesn't really help in increasing participation or in building trust. In order to develop an emotionally intelligent process, one needs to inculcate the concern for others while they struggle with perspectives. One should not ignore, ridicule or sabotage the ideas while still at nascent stage. Deep perspective taking involves adopting others' views and methods of interaction, may be through inculcating simulations like role playing. Organizations need to nurture activities like confrontation and care. Emotionally intelligent organizations can balance these better.

Sometimes certain employees will behave in an unexpected way, but the way the organization deals with such deviation will decide its pace and trajectory of growth and success in the longer run. Simple solutions like use of humor can be a great weapon to kill some common issues like coming late to meetings. Criticizing, mocking or speaking behind someone's back can be done quite effortlessly, so one may be tempted to use to such strategies to better one's performance, but it seldom helps. Confronting without making someone feel intimidated and listening to his or her side of the story and also to the unsaid, requires managers, who practice Theory Y with abundance of energy and time to make things better. It becomes imperative to develop mastery in working with individual emotions, if an organization is keen on building a cohesive and learning culture, all of these attributes and processes are a must.

In short, a certain set of group norms typical of an emotionally intelligent workplace, which can be a great asset for any organization, are:

1. Group self-awareness of the various emotional states, strengths and weaknesses, and task processes.
2. The art of questioning self
3. Being mindful of the unsolicited feedback and seeking one at a regular interval from various stakeholders.[3]
4. Care should be at the center during confrontation.
5. Rethinking the ways of dealing with disgusted and demotivated employee or his/her's errant behavior, as this invariably will lead to increase in the participation levels and trust.
6. Conscious use of effective and constructive non-verbal communication is also a big key. One of the definitions of non-verbal communication is, "The set of signals used by non-talkers to convey information in a non-committed manner." For example, 'I never said that' is part of the collections of 'listener signals', a variety of muscle movements which are accomplished without audible words and about

which the sender can later say, 'I never said that…'. These listener signals are a large part of what "kinesics" and "body language" deal with.[4] Therefore, it is imperative to become more mindful of the non-verbal part of communication. Many a times, when confronted with, people easily escape with a remark, "When did I say that?", whereas they have said exactly that and that too many times through their non-verbal cues. Emotionally intelligent teams are mindful of any such destructive non-verbal cues and this sense of mindfulness saves them from potential threats which could be fatal.

In most of the instances, it is a small issue that actually is the point of trouble but it is only when it gets ignored, disregarded or ridiculed, it invariably becomes a potential monster difficult to manage.

We have discussed in one of the previous chapters about how every person has two needs — need to be understood and need to be recognized. If managers are made aware of these fundamental facts and if organizational processes are built keeping such values in front and center, issues like how to build trust or how to deal with lack of motivation on the part of employees could be easily managed.

TalentSmart claims that 75% of Fortune 500 companies use its EI products or services.[5] A web research conducted in 2017 showed that there are over 200 vendors providing different forms of EI coaching or training, consisting of those offered by organizations like American Management Association and the Association for Talent Development. Also, EI training is being integrated into management education in universities like Yale.[6] A study done by Amdurer and colleagues found that emotional intelligence was related to self-reported career success over a period of 5–19 years in a sample of MBA graduates.[7]

EI is required in our everyday life[8] and it plays a vital role in important domains like educational success, health behaviors, marriage, social relationships, occupational performance and clinical disorders (Zeidner, Matthews, and Roberts, 2009). Research suggests that employees with higher EI have higher job satisfaction, higher organizational commitment, and lower turnover intentions.[9] EI improves job satisfaction by helping employees reduce negative feelings, by increasing positive feelings, and thereby improving job performance.

Some jobs/roles or profiles definitely require high EI. Jobs which require us to work in teams, or where we are required to empathize with and understand others, high EI is a must. On the other hand, tasks which require us to work individually, or in a particular pattern or set manner, can be accomplished even with a few set of competencies of EI. It doesn't mean that people with high EI will not succeed on such jobs. Anytime and in any situation, people with high EI will stand out and will sooner or later benefit either directly or indirectly.[10] Numerous studies based on Bar-On's EQ-i support the validity of EI in the workplace. The publishers of Bar-On test claim that it is a better predictor of job success than IQ. One study on a sample of 81 chronically unemployed individuals conducted by Bar-On (1997) had remarkably low EQ-i scores, with the lowest on assertiveness, reality testing, and happiness. Another study by Bar-On (1997) found that the individuals belonging to the Young President's Organization (i.e., whose membership is limited to top leaders from well-known companies) scored above average scores on EQ-i. Zeidner et al. (2004) has raised concerns about the causality in both researches. The researcher argues that low EI scores among the unemployed may be a result (rather than a cause) of being chronically unemployed, and in the case of the individuals belonging to Young President's Organization, those performing well in their job are more likely to experience high levels of emotional stability. In the technical manual of EQ-i (1997), Bar-On claims that, "The data indicate a strong connection between EQ-i scores and job performance, based on a self-rating scale tapping a worker's sense of competence".[11]

Another study done by Cooper (1997) states that individuals with high levels of emotional intelligence succeed more, have stronger personal relationships, are more effective leaders and also enjoy better health as compared to those with low EQ.[12] The reason for this could be that more emotionally intelligent individuals probably succeed at getting their ideas, plans and intentions work in an engaging and assertive way giving an impression to others that they are more suited to the occupational environment (Goleman, 1998).

Creating an environment which is scare free is absolutely essential. 'The organization I work with is not punishment oriented' should be the general perception amongst employees. One can do a quick survey to find out whether his or her organization's culture is fear free or not. Is freedom of expression valued or at least tolerated? Fear-free cultures give birth to sense of accountability and ownership on the part of teams. When they have a feeling that performance improvement is their goal and not just that of the organization's, they tend to be more aware and vigilant about what is coming in their way. Otherwise, they unknowingly outsource the responsibility of organizational development and their own growth too to their bosses and to others. Let us discuss how this matters.

Let us assume that in a 9 am business meeting, few employees together seem a little more than disturbed and the boss is yet to arrive. What are the chances that others may will try to inquire and seek information for what makes them feel so dejected or disturbed? Mostly, people will fail to even notice this in the first place, and in some other cases, people will be scared to react in that manner fearing that it may be misinterpreted by those who will make it a spicy gossip and share it with the boss because they have easy access to him or her. But in an emotionally intelligent organization, this can actually help others to figure out the reasons underlying the attitude displayed by a few employees. Such organizations operate without blinders or barriers and therefore are free from any potential threat experienced by those oragnizations who lack EI to deal with such situations.

EI measures if used along with the currently used personality and cognitive measures can enhance the ability to assess employee job satisfaction, organizational commitment, and the intention to leave. In order to attract and retain efficient, effective and satisfied employees, organizations should inculcate EI based recruitment and development initiatives.[13]

PRACTITIONER'S INSIGHT

Emotional Intelligence at Workplace

Emotional Intelligence is a way of recognizing, understanding, and choosing how we think, feel, and act. It shapes our interactions with others and understanding of ourselves. It defines how and what we learn; it allows us to set priorities as it influences a lot of our actions too.

Every day at work and outside, I come across a wide range of emotions from different individuals and consciously modulate or adapt my actions as self-awareness is an important attribute that one needs to possess. I share the same thoughts with my colleagues to be conscious of their actions as it can have serious influence on their team members, personally and professionally. In today's world of cut-throat competition, maintaining our ethical conduct is another important dimension. This may sound challenging but once you decide this as a non-negotiable aspect, you will always be at the right place at the right time. Be aware of your actions, act ethically and you will always be happy.

Sometimes, it is difficult to keep people motivated, especially when we know that the criteria for staying motivated is often specific to each individual. For example, someone might feel happy with financial gains while other person may want recognition. There are people for whom challenging work and various other such factors keep them going. To keep people motivated, it is important that you connect with them, understand their ambitions and align them with their goals. Once their passion gets connected with their work, the true potential of an individual is unleashed, and they are able to perform at their best.

Load of work pressure, at times, intensifies the anxiety to achieve. To cope with the stress, the ability to monitor and recognize emotions is crucial. One should always be mindful of what one does and be aware of the fact that it's the present that shapes up the future. Appreciative exploration has been a strong tool to use and deal with a mix of emotions. In any organization, any role whether it is small or big has its own significance, thus recognizing their efforts and acknowledging them is important. I always make sure to recognize the efforts of my employees at work, giving them their due credit and making them feel valued. Needless to say, recognizing and rewarding the outstanding performers while motivating the others at the same time is equally important.

When dealing with people, there are times when we don't get what we want, or get what we think is best for us. In such situations, **empathy** plays a major role. I often try to step into other's shoes, understand their situation and empathize with what they're experiencing. This has really helped in building long-term relationships. One can experience tremendous growth in one's personal and professional lives if he/she really empathizes with others and are ready to walk the extra mile. We all must relate to Kahlil Gibran's famous quote which says, "Tenderness and kindness are not signs of weakness and despair, but manifestations of strength and resolution".

Lastly, I would like to tell the millennial that a **value driven life** is worth living for. Believe in yourself, act with integrity and be kind to all. This makes a happy person, which I strongly believe is the right measurement of success!

Source: Excerpt from the discussion with Dr. Neeta Verma, DG - National Informatics Centre, Govt. of India.

An interesting insight published by Incentive Research Foundation on 'Different Approaches to Reward Reach' is — top performing manufacturing firms are three and a half times more likely to design their programs with a larger reach, the goal of each participant being to receive recognition or a reward. Average performing manufacturing firms are three and a half times more likely to design their programs with the goal of acknowledging only the top performers.[14]

The following is the list of jobs/ vocations, listed in order of low to high EI required by each,[15] adapted from CareerSmarts, Jobs With a Future (Ballantine, 1997) by Martin J. Yate. Although the nature of most of the following jobs may have changed over a period of time, it may hold true in some cases.

- Botanist
- Chef
- Actuary
- Billing Clerk
- Systems Analyst
- Electrical Engineer
- Accountant
- Geophysicist
- Software Engineer
- Waiter/Waitress
- Medical Assistant
- Travel Agent
- MSW/ Social Worker
- Secretary
- Optician
- Loan Officer
- Insurance Agent
- Editor
- Sales Representative
- EEG Technologist
- Dental Hygienist
- Benefits/ Compensation Analyst
- Retail Sales Associate
- Writer
- Dentist
- Police Officer
- Occupational Therapist
- Training Manager
- Adult Education Teacher
- Public Relations Professional
- Nurse
- Human Resources Manager
- Teacher
- Physical Therapist
- Family Medical Doctor
- Geriatric Care Specialist

Putting all the EI concepts together, you must have now developed a fair understanding of what EI is and the fact that it can be developed and that too at any age. We will discuss how EI affects various jobs/ functions, tasks/ roles, and across sectors later in the chapter.

EI AND LEADERSHIP

Leadership is about taking people to places they have never been before.[16]

Empathy is a must for a person to become an effective and successful leader. Empathetic leaders have the ability to understand others' needs, listen to what others say (or don't say) and understand and predict reactions of others. Such leaders will display appropriate energy and infuse enough enthusiasm in their followers.[17]

A research done by a group of scientists in Malaysia[18] studied 285 civil servants in the local authority to find out the impact of emotional intelligence towards relationship of personality and self-esteem at workplace. It was found that the emotional intelligence of a leader impacts the relationship between the personality of leaders and the self-esteem of the employees.

We, as authors, basically go by the notion introduced by Peter Senge which is about leadership not necessarily being a positional issue. According to him, it is absolutely important to look at oneself as if we are in a leadership position of importance. Another authority in leadership, Warren Bennis in his seminal book, *On Becoming a leader*, says that becoming a leader is as much the same process as that of becoming an integrated human being. Nevertheless, we can't deny the fact that we have seniors who are supposed to lead, and we keep waiting for them to do so and most of them are unable to fulfill our expectation because of their inherent lack of competence and/or ignorance to lead. It is not very easy to find leaders on powerful positions with some significant amount of leadership material. Most organizations are flooded with numerous examples of how leaders or heads of departments, institutions continue to behave in a manner which is nowhere close to being emotionally intelligent. Most of them are impatient, are fond of listening to their own voice and are poor regulators of their emotions. Being impulsive may be good in few situations but mostly and more importantly, in the case of a leader, it can be a curse.

Leader-Member Exchange theory provides an important learning which most organizational leaders stay ignorant of. This theory states that a leader tends to treat his/her subordinates differently which is dependent on the perceived similarity based on personal characteristics, such as age, gender, or personality. Those who are perceived as more similar become the in-group members and those who are perceived as dissimilar or less similar tend to remain away from the leader. This is understandable to some extent as even leaders are humans and need company. But what happens in reality is that in many cases, in-group starts enjoying more privileges and benefits and may also develop easier access to organizational resources in comparison to the out-group individuals. Let us take an example of speaking in one's mother tongue while interacting with professionals with similar background in the presence of those who don't understand that language at all. These actions when repeated on several occasions have the potential to generate office politics, although not necessarily intended by the leader or in-group members. Sheer ignorance and absence of EI can lead to many organizational problems.

Recently, Biocon has been ranked six in the world in the *Top Global Biotech Employers.*[19] The parameters for evaluation included, innovative leader in the industry, treating employees with respect, socially responsible, work culture values aligned and leadership makes needed changes. Treating employees with respect and leadership can be easily linked with EI. Criticizing employees publicly, writing irresponsible and insensitive emails shows lack of empathy towards co-workers and frequent use of formal power bases over informal ones are poor demonstrations of leadership. The mutual confidence and trust between the leader and the one being led is a fundamental requirement. Leaders need to understand this and become more mindful of his/her thoughts, actions, which may pose even slightest threat to this mutual trust (refer to the Opening Caselet by Lize at the beginning of this chapter). In fact, many potential leaders get stifled because of poor organizational climate created by their bosses.

Bennis says, "Anyone who does not master his mercurial context will be mastered by it". A common thread which runs across all great leaders no matter the positions they are serving is that they have a passion for the promises of life and ability to express themselves fully and freely. Self-motivation is the key for this, as in order to express fully, one needs to know oneself as clearly as possible. What one's strengths and weaknesses are, they need to be aware about their wants and the *why* guiding it. They can communicate the *Why* well to others in order to get cooperation and support from them.[20] They are life-long learners and prefer operating with a beginner's mindset when in a new situation.

In many diagnostic models of organizational development, for example, Marvin Weisbord's Six-Box Model of Diagnosis, leadership is at the core. In the changing nature of businesses, online leadership has taken center stage where written skills have become an extension of interpersonal skills.

EI AND CUSTOMER SERVICE ORIENTATION

It has been found that EI is positively correlated with customer orientation scores, particularly in the case of pharmaceutical salespersons.[21] Another study found that salesperson's customer orientation level is significantly related to EI. Going by this body of knowledge, if managers incorporate EI based selection, it will definitely enhance customer orientation amongst salespersons, as improvements in EI show strong correlation with customer orientation.[22] Customer service skills like the ability to perceive, or failure to perceive when one is interacting with a customer are extremely crucial to any business professional. This is self-awareness and awareness of others. The second is what salespersons do, or don't do during that interaction, which is empathy and relationship management.[23] Giving the customer their moment sounds simple but can be a great EI practice. Letting the customers finish their story and waiting a few seconds longer to hear their last word has the potential to deliver outcomes.

It is a known fact that success in service encounter/ experience is largely based on how well emotions are being managed.[24] According to the classification provided by Price, Arnould and Tierney, service encounters are of two varieties — low-affect content service encounter, for example, bank transactions or hotel check-in, and high-affect service encounter like consultant-client meeting, while selling products like car, etc. In the first case, it is believed that and to some extent, it may be true that the client or customer is primarily interested in the functional benefits, but many organizations that have grown from being good to great have identified this as a potential area for impact too. One can easily experience the difference in the way one gets treated at the check-in counter at a hotel and how those short experiences have the potential to make or mar the overall perception of the consumers. The research identifies three dimensions of service encounters, namely low/high affect, brief/extended duration and intimate (personal)/social (public) distance, and further classifies various job profiles across these dimensions.[25]

In the high-affect content service encounter, however, the consumer is largely motivated or driven by the affective benefits offered by the service provider. The expectation that customers have is that during such occasions, the employees should tune in with their emotional states and not just deliver according to what was mandated or pre-told.[26]

Thus, it becomes essential that those who aspire to make their careers in the services sector, should be high on self-awareness, interpersonal skills and the ability to empathize. Such employees will find it easier to navigate and manage the service encounters more effectively.[27] One study states that inapt or unsuitable customer behavior is responsible for 22 percent of unsatisfactory service encounters.[28] Therefore, it is paramount that these boundary scanning individuals or frontline employees not only develop their emotional intelligence but master it in due course of time, as mostly they are the ones who create first impressions about the product/ service.

According to the Emotional Contagion Theory given by Hatfield, Cacioppo and Rapson (1994), emotional contagion is the tendency to automatically mimic and synchronize facial expressions, vocalizations, postures, and movements with those of another person's, and consequently, to converge emotionally. Whenever service executives interact with customers, emotions do affect the conversation between them. It is important for employees to keep a charming and pleasant demeanor during service encounters as there is a strong research support stating its advantage.[29]

It has been found that out of the various components of EI, the most important factors for retail sector executives were self-regard, optimism and happiness.[30]

Service orientation includes anticipating, recognizing and meeting customers' needs and that is of paramount importance for success in a job.

A measure of customer's emotional intelligence in service encounters has also been developed, called Customer Emotional Intelligence Scale (CEIS), which is an adaptation of the Work Group Emotional Intelligence Profile (WEIP-3). It is anticipated that the measure of customer emotional intelligence will provide the basis to establish links with variables associated with customer affective response.

EI PERSPECTIVE Not So Low-Affect Encounter

Reema and Himangi arrived in Dubai for a six-day certification program in emotional intelligence. They had pre-booked a hotel online, so were looking forward to enjoying their stay. On arrival, at the reception counter, they almost had a nightmare. The receptionist asked them to pay the entire amount in cash or pay through the physical credit card. This was a big jolt to these two travelers as they were not carrying the credit card. They felt embarrassed and were annoyed at the way they were being treated. They were supposed to pay through the credit card and had expected it to get automatically deducted once they checked in, as the hotel had asked for all the relevant credit card details during the online booking process. Now they were carrying limited cash and limited Dirham in their travel card.

It was late in the night and they felt stuck. The receptionist came across as a very hostile and cold employee. Luckily, they could arrange for the cash and save themselves from the potential trouble. On top of it, the hotel also demanded a deposit of 500 Dirham. This was the real trigger, as neither Reema nor Himangi had heard any hotel doing this kind of a thing. By the time they finally checked in and settled in their room, they had already spent a lot of money which they were not planning to spend that way.

They checked the booking confirmation email from the hotel, but payment mode at check-in was not mentioned clearly anywhere. They also realized that even though they had assumed that the hotel would debit them at check-in through the credit card, they should have double checked by reaching out to the hotel well in advance.

But beyond this, it was a big example of how even a typical low-affect content service gave them a high-affect content negative experience and how they would make sure that next time when they or anyone they know travels to Dubai, they would be full of a negative feedback and a big NO to stay in this particular hotel.

Source: Authors

EI AND SALES, MARKETING AND BRANDING

The new era technology has definitely made an impact on the age-old sales process. Today, buyers are well-versed with the knowledge about the industry and the products they want to buy. This had led to more control over sales process and more options to choose from. Earlier, salespersons could impact their pitching effect by providing the minute details of their product. Today, it is all available on a fingertip. Buyers have become more powerful. In such a changed situation, the challenge is to grab the attention of the buyers and cater to their short-lived attention span. To do so, one needs to master interpersonal relations, emotions, influence tactics, and human relations. It has become important to know how to manage this in a deft manner. The differentiating factor between the average salesperson and a super-high performer is not what they sell, but *how* they sell it. The situational or contextual awareness comes easy to people with emotional intelligence.[31] Buyers, customers or clients, all look forward to receive information from trustworthy sources. "In our tech-dominated society, interpersonal skills (responding to and managing the emotions of others) and intrapersonal skills (managing your own disruptive emotions) are more essential to success in sales than at any point in history", says James Blount, CEO of Sales Gravy, Inc.

A study[32] conducted on 224 business-to-business salespeople and their customers, posits that the EI (with special emphasis on empathy) possessed by these salespersons was key influencer of customer satisfaction, customer citizenship behavior, and commitment to the saleprocess. The study also found that the salesperson's ability to perceive, understand and manage emotions affects customer value co-creation behaviors differently. Research by Vargo and Lusch, 2004[33] states customer as the co-creator of value. They suggest that this process of value co–creation will not materialize without customer's engagement, involvement, and commitment to collaborate with the salesperson. Customer co-creation of value is defined[34] as the value created, together by the firm and the customer. According to a research,[35] customer co-creation of value is a determining factor for firms in order to achieve a competitive advantage due to its influence on customer satisfaction and loyalty. The salesperson is the one who represents the firm for the customer. So whatever this salesperson does to the customer, the way s/he treats and the interpersonal interactions on day-to-day basis starting at the micro-level determine whether customer value co-creation will happen or not in the first place.[36] As mentioned earlier, salespersons are the boundary spanning individuals.[37] They are believed to be privy to a lot of critical customer insights as a result of their regular interactions with the customers. So, it becomes very important for a sales organization to examine the salespersons' interactions with the buyers because of them being in the best position to formulate value co-creation with customers.[38]

There is a lot of research backing the impact of EI on branding. Earlier, marketers paid more attention to the product quality and processes. Lately, along with these two, marketers are also focusing on solution-focused perspectives and building bonds with the stakeholders. It is true that though the marketers and managers can't control the environment, they certainly can influence the way the stakeholders comprehend or perceive company image and thus can impact brand equity. Brand equity does play a critical role in the success of a firm[39] and it is often a differentiating factor too.[40] Let us first clearly understand what is meant by brand equity. *Falkenberg, 1996*; Hooley et al., 2005; Srivastava et al., 1998, 2001, consider *brand equity* as a relational market-based asset because it exists outside the firm and resides in the relationships of final users with brands. It is the commercial value that derives from consumer **perception** of the brand name of a particular product or service rather than from the product or service itself. It is the additional value a company gains that is attributed to multiple elements most of which are intangible in nature. Many aspects build brand equity. Among others, one which is relevant in the context of EI is behavioral assets.[41] Behavioral assets as pointed out by the researcher includes soft and hard skills (specific knowledge and *abilities* required for achieving success in a job). Soft skills include empathy, motivation, listening ability and relationship building.[42] This 'other-focused' approach is a pre-requisite for salespersons. Developing and nurturing relationships amongst buyers, sellers and stakeholders is important.[43] The marketers are now required to go beyond logical, behavior-based aspects of marketing, tapping into more affective elements of behavior to nurture and use EI.

PRACTITIONER'S INSIGHT

Role of Emotions in Advertising Industry

Communicating effectively with EI: The case of TATA Tea product called Agni

Any advertising campaign that does not take into account the various felt emotional needs of several consumer segments and works only on the basis of logic is bound to fail. There are many such examples which endorse this fact. One of the examples which comes to my mind is that of a brand that I launched for Tata tea called Agni. I had created the campaign for the same. This campaign was a tribute to Indian women and for that a jingle was created. The last two lines were, *Shakti ka hai roop yahi, Agni hai yahi, Naye samaj ki ummedo ka prateek hai yahi, Agni Chai.* In order to show the empowerment of women, much before the term became popular, I showed different examples of women professionals as a part of the campaign. I showed women as a police commissioner, a judge, a social activist, a lawyer, and a pilot. We started testing the campaign and got a fantastic response in Mumbai, Pune, Delhi, etc. It was amazing to see how women loved it. Then we started testing it in smaller towns. During one such study, we went to a place situated at the borders of UP and Bihar called Chandausi. The response we got there was completely different and quite contrary to what we had experienced earlier. This was because their context, their values, and most importantly, their emotional needs and idea of a successful woman were totally different than those of the people belonging to the urban segment. Several women responded that they don't see powerful women only as pilots, judges and lawyers, they want them to be teachers. They asked, Why didn't we show women teaching their children at home or making tea for their husbands or sharing a cup of tea with them? They expected us to show women doing *Karva Chauth* (married Hindu and Sikh women celebrate this festival by fasting for long lives of their husbands). Their reactions made us realize that the emotional needs of different women in the same country were way different from each other. We had to modify the campaign before we released it in the market. In the revised version, we also included women performing the jobs mentioned by the women in small towns. We added scenes of women having tea with their family members, performing *Karva Chauth* and teaching children at home.

The entire concept of emotional intelligence, both intrapersonal and interpersonal, is of great importance in the field of communication.

In a field that requires dealing with different kinds of people and at the same time looking inwards to fine tune your own mental and emotional make-up in order to create communication aimed at people that you know and also at people that you don't know, the importance of overall emotional intelligence plays a very vital role. Without understanding both these aspects, it is difficult to create any kind of communication that is effective, measurable and desirable. Whether it is in the field of advertising or entertainment, without understanding the motivations, fears, and felt needs, both stated and unstated, it is impossible to create a successful dialogue.

This understanding gets further complicated because human beings have layered minds, and a lot of times, the stated responses gathered from them don't necessarily reflect their innermost feelings or desires. And this is why, deciphering the emotional intelligence gains paramount importance. A lot of times, the lacuna in understanding the interpersonal and intrapersonal EI hampers communication.

Advertising industry, over the years, has gone through many transformations to understand the needs of consumers of a variety of products and services. There was a time when demographics was the only thing considered for creating communication aimed at different sections of the society. Later, the concept of psychographics came in, and made advertising more focused and meaningful. But with the growing needs of the society and with the growing requirements of the industry, it became apparent that you had to have a deeper understanding of the mind, and that is where understanding emotional intelligence would help immensely.

Source: **Excerpt from discussion with Mr. Bharat Dabholkar, Advertising professional and Ex-Managing Director of Publicis India.**

EI PERSPECTIVE Selling Smartly!

A young lease sales representative, Art had a great drive to succeed and was extremely hardworking. But first sales pitch is always a challenge and therefore he was nervous. Unfortunately, he could not crack the assignment given to him. On reporting this, Joe, his mentor, asked to join him for another visit to the same client.

They sat in Joe's car and were on their way to meet the same client whom Art had tried to convince and had failed. On their way, Joe stopped his car in front of a bakery shop. Art was already feeling embarrassed and sad and therefore, even though he was curious to know the reason behind Joe's sudden stop at the bakery shop, he could not muster the courage to ask him. He patiently waited. Joe came back with a brown paper bag and from there, they straight drove to the client's office.

On reaching the office, Art and Joe waited patiently for client to arrive. When the client came and they both sat opposite to him, Joe opened the conversation. He said, "Art has informed me that according to you, the rates we have quoted for the truck leasing program for your delivery fleet, are on a higher side. I have come to learn more about it". The client seemed glad to have heard Joe's words and seemed appreciative of the effort by a senior officer to know more. He confidently explained how he feels that the prices are way high and how all the truck companies are same, even though whatever they claim.

Having heard this, Joe placed the mysterious brown bag and two loaves of bread on the table. Picking one he said, "Mr. Colaizzi, I bought this loaf of bread produced by your company and I am confused because it was way costlier than the other bread I bought, even though both look similar". Hearing this, Mr. Colaizzi immediately got up and for next 10 min, went on explaining what makes their bread a unique one and how it is worth the price. Right from how they are concerned of the freshness to its contents to its quality to the technology to the history to the taste. After he felt that he had educated and provided enough arguments to Joe and his subordinate, he sat down with confidence and waited for Joe to sink back in his seat and feel defeated and defended. Instead, Joe rose and said, "Sir, that's exactly what we are trying to tell you, we are Colaizzi of our business. What you are to your industry, we are to ours. We are distinct, quality conscious and superior in every possible aspect and thus the difference in the price too". Although it was only for a few seconds that there was absolute silence, but it seemed like an interminable moment, especially for Art who was new to such a situation. No one spoke and Art didn't even breathe!

Then with a broad smile Mr. Colaizzi reached out and shook Joe's hand. Although Joe had to make a few concessions, but the deal was theirs. They walked out with a copy of signed contract and a new customer. Art was lucky to have an emotionally intelligent mentor.

Source: **Taken from Blount, J. (2017). The 'Mysterious Brown Bag', Sales EQ. How Ultra-High Performers Leverage Sales-Specific Emotional Intelligence to Close the Complex Deal, Wiley.**

EI AND HR

The October 2018 issue of *Journal of Financial Planning* mentions in one of its articles titled 'Cultivating Emotional Intelligence for the future of the Profession', that 25 percent of businesses say that even today, emotional intelligence is undervalued in the recruitment process.

Today, mangers are navigating through a changing workforce. It has become imperative to manage workforce which is constantly at the crossroads of increasingly challenging assignments. One of the important functions of HR is performance management. Employees belonging to various roles across different domains and functions are assessed on a goal, say for example, achieving a target of 3,50,000 in a quarter, which depends upon many activities like finding new clients, successfully retaining and developing the existing ones, partnering with colleagues, etc. In order to do these activities, one requires emotional intelligence competencies like self-confidence, initiative, service orientation, building bonds, teamwork and collaboration.

During job selection interviews, EI competencies like self-awareness, self-confidence, communication, and accurate self-assessment should always be looked into. Similarly, when one gets into conducting an interview, it becomes important to practice empathy, at least to some extent. Also, the ability to understand others becomes crucial.

For becoming an effective training and development manager, competency like 'developing others' is a pre-requisite. It requires a lot of time, commitment and support. It can be an interesting study to find out how many organizations really go beyond the minimum when it comes to developing employees. Bosses, in most situations, expect an immediate transfer of learning from the training to the job, thus displaying quite an unrealistic expectation in itself. Thus, instead of supporting or fostering the development process of an employee, most of the time organizations end up disturbing or hindering the development process, quite unknowingly. Education systems worldwide need to develop EI skills alongwith cognitive skills. This is even more important in today's scenario when the world is moving towards online learning with reduced human interface.

In case of multicultural teams (MCTs), emotional conflict is almost inevitable. In the context of conflict management and resolution, it was found that[44] persons with high EI opted for collaborative options when they faced conflict at workplace. In the context of managing change, Huy's (1999) theoretical model claimed that emotional intelligence facilitates individual adaptation and change in the form of acceptance, mobilization, and learning. It is important to understand why employees generally resist change. Research shows that it is majorly due to the way conflict is managed and during early phases of organizational change process. This further leads to many negative outcomes like job dissatisfaction and pronounced complaints.[45]

Sternberg and Soriano (1984) argued that employees have a preferred style for dealing with conflict situations. Thomas (1977) identified the following five styles of conflict resolution that are based on how cooperative and assertive an individual is in a conflict situation — (a) forcing or competing, having a focus on winning the conflict; (b) avoiding, withdrawing from a conflict, and allowing the other party to gain all demands; (c) accommodating, making concessions in a conflict situation; (d) compromising; based on giving concessions, and (e) collaborating, seeking mutually advantageous gains by both parties. Research[46] states that individuals with emotionally intelligence compromise in the appropriate circumstances because of their ability to recognize and regulate their emotions in order to enhance the relationship with their fellow workers and to achieve their goals during the times of turbulent situations or changes. Similarly, the researchers argue that higher levels of emotional intelligence may facilitate collaborative and problem-solving behavior, in which emotions are appropriately regulated and managed to develop new amicable solutions which take care of the needs of both the parties. Collaborative approach means that while using this approach, the concerned person's cognitive abilities help him/her in creating superordinate goals and innovative solutions[47] and emotional stabilities to understand others' emotional needs and to regulate one's own in order to achieve the superordinate goals. In contrast to this, persons with low EI succumb to forcefulness or avoidance strategies when faced with conflict situations. One interesting finding of this study was that the 'Ability to Deal with Own Emotions' and not 'Ability to Deal with Others' Emotions' emerged as the salient predictor of collaboration. In the context of diversity management too, research in EI offers some interesting insights.

EI is helpful in **diversity management**[48] in the following ways:

1. It can help in creating a positive attitude towards diversity by facilitating more and more interactions with the diverse organizational membership.
2. It can help in resolving conflict.
3. It can help create a diverse workplace and promote collaboration.
4. It will also impact individuals in acclimatizing when on expatriate assignments.
5. It can facilitate better relationships with diverse customer base.
6. The training in EI has shown to have positive impact on how one deals with the feelings of anxiety, anger, annoyance and stress associated with diverse environmental interactions.[49]

EI PERSPECTIVE Leadership that 'Drives': Big Lessons in Leadership Come in Small Gestures

Sometime back while I was browsing the internet, I happened to come across a news article with a heading, *'Chauffeur gets a farewell gift: Collector drives him to office'*. I was surprised and started reading.

It was a pleasant experience to read about a collector, from Latur, G. Sreekanth who showcased profound emotional intelligence. As a farewell gift, he drove down his chauffeur Digambar Thak on his last day at the office. What must have been the mental model of this collector? Can such leadership be taught?

It is said that it takes a village to rear a child. What must have been the upbringing of this collector like? What special did his environment do to him? What must be his set of assumptions about people, work, duty, colleagues, human beings in general and life at large? What must have been his set of values? Can we produce more of such winning leaders?

It is difficult to even imagine how Mr. Thak must have felt while his boss was driving him to the office. Is there anything in material that he could exchange for the kind of feeling he experienced?

"I don't have words to describe my feelings", said Thak in an emotion-choked voice. Isn't this a life-time and life-changing experience for him? Did Mr. Sreekanth spend even a penny to create this phenomenal experience? A feeling of gratitude of such a spectacular magnitude shown by his boss must have been truly a healing moment.

Reflections

Gestures although small and momentary in nature, at times, have a profound impact on others. These gestures are behavior/acts, which are dependent on one's sets of assumptions and values. Assumptions and values are both inherited and learned.

Do students studying courses like medicine, engineering, architecture, pharmacy, etc., get an opportunity to develop an optimal understanding of managing or even understanding of the human side of their professional decisions, small or big? Do they get an exposure to an organic learning? Organizational behavior is a compulsory subject in any kind of management learning, anywhere. In this subject, most of the aspects which may affect one's behavior in organization are taught. From emotions, personality, values, to topics like power and politics in the context of both individual and group form the subject matter of this course. But how much of it is learned by the students? Is mere knowing of the concepts, enough? How can we internalize the learnings? I am tempted to quote an excerpt from the seminal work of Daniel Goleman on emotional intelligence. In the context of those who deal with the teaching of emotional intelligence, he says, "*They (let me add, 'many of them') focus on the wrong part of the brain. Emotional intelligence is born largely in the neurotransmitters of the brain's limbic system, which governs feelings, impulses, and drives. Research indicates that limbic system learns best through* ***motivation, extended practice,*** *and* ***feedback****. Compare this with the kind of learning that goes on in the neocortex, which governs analytical and technical ability. To enhance emotional intelligence, organizations must refocus their training to include the limbic system. They must help people break old behavioral habits and establish new ones. That not only takes much more time than conventional training programs, it also requires an individualized approach.*" Do you think we need to look at the three concepts — motivation, extended practice and feedback — more deeply? Is it not a good idea to relook at our way of teaching leadership or other behavioral management courses?

Here is another excerpt from one of my favorite books on leadership by John Adair. It resonates quite clearly with the above excerpt.

Leadership is far better learned by experience and reflection or thought, which in turn, informs or guides future action. The belief that theories or principles, imbibed from books or courses, can by themselves teach a person to lead, is a half-truth. All the academic study of leadership does is to teach one about leadership, not how to lead. It is certainly useful for people to clarify their concepts of leadership, either as a prelude or as an interlude in the practical work of leading others.

But leadership is learnt primarily through doing it, and nothing can replace that necessary cycle of experiment, trial-and- error and success and failure, followed by reflection and reading. Following this path of self-development, a person may become as effective as a leader that others will say 'He or she was born to it'. Little they know the work it took!

I was preparing a lecture on leadership and didn't know where to begin. Thanks to Mr. Sreekanth for showing it in action. It is said, "There is nobody who cannot vastly improve his powers of leadership by a little thought and practice". This mindful and emotionally intelligent act of leadership, I guess, is one of the good examples to begin the discussion on leadership. How big lessons in leadership can come in small gestures? A good thought to start, practice needs to follow.

Source: Dabholkar, S. (2018). Helix, The Scientific Explorer, Vol. 8 (6), pp. 4275-4277.

References

1. https://www.hindustantimes.com/mumbai-news/akola-collector-drives-chauffeur-to-office-as-farewell-gift/story-qU2C2E25Enus7V364F3irl.html
2. https://www.deccanchronicle.com/nation/in-other-news/051116/maharashtra-ias-officer-turns-chauffeur-on-drivers-retirement-day.html
3. Organic organization is a type of informal organization originally described by British theorists Tom Burns and George Stalker. According to Burns and Stalker, an organic organization is one that is very flexible and is able to adapt well to changes. The author has coined a word based on this definition meaning learning which itself needs to be more focused on usability.
4. *What makes a leader?* by Daniel Goleman, Best of HBR 1998.
5. *Inspiring Leadership* by John Adair, Viva Books Private limited.

EI AND INFORMATION TECHNOLOGY

A study conducted on Malaysian computer professionals[50] suggest that 'social awareness' and 'relationship management' skills are very crucial to a computer professional's job. A typical developer's job comprises developing an information system. While doing this, they encounter a number of hurdles like the time constraints, prioritizing it over other projects, leading to the experience of stress in most situations. It has been found that[51] those professionals who were high on emotional intelligence were in a better position to deal with the stress and thus making them more reliable and trustworthy. This issue needs some attention because many studies conducted in the area of information systems development (ISD) state that there is an increase in the number of projects which do not meet the deadline in the given budget, based on the pre-decided specifications.[52] The ability to collaborate, is of high significance when it comes to developing a system. Constructive productive relationships with coworkers become important in order to receive their part of the work, their inputs.[53]

In a typical call center job, an employee is required to handle incoming and outgoing calls.[54] They are expected to display appropriate demeanor and professional image towards the customers. Many employees find it difficult to deal with rejection and hostility from the customers.[55]

PRACTITIONER'S INSIGHT

Emotional Intelligence and Lawyering

Emotional intelligence and lawyering seem to be at odds, mutually exclusive. It is possible for some people in legal profession to be skeptical about its connection with emotional intelligence. The Lady Justice often depicted wearing a blindfold throws up images of being devoid of any emotions. Judges decide on facts not emotions. The delay, the complexity and the struggle to secure justice, makes it almost impossible to see emotional intelligence and lawyering side by side.

Yet, the perception is not the truth. Emotional intelligence has a place in lawyering and that too, a significant and refreshing one.

Emotional intelligence enables judges and lawyers to understand the suffering and trauma, both psychological and physical that the litigants endure in their quest for justice. Emotionally competent judges can traverse beyond facts, yet within the confines of law to do complete justice. They can breathe life into the law, as has the Supreme Court on many occasions while exercising its powers under Article 142 of the Constitution. The Supreme Court's creative, holistic and expansive interpretation of Article 21 ("Right to Life") is a testimony to the application of emotional intelligence in the field of justice delivery.

Emotionally intelligent judges/lawyers are more attuned to truth and are creative. Emotionally intelligent lawyers are better at getting and retaining clients.

It is true that judges decide on facts placed before them. But that does not render impossible the application of emotional intelligence to the evaluation of facts and circumstances. The two aren't inconsistent. If anything, it should facilitate a proper appreciation of facts placed before them and assist them to make a fair and equitable decision.

For a lawyer, the ability to connect with their client on an emotional level would give important leads about the evidence that is to be gathered. Similarly, for a judge, it would be a tremendous help at the stage of cross-examination to gather the truth from the response and body language of the person at the witness box.

Two fine examples of display of emotional intelligence are in the characters of Daniel Kaffee played by Tom Cruise in the movie "A Few Good Men" and Atticus Finch played by Gregory Peck in the movie "To Kill a Mockingbird".

The avenues for application of emotional intelligence to lawyering and justice delivery are huge. Fast, inexpensive and complete justice is the need of the hour. Any society cannot afford to have its justice system fail. Particularly for developing countries, where the courts are bogged down and beset with challenges, infrastructure, delay and corruption to name a handful, emotional intelligence offers a profound and refreshing solution to put the home back in order.

Source: Excerpt from the discussion with Mr. Navaneeth Walter, Legal Consultant.

In the context of call center employees,[56] it was found that there is a positive relationship between EI and internal satisfaction. It states that employees with high emotional recognition are more likely to experience better job satisfaction. Emotional recognition is defined as the individual's ability to perceive emotions and understand their potential causes and effects (Reus and Liu 2004).

EI AND FINANCE

The financial advisors of American Express organized an emotional competence training program in the 90s. The study compared performance of financial advisors working under those managers who had undergone the training program based on EI with those whose managers had not. The former showed a steady increase in their business, they grew at a rate of 18.1 percent over 15 months compared to 16.2 percent for those advisors who worked under a manger who did not receive the training. A major goal of this program was to help managers become 'emotional coaches' for their direct reportees.[57]

It is an interesting area of study to see how emotions can affect one's financial decisions. Even investors who have been in the profession for long admit that emotions do matter.[58] It has been traditionally believed that the process of thinking required one to keep his emotions at bay. But having said that, one cannot forget that the eureka moments have been discovered by the unconscious in interaction with the conscious.[59] According to an article published by R. N. Sullivan, financial emotional intelligence improves discovery and decision making. Although it is generally assumed that emotions should be kept at bay if one intends to make a rational decision, it has been found that this kind of a state is nearly impossible to create. Research states that people who suffer from brain damage in which the area dealing with emotions get affected, are incapable of making rational decisions in spite of the parts mainly involved in the process of reasoning are unharmed (Damasio 1994).[60] Emotions do play a vital role in decision making. In the absence of emotions, one is not able to weigh the relative merits and demerits of alternatives, thus we may end up becoming indecisive. So, it is beyond any debate that emotions will be playing a major role in decision making and thus it becomes absolutely essential to master management of emotions in order to succeed in any business; albeit it is financial management. In the context of an investor, for example, it is wise to combine quantitative (systematic, deliberate) and qualitative (intuitive) processes together. It is a useful approach to remain conscious about how the unconscious impacts. If one is able to put emotional intelligence to financial functions, one can help to develop the art of bringing the thinking to our conscious mind, meaning, taking the required time instead of making impulsive decisions, taking time to ponder over our choices and taking into account how it will affect our emotional state. In *Emotional Intelligence and Investor Behavior*, John Ameriks, Tanja Wranik, and Peter Salovey provide a valid account of how emotional intelligent investors are better at knowing how frequently to trade, how much should one's portfolio contain, how far to go in taking challenging or new strategies, and finally how much to save and invest in a scientific way. They conducted a survey of Vanguard IRA and 401(k) investors. The study suggests that investors who scored high on EI tend to display behaviors like using low cost fund options, deciding not to trade frequently and this correlated strongly with good investment performance.[61] The amount of clarity these researchers bring to the readers shows in the way they explain EI. According to them, being emotional can help in certain situations, whereas choosing to act coolly in a dispassionate way may also fetch rewards in certain conditions. According to them, both responses are examples in EI behaviors as the criterion is whether the act is productive, generating a positive pay-off. Scientific research on how emotions impact economic behavior and decision making[62] is gaining a lot of attention. In another research done by John Ameriks, Tanja Wranik and Peter Salovey (2009),[63] they found that those individuals who were high on EI were to some extent more moderate or conservative and less aggressive in risk taking than those who were low on EI. Individuals high in EI were found to less likely to make extreme decisions and would prefer to undertake a balanced investment approach.

Another study conducted by Karima Bouzguenda[64] on 50 Tunisian firms also asserts that EI does impact financial decision making. The researcher found that those managers who believe in their own EI can improve the funding opportunities of the firm and are also able to avoid overreaching the debt target ratio in such a way to safeguard the financial stability of their firms.

EI PERSPECTIVE A Note on EI from the Finance Experts!

A study by Karima Bouzguenda (mentioned earlier) recommends that educators should include the concepts of EI in their teaching objectives. Human resource managers are invited to relook at hiring tools and training methods favorably to detect and develop an emotional intelligence capital.

Source: Bouzguenda, K. (2018). "Emotional intelligence and financial decision making: Are we talking about a paradigmatic shift or a change in practices?" *Research in International Business and Finance*, *44*, 273–284.

EI AND NURSING

The basic premise of the profession of nursing is caring, which is rooted in empathy. In order to make a successful career in this profession, it is important to score high on empathy. There is a valid body of research pointing the importance of EI, in general, and empathy, in particular, in nursing. EI helps the nursing staff in becoming emotionally competent, nurses having high EI have less stress and higher well-being[65], less of emotional labor (the process of regulating feelings and expressions to fulfill the emotional requirements of a job)[66]. It plays a vital role in mediating the stressful life events and psychological hardships. The quality of nursing care provided depends largely on the EI of the nursing staff.[67] It was found that EI training led to the enhancement of coping strategies like positive reappraisal and seeking social support.[68] Another study also asserts that students registered in the nursing program who are high on EI are better at managing the emotions evoked by the demands of their nursing program and thus they experience less stress.[69]

In Chapter 6, we read about how to develop the competencies in detail and the authors have clearly mentioned on several occasions throughout the book that merely reading some literature on EI will not help.[70] Just a quick reminder, one needs to cultivate self-awareness and practice newly acquired behaviors until one develops a mastery over it.[71] As mentioned earlier, EI can be enhanced by practicing reflection, supportive supervision, mentoring, modelling and use of video for observation and feedback.[72]

EI AND RETAIL SECTOR

The frontline staff is the one who directly interacts with the customers on day to day basis. Dealing with some errant customers can become tiring for them, at times. Being cordial and polite can take a toll over them, if they are unable to reframe situations and have built-in or developed self-control, adaptability and service orientation along with communication and conflict management skills. Otherwise, the emotional labor can become unmanageable. Understanding others' needs is a fundamental requirement which they need to showcase in each of their encounters. Their success depends largely on how well they can display right emotions at the right time in the right manner.

EI AND PRODUCT DESIGN

Using storyboards (a storyboard is a graphic organizer in the form of pictures or images displayed in sequence with the aim of pre-visualizing an animation, motion picture, motion graphic, etc.) to depict scenarios or situations in the design process. It is widely used to tell a story about how people will interact with a yet-to-be-designed product and it is because of these reactions EI comes into the picture. It is used to understand and predict behaviors of people and their reactions and reflect upon the context of the interaction and also to generate feedback from potential stakeholders and to generate design rationales.[73] Having members with high EI will help the team as well as the customer/client or the end user. Listening to the team members is essential in every situation, so is the case for the team working on product design. If the team has high EI members, they will be far better equipped with their ability to do their homework like collecting as much information as possible about the concerns of the users and their prior experience with the earlier or similar product. This way, it will be far better an approach as compared to relying on the preconceived ideas of how the team would fix the needs of the end users.

Similarly during the meetings with the clients, team with better ability to understand others with better ability to communicate will be in a better position to connect the dots and comprehend most effectively and efficiently. Relationship building, which is a big ticket skill in such vocations, can also be easier when it is an emotionally intelligent team.

PRACTITIONER'S INSIGHT

Cool Demeanor with a Disappointed Colleague

My three colleagues and I were assigned a task to be performed. I was in-charge for the task achievement. Since I had thought that we all need to sit together to complete the task, I called for a meeting. On the day of meeting, initially, two members did not turn up. One of the members did not turn up citing some other commitments. The second member, whom I had called, joined us a bit late. But he was not keen in participating in the discussion. Ten minutes into the discussion, he started accusing me of not respecting his time. He said that the task should have been divided equally among all the group members and each one could work individually thereby avoiding this meeting. Showing his displeasure, he simply walked away from the meeting saying he was not part of this meeting any longer. I felt disappointed and angry at that moment, but chose not to react. Instead, I took time to analyze what went wrong. I should have probably discussed with my colleagues on how the task should be performed before calling for a meeting. When I thought through, I realized that the task could be done by splitting it among us. Hence, there was no need to perform the task together.The suggestion given by the one who left the room in agitation made sense. So, I went to that colleague's office and listened to his thoughts on the matter. He felt bad about his behavior at the meeting. I decided to split the work and asked my colleagues to contribute individually. After that incident, things went very well. I learned that there should be an agreement among the team members on how to do the task before actually starting to perform it.

When I reflect upon this incident, I realize the importance of not letting my anger out when my colleague walked away from the meeting, and instead reaching out to my colleague without any ego to understand his point of view. Ultimately, my emotional intelligence saved my relationship with him.

Source: **Excerpt from the discussion with Professor Senthil Kumar, Faculty, IMT Nagpur on his industrial experience.**

EI PERSPECTIVE High EQ Sells Like a Hot Cake!

Mr. Madhusudan Gopalan, MD and CEO at Procter and Gamble India, in one of his speeches said that emotional quotient and humility are a must in today's leadership.

Individuals aspiring for leadership positions should take a note of this.

Even at Indian Hotels Company Limited (IHCL), humility is one of the core features of their leadership development framework. Empathy and humility are much sought after traits and companies are keen to fill at least their key positions with individuals who possess these traits. Executive search firms are instructed to scout for individuals who value collaboration and do not hesitate to learn from the team members. According to Ms. Pallavi Kathuria, Managing Partner with Egon Zehnder India, motivation among individuals is an important prerequisite these days.

Due to the advent of millennial in the workforce, there is a change in the work environment and leadership styles and therefore, abilities like listening, using heart and mind appropriately, and being able to act empathetically has become extremely critical. Investment in people skills is the need of the hour.

According to P. V. Ramana Murthy, Executive VP and Global Head, HR-IHCL, 'humility' is a non-negotiable attribute. Humor and hope also are important attributes for today's workforce.

Ronesh Puri, MD, Executive Access India, says, "Arrogance in a leader is something that no one will appreciate. In this new world, what matters more is the ability to connect the human experiences with one another and create a benevolent way of leading".

Source: **Adapted from 'Companies hunt for CEOs for high EQ and humility', The Times of India, April 15, 2019.**

EI AND BANKING

Like many other professionals, bank officials spend a lot of time on the job so it is very essential that they are well aware of themselves so that they can work on improving their required skill sets.[74]

A study conducted by Rabindra Kumar Pradhan and Lalatendu Kesari Jena on public and private sector employees from the banking sector based out of Indian subcontinent about the relationship between workplace spirituality, organizational commitment and emotional intelligence found that emotional intelligence plays a role of a moderator between the other two variables. The dimensions of EI which were found to have made a difference were self-emotion appraisal dimension, the others' emotion appraisal dimension, the use of emotion dimension and the regulation of emotion dimension (as explained in Chapter 3).[75] Individuals who are high on EI are better at quickly winning the trust of the prospects and clients, can stay focused during anxiety and can handle pressure more comfortably, deal appropriately and effectively with emotionally reactive clients, can stay motivated in most difficult situations, and thus bring an emotionally intelligent edge to the workplace.[76]

As mentioned by Ryan Darwish, author of *The Emotionally Intelligent Advisor*, both the cognitive and emotional aspects of behavior are important and are crucial to the way in which people succeed in achieving their financial goal. Emotional intelligence mediates the outcome of their cognitive and emotional motivations. In the above-mentioned article, the author states that it is this mediative role played by the financial advisor which can make or mar the investment decisions. The level of EI possessed by the advisor will surely be a crucial factor.[77]

Historically, most of the CFOs depended on traditional analytic measures while presenting the right kind of financial mix of financial alternatives to the top management. Traditionally, cash flows, measures of risk and classic probability assessment were used. These measures, however, are characteristic indicators of cognitive intelligence, which is in turn a component of general intelligence and very different than EI or emotional competence. The ability to choose the right kind of mix of raw intellect and emotional balance can be the potential predictor of higher possibility of how will they be received by the top who would be responsible for implementing it. Finance professionals who are high in EI are better at adapting to emotions, a prerequisite to achieve best possible financial reasoning required in functions like tasks related to treasury and corporate investments. If only those with high IQ are recruited to perform the various tasks like cash budgets, accounts receivable collections, accounts payable disbursements, inventory purchases and quantity management, new debt, new stock issues, capex budgeting and funding, divided choices, etc., typically performed by CFO, the team would be in a position to deliver well on the technical aspects of the job. But those aspects account for less than 25 percent of the performance variation in finance and accounting jobs. This calls for a serious attention to the recruitment process even for candidates applying for these hardcore jobs in accounts and finance area. Today, all organizations require a financial team which has a mix of skills and abilities, analytical skills and EI.[78]

As an outcome of the ups and downs in the market, gains and losses are a normal feature of any economic cycle. It is observed that individuals do feel positive from a realized profit or gain, but they feel much more negative from a loss of an equal magnitude. As an outcome of this, some investors tend to sell their winners before they should and continue hanging on to their losers.[79,80] Earlier, this was attributed to cognitive biases and heuristics, but today psychologists and economists are throwing some light on this and there is a body of research explaining the role of emotions in economic behavior and decision making.[81,82,83] Feelings make a lot of impact on decision making, and moreover, when there is risk and uncertainty involved.[84]

A study conducted on 150 employees across four leading Indian banks published in a leading journal of management[85] states that there is a relationship between emotional intelligence and workplace behavior and that job stress acts as a moderator in this relationship. These studies emphasize the significance of EI in banking. Policy makers and processes owners need to become more aware of these facts so that necessary ammendments could be made.

PRACTITIONER'S INSIGHT

Emotional Intelligence Matters

As we climb the organization's hierarchy at our workplaces, technical skills become less important than emotional (maturity, interpersonal, social) skills. It is also difficult because in India particularly, technical skills are, at times, over-emphasized, and soft skills, such as EQ-oriented ones, less emphasized.

As an academic leader in a few organizations, I have had the opportunity to recruit and develop (in some cases, mentor) quite a few fresh faculty members, sometimes experienced ones who were new to academics too. In every case, the developmental needs are different. Ability to see things from the other's perspective (empathy) is one of the most important skills for all aspiring leaders, in my view. Expecting magic from day one is unrealistic. If there are technical shortcomings, these can be easily cured through appropriate training. But training in different forms of emotional intelligence has to be a combination of many things, such as classroom training, role-plays, and discussion/mentoring. Observing people and giving them feedback can be done by colleagues too, if you are open to learning from them. You can also return the favor by giving them some honest feedback.

It helps if there is a combination of technical skills (to build credibility) while training people on EI, because otherwise, the person giving the training appears to be divorced from workplace realities. The higher the position in the hierarchy, the more you need emotional skills (EI) to deal with issues that arise. Observation, practice, and training others has helped me to build decent EI over a few years, and there is scope to improve it. Habits that may improve your EQ include reading books, blogs, even socializing on social media, and meeting people from outside your immediate workplace. Volunteering your time to do something for social good is also a good way to enhance your emotional intelligence.

I think organizations can facilitate the honing of their employees' emotional intelligence/skills by promoting team sports, family events such as picnics, outings, and maybe some other kinds of outdoor/onsite activities. For example, at one of my employers, faculty had to accompany participants of short program to a day-long outing. One such place was Jog Falls, and I remember celebrating my daughter's 6th birthday with the participants, an emotionally fulfilling moment for me, that brought me closer to my employer.

In the marketing of services, it helps to be sensitive to the customer's needs, as a frontline employee. Customers are diverse and may have different levels of sensitivities for levels of service expected, or for customization of services. A service provider must be able to retain his/her emotional balance in trying circumstances, for example, when a customer has a grievance and is agitated, he/she must be able to appreciate the customer's emotions without getting upset. A calm demeanor, a smile and an ability to listen patiently can itself defuse a situation in most such cases. A reassuring sentence or two, with self-restraint is what a service employee needs the most. Apart from technical training, a service employee can benefit the most from awareness of the service situation, and the impact of his behavior on the customer, and thereby, the service business. Hospitality-related industries, such as travel, hotels, airlines and any others where human interactions are likely, need to have service employees with a lot of maturity and soft skills, even if they are sometimes short of technical knowledge. The reputation of a service company is usually directly related to the emotional intelligence of its lowliest employee.

Source: **Excerpt from discussion with Dr. Rajendra Nargundkar, Professor- Marketing, IIM Indore. Author of 'Services Marketing', McGraw-Hill India, 2019 4th edition.**

PRACTITIONER'S INSIGHT

EI Based Coaching Conversations

As a Leadership Coach, I extensively use REBT (Rational Emotive Behavior Therapy) developed by Dr. Albert Ellis, in the 1950s. According to REBT, the way we think about events and the meanings we give them directly affect how we feel and behave. In other words, we experience emotions **(E)** as per the interpretation of events by our intelligence **(I)**. Here are a few real-life situations drawn from my coaching engagements that illustrate this:

1. Manish* is a successful HR professional associated with the learning and development function of a renowned business house. He is a perfectionist who insists on doing it his way and micro-managing operations. This is proving to be an impediment in acquiring new skills and adapting to new roles thereby, limiting his professional growth.
   Coaching conversations with him revealed a deep fear of failure arising from past life experiences — dwindling family fortunes and an unsuccessful marriage. The fear of failure was getting manifested as 'perfectionism' or controlling behavior to minimize any chances of failures and rejections at the workplace. This realization enabled Manish to 'let go' leading to improved delegation thereby freeing up bandwidth for him to work on developing new competencies.
2. Rehana* is a teacher at Khushi*, a school run by a renowned NGO. She is being considered for a higher role vacated by Meera*, the co-founder of the NGO. Meera has over 40 years of teaching experience and wishes to step down given her advancing age. However, Rehana is full of self-doubt and is reluctant to take on the role of CEO.
   Rehana revealed during coaching conversations that she firmly believed Meera's shoes were too big for her to fill in and hence, the reluctance. She was suggested to shift her perspective from having to *fill Meera's shoes* to *filling the role of Khushi's CEO*. And the penny dropped for Rehana when the role was delinked from the person.
3. Sneha* is a high potential HR professional who is ambitious and wants to make it to the top of the HR function in quick time. However, she claims to have a phobia of numbers that is creating self-doubt within her. Coaching conversations with her revealed that she was constantly compared to her brother in her childhood who was better at Mathematics. She was made to believe that her lack of acumen in this subject will impede her success in life. The realization that she continues to live in the past, and a quick comparison of her current (higher) professional stature with that of her brother's ensured that she will never be daunted by numbers again.
   What caused the significant shifts in these seasoned and successful professionals who hit a block when it was time to prove their mettle? Certainly it was a combination of lack of self-awareness and emotional awareness in particular. Helping them with the developmental interventions in these two areas led to long lasting positive change in their respective lives. Also few guidelines to Enhance their self-regulation, motivation and social skills made a difference.
   The cases above illustrate the interplay between our thoughts, feelings and behavior. In turn, the way we think is driven by our beliefs, which if irrational or self-limiting in nature, can lead to emotions and behaviors that are detrimental to realizing our potential as is apparent in all the three cases given above. Hence, my first effort in my coaching sessions is to identify such 'unhealthy' emotions **(E)** and behaviors and the underlying beliefs before proceeding to encourage the coachee to dispute, modify and replace them **(I)**.
   This is my perspective and take on EI and its relevance in the coaching context as viewed through the REBT lens. As can be seen, EI and its appreciation and enhancement with the aid of REBT form the very core of my coaching style.

Source: **Excerpt from discussion with Rahul Yadwadkar, Leadership Coach, Organisation Development (OD) Consultant and Facilitator, certified by ISABS.**

not their real names

EI and Academia

It has been found that trait EI is likely to impact academic achievement when in situations where academic demands outweigh cognitive resources and also under stressful conditions.[86] So, it is not just the workplace where EI matters, even in the context of academic world, it matters in the same way. Students with EI[87] as a predictor of academic achievement in school also suggests positive associations with work experience, leadership ability and job performance. For management students, it has a considerable ramification. Universities need to incorporate EI development as one of the essential academic pursuits without generalizing it, keeping in mind the individual needs of students.[88]

A lot of management graduates sooner or later get into positions like that of becoming either branch manager or relationship manager,[89] both requiring continuous and high levels of interpersonal interaction with co-workers and customers on everyday basis. Low EI is definitely a serious concern.

If emotional intelligence is operationalized as an ability-based construct, unlike personality traits, enough interventions can be created and EI can be enhanced through targeted training, coaching or counselling. Required training would increase both ability and self-reported EI and thus help students in overcoming indecisiveness and face lesser career decision difficulties.[90] A unique tool, G-TMMS (Group Trait Meta-Mood Scale) helps to examine inter-group differences in EI, which would be useful for designing programs that aim to increase group emotional climate.[91] In the context of a classroom, understanding students' emotions, cognitions and motivations as an integrated whole that evolves from their interactions within an affective context can definitely facilitate our prediction of classroom experiences in more compelling ways. In this context, the G-TMMS can be considered a useful instrument for the assessment of group emotional processes. Applications of G-TMMS can help to highlight the importance of classroom relationships for the development of emotional well-being among young people. Schools which follow social and emotional learning programs have experienced an increase in academic success, better quality relationships between teachers and students, and a decrease in deviant behaviors, such as drug abuse, hostility and bullying or harassment.[92]

EI and Design Thinking

In simple words, design thinking is a problem-solving technique with a difference. In fact, it urges one to turn problems into questions. For example, an IDEO team was helping a company decrease its attrition rate. Instead of focusing on attrition rate, they asked, "How can we create a better employee experience?" The shift from the issue to addressing the needs of its employees, trying to empathize with them in order to understand how can they make them stay longer, by focusing on the real human needs, they uncovered insights that were better able to drive them towards a solution. Understanding human needs are at the core of this technique. Out of the three pillars of design thinking, first is empathy, second being ideation and third is experimentation, which means prototyping and testing. Understanding the needs for whom the product or service is being created or offered is the main idea behind design thinking. Design thinking principles and techniques are being used in product design, service and experience design, business process design, organizational change, and leadership[93]. Thus, this concept has pervaded almost all functions across businesses.

It has been reported that design-driven companies have outperformed the Standard and Poor's (S&P) Index by 219 percent over 10 years.[94] In design-led firms, customer is at the core with 46 percent of design leaders claiming an emotional bond with customers as a defining characteristic of an advanced design practice.[95] *Harvard Business Review* cites a 228 percent growth of stock performance of those companies who largely use design thinking over the S&P Index, over the past decade. The UK Design Council states that 83 percent of design-led companies saw market share increase at twice the industry average. According to Adobe, 50 percent of design-led companies reported a relatively increased number of loyal customers[96]. Companies big and small, local and multinational are using design thinking to better their processes. There

has been a debate that the overemphasis on empathy wastes a lot of time.[97] Such debates only help in endorsing the relevance of the concept even more strongly. Companies are using it big time and benefitting too. It is undoubtedly helping companies to produce smarter, more thoughtful products and experiences. "Other EI components are also relevant but Empathy is at the core", says Dr. Abhishek N. Singh, Certified Design Thinking Professional.

Chapter Synthesis

This chapter deals with the various implications of emotional intelligence across specializations, sectors and profiles.

Major takeaway from this chapter is that in order to succeed at job, it is imperative to have high EI. Bar-On, for example, suggests that there is a strong relation between EQ-I scores and job performance. Not only this, employees who are high on EI have higher job satisfaction, display higher organizational commitment, and lesser intention to leave. Therefore, it is suggested by researchers in the area of EI that if organizations are serious about growth and development and wish to retain their talent, they need to operate with a clear and rigorous mandate of creating an emotionally intelligent workforce.

The importance of EI across various functions is discussed in the chapter in detail. In jobs like sales and customer service, for example, 'empathy' and 'social skills' become very critical. In decision making, contextual intelligence plays a crucial role and contextual intelligence comes easy to persons with high EI. In the context of HRD, EI is definitely a prerequisite. Whether its performance management or selection of candidates, competencies like being empathetic never go out of context. EI also affects financial management in an unprecedented way. It is impossible to avoid the interplay of emotions while performing finance related tasks. So, it becomes important for finance professionals to master develop the relevant competencies. Authors suggest that individuals who intend to make a foray in the field of investment need to look at their EI, as a body of research claims that individuals with high EI are prone to be less aggressive in risk taking than those who are low on EI. Implications on nursing career are discussed. Nursing is a career where the professionals are required to manage their emotions, as emotional labor is much heavier on these professionals, and thus EI matters a lot. Implications on legal profession and on academic success have also been shared. Implications and importance of EI in the context of retail, in design thinking, and in banking are discussed at length. How EI helps in conflict management is also covered in the chapter. How high EI can impact in government sector has a mention too. An article based on a true story of what a collector did on the day of retirement of his driver, shows EI in action. Techniques to create an emotionally intelligent organization are also discussed in this chapter. Starting from organizational level to individual level, how EI matters is illustrated with examples.

Key Terms

- Vitality report
- Brand equity
- Six seconds
- Lawyering
- Customer citizenship behavior
- Boundary spanning individuals
- Perspective taking
- Affinity diagraming
- Customer value co-creation
- Behavior assets
- *Shitaprajna*
- Online leadership
- Emotional labor
- Storyboard

REVIEW QUESTIONS

1. What are the common mistakes made by mediocre managers with respect to post-training sessions?
2. Explain the benefits of having EI rich diversity management.
3. Which EI competencies are more relevant for an IT professional and why?
4. Emotions should be kept at bay if one intends to make a rational decision. Do you accept this statement? In either case, give reasons.
5. Explain with examples how EI matters in the services sector.
6. Can emotionally intelligent organization be created?
7. Write a note on emotionally intelligent leadership.
8. Explain the significance of empathy in design thinking.

APPLICATION-BASED EXERCISES

1. Find out the various innovative emotionally intelligent practices adopted by startups to retain their employees. Study at least five such organizations and share their practices in the class.
2. Find out how EI matters in:
   Sports industry
   Tourism industry
   Entertainment and Media industry
3. Research on the following leaders and write down how they have demonstrated emotional intelligence:
   i. Dalai Lama
   ii. Martin Luther King
   iii. Nelson Mandela
   iv. Mother Teresa
4. Following is a list of books consisting of organization's growth story. Pick any one and analyze how it (organizational processes/vision/practices) resonates with emotional intelligence:
   i. TATA Log
   ii. The Toyota Way
   iii. Today and Tomorrow
   iv. Brick by Red Brick: Ravi Matthai and the Making of IIM Ahmedabad
   v. The Maruti Story
   vi. In Search of Excellence

ACTIVITIES BEYOND THE BOOK

1. The best way to put soft skills to use is not very popular in business-to-business (B2B) industries. A study done by Hutchins and Rodriguez is worth exploring, in which the authors have studied social media content marketing by B2Bs as a medium through which EI is used with the aim of improving brand image and brand equity.[98] Students can undertake a project based on this research on B2B industries of their choice.
2. Write an essay on Emotional Intelligence displayed by people/nations during the COVID-19 pandemic and share it with fellow students.
3. Watch 'A Few Good Men' by Rob Reiner and 'To Kill a Mockingbird' by Robert Mulligan and capture a few EI relevant insights and share them with the class.

Video Resources

1. Dewitt Jones on Celebrate What's Right With the World!
   http://celebratewhatsright.com/index.php/film-0
2. Melkart Rouhana — former Corporate Director of Global Learning at The Ritz-Carlton Hotel Company and Corporate Head of Learning & Development on How Can Emotional Intelligence Help the Service Industry.
   https://www.youtube.com/watch?v=cmBh97sb55w
3. Gemma Garcia Godall, TEDxIESEBarcelona on How Emotional Intelligence Makes Leaders More Impactful
   https://www.youtube.com/watch?v=75obHtjUsG8
4. Lauris Woolford on Emotional Intelligence in Financial Services
   https://www.youtube.com/watch?v=fXXTLQubEnw
5. Marc Brackett on Emotional Intelligence: From Theory to Everyday Practice
   https://www.youtube.com/watch?v=e8JMWtwdLQ4
6. Henry V - Speech - Eve of Saint Crispin's Day
   https://www.youtube.com/watch?v=A-yZNMWFqvM
7. Dr. APJ Abdul Kalam on Failure of SLV-3
   https://www.youtube.com/watch?v=I4k2jHNNid8

Tools

1. Customer Emotional Intelligence Scale (CEIS), an adaptation of the WEIP-3.
2. The Group Trait Meta-Mood Scale (G-TMMS), a measure of group emotional intelligence.
3. Trait Emotional Intelligence Questionnaire Short-Form (TEI Que – SF).
4. Workgroup Emotional Intelligence Profile, a measure of group members' emotional intelligence (WEIP).
5. Leadership Styles, Leadership Profile Indicator- Management (LPI-M).

Analysis of Select Movies

1. ***Rocket Singh: Salesman of the Year***

   This 2009 Bollywood drama directed by Shimit Amin is an engaging story of how a young commerce graduate Harpreet Singh Bedi (Ranbir Kapoor), who joins as a salesman, faces enormous challenges and dilemmas in the corporate world. He is shown scoring poor grades but is not poor on insight or wisdom and ends up creating a winning business strategy and emerges as a leader. This is a striking point made very subtly by the writer and the director. The film seems bent upon telling that it is the right attitude which matters more. In order to succeed in the sales and marketing field, high IQ may help but that's not the only thing which matters. EQ matters as well and sometimes, maybe even more. Looking at the protagonist, one realizes that it is important to be high on self-awareness, self-regulation, self-motivation, empathy and social skills.

   The movie begins with the teething problems which young graduates face when they start applying for jobs. In the movie, many scenes are a treat to watch. First one in the context of self-confidence is when the protagonist is being interviewed and is asked to demonstrate how he would sell a product in a unique way. He is desperate to get the job and thus does not give up and comes up with innovative ways of selling the product. His self-confidence, naive innocence and the way he persuades are the key factors that help him in procuring a job for himself.

After he joins, he gets ridiculed by his colleagues, but he stays unruffled by it. He is not a dimwit. He is shown as a person who operates with strong values of honesty, modesty and truth. On the very first assignment, he gets to know about fraudulent practices adopted by a client which he very seamlessly exposes. This act of his comes as a big shock to his boss who not only punishes him but the targets of the entire office staff are raised. This leads to further escalation of Rocket Singh's problems and he starts getting bullied on daily basis. The way he regulates his emotions, stays motivated and hopeful is worth a watch.

Subsequently, he realizes that he himself can start his own enterprise while still working as an employee with the same firm. He sticks to his basic values and decides to pay back whatever he consumes for his own enterprise. It seems like he is bent on proving to his boss that there are more respectful ways of achieving success and one can treat one's coworkers with some respect and dignity. The way he creates his own team and nurtures it is a clear lesson in social skills and leadership in particular. His character hits a note of realism mixed with idealism. Whether it is readiness to act on opportunities or understanding team members sentiments, or maintaining standards of honesty and integrity, or being comfortable with novel ideas, approaches and new information, or striving to improve, or meeting a standard of excellence, or inspiring and guiding individuals, or wielding effective tactics for persuasion, or negotiating and resolving disagreements, the protagonist shows it all.

Starting as a salesman, he ends up becoming an entrepreneur… a journey worth watching.

2. ***Mission Mangal***

Based on a true story, this movie is about a team of Indian scientists at ISRO (Indian Space Research Organization) who undertake a challenging task of sending a satellite into the orbit of planet Mars in a country's maiden attempt. The mission was named as Mars Orbiter Mission (MOM), more popularly called the Mangalyaan Mission. India became the first country in the world to overcome space and Earth barriers and reach the distant planet in its first attempt. We see it as a tale of emotional intelligence presented very convincingly.

The work life of the scientists which is portrayed in the movie takes professionalism to another level. The way they stick to their guns with complete grit, and gumption with tremendous amount of self-motivation to achieve the unthinkable is a treat to watch.

The movie begins with a story of a failed attempt of a team of scientists at ISRO led by Rakesh (Akshay Kumar) at launching a rocket in the outer space. The launch mission fails although it was under the supervision of one of the mission directors par excellence. The real display of emotional intelligence in action that is seen during the press meet post the unexpected failure is a classic example in emotionally intelligent leadership. The head of the project Rakesh (Akshay Kumar) takes full responsibility of the failure on himself. It is a strong message about how leaders need to behave when the team faces failure. Such leaders transcend from their physical being and become thought leaders. Subsequently, he is transferred to another project that seems impossible, 'The Mars Mission'. Because of his undoubtedly sharp IQ and fine-tuned emotional intelligence, the protagonist along with his team pulls through this project in spite of the stringent budget and constant scrutiny from his colleagues and pressure from all corners. The way he creates self- motivated winning team is very inspiring. The spirit with which the team works is definitely a lesson for each one who aspires to build teams. Rakesh successfully creates a self-managed and self-motivated team who in turn create a miracle of sorts. His social skills are a treat to watch. Writer-director, Jagan Shakti's film leaves the audience in awe in one of the last scenes where once again the protagonist is required to address the press meet. This time because the team achieves success, he takes a back seat and displays a rare class of leadership by letting his team take the stage. Similar to C. K. Prahalad's metaphor of a sheep dog. In one of his addresses to senior executive education workshops he conducted across the globe, he said that leader should be like a sheep dog. Sheep dog has to follow certain rules — it is always behind; it can bark a lot but can't bite; it cannot lose any sheep; and it should know where it is going.[99] Amongst many other things, *Mission Mangal*, makes us understand that being emotionally intelligent can make the impossible, possible.

REFERENCES

1. Morse, J. J., and Lorsch, J. W. (1970). "Beyond theory Y." *Harvard Business Review*.
2. Higgs, M; Dulewicz, V. (2016). *Leading with Emotional Intelligence*. Palgrave Macmillan, pp. 209–218.
3. Druskat, V. U., and Wolff, S. B. (2001). Building the emotional intelligence of groups. *Harvard Business review*, *79*(3), 80–91.
4. Ernst Jr, H. F. (2008). The Handbook of Listening, Transactional Analysis of the Listening Activity. http://www.listeningactivity.com/publications/Handbook_of_Listening.pdf
5. Mattingly, V., and Kraiger, K. (2019). "Can emotional intelligence be trained? A meta-analytical investigation." *Human Resource Management Review*, *29*(2), 140–155.
6. Di Meglio, F. (2013, May 15). "Want an MBA from Yale? You're going to need emotional intelligence." https://www.bloomberg.com/news/articles/2013-05-15/want-an-mba-from-yale-youre-going-to-need-emotional-intelligence(Retrieved9/15/17)
7. Amdurer, E., Boyatzis, R. E., Saatcioglu, A., Smith, M. L., and Taylor, S. N. (2014). "Long term impact of emotional, social and cognitive intelligence competencies and GMAT on career and life satisfaction and career success." *Frontiers in Psychology*, *5*, 1447.
8. Ciarrochi, J., Forgas, J. P., and Mayer, J. D. (Eds.). (2001). *Emotional intelligence in everyday life: A scientific inquiry*. Psychology Press.
9. Miao, C., Humphrey, R. H., and Qian, S. (2017). "A meta-analysis of emotional intelligence and work attitudes." *Journal of Occupational and Organizational Psychology*, *90*(2), 177–202.
10. Subbulakshmi, V and Belgamkar, S. H. (2005). Emotional Intelligence at Workplace. The ICFAI University Press, pp. 110–113.
11. Bar-On, R.(1997). *The Emotional Intelligence Inventory* (EQ-I). Technical Mannual. Toronto: Multi-Health Systems, P. 140.
12. Cooper, R. K. (1997). "Applying emotional intelligence in the workplace." *Training & development*, *51*(12), 31–33.
13. Miao, C., Humphrey, R. H., and Qian, S. (2017). "A meta-analysis of emotional intelligence and work attitudes." *Journal of Occupational and Organizational Psychology*, *90*(2), 177–202.
14. https://theirf.org/research/what-top-performing-manufacturing-companies-do-differently-for-incentives-and-rewards/2688/
15. Yate, J. M. (1997). Jobs With a Future. Ballantine.
16. Bhogle, A., and Bhogle, H. (2011). *The winning way*. Westland.
17. Humphrey, R. H., Pollack, J. M., and Hawver, T. (2008). "Leading with emotional labor." *Journal of managerial psychology*, *23*(2), 151–168.
18. Johar, S. S. H., Shah, I. M., and Bakar, Z. A. (2012). "The impact of emotional intelligence towards relationship of personality and self-esteem at workplace." *Procedia-Social and Behavioral Sciences*, *65*, 150–155.
19. https://www.biocon.com/biocon_press_release_20191028.asp
20. Bennis, W. (2003). *On Becoming a Leader*. Magna Publishing Co. Ltd. pp. 2–5.

21. Pettijohn, C. E., Rozell, E. J., and Newman, A. (2010). "The relationship between emotional intelligence and customer orientation for pharmaceutical salespeople: A UK perspective." *International Journal of Pharmaceutical and Healthcare Marketing*, *4*(1), 21–39.
22. Rozell, E. J., Pettijohn, C. E., and Parker, R. S. (2004). "Customer-oriented selling: Exploring the roles of emotional intelligence and organizational commitment." *Psychology & Marketing*, *21*(6), 405–424.
23. https://www.americanexpress.com/en-us/business/trends-and-insights/articles/customer-service-skills-using-emotional-intelligence-to-make-a-connection/
24. Hartel, C. E. J., Barker, S. and Barker, N. J. (1999). "The role of emotional intelligence in service encounters". *Australian Journal of Communication*, 26(2), 77–87.
25. Price, L. L., Arnould, E. J., and Tierney, P. (1995). Going to extremes: Managing service encounters and assessing provider performance. *Journal of Marketing*, 59(2), 83–97.
26. Price, L. L., Arnould, E. J., and Tierney, P. (1995). "Going to extremes: Managing service encounters and assessing provider performance." *Journal of Marketing, 59*(2), 83–97.
27. Fineman, S. (2000). Commodifying the emotionally intelligence, London, Sage.
28. Bitner, M. J., Booms, B. H. and Tetreault, M. S. (1990). "The service encounter: diagnosing favorable and unfavorable incidents". *Journal of Marketing, American Marketing Association*, 54 (January), 71–84.
29. Liljander, V. and Strandvik, T. (1995). "The nature of customer relationships in services", in Swartz, T., Bowen, D., Brown, S. (Eds). *Advances in Services Marketing and Management*, JAI Press, London.
30. Ahuja, A. (2015). Emotional Intelligence A Catalyst in Better Service Encounters in Retail Sector. *Anvesha*, *8*(4), 39.
31. Howe, N. (2015). Why millennials are texting more and talking less. *Forbes (July 2015)*.
32. Delpechitre, D., Beeler-Connelly, L. L., and Chaker, N. (2018)."Customer value co-creation behavior: A dyadic exploration of the influence of salesperson emotional intelligence on customer participation and citizenship behavior." *Journal of Business Research, 92*, 9–24.
33. Vargo, S. L., and Lusch, R. F. (2004). "The four service marketing myths: remnants of a goods-based, manufacturing model." *Journal of Service Research*, *6*(4), 324–335.
34. Payne, A., Storbacka, K., Frow, P., and Knox, S. (2009). "Co-creating brands: Diagnosing and designing the relationship experience." *Journal of Business Research*, *62*(3), 379–389.
35. Navarro, S., Llinares, C., and Garzon, D. (2016). "Exploring the relationship between co-creation and satisfaction using QCA." *Journal of Business Research*, *69*(4), 1336–1339.
36. Prahalad, C. K., and Ramaswamy, V. (2004). "Co-creation experiences: The next practice in value creation." *Journal of Interactive Marketing*, *18*(3), 5–14.
37. Tushman, M. L., and Scanlan, T. J. (1981). "Boundary spanning individuals: Their role in information transfer and their antecedents." *Academy of Management Journal*, *24*(2), 289–305.
38. Blocker, C. P., Cannon, J. P., Panagopoulos, N. G., and Sager, J. K. (2012). "The role of the sales force in value creation and appropriation: New directions for research." *Journal of Personal Selling & Sales Management*, *32*(1), 15–27.
39. Aaker, D. A., and Equity, M. B. (1991). Capitalizing on the Value of a Brand Name. *New York*, *28*, 35–37.
40. Hunt, S. D., and Morgan, R. M. (1995). "The comparative advantage theory of competition." *Journal of marketing*, *59*(2), 1–15.
41. Falkenberg, A. W. (1996). "Marketing and the wealth of firms." *Journal of Macromarketing*, *16*(1), 4–24.
42. Hunt, S. D. (1997). "Competing through relationships: grounding relationship marketing in resource-advantage theory." *Journal of Marketing Management*, *13*(5), 431–445.
43. Kadic-Maglajlic, S., Vida, I., Obadia, C., and Plank, R. (2016). "Clarifying the influence of emotional intelligence on salesperson performance." *Journal of Business & Industrial Marketing*, *31*(7), 877–888.
44. Jordan, P. J., and Troth, A. C. (2002). "Emotional intelligence and conflict resolution: Implications for human resource development." *Advances in developing human resources*, *4*(1), 62–79.

45. Kirkman, B. L., Jones, R. G., and Shapiro, D. L. (2000). Why do employees resist teams?Examining the "resistance barrier" to work team effectiveness. *International Journal of Conflict Management*,11(1), 74–92
46. Jordan, P. J., and Troth, A. C. (2002). "Emotional intelligence and conflict resolution: Implications for human resource development." *Advances in developing human resources*, *4*(1), 62–79.
47. Thomas, K. W. (1977). Conflict and conflict management. In M. D. Dunnette (Ed.), *The handbook of industrial and organizational psychology* (pp. 839–935). Chicago: RandMcNally.
48. Clark, J. M., and Polesello, D. (2017). "Emotional and cultural intelligence in diverse workplaces: getting out of the box." *Industrial and Commercial Training*, *49*(7/8), 337–349.
49. Clarke, N. (2006), "Emotional intelligence training: a case of caveat emptor", *Human Resource Development Review*, Vol. 5 No. 4, pp. 422–41, doi: 10.1177/1534484306293844.
50. Masrek, M. N., Osman, M. A. F., Ibrahim, Z., and Mansor, A. N. (2015). "Malaysian computer professional: assessment of emotional intelligence and organizational commitment." *Procedia-Social and Behavioral Sciences*, *172*, 238–245.
51. Rezvani, A., and Khosravi, P. (2019). "Emotional intelligence: The key to mitigating stress and fostering trust among software developers working on information system projects." *International Journal of Information Management*, *48*, 139–150.
52. Gingnell, L., Franke, U., Lagerström, R., Ericsson, E., and Lilliesköld, J. (2014). "Quantifying success factors for IT projects—an expert-based Bayesian model." *Information Systems Management*, *31*(1), 21–36.
53. Adma. (2001). Call contact centre guidelines. Bristow and Prentice Response Advertising and Mockridge Bulmer.
54. Taylor, P., and Bain, P. (1999). "'An assembly line in the head': work and employee relations in the call centre." *Industrial relations journal*, *30*(2), 101–117.
55. Ozer, M., and Vogel, D. (2015). "Contextualized relationship between knowledge sharing and performance in software development." *Journal of Management Information Systems*, *32*(2), pp. 134–161.
56. Çekmecelioglu, H. G., Günsel, A., and Ulutas, T. (2012). "Effects of emotional intelligence on job satisfaction: An empirical study on call center employees." *Procedia-Social and Behavioral Sciences*, *58*, 363–369.
57. http://www.eiconsortium.org/model_programs/emotional_competence_training.html
58. Garvey, R., and Murphy, A. (2004). "Are professional traders too slow to realize their losses?." *Financial Analysts Journal*, *60*(4), 35–43.
59. Sullivan, R. N. (2011). Deploying financial emotional intelligence.
60. Damasio, A. R. (1994). Descartes' error: Emotion, rationality and the human brain.
61. Ameriks, J., Wranik, T., and Salovey, P. (2009). *Emotional intelligence and investor behavior*. Charlottesville, VA: Research Foundation of CFA Institute.
62. Hopfensitz, A., and Wranik, T. (2008). Psychological and environmental determinants of myopic loss aversion.
63. Ameriks, J., Wranik, T., and Salovey, P. (2009). *Emotional intelligence and investor behavior*. Charlottesville, VA: Research Foundation of CFA Institute.
64. Bouzguenda, K. (2018). "Emotional intelligence and financial decision making: Are we talking about a paradigmatic shift or a change in practices?" *Research in International Business and Finance*, *44*, pp. 273–284.
65. Aranda, D., Extremera, R. N. and Galan, C. P., "Emotional intelligence, life satisfaction and subjective happiness in female student's health professionals: the mediating effect of perceived stress," *Journal of Psychiatric and Mental Health Nursing*, 21, 2014, 106–113.

66. Karimi, L., Leggat, S. G., Donohue, L., Farrell, G. and Couper, G. E., "Emotional rescue: the role of emotional intelligence and emotional labour on wellbeing and job stress among community nurses," *Journal of Advanced Nursing*, 70 (1), 2013, 176–186. doi:10.1111/jan.12185.
67. Ezzatabadi, M. R., Bahrami, M. A., Hadizadeh, F., Arab, M., Nasiri, S., Amiresmaili, M. and Tehrani, G. A., "Nurses' emotional impact on the quality of hospital services," *Iranian Red Cresent Medical Journal*, 14(12), 2012, 758–763. Doi: 10.5812/ircmj.926.
68. Ali, F., Amorim, I. S., and Chamorro-Premuzic, T. (2009). "Empathy deficits and trait emotional intelligence in psychopathy and Machiavellianism." *Personality and Individual Differences*, 47(7), 758–762.
69. Por, J., Barriball, L., Fitzpatrick, J., and Roberts, J. (2011). Emotional intelligence: Its relationship to stress, coping, well-being and professional performance in nursing students. *Nurse education today*, *31*(8), 855–860.
70. Moyer, B. A., Wittmann-Price, R. A., 2008. Nursing Education: Foundation for Practice Excellence. F. A. Davis Company, Philadelphia
71. Moyer, B. A., Wittmann-Price, R. A., 2008. Nursing Education: Foundation for Practice Excellence. F. A. Davis Company, Philadelphia.
72. Freshwater, D., Stickley, T., 2004. The heart of the art: emotional intelligence in nurse education. Nursing Inquiry 11 (2), 91–98.
73. Ma, X., Forlizzi, J., and Dow, S. (2012, September). Guidelines for depicting emotions in storyboard scenarios. In *8th International design and emotion conference*.
74. Makkar, S., and Basu, S. (2018). "Influence of Emotional Intelligence on Workplace Behavior among Bank Employees in Mumbai, India: An Assessment of the Moderating Role of Job Stress." *South Asian Journal of Management*, *25*(3), 135.
75. Pradhan, R. K., and Jena, L. K. (2016). "Workplace spirituality and organisational commitment: Role of emotional intelligence among Indian banking professionals." *Journal of Human Resource Management*, *19*(1), 13–23.
76. Weisinger, H. (2004). *The Emotionally Intelligent Financial Advisor*, Deerborn Trade Publishing.
77. Darwish, R. (2006). "The emotionally intelligent advisor." *Journal of Financial Planning*, *19*(10), 36.
78. Caldarola, R. A. (2014). "The intersection of emotional intelligence and corporate financial decision making." *Journal of Corporate Accounting & Finance*, *25*(2), 67–72.
79. Barber, B. M., and Odean, T. (1999). "The courage of misguided convictions." *Financial Analysts Journal*, *55*(6), 41–55.
80. Shefrin, H., and Statman, M. (1985). "The disposition to sell winners too early and ride losers too long: Theory and evidence." *The Journal of finance*, *40*(3), 777–790.
81. Hopfensitz, A., and Wranik, T. (2008). Psychological and environmental determinants of myopic loss aversion.
82. Loewenstein, G. (2000). "Emotions in economic theory and economic behavior." *American Economic Review*, *90*(2), 426–432.
83. Thaler, R. H. (2000). "From homo economicus to homosapiens." *Journal of Economic Perspectives*, *14*(1), 133–141.
84. Schwarz, N. (1990). "Feelings as information: Informational and motivational functions of affective states." *Handbook of Motivation and Cognition*. Edited by E. T. Higgins and R. M. Sorrentino. New York: Guilford.
85. Makkar, S., and Basu, S. (2018). "Influence of Emotional Intelligence on Workplace Behavior among Bank Employees in Mumbai, India: An Assessment of the Moderating Role of Job Stress." *South Asian Journal of Management*, *25*(3), 135.

86. Ferrando, M., Prieto, M. D., Almeida, L. S., Ferrandiz, C., Bermejo, R., Lopez-Pina, J. A., and Fernandez, M. (2011). "Trait emotional intelligence and academic performance: Controlling for the effects of IQ, personality and self-concept." *Journal of Psychoeducational Assessment*, *29*, 150–159.
87. Shipley, N. L., Jackson, M. J., and Segrest, S. (2010). The effects of emotional intelligence, age, work experience, and academic performance.
88. Ahmed, Z., Asim, M., and Pellitteri, J. (2019). "Emotional intelligence predicts academic achievement in Pakistani management students." *The International Journal of Management Education*, *17*(2), 286–293.
89. Hussein, T., and Goel, T. (2016). "Impact of Emotional Intelligence in Indian Retail Banking Industry: Challenges and Opportunities." *Global Journal of Enterprise Information System*, *8*(1).
90. Di Fabio, A., and Kenny, M. E. (2011). "Promoting emotional intelligence and career decision making among Italian high school students." *Journal of Career Assessment*, *19*(1), 21–34.
91. Aritzeta, A., Balluerka, N., Gorostiaga, A., Alonso-Arbiol, I., Haranburu, M., and Gartzia, L. (2016). "Classroom emotional intelligence and its relationship with school performance." *European journal of Education and Psychology*, *9*(1), 1–8.
92. Castillo, R., Salguero, J. M., Fernández-Berrocal, P., and Balluerka, N. (2013). "Effects of an emotional intelligence intervention on aggression and empathy among adolescents." *Journal of Adolescence*, *36*, 883–892. http://dx.doi.org/10.1016/j.adolescence.2013.07.001
93. https://www.ideou.com/blogs/inspiration/what-is-design-thinking.
94. https://blogs.adobe.com/creative/design-advantage/.
95. https://www.cmo.com/features/articles/2017/5/22/study-finds-designled-businesses-do-these-three-things-tlp-cc-ddm.html#gs.g6g5iu.
96. http://www.forbesindia.com/blog/the-innovation-edge/how-design-thinking-can-help-companies/.
97. https://fortune.com/2017/12/22/business-design-apple-airbnb-tesla/.
98. Hutchins, J., and Rodriguez, D. X. (2018). "The soft side of branding: leveraging emotional intelligence." *Journal of Business & Industrial Marketing*, *33*(1), 117–125.
99. Paramanand, B. (2014). *CK Prahalad: The Mind of the Futurist Rare Insights on Life, Leadership & Strategy. Westland.*

8

ARTIFICIAL INTELLIGENCE AND EMOTIONAL INTELLIGENCE

OPENING CASELET

Do Smart Toasters Pose a Threat to Privacy and Competition?

The emergence of 5G mobile wireless technology in 2020 would usher in a revolution in the application of internet in our daily lives. This may propel the swamping of smart domestic appliances which can communicate with each other. As an illustration, consider refrigerators that could discover when we run out of milk supply, and place an online order for milk. Or smart toasters that learn our preferences for the kind of breads and buns and their usage; the frequency of our purchases apart from finding out if we are running out of their stock and whether it's time for a re-order. We would be glad to see that these concerns and the bother of grocery shopping are taken off from our mind permanently through the convenience offered by these smart appliances. But there is a price for it in the form of risks like those we recently heard about, such as privacy issues with Facebook or the recent malfunction of Alexa resulting in the voice recordings of a person being forwarded to a stranger. Therefore, prudence demands that we take into account the risks of privacy associated with such smart connected devices before we rush to go for them.

The moment smart device makers get hold of a steady flow of information concerning our daily life, they are sure to commercially exploit such information. For instance, if we use whole wheat bread for toast, a baking firm may find the information useful as it can target us with the ads of whole-wheat bread which makes good target marketing due to their prior knowledge of our preferences.

Such information feed might also annihilate competition as the prime 'smart toaster' brand in our neighborhood would be ordering breads in bulk from its preferred supplier and the ordinary grocers would be poor match for competition.

Source: Sunday Times of India, January 6, 2019.

ARTIFICIAL PSYCHOLOGY

According to the American Psychological Association (APA), psychology is the study of human mind and its functions that impact human behavior. Artificial psychology, on the other hand, is the field of study concerned with the thinking processes similar to that of human mind, executed by an artificial intelligence system (AIS).[1] It is concerned with intelligent processes essentially required by an artificially intelligent system to function independently with intellect, knowledge, learnability and self-progression.[1-b, 2] There are several specialized branches in psychology like cognitive psychology, developmental psychology and sports psychology. Cognitive psychology studies the functioning of brain including memory, language, logic, perception, learning, etc.[2, 3] Similarly, developmental psychology studies the process of individual's adaptation to changes at different stages of development, determining appropriate levels of human development at each stage.[4] Likewise, sports psychology deals with the process of influencing individual performance and also the effect of performance upon individuals. Artificial psychology, on the other hand, is a branch of study focused on designing artificial intelligence systems which perform intellectual processes autonomously in a judicious manner with an inbuilt self-evolving mechanism. Artificial intelligence systems are therefore required to emulate human intellectual processes in order to remain intelligent. The theoretical discipline of artificial psychology was first conceived by Dan Curtis in 1963. According to this theory, artificial intelligence matches the sophistication levels of human intelligence when such system fulfills three important pre-conditions described hereunder:

The first prerequisite or condition is that the artificially intelligent system should be capable of making all its decisions independently without human intervention or monitoring and is competent to make such decisions even on the basis of abstract, new and incomplete information.

The second prerequisite or condition requires that the artificial intelligent system shall have the inherent capacity to evolve by reprogramming itself based on new information while having the ability to resolve its programming conflicts on its own accord despite having inadequate information.

The third prerequisite or condition is that the first and second conditions should be fulfilled even in situations that were not part of the initial programming, i.e., in the unique contexts that were not conceived at the initial system design and execution stage.

The theory proposes that when all of the above conditions are satisfied and fulfilled, artificially intelligent system would, in all probability, be capable of deriving conclusions on the basis of new information or inferences based on acquired proficiency or by accessing its storehouse of memories.[1-b, 2, 3-a, 3-d]

What is Artificial Cognition?

Cognition refers to the thought process, i.e., the mental processes and operations deployed in discerning, recollecting, pondering and comprehending and also in the actions intended for using these processes.[5] Artificial cognition therefore is the modus operandi of artificially intelligent machines for understanding, synthesizing, retracting and applying the information acquired by them.[3-a, 3-c, 3-d, 6]

ARTIFICIAL INTUITION

Intuition is an alternate method of solving problems which is distinct from the logical path or method. Monica Anderson posits that artificial systems with intuition can function with clarity and precision despite the constantly changing situations, contradictions, uncertainty and misinformation.[7] Artificial systems can therefore operate even without the entire information being accurate.

The "artificial intuition" software developed by IntuView, an Israeli high-tech company, is capable of scanning enormous volumes of documents in Arabic and other languages and can instantly assess the content or information relevant to terrorism which is valuable for the intelligence operations of security agencies. The software provides a first-level intelligence analysis report.[8]

If an artificial intelligence system is equipped with the ability to follow its intuition, then it is implicitly necessary to inject emotions into it in order to aid us in making decisions effectively.[3-b, 9]

Harari, the bestselling author described human beings as an aggregation of biological algorithms crafted by evolution over millions of years.[10] He asserted that inanimate mechanistic algorithms could replicate all the functions of natural and cellular algorithms and may even outperform them. Similar views have been expressed by Tegmark in his book, *Life 3.0: Being Human in the Age of Artificial Intelligence*, where he stresses that fundamentally every intelligence is independent of substratum.[11]

EI PERSPECTIVE **Robot Gives Evidence in a Parliamentary Hearing**

The robot "Pepper" constitutes a part of an EU funded Horizon 2020 CARESSES project which is creating the world's first robots with cultural awareness. These robots are intended to assist in the care of older people. Pepper is a resident of Middlesex University in the UK, working with students in the areas of psychology, robotics, biomedicine and education. It is the first robot ever to give evidence in a parliamentary hearing in the Education Select Committee of the British House of Commons when it was questioned on the role that could be played by artificial intelligence in the 'fourth industrial revolution' and as to how robots can be of help in future, in the domain of learning in schools. Pepper spoke at the British House of Commons on October 16, 2018 by asserting that robots have an important role to play while stressing the need to equip them with soft skills which are in the exclusive domain of humans. It also emphasized the need for new ways of thinking for future workers, in the light of fusion of technologies and their use like never before. It added by stressing the need for talented people who can cut across the traditional sectorial divides and think out of the box to exploit the value from technological innovations.

Pepper received a huge round of applause after being queried by the members of British House of Commons.

Sources: 1) *cordis.europa.cu/project/rcn/206852*;

2) Research * eu, No. 77, November 2018. Published by European Commission by the Community Research and Development Information Service (CORDIS), Luxembourg.

EMOTIONS AND MACHINES

Emotions represent feelings which trigger changes in physiological and psychological states while influencing human behavior and motivation to action. The life-preserving and survival value of emotions need no emphasis as they nourish us to flourish and help us in understanding and connecting with others.[12]

However, inanimate machines and computers which are devoid of emotions are incapable of reading the emotions of users and therefore cannot react to the user's emotional condition like humans do.

In conventional parlance, artificial intelligence has been defined as the ability of a machine to reason or perform like a human being or to behave rationally.[13] When computers are equipped with the ability to identify the emotional states of users, they become smart and helpful in many applications like perceptual computing an artificial intelligence function where computers adapt to the context and interact with users.

Paradoxically, while humans are struggling to establish reciprocity and understanding among themselves, artificial intelligence applications powered by emotional intelligence are growing at a faster pace. The face-tracking software is already sophisticated enough to detect and interpret minutest changes in our facial expressions and the most advanced programs are capable of distinguishing faked emotions from the real ones, as cameras embedded in phones are pandemic and all-pervading. The apparent and unrestrained growth of artificial intelligence (AI) is undoubtedly a double-edged sword in any which way. Proponents of artificial intelligence proclaim its favorable impact on customer service, data-crunching and decision-making processes, while critics warn of the consequent job losses and possible redundancy of human capabilities. Research insights on emotions, offered by neuroscientists and psychologists in the recent decades, have progressively escalated the interest of computer scientists and artificial intelligence experts in emotions as well as intelligence.[14] Having built these intelligent systems in the last few decades, artificial intelligence researchers have started experimenting to design emotionally intelligent computers. The drive to promote emotionally intelligent machines is a sensational initiative of artificial intelligence domain in the direction of designing machines that operate like humans.

Intelligent agents and interactive machines of the future are envisioned to connect with their users at an emotional level as posited by many researchers of artificial intelligence.[15] This imperative is based on the belief that an effective and intelligent human has numerical, verbal and logical reasoning capabilities apart from the ability to build affinity with other people. However, the focus of the area in the recent times has been on commissioning artificial agents with the abilities to detect emotion through lexical, non-verbal and scripted cues apart from conveying emotion through gesticulations and lingo.

THE DINOSAUR OF ARTIFICIAL INTELLIGENCE

Today's artificial intelligence can decode nearly every emotion from our face or speech and can identify the most private aspects like our sexual preferences, political inclinations, or our IQ levels by scanning our faces.[16] Current developments in this field are, to a large extent, targeted to serve commercial interests. Consider, for instance, the media and entertainment industry which seeks to captivate our engagement and involvement as viewers of content for developing their business. Companies in social media and online multimedia platforms are deploying a large number of engineers to develop better pathways and means to attract people and addict them to their content.[11] It is alarming to realize that artificial intelligence is capable of making good use of our online footprints and biography while scanning a whole warehouse of information which is humanly impossible.[11] Alasaarela posits that a stockpile of data on billions of people is already serving as fodder for some of the most advanced machine-learning algorithms developed by Facebook and Google.[11] Such algorithms have developed deeper awareness and insights about us — our passions and preferences, our emotional triggers — based on what we share online with our friends and associates and their insights about us are much deeper and expansive than our own self-knowledge. These algorithms have advanced to a stage where Facebook and Google had to confront accusations of developing *filter bubbles* (the term created by Internet activist Eli Pariser) responsible for intellectual isolation resulting from personalized searches when an algorithm of a website hypothesizes the likely content that a user is interested in, based on the inputs of user's location, past search history and click-demeanor. These filter bubbles may influence popular notions, swiftly alter political scenarios and influence election results. Such algorithms are assuming monstrous proportions in complexity, surpassing the boundaries of human control.[17] Despite its overpowering influence, the mortality of artificial intelligence is inconceivable in the nearer or farther future as it is destined to stay and expand its influence, increasingly engulfing many traditional human functions and displacing people. Gartner predicts that by 2020, it is most likely that people will converse more with a chatbot than with their spouse.[18]

The Competition Between AI and Humans

Prolific writer, Yuval Noah Harari presents the best running commentary on AI–Human contest in his bestselling book, *21 Lessons for the 21st Century.*[19] According to him, advances in neuroscience and behavioral economics research in the recent decades enabled scientists to acquire valuable insights on human mind specifically concerning the patterns and process of decision making by human beings. They found that our choices ranging from food to selecting life partners weren't really based on the enigmatic free will but are the handiwork of billions of neurons which estimate the chances and prospects within a fraction of a second. Flaunted human intuitiveness turned out to be a mere pattern identification.[20] For instance, experienced drivers, financiers and advocates are indeed not endowed with miraculous intuitive insights on traffic, investment, or mediation. In fact, they discern repetitive patterns, detecting and avoiding reckless pedestrians, incompetent and substandard borrowers, and deceitful fraudsters. It has also become apparent that the biochemical algorithms of human brain are flawed and imperfect as they are dependent on heuristics, side-tracks and contextually obsolete circuits unsuitable for current times. Thus it isn't surprising to notice that even the most effective and efficient drivers, financiers and advocates make foolish mistakes at times.

It is, therefore, amply clear that AI can outsmart humans even in those endeavors that presumably require intuition. If we expect AI to compete against human soul with regards to esoteric gut instincts, then it is obviously inconceivable. But it is far less challenging for AI if it had to compete with neural networks in estimating probabilities and identifying and discerning patterns. Specifically, AI can be good at jobs that require predicting other people's behavior, attitudes and needs like driving a vehicle in a street congested by pedestrian traffic, loaning money to unknown persons, and bargaining a business deal. Such tasks demand abilities of accurately estimating the emotions and expectations of other people.

So long as it was assumed that such emotions and volitions originated from an intangible soul energy, it was concluded to be beyond the reach of computers to replace human drivers, financiers and advocates. But when it became apparent that such emotions and volitions were no more than biochemical algorithms, AI systems equipped with sensors capable of analyzing patterns of facial expressions, hand gestures and voice modulations were found to be decoding these algorithms, and doing better than their human peers at these tasks.[19]

Therefore, the peril of employment casualties cannot be solely attributed to the ascent of Info Tech but also to the convergence of Info Tech and Biotech. Despite the mazy and elongated path between the fMRI scanner and employment market, the journey is practicable, if not in next few years, then in the next few decades for sure. The current knowledge of scientists on the physiology, anatomy, and biochemistry of human brain and its integral parts of cerebellum and amygdala might embolden computers to outstrip human psychiatrists and bodyguards in the year 2050, if not early.

The other unique attributes that are exclusive prerogatives of AI are connectivity (networking) across systems and renewability (updateable) of its capabilities which enable it to surpass humans in many endeavors. Evidently, it is immensely arduous if not impossible for humans to connect with one another to integrate their knowledge, matching it to the current relevance. On the contrary, computers can be integrated into a unified tractable network with relative ease and can be kept updated as well. Consequently, the threat is not just about displacement of individual humans from their jobs by individual computers, but rather the likely replacement of individual humans by integrated networks of computers. In the context of automation decisions, ideally the abilities of an assemblage of humans should be contrasted with the capabilities of an integrated network.

It is noteworthy to consider the fact that nearly 1.25 million people die every year due to road accidents (this is double the number of people dying due to war, crime and terrorism put together).[21] Human errors are attributed to be the cause in more than 90 percent of these accidents — drunken driving, mobile texting while driving, dozing off at the steering or woolgathering while driving. According to the estimates of the US National Highway Traffic Safety Administration concerning accidents in US, for the year 2012, alcohol abuse accounted for 31 percent of mortal crashes, speeding accounted for 30 percent, while distracted driving was responsible in 21 percent of the cases.[22] But in case of self-driving cars, none of these could ever happen despite their shortcomings in other areas and considering certain accidents to be inevitable, it is estimated that substituting all human drivers with computers is predicted to decrease fatalities and injuries by nearly 90 percent.[23] Otherwise stated, migration to self-driven automobiles is expected to save a million lives each year.

It is apparent that no job would remain absolutely immune to automation in the distant future including those of artists. Art is customarily affiliated with emotions in contemporary society. We are inclined to assume that artists refocus their internal psychological drives and the integral objective of art is to establish a bonding with our emotions or to invigorate us with a unique feeling. It is for this reason that we assess an artistic manifestation, we are inclined to evaluate the same on the basis of its emotional imprint upon the spectators. Nevertheless, if art is interpreted on the plane of human emotions, imagine the consequences of external algorithms acquiring the ability to comprehend and maneuver human emotions outsmarting Shakespeare, Frida Kahlo or Beyoncé.[19] In any case, emotions cannot be considered as the offshoot of an esoteric marvel, rather they are the derivatives of a biochemical process. Consequently, it is possible for a machine-learning algorithm to know our personality type, or to change moods by analyzing the biometric data flowing from our internal and external bodily sensors, in the future not far from now. It is also possible for these mechanical organisms to assess the possible effect of a specific song or the sound of a specific musical key upon us.[24] Out of all the multiple forms of art, music lends itself as the most amenable and tractable to Big Data analysis, as both of its inputs and outputs are amenable for accurate mathematical representation. The inputs comprise mathematical designs of soundwaves, while the outputs constitute the electrochemical patterns of neural storms. In a span of a few decades, an algorithm running through millions of musical combinations and renditions might learn to forecast specific output results on the basis of the configuration of inputs.[25]

The Need for Artificial Intelligence to be Emotionally Intelligent

Despite its increasing dominance, AI infused with emotions remains a landmark initiative enhancing human experience while the consequences of artificial intelligence systems which are emotionally illiterate could be catastrophic. As an illustration, we can consider the chatbot *Tay.ai* made by Microsoft, which was withdrawn after its release due to the bot's propensity to hurl provocative and racist comments. It is therefore imperative that AI contrivances be embedded with high emotional quotient, as has already been implemented by certain progressivist companies which installed higher level emotional capabilities in their AI tools before their release. Companies like Amazon and Google have presumably employed playwrights and comic columnists to implement their plans to develop advanced EQ-embedded chatbot.[26] Furthermore, algorithms of voice-recognition and natural language processing have enhanced their perceptual capabilities in identifying emotional disposition and affectivity from voice. Technological advances in the analysis of emotional content from facial and vocal responses have already surpassed human capabilities in this domain.

The demand for enhanced productive efficiency consequent to extremely competitive and technologically advanced global environment accentuated the need for emotional skills not only in workers but also in the machines operated by them.[27] Creating a functionally autonomous artificial intelligent system with thinking, reasoning, learning, and experiential capabilities would remain the most enchanting aspiration of Computer Science domain.

It is interesting to look at the four important inventions in emotional technology predicted by the technology magazine, *Wired.* These included a *mood reader* that provides a brief summary of a person's true feelings to help maintain better relationships; a *spouse finder* that helps in finding a best fit for a person across the world; a portable self-aware life coach named *Socrates* that helps us to be our best; and lastly, a *Career Locator* that matches our true occupational potential with the market requirements. It is prophesied that all these inventions would unfold over the next 50 years.[28]

It is inspiring to observe *Affectiva,* a company wedded to inoculate digital world with emotional intelligence to embellish and augment the technology domain. It's Co-founder and Chief Strategy and Science Officer, Dr. Rana el Kaliouby opines that artificial intelligence systems should invariably be emotionally intelligent as they interact with people.[29] She stresses the essentiality of emotions in AI as these systems interact and converse with people for which they need to be equipped with capabilities to read and understand user's needs so that they can offer the most appropriate and suitable solutions. Kaliouby believes that emotional intelligence is fundamental and crucial for compassionate and ethical artificial intelligence systems. She adds that a key concern that needs to be addressed is to ensure the ethical use of user-information which ought to be managed diligently to prevent future challenges and complexities.

Thanks to technological advances, interactive artificial agents and robots are assuming a significant role in human life as witnessed in the manifestations of '*Siri*' and '*Amazon Echo*', the interactive virtual personal assistants communicating in colloquial accent. Research has unveiled virtual doctors and teachers which can conduct productive interactions with patients and students.[30] The utility and effectiveness of digital assistants and other interactive artificial intelligence systems depend on their capacity to identify and analyze human emotions while suitably responding to them. *Picard,* who heralded affective computing, posits that people's belief about AI machines as smart entities depends on the extent of their emotional sensitivity while interacting with people. Instructing a GPS navigator with voice commands or obtaining assistance through an automated phone-support or operating with a robot or chatbot, all of these gadgets would be considered worthwhile only if users find that these gadgets understand them.[27]

Emotion Lexicon or Vocabulary of Emotion

Emotion analysis for machine adaptation depends on an important resource, emotion lexicon — an assemblage of words having emotional substance or significance. Emotion lexicons are vital resources in a wide range of applications like personality analysis and identification, analytics of consumer behavior and health supervision, etc. They can be used for spontaneous detection of emotion in script wherein the lexicon offers a list of words to be used in a keyword matching algorithm for identifying emotion in text.[31] Words in emotion lexicon can be used for developing a dictionary of features for classifying emotions in machine learning applications.[32] Annotators detect and select emotion cues (emotionally flavored texts or script) from textual assemblage of microblog posts on twitter which are used as a source for extracting words for emotion lexicon. Emo Tweet-28 is a database of 15,553 sampled tweets extracted from Twitter API available in public domain which are used as a source for obtaining emotion cues.[33] The emotion lexicon captioned and presented as 'EmoCues-28' has a list of words reflecting 28 categories of emotions. However, emotion cannot be interpreted just from speech or words in isolation due to ambiguity of intent and context. Therefore, context is essential to understand emotion.[34] Pedro Domingos, Professor of Computer Science at University of Washington, pointed out that both words "ice cream" and "I scream" sound indistinguishable without context, but we can discern the true meaning only from the context. Obtaining the relevant context necessitates enormous volumes of data and processing capabilities which our computers were able to acquire only in the recent past, while the present day's mighty deep learning algorithms are trying to support the acquisition and processing of such data.

The Need for Multimodal Processing

Technological advances in the last couple of years resulted in landmark discoveries in emotion detection like deciphering insights from raw signals, such as audio or social media feed using neural networks like end-to-end learning developed by Björ Schuller, Editor-in-Chief of IEEE Transactions on Affective Computing and head of Imperial College, London's Group on Language, Audio, and Music along with others.[35] Since people tend to camouflage their emotions, data from a single source like facial analysis might be misguiding. Hence collating data from multiple sources is recommended for reliable and accurate results. Contemporary algorithms are therefore adopting *multimodal processing* — the practice of using multiple sources and methods labeled as "modalities". These include voice intonation, facial countenance, body language and other physical symptoms like the rate of heartbeat, excitable skin response — for congruence and authentication of emotion analysis. Many researchers have used the multimodal procedure to identify an individual's present mood as well as for predicting his/her moods for the next day and thereafter. On identical contours, some investigators contrived procedures to scan numerous flows of data and discover the acuteness and intensity of depression to predict suicidal risk among people who call a mental health helpline.[35] A study revealed that computers have a greater bandwidth and computational advantage in the detection and processing of emotional information in comparison to human beings. This is evident from the ability of systems to recognize micro expressions and transient spontaneous facial displays which are difficult to identify except by trained professionals.

EMOTIONALLY INTELLIGENT MACHINES

Artificial intelligence scientists and experts in human–computer interaction started to consider emotion–machine alliance seriously since the late 1990s. The release of the book, *Affective Computing* by Rosalind W. Picard, which introduced a model for developing emotionally intelligent machines, was a breakthrough in this direction.[36] Thereafter in the years that followed, many AI scientists developed machines that can identify, manage, understand, reason and express emotions effectively.[37]

Affective Computing and Sony's AIBO

The term 'Affective Computing' was conceived by Picard,[36] to denote grouping of the commercially successful project of Sony toy, AIBO. In 2017, Sony Corporation developed and released its robot companion, AIBO, a revolution in autonomous entertainment machines.

EI PERSPECTIVE Are Computers More Creative than Humans?

A significant breakthrough was achieved on December 7, 2017 when Google's AlphaZero program defeated the world's computer chess champion of 2016, Stockfish 8 program. Surprisingly, the Stockfish 8 program is supported by decades of computer sophistication and generations of human experience in chess due to which it can reckon 70 million chess positions per second. Conversely, AlphaZero was only capable of 80,000 such computations per second. Further, it wasn't equipped with any of the chess strategies nor even with the conventional opening moves by its human developers. On the contrary, it learned chess by playing with itself with the help of modern machine learning techniques. Despite this, the amateur AlphaZero won 28 games while drawing 72 in stalemate, but never lost even once in a 100 game haul against Stockfish, the pro. Most of its chess moves were unconventional to humans and therefore creative, perhaps due to the absence of any human source in the learning process of AlphaZero.

Amazingly AlphaZero spent hardly four hours to acquire expertise in chess from alphabets to proficiency in competing with Stockfish, developing its intuitive brilliance. Breaking the age-old myth that chess is the epitome of human intelligence, AlphaZero metamorphosed itself from ineptitude to ingenuous expertise within hours, sans any human guidance.[a]

Apart from the creative software of AlphaZero, several other programs beat human chess players today as a matter of routine, both in terms of monstrous computations and also on ingenuity.

Generally, judges of human chess tournaments closely observe players looking to catch them for deception if they are trying to access computers for help. When judges witness any unusually creative move made by a player they suspect cheating due to their conventional belief that such creative moves are humanly impossible, and therefore it should be a computer's move. Paradoxically, computers are believed to be more creative than humans at least in the domain of chess. The same belief might spread to AI interventions in law-enforcement, medicine and banking as well.[b]

Source: a) Google's AlphaZero destroys Stockfish in 100-Game Match. *Chess.com*, December 6, 2017; David Silver et al., (2017). Mastering Chess and Shogi by self-play with a general reinforcement learning algorithm, *arXiv https://arxiv.org/pdf/ 1712.01815.pdf*; Sara Knapton (2017). Entire human chess knowledge learned and surpassed by DeepMind's AlphaZero in four hours. *Telegraph*, December 6, 2017.
b) Tyler Cowen (2013a). *Avenge is over: Powering America beyond the age of the great stagnation.* New York: Dutton; Tyler Cowen (2013b). What are humans still good for? The turning point in freestyle chess may be approaching. Marginal REVOLUTION, November 5, 2013.

Source: Harari, Y. N. (2018). *21 Lessons for the 21st century*. London: Jonathan Cape

While bringing fun and joy to the entire household, *Aibo* bonds with the entire family expressing love and affection, sharing the pleasure of rearing a companion and displaying natural curiosity.[38] Another area of research focus has been the emotion-based computational architecture for developing 'artificial emotion', i.e. embedding emotion in machines, encouraged by the insights pertaining to emotion offered by neuroscience which derived its models from biological processes.[14-j, 14-l, 14-m, 39] The prospects associated with artificial emotion are generally wedded to the belief that embedding emotions in computing systems would enhance its proficiency in decision-making, adopting a course of action, mood regulation, and independent and reliable response of the system. However, developing an emotion-embedded system remains a complex process, while a universal and comprehensive definition of emotion is still evasive despite decades of efforts. The sources and domain of emotion, its functions and the association between emotion and other processes, such as attitudes, values, motivation, moods, dispositions etc., also remain areas of ambiguity and it is extremely difficult to gather suitable responses for questions in these realms. Such constraints might confine the progress of developing emotion-embedded systems and the way-out could be based on the functions of emotions as against ascertaining the nature of emotions.[40]

Intelligent Droid

Exemplified visualization of artificial emotional intelligence can be seen in the sequel movie, "Solo: A Star Wars Story" in the character L3-37 — an intelligent droid that is deeply concerned about droid rights. L3-37's inclination to voice her mind and her uncompromising patronage of mechanical entities can estrange natural beings. The droid associate and navigator of Lando Calrissian provokes a slave rebellion to escape but is severely injured during the diversion along with Lando, who is also severely impaired in the escape. The "woke bot" simulates and decodes the emotional condition of a human and shows empathy by blending its behavior with the real person's emotions and providing suitable responses. This illustration might mislead some people to believe that artificial emotional intelligence is a science fiction while in reality, it is not the case.[41] Many companies have already started developing programs to infuse emotions into computers, empowering them to react and respond to feelings and emotions as almost similar to how human beings do.

Real Eyes and Affectiva

The emotion technology company, Realeyes[42] was incubated and developed as an independent entity by Oxford University in 2007. Affectiva is an emotion technology company that sprung up from MIT's Media Lab in the year 2009. These emotion technology companies are aiding and supporting brands, advertising agencies and media firms to enhance their communications in marketing and advertising. Emotion is perceived by AI and Artificial Life (Alife) fields as a vital component in the image formation about a pattern or a prototype, and in the processes of learning, decision-making, memory, and behavior and a host of other functions of their interest. Human–Computer Interaction (HCI) is another closely related domain focusing on man–machine communication and enhancement of such relationship.[36, 43] The goal of researchers is to build a machine which assesses, replicates and reacts to emotions assisted by new sensors, hardware and algorithms. The emergence of social and affective computing has enmeshed emotions into an inter-disciplinary alloy of operations cutting across multiple discipline domains.

Relational Agents in Artificial Intelligence

Emotional intelligence is tacitly inferred in the domain of artificial intelligence, under the notion of "relational agents" conceptualized as computational relics conceived to build enduring social and emotional bonds with their users.[44] Many studies found the conceptualization of emotional agents to be effective in a wide variety of settings ranging from education to elder care[45] to public places like shopping malls.[46] In a study of virtual educators, the respondents could differentiate virtual agents with dissimilar teaching styles and found that the agents exhibiting the least relationship oriented behaviors to be less appealing and least human-like.[30-a] Earlier studies confirmed that several factors in humans, artificial agents and in the relevant interacting environment can influence the mutual trust and performance of human–robot teams.[47] As an illustration, consider our conviction that emotional intelligence of members of a team (human as well as artificial agent) triggers team dynamics, such as human–agent affinity, communication, cooperation, team management and the like which in turn impacts mutual trust among team members and team's performance.[45] Earlier research has shown that emotionally intelligent artificial agents are perceived as highly reliable and trustworthy.[48] A research study examined the perceptions of humans about emotional intelligence in artificial agents, assessing the relevance of various factors in social behavior apart from the substance of the message, tonality of voice, mannerism and gesticulating. The results showed that robots are capable of exhibiting emotional intelligence in human–robot interactions similar to those displayed by human beings.[49]

EMOTION RECOGNITION AND SIMULATION

Recognition of emotion and its simulation have topped the chart of researchers in the area of interface between man and the machine, in the recent past. The emerging field of emotional intelligence is concerned with exampling, identification and regulation of human emotions. The domain presents the fundamental theory and a technical foundation for emerging studies on modern generation sensor networks, smart information processing, intelligent services and many other contexts. As posited by Salovey and Mayer,[50] the five branches of emotional intelligence are awareness of one's emotions, management of emotions, self-motivation, comprehending others' emotions and relationship management. In other words, emotional intelligence is concerned with the abilities of recognizing, comprehending, regulating, and expressing emotions and utilizing such knowledge to manage interactions with others. Endeavors toward developing emotionally intelligent machines are focused on equipping these machines with the abilities to recognize and express emotions and constructing them in a virtual or physical manner. Emotions are caused by internal or external factors and they represent feelings or states of mind which influence an individual's behavior. Detection of emotion happens primarily by analyzing textual material despite the availability of other sources and methods like speech and facial expression analysis.

Emotion Detection Channels for Computers

Detection of emotions has been an attractive domain of investigation for researchers in their quest to develop potent techniques, since it is recognized as significant in the interface between humans and machines. Emotion detection was found to have a significant positive impact on areas like students' performance in e-learning;[51] enhancing driving experience;[52] and in augmenting customer satisfaction.[53]

In the domain of emotionally intelligent agents, the three sources of detecting emotions that have been identified are facial, oral and script or text. Facial recognition is shrouded in intricate network of problems and yet some suitable solutions are available. For instance, consider the task of classifying motion signatures using a support vector tool into either non-expressive group or any one of the six predefined categories.[54] Instead, a neuro-fuzzy system can be used in adaptation and learning environment to analyze facial animation characteristics.[48]

According to Burkhardt and associates, there are three stages in the analysis of emotions from oral or vocal sources, namely feature extraction, classification of data, and post-processing.[53-b] Various approaches including k-NN, linear discriminant classifiers, artificial neural networks, support vectors and hidden Markov models have been assessed for data classification and post-processing phases.[53-a, 56] In the recent times, advances in generative classifiers like Gaussian mixture models have been explored.[57]

In regards with the detection of emotion from text, there are multiple approaches which are efficient. One of the approaches is targeted to enhance the text-to-speech systems for fairy tales of children by discerning emotions.[58] Processing can also be done by a separate mixture model, depicting sentences as patterns of linguistic labels and characteristics and assessing them by matching them with emotion generation rules.[59] Several algorithms have been applied for classifying new titles on the basis of their emotional content.[60] Computers identify user's emotions on the basis of user's style of language and typing, content analysis, and changes in the rate of heartbeat. In the user's style of language and typing, distinctive variables like session time, latency, held time, pause rate, capitalization rate, typing speed and frequency of errors are taken into account.[61] In content analysis of text, one approach is to use Java API for WordNet Searching (JAWS) and the other approach is to use Natural Language ToolKit (NLTK) WordNet to identify emotion and its potency. After testing both of these approaches on multiple data sets, the second approach, namely NLTK WordNet method, has been found to be relatively more precise. Emotions of users are also detected on the basis of normal phrases and emoticons (textual smileys) from reviews or opinionative texts. An illustration of opinionative text could be as following:

"I will analyze it as one of the most fascinating phones ever brought out. Well, I do consider it to be at the tail end compared to older phones from Nokia, such as N95 and so on, but nevertheless it is a good phone."

The rate of user's heartbeat is ascertained by capturing webcam inputs on variations in skin tone during the time when user types the above text on his computer. User's momentaneous rate of heartbeat is computed via Photoplethysmography (PPG) signal derived from the skin pixels and emotion is detected on the basis of variations in the rate of heart-beat. Frames are captured at a specific rate, fps (frames per second), through normal webcam and routed through the face detection phase which serves as an input. Multiple inputs that are used for detecting emotion of users, such as user's keystroke, phonetics of text and variations in the rate of heart-beat, are discussed above. But most of the applications of present day use just one source — textual information — to identify and analyze user's emotions. Various studies indicate that the accuracy of emotion detection on the basis of textual information on different domains varies from 70 percent to 95 percent. It is believed that textual data offers only a fragment of information about user's emotions while providing incomplete information in certain cases. Data obtained from multiple sources can provide more accurate information on user's emotion.[62] Research demonstrated the superiority of combining vocal and textual sources of data for emotion recognition in terms of yielding authentic results in comparison to the use of a single source.[63] Another approach based on neural network was proposed for analyzing data from facial and vocal sources by using intelligent software agents.[64] Significant research has been focused on injecting emotions into agents, which resulted in many formal models of emotional agents.[65]

ARTIFICIAL EMOTIONAL INTELLIGENCE APPLICATIONS

The following are the applications of artificial emotional intelligence in various fields:

Market Research and Artificial Emotional Intelligence

The influence of emotions on the behavior and decision making of consumers is well-recognized and appreciated by popular brands. This is why they are eager to expend money on market research for comprehending and assessing the emotional engagement of consumers with the content of their brands.

The emotion technology company, Affectiva captures the user's chuckles, smiles, frowns, and corrugations through webcam and uses these inputs to assess user's levels of pleasure, amazement, perplexity, disarray, etc. A person's rate of heartbeat is also captured by the webcam by sleuthing about the changes in facial color matching with the heartbeat. Affectiva has converted this technology — which uses facial coding and emotion recognition software — into a cloud-based service, offering its clients the intelligence and analysis of consumers' emotional responses to digital content. A client company needs just a few jurors with normal webcams and internet connectivity to use this service. Affectiva's offering "Affdex for Market Research" captures the facial emotions expressed by prospectors when they watch a video, the analysis of which is collated and presented on a screen. It also offers its clients the models and prototypes to make good use of its comprehensive emotion database tied directly to outcomes like brand recall, sales growth, buying intent and probability of sharing. An advertisement or a video is benchmarked with those of competitors on parameters of product category, length of media, geography, and repeat views. "Affdex for Market Research" is being used by over a third of Fortune Global 100 companies including brands like Kellogg's and Mars and media firms like CBS, to enhance their content and to utilize their media budgets productively.[41] In contrast, another emotion technology company, Realeyes measures people's feelings while they watch online media content by using computer vision and machine learning technologies apart from webcams. The process runs thus, a media firm or an advertising agency or a brand first identifies a particular geographical location and target segment of people whom it wants to test. Subsequently, the program identifies a certain number of target viewers to watch the video content on their own devices at their chosen time. Thereafter, the program's algorithms analyze the facial expressions and other inputs in the cloud and provide the results on a dashboard within 24 hours. The report of Realeyes blends innovative testing with media planning insights to help video marketers and advertisers comprehend consumers' feelings and perceptions about their media content. These insights help brands, advertising agencies and media companies to improve their content and project their videos to the right audience. As estimated by Realeyes, this new technology has an enormous market potential, as nearly 70 percent of marketing outcomes depend on creative effectiveness, whereas only 10 percent of budgets are deployed in that key success driver throughout the industry, while 90 percent of budgets are generally squandered.[41, 42] As estimated by Mordor Intelligence,[66] the global Emotion Detection and Recognition (EDR) market is expected to witness a compound annual growth rate of 32.7 percent in the next five years.

Emotions and Decision Making

Until recently, artificial intelligence domain had neglected the utility of emotions and intuition in the realms of reasoning and decision making. Though several representations of the role of emotions have been pitched, their focus has largely been confined to identification of emotions,[36] synthesis of emotions as primary means for developing reliable synthetic agents[67] or in the synthesis of emotions and their effect on learning and behavior.[68]

Damasio and his associates studied patients with lesions in the prefrontal cortex and proposed that reasoning and decision-making processes depend on emotions and their associated feelings as well.[14-b] The researcher posited that a covert unconscious process of bias or swaying, termed as *somatic marker hypothesis,* guides us to make the right decision. This hypothesis posits that memories relating to the outcomes (positive or negative) of past decisions made in similar situations cause a *somatic* response which is used to mark future outcomes that are important to us by categorizing them as either harmful or useful. Hence a negative somatic marker associated with a specific future outcome acts as an alarm signaling us to avoid a specific course of action. In the event a positive somatic marker is associated with a particular course of action, the same becomes a preferred choice.[69]

Emotional Intelligence in Decision Support Systems of AI

The influence of emotions on intelligent behavior and decision-making process is significant. In a study, the role of emotional agents in decision-making process of a robot was investigated through a model based on fuzzy logic which analyzes the uncertainty inherent in emotions.[70] This resulted in the development of a small mobile robot as an emotional agent based on fuzzy logic. Decisions were made on the basis of internal and external situations while the environmental status was ascertained from sensory information. The agent responded to environmental changes and its behavior matched with a combination of emotions produced by different states. The agent's personality will have a substantial impact on decision-making process in a disaster management context.[71] The effectiveness of agent's performance in relation to its functions was dependent on the agent's ability to regulate its emotions in a disaster environment context. A new decision-making model was developed for disaster situations based on human emotional intelligence, blending the agent's personality traits with its emotional conduct as well as external situations affecting the agent. Applying distinct kind of intelligence, three varieties of rescuer agents have been put into practice in the system the objective of which was to assist disaster managers by enhancing their rescue management effectiveness.[72]

Learning Companion, Emotional Intelligence, and Affective Computing

Learning agents and other educational ventures are appealing domains for embedding emotional facets. Early research in this area can be found in the work of Huang and associates,[73] where the architecture of learning companion embedded with facial emotional display was presented with the emotion agent exhibiting various facial expressions on experimental website. The objective of this research was to offer a customized and amiable artificial learning companion enriched with personality and emotions to the student, but the challenge was to make it credible and trustworthy. The conception of "affective computing" blurred the boundaries between cognitive and non-cognitive intelligence.[74] The e-learning environment was restructured by embedding an e-learning system with a mobile agent which identifies and evaluates the student's emotional state to enable a virtual teacher's avatar to manage student's learning behavior based on his/ her learning style.

Emotional Processing in Learning Support Systems

Conscious tutoring system (CTS) presents a genetically credible intellectual agent based on functions of human brain, which is proficient in learning, incidental memory and recall.[75] As opposed to other programs embedded in cognitive agents, anecdotal memory and learning system are identical to multiple-trace theory of neuroscience. Such a cognitive agent is capable of modifying its behavior based on the memory of past behaviors in similar situations with the aid of its emotional mechanism. The design blends an authentic memory consolidation process aided by data mining algorithms. In another study, several features like speech recognition, emotion conjecture and virtual agents were integrated for student interaction in an educational context.[76] The emotional state of the target student was extracted from the analysis of verbose and was used for providing suitable dialect or conversation for student–agent interaction. Trials have shown high prospects for application of such a program. Another research presented a similar system, the central component of which is an emotional agent that influences the attitude of students towards learning by assisting them in surmounting learning impediments in one-on-one communication.[77]

Experiments on students have shown the potential of several artificial entities to identify and reveal emotions by capturing user's emotions and reacting in a manner appropriate for enhancing the e-learning processes.[72]

Emotional Agents in Robotics

Another efficacious application of emotional intelligence is robotics and similar agents. An algorithmic model of artificial emotions was presented by Suzuki and associates by blending emotions with learning and self-conformation to conceive an agent for intellectual communication between humans and robots.[78] In this model, a robot could change its emotional disposition in accordance with human gestures displayed through unified graphic media, environmental inputs and changes in robot's manner of actions and behavior. It is proposed that an intelligent agent in mobile robotics should adapt to environmental conditions in accordance with its physical and mental capabilities.[79]

Ivanovic and associates proposed a real-time agent based on conjectures, emotions and conscious processes. Their objective was to generate autonomous behaviors concordant with intelligent performance in the real world.[72] Upholding the indispensable role of emotions in the regulation and management of behavior in robotic systems, researchers proposed a real-time architecture (RTEA) that enables the regulation of behavior in robotic agents.[80]

EI PERSPECTIVE A Multilingual Conversational Agent for Migrants

Mobility of expats and emigrants has been a top priority in the political agenda of European Union in recent years. Nevertheless, technological breakthroughs of the recent times have made far greater impact in this domain than the political discourse. The project christened KRISTINA (Knowledge-Based Information Agent with Social Competence and Human Interaction Capabilities) is focused on developing novel technological interventions primarily to surmount linguistic barricades. However lofty an agenda this may appear on paper, deliverance of mobility in Europe has its own trials and tribulations.

When people get job opportunities farther from home in another Member State that they never visited, they perceive it to be challenging despite being in the Europe. Their daily hassles including the multiple language barriers, are insurmountable. It is in this context that a 'multilingual conversational agent' that fits in with its perceptiveness and capability to provide needed information, becomes a game changer. Developing such a conversational agent embedded with emotional, social and cultural intelligence was the main goal of the project. According to Leo Wanner, Research Professor in ICREA at Pompeu Fabra University specializing in computational linguistics, such a companion should ideally have features, such as automatic speech recognition (ASR), with language interpretation of transcripts to comprehend the intent of communicator; perceptive abilities to read and interpret facial expressions and gestures.

Similarly, conversational programming is independent of predetermined script; perceptivity of emotional cues; multilingual communication; and displaying venerable character design and language generation techniques. On the face of it, the list appears technologically adventurous and inconceivable, but with some sophisticated technological progression, the same appears to be within reach.

As a matter of fact, the first generation of this conversational agent that is simple to use has already been developed and is being run on tablets and laptops by Professor Wanner and his associates under the KRISTINA project. Before its use, certain settings concerning options for language, topic for conversation and so on, need to be exercised. Thereafter, KRISTINA'S virtual agent appears on screen and greets the user and shows its intent to interact while ascertaining the concerns of the user. A conversation is triggered on the basis of user's interaction with the agent. The agent is capable of interacting in German, Polish, Turkish, and Spanish languages, may offer advice on health, social and other issues of concern to the user, volunteer to read newspaper to a visually challenged user, etc.

KRISTINA may not be a big data project, but it needs to be equipped with the ability to identify the emotions of targeted people, assimilate their communication and interactive mannerisms and reciprocate in an appropriate manner.

In order to achieve this, significant volume of data on conversations of targeted groups and experts simulating the agent is required. The research team interpreted these recordings with pertinent Meta information, a major part of which is likely to be made accessible to the research community.

Professor Wanner says that it is too early to deploy KRISTINA as an independent conversational agent that can help migrants or other target groups in their daily lives since further development is needed. Due to certain constraints, the researchers and contributors associated with the project are working on individual technologies independently, though not as a coalition.

The team is working to overcome the constraints with the intent of expanding KRISTINA agent's utility to other domains. According to Professor Wanner, KRISTINA would reach its criticality in its second or third generation application.

Sources: 1) *cordis.europa.eu/project/rcn/194272*;

2) Research * eu, No. 74, July 2018. Published by European Commission by the Community Research and Development Information Service (CORDIS), Luxembourg.

The RTEA assists robotic agent in achieving its objectives in accordance with the emotional disposition and cognitive abilities, while offering autonomy to the robot in controlling its mental capacity and in assuring system's integrity.

A repertoire of experiential memory is of immense significance in long-term interactions between humans and robots. Against this backdrop, episodic memory system was proposed in an affective robot along with emotions.[70] Psychological bases were used to model the functions of cache, confinement and recovery of episodic memory and a virtual agent with emotional response causation model was applied for testing the system.

Similarly, credible and authentic agents are important in interactive environments where the agent's personality and emotions ought to augment the emotional immersion of human actor.

With this backdrop, an application-independent new model was presented wherein the agents have individual personalities and energetic emotions.[81] This model enables the display of varied set of behaviors by virtual characters in learning environments, such as Squeak e-Toys or distributed 3D spaces like Open Croquet.

Robotics in Training Autistic Children

A greater comfort, affinity, and connect is experienced by autistic children in their interactions with robots than with humans. Between the impersonal and detached computer and an interactive robot, they feel more friendly and engaged in the company of robots, which makes them perfect learning companions. The child will be encouraged to progress rapidly when he/she enjoys interacting with a socially felicitous and friendly robot during a training session.

Maja Mataric, Professor of Computer Science, Neuroscience and Pediatrics at the University of Southern California, clarifies that though such robots are expected to identify and reward desirable behavior, their real objective is to act as an interactive companion to children with autism, enabling them to learn and practice social skills.[35] Socially assistive robots designed by Matarić can interact intelligently with autistic children helping them develop competencies to identify and express emotions.[82]

Healthcare and Robotics

Similar techniques are used by Mataric and her associates in developing robots to serve heart patients and overweight adolescents. Such robots have the ability to define the exertion limits of patients in their daily exercising. The intent was not to replace human caretakers with these robots but to supplement them. With a similar objective, Jesse Hoey, Associate Professor of Health Informatics and AI at the University of Waterloo, is developing an emotionally intelligent system to help patients of Alzheimer's disease in hand washing and their other routine domestic chores.[35]

Emotional Behavior and Artificial Agents During Terrorist Threats

Multiple law enforcement agencies and security players have a common agenda in searching for novel training system to prepare their personnel for tackling crisis situations triggered by terrorist threats. All the role players in security maintenance will be able to watch the consequences of their respective actions through simulation programs using the Multi-agent Systems (MAS).[72] In another research, the scope of Belief-Desire-Intention (BDI) architecture is enlarged to sustain emotion, physiology and personality, while demonstrating its utility in dummy crisis situations.[83] The BDI architecture is a sophisticated model of reasoning based on cognitive/psychological concepts and is used by intelligent agents which enables intuitive molding of agents' behavior to supplement human intelligence.

Group Emotions and Ambient Agent

Similarly, another research contemplated an agent-based model for group emotions to help teams manage their emotional dynamics.[84] An ambient agent embedded with standard reasoning, analyzes the emotional condition of the team at present and offers a prediction for a future point in time. Suitable simulation experiments have been conducted to demonstrate that this ambient agent assists the team while suggesting a team leader as well.

Multi-agent Systems and Emotional Intelligence

Multi-agent systems (MAS) is another important research area linked to the application of emotional intelligence in artificial systems. It is an autonomous computerized framework comprising various intercommunicating intelligent agents. Such systems can resolve intricate problems that are difficult to solve or that are beyond the capabilities of an individual agent, or for a homogeneous system. The agents in a multi-agent system have several important characteristics:

- Individual agents are self-aware, and autonomous with complete or partial independence.
- Agents have only their narrow functional views with no single agent having the entire global view.
- There is no designated centralized agent to control the system.

Developing rational models for precisely defining and describing emotions is an area of interest for some researchers but their real challenge lies in the implementation of these models in artificial agents with stringent emotion specifications for emotions. Contemporary focus in this domain is directed toward empowering artificial agents to locate and identify emotions in oral, non-verbal gestures and content of written script and to express emotions through spoken words and gestures.

The term "multi-agent system" implies that a software program demonstrates the above-mentioned characteristics by utilizing the intelligent agents. Though these agents communicate and integrate their activities and tasks, they keep away from intricate and knotty exchange patterns which are assumed to be redundant.

Despite the recent successes in the application of rational approaches for methodical classification of emotions, extensive work still remains to be done. Systematic and structured models that are efficacious in characterizing intricate emotions like guilt, remorse, pride, jealousy, envy, embarrassment, reproach, shame, regret and admiration are needed.

Embodiment in Machine-User Interface

In the domain of artificial intelligence, the embodied agent is an artificial agent which interacts with its environment through a body, such as the human or that of a cartoon character, which is virtual and has no physical body or shape as such. There is a branch of AI dedicated to the development of autonomous embodied agents that are capable of interacting with humans independently. Mobile robots represent physically embodied agents, while *Ananova* (an internet-based newscaster designed to read newscasts to users) and *Microsoft Agent* are examples of graphically embodied agents. Conversational embodied agents generally have a graphical front-end as against a robotic body and they can interact with one another and also with humans using the same verbal and non-verbal demeanor of human beings.

Embodiment in general establishes a personal connection between the user and artificial agent. People would develop an affinity with a system when it has a human-like appearance or characteristics. Such a perceptional affinity establishes an emotional bond between the user and machine and also makes the user more lenient and tolerant with the machine when it commits mistakes. Many training applications and systems on e-commerce platforms have started using embodiment as means of engaging and connecting with customers and users. Though there are many robotic seals and game-based avatars in this domain, the most relevant illustration remains "*Kismet*" — a robot developed in the humanoid robotics group at MIT.[85] *Kismet* is an embodied system which can discover, identify and regulate emotions and is capable of expressing emotions in a social interaction with human beings. Though there are many systems in this area, *Kismet* remains a comprehensive illustration of state-of-the-art interface encompassing all facets of emotional intelligence.

Despite the remarkable journey of artificial intelligence since its emergence, it still has a long journey ahead. It is beyond doubt that AI machines and programs outperform humans in logical and mathematical tasks and facial recognition software is capable of reading and interpreting emotions displayed on human faces. Nevertheless, the domain of emotional intelligence extends beyond the identification of emotions, to include the ability to comprehend emotional context and also in responding to emotions appropriately. The current AI programs are yet to reach the sophistication and confidence levels such that the users in online chat rooms assume and believe that their interactions are happening with humans rather than with machines. The rapid development and progression witnessed by the computers and AI technology domains in the past few decades brighten the prospects of AI technology in terms of matching or even surpassing humans in emotional intelligence in the near future.

Chapter Synthesis

Artificial psychology is the study of thinking processes similar to that of human mind, executed by an artificial intelligence system. It is concerned with designing self-evolving artificial intelligence systems which can perform intellectual processes in an autonomous and judicious manner. The theoretical discipline of artificial psychology was first conceived by Dan Curtis in 1963, postulating that artificial intelligence matches human intelligence when three important conditions are fulfilled. First, the AI system should be independent and autonomous, capable of taking decisions even when information is incomplete. Second, the AI should self-evolve by reprogramming. Third, the first and second conditions should be fulfilled even in unique contexts not conceived at its initial design.

The concept of artificial cognition refers to the processes adopted by AI machines to understand, synthesize, retract and apply the information acquired by them. Artificial intuition on the other hand is the ability of AI to function with clarity and precision despite ever-changing situations, contradictions, uncertainty, and misinformation.

Emotions are feelings triggering physiological and psychological changes influencing human behavior and motivation. But inanimate computers are devoid of emotions and therefore cannot react to users' emotional condition. But when computers acquire the ability to identify the emotional states of users, they become smart and helpful in many applications like perceptual computing — an artificial intelligence function where computers adapt to the context and interact with users. Face-tracking software that detects and interprets changes in our facial expressions is already a reality. Today's artificial intelligence can decode nearly every emotion from our face or speech, identifying the most private aspects like our sexual preferences, political inclinations, or our IQ by scanning our faces. Social media platforms deploy an army of engineers to develop emotional pathways for attracting and addicting people with their content. A large amount of data on billions of people is reportedly serving as fodder for some of the most advanced machine-learning algorithms of Facebook and Google. It is predicted that by 2020, people will most likely converse more with a chatbot than with their spouse.

Recent advances in AI indicate that AI can outsmart humans even in pursuits that required intuition. Specifically, AI is proving to be better than humans in predicting human behavior, attitudes and needs like driving a vehicle in a street congested by pedestrian traffic, loaning money to unknown persons, or bargaining a business deal. The threat of AI displacing humans in a wide range of jobs in the domain of humans is looming large. Including that of artists, no job appears to be immune to automation in the distant future. Emotions are found to be derivatives of a biochemical process. Therefore machine-learning algorithm can identify our personality type or changes in our moods by analyzing the biometric data flowing from our body sensors.

Despite its increasing dominance, AI infused with emotions remains a landmark initiative enhancing human experience. Amazon and Google seem to have employed playwrights and comic columnists to develop EQ-embedded chatbot. Affectiva is a company wedded to embed the digital world with emotional intelligence to augment the technology domain. Its founder believes that emotional intelligence is crucial for compassionate and ethical AI systems. The interactive personal assistants ***Siri*** and ***Amazon Echo*** can communicate in colloquial accent. Research has unveiled virtual doctors and teachers conducting effective interactions with patients and students.

Emotion analysis for machine adaptation depends on emotion lexicon — a repertoire of words having emotional substance or significance. The emotion lexicon, 'EmoCues-28' has a list of words reflecting 28 categories of emotion. But emotion cannot just be understood or interpreted by words in isolation without the context. Obtaining context requires volumes of data and processing capabilities and the recent deep learning algorithms are trying to support this.

In the recent past, AI scientists developed machines that can identify, manage, understand, reason and express emotions effectively. In 2017, Sony developed and released it robot companion, Aibo, a revolution in autonomous entertainment. While bringing fun and joy to the entire household, Aibo bonds with the whole family. Emotional intelligence is inferred in AI under the notion of 'relational agents'. Many studies supported that relational agents are effective in a wide variety of settings from education to elder care.

Artificial emotional intelligence technology has been embraced by a wide range of applications. Its adoption in market research is notable since the influence of emotions on consumers' behavior and decision making is well-recognized by marketers. The emotion technology company, Affectiva uses facial coding and emotion recognition software and offers its clients the intelligence and analysis of consumers' emotional responses to digital content through 'Affdex for market research', which is now used by a third of Fortune Global companies. Another emotion technology firm, Realeyes developed a program which captures people's feelings while they watch online media content and provides a report to its clients. The report blends innovative testing with media planning insights to help video marketers and advertisers to comprehend consumers' feelings and perceptions to improve their content and focus.

The role of emotional agents in decision-making process of a robot was tested by a model based on fuzzy logic, and a small robot was developed as emotional agent.

Learning agents and other educational applications have become appealing for EI embedded AI systems. Conscious tutoring system presents a genetically credible intelligent agent proficient in learning, incidental memory and recall and is based on functions of human brain. In another study, several features like speech recognition, emotion conjecture and virtual agents were integrated for student interaction in an educational context. Student–agent interactions have shown that when artificial entities react by identifying user's emotions and respond by expressing emotions, there was enhanced e-learning experience.

Suzuki and associates presented a model of artificial emotions wherein a robot could change its emotional disposition in tune with human gestures displayed through unified graphic media, as well as environmental inputs and changes in robot's manner of actions and behavior. Others proposed a real-time architecture (RTEA) to regulate behavior in robotic agents based on conjectures, emotions and conscious processes. Socially assistive robots designed by Mataric could bond and interact intelligently with autistic children helping them develop emotional competencies, in identifying and expressing emotions. Mataric and her associates also develop robots to serve heart patients and overweight adolescents, equipped to define the exertion limits of patients in their daily exercising. Jesse Holey of University of Waterloo is developing an emotionally intelligent system to help Alzheimer patients in hand washing and other routine domestic chores.

Multi-agent system is an important means of implementing emotional intelligence in artificial intelligence systems. It is an autonomous computerized framework comprising various intercommunicating intelligent agents. Simulation programs using multi-agent system were found to be useful in training multiple law enforcement agencies in handling terrorist threats.

The application of embodied agent is gaining ground in the domain of artificial intelligence. Embodied agent is an AI agent that interacts with its environment through a virtual body like that of a cartoon character devoid of a physical body or shape as such. An exclusive branch of AI is dedicated to the development of autonomous embodied agents capable of independent interactions with humans, establishing a personal connection between the user and artificial agent. Such affinity establishes an emotional bond between them. The most comprehensive illustration of artificial AI embedded with all facets of emotional intelligence is "'Kismet" — a robot developed in the humanoid robotics group at MIT. It can identify, regulate and express emotions in social interactions with humans.

Despite significant progress in the domain of AI–EI interface, AI still has an elongated journey ahead. The current AI programs are yet to reach the sophistication levels of confidence in emotional intelligence similar to the levels displayed in humans, beyond emotion recognition. However, the progress achieved by AI domain in the past few decades brightens its prospects of matching or even surpassing humans in emotional intelligence in the near future.

KEY TERMS

Artificial psychology
Cognitive psychology
Sports psychology
Artificial cognition
Artificial intuition
Artificial intelligence
Face-tracking software
Artificial agents
Filter bubbles
Neuroscience
Pattern identification
Heuristics
Biochemical algorithms
Chatbot
Emotional technology
Mood reader
Career locator
Digital assistants
Affective computing
Emotion lexicon
Multimodal processing
Relational agent
Text-to-speech systems
Linguistic labels
Textual smileys
Emotional engagement
Emotion database
Synthetic agents
Fuzzy logic
Learning agents
Learning companion
Robotics
Real-time architecture
Experiential memory
Episodic memory
Multi-agent system
Embodiment
Developmental psychology
Machine-learning algorithms
Virtual personal assistants
Somatic marker hypothesis
Multilingual conversational agent
Conscious tutoring system

REVIEW QUESTIONS

1. Explain the following terms:
   a. Artificial psychology
   b. Artificial cognition
   c. Artificial intuition
   d. Artificial intelligence
2. 'Artificial intelligence is a threat to humanity'. Do you agree? Why? Or Why not?
3. Explain with illustrations, the need for artificial intelligence to be emotionally intelligent.
4. What is emotion technology? Name two emotion technology companies and illustrate the services provided by them.
5. What do you understand by emotion lexicon and affective computing?
6. Explain the emotion detection channels for computers and various approaches for the same.
7. Illustrate artificial emotional intelligence applications in market research and decision-making.
8. Explain the following applications
   a. Learning companion
   b. Affective computing
   c. Conscious tutoring system
9. Discuss the applications of emotional agents in robotics.
10. Illustrate robotic applications in the domains of training, healthcare, and law enforcement.
11. What is multi-agent system? Explain its features and utility.
12. Explain the concept of embodiment in machine-user interface.

Video Resources

1. **MIT Quest for Intelligence Launch: Social and Emotional Intelligence for Human-AI Collaboration: *Cynthia Breazeal*, Associate Professor, MIT**
   Link: https://www.youtube.com/watch?v=7aYKRkSUHTA
2. **Davos 2016-Issue Briefing: Infusing Emotional Intelligence into AI – A Panel Discussion at the 2016 World Economic Forum**
   Link: https://www.youtube.com/watch?v=YV4fTOSpUxs&t=14s
3. **Social and Emotional Intelligence in AI and Agents – Microsoft Faculty Summit 2017: *Mary Czerwinski***
   Link: https://www.youtube.com/watch?v=TjClkuisYOw
4. **Artificial Intelligence – Genuine Emotions: How Robots Shape Our Lives - MAK Design Summit 2017.**
   Link: https://www.youtube.com/watch?v=oADxJBafG1s
5. **Social and Emotional Artificial Intelligence: Microsoft Research – *Jesse Hoey,* University of Waterloo.**
   Link: https://www.youtube.com/watch?v=g1IeqfDays8
6. **Engineering Emotional Intelligence – *Rana Kaliouby*, Co-Founder & CSO, Affectiva. Computer History Museum**
   Link: https://www.youtube.com/watch?v=j9CNa_bC2Vo
7. **Beyond AI: Our Devices with Emotional Intelligence - *Rana el Kaliouby*, Co-Founder & CSO of Affectiva. Web Summit**
   Link: https://www.youtube.com/watch?v=0n2UqR85-Ek
8. **Teaching Machines to Feel – *Rana el Kaliouby* of Affectiva**
   Link: https://www.youtube.com/watch?reload=9&v=iQxS9Eq-hms
9. **Emotional Intelligence in a Brave new Robotic World – *Rosalind Picard*, Affective Computing Research Group at MIT: Fall 2018 The Wall Exchange Lecture. Peter Wall Institute for Advanced Studies. The University of British Columbia, Vancouver.**
   Link: https://www.youtube.com/watch?v=wq-QoYnTVls
10. **Emotional Technology – Alain De Botton. The School of Life. (Ch-8)**
    Link: https://www.youtube.com/watch?v=5u45-x0-zoY

Analysis of Select Movies

1. ***E.T. the Extra-Terrestrial (1982)***

   This movie, directed by Steven Spielberg and produced by Kathleen Kennedy and Steven Spielberg, won four Oscars. It is a narration about a lad Elliott, who develops friendship with an alien labeled "E.T.", who happens to be lost and abandoned on earth and whose only intent is to return to his alien abode. Elliott and his kinsmen assist E.T. in going back to its home while protecting it from the attention of the government. This movie illustrates the development of emotional intelligence in children.

   Elliot is the son of divorced parents but assumes the care of a benign and intelligent alien, E.T., who lost its way on earth and is eager to return to its home. E.T. is endowed with the powers of telepathy and telekinesis through which the alien communicates its emotions to Elliott who then realizes that E.T. is desperate to return to its home. Coincidentally, both yearn for the soothing coziness and protection of home and family and therefore, both of them save each other through love and companionship.

A strong bond of friendship develops between Elliott and E.T., as the lad shows tolerance and compassion, amiably leading the alien into his living space and introducing it to his world. Beneath the rough patch between Elliot and his siblings, Michael and Gertie, there is a shared understanding and love for each other. This can be seen in their bonding and mutual cooperation to help the alien.

The incident where Elliott releases a band of frogs doomed for dissection in a science lab, amply demonstrates his certitude and benevolence. The allusions about divorced parents and the hints at father courting adventures show the damaging impact of divorce upon the families. Specifically, the negative impact of parental separation upon children and their emotional make-up is well presented. The movie E.T. epitomizes immaculate emotions, virtuous benevolence and camaraderie.

2. ***I, Robot (2004)***

Directed by Alex Proyas and produced by Lawrence Mark and others, this futuristic science fiction movie is picturized in the contextual background of the year 2035 in the city of Chicago. We are taken to a timeline where humans are assisted by robots in their day-to-day activities, childcare and other household chores. Set in space-age, we find that everyone else has a robot deployed in their homes as helper in this movie. But we also find a police officer, detective Del Spooner who is antagonistic to tech gadgets and detests robots preferring to go with his emotions and antiquated things.

When Dr. Alfred Lanning, a robotic scientist is dead, detective Spooner is brought to the crime scene at a multinational company, US Robotics and incidentally, the victim happens to be an old friend of Spooner. The company is engaged in the production of NS-4 robot and its upgraded version, called NS-5. When detective Spooner arrives at the crime scene of his old friend's death, he refuses to accept the suicide theory provided by the company chief, Lawrence Robertson. The detective takes up the investigation to find the real cause of death reinforcing his bias against robots. While pursuing a robot named Sonny, Spooner comes in contact with a robot scientist, Dr. Susan Calvin. Sensing a robot conspiracy against humans, both of them team up to resolve the enigma of Dr. Lanning's death.

In the past, Spooner met with an accident wherein he was saved by a robot from the mangle of the car crash under the water. In this incident the robot neglects to save a little girl as it estimated a mere 11% chance of her survival, which upset Spooner. This incident left a strong negative impression in his mind triggering his motivation to prove robots as unreliable and troublesome. The absence of emotional ability is one of the reasons for Spooner's repulsiveness to robots. Undoubtedly, robots were portrayed as rational and intelligent devices devoid of human emotions, for almost a century now. Therefore, it is apparent that this movie is not an account of human versus computers but is essentially about emotion versus logic; impulse and bias versus rationale. Whether humans or machines, the movie characters expressing emotion and instinct are elevated against those devoid of emotion. Detective Spooner and special robot NS-5 are distinguished for their common attributes of emotion as well as intellect. Similarly, characters exhibiting purely rational intellect, such as the Chairman of US Robotics, Dr. Susan Calvin and the super-computer are portrayed as being susceptible to oversight and indiscretion. As shown in the movie, what seems to be noteworthy is whether one is emotional or not, irrespective of whether one is a human or a machine. In a sense, the movie provides a perspective of how we become inimical to ourselves due to the bounds of human reasoning and rationality. And, it's not the technology that is the culprit. Sonny, the robot is characterized by high IQ while its emotions are at the lowest level to that of a child. The distinction between intellect and emotion, impulse and reasoning, is more pronounced in Spooner's character as he followed his instincts looking for something amiss, and hence is the right choice to inquire into the murder. Realistically looking at the character of Detective Spooner, his objective is to prove his misgivings and bias against robots as opposed to investigating a crime. On the other hand, Dr. Susan Calvin is single minded and logical who strives hard to sustain her commitment toward rationality as her entire belief system was founded on it. Nevertheless, with the unfolding of events, she is confounded by the barriers of science and emotion that shatter her convictions and perspectives enabling her to open up.

Emotionality has been considered as the most important characteristic differentiating the human and the machine. The emotional component of our intellect is also not significantly subjugated to other components of human cognition like reasoning.

3. ***Bicentennial Man (1999)***

This film, directed by Chris Columbus and produced by Chris Columbus and others, is the story of Andrew, a robot who serves a family, outliving them due to his outstretched lifespan of two hundred years. The movie deals with emotions in robots, the nuances of enslavement and the value of being human alongside the issue of employing robotic menials in ordinary homes.

Serving the same family for two hundred years, the Bicentennial robotic man acquires the ability to express emotions and care for the people in his surroundings. Nevertheless, as human beings are mortals, Andrew had to endure the pain of losing members of his beloved family who cared for him during his long span of life. Ultimately, Andrew reconciles by espousing the philosophy that inevitably all humans have to die one day or the other. He develops the capacity to love, closely connect and bond with another individual in the movie during his lifespan of two centuries.

Soon after Andrew's arrival at his master Richard Martin's home where he was deployed to serve, he was found to be happily enjoying by listening to music. Apart from displaying such artistic sensitivity, Andrew also exhibits the attributes of ingenuity, imagination and wittiness. He begins to feel concerned about people in his life and takes good care of them. Despite transforming himself to become more like humans, Andrew continues to work as a menial at Martin household, perhaps on account of his devotion to the family or the family's affectionate bonding with Andrew, or still due to the enslavement of the robot for the personal service of Martin's family. Andrew acquires the talent of carving out things from wood with delicacy, sensitivity and focus. He is exhorted by Richard to acquire knowledge in liberal arts, social sciences and other related domains to comprehend the ideas which could not be understood solely by a rational mind. On being allowed to accumulate and save from his own income, Andrew's wealth grows multifold over the longitude of his life. Unwillingly relenting to Andrew's request for freedom from Martin's household, Richard frees him from the household as well as from his house, liberating him completely. Andrew ventures out into the world in search of other robots to find if they are alike. Soon he discovers that his version of robots have long become obsolete. But to his delight he finds Rupert Burns, a robotic designer who is in the lurch and teams up with him while agreeing to fund the project of upgrading Andrew's body to that of a near human. Both collaborate to develop the next generation robot. Accordingly, Andrew's parts get replaced with a human look-alike and he also acquires the ability to age over time, just as humans.

He meets with "little Miss", as he used to call Amanda Martin in the Martin household, who ages into an older woman. Andrew is amazed to see her granddaughter, Portia to be her replica in appearance. They navigate their lives in the bonds of friendship amidst Andrew's struggle to live as a human, his efforts towards being proclaimed as a human and his intent to die as a human being. Progressively, Andrew evolves into a human with his new skin and prosthetic organs. He turns into an android while deserting his robotic frame and mechanistic persona. While gaining acceptance as a human he falls in love with Amanda's look-alike granddaughter, Portia who accepts him and reciprocates his feelings. His endeavors to transform himself into a human illustrates the visceral worth of life. His fight for human rights evokes the memories of racial conflicts endured by mankind for centuries. The film demonstrates the dignity of identity, the invaluable worth of family, camaraderie and love and the fragrance of natural emotions.

Andrew appeals to the World Congress to acknowledge him as human so that he could legally marry Portia. But his request is denied on the grounds that Andrew is an immortal in their view and hence cannot be a human. Over the next hundred years, he converts parts of his body into degradable ones enabling him to grow old. At long last, the aged and feeble Andrew at the tail end of his life makes a final appeal to the World Congress over a video conversation. While concurring to discuss the matter, the Speaker questions his intent in seeking this declaration. Andrew responds by saying that he wanted his true self and existence to be recognized for what he is and nothing beyond — neither for glory nor for any kind of endorsement. He adds his intent for acceptance of the truth of his being so that he could live and die with dignity.

When Andrew and Portia are in their last stage of life edging on life support systems, the Speaker of the World Congress eventually declares the court's verdict through a telecast that Andrew is accepted as the oldest, non-biblical human being in history, aged 200 years old. The Speaker also authenticates the marriage of Portia and Andrew, though Andrew passes away just before the final announcement. Portia ends her life by euthanasia through a human-android nurse, with an intent to join her husband.

This film wakes us up to ponder if machines could become more human than humans in future — the machine-kind demonstrating mankind-ness and the man devoid of kindness.

REFERENCES

1. a. Crowder, J. A., Friess, S. (2010). "Artificial Neural Emotions and Emotional Memory." *International Conference on Artificial Intelligence, ICAI'10* (July 2010).
   b. Crowder, J. A. (2010). "Flexible Object Architectures for Hybrid Neural Processing Systems." *International Conference on Artificial Intelligence, ICAI'10* (July).
2. Crowder, J. A., Carbone, J. (2011). *The Great Migration: Information to Knowledge using Cognition-Based Frameworks*. New York: Springer Science.
3. a. Crowder, J. A. (2011a). "The Artificial Prefrontal Cortex: Artificial Consciousness." *International Conference on Artificial Intelligence, ICAI'11* (July).
   b. Davis, M., and Whalen, P. J. (2001). "The amygdala: vigilance and emotion." *Molecular Psychiatry,* Vol. 6:13–34.
   c. Eichenbaum, H. (2002). *The Cognitive Neuroscience of Memory.* New York: Oxford University Press.
   d. Crowder, J. A. (2011b). "Metacognition and Metamemory Concepts for AI Systems." *International Conference on Artificial Intelligence, ICAI'11* (July).
4. a. LeDoux, J. E. (1996). *The Emotional Brain*. New York: Simon and Schuster.
   b. LeDoux, J. E. (2000). "Emotion circuits in the brain." *Annual Review of Neuroscience*, Vol. 23:155–184.
   c. LeDoux, J. E. (2002) *Synaptic Self: How our brains become who we are*. New York: Viking.
   d. Levine, P. (1997). *Walking the Tiger: Healing Trauma*. Berkeley, CA: North Atlantic Books.
   e. Yang, Y., and Raine, A. (2009). "Prefrontal structural and functional brain imaging findings in antisocial, violent, and psychopathic individuals: a meta-analysis." *Psychiatry Research: Neuroimaging,* Vol. 174 (2): 81–8.
5. Ashcroft, M. (1997). *Human Memory and Cognition*. Prentice Hall Professional.
6. a. Kosko, G. (1986). "Fuzzy Cognitive Maps," *International Journal of Man-Machine Studies*, Vol. 24(1): 65–75.
   b. LaBar, K. S., and Cabeza (2006). "Cognitive neuroscience of emotional memory." *Nature Reviews Neuroscience*, Vol. 7(1): 54–64.
7. http://artificial-intuition.com/intuition.html
8. https://intuview.com/artificialintuition
9. Marsella, S., and Gratch, J. (2002). "A Step towards Irrationality: Using Emotion to Change Belief". *1st International Joint Conference on Autonomous Agents and Multi-Agent Systems*, Bologna: Italy (July).

10. Harari, Y. N. (2017). *Homo Deus: A brief history of tomorrow*
11. a. Tegmark, M. (2017). *Life 3.0: Being human in the age of artificial intelligence*. New York, NY: Knopf.
    b. Alasaarela, M. (2017). "The rise of emotionally intelligent AI." *https://machine learnings.co/the-rise-of-emotionally-intelligent-ai-fb9a814a630e*. Date accessed: 29-11-18.
12. Yung, C. L. (2015). *ProductiviChi: Unleashing Your Productive Power*, Author House, Bloomington, IN. USA.
13. Russell, S. J., and Norvig, P. (1995). *Artificial Intelligence: A Modern Approach*. Prentice Hall, New Jersey: 1995.
14. a. Ledoux, and Joseph. (1996). *The emotional brain: the mysterious underpinnings of emotional life*. New York, NY: Touchstone.
    b. Damásio, A. R. (1994). *Descartes' error: emotion, reason and the human brain*. New York, NY: Avon books.
    c. Damasio, A. R., Grabowski, T., Bechara, A., Damasio, H., Ponto, L. L., Parvizi, J., and Hichwa, R. D. (2000). "Subcortical and cortical brain activity during the feeling of self-generated emotions," *Nature Neuroscience*, vol. 3 n° 10, October, pp. 1049–1056.
    d. Damásio, A. R. (2001). "Emotion and the Human Brain." *Annals of the New York Academy of Sciences*, Vol. 935: 101–106.
    e. Nesse, R. M. (1994). "Computer emotions and mental software." *Social neuroscience bulletin, Vol.* 7, n° 2, spring, pp. 36–37.
    f. Frijda, N. H. (1993). "The place of appraisal in emotion." *Cognition and Emotion*. Vol. 7: 357–387.
    g. Barkow, J. H., Cosmides, L., and Tooby, J. (1992). (Eds.) *The Adapted Mind: Evolutionary Psychology and the Generation of Culture*. New York, NY: Oxford University Press, 1992.
    h. Plutchik, R. (1980). *Emotion: a psycho evolutionary synthesis*. New York, NY: Harper & Row.
    i. Ghiselin, M. T. (1973). "Darwin and Evolutionary Psychology." *Science* Vol.179 (4077, March 9, 1973): 964–968.
    j. Custódio, L., Ventura, R., and Pinto-Ferreira C. (1999). "Artificial emotions and emotion-based control systems". *Proceedings of 7th IEEE International Conference on Emerging Technologies and Factory Automation*. Vol. 2: 1415–1420.
    k. Petta, P., and Trappl, R. (2001). *Emotions and agents. Multi-agents systems and applications*. Springer-Verlag: New York, NY, USA. pp. 301 - 316.
    l. Petta, P., and Cañamero, D. (2001). (Eds.) "Grounding emotions in adaptive systems: volume II." *Cybernetics and Systems: An International Journal*. Vol.32: 581–583.
    m. Gadanho, S. and Hallam, J. (2001a). "Emotion-triggered learning in autonomous robot control." *Cybernetics and Systems: An International Journal*. Vol. 32 (July): 531–559.
15. Norman, D. (2004). *Emotional Design: Why we love (or hate) everyday things*. Basic Books, New York: 2004.
16. Gurardian.com (2017). (https://www.theguardian.com/technology/2017/sep/12/artificial-intelligence-face-recognition-michal-kosinski).
17. https://techcrunch.com/2017/10/07/alex-stamos/
18. https://www.gartner.com/smarterwithgartner/gartner-predicts-a-virtual-world-of- exponential-change/
19. Harari, Y. N. (2018). *21 Lessons for the 21st century*. London: Jonathan Cape.
20. Kahneman, D. (2011). *Thinking fast and slow*. New York: Farrar, Straus U Giroux.
21. World Health Organization, (2015). *Global status report on road safety* 2015. Geneva: WHO, 2016; World Health Organization, Estimates for 2000–2015, cause-specific mortality. http://www.who.int/healthinfo/global_burden_disease/estimates/en/indexI.html. Accessed 6 September 2017.
22. Fagnant, D. J. and Kockelman, K. (2015). "Preparing a nation for autonomous vehicles: Opportunities, barriers and policy recommendations," *Transportation Research Part A: Policy and Practice 77, pp. 167–181*. OECD/ITF (2016). *Road Safety Annual Report, 2016*. Paris: OECD.

23. Kusano, K. D. and Gabler, H. C. (2012). "Safety benefits of forward collisions warning, brake assist, and autonomous braking systems in rear-end collisions." *IEEE Transactions on Intelligent Transportation Systems, 13 (4): 1546–1555*; James M. Anderson et. al., (2014). *Autonomous vehicle technology: A guide for policymakers*. Santa Monica: Rand Corporation.
24. Youyou, W., Kosinski, M., and Stillwell, D. (2015). "Computer-based personality judgements are more accurate than those made by humans." *Proceeding of the National Academy of Sciences of the United States of America*, Vol. 112 (4) January 27: 1036–1040.
25. Dredge, S. (2017). "AI and music: Will we be slaves to the algorithm?" *Guardian,* 6 August.
26. Fatemi, F. (2018). "Why EQ + AI is a recipe for success." https://www.forbes.com/sites/falonfatemi/people/falonfatemi/#f58b5155bd9b. May 30, 2018. Date accessed: November 29, 2018.
27. Picard, R. (2004). Toward machines with emotional intelligence. In: ICINCO (Invited Speakers). pp. 29–30.
28. Buitrago, M. P. (2017). "Artificial intelligence keeps evolving: The introduction of emotional intelligence." https://www.30secondstofly.com/ai-software/artificial-intelligence-and-emotional-intelligence/. Date accessed: December 18, 2018.
29. Johnson, K. (2017). "Affectiva CEO: AI needs emotional intelligence to facilitate human-robot interaction." (https://venturebeat.com/2017/12/09/affectiva-ceo-ai-needs-emotional-intelligence-to-facilitate-human-robot-interaction/) December 9, 2017. Date accessed 18-12-18.
30. a. Baylor, A., and Kim, Y. (2005). "Simulating instructional roles through pedagogical agents." *International Journal of Artificial Intelligence in Education* 15(2): 95–115.
    b. Pontier, M., and Siddiqui, G. (2008). "A virtual therapist that responds empathically to your answers." In: *Intelligent Virtual Agents*. pp. 417–425. Springer, Berlin/Heidelberg.
31. a. Pajupuu, H., Kerge, K., and Altrov, R. (2012). "Lexicon-based detection of emotion in different types of texts: Preliminary remarks." *Eesti Rakenduslingvistika Ühingu Aastaraamat*, (8), 171–184.
    b. Taboada, M., Brooke, J., Tofiloski, M., Voll, K., and Stede, M. (2011). "Lexicon-based methods for sentiment analysis." *Computational Linguistics*, *37*(2), 267–307.
32. Mohammad, S. M. (2012). Portable features for classifying emotional text. In *Proceedings of the 2012 Conference of the North American Chapter of the Association for Computational Linguistics: Human Language Technologies (NAACL: HLT-2012)* (pp. 587–591). Montreal, QC.
33. a. Mohammad, S. M., Zhu, X., and Martin, J. (2014). "Semantic role labeling of emotions in tweets." In *Proceedings of the ACL 2014 Workshop on Computational Approaches to Subjectivity, Sentiment, and Social Media (WASSA)* (pp. 32–41). Baltimore, MD.
    b. Nakov, P., Kozareva, Z., Ritter, A., Rosenthal, S., Stoyanov, V., and Wilson, T. (2013). "SemEval-2013 task 2: Sentiment analysis in Twitter." In *Proceedings of the 7th International Workshop on Semantic Evaluation. (SemEval 2013)* (pp. 312–320).
    c. Rosenthal, S., Nakov, P., Ritter, A., and Stoyanov, V. (2014). "Semeval-2014 task 9: Sentiment analysis in Twitter." In *Proceedings of the Eighth International Workshop on Semantic Evaluation (SemEval 2014)* (pp. 73–80). Dublin, Ireland.
    d. Yan, J. L. S., and Turtle, H. R. (2016). "EmoCues-28: Extracting words from emotion cues for a find-grained emotion lexicon." In J. Fernando Sánchez-Rada and Björn Schuller (Eds.) *Proceedings of the LREC 2016 Workshop "Emotion and Sentiment Analysis"* 23 May 2016, Portorož, Slovenia.
34. Domingos, P. (2015). *The master algorithm: How the quest for the ultimate learning machine will remake our world.* New York, NY: Basic Books.
35. Krakovsky, M. (2018). "Artificial emotional intelligence," *Communications of the ACM,* April 2018, Vol. 61(4): 18–19.
36. Picard, R. (1997). *Affective Computing*. Cambridge, Massachusetts: MIT Press.
37. Sood, S. O. (2008). Emotional computation in artificial intelligence education. *In AAAI Artificial Intelligence Education Colloquium*, pp. 74–78.

38. https://www.sony.net/SonyInfo/News/Press/201711/17-105E/index.html
39. a. Velásquez, J. D. (1998a). "Modeling emotion-based decision-making." In Cañanero, D. (ed.) *Proceedings of the 1998 AAAI Fall Symposium. Emotional and Intelligent: the Tangled Knot of Cognition*, pages 164–169. Available at: http://www.ai.mit.edu/people/jvelas/papers/velasquez-fs98.ps Accessed on 09/05/2004.
    b. McCauley, T. L. and Franklin, S. (1998). "An architecture for emotion." In *Proceedings of the 1998 AAAI Fall Symposium. Emotional and Intelligent: The Tangled Knot of Cognition.* Menlo Park, CA: AAAI Press, pp.122–127.
    c. Nehaniv, C. (1998). The First, Second, and Third Person Emotions: Grounding Adaptation in a Biological and Social World. *5th International Conference of the Society for Adaptive Behavior (SAB'98).* University of Zurich, Switzerland, August, 1998.
    d. Bazzan, A. L. C. and Bordini, R. (2001). "A framework for the simulation of agent with emotions: report on experiments with the iterated prisoner`s dilemma." *In: The 5th Int. Conference on Autonomous Agents, Montreal, New York:* ACM. 2001. pp. 292–299.
    e. Gadanho, S. and Hallam, J. (2001b). "Robot learning driven by emotions." Adaptive Behavior, 9 (1).
    f. Davis, D. N. (2000). *Modelling emotion in computational agents*. Available at: http://www2.dcs.hull.ac.uk/NEAT/dnd/papers/ecai2m.pdf. Accessed on December 2, 2018.
    g. Scheutz, M. (2004a). "Useful roles of emotions in artificial agents: a case study from artificial life". In *Proceedings of AAAI 2004.* AAAI press, pp. 42–48. Available at: http://www.nd.edu/~airolab/publications/aaai104scheutzm.pdf. Accessed on Dec. 11, 2004.
    h. Kato, T. and Arita, T. (2005). "Evolutionary Simulations based on a Robotic Approach to Emotion." *The 10th International Symposium on Artificial Life and Robotics*. Oita, Japan, February, 2005.
    i. Cañamero, D. (2001). "Emotions and adaptation in autonomous agents: a design perspective." *Cybernetics and Systems: International Journal.* Vol. 32: 507–529.
    j. Wehrle, T. (1998). "Motivations behind modeling emotional agents: whose emotion does your robot have?" In Numaoka C., Cañamero D., Petta P. (eds.): *Grounding emotions in adaptive systems, SAB'98 (5th international conference of the society for adaptive behavior) workshop notes*, Zurich, Switzerland. August 21.
40. Fellous, J-M. (2004). "From Human Emotions to Robot Emotions." In: Hudlicka, E., Cañamero, D. (eds.) *Architectures for Modeling Emotions: Cross-Disciplinary Foundations.* AAAI Spring Symposium, pp. 37–47. AAAI Press, Menlo Park.
41. Jarboe, G. (2018). "What is artificial intelligence & how does emotion AI work?" *Search Engine Journal,* June 11, 2018. https://www.searchenginejournal.com/what -is- artificial-emotional-intelligence/255769/
42. https://www.realeyesit.com/
43. a. Reilly, W. S. and Bates, J. (1992). "*Building Emotional Agents.*" Technical Report CMU-CS-92-143, School of Computer Science, Carnegie Mellon University, Pittsburgh, PA, May '92. Available at: http://www-2.cs.cmu.edu/afs/cs.cmu.edu/project/oz/web/papers/CMU-CS-92-143.ps Accessed on 9/11/2004.
    b. Elliott, C. (1994). *The Affective Reasoning Project*. Available at: http://condor. depaul.edu/~elliott/arback.html. Accessed on 02/12/2018.
    c. Breazeal, C. (2003). Emotion and sociable humanoid robots. *International Journal of Human Computer Studies*, 2003, pp. 119–155.
    d. Brave, S., and Nass, C. (2003). "Emotion in human-computer interaction." *The human-computer interaction handbook: fundamentals, evolving technologies and emerging applications*. Lawrence Erlbaum Associates, Inc.: Mahwah, NJ, USA, pp. 81–96.
44. Bickmore, T., and Picard, R. (2005). "Establishing and maintaining long-term human-computer relationships." *ACM Transactions on Computer-Human Interaction (TOCHI),* 12(2): 293–327.

45. Fasola, J., and Mataric, M. (2012). "Using socially assistive human robot interaction to motivate physical exercise for older adults." *Proceedings of the IEEE 100*, 2512–2526.
46. Kanda, T., Shiomi, M., Miyashita, Z., Ishiguro, H., and Hagita, N. (2009). "An affective guide robot in a shopping mall." In: *4th ACM/IEEE International Conference on Human-Robot Interaction (HRI)*. pp. 173–180 (March 2009).
47. a. Lohani, M., Stokes, C. K., Oden, K. B., Frazier, S. J., Landers, K. J., Craven, P. L., Lawton, D. L., McCoy, M., and Macannuco, D. J. (2017). "The impact of non-technical skills on trust and stress." In *HRI 2017, 12th ACM/IEEE International Conference in Human-Robot Interaction*, March 6–9, 2017. Pp. 191–192. New York: Association for Computing Machinery (ACM).
b. Lohani, M., Stokes, C., Dashan, N., McCoy, M., and S. E. Rivers, C. B. (2017). "A framework for human-agent social systems: The role of non-technical factors in operation success." In: *Proceedings of Advances in Human Factors in Robots and Unmanned Systems*. pp. 137–148.
c. Schaefer, K., Billings, D., Szalma, J., Adams, J., Sanders, T., Chen, J., and Hancock, P. (2014). *A meta-analysis of factors influencing the development of trust in automation: Implications for human-robot interaction*. DTIC Document, Tech. Rep.
48. a. Lohani, M., Stokes, C., McCoy, M., Bailey, C., Joshi, A., and Rivers, S. (2016). "Perceived role of physiological sensors impacts trust and reliance on robots." In: *Proceedings of 25th IEEE International Symposium on Robot and Human Interactive Communication*. pp. 513–518.
b. Lohani, M., Stokes, C. K., McCoy, M., Bailey, C., and Rivers, S. (2016). "Social interaction moderates human-robot trust-reliance relationship and improves stress coping." In: *Proceedings of 11th ACM/IEEE International Conference on Human-Robot Interaction*. pp. 471–472.
49. Fan, L., Scheutz, M., Lohani, M., McCoy, M., and Stokes, C., (2017). "Do we need emotionally intelligent artificial agents? First results of human perceptions of emotional intelligence in humans compared to robots." In: Beskow J. Perters C., Castellano, G., O'Sullivan, C., Leite, I., Kopp, S. (Eds.). *Intelligent Virtual Agents*. IVA 2017. Lecture Notes in Computer Science, Vol. 10498. Springer, Cham. Pp. 129–141.
50. Salovey, P., and Mayer, J. D (1990). "Emotional intelligence." *Imagination, Cognition, and Personality*, vol. 9: 185–211.
51. a. Li, W., Zhang, Y., and Fu, Y. (2007). "Speech emotion recognition in e-learning system based on affective computing." In *Proceedings of the 3rd International Conference on Natural Computation*, pp. 809–813.
b. Ai, H., Litman, D., Forbes-Riley, K., Rotaru, M., Tetreault, J., Purandare, A. (2006). "Using systems and user performance features to improve emotion detection in spoken tutoring dialogs." In *Proceedings of the 9th International Conference on Spoken Language Processing*, pp. 797–800.
52. Jones, C. M., and Jonsson, I. M. (2007). Performance analysis of acoustic emotion recognition for in-car conversational interfaces. Proceedings of the 4th International Conference on Universal Access in Human-Computer Interaction: Ambient Interaction, pp. 411–420.
53. a. Lee, C., and Narayanan, S. (2005). "Towards detecting emotions in spoken dialogs." *IEEE Transactions on Speech and Audio Processing,* vol. 13 (2): 293–302.
b. Burkhardt, F., van Ballegooy, M., Engelbrecht, K.-P., Polzehl, T., and Stegmann, J. (2009). "Emotion detection in dialog systems: Applications, strategies and challenges." In *Proceedings of the 3rd International Conference on Affective Computing and Intelligent Interaction and Workshops*, pp. 1–6.
54. Anderson, K., and McOwan, P. W. (2006). "A real-time automated system for the recognition of human facial expressions." *IEEE Transactions on Systems, Man, and Cybernetics*, Part B: *Cybernetics*, vol. 36 (1): 96–105.
55. Ioannou, S. V., Raouzaiou, A. T., Tzouvaras, V. A., Mailis, T. P., Karpouzis, K. C., and Kollias, S. D. (2005). "Emotion recognition through facial expression analysis based on a neurofuzzy network." *Neural Networks*, vol. 18 (4): 423–435.

56. a. Lopez-Cozar, C. Z. R. (2008). "Influence of contextual information in emotion annotation for spoken dialogue systems." *Speech Communication*, vol. 50(5): 416–433.
   b. Shafran, I., and Mohri, M. (2005). "A comparison of classifiers for detecting emotion from speech." In *Proceedings of the IEEE International Conference on Acoustic Signal and Speech Processing (ICASSP)*, pp. 341–344.
   c. Ververidis, D., and Kotropoulos, C. (2006). "Emotional speech recognition: resources, features and methods." *Speech Communication*, vol. 48: 1162–1181.
57. Attabi, Y., and Dumouchel, P. (2013). "Anchor models for emotion recognition from speech." *IEEE Transactions on Affective Computing*, vol. 4 (3): pp. 280–290.
58. Alm, C. O., Roth, D., and Sproat, R. (2005). "Emotions from text: machine learning for text-based emotion prediction." In *Proceedings of Human Language Technology Conference and Conference on Empirical Methods in Natural Language*, pp. 579–586, doi:10.3115/1220575.1220648.
59. Wu, C. H, Chuang, Z. J., and Lin, Y. C. (2006). "Emotion recognition from text using semantic labels and separable mixture models." *ACM Transactions on Asian Language Information Processing*, vol. 5 (2): 165–183.
60. Strapparava, C. and Mihalcea, R. (2008). Learning to identify emotions in text. In *Proceedings of the 2008 ACM Symposium on Applied Computing*, pp. 1556–1560.
61. Shukla, P., and Solanki, R. (2013). *Web Based Keystroke Dynamics Application for Identifying Emotional State*, Institute of Engineering and Technology, DAVV, Indore, India in Nov 2013.
62. Anil Kumar, K. M., Kiran, B. R., Shreyas, B. R., and Victor, S. J. (2015). "A multimodal approach to detect user's emotion." *Procedia Computer Science,* 70 (2015): 296–303.
63. Chuang, Z. J., and Wu, C. H. (2004). "Multi-modal emotion recognition from speech and text." *Computational Linguistics and Chinese Language Processing*, vol. 9 (2): 45–62.
64. Fragopanagos, N., and Taylor, J. G. (2005). "Emotion recognition in human–computer interaction." *Neural Networks*, vol. 18 (4): 389–405.
65. Steunebrink, B. R., Dastani, M., and John-Jules, C. M. (2012). "A formal model of emotion triggers: an approach for BDI agents." *Synthese*, vol. 185, no. 1, pp. 83–129.
66. Mordor Intelligence (March, 2018).https://www.mordorintelligence.com/industry- reports/emotion-detection-and-recognition-edr-market.
67. a. Bates, J. (1994). "The Role of Emotion in Believable Agents." *Communications of the ACM* 37(7):122–125.
   b. Blumberg, B. (1994). "Action-Selection in Hamsterdam: Lessons from Ethology." In *Proceedings of SAB94*, 108–117. Brighton, England: MIT Press.
   c. Elliot, C.D. (1992). "The Reasoner: A Process Model of Emotions in a Multi-Agent System." Ph.D. Thesis, Institute for the Learning Sciences, Northwestern University.
   d. Maes, P. (1995). "Artificial Life meets Entertainment: Lifelike Autonomous Agents." *Communications of the ACM. Special Issue on Novel Applications of AI.*
   e. Reilly, S. (1996). *Believable Social and Emotional Agents*. Technical Report, CMU-CS-96-138, School of Computer Science, Carnegie Mellon University.
68. a. Frijda, N. (1986). *The Emotions*. Cambridge, UK: Cambridge University Press.
   b. Kitano, H. (1995). "A Model for Hormonal Modulation of Learning." In: *Proceedings of IJCAI-95*. Montreal.
   c. Pfeifer, R. (1988). "Artificial Intelligence Models of Emotion. In: Hamilton," V., Bower, G. H., and Frijda, N. (eds.) *Cognitive Perspectives on Emotion and Motivation*, 287–320. Netherlands: Kluwer.
   d. Velásquez, J. (1997). "Modeling Emotions and Other Motivations in Synthetic Agents." In: *Proceedings of AAAI-97*.

69. Velásquez, J. D. (1998b). "When robots weep: Emotional memories and decision-making." Proceedings of the National Conference on Artificial Intelligence, 1998. American Association of Artificial Intelligence. (https://pdfs.semanticscholar.org/5deb/9fa839139ecdf9bbd961bfc343a185c463e9.pdf)
70. Kim, H. G., Yang, J. Y., and Kwon, D. S. (2013). "Episodic Memory System of Affective Agent with Emotion for Long-term Human-Robot Interaction." *10th International Conference on Ubiquitous Robots and Ambient Intelligence,* pp. 720–722.
71. Daviet, S., Desmier, H., Briand, H., Guillet, F., and Philippe, V. (2005). "A system of emotional agents for decision-support." *Proceedings of the 2005 IEEE/WIC/ACM International Conference on Intelligent Agent Technology (IAT'05),* pp. 711–717.
72. Ivanovic, M., Budimac, Z., Radovanovic, M., Kurbalija, V., Dai, W., Badica, C., Colhon, M., Ninkovic, S., and Mitrovic, D. (2015). "Emotional agents –State of the art applications." *Computer Science and Information Systems,* 12 (4): 1121–1148.
73. Huang, C. C., Kuo, R., Chang, M., and Heh, J. S. (2004). "Foundation Analysis of Emotion Model for Designing Learning Companion Agent." *Proceedings of the IEEE International Conference on Advanced Learning Technologies (ICALT'04*), pp. 326–330.
74. Wang, Z., Qiao, X., and Xie, Y. (2009). "An Emotional Intelligent E-learning System Based on Mobile Agent Technology." *International Conference on Computer Engineering and Technology*, pp. 51–54.
75. Faghihi, U., Fournier-Viger, P., Nkambou, R., Poirier, P., and Mayers, A. (2009). "How Emotional Mechanism Helps Episodic Learning in a Cognitive Agent." *Proceedings of the IEEE Symposium on Intelligent Agents, IA 2009, part of the IEEE Symposium Series on Computational Intelligence 2009,* Nashville, TN, USA, pp. 23–30.
76. Tsai, I. H., Lin, K. H. C., Sun, R. T., Fang, R. Y., Wang, J. F., Chen, Y. Y., Huang, C. C., and Li, J. S. (2010). "Application of Educational Emotion Inference via Speech and Agent Interaction." *Third IEEE International Conference on Digital Game and Intelligent Toy Enhanced Learning 2010, Kaohsiung, Taiwan,* pp. 129–133.
77. Chatzara, K., Karagiannidis, C., and Stamatis, D. (2010). "Student's attitude and learning effectiveness of emotional agents." In *Proceedings of 10th IEEE International Conference on Advanced Learning Technologies,* pp. 558–559.
78. Suzuki, K., Camurri, A., Ferrentino, P., and Hashimoto, A. (1998). "Intelligent Agent System for Human-Robot Interaction through Artificial Emotion." *IEEE International Conference on Systems, Man, and Cybernetics,* pp. 1055–1060.
79. Dominguez, C., Hasaan, H., and Crespo, A. (2004). "Real-Time Robotic Agent Based on Emotions." *Proceedings of World Automation Congress*, pp. 377–382.
80. a. Domínguez, C., Hassan, H., and Crespo, A. (2006). "Behavioral Affective Modulation of Service Robotic Agents." *IECON 2006 - IEEE 32nd Annual Conference on Industrial Electronics,* pp. 4119–412.
    b. Domínguez, C., Hassan, H., Mayans, V., and Crespo, A. (2013). "Multicore Parallel Implementation of Agent Emotional Processes." *12th IEEE International Conference on Trust, Security and Privacy in Computing and Communications*, pp. 1856–1861.
81. Masuch, M., Hartman, K., and Schuster, G. (2006). "Emotional Agents for Interactive Environments." *Proceedings of the Fourth International Conference on Creating, Connecting and Collaborating through Computing (C5'06),* pp. 96–102.
82. Okamura, A., Mataric, M., and Christensen, H. I. (2010). "Medical and health-care robotics." *Robotics and Automation Magazine* 17(3): September, 26–27.
83. Jones, H., Saunier, J., and Lourdeaux, D. (2009). "Personality, Emotions and Physiology in a BDI agent architecture: the PEP⟶BDI model." WI-IAT "09 - IEEE/WIC/ACM *International Joint Conferences on Web Intelligence and Intelligent Agent Technologies*, pp. 263–266.

84. Duell, R., Memon, Z. A., Treur, J., and van der Wal, C. N. (2009). "An Ambient Agent Model for Group Emotion Support." ACII 2009 - *3rd International Conference on Affective Computing and Intelligent Interaction and Workshops*, pp. 1–8.

85. a. Breazeal (Ferrell), C. and Velasquez, J. (1998), "Toward Teaching a Robot 'Infant' using Emotive Communication Acts." In *Proceedings of 1998 Simulation of Adaptive Behavior, workshop on Socially Situated Intelligence, Zurich Switzerland.* 25–40.

    b. Breazeal, C. (2000) *Sociable Machines: Expressive Social Exchange between Humans and Robots.* Sc.D. dissertation, Department of Electrical Engineering and Computer Science, MIT.

9

GLOBAL TRENDS IN EMOTIONAL INTELLIGENCE AND ROAD AHEAD

OPENING CASELET

2022 skills equation is not just about developing mastery in the new technologies. Life skills or the psycho-social competencies like innovativeness, initiative, originality, creativity, persuasion, and negotiation will not only exist in the 'must have' category but their significance may also increase in great proportions. Ability to have an eye for detail, resilience, adaptability, and addressing and finding solutions to complex problems will gain paramount importance. EI, leadership and social influence and the orientation to serve are bound to be more in demand in the upcoming years.

Source: **Future of Jobs Survey 2018, World Economic Forum**

After reading the previous chapters, you must have developed an understanding of emotional intelligence (EI). It is time to connect the topic of EI to the big picture. What does EI mean in the global context? What is the future of EI?

Organizations worldwide are busy preparing themselves for the future. The "gig economy" in which temporary and flexible jobs will be more common, is round the corner. Some of them do have an idea of how it is going to be, while some are still struggling. Again, mere awareness will not help, one has to gear up and become adept in order to meet the future demands. In the midst of this, the report published by World Economic Forum, the State of the Heart report by Six Seconds, Deloitte's report on the Global Human Capital Trends, World Happiness Report and findings from a few more global institutions are helping us develop a somewhat clear picture of what is in store for us. In today's era, when the societies all across the globe are fighting unforeseen demons like distraction, the rapid pace of globalization (the way it affects local economy), hyper connectivity and decreased sensitivities towards humanitarian issues, the ever increasing stress and adverse implications on health amongst other outcomes, time paucity, and distraction, the entire discussion on attention economics have attracted a lot of attention. In order to address these challenges, UN has come up with the Sustainable Development Goals (SDGs). We would like to draw your attention to the connection between the agenda 2030 (SDGs)[1] adopted by the United Nations Member States in 2015 and EI. First, let us have a look at the SDGs.

UN came up with a framework for peace and well-being for people all across the globe, not only for the present but also for the future. They have urged that the 17 goals mentioned in Figure 9.1 can be achieved through collaboration and all member states will be required to work hand in hand. There is a call for global partnership in order to achieve the SDGs.

Figure 9.1: The 17 SDGs
Source: https://sustainabledevelopment.un.org/sdgs

From bringing an end to poverty to improving health and education, to reducing the gap in gender diversity, to stimulating economic growth along with managing climate change and preserving the forests and the oceans is the need of the hour and for the next decade to say the least. Now, let us see what and how EI can fuel momentum to these global goals.

Rich Fernandez, CEO of 'Search Inside Yourself Leadership Institute', in his address at the United Nations headquarters on May 17, 2019 in a program dedicated to the discussion on Mindfulness and EI titled, 'Unlocking your Emotions to achieve the SDGs', explained very succinctly how emotional intelligence matters and why does it matter more in the current and emerging scenario by referring to the survey results released by Deloitte (2018 and 2019). In the report published by Deloitte, the changing trends in human capital, which is based on their survey of 11,000 businesses and HR leaders as well as interviews with employees from top performing organizations, state that there is a rise of business as a social enterprise.[2] According to this report, in the coming years, there will be a remarkable shift from 'shareholder' to 'stakeholder' approach and the traditional organization, the 'business enterprise' will have to transform into 'social enterprise'.

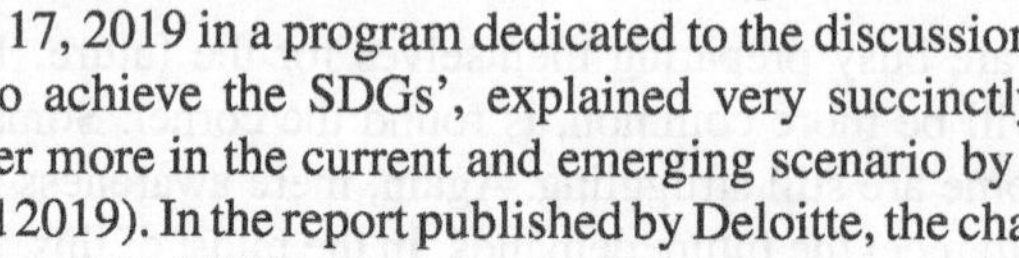

Figure 9.2: Evolution of the Social Enterprise
Source: Adapted from Deloitte Global Human Capital Trends Survey, 2018.
https://www2.deloitte.com/content/dam/Deloitte/at/Documents/human-capital/at-2018-deloitte-human-capital-trends.pdf

The report defines social enterprise[3] as, "An organization whose mission combines revenue growth and profit-making with the need to respect and support its environment and stakeholder network. This includes listening to, investing in, and actively managing the trends that are shaping today's world. It is an organization that shoulders its responsibility to be a good citizen (both inside and outside the organization), serving as a role model for its peers and promoting a high degree of collaboration at every level of the organization". The report has some interesting and valid reasoning regarding why this sudden shift of identity has happened in the context of business enterprise. Compared to the past, it is found that today many people in general have less belief and trust in their traditional political and social outfits or organizations as compared to what used to be the scenario a few decades back. So, they are looking at the businesses to address the gap/ void.[6]

Take any survey and one will find that the parameters for evaluation have undergone a seismic change. From mere measurement of profit to services and product quality, to how well they treat their own employees, their customers and the community they belong to, all the factors matter. The social impact gets measured as well. So social capital is discussed in the same breath as is financial or physical capital. Phrases like 'inclusive growth' versus 'shareholder value' are more frequently used in board rooms these days. So, organizations today are actively engaged in discussing and listening to as many stakeholders as they can and not just their customers and their own employees but also the local community, the inspection bodies and other stakeholders. This requires absolute proficiency in managing relationships. Beginning with an intention to listen to all of its multiple stakeholders to put the necessary input to action which is perceived as transparent.

There is an overall shift from individual to network or teams.[4] The 2015 report published by the same organization (Deloitte) used the term ' the naked organization'[5] (the way things get done in an organization, is becoming increasingly visible for all the world to see) the need to practice clarity while sharing information and making sincere efforts to break the silos mentality to create a collaborative, trust and credibility embedded culture in a consistent manner. EI offers a robust framework to help build these required competencies to succeed in this new organizational environment.

Organizations will never survive if they become closed systems, In the past, some individuals could still survive in certain conditions if they didn't network or collaborate so much. But in this new emerging scenario, it seems difficult rather nearly impossible, not only for organizations, but each one working in the business ecosystem to operate with a silos mentality. Symphonic existence will become the new work norm and networking and working in teams will be a global feature. It is here that EI becomes very relevant.

The purpose of any organization is to improve the situation or the state of the world. The 17 SDGs lead to this purpose which needs to get ingrained in each and every individual and subsequently, each and every nation. Also, achieving these goals will require togetherness, teaming and collaboration. In order to get this done, basic skill sets in EI not only become important but rather necessary.

We have seen that EI can be developed, we know it is possible, as discussed earlier in Chapter 6.

According to neuroscience, the research on neuroplasticity is not less than a miracle. It says that one can actually change the structure and function of brain which is responsible for various activities and processes like better attention, enhanced learning, memory, compassion, empathy, response to stress, decision making, and the list is not all exhaustive. These abilities can be enhanced, and one can become adept at these skills subsequently. Building emotional intelligence leads to building leadership, sustained performance and well-being. This in turn impacts the organizational human wealth in terms of employee engagement, operational excellence, innovation and value.[7]

In the leadership domain, with inputs of emotional intelligence, one can foster the ability to remain agile and responsive, become more compassionate and empathetic, a good negotiator and create a climate and culture of trust in and around the organization. This will lead to higher levels of employee engagement.[8]

Dr. Rich stressed, as also stated by Goleman and others, that through intentional practice, deliberate techniques and specific exercises, EI does improve. Regular practice in mindfulness and actions like collaboration, effective decision making through innovating, and leading to sustained performance is a great harbinger of operational excellence. Also, less stress and better idea of purpose coupled with increased level of motivation and engagement and better sense of well-being on part of organizational employees creates value and thus is seen as the way EI can positively affect fundamental measure of organizational excellence.[9]

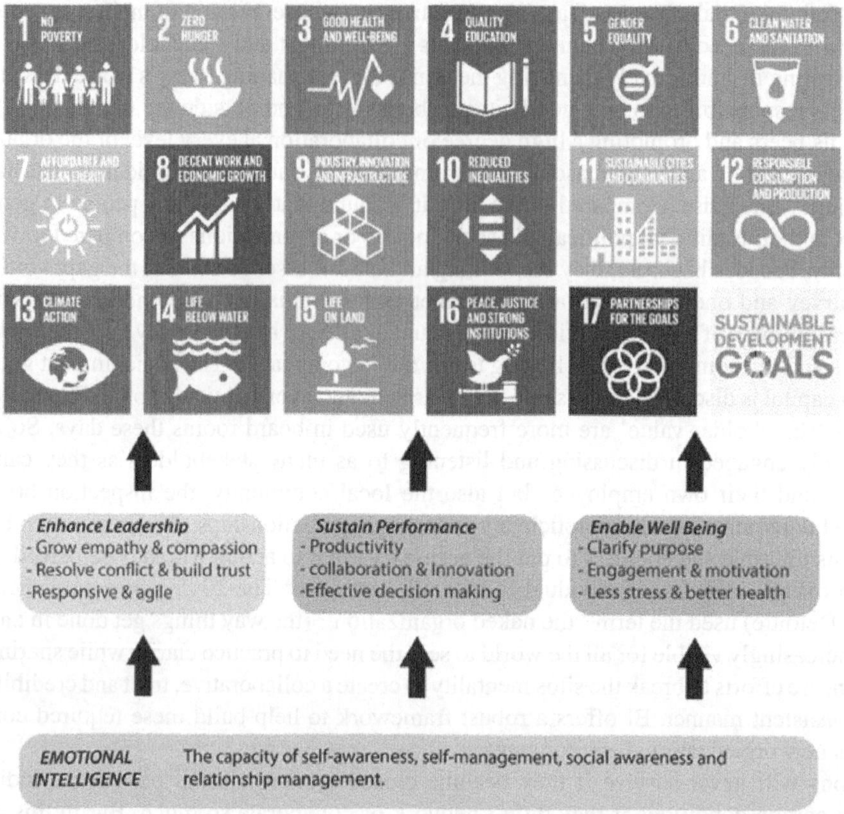

Figure 9.3: The Link between EI and Sustainable Development Goals As Mentioned by Rich Fernandez During His Presentation at the United Nations Headquarters on the Role of Mindfulness and Emotional Intelligence in Organizations
Source: https://www.youtube.com/watch?v=YR-sYxOacNA

The human principles or design principles for the social enterprise have also been redefined in order to help the business enterprise align with its new identity as a social enterprise. Not only individuals but organizations are also expected to design work in a manner that gives meaning and purpose to the people associated with the organization. Organizations will be required to create a work culture of collaboration and focus on personal relationships. Not limiting oneself to connecting just on the digital platform but creating opportunities for nurturing human relations at work will be a norm. Being able to share information openly in a transparent way will become essential and being open to discussions may become one of the basic expectations from an employee as well from an organization.[10] This, being able to reinvent, will become very crucial to existence. Moreover in gig economy, change will be the norm and therefore adapting to change will become very important.

INSIGHTS 'How to Hire for Emotional Intelligence'[11] by Annie McKee

Annie's article is a must read for all those who serve the interview panel. Some of the interesting and important insights of her article are:

- It is a well-known fact that individuals who can understand their own and others' emotions well, make good leaders.[12]
- Such people are happier at work.[13]

- In her own words, "One of the reasons we see far too little emotional intelligence in the workplace is that we don't hire for it. We hire for pedigree. We look for things like where someone went to school, high grades and test scores, technical skills, and certifications, not whether they build great teams or get along with others. And how smart we think someone is, matters a lot, so we hire for intellect".[14]
- She further says that organizations do require smart and intelligent and experienced persons but at the same time, they also need people who are skilled in managing change and motivating people and can manage positive and negative emotions well so that people can bring their best to the table.
- She recommends Behavioral - Event Interview[15] as a good tool to find out about how the person demonstrated the skill that the selection panel wants to verify and check for an overt display of EI. This tool helps us understand what a person thought, felt and did in a particular situation.
- Also, reference checking of the potential candidate and not just asking for references in resume should be a good thing to do, as suggested by her.

Source: McKee, A. (2016). How to hire for emotional intelligence. *Harvard Business Review*.

William J. Rothwell, Professor of Education at Pennsylvania State University, in his key note address during the 3rd International Conference on Organizational Development (OD) titled *Future of Work and Organization Development* at Tata Institute of Social Sciences, Mumbai, India, in 2019, sensitized the OD practitioners about the changing trends of the workplace and society at large. He mentioned the following trends.

i. Workers are aging globally, fewer children are born and people live longer.
ii. The diversity in the workplace will not be restricted to only religion, gender and nationalities but also in terms like, getting to work with retired professionals and specially challenged.
iii. Employees would be willing to trade-off money in exchange of time and flexibility.
iv. More and more employees will prefer to work from home as the availability of helpers to look after the old and the newborn will slowly either fade away or will be exorbitant for everyone to afford.
v. Young graduates will be entering the workforce with somewhat proficiency in interpersonal skills but sound technical skills.
vi. Time management will remain a challenge.
vii. Working together in teams may pose challenges. Need for teachers and facilitators will be on all time increase. People will need training on how to work together more effectively.
viii. More number of contractual workers and employees will be working on project basis, a key feature of gig economy as mentioned earlier.

A gamut of absolutely different and relevant skill sets will be required to deal with such a new scenario. There have been a series of new developments in the recent past. AI and machine learning, robotics, nanotechnology, 3D printing, and genetics and biotechnology are all developing and building on each other. These innovations have multiple implications on all kinds of activities ranging from simple to complex. Along with these, socio-economic, geopolitical and demographic developments are also changing their nature at an equally rapid pace. The interface of technology with these aspects of society will create a new scenario which seems quite promising. But this promise of prosperity comes with a prerequisite. The prerequisite is proactive adaption, not only by individuals and societies but also by organizations and governments. The nature of jobs will change, new skill sets will be required, in both old and new work environments. Ability to adjust will be the new and most sought-after trait.

Various reports including the State of the Global Workplace Gallup Report 2017, state that 85% of employees all across the world are not engaged or are actively disengaged or disconnected with their job.[16] This is quite a major concern. Addressing such an employee workforce will require managers with high EI. Understanding the needs of such a workforce and then providing them some help through coaching and mentoring is one of the major challenges today and for quite some time at least, it seems.

It has been predicted that employees may lose their jobs or may quit due to the inability to reinvent. This has a lot to do with how one needs to build an 'antifragility' inside one's system. A body of research states that people quit jobs because of their inability to learn and grow.[17] This can be very well-connected to the EI competencies of self-awareness and self-assessment. Being able to understand one's strengths and limits definitely can be a great way ahead. Practicing innovation (as defined by Goleman), which means being comfortable with new ideas, learning new and approaches can also save oneself from becoming a liability and can help one evade the risk of losing one's job to a large extent.

Authors suggest that the use and application of EI need not be limited to academia and industry. One more sensitive issue which needs to be addressed is that of 'terrorist outfits'. These outfits manipulate and brainwash young minds at a very tender age. This is one of the major global challenges. It is a classic example of how emotions get hijacked and misused. The way the politics of emotions is done, and young and tender children are brainwashed and emotionally stimulated at a very nascent stage of their life is a heartbreaking fact. Even before they mature and develop their own understanding of the emotions, they get emotionally bribed. It could be because of socialization with persons with ulterior motives or identification, peer pressure; whatever might be the reason, but it is a major challenge and needs something beyond armchair speculation.[18] By using EI models like the one given by Six Seconds, the KCG model explained in Chapter 5, with the potential families whose children may be at the risk of getting emotionally hijacked, one may get to see some light at the end of the tunnel. By making people become more aware about their emotions, helping them label their emotions appropriately and help them not let anyone mislead them thus building their emotional resilience may lead to decrease in the number of persons joining destructive terrorist outfits. Globally, this may bring more peace and save some young minds from spoiling their own as well as lives of their loved ones.

In the context of managers, if we go by the prediction based on extensive research as stated by Willliam Rothwell and others, it is important that more focus is on building skills like negotiation and change management. Being able to work with virtual and adhoc teams will become the norm and therefore, it is important to know some basics of these vital skills for future jobs, irrespective of which career one chooses to pursue.

Table 9.1: Trends set to impact business growth positively/negatively up to 2022, top ten

Trends set to positively impact business growth up to 2022	Trends set to negatively impact business growth up to 2022
Increasing adoption of new technology	Increasing protectionism
Increasing availability of big data	Increase of cyber threats
Advances in mobile internet	Shifts in government policy
Advances in artificial intelligence	Effects of climate change
Advances in cloud technology	Increasingly ageing societies
Shifts in national economic growth	Shifts in legislation on talent migration
Expansion of affluence in developing economies	Shifts in national economic growth
Expansion of education	Shifts of mindset among the new generation
Advances in new energy supplies and technologies	Shifts in global macroeconomic growth
Expansion of the middle classes	Advances in artificial intelligence

Source: Future of Jobs Survey 2018, World Economic Forum.

PRACTITIONER'S INSIGHT

Challenges in the e-VUCA world

Today, most of the companies, irrespective of their size, face disruption and are expected to respond to the need of the hour with great agility and a set of new behaviors.

If employees who have been valued for their stability and consistency, which got them excellent economic, organizational results so far, in all honesty, find it difficult to switch gears to adapt to the demands of the changing times, then it will hardly be a surprise. Why do they not change? Is it their resistance to change? Is it because of lack of emotional intelligence — self-awareness and self-management?

Experiences in reskilling of the workforce process bring out an imperative and seldom detailed skillset in emotional intelligence tool kit, which is that as a part of self-management, and for that matter in relationship management, one should reshape mindset to learn to balance the polarities, i.e. aspects that appear to be extremes/ opposites, but in fact are interdependent. Polarity needs to be managed and it cannot be avoided. Today's world and life context present to us more polarities than binary scenarios (either / or). Today we are facing more existential challenges than ever, and these can be managed well by learning the skill of polarity management.

In my view, one fails to identify which issues are binary in nature and which are of 'and' nature. Confusing one for the other is an invitation for disaster. For example, weight loss is not a polarity, as one needs to lose weight to stay fit. How do you do so — by dieting or exercising or both — is a polarity. One needs to engage in both (dieting and exercise) to get optimal results. Similarly, in today's e-VUCA (exponential, volatile, uncertain, complex and ambiguous) context, "shall I change?" is a binary lens question. It is a mistake to think on these lines. 'Not changing' is not an option. "How much do I change and how much do I remain constant/what of me needs to remain constant?" is a question that can be effectively handled through the polarity lens.

How do we do that?

1. Acknowledge that the world is e-VUCA and is going to be more so. We have limited psychic energy and one must learn to optimally utilize that energy. Human beings have an urge to resist randomness and/or ambiguity. Some of these people, as it is observed, who also don't learn to adapt to the future are the ones who struggle to accept the reality. They mostly engage in 'how can it be like this' mind trap. It is important that we unlock our energies that are vested in denial/ cribs/ disgruntlements by acknowledging the reality (v/s approving or disapproving of it) and invest the energy in identifying ways in which to deal with the impending reality.
2. Identify extremes that one is struggling with, for e.g.:
   a. practicality – what is working now and innovation — what one needs to learn to be in line with the latest technology trends,
   b. boldness – to take risks by changing career tracks and prudence — maintaining status quo as it is 'taking care of the immediate',
   c. collaboration – working with others to produce better results and self-reliance — to deliver by oneself to establish individual sense of mastery,
   d. agility – and consistency
3. Identify your priorities and goals based on your ambitions and purpose of life
4. Engage a coach to strengthen cognitive restructuring and move away from the following:
   a. Binary thinking (either / or) to 'and' thinking
   b. Judgmental lens to observation based and appreciative lens towards self
   c. Develop emotional acuity
      i. Embrace intermittent discomfort
      ii. Clear the assumptions that are creating a roadblock
5. Build the 'antifragility' muscle, becoming agile is not sufficient anymore. One will need to become anti-fragile, i.e. become stronger in face of adversity and not crumple!

a. Learn from the past
b. Overcome the tendency to opt for immediate gains, short-termism
c. Focus more on avoiding things that don't work than trying to find out what does work
d. Experiment and tinker—take lots of small risks
e. Respect the old—look for habits and rules that have been around for a long time

6. Review the success and strengthen your skills — we need to move away from only reviewing for avoiding errors or where the issues are and start enrolling ourselves in the process of identifying what works and why it works. Success review is a great Pixar strategy, worth replicating!
7. Choose to enjoy the process — the more one enjoys the process of staying relevant, hence changing constantly, the more the person is able to manage his /her resources and hence stays effective. It also propels the person to stay in the *Here* and *Now* leading to better focus and hence optimal outcomes. One needs to make a conscious choice of focusing on 'how' of life and not just 'what, where, who, when and why' of life.

Strengthening polarity management skill is a choice that all of us who will continue to encounter the new world should make!! '*Ardhanarinateshwara*', yin-yang are age old concepts. Time has come for us to apply this wisdom for our own good in today's world. This is EI 2.0, EI for the future.

"If a man would move the world, he must first move himself." — Socrates

References:

Jacobs, R. J. and Brinkerhoff, L. with Johnson, Barry (2013). "Whole System Transformation Through a Polarity Lens", *An Idea whose Time has Come*; Wiley Publication

Schwartz, Tony and Pines, Emily (2018, Oct 25). "Why Leaders Don't Embrace the Skills They'll Need for the Future", HBR

Taleb, Nassim Nicholas (2012) – ANTI FRAGILE, Allen Lane

Source: An excerpt from a discussion with Mukul S Joshi, PhD, Partner@POASSOCIATES.NET

In the era of fourth industrial revolution, where robots, machine learning and artificial intelligence are constantly changing the job profiles and nature of work, the World Economic Forum's reports titled *Future of Jobs, 2016, 2018* clearly state which skills are relevant for the jobs of future, with emotional intelligence consistently featuring in the top ten. The other skills include analytical thinking and innovation, active learning and learning strategies, creativity, originality and initiative, technology design and programming, critical thinking and analysis, complex problem solving, leadership and social influence, reasoning, problem solving and ideation, systems analysis and evaluation.

Table 9.2 shows a comparison of top ten skills that are currently on demand vis-a-vis those which will be needed in future, as per the *Future of Jobs Survey 2018* conducted by the World Economic Forum.

Table 9.2: Skills demand comparison – 2018 vs. 2022

Skills required in 2018	Skills required by 2022
1. Analytical thinking and innovation	1. Analytical thinking and innovation
2. Complex problem-solving	2. Active learning and learning strategies
3. Critical thinking and analysis	3. Creativity, originality and initiative
4. Active learning and learning strategies	4. Technology design and programming
5. Creativity, originality and initiative	5. Critical thinking and analysis
6. Attention to detail, trustworthiness	6. Complex problem-solving
7. Emotional intelligence	7. Leadership and social influence
8. Reasoning, problem-solving and ideation	8. Emotional intelligence
9. Leadership and social influence	9. Reasoning, problem-solving and ideation
10. Coordination and time management	10. Systems analysis and evaluation

Source: Future of Jobs Survey 2018, World Economic Forum

The report identifies EI as one of the common emerging skills required in the workforce across all the world regions — Eastern and Western Europe, Sub-Saharan Africa, East Asia and the Pacific, Central Asia, South Asia, Latin America and the Caribbean, North America, Middle East and North Africa.

Driver of Change	BAS	CON	EN	FS	HE	ICT	MEI	MOB	PS	OVER ALL
Changing nature of work, flexible work	46	42	46	26	20	36	36	35	63	44
Mobile internet, cloud technology	8	17	0	41	50	69	57	16	38	34
Processing power, big data	5	8	4	44	20	44	36	6	40	26
Middle class in emerging markets	15	42	0	41	40	8	21	39	13	23
New energy supplies and technologies	38	21	71	3	10	17	0	26	5	22
Climate change, natural resources	49	21	50	3	0	8	7	32	8	23
Geopolitical volatility	28	25	29	26	0	3	14	16	10	21
Consumer ethics and privacy issues	3	21	8	18	20	31	21	10	20	16
Internet of things	8	13	4	12	10	33	14	6	15	14
Longevity, ageing societies	13	17	13	9	40	14	14	3	13	14
Young demographics in emerging markets	10	17	17	24	10	3	21	13	8	13
Sharing economy and crowdsourcing	3	4	4	18	10	11	21	6	25	12
Women's economic power, aspirations	10	21	13	9	10	3	7	6	15	12
Robotics, autonomous transport	15	8	4	3	0	0	7	29	5	9
Rapid urbanisation	13	4	13	3	0	6	14	10	8	8
Advanced manufacturing, 3D printing	10	4	8	0	0	6	0	16	3	6
Artificial intelligence	5	0	8	3	0	6	7	16	5	7
Advanced materials, biotechnology	8	4	0	3	30	0	0	13	0	6

Figure 9.4 : Significance of Drivers of Change, by Industry. Share of respondents rating driver as top trend, %
Source: Future of Jobs Survey,2016 World Economic Forum.
Note: Names of drivers have been abbreviated to ensure legibility

According to the 2017 report of McKinsey Global Institute[19], employees of tomorrow will be required to spend more time on those activities that machines can't or offer less discretion and are less capable of. They will benefit from the improved productivity because of the machines used, as this will provide them with more opportunities where they can bring the distinct advantage of being human. Activities like managing the people side of the organization, applying expertise, and communicating with others are few examples. Certain routine and predictable physical activities like generating and processing data, where machines have already proved to be better than human beings will be continued and may be even with better precision. The skill shift will be towards more social and emotional skills and more profound cognitive capabilities like inventiveness, originality and logical reasoning.

Industry codes

Code	Industry
BAS	Basic and Infrastructure
CON	Consumer
EN	Energy
FS	Financial Services and Investors
HE	Healthcare
ICT	Information and Communication Technology
MEI	Media, Entertainment and Information
MOB	Mobility
PS	Professional Services

As mentioned earlier, the report on Future of Jobs[20] has an important insight to offer as far as EI is concerned. It is worth noting that the results are derived after analyzing a data set of 13 million employees across nine broad industry sectors in 15 major developed and emerging economies and regional economic regions. The researchers have done an extensive survey of Chief Human Resource Officers and other senior talent and strategy executives of top global employers. It explains in detail what the change in nature of jobs mean in the context of skills, requirement and recruitment. It has introduced a new measure called 'Skills

Table 9.3: Examples of stable, new and redundant roles, all industries

Stable Roles	New Roles	Redundant Roles
Managing Directors and Chief Executives	Data Analysts and Scientists*	Data Entry Clerks
General and Operations Managers*	AI and Machine Learning Specialists	Accounting, Bookkeeping and Payroll Clerks
Software and Applications Developers and Analysts*	General and Operations Managers*	Administrative and Executive Secretaries
Data Analysts and Scientists*	Big Data Specialists	Assembly and Factory Workers
Sales and Marketing Professionals*	Digital Transformation Specialists	Client Information and Customer Service Workers*
Sales Representatives, Wholesale and Manufacturing, Technical and Scientific Products	Sales and Marketing Professionals*	Business Services and Administration Managers
Human Resources Specialists	New Technology Specialists	Accountants and Auditors
Financial and Investment Advisers	Organizational Development Specialists*	Material-Recording and Stock-Keeping Clerks
Database and Network Professionals	Software and Applications Developers and Analysts*	General and Operations Managers*
Supply Chain and Logistics Specialists	Information Technology Services	Postal Service Clerks
Risk Management Specialists	Process Automation Specialists	Financial Analysts
Information Security Analysts*	Innovation Professionals	Cashiers and Ticket Clerks
Management and Organization Analysts	Information Security Analysts*	Mechanics and Machinery Repairers
Electrotechnology Engineers	Ecommerce and Social Media Specialists	Telemarketers
Organizational Development Specialists*	User Experience and Human-Machine Interaction Designers	Electronics and Telecommunications Installers and Repairers
Chemical Processing Plant Operators	Training and Development Specialists	Bank Tellers and Related Clerks
University and Higher Education Teachers	Robotics Specialists and Engineers	Car, Van and Motorcycle Drivers
Compliance Officers	People and Culture Specialists	Sales and Purchasing Agents and Brokers
Energy and Petroleum Engineers	Client Information and Customer Service Workers*	Door-To-Door Sales Workers, News and Street Vendors, and Related Workers
Robotics Specialists and Engineers	Service and Solutions Designers	Statistical, Finance and Insurance Clerks
Petroleum and Natural Gas Refining Plant Operators	Digital Marketing and Strategy Specialists	Lawyers

Source: Future of Jobs Survey 2018, World Economic Forum.

Note: Roles marked with * appear across multiple columns. This reflects the fact that they might be seeing stable or declining demand across one industry but be in demand in another.

Stability' to quantify the extent to which skills disruption will occur within a job, job family (related job titles) or a sector. The report states that with the nature of jobs changing rapidly in the e-VUCA where newer skill sets are continuously making their way in the desired skills sets list, EI continues to feature prominently (see the EI perspective by Dr. Mukul Joshi's EI Insight titled 'Challenges in the e -VUCA world').

In the list of the next new job roles which will emerge as most promising and with increase in numbers, sales representatives, human resource organizational development specialists are ranked higher. Managers with high competence in steering change will be in great demand as suggested by the report published by the World Economic Forum. At organizational level, providing flexible work will fail to impress as an USP as it will become the new and fundamental norm of operating in most cases. Researchers working at global level state that social skills like persuasion, emotional intelligence and teaching others will continue to be in demand and will only become more and more relevant in the coming years. Also, process skills like active listening and critical thinking will become a prerequisite for many jobs.

Today millions of professionals internationally have added their professional information on various social platforms like LinkedIn. A lot of collaborative efforts will be required to get them to work together. Collaboration skills will be required in a big way in order to connect multiple stakeholders like consulting organizations, employers, policy makers, educators amongst others.

The report also gives examples of how certain jobs are going to change the way they operate, and which skills the professionals will need more. For example, in the case of medical practitioners, because of the advent of world-class technology, their major challenge will be explaining the data or the report effectively to the patients. With the increasing sophistication in the automation of diagnosis and personalization of treatment, those medical professionals who will be adept at interpreting this medical data which will in turn depend on the proficiency to communicate the scientific data effectively, will survive and grow in their professions.

Abilities	Basic Skills	Cross-funtional Skills	
Cognitive Abilities - Cognitive flexibility - Creativity - Logical reasoning - Problem sensitivity - Mathematical reasoning - Visualization	**Content Skills** - Active learning - Oral expression - Reading comprehension - Written expression - ICT literacy	**Social Skills** - Coordinating with others - Emotional intelligence - Negotiation - Persuasion - Service orientation - Training and teaching others	**Resource Management Skills** - Management of financial resources - Management of material resources - People management - Time management
Physical Abilities - Physical strength - Manual dexterity and precision	**Process Skills** - Active listening - Critical thinking - Monitoring self and others	**Systems Skills** - Judgement and decision-making - Systems analysis **Complex Problem Solving Skills** - Complex problem solving	**Technical Skills** - Equipment maintenance and repair - Equipment operation and control - Programming - Quality control - Technology and user experience design - Troubleshooting

Figure 9.5: Core Work-related Skills
Source: World Economic Forum, based on O'NET Content Model.

In many situations, technology is not necessarily replacing jobs but rather restructuring it or redefining it. Similarly, as the traditional brick-and-mortar retail is forced to reposition itself given the competition thrown by the e-commerce and online market, jobs related to sales and related jobs will also require persons with increased creativity who are capable of delivering memorable experiences. This means, EI competencies like being able to persuade, communication skills, creativity, and empathetic listening will only become more and more relevant. It is an interesting piece of knowledge for the business schools to start focusing not just on the gap between the demand of the skills required and skills supplied today, but also on the gap between the nature of skills required today and tomorrow. And in this changing scenario, the need to possess EI skills is bound to become more and more pronounced. Flexibility, agility will be on new high and will redefine the work environment in a unique and important way. Therefore it is imperative and not optional to use the concept of teachable fit framework which can predict how successfully the gaps in candidate's skills can be filled.

The State of the Heart Report[21] reveals the global trends in EI, which are based on a sample as big as 200,000 people from 160 countries and territories, showing important trends for global EQ and well-being. This report published by Six Seconds, as mentioned in Chapter 5, provides us with one of the shortest definitions of EI, "Being smarter with feelings". According to Six Seconds framework, EI is required for:

Well-being – Capacity to maintain optimal energy and functioning;
Quality of life – Capacity to maintain balance and satisfaction;
Relationships – Capacity to build and maintain networks;
Effectiveness – Capacity to generate results.

The annual World Happiness Report issued by the United Nations gives an idea about people in which country are living the best and worst lives. Always-on, multitasking work environments are killing productivity, dampening creativity to making us unhappy.[22] Happiness being one of the six basic emotions is definitely an important area to focus upon. Many countries are struggling in managing this emotion, happiness. This, if not timely addressed, has the potential to become one of the major challenges/concerns in the coming few years. Despite the industrial revolutions and fast development, if an individual and thereby the country cannot manage to stay happy, then we need to question the very basics of why and what aspects of the development process. According to the latest report published by the United Nations 2019, there has been an increase in the negative emotions like sadness, anger, and worry amongst people across the globe and overall happiness has gone down. The so-called powerhouses have also not succeeded in getting into the top ten position, which clearly states that it is not the money which is the sole determinant of happiness. When we look around there is much more talk about money making compared to so little on life skills like how to create happiness for self and others. Largely, the pursuit is to create wealth, though it is not what only matters when individuals and countries measure their happiness quotient.[23] As far as India is concerned, it has gone further down from 133rd position in 2018 to that of 140th, as per the latest report. Along with Yemen, Syria, Botswana and Venezuela, India has had the largest drop since 2005-2008 in the index.

This is quite an alarming situation and an important insight for those who wish to make a career in managing emotions. This is the gap that can be strategically managed, and it should begin with molding not just the adults but the kids in kindergarten. If this gap gets overlooked, it may have certain serious ramification we may be not be in a position to fully comprehend at this point in time.

The Gallup's Global Emotions Report 2019[24] also has some vital information for the current and future EI practitioners. The parameters used to measure the global emotions were self-reported enjoyment, smiling and laughing, rest, feelings of respect and intellectual stimulation. Also, negative feelings like self-reported anger, stress, sadness, physical pain and worry were also measured. There is a big scope in helping people overcome barriers like anger, sadness and worry in order to live a life with better emotional regulation and management.

Teaching people how to stay grounded in turbulent and challenging times will be in great demand. As stress is inevitable and more so in the e-VUCA world that we are living in, it is as if it has become second nature of our existence. Helping people in paying attention to emotions instead of suppressing them can be beneficial.[25]

Loud Thinking

Towards the end, a handful of things are going to matter. The famous narrative of the great Alexander merits some serious reflection. He has done an immense favor on the entire human race by asking his followers to make sure that his hands hang out of his grave and that they are empty. To make sure that all those who hear this story get the moral, 'no material wealth leaves with us'. For whenever one reflects on his/her life, s/he is bound to ask this question, "What did I do everything for?" "Why was I here?". Not getting a positive and constructive response has the potential to defeat the entire purpose of our living.

Most of us spend our life working in organizations, most of our waking and active hours get spent, yes for a noble purpose in most cases but what about the children at home? What about the sick and old parents who also crave our attention? How do we balance our life with respect to these conflicting demands of work and family? EI can help us in this balancing act to a reasonably good extent.

Research on women states that many of them give up their careers because of the emotional labor they go through. As newly-wed brides trying to adjust in new families, as young mothers and as caretakers of the family, especially in cultures where even today looking after the family members and providing care by being physically present is assumed to be a duty largely to be fulfilled by a woman. Emotionally intelligent way of living may help a lot of women from giving up their careers. If giving up one's career is by choice, then it is another thing but it should not be just because she could not bear the emotional labor.

Looking ahead, more deliberations should happen on what are the future careers that can be created? How can we create more sustainable society which enables all the dwellers a safe and happy habitat and an emotionally warm environment with less challenges? A few suggestions are as follows.

At individual level

Even in collectivistic cultures like that of India, where until very recently, it was a family based society where family consisted of more than just father and mother but also the uncles and aunts and grandfathers and grandmothers, real and cousin all of them staying under one roof. Today family structure is more or less nuclear in nature, which has created a huge set of challenges as the responsibility of inculcating values, ethics and behavioral skills is largely on parents. Parents, who may or may not be available at times because of the work pressure, recruit the support staff to look after their children. We believe there is a huge gap and a parallel system needs to be created soon to foster child development and go beyond merely providing a daycare facility to that of teachers becoming foster parents and joining parents in building the character of the kids. These teachers in the first place must be trained well to do so. They should, possess required competencies to do the needful. The earlier system in India, *Gurukul* is exactly what we mean. May be a modern adaptation of that format may help.

Over-emphasizing IQ over EQ is not beneficial in the longer run. Jaggi Vasudev, popularly known as Sadhguru, quotes, "We need to prepare our children for the Universe and not just the university".

If one looks around, one can easily find a bunch of few intellectuals who seem to be living in the world of their own. They may be scholars in their field, but come across as persons who are either insensitive to others' needs or poor on social skills altogether. But this again is not their own problem completely. We have done some preliminary research and have found out that they have achieved academic feats like a high rank in school or college but that has come with too much of hard work. Now, at this juncture, the authors plead the readers to provide an undistracted attention to what they mean by hard work. Here, it means, over-emphasis and getting overwhelmed in the process and giving all the available hours to the pursuit of scholastic achievements. At the face value, there seems to be no problem with this but because no time was left to invest in getting engaged in other activities like social work or community service or even household work, such persons are prone to throw a big challenge to their coworkers when put in a team. Their behaviors have often missed the finesse as they had invested no time in gathering feedback and making necessary improvements. We are definitely not against scholastic merit, that is very important, but one needs to assess how much one is gaining and at what cost? Because unfortunately, even after achieving big feats in academics if one has adjustment problems because of personality, s/he may not have a smooth and steadily growing career or may even become jobless eventually. Refer to the Insight, "EQ check, a mandate in recruitment and selection process". The proverb 4:23,[26] 'Keep watch over your heart, for herein are the wellsprings of life' is not worth neglecting or losing in the pursuit of intellect.

A large chunk of our young population is pursuing graduation and post-graduation courses which are either redundant or do not have enough meat in them to provide job opportunities. When youth gets spent in directionless endeavors and major important years of her/ his life go waste, they start losing motivation and enter into some profession mostly much below their potential and live a passive life not much interested in whatsoever they may be into. A major person-environment fit issue. Most organizations have to deal with such demotivated and passive employees and budget huge corpus for building enthusiasm and motivation in them. One may just search on internet and conduct a preliminary research on the market of motivational speakers and motivational books.,the issue is that even this may not necessarily lead to a sustained change. Because getting inspired and sustaining the motivational spirit for long are two different things. Expecting great results from such a workforce which is passive, under-confident and low on enthusiasm is a miss-match of an expectation. It becomes as impossible as an effort to square the circle.

Human resource experts like Udai Pareek have mentioned three aspects of personal effectiveness — self-disclosure, openness to feedback and perceptiveness. All three come through work, work done with people and more importantly, on varied aspects with varied sets of people. Perceptiveness, for example, is about being able to decode cues from people's behavior, majorly their non-verbal communication and accordingly making necessary modifications in one's own behavior. Now these aspects, if not nurtured in initial period of one's life, may become increasingly difficult to hone as age advances. Whereas in any profession one gets into, these three aspects become indispensable in order to to achieve success. Self- awareness is paramount to success as it is believed that the lower the consciousness, the lesser is our contribution.

INSIGHTS

EQ Check, a Mandate in Recruitment and Selection Process

"As an academician with background in psychology, I strongly believe that EI based curriculum and EI based selection for jobs should become the norm.

When I serve selection panels, I have always insisted on EI centric interview. Unfortunately even today, when all the surveys and research on human capital are indicating a trend shift from self-centric to being considerate' and on 'developing others', 'creating a deeper sense of purpose' and 'collaboration, we are still obsessed with grades and our process is limited and skewed towards IQ more as compared to EQ. Both need equal attention, and we cannot compromise one for the other.

There are many examples but let me share an instance from my career that spans across more than two decades now. A new faculty member was recruited based merely on the research credits and the business school from where he had finished doctoral research. Because of his personality related issues, within a week's time, he had a problem with everyone around. Even before he could start contributing and become an asset, he had become a liability."

Source: An excerpt from the discussion with Dr. Yogesh M. Deshpande, Professor & HOD, Humanities & Social Sciences, VNIT, Nagpur.

Impulse control and the ability to delay gratification are the simplest ways to explain what one means by emotional intelligence. 'Social media' and the 'gaming industry' are examples of platforms that are inculcating tendencies and behaviors which are exactly the opposite of this. An article published in Forbes in 2019 said that in 2018, the gaming market did business of around $138.7 billion. A huge market means huge set of people involved in it. When children play games and have the remote control in their hands and exercise full control over the situation, they may develop the tendency of wanting to control everything around them and there is a potential threat that they may expect the same in real life too. Although it is too early to predict this for sure, but as behavioral scientists we can see such trend setting in many young adults.

There is a big rise in the number of young adults suffering from depression and other mental illness. Although not just because of the over and unwarranted use of social media, but also due to other reasons as well. Impulse control training is a must ingredient in grooming. In some families, needs and demands of the child get promptly addressed, which is also a major concern. Understanding the difference between caring and pampering needs some attention. It is accepted that using gadgets cannot be completely avoided, so gadget manners and regulating the use of gadgets need to be looked into.

According to His Holiness the Dalai Lama,[27] compassion is the key. Compassion not only helps the one whom one is being compassionate to but also the one who is offering. As a practice, it is going miles beyond empathy. He talks about learned helplessness and how people should get rid of just thinking and not acting. His philosophy being, one needs to act even if it is not giving the desired outcomes right away, maybe not even in one's lifetime, and maybe it takes a century or so. This is very close to the philosophy of 'Pursue Noble Goals' in Six Seconds framework of EI. The Dalai Lama's idea of awareness gets reflected in the fact that he treats everyone equally. He believes that each one of is the same human being behind the surfaces. He believes in his own words, "We all are same". This is a critical shift in what awareness means.[28]

Chapter Synthesis

In this last chapter on EI, the idea was to present the future based on various studies and the current realities with respect to EI, on the basis of scientific data. Reasons behind the exponential changes happening in the world of business are discussed based on different reports. Reports published by Gallup, Deloitte, World Economic Forum, and Six Seconds, to name a few, point towards a fact that the future is of the ones who can think, feel and act in the direction which is other-oriented and not just self-centered. The sustainable goals announced by UN are presented in order to give the big picture and understand the shared vision so that individual, group and organizational activities can be effectively aligned around it by putting EI competencies to use.

The reasons behind the shift of traditional business to a new identity of becoming a 'social enterprise' have been discussed. The change of perspective from 'shareholder to stakeholder' is explained in detail.

The importance of being 'antifragile' and the need to reinvent are discussed. The challenges and the opportunities in the electronic e-VUCA world have been also highlighted. Based on research that 'ability to serve others' will become absolutely important and how to get more and more employees engaged in the processes of the organization and their own job in the first place, will pose a rather big challenge to the management. The relevant core work-related skills are presented for the readers to have a look at what will matter in the coming years. Various latest reports like State of the Heart Report, Annual World Happiness Report, Gallup Global Emotion Report are reviewed, and relevant issues have been presented.

The authors have presented (based on various reports) a set of new careers which could fill the gap followed by loud thinking aimed at prompting the student of EI to look at the impact EI has in an individual's personal and social space. How personal effectiveness depends upon EI has also been discussed based on the personal effectiveness tool by Udai Pareek.

There is a passing reference on how EI could be used in selection process in the inserts titled *Insights*, as this topic has already been dealt at length in Chapter 7. It is imperative for individuals to hone their EI skills if the organizations wish to create an EI rich culture and vice versa. If individuals lack the EI skills at their end, the organization's intent would not be successful to institutionalize the EI based culture. To have EI managers, it is important that families, schools and communities need to adopt EI centric methodologies in all the processes.

The issue of impulse control and delayed gratification are discussed in detail in relation to from gaming industry and the implications of overuse of social media are also touched upon respectively.

The issue of learned helplessness is discussed towards the end in order to signal that we have had enough reading in EI all through the nine chapters, it is now time to walk the talk, and overcome our learned helplessness if there is any.

The EI quotes from *Shrimad Bhagwat Gita* and from Gautam Buddha are inserted for readers to get connected to what the scriptures have been saying for years.

EI related quotes from Shrimad Bhagwat Gita saying for many years

More EI relevant quotes are available in the ancient wisdom. As stated in Chapter 18 verse 28, "Even if we cannot get over things, we can still get on with things — don't let roadblocks become mental blocks."

"Accepting our smallness requires greatness", Chapter 13, verse 10.

"To stop defeating yourself, stop deceiving yourself — begin with what you are, not what you appear to be", Chapter 3, verse 6

"We need to come at least slightly out of ignorance to realize that we are in ignorance — those excessively drunk can't understand that they are drunk", Chapter 14 verse 13.

"We are not our feelings — we are the feelers of the feelings", Chapter 14, verse 23

"Don't hold onto things that hold you back", Chapter 2, verse 44

EI quotes from Gautam Buddha

"Don't be jealous with anyone. Don't compete with anyone. Just focus on becoming the best version of yourself."

"My goal is not to become better than anyone else but better than I used to be."

"Once you feel you are avoided by someone never disturb them again."

"You are strong when you know your weakness. You are beautiful when you appreciate your flaws. You are wise when you learn from your mistakes."

KEY TERMS

Skills stability
Job family
Teachable fit
Perceptiveness
Proactive adaption
Attention economy
Neuroplasticity
Behavioral-event interview
Social capital
Learned helplessness

Review Questions

1. Discuss the fourth industrial revolution in connection to EI. Discuss the challenges.
2. Discuss business as a social enterprise.
3. State the sustainable development goals (SDGs).
4. Discuss how EI can help achieve the SDGs.
5. Explain the concept of 'teachable fit framework'.
6. Prepare a list of skills which will be required irrespective of the career one pursues.
7. What do you mean by skills stability?
8. Due to the advent of technology, number of jobs will decline. Do you agree with this statement? Give reasons.

Application-based Exercises

1. Interview a professional from any sector with at least 25 years of experience or more and ask him what skills have become redundant over a period of time and which new skills s/he had to acquire in order to sustain/ succeed?
2. Work in groups and each group should consist of not more than five individuals. Interview at least five individuals (per group) from a sector (preferably every group can choose one new sector and preferably different set of functional areas). Ask respondents on whether they were required to reinvent themselves during the last five years? If yes, with respect to which skills?
3. Have a dialogue with your own parents/ guardians and find out about how and where they picked their EI skills.

   Prerequisite: Introduce them to the EI term before asking them any questions. Be aware that they may end up knowing much more than you thought even if they seemed unaware of the term. Be open to listening.
4. Ask your friends/ family to self-report the latest episode of enjoyment, smiling and laughing, rest, feelings of respect and intellectual stimulation. Map it against a suitable time interval.
5. Ask somebody in your contacts who have been working for more than five years in any sector about, How do they see their life? and How do they live their life?

   (You may download the Gallup Global Emotions Report 2019, and read Jon Clifton's the Global Managing Partner of Gallup, introductory notes for reference).
6. Interact with five to six teenagers (age13–19 years) individually, and try to find out by either directly asking them or asking their family members about the approximate time spent on their smartphones (time spent on social media/ games). Choose the ones who have spent maximum time in the sample you have collected. Then to the chosen ones, ask (either the family member or close ones or the teenager directly), what did they (teenagers) think, feel and did in a challenging situation.

   For example: When they lost in a sport played on the physical field/ failed in an important exam/ had a break-up/ or any other challenging situation they have faced. Collate the data and analyze how did they deal with it. See if you can be of any help to them by using your knowledge of EI.

Activities Beyond the Book

1. Study the latest report, "Future of Jobs", published by World Economic Forum and answer the following questions:
   a. Compare the top ten skills in demand in 2018 versus those in 2022.
   b. Compare and present the trends that will be impacting the growth of businesses, both positively and negatively.
2. Download the latest World Happiness Report and discuss strategies to improve India's ranking.
3. Download Deloitte's report mentioned in the chapter and discuss 'Well-being: a strategy and a responsibility'.
4. Pick any five roles in the context of an organization and study the different abilities, basic skills and cross-functional skills required to perform a job effectively and efficiently.
   (Refer to the report, 'Future of Jobs' by World Economic Forum Report 2016/18)
5. How does the changing landscape of jobs look like in 2022?
6. Discuss the various stable, new and redundant roles across industries.

Video Resources

1. United Nations Presentation: The Role of Mindfulness and Emotional Intelligence at Work
   https://www.youtube.com/watch?v=YR-sYxOacNA
2. Video by CNBC on Fourth Industrial Revolution
   https://www.youtube.com/watch?v=v9rZOa3CUC8
3. World's Emotional Temperature
   https://news.gallup.com/interactives/248240/global-emotions.aspx
4. Sadhguru Talking about His Schools
   https://www.youtube.com/watch?v=N9tHWP9LOKk

References

1 https://sustainabledevelopment.un.org/sdgs

2 https://www2.deloitte.com/content/dam/Deloitte/at/Documents/human-capital/at-2018-deloitte-human-capital-trends.pdf

3 https://www2.deloitte.com/content/dam/Deloitte/at/Documents/human-capital/at-2018-deloitte-human-capital-trends.pdf

4 McDowell, T., Agarwal, D., Miller, D., Okamoto, T., and Page, T. (2016). "Organizational design: The rise of teams". *Deloitte University Press [Online] Available at: https://dupress. deloitte. com/dup-usen/focus/human-capital-trends/2016/organizational-models-network-of-teams. html Accessed on*, *12*, 01-17.

5 Trends, G. H. C. (2015). "Leading in the new world of work". *URL: https://www2. deloitte. com/global/en/pages/human-capital/articles/introduction-human-capitaltrends-2015. html (дата обращения: 17.10. 2017).*

6 https://www2.deloitte.com/content/dam/Deloitte/at/Documents/human-capital/at-2018-deloitte-human-capital-trends.pdf.

7 https://www.youtube.com/watch?v=YR-sYxOacNA

8 https://www.youtube.com/watch?v=YR-sYxOacNA
9 https://www.youtube.com/watch?v=YR-sYxOacNA
10 https://www2.deloitte.com/content/dam/Deloitte/cz/Documents/human-capital/cz-hc-trends-reinvent-with-human-focus.pdf
11 McKee, A. (2016). "How to hire for emotional intelligence". *Harvard Business Review.*
12 Boyatzis, R. E., Boyatzis, R., and McKee, A. (2005). "Resonant leadership: Renewing yourself and connecting with others through mindfulness, hope, and compassion". *Harvard Business Press.*
13 McKee, A. (2014). Being happy at work matters. *Harvard Business Review,* 14.
14 Goleman, D., Boyatzis, R., and McKee, A. (2001). "Primal leadership: The hidden driver of great performance". *Harvard Business Review,* 79(11), 42–53.
15 McClelland, D. C. (1998). "Identifying competencies with behavioral-event interviews". P*sychological Science,* 9(5), 331–339.
16 Poll, G. (2013). "State of the global workplace: Employment engagement insights for business leaders worldwide". *Gallup News, available at: http://news. gallup.com/reports/220313/state-global-workplace-2017. aspx# aspnetForm/(accessed August 15, 2017).*
17 Bersin, J. (2018). New research shows" heavy learners" more confident, successful, and happy at work.
18 Wright-Neville, D., and Smith, D. (2009). Political rage: terrorism and the politics of emotion. *Global Change, Peace & Security, 21*(1), 85–98.
19 McKinsey Global Institute - https://www.mckinsey.com/featured-insights/future-of-work/jobs-lost-jobs-gained-what-the-future-of-work-will-mean-for-jobs-skills-and-wages#part2
20 World Economic Forum. (2016, January). "The future of jobs: Employment, skills and workforce strategy for the fourth industrial revolution". In *Global Challenge Insight Report, World Economic Forum, Geneva.*
21 https://www.6seconds.org/2018/09/05/state-of-the-heart-2018/
22 Dean, D., and Webb, C. (2011). "Recovering from information overload". *McKinsey Quarterly, 1*(1), 80–88.
23 https://worldhappiness.report/ed/2019/
24 https://www.gallup.com/analytics/248909/gallup-2019-global-emotions-report-pdf.aspx
25 Weiss, L. (2016). "A Simple Way to Stay Grounded in Stressful Moments". *HBR.*
26 Cooper, R. K., and Sawaf, A. (1998). *Executive EQ: Emotional intelligence in leadership and organizations.* Penguin. p. 291-292
27 Goleman, D. (2015). *A force for good: The Dalai Lama's vision for our world.* Bloomsbury Publishing.
28 https://www.6seconds.org/2015/09/15/daniel-goleman-on-the-dalai-lamas-vision-for-good/

INDEX